THE Scholarship BOOK

FOURTH EDITION

Daniel J. Cassidy

President, National Scholarship Research Service (NSRS)

PRENTICE HALL
Englewood Cliffs, New Jersey 07632

Prentice-Hall International (UK) Limited, *London*
Prentice-Hall of Australia Pty. Limited, *Sydney*
Prentice-Hall Canada, Inc., *Toronto*
Prentice-Hall Hispanoamericana, S.A., *Mexico*
Prentice-Hall of India Private Limited, *New Delhi*
Prentice-Hall of Japan, Inc., *Tokyo*
Simon & Schuster Asia Pte. Ltd., *Singapore*
Editora Prentice-Hall do Brasil, Ltda., *Rio de Janeiro*

10 9 8 7 6

Library of Congress Cataloging-in-Publication Data

Cassidy, Daniel J.
The scholarship book : the complete guide to private scholarships, grants, and loans for undergraduates / Daniel J. Cassidy.—4th ed.
p. cm.
Includes indexes.
ISBN 0-13-799545-8.—ISBN 0-13-799537-7
1. Scholarships—United States—Directories. 2. Student aid—United States—Directories. 3. Associations, institutions, etc.—United States—Charitable contributions—Directories. I. Title.
LB2337.2.C37 1993 93-5030
378.3'4'0973—dc20 CIP

0-13-799545-8 {PAPER}

0-13-799537-7 CASE

PRENTICE HALL
Career & Personal Development
Englewood Cliffs, NJ 07632
A Simon & Schuster Company

On the World Wide Web at http://www.phdirect.com

Printed in the United States of America

I want to thank all of those who have made this fourth edition of THE SCHOLARSHIP BOOK a reality. My sincere thanks and gratitude to:

The staff at NSRS

especially:

My wife Deirdre Carlin Cassidy, Vice President/Controller

Research & Computer Engineering

William L. Sheppard, Director of Research
Richard Merwin, Computer Systems

Administration & Public Relations

Joe Gargiulo, Public Relations Director
Christina D. Kaufman, Executive Secretary
Julanne C. Lorimor, Secretary

A Very Special Thank You to
Jim Eason
KGO Radio, San Francisco
The man who made NSRS possible

And, at Prentice Hall

Thank you to

Joe Tessitore
President
Career & Personal Development Division

Tom Power
Senior Editor

Roseann Wright
Editorial Assistant

Barbara Palumbo
Manager/Desktop

Jacqueline Roulette
Production Editor

Preface

INTRODUCTION

The information in *The Scholarship Book* was compiled from the data base of the largest Private Sector financial aid research service in the world. Located in Santa Rosa, California, NATIONAL SCHOLARSHIP RESEARCH SERVICE (NSRS) began tracking Private Sector scholarships in the late 1970s, using a specialized computer system. Prospective college students and present undergraduates will find the information in this book valuable in directing their applications and broadening their prospects for scholarship selection.

THE FACTS

According to the Association of Fund Raising Counsel, more than 80% of the grant applications that went to the 23,000 foundations in the United States were either misdirected or filled out improperly. The National Commission on Student Financial Assistance, a U.S. Congressional Subcommittee, found that while there was more than $7 billion available to students from corporations, only $400 million was used! Some $6.6 billion went unclaimed, not because people were unqualified but because they didn't know where to look. To put that figure in a more understandable perspective, the unused portion of available funds would amount to $600 for each of the 15 million collegebound students in the United States alone. There is a great need to organize this "paper-chase" of information into a workable source for today's student. Utilizing the data collected here students will have a broad base of information to convert to their advantage. The monies are there. Apply for them!

PRIVATE SECTOR FUNDS

Philanthropy in the United States is alive and well. More than 65% of the available scholarships, fellowships, grants and loans are from the Private Sector. These funds, which totaled $56 billion in 1987 increased to a whopping $151 billion in 1992. Of that amount 15%, or $20 billion, goes into the United States educational system. An additional $20 billion is dispersed worldwide.

That amount increases daily. The interest alone on a properly invested $2 million is easily $200,000 annually. Private Sector resources for higher education are as varied as the awards themselves.

Many scholarships are renewable. You simply sign for them year after year. Others allow you to "piggy-back" several individual scholarships. The average undergraduate scholarship is $4,000 per year, ranging from a low of $100 to a high of $20,000. Graduate level fellowships range from $10,000 to $60,000. Some research projects can yield a quarter of a million dollars or more. As inflation spirals, so do the costs of education and the need for financial assistance.

INVESTIGATE THE POSSIBILITIES

Don't think you can't apply because your parents earn too much money; 80% of the Private Sector does not require a financial statement or proof of need. Don't think that application deadlines occur only in the fall; Private Sector deadlines are passing daily because often they are set to coincide with the tax year or organizational meeting dates. Don't believe that grades are the only consideration for an award; many application questions deal with personal, occupational, and educational background, organizational affiliation, talent, or ethnic origins; 90% are not concerned with grades. Don't be concerned with age; 42% of all college students are over the age of 25 and many organizations are interested in the reentry student and the mid-career development student. The Business and Professional Woman's Foundation awards hundreds of scholarships to applicants who must be older than 25 or even 35. There is a scholarship at the California State Colleges for students over the age of 60.

PLAN TO COMPETE AND QUALIFY

The plan is simple: use this book and every other resource you can find. Inquire at your institution's financial aid office about government assistance and private endowments. If you are a high school sophomore, write to ten or more schools. Choose a good range of institutions that interest you, both large and small; public and private. Request the application materials and catalogs: many private endowments are available in the form of scholarships and fellowships bequeathed by alumni. A significant number of these go unclaimed because qualified students do not know they exist! The information is available but the commitment belongs to the individual.

The Private Sector is easily accessed with this book. The student can use its tables to cross reference the scholarships applicable to his or her personal background and educational goals. Choose twenty or more sources and request application forms and any pertinent materials. Some have specific requirements for applicants such as a personal interview, the submission of an essay or related work, or a promise to work for the company on completion of study and/or the earning of a degree. Others may have paid internships or work advancement programs. Still others may simply require that you fill out an application form.

The money is there. Billions go unclaimed. The student who does not take the time to inquire loses every advantage. You might even give consideration to overseas study. The opportunity to study abroad is exciting — the rewards incalculable. Information is merely a passage waiting to be used. There are moments in every life akin to the lines from the poem, The Road Not Taken:

"Two roads diverged in a wood, and I-
I took the one less traveled by,
And that has made all the difference."
—Robert Frost

JUST FOR FUN: A POTPOURRI OF SCHOLARSHIPS

1. Now here's a house with equity. *Morehouse College* received $1 million from talk show host Oprah Winfrey to establish the **Oprah Winfrey Endowed Scholarship.** K24/R128
2. If you're a Mexican American between the ages of 17 and 22 and live in the Golden State, you just might strike gold with the $1,500 **Vikki Carr Scholarship**. K19/R85
3. Your tuition troubles could be gone with the wind! If you are a lineal descendant of a worthy Confederate soldier, contact the **United Daughters of the Confederacy** about their $400 to $1,500 scholarships. K22/R7
4. If you or your parents are actively involved in Harness Racing, you just might hitch yourself to one of the **Harness Tracks of America** scholarships worth $2,500 to $3,000. K18/R147
5. If you're the child of a full time *Chrysler Corporation* employee, you "auto" apply to the **Lee Iacocca Scholarship Program.** You could drive away with up to $5,000 for undergraduate study. K21/R7
6. Don't let financial woes cast a pall over your dreams. Bury those worries with a **Hilgenfeld Foundation for Mortuary Education** scholarship! It's available to qualified individuals interested in the funeral service or funeral education fields. K99/R5
7. *Jen unu mil pundo—nun EK!* (Here's a thousand pounds—now go!) If you understood that you might be eligible for a **Norwich Jubilee Esperanto Foundation** scholarship paying 1,000 pounds sterling to study Esperanto in the United Kingdom. K73/R10
8. Migrant farmworkers and their children can reap the benefits of an education with a **Boces Geneso Migrant Center** scholarship. Most of the awards are for undergraduate study but some support high school graduation. K19/R142
9. For students whose ancestors put their John Hancocks on the Declaration of Independence, the **Descendants of the Signers of the Declaration of Independence** have scholarships worth $1,200 to $2,000. K19/R152
10. Investigating scholarship possibilities? The **Association of Former Agents of the U.S. Secret Service** offers scholarships of $500 to $1,500 to undergraduate law enforcement and police administration students. You do have to give your real name, but fingerprints won't be necessary. K95/R32

RECOMMENDATIONS

By using this book to track down all your potential sources of funding, you may need additional help. Following are some excellent sources that NSRS recommends:

THE INSTITUTE OF INTERNATIONAL EDUCATION (IIE)

ACADEMIC YEAR ABROAD, $39.95. The most complete guide to planning study abroad describes over 1900 postsecondary study programs outside the USA. Concise descriptions provide the information you need on costs, academic programs and credits, dates and applications, and more. K11/R60

VACATION STUDY ABROAD, $31.95. Describes over 1450 summer or short term study-abroad sponsored by United States colleges and universities and foreign institutions. K11/R58

All orders must be prepaid. IIE pays domestic postage. If you have questions write or phone:

Institute of International Education (IIE)
Publications Service, IIE
809 United Nations Plaza, New York, NY 10017

(212) 984-5330

MAKING IT THROUGH COLLEGE, $1.00. Handy booklet describing how to make it through college. Includes information on how to cope with competition, getting organized, study techniques, solving work overloads and much more. K11/R16

Write to:

Professional Staff Congress
25 West 43rd Street, 5th Floor
New York, NY 10036

NEED A LIFT? $2. Outstanding guide to education and employment opportunities. Contains complete information on the financial aid process (how, when and where to start), scholarships, loans, and career information addresses. K11/R24

Write to:

American Legion Education Program
P.O.Box 1050
Indianapolis, IN 46206

COLLEGE FINANCIAL AID EMERGENCY KIT, $5.50 (prepaid). 40-page booklet filled with tips on how to meet the costs of tuition; room and board; and fees. Tells what is available; whom to ask and how to ask!K11/R66

Write to:

Sun Features Inc.
Box 368-K
Cardiff, CA 92007

FISKE GUIDE TO COLLEGES, $16. Describes the 265 top-rated four year colleges in the USA and rates for academics; social life and quality of life. K11/R28

Write to:

Times Books
400 Hahn Road
Westminster, MD 21157

INDEX OF MAJORS, $15.95. Describes over 500 major programs of study at 3000 undergraduate and graduate schools. Also lists schools with religious affiliations, special academic programs and special admissions procedures. K11/R95

Add $3.00 postage. Write to:

College Board Publications
P.O.Box 886
New York, NY 10101

PETERSON'S GUIDE TO FOUR-YEAR COLLEGES, $18.95. Detailed profiles of over 1900 accredited four year colleges in the USA and Canada. Also includes entrance difficulty directory; majors directory and college cost directory. K11/R98

INTERNSHIPS, $14.95. Are you a college student? Looking for your first job? Reentering the work force? Thinking about making a career change? Or just taking a break before higher education and would like to try a particular career field? This book lists over numerous job training opportunities, arranged by career field and indexed geographically. K11/R92

"If you are somewhat undecided on the question of a career, simply browsing through the myriad possibilities may spark an unexpected interest."— Business Week

Write to:

Peterson's Inc.
Dept. 7707, PO Box 2123
Princeton, NJ 08543

Add $2.50 for domestic postage.

COLLEGE DEGREES BY MAIL, $21.95 plus $2.50 shipping and handling. John Bear, Ph.D., describes every approach known to earning a degree without ever taking a single traditional course! It lists 100 reputable colleges that offer bachelors, masters, doctorates and law degrees through home study. The book also lists colleges reputed to be diploma mills and cautions against them. K11/R102

HAPPIER BY DEGREES, $8.95. The complete guide for women returning to college or just starting out. It is the kind of resource that you can depend on for everything from financial aid to using campus programs. A step-by-step guide for selecting the right college and incorporating a student role into an already busy life; and concludes with advice on making your career choice. K11/R61

"I have never seen a more useful guide to the puzzling world of academia."—Carolyn See, Professor, Loyola Marymount University

This is my most recommended book for women attending college today; it is full of good advice. Pam has done a great job!

Include $1.25 for shipping and handling. Write to:

Ten Speed Press
PO Box 7123
Berkeley, CA 94707

WHERE THE INFORMATION IN THIS BOOK CAME FROM

The information for this book was compiled from the data base of the largest Private Sector college financial aid research service in the world: National Scholarship Research Service (NSRS) located in Santa Rosa, California.

Since the late 1970s, NSRS has been using computers to research and update information on potential sources of financial assistance for college students. Many thousands of students have used NSRS's services to locate sources offering financial aid.

NATIONAL SCHOLARSHIP RESEARCH SERVICE

NSRS's computer stores information on thousands of Private Sector aid programs for all levels of college study: from high school seniors just entering college to post doctoral researchers.

Applicants for NSRS's services first complete a biographical questionnaire, indicating their particular area(s) of interest. This information is entered into the computer which searches NSRS's files for the scholarships the applicant may qualify for. Since each applicant has a different background and each of the thousands of aid programs have different requirements, this computer search can save valuable time and often provides students with potential sources of aid that they might never have considered applying for.

If you consider that all the financial aid programs listed in this book are constantly changing, with new application dates, qualifying requirements, etc., you may want to utilize this company's services.

Since NSRS is a privately owned company, there is a modest fee for its services. For a product list, write or call:

NATIONAL SCHOLARSHIP RESEARCH SERVICE (NSRS)
Box 6609
Santa Rosa, California 95406-0609

Phone: (707) 546-6777

IMPORTANT NOTE: This book is an abridged version of the National Scholarship Research Service data base. For a more comprehensive search of NSRS's data base write to NSRS at the address above. Every effort has been made to supply you with the most accurate and up to date information possible but even as this book goes to print, awards are being added and application requirements are being changed by sponsoring organizations. Such circumstances are beyond our control.

Since the information we have supplied may not reflect the current status of any particular award program you are interested in, you should use this book only as a guide. Contact the source of the award for current application information.

If questions arise during your search for educational funding, you are welcome to call an NSRS counselor at 707/546-6781.

Use this sample letter as a guide to create your own letter requesting information. Photocopy your letter and address the envelopes for mailing. Remember to apply well in advance of the deadlines. You should keep a calendar to keep track of them.

Scholarship Program Office
ABC Foundation
100 Street Name
Any City, Any State 00000

I am a student at __________________ and will be applying for admission to college next year. I would appreciate receiving application forms for any scholarships you might offer.

Enclosed is a stamped, self-addressed business size envelope for your convenience in replying.

Sincerely,

James Maurice Cassidy
2280 Airport Boulevard
Santa Rosa, California 95403

(707) 546-6777

How to Use This Book

Each award, book and resource listed in THE SCHOLARSHIP BOOK has a record number preceding it. All of our indexes are based on these record numbers.

Here is a short guide to finding the information you need:

"QUICK FIND" INDEX:

Most private-sector awards have certain eligibility qualifications. We have selected several of the most common requirements for this "quick find" index.

Here you can find awards targeted for people with physical handicaps, for people of a particular race or family ancestry, for people who will be studying in a particular state and much more. Simply go through each of the tables and write down the reference numbers that apply to you. Then proceed to those sources and read each one carefully to see if you qualify.

FIELD OF STUDY INDEX

Since the awards listed in this book also are based on your intended field of study, we have structured this index along the lines of a college catalog.

First, look under your particular field of study. (School of Business, for instance.) Then look under your area of interest (Accounting) and finally, under your specific subject (Banking). In this section you will find record numbers that reference both financial aid awards and other resources that can help you in your career. Again, since there might be several eligibility requirements you must meet in order to be able to qualify for any listed award be sure you read each listing carefully and meet the requirements of the award before requesting an application.

SCHOLARSHIP AND AWARD LISTINGS

Each listing contains a very condensed description of the award, its eligibility requirements, deadline dates and where to get more information or an application.

You will notice a large "general" section. These are awards that do not usually specify a particular field of study in their eligibility requirements. You need to use the indexes provided and read each listing carefully to see if you might qualify for one of these awards.

Use the information we have provided only as a guide. Write to the source for a complete description of qualifications.

HELPFUL PUBLICATIONS

This section of THE SCHOLARSHIP BOOK contains a selection of helpful books and pamphlets. These publications are excellent sources of information on a wide variety of college and financial aid subjects.

If you discover a publication you find particularly helpful, let us know so we can share the information with others.

CAREER INFORMATION

This is a list of organizations that can help you decide where to study, give you information on job opportunities available in your field of study and much more. We encourage you to write to these organizations for information.

ALPHABETICAL INDEX

A to Z, this index lists the reference number of every award, book and career organization that is included in this book.

Quick Find Index

CONTINENT OF INTENDED STUDY

COUNTRY OF INTENDED STUDY

COUNTRY OF RESIDENCE

CURRENT GRADE POINT AVERAGE

CURRENT SCHOOL PROGRAM

DEGREES RECEIVED

ETHNIC BACKGROUND

EXTRACURRICULAR ACTIVITIES

FAMILY ANCESTRIES

FOREIGN LANGUAGES SPOKEN

HONORS/AWARDS/CONTESTS

LEGAL CITY OF RESIDENCE

LEGAL CONTINENT OF CITIZENSHIP

LEGAL COUNTRY OF CITIZENSHIP

LEGAL COUNTY OF RESIDENCE

LEGAL STATE/PROV OF RESIDENCE

MARITAL STATUS

OCCUPATIONAL GOALS

OCCUPATIONS

ORGANIZATIONS

PHYSICAL HANDICAPS

PRE/CUR/FUT SCHOOLS

RELIGIOUS AFFILIATION

SEX

SORORITY/FRATERNITY

STATE/PROVINCE INTENDED STUDY

UNIONS

UNUSUAL CHARACTERISTICS

Field of Study Index

SCHOOL OF BUSINESS

BUSINESS ADMINISTRATION

SCHOOL OF EDUCATION

EDUCATION

SCHOOL OF ENGINEERING

AERONAUTICS

ARCHITECTURE

CIVIL ENG

COMPUTER SCIENCE

ELECTRICAL ENG

ENGINEERING TECH

MECHANICAL ENG

SCHOOL OF HUMANITIES

AREA STUDIES

ART

ENGLISH LANG / LIT

FOREIGN LANGUAGE

PERFORMING ARTS

PHILOSOPHY

SCHOOL OF NATURAL RESOURCES

AGRICULTURE

EARTH SCIENCE

ENVIRO STUDIES

MARINE SCIENCE

NATURAL HISTORY

SCHOOL OF SCIENCE

BIOLOGY

CHEMISTRY

MATHEMATICS

MEDICAL DOCTOR

MEDICAL RELATED DISCIPLINES

MEDICAL RESEARCH

MEDICAL TECHNOLOGIES

NURSING

NUTRITION

SCHOOL OF SOCIAL SCIENCE

COMMUNICATIONS

HISTORY

LAW

POLITICAL SCIENCE

PSYCHOLOGY

SOCIOLOGY

SCHOOL OF VOCATIONAL ED

Scholarship and Awards Listings

BUSINESS ADMINISTRATION

1

AMERICAN ACCOUNTING ASSOCIATION (ARTHUR H CARTER SCHOLARSHIPS)
5717 BESSIE DR
SARASOTA FL 34233
813/921-7747; FAX 813/923-4093
AMOUNT: $2500
DEADLINE(S): APR 1
FIELD(S): ACCOUNTING
OPEN TO UNDERGRADUATE AND MASTER'S DEGREE CANDIDATES FOR STUDY AT ACCREDITED USA INSTITUTIONS OFFERING ACCOUNTING DEGREES. MUST HAVE COMPLETED AT LEAST 2 YEARS OF UNDERGRAD STUDY AND HAVE AT LEAST 1 FULL YEAR OF STUDY REMAINING.
SELECTIONS BASED ON MERIT NOT NEED. 50 AWARDS PER YEAR. APPLICATIONS SHOULD BE OBTAINED FROM DEAN OF ACCOUNTING AT INDIVIDUAL COLLEGES.

2

AMERICAN ASSOCIATION OF AIRPORT EXECUTIVES - NORTHEAST CHAPTER (WILFRED M. "WILEY" POST JR. AAE AVIATION SCHOLARSHIP)
PO BOX 1253
ROCKVILLE MD 20849
WRITTEN INQUIRY
AMOUNT: $1000 MINIMUM
DEADLINE(S): DEC 31
FIELD(S): AVIATION MANAGEMENT
OPEN TO COLLEGE SENIORS OR JUNIORS WHO ARE WORKING TOWARD A BA OR BS DEGREE WHO ASPIRE TO A CAREER IN AVIATION/AIRPORT MANAGEMENT. THOSE SEEKING TO BECOME PROFESSIONAL PILOTS ARE -NOT- ELIGIBLE.
APPLICATION FORMS ARE AVAILABLE THROUGH COLLEGES AND UNIVERSITIES OFFERING AVIATION MANAGEMENT DEGREE PROGRAMS. WRITE FOR COMPLETE INFORMATION.

3

AMERICAN COLLEGE FOR THE APPLIED ARTS (EMILIO PUCCI SCHOLARSHIPS)
3330 PEACHTREE RD NE; ADMISSIONS OFFICE
ATLANTA GA 30326
404/231-9000
AMOUNT: $1000 (DISTRIBUTED OVER 6 QTRS)
DEADLINE(S): MAY 1
FIELD(S): FASHION DESIGN; MERCHANDISING; INTERIOR DESIGN; COMMERCIAL ART; BUSINESS ADMINISTRATION
SCHOLARSHIPS ARE FOR HIGH SCHOOL STUDENTS WHO ARE INTERESTED IN EITHER A 2-YEAR OR 4-YEAR PROGRAM AT ONE OF THE AMERICAN COLLEGES FOR THE APPLIED ARTS IN ATLANTA; LOS ANGELES OR LONDON. SCHOLARSHIP IS APPLIED TOWARD TUITION.
WRITE FOR APPLICATIONS AND COMPLETE INFORMATION.

4

AMERICAN HUMANICS INC (LOAN FUND)
4601 MADISON AVE - SUITE B
KANSAS CITY MO 64112
816/561-6415; 800/343-6466; FAX 816/531-3527
AMOUNT: UP TO $2000/YEAR
DEADLINE(S): NONE SPECIFIED
FIELD(S): YOUTH & HUMAN SERVICES AGENCY ADMINISTRATION
LOANS OPEN TO UNDERGRADUATES WHO ARE SATISFACTORILY PARTICIPATING IN ONE OF 15 AMERICAN HUMANICS PROFESSIONAL CERTIFICATION PROGRAMS AT COLLEGES & UNIVERSITIES THROUGHOUT THE USA.
APPLICANTS MUST DESIRE TO WORK PROFESSIONALLY IN VOLUNTARY NON-PROFIT YOUTH & HUMAN SERVICE AGENCIES. WRITE FOR COMPLETE INFORMATION.

5

AMERICAN INDIAN SCIENCE & ENGINEERING SOCIETY (SANTA FE PACIFIC FOUNDATION SCHOLARSHIPS)
1630 30TH ST - SUITE 301
BOULDER CO 80301
303/492-8658

AMOUNT: UP TO $2500 PER YEAR FOR 4 YEARS
DEADLINE(S): MAR 15
FIELD(S): BUSINESS; ENGINEERING; SCIENCE; HEALTH ADMINISTRATION

OPEN TO GRADUATING HIGH SCHOOL SENIORS WITH 1/4 DEGREE OR MORE INDIAN BLOOD. MUST RESIDE IN KS; OK; CO; AZ; NM OR SAN BERNARDINO COUNTY CA (AT&SF RAILWAY SERVICE AREA). 2 OF THE 5 SCHOLARSHIPS ARE DESIGNATED FOR NAVAJO TRIBE MEMBERS.

MUST PLAN TO ATTEND A 4 YEAR POST-SECONDARY ACCREDITED EDUCATIONAL INSTITUTION. WRITE FOR COMPLETE INFORMATION.

6 ———

AMERICAN INSTITUTE FOR ECONOMIC RESEARCH (SUMMER FELLOWSHIPS; IN-ABSENTIA AWARDS)

DIVISION ST
GREAT BARRINGTON MA 01230
413/528-1217
AMOUNT: TUITION; ROOM & BOARD; $125 PER WEEK STIPEND
DEADLINE(S): MAR 31
FIELD(S): ECONOMICS

SUMMER FELLOWSHIPS IN ECONOMIC SCIENCE AT THE INSTITUTE OPEN TO UNDERGRADUATES WHO HAVE COMPLETED THEIR JUNIOR YEAR & GRADUATE STUDENTS. PREFERENCE TO GRADUATE STUDENTS & USA CITIZENS. FOREIGN STUDENTS MUST BE FLUENT IN ENGLISH.

SUCCESSFUL SUMMER FELLOWS ARE ELIGIBLE FOR IN-ABSENTIA AWARDS WHICH WILL PAY TOTAL OR PARTIAL TUITION OR MONTHLY STIPEND FOR ALL OR PART OF THE FOLLOWING ACADEMIC YEAR; OR BOTH. WRITE FOR COMPLETE INFORMATION.

7 ———

AMERICAN INSTITUTE OF CERTIFIED PUBLIC ACCOUNTANTS (MINORITY SCHOLARSHIP PROGRAM)

1211 AVENUE OF THE AMERICAS
NEW YORK NY 10036
212-575-7641
AMOUNT: UP TO $2000 PER YEAR
DEADLINE(S): JUL 1; DEC 1
FIELD(S): ACCOUNTING

SCHOLARSHIPS OPEN TO AMERICAN MINORITY GROUP MEMBERS. AWARDS SUPPORT UNDERGRADUATE STUDY AT ACCREDITED COLLEGES & UNIVERSITIES. USA CITIZEN OR LEGAL RESIDENT.

400 SCHOLARSHIPS PER YEAR. RENEWABLE. WRITE FOR COMPLETE DETAILS.

8 ———

AMERICAN INSTITUTE OF POLISH CULTURE INC. (SCHOLARSHIPS)

1440 79TH STREET CAUSEWAY; SUITE 117
MIAMI FL 33141
305/864-2349
AMOUNT: $2500
DEADLINE(S): JAN 15
FIELD(S): JOURNALISM/PUBLIC RELATIONS

SCHOLARSHIPS TO ENCOURAGE YOUNG AMERICANS OF POLISH DESCENT TO PURSUE THE ABOVE PROFESSIONS. AWARD CAN BE USED AT ANY ACCREDITED AMERICAN COLLEGE. THE RULING CRITERIA FOR SELECTION ARE ACHIEVEMENT/TALENT & INVOLVEMENT IN PUBLIC LIFE.

AWARDS RENEWABLE. FOR FULL-TIME STUDY ONLY. CONTACT PROF. ZDZISLAW WESOLOWSKI AT ADDRESS ABOVE FOR COMPLETE INFORMATION.

9 ———

AMERICAN INSTITUTE OF REAL ESTATE APPRAISERS (THE APPRAISAL INSTITUTE SCHOLARSHIPS)

875 N MICHIGAN AVE; SUITE 2400
CHICAGO IL 60611
312/335-4100
AMOUNT: $2000 FOR UNDERGRADS; $3000 FOR GRADS
DEADLINE(S): MAR 15
FIELD(S): REAL ESTATE; ECONOMICS; APPRAISING

SCHOLARSHIPS OPEN TO UNDERGRADUATE AND GRADUATE STUDENTS WHO ARE ENROLLED IN A COLLEGE OR UNIVERSITY ACCREDITED BY THE AMERICAN ASSEMBLY OF COLLEGIATE SCHOOLS OF BUSINESS. USA CITIZEN.

APPROXIMATELY 50 AWARDS PER YEAR. WRITE FOR COMPLETE INFORMATION.

10

AMERICAN MANAGEMENT ASSOCIATION (OPERATION ENTERPRISE - TRAINING SEMINARS)
135 W 50TH ST
NEW YORK NY 10020
315-824-2000
AMOUNT: VARIES
DEADLINE(S): DEC 1; APR 1
FIELD(S): MANAGEMENT SEMINARS
FULL & PARTIAL SCHOLARSHIPS ARE AVAILABLE FOR HIGH SCHOOL & COLLEGE STUDENTS TO ATTEND 6-10 DAY TRAINING SEMINARS ON PRACTICAL LEADERSHIP & MANAGEMENT SKILLS. PROMINENT EXECUTIVES SERVE AS GUEST FACULTY.
WRITE FOR COMPLETE INFORMATION.

11

AMERICAN PRODUCTION AND INVENTORY CONTROL SOCIETY INC. (INTERNATIONAL STUDENT PAPER COMPETITION)
500 WANNANDALE RD
FALLS CHURCH VA 22046
703/237-8344
AMOUNT: $150 $100 $50 REGION LEVEL; $500 $300 $200 SOCIETY LEVEL
DEADLINE(S): MAY 15 (APPLY THROUGH LOCAL CHAPTER)
FIELD(S): BUSINESS ADMINISTRATION; MANAGEMENT; RESOURCE MANAGEMENT
PRIZE FOR BEST PAPER DEALING WITH OPERATIONS MANAGEMENT; PRODUCTION MANAGEMENT; INDUSTRIAL MANAGEMENT OR BUSINESS ADMINISTRATION. OPEN TO FULL OR PART TIME UNDERGRADUATE OR GRADUATE STUDENTS.
WRITE FOR COMPLETE INFORMATION.

12

AMERICAN SOCIETY OF TRAVEL AGENTS (ASTA SCHOLARSHIP FOUNDATION SCHOLARSHIP FUNDS)
1101 KING ST
ALEXANDRIA VA 22314
703/739-2782
AMOUNT: $250 - $3000
DEADLINE(S): JUN 11
FIELD(S): TRAVEL & TOURISM
FOUNDATION ADMINISTERS VARIOUS SCHOLARSHIP FUNDS WHICH ARE OPEN TO STUDENTS ENROLLED IN ACCREDITED PROPRIETARY SCHOOLS; 2-YEAR OR 4-YEAR UNDERGRADUATE SCHOOLS OR GRADUATE SCHOOLS. AT LEAST 3.0 GPA (4.0 SCALE). USA OR CANADIAN CITIZEN.
EACH FUND HAS SPECIFIC ELIGIBILITY REQUIREMENTS & SOME AWARDS ARE RENEWABLE. WRITE FOR COMPLETE INFORMATION.

13

AMERICAN WOMEN IN RADIO & TELEVISION (HOUSTON INTERNSHIP PROGRAM)
APRILLE MEEK; AWRT-HOUSTON; PO BOX 980908
HOUSTON TX 77098
WRITTEN INQUIRY
AMOUNT: $500 PER YEAR
DEADLINE(S): MAR 1
FIELD(S): RADIO; TELEVISION; FILM & VIDEO; ADVERTISING; MARKETING
INTERNSHIPS OPEN TO STUDENTS WHO ARE JUNIORS; SENIORS OR GRADUATE STUDENTS AT GREATER HOUSTON AREA COLLEGES & UNIVERSITIES.
WRITE FOR COMPLETE INFORMATION.

14

APPRAISAL INSTITUTE (EDUCATION TRUST SCHOLARSHIPS)
875 N MICHIGAN AVE - STE 2400
CHICAGO IL 60611
312/335-4136; FAX 312/335-4000
AMOUNT: $3000 GRADUATES; $2000 UNDERGRADS
DEADLINE(S): MAR 15
FIELD(S): REAL ESTATE APPRAISAL; LAND ECONOMICS; REAL ESTATE OR ALLIED FIELDS
OPEN TO USA CITIZENS FOR GRADUATE OR UNDERGRADUATE STUDY IN THE ABOVE FIELDS. AWARDS ARE MADE ON THE BASIS OF ACADEMIC EXCELLENCE. APPLICATIONS WILL BE DISTRIBUTED STARTING SEP 1.
APPROX 50 SCHOLARSHIPS PER YEAR. WRITE FOR COMPLETE INFORMATION.

15

APPRAISAL INSTITUTE EDUCATION TRUST (SCHOLARSHIP PROGRAM)
875 N MICHIGAN AVE; SUITE 2400
CHICAGO IL 60611
312/335-4100
AMOUNT: $2000 AND $3000
DEADLINE(S): MAR 15

FIELD(S): REAL ESTATE

OPEN TO UNDERGRADUATE & GRADUATE STUDENTS MAJORING IN REAL ESTATE APPRAISAL; LAND ECONOMICS; REAL ESTATE OR ALLIED FIELDS. AWARDS ARE BASED ON ACADEMIC EXCELLENCE.

50 AWARDS PER YEAR. WRITE FOR COMPLETE INFORMATION.

16

CALIFORNIA ASSOCIATION OF REALTORS (CAR SCHOLARSHIP FOUNDATION)

525 S VIRGIL AVE
LOS ANGELES CA 90020
213/739-8200

AMOUNT: $750 - 2 YEAR COLLEGES; $1500 - FOUR YEAR COLLEGES

DEADLINE(S): NONE SPECIFIED

FIELD(S): REAL ESTATE

OPEN TO CALIFORNIA RESIDENTS WHO ARE USA CITIZENS OR PERMANENT RESIDENTS AND ARE INTENT ON ENTERING THE FIELD OF REAL ESTATE. MUST BE AT LEAST A SOPHOMORE IN A TWO YEAR OR FOUR YEAR COLLEGE WITH AT LEAST A 2.5 GPA.

RENEWABLE. PREFERENCE TO STUDENTS WHO SHOW FINANCIAL NEED. WRITE FOR COMPLETE INFORMATION.

17

CDS INTERNATIONAL INC. (CONGRESS-BUNDESTAG YOUTH EXCHANGE PROGRAM)

330 SEVENTH AVE
NEW YORK NY 10001
212/760-1400; FAX 212/268-1288

AMOUNT: TRAVEL; TUITION; INSURANCE; HOST FAMILY PAYMENT

DEADLINE(S): DEC 31

FIELD(S): BUSINESS; VOC/TECH FIELDS

YEAR LONG WORK/STUDY PROGRAMS IN GERMANY FOR USA CITIZENS AGE 18-24 AND IN THE USA FOR GERMAN CITIZENS AGE 18-21. PROGRAM FOR AMERICANS INCLUDES 2 MONTHS LANGUAGE STUDY; 4 MONTHS STUDY IN A TECH OR PROFESSIONAL SCHOOL & 6 MONTH INTERNSHIP.

PROFESSIONAL TARGET AND APPLICABLE WORK EXPERIENCE REQUIRED. PARTICIPANTS MUST PROVIDE THEIR OWN SPENDING MONEY OF $300-$350 A MONTH. WRITE FOR COMPLETE INFORMATION.

18

CHARLES PRICE SCHOOL OF ADVERTISING AND JOURNALISM INC. (SCHOLARSHIP PROGRAM)

1700 WALNUT ST
PHILADELPHIA PA 19103
215/546-2747

AMOUNT: $500 - $1000

DEADLINE(S): VARIES

FIELD(S): ADVERTISING/JOURNALISM/PUBLIC RELATIONS

SCHOLARSHIPS FOR STUDY IN ABOVE FIELDS -AT- CHARLES PRICE SCHOOL OF ADVERTISING & JOURNALISM. UNDERGRADUATE JUNIORS AND SENIORS AND GRADUATE STUDENTS MAY APPLY. USA CITIZEN.

6 SCHOLARSHIPS PER YEAR. WRITE FOR COMPLETE INFORMATION.

19

CLUB FOUNDATION (SCHOLARSHIP AWARDS)

1733 KING STREET
ALEXANDRIA VA 22314
703/739-9500; FAX 703/739-0124

AMOUNT: VARIES

DEADLINE(S): MAY 1

FIELD(S): MANAGEMENT

OPEN TO STUDENTS WHO HAVE COMPLETED THEIR FRESHMAN YEAR AT AN ACCREDITED USA COLLEGE OR UNIVERSITY AND ARE INTERESTED IN A CAREER IN PRIVATE CLUB MANAGEMENT. APPLICANTS SHOULD HAVE 2.5 OR BETTER GPA. AWARDS ARE NOT BASED SOLELY ON NEED.

WRITE FOR COMPLETE INFORMATION.

20

COLLEGE OF INSURANCE (SCHOLARSHIPS)

101 MURRAY STREET; ADMISSIONS OFFICE
NEW YORK NY 10007
212/962-4111

AMOUNT: UP TO $1800 PER SEMESTER

DEADLINE(S): MAY FOR FOLLOWING SEPTEMBER

FIELD(S): INSURANCE MANAGEMENT; ACTUARIAL SCIENCE

AWARDS TENABLE AT THE COLLEGE OF INSURANCE ONLY. OPEN TO APPLICANTS WHO ARE USA CITIZENS; HIGH SCHOOL GRADUATE; 3 YEARS C.P. MATH; SAT-1000 OR ACT 24 COMPOSITE.

50 SCHOLARSHIPS PER SEMESTER. RENEWABLE. WRITE FOR COMPLETE INFORMATION.

21

COLORADO SOCIETY OF CPA'S (EDUCATIONAL FOUNDATION SCHOLARSHIPS FOR H.S. SENIORS)
7720 E BELLEVIEW AVE; BLDG 46B
ENGLEWOOD CO 80111
303/773-2877
AMOUNT: $750
DEADLINE(S): MAR 1
FIELD(S): ACCOUNTING
COLORADO RESIDENTS. OPEN TO HIGH SCHOOL SENIORS WITH AT LEAST 3.75 GPA WHO INTEND TO MAJOR IN ACCOUNTING AT COLORADO COLLEGES & UNIVERSITIES WHICH OFFER AN ACCREDITED ACCOUNTING MAJOR.
FINANCIAL NEED IS A CONSIDERATION. WRITE FOR COMPLETE INFORMATION.

22

COLORADO SOCIETY OF CPA'S (EDUCATIONAL FOUNDATION SCHOLARSHIPS FOR UNDERGRADUATES)
7720 E BELLEVIEW AVE; BLDG 46B
ENGLEWOOD CO 80111
303/773-2877
AMOUNT: $500/SEMESTER
DEADLINE(S): JUN 1; NOV 30
FIELD(S): ACCOUNTING
OPEN TO UNDERGRADUATES WHO HAVE COMPLETED AT LEAST THEIR 1ST YEAR; HAVE 3.0 OR BETTER GPA & ARE MAJORING IN ACCOUNTING AT ONE OF THE 13 COLORADO COLLEGES & UNIVERSITIES WHICH OFFER ACCREDITED ACCOUNTING MAJORS.
SCHOLARSHIPS ARE AWARDED EACH SEMESTER & ARE RENEWABLE WITH RE-APPLICATION. FINANCIAL NEED IS A CONSIDERATION. WRITE FOR COMPLETE INFORMATION.

23

DAUGHTERS OF THE AMERICAN REVOLUTION (ENID HALL GRISWOLD MEMORIAL SCHOLARSHIP PROGRAM)
OFFICE OF THE COMMITTEES; 1776 'D' ST NW
WASHINGTON DC 20006
202/879-3292
AMOUNT: $1000
DEADLINE(S): FEB 15
FIELD(S): HISTORY; POLITICAL SCIENCE; GOVERNMENT; ECONOMICS
OPEN TO UNDERGRADUATE JUNIORS & SENIORS ATTENDING AN ACCREDITED COLLEGE OR UNIVERSITY IN THE USA. AWARDS ARE JUDGED ON THE BASIS OF ACADEMIC EXCELLENCE AND FINANCIAL NEED. USA CITIZEN.
DAR AFFILIATION IS NOT REQUIRED BUT APPLICANTS MUST BE SPONSORED BY A LOCAL DAR CHAPTER. NOT RENEWABLE. WRITE FOR COMPLETE INFORMATION. SEND SELF-ADDRESSED STAMPED ENVELOPE.

24

DECA (HARRY A. APPLEGATE SCHOLARSHIPS)
1908 ASSOCIATION DRIVE
RESTON VA 22091
703/860-5000
AMOUNT: VARIES
DEADLINE(S): MAR 1
FIELD(S): MARKETING
OPEN TO HIGH SCHOOL SENIORS OR GRADUATES WHO ARE MEMBERS OF DECA. SCHOLARSHIPS ARE FOR UNDERGRADUATE STUDY AT ACCREDITED COLLEGES OR UNIVERSITIES. USA CITIZEN.
SCHOLARSHIPS ARE RENEWABLE. WRITE FOR COMPLETE INFORMATION.

25

DEVRY INC (SCHOLARSHIP PROGRAM)
ONE TOWER LANE
OAKBROOK TERRACE IL 60181
708/571-7700; 800/323-4256
AMOUNT: FULL TUITION (40); 1/2 TUITION (80)
DEADLINE(S): MAR 22
FIELD(S): ELECTRONICS ENGINEERING TECHNOLOGY; COMPUTER INFORMATION SYSTEMS; BUSINESS OPERATIONS; TELECOMMUNICATIONS MANAGEMENT; ACCOUNTING
40 FULL-TUITION & 80 1/2 TUITION UNDERGRADUATE SCHOLARSHIPS. OPEN TO USA HIGH SCHOOL GRADUATES WHO WISH TO ENROLL IN A FULLY ACCREDITED BACHELOR OF SCIENCE DEGREE PROGRAM AT ONE OF THE DEVRY INSTITUTES LOCATED THROUGHOUT NORTH AMERICA.
AWARDS RENEWABLE PROVIDED 2.5 GPA IS MAINTAINED. CONTACT YOUR GUIDANCE COUNSELOR; NEAREST DEVRY INSTITUTE OR ADDRESS ABOVE FOR COMPLETE INFORMATION.

26

EAA AVIATION FOUNDATION (SCHOLARSHIP PROGRAM)

WHITMAN REGIONAL AIRPORT; PO BOX 3065
OSHKOSH WI 54903
414/426-4888

AMOUNT: $200 TO $1500
DEADLINE(S): APR 1
FIELD(S): AVIATION

TEN DIFFERENT SCHOLARSHIP PROGRAMS OPEN TO WELL ROUNDED INDIVIDUALS INVOLVED IN SCHOOL AND COMMUNITY ACTIVITIES AS WELL AS AVIATION. APPLICANTS' ACADEMIC RECORDS SHOULD VERIFY THEIR ABILITY TO COMPLETE THEIR EDUCATIONAL PROGRAM.

FINANCIAL NEED IS A CONSIDERATION. WRITE FOR COMPLETE INFORMATION.

27

EMPIRE COLLEGE (DEAN'S SCHOLARSHIP)

3033 CLEVELAND
SANTA ROSA CA 95403
707/546-4000

AMOUNT: $250 - $1500
DEADLINE(S): APR 15
FIELD(S): COURT REPORTING; ACCOUNTING; SECRETARIAL; LEGAL; MEDICAL (CLINICAL & ADMINISTRATIVE); TRAVEL & TOURISM; GENERAL BUSINESS

OPEN TO HIGH SCHOOL SENIORS WHO MEET ADMISSION REQUIREMENTS AND WANT TO ATTEND EMPIRE COLLEGE IN SANTA ROSA CALIF. USA CITIZENSHIP REQUIRED.

TEN SCHOLARSHIPS PER YEAR. CONTACT MS. MARLENE MARELLO - HIGH SCHOOL DIRECTOR - FOR COMPLETE INFORMATION.

28

FIRST INTERSTATE BANK OF WASHINGTON (SCHOLARSHIP PROGRAM)

PO BOX 160; MS 803
SEATTLE WA 98111
206/292-3482

AMOUNT: $1000 - $1500
DEADLINE(S): ESTABLISHED BY INSTITUTIONS MAKING AWARDS
FIELD(S): BUSINESS; FINANCE; ECONOMICS

OPEN TO WASHINGTON STATE RESIDENTS WHO ARE ENTERING SPECIFIED COLLEGES IN WASHINGTON STATE AS FRESHMEN. MUST EXHIBIT NEED FOR FINANCIAL AID AND DEMONSTRATE ACADEMIC OR EXTRACURRICULAR ACHIEVEMENT IN BUSINESS; FINANCE OR ECONOMICS.

APPLY DIRECTLY TO FINANCIAL AID OFFICE OF COLLEGE OR UNIVERSITY.

29

FUND FOR AMERICAN STUDIES (INSTITUTES ON POLITICAL JOURNALISM; BUSINESS & GOVERNMENT AFFAIRS & COMPARATIVE POLITICAL & ECONOMIC SYSTEMS)

1526 18TH ST NW
WASHINGTON DC 20036
202/986-0384

AMOUNT: UP TO $3500
DEADLINE(S): JAN 11 EARLY DECISION; MAR 15 GENERAL APPLICATION DEADLINE
FIELD(S): POLITICAL SCIENCE; ECONOMICS; JOURNALISM; BUSINESS ADMINISTRATION

SCHOLARSHIPS COVER COST TO ATTEND ANNUAL 6-WEEK SUMMER INSTITUTE AT GEORGETOWN UNIV. COURSES ARE WORTH 6 CREDITS & INCLUDE FOREIGN POLICY LECTURES; MEDIA DIALOGUE SERIES; SITE BRIEFINGS & CAREER DAYS. OPEN TO COLLEGE SOPHOMORES & JUNIORS.

APPROX 100 AWARDS PER YEAR. FOR FUND'S PROGRAMS ONLY. WRITE FOR COMPLETE INFORMATION.

30

GLENN CARRINGTON FOUNDATION (ALASKA SCHOLARSHIP TO BENEFIT NATIVE ALASKANS)

927 LARKSPUR RD
OAKLAND CA 94610
510/763-9762

AMOUNT: UP TO $2000
DEADLINE(S): MAR 1
FIELD(S): BUSINESS; EDUCATION; ENVIRONMENT; POLITICAL SCIENCE; COMMUNICATIONS

OPEN TO ALASKA RESIDENTS COMMITTED TO HELPING NATIVE ALASKANS GOVERN; EDUCATE; DEVELOP BUSINESSES AND IMPROVE THEIR MANAGEMENT ABILITIES. MUST DEMONSTRATE PERSONAL AND FAMILY FINANCIAL NEED.

WRITE FOR COMPLETE INFORMATION.

31

GOLDEN GATE RESTAURANT ASSOCIATION (DAVID RUBENSTEIN MEMORIAL SCHOLARSHIP FOUNDATION AWARDS)
291 GEARY ST; SUITE 600
SAN FRANCISCO CA 94102
415/781-5348
AMOUNT: $1000 - $1500
DEADLINE(S): MAR 31
FIELD(S): HOTEL & RESTAURANT MANAGEMENT/FOOD SCIENCE
OPEN TO STUDENTS WHO HAVE COMPLETED THE FIRST SEMESTER OF COLLEGE AS A FOODSERVICE MAJOR AND HAVE A 2.75 OR BETTER GPA (4.0 SCALE) IN HOTEL & RESTAURANT COURSES.
SEVEN AWARDS PER YEAR. WRITE FOR COMPLETE INFORMATION.

32

GOLDEN STATE MINORITY FOUNDATION (MINORITY FOUNDATION SCHOLARSHIP)
1999 W ADAMS BLVD
LOS ANGELES CA 90018
213/731-7771
AMOUNT: UP TO $2000
DEADLINE(S): QUARTERLY
FIELD(S): BUSINESS ADMINISTRATION
OPEN TO MINORITY CALIFORNIA RESIDENTS WHO ATTEND CALIFORNIA COLLEGES & UNIVERSITIES. AWARDS SUPPORT STUDY AT THE UNDERGRADUATE JUNIOR/SENIOR OR GRADUATE LEVELS. MAINTAIN GPA OF 3.0 OR BETTER. USA CITIZEN OR LEGAL RESIDENT.
MAY NOT WORK MORE THAN 25 HOURS A WEEK. INCOME MUST BE INSUFFICIENT TO COVER EXPENSES. APPROX 75 AWARDS PER YEAR. WRITE FOR COMPLETE INFORMATION.

33

GRIFFITH FOUNDATION FOR INSURANCE EDUCATION (GAMMA IOTA SIGMA SCHOLARSHIPS)
941 CHATHAM LANE - SUITE 210
COLUMBUS OH 43221
614/442-8357
AMOUNT: $500
DEADLINE(S): NONE
FIELD(S): INSURANCE; RISK MANAGEMENT; ACTUARIAL SCIENCE
OPEN TO UNDERGRADUATES AT UNIVERSITIES WITH CHAPTERS OF GAMMA IOTA SIGMA INSURANCE FRATERNITY WHO ARE MEMBERS OF THE GAMA IOTA SIGMA CHAPTER.
APPLICATION MUST BE MADE THROUGH FACULTY ADVISOR.

34

HILLSDALE COLLEGE (FREEDOM AS VOCATION SCHOLARSHIP)
33 E COLLEGE ST
HILLSDALE MI 49242
517/437-7341
AMOUNT: VARIES
DEADLINE(S): NONE SPECIFIED
FIELD(S): BUSINESS; HISTORY; POLITICAL SCIENCE & ECONOMICS
OPEN TO HILLSDALE COLLEGE UNDERGRADUATES WHO MAINTAIN A 3.0 OR BETTER (4.0 SCALE) GPA AND COMMIT TO A SERIES OF COURSES IN THE ABOVE FIELDS. STUDENT MUST RANK IN TOP 20% OF CLASS AND TOP 10% OF TEST SCORES.
STUDENTS MUST POSSESS EXCELLENT COMMUNICATIONS AND PUBLIC SPEAKING SKILLS; LEADERSHIP SKILLS AND DEMONSTRATE OUTSTANDING CHARACTER AND CITIZENSHIP. WRITE FOR COMPLETE INFORMATION.

35

HOTEL EMPLOYEES & RESTAURANT EMPLOYEES INTERNATIONAL UNION (ED. S. MILLER SCHOLARSHIP)
1219 28TH STREET NW
WASHINGTON DC 20007
202/393-4373
AMOUNT: $3500
DEADLINE(S): FEB 28
FIELD(S): INDUSTRIAL & LABOR RELATIONS
OPEN TO H.E.R.E. UNION MEMBERS; THEIR WARDS; CHILDREN & GRANDCHILDREN. MUST HAVE BEEN UNION MEMBER AT LEAST 1 YEAR PRIOR TO NOV 1 OF THE APPLICATION YEAR. APPLICATION REQUESTS ARE IN OCT NOV & DEC EDITIONS OF "CATERING INDUSTRY EMPLOYEE."
CANDIDATES LIVING EAST OF THE MISSISSIPPI APPLY IN ODD NUMBERED YEARS & ATTEND CORNELL. THOSE WEST OF THE MISSISSIPPI APPLY IN EVEN NUMBERED YEARS & ATTEND UCLA. RENEWABLE. WRITE FOR COMPLETE INFORMATION.

36

INDEPENDENT ACCOUNTANTS INTERNATIONAL EDUCATIONAL FOUNDATION INC (ROBERT KAUFMAN MEMORIAL SCHOLARSHIP AWARD)
9200 S. DADELAND BLVD; SUITE 510
MIAMI FL 33156
305/661-3580
AMOUNT: $250 - $5000
DEADLINE(S): FEB 28
FIELD(S): ACCOUNTING
OPEN TO STUDENTS WHO ARE PURSUING OR PLANNING TO PURSUE AN EDUCATION IN ACCOUNTING AT RECOGNIZED ACADEMIC INSTITUTIONS THROUGHOUT THE WORLD. MUST DEMONSTRATE FINANCIAL NEED FOR LARGER SUMS; NOT REQUIRED FOR $250 HONORARY TEXTBOOK AWARD.
UP TO 20 SCHOLARSHIPS PER YEAR. WRITE FOR COMPLETE INFORMATION.

37

INTERNATIONAL ASSOCIATION OF FIRE CHIEFS FOUNDATION (SCHOLARSHIP PROGRAM)
1329 18TH STREET NW
WASHINGTON DC 20036
202-833-3420
AMOUNT: $250
DEADLINE(S): AUG 15
FIELD(S): BUSINESS & URBAN ADMINISTRATION; ENGINEERING; FIRE SCIENCE
OPEN TO MEMBERS OF A FIRE SERVICE OF A STATE; COUNTY; PROVINCIAL; MUNICIPAL; COMMUNITY; INDUSTRIAL OR FEDERAL FIRE DEPARTMENT.
18 SCHOLARSHIPS PER YEAR. RENEWABLE. WRITE FOR COMPLETE DETAILS.

38

KARLA SCHERER FOUNDATION (SCHOLARSHIPS)
400 RENAISSANCE CENTER; SUITE 500
DETROIT MI 48243
313/259-4520
AMOUNT: VARIES
DEADLINE(S): NONE
FIELD(S): FINANCE; ECONOMICS
OPEN TO WOMEN WHO PLAN TO PURSUE CAREERS IN FINANCE AND/OR ECONOMICS. SEND LETTER STATING WHAT SCHOOL YOU ATTEND OR PLAN TO ATTEND; THE COURSES YOU PLAN TO TAKE AND HOW YOU WILL USE YOUR EDUCATION IN YOUR CHOSEN CAREER.
SCHOLARSHIPS ARE FOR UNDERGRADUATE OR GRADUATE STUDY AND ARE RENEWABLE. INFORMATION DESCRIBED ABOVE SHOULD ACCOMPANY REQUEST FOR APPLICATION PACKAGE.

39

MARYLAND ASSOCIATION OF CERTIFIED PUBLIC ACCOUNTANTS (SCHOLARSHIP PROGRAM)
PO BOX 4417
LUTHERVILLE MD 21094
410/296-6250; 800/782-2036
AMOUNT: $1000 PER YEAR
DEADLINE(S): APR 15
FIELD(S): ACCOUNTING
OPEN TO MARYLAND RESIDENTS WHO ARE IN THEIR JUNIOR OR SENIOR YEAR AT MARYLAND COLLEGES OR UNIVERSITIES AND ARE ACCOUNTING MAJORS. A CUMULATIVE 3.0 OR BETTER GPA (4.0 SCALE) IS REQUIRED. MUST DEMONSTRATE FINANCIAL NEED.
WRITE FOR COMPLETE INFORMATION.

40

MOONEY AIRCRAFT PILOTS ASSOCIATION SAFETY FOUNDATION (AL AND ART MOONEY SCHOLARSHIP PROGRAM)
MARK BUNZEL; AVTEX CORP; 2105 S. BASCOM AV #290
CAMPBELL CA 95008
408/245-2374
AMOUNT: $1000
DEADLINE(S): JUL 1
FIELD(S): AVIATION (FLIGHT SAFETY)
OPEN TO STUDENTS HAVING A CAREER OBJECTIVE WHICH WOULD PROMOTE FLIGHT SAFETY WHO HAVE COMPLETED HALF OF THEIR COURSE OF STUDY. MUST BE A MEMBER OF MAPA OR BE SPONSORED BY A MEMBER. ESSAY ON HOW CAREER WILL PROMOTE FLIGHT SAFETY IS REQUIRED.
CANDIDATES SHOULD HAVE 3.0 OR BETTER GPA. CONTACT DENNIS MCGUIRE AT ABOVE ADDRESS FOR APPLICATION FORM AND COMPLETE INFORMATION.

41

NATIONAL ASSOCIATION OF PLUMBING-HEATING-COOLING CONTRACTORS EDUCATIONAL FOUNDATION (NAPHCC SCHOLARSHIP PROGRAM)
PO BOX 6808
FALLS CHURCH VA 22046
703/237-8100
AMOUNT: $2500
DEADLINE(S): APR 1
FIELD(S): PLUMBING; HEATING; COOLING; CONSTRUCTION; BUSINESS ADMINISTRATION

SCHOLARSHIPS ARE AVAILABLE TO HIGH SCHOOL SENIORS AND INCOMING FRESHMEN WHO ARE ENROLLED IN BA PROGRAMS. STUDENTS MUST HAVE A SPONSOR WHO HAS BEEN A MEMBER IN GOOD STANDING IN THE NAPHCC FOR AT LEAST TWO YEARS. USA CITIZEN.

SCHOLARSHIPS RENEWABLE. WRITE FOR COMPLETE INFORMATION.

42

NATIONAL ASSOCIATION OF WATER COMPANIES - NEW JERSEY CHAPTER (SCHOLARSHIP)
C/O NJ-AMERICAN WATER CO - EASTERN DIV 661 SHREWSBURY AVE
SHREWSBURY NJ 07702
908/842-6900; FAX 908/842-7541
AMOUNT: $2500
DEADLINE(S): APR 1 (POSTMARK)
FIELD(S): BUSINESS ADMINISTRATION; BIOLOGY; CHEMISTRY; ENGINEERING

OPEN TO USA CITIZENS WHO HAVE LIVED IN NJ AT LEAST 5 YEARS AND PLAN A CAREER IN THE INVESTOR-OWNED WATER UTILITY INDUSTRY IN DISCIPLINES SUCH AS THOSE ABOVE. MUST BE UNDERGRAD OR GRADUATE STUDENT IN A 2 OR 4 YEAR NJ COLLEGE OR UNIVERSITY.

GPA OF 3.0 OR BETTER REQUIRED. WRITE FOR COMPLETE INFORMATION.

43

NATIONAL CUSTOMS BROKERS & FORWARDERS ASSN OF AMERICA INC (NCBFAA SCHOLARSHIP)
ONE WORLD TRADE CENTER; SUITE 1153
NEW YORK NY 10048
212/432-0050
AMOUNT: $5000
DEADLINE(S): FEB 1
FIELD(S): INTERNATIONAL BUSINESS - CUSTOMS BROKERAGE OR FREIGHT FORWARDING

OPEN TO FAMILY MEMBERS AND EMPLOYEES OF REGULAR NCBFAA MEMBERS WHO ARE INTERESTED IN A CAREER IN CUSTOMS BROKERAGE OR FREIGHT FORWARDING. APPLICANTS MUST HAVE A 2.0 OR BETTER GPA AND SUBMIT A 1000 TO 1500 WORD ESSAY.

WRITE FOR COMPLETE INFORMATION.

44

NATIONAL DEFENSE TRANSPORTATION ASSOCIATION - SAN FRANCISCO BAY AREA CHAPTER (NDTA SCHOLARSHIP)
PO BOX 24676
OAKLAND CA 94623
WRITTEN INQUIRY
AMOUNT: $1000
DEADLINE(S): MAY 1
FIELD(S): TRANSPORTATION

OPEN TO USA CITIZENS STUDYING IN THE FIELD OF BUSINESS; ENGINEERING; PLANNING OR ENVIRONMENT IN PREPARATION FOR A CAREER RELATED TO TRANSPORTATION. FINANCIAL NEED WILL BE CONSIDERED.

WRITE FOR COMPLETE INFORMATION.

45

NATIONAL ELECTRONIC DISTRIBUTOR ASSOCIATION EDUCATION FOUNDATION (NEDA SCHOLARSHIPS)
35 E WACKER DR; SUITE 3202
CHICAGO IL 60601
312/558-9114
AMOUNT: $1000
DEADLINE(S): JUN 15
FIELD(S): INDUSTRIAL DISTRIBUTION; BUSINESS ADMINISTRATION; MARKETING

OPEN TO FULL-TIME UNDERGRADUATE STUDENTS MAJORING IN A DISCIPLINE RELATED TO ELECTRONIC DISTRIBUTION SUCH AS THE ABOVE AREAS. AWARDS TENABLE AT RECOGNIZED COLLEGES & UNIVERSITIES IN THE USA. USA CITIZEN.

20-25 AWARDS PER YEAR. RENEWABLE UP TO 4 YEARS. WRITE FOR COMPLETE INFORMATION.

46

NATIONAL ITALIAN AMERICAN FOUNDATION (A.P. GIANNINI SCHOLARSHIP)

DR. M. LOMBARDO; EDUCATION DIRECTOR; 666 11TH ST. NW; SUITE 800
WASHINGTON DC 20001
202/638-2137
AMOUNT: $1000
DEADLINE(S): LL03-92
FIELD(S): BANKING; INTERNATIONAL FINANCE
OPEN TO UNDERGRADUATE OR GRADUATE STUDENTS OF ITALIAN HERITAGE WHO ARE MAJORING IN BANKING OR INTERNATIONAL FINANCE. MUST SUBMIT EVIDENCE OF FINANCIAL NEED AND ESSAY (TYPED; 1 PAGE MAXIMUM) DESCRIBING ITALIAN BACKGROUND.
WRITE FOR COMPLETE INFORMATION.

47

NATIONAL ITALIAN AMERICAN FOUNDATION (STELLA SCHOLARSHIP)

DR. M. LOMBARDO; EDUCATION DIRECTOR; 666 11TH ST NW; SUITE 800
WASHINGTON DC 20001
202/638-2137
AMOUNT: $1000
DEADLINE(S): MAY 31
FIELD(S): BUSINESS
OPEN TO UNDERGRADUATE OR GRADUATE BUSINESS MAJORS OF ITALIAN HERITAGE. APPLICATION REQUIRES EVIDENCE OF FINANCIAL NEED AND AN ESSAY (1 TYPED PAGE MAXIMUM) DESCRIBING APPLICANT'S ITALIAN BACKGROUND.
WRITE FOR COMPLETE INFORMATION.

48

NATIONAL SOCIETY OF PUBLIC ACCOUNTANTS SCHOLARSHIP FOUNDATION (SCHOLARSHIPS)

1010 NORTH FAIRFAX ST
ALEXANDRIA VA 22314
703/549-6400; FAX 703/549-2984
AMOUNT: $500 - $1000
DEADLINE(S): MAR 10
FIELD(S): ACCOUNTING
OPEN TO FULL TIME ACCOUNTING STUDENTS IN THEIR 2ND, 3RD OR 4TH YEAR IN AN ACCREDITED TWO OR FOUR YEAR COLLEGE IN THE USA. MUST MAINTAIN AN OVERALL GRADE POINT AVERAGE OF 3.0 (4.0 SCALE).
APPROX 22 AWARDS PER YEAR. SELECTION BASED ON ACADEMIC ATTAINMENT; LEADERSHIP ABILITY AND FINANCIAL NEED. WRITE FOR COMPLETE INFORMATION.

49

NATIONAL URBAN LEAGUE INC (NUL-KRAFT SCHOLARSHIP/INTERN PROGRAM FOR MINORITY STUDENTS)

500 EAST 62ND ST; 10TH FLOOR; DIRECTOR OF EDUCATION
NEW YORK NY 10021
212-310-9000
AMOUNT: $1000-5000 PER YEAR
DEADLINE(S): MAR 28
FIELD(S): ENGINEERING/SALES/MARKETING/MANUFACTURING OPERATIONS/FINANCE/BUSINESS ADMINISTRATION
OPEN TO MINORITY UNDERGRADUATE STUDENTS AT ACCREDITED INSTITUTIONS WHO ARE IN TOP 25% OF THEIR CLASS & WILL BE ENTERING THEIR 3RD OR JUNIOR YEAR AT THE TIME THE AWARD COMMENCES. US CITIZEN OR LEGAL RESIDENT.
10 AWARDS PER YEAR. WRITE FOR COMPLETE INFORMATION.

50

NELLIE MARTIN CARMAN SCHOLARSHIP TRUST (SCHOLARSHIPS)

1121 244TH ST; SW #65
BOTHELL WA 98021
206/486-6575
AMOUNT: UP TO $1000
DEADLINE(S): MAR 15
FIELD(S): ALL FIELDS OF STUDY EXCEPT THOSE NOTED BELOW
OPEN TO SENIORS IN KING; PIERCE & SNOHOMISH COUNTY (WA) HIGH SCHOOLS WHO HAVE LIVED IN WASHINGTON AT LEAST 5 YRS. FOR UNDERGRADUATE STUDY IN WASHINGTON IN ALL FIELDS EXCEPT MUSIC; SCULPTURE; DRAWING; INTERIOR DESIGN & HOME ECONOMICS.
APPLICATIONS AVAILABLE ONLY THROUGH HIGH SCHOOLS. NOMINATION BY HS COUNSELOR IS REQUIRED. AWARDS ARE RENEWABLE. USA CITIZEN.

51

NEW YORK CITY DEPT. OF PERSONNEL (GOVERNMENT SCHOLARS INTERNSHIP PROGRAM)
2 WASHINGTON ST. 15TH FLOOR
NEW YORK NY 10004
212/487-5698
AMOUNT: $2500
DEADLINE(S): JAN 27
FIELD(S): PUBLIC ADMINISTRATION; URBAN PLANNING; GOVERNMENT; PUBLIC SERVICE; URBAN AFFAIRS
10-WEEK SUMMER INTERN PROGRAM OPEN TO UNDERGRADUATE SOPHOMORES; JUNIORS & SENIORS. PROGRAM PROVIDES STUDENTS WITH UNIQUE OPPORTUNITY TO LEARN ABOUT NY CITY GOVERNMENT. INTERNSHIPS AVAILABLE IN VIRTUALLY EVERY CITY AGENCY & MAYORAL OFFICE.
WRITE FOR COMPLETE INFORMATION.

52

NEW YORK CITY DEPT. OF PERSONNEL (URBAN FELLOWS PROGRAM)
2 WASHINGTON ST.; 15TH FLOOR
NEW YORK NY 10004
212/487-5698
AMOUNT: $17000 STIPEND
DEADLINE(S): JAN 26
FIELD(S): PUBLIC ADMINISTRATION; URBAN PLANNING; GOVERNMENT; PUBLIC SERVICE; URBAN AFFAIRS
FELLOWSHIP PROGRAM PROVIDES ONE ACADEMIC YEAR (9 MONTHS) OF FULL-TIME WORK EXPERIENCE IN URBAN GOVERNMENT. OPEN TO GRADUATING COLLEGE SENIORS AND RECENT COLLEGE GRADUATES. USA CITIZEN.
WRITE FOR COMPLETE INFORMATION.

53

NORTHERN VIRGINIA BOARD OF REALTORS INC (EBNER R. DUNCUN SCHOLARSHIP PROGRAM)
8411 ARLINGTON BLVD
FAIRFAX VA 22116
703/207-3200
AMOUNT: $500 - $1000
DEADLINE(S): APR 30
FIELD(S): REAL ESTATE
FOR NORTHERN VIRGINIA RESIDENTS ONLY. PURPOSE OF THIS PROGRAM IS TO RECOGNIZE & ENCOURAGE THOSE SERIOUS STUDENTS WITH POTENTIAL FOR PROFESSIONAL DEVELOPMENT & CONTRIBUTIONS TO THE REAL ESTATE COMMUNITY TO CONTINUE THEIR COLLEGE EDUCATION.
AWARDS SUPPORT UNDERGRADUATE OR GRADUATE STUDY AT RECOGNIZED COLLEGES & UNIVERSITIES IN NORTHERN VIRGINIA. WRITE FOR COMPLETE INFORMATION.

54

OREGON AFL-CIO (SCHOLARSHIP CONTEST)
AMY KLARE; 1900 HINES ST SE
SALEM OR 97302
503/585-6320
AMOUNT: $3000; $1000; $750; $600
DEADLINE(S): FEB 15
FIELD(S): LABOR STUDIES
OPEN TO GRADUATING SENIORS FROM ANY ACCREDITED HIGH SCHOOL IN OREGON FOR UNDERGRADUATE STUDY AT ANY ACCREDITED USA COLLEGE OR UNIVERSITY OR AT AN OREGON COMMUNITY COLLEGE OR TRADE SCHOOL.
CANDIDATES MUST TAKE A WRITTEN EXAM ON LABOR HISTORY AND LABOR ISSUES. FINALISTS WILL BE CHOSEN ON EXAM SCORE; FINANCIAL NEED AND HIGH SCHOOL GPA. WRITE FOR COMPLETE INFORMATION.

55

PACIFIC GAS & ELECTRIC CO. (SCHOLARSHIPS FOR HIGH SCHOOL SENIORS)
77 BEALE ST; ROOM 2837
SAN FRANCISCO CA 94106
415/973-1338
AMOUNT: $1000 - $4000
DEADLINE(S): NOV 15
FIELD(S): ENGINEERING; COMPUTER SCIENCE; MATHEMATICS; MARKETING; BUSINESS; ECONOMICS
HIGH SCHOOL SENIORS IN GOOD ACADEMIC STANDING WHO RESIDE IN OR ATTEND HIGH SCHOOL IN AREAS SERVED BY PG&E ARE ELIGIBLE TO COMPETE FOR SCHOLARSHIPS AWARDED ON A REGIONAL BASIS. NOT OPEN TO CHILDREN OF PG&E EMPLOYEES.
36 AWARDS PER YEAR. APPLICATIONS & BROCHURES ARE AVAILABLE IN ALL HIGH SCHOOLS WITHIN PG&E'S SERVICE AREA AND AT PG&E OFFICES.

56

REAL ESTATE EDUCATORS ASSN (REEA - HARWOOD SCHOLARSHIP PROGRAM)
111 E WACKER DR; #200
CHICAGO IL 60601
313/616-0800
AMOUNT: $250
DEADLINE(S): DEC 6
FIELD(S): REAL ESTATE
OPEN TO UNDERGRADUATE STUDENTS (WHO HAVE COMPLETED AT LEAST 2 SEMESTERS) & GRADUATE STUDENTS. CRITERIA ARE FULL-TIME STUDY AT ACCREDITED USA SCHOOL; AT LEAST 3.2 GPA & INTENT TO PURSUE CAREER IN REAL ESTATE.
10 SCHOLARSHIPS PER YEAR. WRITE FOR COMPLETE INFORMATION.

57

SACRAMENTO ASSOCIATION OF REALTORS (EUGENE L. WILLIAMS SCHOLARSHIP)
2003 HOWE AVE
SACRAMENTO CA 95825
916/922-7711; FAX 916/922-1221
AMOUNT: $500 - $1000
DEADLINE(S): NONE SPECIFIED; SCHOLARSHIPS AWARDED IN EARLY APRIL
FIELD(S): REAL ESTATE AND RELATED FIELDS
OPEN TO STUDENTS OF NOT LESS THAN SOPHOMORE STANDING AT SACRAMENTO CITY COLLEGE; CSU SACRAMENTO OR AMERICAN RIVER COLLEGE. ALL APPLICANTS ARE INTERVIEWED AND MUST SUBMIT A STATEMENT OF WHY THEY ARE PLANNING A REAL ESTATE CAREER.
WRITE FOR COMPLETE INFORMATION.

58

SAN FRANCISCO BAY AREA CHAPTER - NATIONAL DEFENSE TRANSPORTATION ASSN (NDTA MERIT SCHOLARSHIP)
BOX 24676
OAKLAND CA 94623
WRITTEN INQUIRY
AMOUNT: $2000
DEADLINE(S): MAR 31
FIELD(S): BUSINESS; ENGINEERING; PLANNING; ENVIRONMENT (AS RELATED TO TRANSPORTATION)
OPEN TO USA CITIZENS ENROLLED IN AN ACCREDITED UNDERGRADUATE DEGREE OR VOCATIONAL PROGRAM IN ABOVE FIELDS WHO PLAN TO PURSUE A CAREER RELATED TO TRANSPORTATION. FINANCIAL NEED WILL BE CONSIDERED.
WRITE FOR COMPLETE INFORMATION.

59

SISTERS OF SALISAW FOUNDATION (SCHOLARSHIP)
911 BARTLETT PL
WINDSOR CA 95492
WRITTEN INQUIRY
AMOUNT: $500
DEADLINE(S): AUG 1
FIELD(S): BUSINESS
OPEN TO CHILDREN OF MIGRANT FARM LABORERS RESIDING IN WINDSOR CA WHOSE FAMILY MIGRATED TO CALIFORNIA FROM SALISAW OK DURING THE DUST BOWL ERA OF THE 1930'S. FAMILY MUST HAVE WORKED AT LEAST SIX MONTHS IN THE HERNESTO ONEXIOCA VINEYARDS.
FOR UNDERGRADUATE OR GRADUATE STUDY LEADING TO A DEGREE IN BUSINESS. WRITE FOR COMPLETE INFORMATION.

60

SOCIETY OF ACTUARIES (ACTUARIAL SCHOLARSHIPS FOR MINORITY STUDENTS)
475 N MARTINGALE RD; SUITE 800
SCHAUMBURG IL 60173
708/706-3500
AMOUNT: VARIES
DEADLINE(S): MAY 1
FIELD(S): ACTUARIAL SCIENCE
OPEN TO STUDENTS WHO ARE MEMBERS OF ETHNIC MINORITIES AND ARE ENROLLED OR ACCEPTED IN AN ACTUARIAL SCIENCE PROGRAM AT AN ACCREDITED COLLEGE OR UNIVERSITY. MUST DEMONSTRATE FINANCIAL NEED AND BE A USA CITIZEN OR LEGAL RESIDENT.
AMOUNT VARIES ACCORDING TO STUDENT'S NEED AND CREDENTIALS. APPROXIMATELY 40 AWARDS PER YEAR. WRITE FOR COMPLETE INFORMATION.

61

SOIL AND WATER CONSERVATION SOCIETY OF AMERICA (DONALD A WILLIAMS SCHOLARSHIP)
7515 NORTHEAST ANKENY ROAD
ANKENY IA 50021

515/289-2331; FAX 515/289-1227
AMOUNT: $1200
DEADLINE(S): APR 1
FIELD(S): BUSINESS ADMINISTRATION; CONSERVATION
SCHOLARSHIP OPEN TO SOCIETY MEMBERS WHO ARE CURRENTLY EMPLOYED IN NATURAL RESOURCE RELATED FIELD AND WISH TO RETURN TO SCHOOL TO IMPROVE THEIR TECHNICAL OR ADMINISTRATIVE SKILLS. ATTAINMENT OF DEGREE NOT REQUIRED.
APPLICANTS WHO HAVE NOT RECEIVED A BACHELOR'S DEGREE WILL BE GIVEN PREFERENCE. MUST SHOW REASONABLE FINANCIAL NEED. WRITE FOR COMPLETE INFORMATION.

62

STATE FARM COMPANIES FOUNDATION (EXCEPTIONAL STUDENT FELLOWSHIP)
1 STATE FARM PLAZA
BLOOMINGTON IL 61710
WRITTEN INQUIRY
AMOUNT: $3000
DEADLINE(S): FEB 28
FIELD(S): ACCOUNTING; BUSINESS ADMINISTRATION; ACTUARIAL SCIENCE; COMPUTER SCIENCE; ECONOMICS; FINANCE; INSURANCE; INVESTMENTS; MARKETING; MATHEMATICS; STATISTICS
OPEN TO CURRENT FULL TIME COLLEGE JUNIORS AND SENIORS MAJORING IN ANY OF THE FIELDS ABOVE. ONLY STUDENTS NOMINATED BY THE COLLEGE DEAN OR A DEPARTMENT HEAD QUALIFY AS CANDIDATES. APPLICATIONS WITHOUT NOMINATIONS WILL NOT BE CONSIDERED.
USA CITIZEN. GPA OF 3.4 OR BETTER (4.0 SCALE) IS REQUIRED. 50 FELLOWSHIPS PER YEAR. WRITE FOR COMPLETE INFORMATION.

63

STATE FARM COMPANIES FOUNDATION (EXCEPTIONAL STUDENT FELLOWSHIP AWARDS)
ONE STATE FARM PLAZA; SC-3
BLOOMINGTON IL 61710
309/766-2039
AMOUNT: $3000
DEADLINE(S): FEB 15
FIELD(S): BUSINESS RELATED FIELDS; COMPUTER SCIENCE; PRELAW; MATHEMATICS
OPEN TO EXCEPTIONAL CURRENT JUNIOR OR SENIOR UNDERGRADUATES IN THE ABOVE FIELDS. MUST BE NOMINATED BY DEAN OR DEPARTMENT HEAD. US CITIZEN. MUST BE COLLEGE JUNIOR OR SENIOR AT TIME OF APPLICATION.
50 FELLOWSHIPS PER ACADEMIC YEAR. APPLICATIONS AND NOMINATIONS AVAILABLE NOV 1. WRITE FOR COMPLETE INFORMATION.

64

STATLER FOUNDATION (SCHOLARSHIPS)
107 DELAWARE AVE; SUITE 508
BUFFALO NY 14202
716/852-1104
AMOUNT: $500 PER YEAR
DEADLINE(S): APR 15
FIELD(S): FOOD MANAGEMENT; CULINARY ARTS; HOTEL-MOTEL MANAGEMENT
OPEN TO UNDERGRADUATE OR GRADUATE STUDENTS WHO ARE ACCEPTED TO OR ENROLLED FULL TIME AT A USA INSTITUTION IN AN ACCREDITED PROGRAM OF STUDY IN ANY OF THE ABOVE AREAS.
APPROX 900 AWARDS PER YEAR. RENEWABLE. WRITE FOR COMPLETE INFORMATION.

65

TRANSPORTATION CLUBS INTERNATIONAL (CHARLOTTE WOODS MEMORIAL SCHOLARSHIPS)
1275 KAMUS DR; SUITE 101
FOX ISLAND WA 98333
206/549-2251
AMOUNT: $1000
DEADLINE(S): APR 15
FIELD(S): TRANSPORTATION; TRAFFIC MANAGEMENT
OPEN TO TCI MEMBERS & DEPENDENTS WHO ARE IN THEIR SOPHOMORE YEAR AT AN ACCREDITED COLLEGE OR UNIVERSITY. MUST BE ENROLLED IN A PROGRAM IN TRANSPORTATION; TRAFFIC MANAGEMENT OR RELATED AREA & CONSIDERING A CAREER IN TRANSPORTATION.
SEND SELF-ADDRESSED STAMPED (BUSINESS SIZE) ENVELOPE FOR COMPLETE INFORMATION.

66

TRANSPORTATION CLUBS INTERNATIONAL (HOOPER MEMORIAL SCHOLARSHIPS)
1275 KAMUS DR; SUITE 101
FOX ISLAND WA 98333
206/549-2251
AMOUNT: $1000
DEADLINE(S): APR 15
FIELD(S): TRANSPORTATION; TRAFFIC MANAGEMENT
OPEN TO SOPHOMORE STUDENTS ENROLLED IN AN ACCREDITED COLLEGE OR UNIVERSITY IN A DEGREE OR VOCATIONAL PROGRAM IN TRANSPORTATION; TRAFFIC MANAGEMENT OR RELATED AREA & CONSIDERING A CAREER IN TRANSPORTATION.
SEND SELF-ADDRESSED STAMPED ENVELOPE (BUSINESS SIZE) FOR COMPLETE INFORMATION.

67

TRANSPORTATION CLUBS INTERNATIONAL (MEXICO TRAFFIC & TRANSPORTATION SCHOLARSHIPS)
1275 KAMUS DR; SUITE 101
FOX ISLAND WA 98333
206/549-2251
AMOUNT: $500
DEADLINE(S): APR 15
FIELD(S): TRANSPORTATION; TRAFFIC MANAGEMENT
OPEN TO STUDENTS OF MEXICAN NATIONALITY WHO ARE ENROLLED IN A MEXICAN INSTITUTION OF HIGHER LEARNING IN A DEGREE OR VOCATIONAL PROGRAM IN THE ABOVE OR RELATED AREAS.
WRITE FOR COMPLETE INFORMATION.

68

TRANSPORTATION CLUBS INTERNATIONAL (MICHIGAN TRANSPORTATION SCHOLARSHIPS)
1275 KAMUS DR; SUITE 101
FOX ISLAND WA 98332
206/549-2251
AMOUNT: $1000
DEADLINE(S): APR 15
FIELD(S): TRANSPORTATION; TRAFFIC MANAGEMENT
OPEN TO COLLEGE SOPHOMORES WHO HAVE ATTENDED SCHOOL IN MICHIGAN AT ANY LEVEL (EVEN ELEMENTARY) & ARE NOW ENROLLED IN AN ACCREDITED INSTITUTION OF HIGHER LEARNING IN A DEGREE OR VOCATIONAL PROGRAM IN THE ABOVE OR RELATED AREAS.
SEND SELF-ADDRESSED STAMPED ENVELOPE (BUSINESS SIZE) FOR COMPLETE INFORMATION.

69

TRANSPORTATION CLUBS INTERNATIONAL (TEXAS TRAFFIC & TRANSPORTATION SCHOLARSHIPS)
1275 KAMUS DR; SUITE 101
FOX ISLAND WA 98333
206/549-2251
AMOUNT: $1000
DEADLINE(S): APR 15
FIELD(S): TRANSPORTATION; TRAFFIC MANAGEMENT
OPEN TO STUDENTS WHO HAVE GRADUATED FROM A TEXAS HIGH SCHOOL & ARE NOW IN THEIR SOPHOMORE YEAR AT AN ACCREDITED COLLEGE OR UNIVERSITY IN A DEGREE OR VOCATIONAL PROGRAM IN THE ABOVE OR RELATED FIELDS.
SEND SELF-ADDRESSED STAMPED ENVELOPE (BUSINESS SIZE) FOR COMPLETE INFORMATION.

70

TYSON FOUNDATION INC. (SCHOLARSHIP PROGRAM)
2210 OAKLAWN
SPRINGDALE AR 72764
501/756-4955
AMOUNT: UP TO $1000/SEMESTER
DEADLINE(S): JUN 21
FIELD(S): BUSINESS; AGRICULTURE; ENGINEERING; COMPUTER SCIENCE; NURSING
OPEN TO USA CITIZENS WHO LIVE IN THE VICINITY OF TYSON FOOD FACILITIES AND MAINTAIN A 2.5 GPA. MUST WORK AND CARRY AT LEAST 12 SEMESTER HOURS OR EQUIVALENT. FOR UNDERGRADUATE STUDY AT SCHOOLS IN USA.
RECIPIENTS SIGN A PLEDGE EITHER TO REPAY THE SCHOLARSHIP MONEY OR HELP ANOTHER DESERVING STUDENT NOT RELATED BY BLOOD OR MARRIAGE TO ATTEND COLLEGE. WRITE FOR COMPLETE INFORMATION.

71

U.S. DEPT. OF EDUCATION (INDIAN FELLOWSHIP PROGRAM)
400 MARYLAND AVENUE SW; RM 2177; MAIL STOP 6335
WASHINGTON DC 20202
202/401-1902
AMOUNT: $1000 - $34000 (AVERAGE $13000)
DEADLINE(S): FEB 7
FIELD(S): BUSINESS ADMIN; ENGINEERING; NATURAL RESOURCES & RELATED AREAS
FELLOWSHIPS FOR AMERICAN INDIANS OR ALASKAN NATIVES WHO ARE US CITIZENS AND SEEKING UNDERGRADUATE OR GRADUATE DEGREES IN THE ABOVE FIELDS AT ACCREDITED INSTITUTIONS IN USA.
APPROXIMATELY 90 CONTINUATION AND 35 NEW AWARDS PER YEAR. WRITE FOR COMPLETE INFORMATION.

72

WILLIAM RANDOLPH HEARST FOUNDATION (U.S. SENATE YOUTH PROGRAM)
90 NEW MONTGOMERY ST; SUITE 1212
SAN FRANCISCO CA 94105
415/543-4057; FAX 415/243-0760
AMOUNT: $2000 + ALL EXPENSES PAID WEEK IN WASHINGTON DC
DEADLINE(S): NONE SPECIFIED
FIELD(S): US GOVERNMENT; HISTORY; POLITICAL SCIENCE; ECONOMICS
OPEN TO ANY HIGH SCHOOL JUNIOR OR SENIOR WHO IS SERVING AS AN ELECTED STUDENT BODY OFFICER AT A USA HIGH SCHOOL. STUDENT RECEIVES A WEEK'S STAY IN WASHINGTON AS GUEST OF THE SENATE AND A $2000 SCHOLARSHIP.
STUDENT MUST BECOME A CANDIDATE FOR A DEGREE AT AN ACCREDITED USA COLLEGE OR UNIVERSITY WITHIN TWO YEARS OF HIGH SCHOOL GRADUATION. USA PERMANENT RESIDENT. CONTACT HIGH SCHOOL PRINCIPAL FOR COMPLETE INFORMATION.

73

Y'S MEN INTERNATIONAL (U.S. AREA - ALEXANDER SCHOLARSHIP-LOAN FUND)
BILL WARD; AREA SERVICE DIRECTOR; 17909 MANHATTAN PL.
TORRANCE CA 90504
WRITTEN INQUIRY ONLY
AMOUNT: UP TO $1500 PER YEAR
DEADLINE(S): MAY 1; OCT 1
FIELD(S): BUSINESS ADMINISTRATION; YOUTH LEADERSHIP
OPEN TO UNDERGRADUATES. REPAYMENT IS WAIVED FOR THOSE WHO AGREE TO WORK FOR YMCA AFTER GRADUATION FOR AT LEAST A YEAR FOR EACH YEAR OF FUNDING. HISTORY OF PREVIOUS YMCA PARTICIPATION IS HELPFUL. USA CITIZEN OR LEGAL RESIDENT.
12 TO 16 SCHOLARSHIPS PER YEAR. RENEWABLE. WRITE FOR COMPLETE INFORMATION.

74

YOUNG PRINTING EXECUTIVES CLUB (SCHOLARSHIP FUND)
C/O JWP GROUP; 220 E 42ND ST; #402
NEW YORK NY 10017
212/687-8805; FAX 212/687-8826
AMOUNT: $2500 PER YEAR
DEADLINE(S): MAY 15 - JUN 1
FIELD(S): PRINTING MANAGEMENT
OPEN TO RESIDENTS OF NEW YORK; NEW JERSEY & CONNECTICUT WHO ARE ENROLLED AT THE ROCHESTER INSTITUTE OF TECHNOLOGY. APPLICANTS SHOULD HAVE AT LEAST A 3.0 GPA & BE COMMITED TO A CAREER IN THE TRI-STATE AREA.
RENEWABLE UP TO 4 YEARS. WRITE FOR COMPLETE INFORMATION.

EDUCATION

75

ALASKA COMMISSION ON POST-SECONDARY EDUCATION (PAUL DOUGLAS SCHOLARSHIP-LOAN PROGRAM)
BOX 110505
JUNEAU AK 99811
907/465-2962 EXT 106
AMOUNT: $5000 PER YEAR FOR UP TO 4 YEARS
DEADLINE(S): MAY 30
FIELD(S): EDUCATION
ALASKA RESIDENTS. FEDERALLY FUNDED PROGRAM TO ENCOURAGE OUTSTANDING H.S. SENIORS & UNDERGRADUATE STUDENTS TO PURSUE TEACHING CAREERS AT THE ELEMENTARY OR SECONDARY LEVELS.
RECIPIENTS ARE REQUIRED TO TEACH 2 YEARS FOR EACH YEAR OF FUNDING OR 1/2 THAT FOR TEACHING IN A CRITICAL TEACHER SHORTAGE AREA. WRITE FOR COMPLETE INFORMATION.

76

AMERICAN ASSOCIATION OF UNIVERSITY WOMEN (ELEANOR ROOSEVELT TEACHING FELLOWSHIPS)
1111 16TH ST NW
WASHINGTON DC 20036
202/728-7603; FAX 202/872-1430
AMOUNT: $1000 - $10000
DEADLINE(S): JAN 11
FIELD(S): TEACHING
OPEN TO FEMALE PUBLIC SCHOOL TEACHERS IN GRADES K-12 WHO ARE USA CITIZENS OR PERMANENT RESIDENTS AND HAVE DEMONSTRATED THEIR COMMITMENT TO CREATING EDUCATIONAL EQUITY FOR GIRLS.
MUST HAVE AT LEAST FIVE CONSECUTIVE YEARS OF FULL TIME TEACHING EXPERIENCE AND INTEND TO RETURN TO THE CLASSROOM AFTER THE FELLOWSHIP. WRITE FOR COMPLETE INFORMATION.

77

AMERICAN FOUNDATION FOR THE BLIND (DELTA GAMMA FOUNDATION FLORENCE HARVEY MEMORIAL SCHOLARSHIP)
15 WEST 16TH ST
NEW YORK NY 10011
212/620-2000; TDD 212/620-2158
AMOUNT: $1000
DEADLINE(S): APR 1
FIELD(S): REHABILITATION AND/OR EDUCATION OF THE VISUALLY IMPAIRED AND BLIND
OPEN TO LEGALLY BLIND UNDERGRADUATE AND GRADUATE COLLEGE STUDENTS OF GOOD CHARACTER WHO HAVE EXHIBITED ACADEMIC EXCELLENCE AND ARE STUDYING IN THE FIELD OF EDUCATION AND/OR REHABILITATION OF THE VISUALLY IMPAIRED AND BLIND.
MUST BE USA CITIZEN. WRITE FOR COMPLETE INFORMATION.

78

AMERICAN FOUNDATION FOR THE BLIND (RUDOLPH DILLMAN MEMORIAL SCHOLARSHIP)
15 WEST 16TH ST
NEW YORK NY 10011
212/620-2000; TDD 212/620-2158
AMOUNT: $2500
DEADLINE(S): APR 1
FIELD(S): REHABILITATION; EDUCATION OF BLIND & VISUALLY IMPAIRED
OPEN TO LEGALLY BLIND UNDERGRADUATE OR GRADUATE STUDENTS ACCEPTED TO OR ENROLLED IN AN ACCREDITED PROGRAM WITHIN THE BROAD AREAS OF REHABILITATION AND/OR EDUCATION OF THE BLIND AND VISUALLY IMPAIRED. USA CITIZEN.
THREE AWARDS PER YEAR. WRITE FOR COMPLETE INFORMATION.

79

AMERICAN FOUNDATION FOR THE BLIND (TELESENSORY SCHOLARSHIP)
15 WEST 16TH ST
NEW YORK NY 10011
212/620-2000; TDD 212/620-2158
AMOUNT: $1000
DEADLINE(S): APR 1
FIELD(S): REHABILITATION; EDUCATION OF BLIND & VISUALLY IMPAIRED
OPEN TO LEGALLY BLIND UNDERGRADUATE & GRADUATE STUDENTS ACCEPTED TO OR ENROLLED IN AN ACCREDITED PROGRAM WITHIN THE BROAD AREAS OF REHABILITATION AND/OR EDUCATION OF THE BLIND AND VISUALLY IMPAIRED. USA CITIZEN.
WRITE FOR COMPLETE INFORMATION.

80

BOY SCOUTS OF AMERICA-DR. HARRY BRITENSTOOL SCHOLARSHIP COMMITTEE (GREATER NEW YORK CITY COUNCILS' SCHOLARSHIPS)
345 HUDSON STREET
NEW YORK NY 10014
212/242-1100
AMOUNT: VARIES
DEADLINE(S): JUN 1
FIELD(S): YOUTH LEADERSHIP
UNDERGRADUATE SCHOLARSHIPS OPEN TO STUDENTS WHO HAVE BEEN NYC BOY SCOUT OR EXPLORER SCOUT FOR AT LEAST LAST 2 YEARS. SHOW ACADEMIC EXCELLENCE; FINANCIAL NEED; SERVICE TO GREATER NYC COUNCILS AND STRONG SCOUTING HISTORY. USA CITIZEN.
WRITE FOR COMPLETE INFORMATION.

81

BUSINESS AND PROFESSIONAL WOMEN'S FOUNDATION (CAREER ADVANCEMENT SCHOLARSHIPS)
2012 MASSACHUSETTS AVE NW
WASHINGTON DC 20036
202/293-1200
AMOUNT: $500 - $1000
DEADLINE(S): APR 15 POSTMARK (APPS AVAILABLE ONLY OCT 1 - APR 1)
FIELD(S): COMPUTER SCIENCE; EDUCATION; PARALEGAL; ENGINEERING; SCIENCE (EXCEPT HEALTH CARE)
OPEN TO WOMEN (30 OR OLDER) WITHIN 12-24 MONTHS OF COMPLETING UNDERGRAD OR GRAD STUDY IN USA (INCLUDING PUERTO RICO & THE VIRGIN ISLANDS). SHOULD LEAD TO ENTRY OR REENTRY INTO THE WORK FORCE OR IMPROVE CAREER ADVANCEMENT CHANCES.
MUST SHOW FINANCIAL NEED. SEND SELF-ADDRESSED STAMPED ($.52) #10 ENVELOPE FOR APPLICATION & COMPLETE INFORMATION. NOT FOR STUDY AT DOCTORAL LEVEL.

82

CALIFORNIA SCHOOL LEADERSHIP ACADEMY (DR. ROBERT F. ALIOTO SCHOLARSHIP AWARD)
313 W WINTON AVE; SUITE 373
HAYWARD CA 94544
415/887-8808
AMOUNT: $1000
DEADLINE(S): JUN 1
FIELD(S): EDUCATION
OPEN TO A GRADUATING SALINAS (CA) HIGH SCHOOL SENIOR WHO PLANS TO PURSUE A CAREER IN EDUCATION. MUST HAVE 3.0 OR BETTER GPA AND SUBMIT 300 WORD ESSAY ON WHY APPLICANT WANTS TO BECOME A TEACHER.
WRITE FOR COMPLETE INFORMATION.

83

CALIFORNIA STUDENT AID COMMISSION (PAUL DOUGLAS TEACHER SCHOLARSHIP PROGRAM)
PO BOX 510624
SACRAMENTO CA 94245
916/322-2294
AMOUNT: UP TO $5000 PER YEAR FOR UP TO 4 YEARS
DEADLINE(S): JUL 1
FIELD(S): EDUCATION
CALIFORNIA RESIDENT. FEDERALLY FUNDED PROGRAM OPEN TO TOP HIGH SCHOOL SENIORS & COLLEGE STUDENTS WHO DEMONSTRATE COMMITMENT TO PURSUING TEACHING CAREERS. FOR UNDERGRADUATE & TEACHER PREPARATION STUDY AT ELIGIBLE CALIF SCHOOLS.
USA CITIZEN OR ELIGIBLE NON CITIZEN. RECIPIENTS AGREE TO TEACH 2 YEARS FULL TIME (ANYWHERE IN USA) FOR EACH YEAR THE SCHOLARSHIP IS RECEIVED. RENEWABLE. CONTACT COLLEGE COUNSELOR; FINANCIAL AID OFFICE OR ADDRESS ABOVE.

84

CHARLES E. SAAK TRUST (EDUCATIONAL GRANTS)
C/O WELLS FARGO BANK TRUST DEPT; 2222 W. SHAW; #11
FRESNO CA 93711
WRITTEN INQUIRY ONLY
AMOUNT: VARIES
DEADLINE(S): MAR 31
FIELD(S): EDUCATION; MEDICINE
UNDERGRADUATE GRANTS FOR RESIDENTS OF THE PORTERVILLE-POPLAR AREA OF TULARE COUNTY CALIF. MUST CARRY A MINIMUM OF 12 UNITS; HAVE AT LEAST A 2.0 GPA; BE UNDER AGE 21 AND DEMONSTRATE FINANCIAL NEED.
APPROXIMATELY 100 AWARDS PER YEAR; RENEWABLE WITH REAPPLICATION. WRITE FOR COMPLETE INFORMATION.

85

CIVIL AIR PATROL (CAP UNDERGRADUATE SCHOLARSHIPS)
NATIONAL HEADQUARTERS
MAXWELL AFB AL 36112
205/293-5332
AMOUNT: $750
DEADLINE(S): MAR 15
FIELD(S): HUMANITIES; SCIENCE; ENGINEERING; EDUCATION
OPEN TO CAP MEMBERS WHO HAVE RECEIVED THE BILLY MITCHELL AWARD OR THE SENIOR RATING IN LEVEL II OF THE SENIOR TRAINING

PROGRAM. FOR UNDERGRADUATE STUDY IN THE ABOVE AREAS.
WRITE FOR COMPLETE INFORMATION.

86

CIVITAN INTERNATIONAL FOUNDATION (DR. COURTNEY W. SHROPSHIRE GRANT)
PO BOX 130744
BIRMINGHAM AL 35213
205/591-8910
AMOUNT: $1000 - $1500
DEADLINE(S): FEB 20
FIELD(S): FIELDS RELATING TO MENTAL RETARDATION OR OTHER DEVELOPMENTAL DISABILITIES
OPEN TO UNDERGRADUATE JUNIORS & SENIORS & MASTER'S CANDIDATES ENROLLED IN AN ACCREDITED COLLEGE OR UNIVERSITY WHO PLAN A CAREER IN THE DISTINCTIVE AREA ABOVE. MUST AGREE TO UPHOLD CIVITAN IDEALS. INTERVIEW BY CIVITAN MEMBER REQUIRED.
20-40 AWARDS PER YEAR. WRITE FOR COMPLETE INFORMATION. INCLUDE A SELF-ADDRESSED BUSINESS SIZE ENVELOPE WITH POSTAGE SUFFICIENT FOR A 2-OUNCE FIRST CLASS MAILING.

87

EASTER SEAL SOCIETY OF IOWA (SCHOLARSHIPS & AWARDS)
PO BOX 4002
DES MOINES IA 50333
515/289-1933
AMOUNT: $400 - $600
DEADLINE(S): APR 15
FIELD(S): PHYSICAL REHABILITATION; MENTAL REHABILITATION; & RELATED AREAS
OPEN TO IOWA RESIDENTS WHO ARE FULL-TIME UNDERGRADUATE SOPHOMORES; JUNIORS; SENIORS OR GRADUATE STUDENTS AT ACCREDITED INSTITUTIONS; PLANNING A CAREER IN THE BROAD FIELD OF REHABILITATION; FINANCIALLY NEEDY & IN TOP 40% OF THEIR CLASS.
6 SCHOLARSHIPS PER YEAR. RENEWABLE. WRITE FOR COMPLETE INFORMATION.

88

FLORIDA DEPT. OF EDUCATION (CHALLENGER ASTRONAUTS MEMORIAL SCHOLARSHIP PROGRAM)
OFFICE OF STUDENT FINANCIAL ASSISTANCE; KNOTT BLDG
TALLAHASSEE FL 32399
904/488-4095
AMOUNT: $4000 PER YEAR
DEADLINE(S): MAR 1
FIELD(S): LIBERAL ARTS; EDUCATION
FLORIDA RESIDENT FOR AT LEAST 1 YEAR FOR PURPOSES OTHER THAN EDUCATION. OPEN TO FLORIDA HIGH SCHOOL SENIORS WHO PLAN TO COMPLETE AN UNDERGRADUATE DEGREE IN LIBERAL ARTS OR PURSUE A TEACHING CAREER.
MUST BE NOMINATED BY DISTRICT SCHOOL BOARD BASED ON ACTIVITIES; RECOMMENDATIONS AND ESSAY ON 'THE CHALLENGE OF SPACE.' WRITE FOR COMPLETE INFORMATION.

89

FLORIDA DEPT. OF EDUCATION (CRITICAL TEACHER SHORTAGE SCHOLARSHIP LOAN PROGRAM)
OFFICE OF STUDENT FINANCIAL ASSISTANCE; 1344 FLORIDA EDUCATION CENTER
TALLAHASSEE FL 32399
904/487-0049
AMOUNT: $4000 PER YEAR FOR A MAXIMUM OF TWO YEARS
DEADLINE(S): MAR 15 POSTMARK
FIELD(S): TEACHER EDUCATION
FOR FULL-TIME UNDERGRAD JUNIOR OR SENIOR OR GRADUATE STUDENT ENROLLED IN A STATE APPROVED TEACHER EDUCATION PROGRAM IN A FLORIDA INSTITUTION. CANDIDATES SHOULD BE PURSUING A DEGREE IN A DESIGNATED CRITICAL TEACHER SHORTAGE FIELD.
LOAN IS REPAID BY TEACHING IN FLORIDA OR IN CASH. 376 AWARDS PER YEAR. WRITE FOR COMPLETE INFORMATION.

90

FLORIDA DEPT. OF EDUCATION (FLORIDA TEACHER-STUDENT LOAN FORGIVENESS PROGRAM)
OFFICE OF STUDENT FINANCIAL ASSISTANCE; 1344 FLORIDA EDUCATION CENTER

TALLAHASSEE FL 32399
904/487-0049
AMOUNT: SEE BELOW
DEADLINE(S): MAR 1
FIELD(S): TEACHER-FLORIDA CRITICAL SHORTAGE AREA
OPEN TO CERTIFIED FLORIDA PUBLIC SCHOOL TEACHERS. PROGRAM PROVIDES REPAYMENT OF EDUCATION LOANS IN RETURN FOR TEACHING IN DEPT OF ED DESIGNATED CRITICAL TEACHER SHORTAGE AREAS IN FLORIDA PUBLIC SCHOOLS.
UP TO $2500 PER YEAR FOR 4 YEARS FOR TEACHERS WITH UNDERGRADUATE DEGREES; UP TO $5000 PER YEAR FOR UP TO 2 YEARS FOR TEACHERS WITH GRADUATE DEGREES. APPLICATIONS MUST BE SUBMITTED BY JULY 15 AFTER FIRST ACADEMIC YEAR OF TEACHING.

91

GLENN CARRINGTON FOUNDATION (ALASKA SCHOLARSHIP TO BENEFIT NATIVE ALASKANS)
927 LARKSPUR RD
OAKLAND CA 94610
510/763-9762
AMOUNT: UP TO $2000
DEADLINE(S): MAR 1
FIELD(S): BUSINESS; EDUCATION; ENVIRONMENT; POLITICAL SCIENCE; COMMUNICATIONS
OPEN TO ALASKA RESIDENTS COMMITTED TO HELPING NATIVE ALASKANS GOVERN; EDUCATE; DEVELOP BUSINESSES AND IMPROVE THEIR MANAGEMENT ABILITIES. MUST DEMONSTRATE PERSONAL AND FAMILY FINANCIAL NEED.
WRITE FOR COMPLETE INFORMATION.

92

ILLINOIS CONGRESS OF PARENTS AND TEACHERS (LILLIAN E. GLOVER ILLINOIS PTA SCHOLARSHIP PROGRAM)
901 S SPRING ST
SPRINGFIELD IL 62704
217/528-9617
AMOUNT: $500 - $1000
DEADLINE(S): MAR 1
FIELD(S): EDUCATION
ILLINOIS RESIDENTS. OPEN TO GRADUATING PUBLIC HIGH SCHOOL SENIORS WHO PLAN TO MAJOR IN EDUCATION AT ACCREDITED COLLEGE OR UNIVERSITY IN USA AND ARE IN THE UPPER 20% OF THEIR CLASS.
52 AWARDS PER YEAR. APPLICATIONS ARE AVAILABLE AFTER JAN 1. WRITE FOR COMPLETE INFORMATION.

93

INDIANA STATE STUDENT ASSISTANCE COMMISSION (MINORITY TEACHER & SPECIAL EDUCATION TEACHER SCHOLARSHIP PROGRAM)
150 W. MARKET ST; 5TH FLOOR
INDIANAPOLIS IN 46204
317/232-2350
AMOUNT: $1000 - $4000
DEADLINE(S): VARIES WITH COLLEGE
FIELD(S): EDUCATION
OPEN TO BLACK OR HISPANIC RESIDENTS OF INDIANA OR INDIANA RESIDENTS WORKING TOWARD A CERTIFICATE IN SPECIAL EDUCATION. FOR FULL TIME UNDERGRADUATE OR GRADUATE STUDY AT AN INDIANA COLLEGE. GPA OF 2.0 OR BETTER (4.0 SCALE) IS REQUIRED.
MUST DEMONSTRATE FINANCIAL NEED (FAF). WRITE FOR COMPLETE INFORMATION.

94

INDIANA STATE STUDENT ASSISTANCE COMMISSION (PAUL DOUGLAS TEACHER SCHOLARSHIP PROGRAM)
150 W. MARKET ST; 5TH FLOOR
INDIANAPOLIS IN 46204
317/232-2350
AMOUNT: $5000
DEADLINE(S): MAR 1
FIELD(S): EDUCATION
OPEN TO INDIANA RESIDENTS FOR UNDERGRADUATE OR GRADUATE STUDY LEADING TO A TEACHING CREDENTIAL. MUST BE IN TOP 10% OF HIGH SCHOOL GRADUATING CLASS OR (IF IN COLLEGE) HAVE 3.0 OR BETTER GPA (4.0 SCALE).
USA CITIZEN. WRITE FOR COMPLETE INFORMATION.

95

INTERNATIONAL ORDER OF THE ALHAMBRA (SCHOLARSHIP FUND AND ENDOWMENT FUND)
4200 LEEDS AVE

BALTIMORE MD 21229
301/242-0660
AMOUNT: VARIES
DEADLINE(S): JAN; APR; JUL; OCT
FIELD(S): SPECIAL EDUCATION
OPEN TO UNDERGRADUATE STUDENTS WHO WILL BE ENTERING THEIR JUNIOR OR SENIOR YEAR IN AN ACCREDITED PROGRAM FOR TEACHING THE MENTALLY RETARDED & THE HANDICAPPED. AVAILABLE TO GRADUATE STUDENTS IN CANADA & THE STATES OF CALIFORNIA & VIRGINIA.
USA CITIZENSHIP REQUIRED. WRITE FOR COMPLETE INFORMATION.

96

IOWA COLLEGE STUDENT AID COMMISSION (PAUL DOUGLAS TEACHER SCHOLARSHIPS)
201 JEWETT BUILDING; 9TH & GRAND AVE
DES MOINES IA 50309
515/281-3501
AMOUNT: $5000 PER YEAR (4 YEAR MAXIMUM)
DEADLINE(S): NONE SPECIFIED
FIELD(S): EDUCATION
OPEN TO IOWA HIGH SCHOOL SENIORS WHO HAVE APPLIED TO IOWA STATE SCHOLARSHIP PROGRAM; ARE IN TOP 10% OF THEIR CLASS & WANT TO TEACH IN SPECIFIC AREAS OF NEED AT ELEMENTARY OR SECONDARY LEVEL. SHOW FINANCIAL NEED.
MUST BE USA CITIZEN OR LEGAL RESIDENT AND AGREE TO TEACH FOR 2 YEARS FOR EACH YEAR OF FUNDING. CONTACT YOUR COUNSELOR OR WRITE TO ADDRESS ABOVE FOR COMPLETE INFORMATION.

97

MARYLAND HIGHER EDUCATION COMMISSION (SHARON CHRISTA MCAULIFFE CRITICAL SHORTAGE TEACHER PROGRAM)
STATE SCHOLARSHIP ADMINISTRATION 16 FRANCIS ST.
ANNAPOLIS MD 21401
410/974-5370
AMOUNT: UP TO $8000 FOR TUITION; FEES & ROOM & BOARD
DEADLINE(S): DEC 31
FIELD(S): EDUCATION (CRITICAL SHORTAGES DETERMINED ANNUALLY)
MARYLAND RESIDENT. PROGRAM FOR PERSONS WHO AGREE TO TEACH IN CRITICAL SHORTAGE AREA IN MARYLAND FOR UP TO 1 YEAR FOR EACH YEAR OF FUNDING. FOR FULL OR PART TIME UNDERGRAD OR GRAD STUDY AT MARYLAND DEGREE GRANTING INSTITUTION.
RENEWABLE IF 3.0 GPA IS MAINTAINED. WRITE FOR COMPLETE INFORMATION.

98

MINNESOTA FEDERATION OF TEACHERS (FLORA ROGGE COLLEGE SCHOLARSHIP)
168 AURORA AVE
ST PAUL MN 55103
612/227-8583
AMOUNT: $1000
DEADLINE(S): FIRST FRIDAY IN MARCH
FIELD(S): EDUCATION
OPEN TO MINNESOTA HIGH SCHOOL SENIORS AND TO GRADUATES OF MN HIGH SCHOOLS FOR STUDY AT ANY ACCREDITED COLLEGE OR UNIVERSITY. APPLICATION FORM IS AVAILABLE FROM HIGH SCHOOL COUNSELOR OR PRINCIPAL AND INCLUDES STATEMENT OF FINANCIAL STATUS.
WRITE FOR COMPLETE INFORMATION.

99

MISSISSIPPI BOARD OF TRUSTEES OF STATE INSTITUTIONS OF HIGHER LEARNING (WILLIAM WINTER TEACHER EDUCATION PROGRAM)
3825 RIDGEWOOD RD
JACKSON MS 39211
601/982-6570
AMOUNT: UP TO $3000 PER YEAR
DEADLINE(S): MAR 31
FIELD(S): TEACHER (CRITICAL SHORTAGE SUBJECT AREAS)
OPEN TO FULL TIME UNDERGRADUATE STUDENTS IN A MISSISSIPPI COLLEGE OR UNIVERSITY WHO ARE IN A TEACHER EDUCATION PROGRAM WHICH WILL LEAD TO 'CLASS A' CERTIFICATION.
RECIPIENTS MUST AGREE TO TEACH IN A CRITICAL SHORTAGE AREA IN MISSISSIPPI UPON COMPLETION OF THE PROGRAM.

100

NATIONAL COLLEGIATE ATHLETIC ASSOCIATION (NCAA ETHNIC MINORITY INTERNSHIP PROGRAM)
6201 COLLEGE BLVD

OVERLAND PARK KS 66211
913/339-1906
AMOUNT: $1300 PER MONTH (INCLUDES $200 HOUSING ALLOWANCE)
DEADLINE(S): FEB 15
FIELD(S): SPORTS ADMINISTRATION; COACHING; OFFICIATING
INTERNSHIPS OF APPROXIMATELY ONE YEAR AT THE NCAA NATIONAL OFFICE OPEN TO MEMBERS OF ETHNIC MINORITIES WHO HAVE COMPLETED THE REQUIREMENTS FOR AN UNDERGRADUATE DEGREE AND HAVE DEMONSTRATED AN INTEREST IN A CAREER IN THE ADMINISTRATION OF ATHLETICS.
WRITE FOR COMPLETE INFORMATION.

101

NATIONAL FEDERATION OF THE BLIND (BLIND EDUCATOR OF TOMORROW AWARD)
814 4TH AVE
GRINNELL IA 50112
515/236-3366
AMOUNT: $2500
DEADLINE(S): MAR 31
FIELD(S): ELEMENTARY; SECONDARY; OR POST SECONDARY TEACHING
OPEN TO LEGALLY BLIND STUDENT WHO IS PURSUING OR PLANNING TO PURSUE A FULL TIME POST-SECONDARY COURSE OF STUDY THAT LEADS TO A CAREER IN ELEMENTARY; SECONDARY OR POST-SECONDARY TEACHING.
AWARD IS BASED ON ACADEMIC EXCELLENCE; SERVICE TO THE COMMUNITY AND FINANCIAL NEED. WRITE FOR COMPLETE INFORMATION.

102

NATIONAL STRENGTH & CONDITIONING ASSN (CHALLENGE SCHOLARSHIPS)
PO BOX 81410
LINCOLN NE 68501
402/472-3000
AMOUNT: $1000
DEADLINE(S): APR 17
FIELD(S): FIELDS RELATED TO STRENGTH & CONDITIONING
OPEN TO NATIONAL STRENGTH & CONDITIONING ASSN MEMBERS. AWARDS ARE FOR UNDERGRADUATE OR GRADUATE STUDY.
WRITE FOR COMPLETE INFORMATION.

103

NELLIE MARTIN CARMAN SCHOLARSHIP TRUST (SCHOLARSHIPS)
1121 244TH ST SW; #65
BOTHELL WA 98021
206/486-6575
AMOUNT: UP TO $1000
DEADLINE(S): MAR 15
FIELD(S): ALL FIELDS OF STUDY EXCEPT THOSE NOTED BELOW
OPEN TO SENIORS IN KING; PIERCE & SNOHOMISH COUNTY (WA) HIGH SCHOOLS WHO HAVE LIVED IN WASHINGTON AT LEAST 5 YRS. FOR UNDERGRADUATE STUDY IN WASHINGTON IN ALL FIELDS EXCEPT MUSIC; SCULPTURE; DRAWING; INTERIOR DESIGN & HOME ECONOMICS.
APPLICATIONS AVAILABLE ONLY THROUGH HIGH SCHOOLS. NOMINATION BY HS COUNSELOR IS REQUIRED. AWARDS ARE RENEWABLE. USA CITIZEN.

104

NORTH CAROLINA ASSOCIATION OF EDUCATORS (MARY MORROW SCHOLARSHIP)
PO BOX 27347; 700 S SALISBURY ST
RALEIGH NC 27611
919/832-3000
AMOUNT: $1000
DEADLINE(S): JAN 9
FIELD(S): EDUCATION - TEACHING
AWARDS GIVEN IN JUNIOR YEAR TO STUDENTS IN AN ACCREDITED NORTH CAROLINA UNDERGRADUATE INSTITUTION FOR USE IN THEIR SENIOR YEAR. RECIPIENTS MUST LIVE IN NORTH CAROLINA & AGREE TO TEACH IN THE STATE FOR AT LEAST 2 YEARS AFTER GRADUATION.
FINANCIAL NEED IS A CONSIDERATION. 4-7 SCHOLARSHIPS PER YEAR. APPLY IN JUNIOR YEAR OF COLLEGE. WRITE FOR COMPLETE INFORMATION.

105

NORTH CAROLINA DEPARTMENT OF PUBLIC INSTRUCTION (SCHOLARSHIP LOAN PROGRAM FOR PROSPECTIVE TEACHERS)
116 W EDENTON ST; OFFICE OF TEACHER EDUCATION
RALEIGH NC 27603
919/733-0701

AMOUNT: UP TO $2000 PER YEAR
DEADLINE(S): FEB 10
FIELD(S): EDUCATION - TEACHING
OPEN TO NC STUDENTS INTERESTED IN TEACHING IN NC PUBLIC SCHOOLS. AWARDS ARE BASED ON ACADEMIC PERFORMANCE; SCORES ON STANDARDIZED TESTS; CLASS RANK; CONGRESSIONAL DISTRICT; AND RECOMMENDATIONS. USA CITIZENSHIP REQUIRED.
200 AWARDS PER YEAR. WRITE FOR COMPLETE INFORMATION.

106

OHIO BAPTIST EDUCATION SOCIETY (SCHOLARSHIPS)
PO BOX 288
GRANVILLE OH 43023
614/587-1531
AMOUNT: VARIES
DEADLINE(S): APR 1
FIELD(S): PULPIT MINISTRY; CHRISTIAN LEADERSHIP EDUCATION; CHURCH MUSIC
OHIO RESIDENT. MEMBER OF AN AMERICAN BAPTIST CHURCH IN OHIO. SHOULD BE COMPLETING SECOND YEAR OF UNDERGRADUATE STUDY AT AN ACCREDITED INSTITUTION. US CITIZEN OR LEGAL RESIDENT.
MUST DEMONSTRATE FINANCIAL NEED. NUMBER OF AWARDS DEPENDS ON THE INCOME FROM THE SMALL ENDOWMENT OF THE SOCIETY. WRITE FOR COMPLETE INFORMATION.

107

OREGON PTA (TEACHER EDUCATION SCHOLARSHIPS)
531 S E 14TH
PORTLAND OR 97214
503/234-3928
AMOUNT: $250
DEADLINE(S): MAR 1
FIELD(S): EDUCATION
OPEN TO OUTSTANDING STUDENTS WHO ARE OREGON RESIDENTS AND ARE PREPARING TO TEACH IN OREGON AT THE ELEMENTARY OR SECONDARY SCHOOL LEVEL. THE SCHOLARSHIPS MAY BE USED TO ATTEND ANY OREGON PUBLIC COLLEGE.
WRITE FOR COMPLETE INFORMATION.

108

PENNSYLVANIA HIGHER EDUCATION ASSISTANCE AGENCY (PAUL DOUGLAS TEACHER SCHOLARSHIP PROGRAM)
PO BOX 8118
HARRISBURG PA 17105
717/975-3320
AMOUNT: $5000 PER YEAR FOR UP TO 4 YEARS
DEADLINE(S): MAY 1
FIELD(S): EDUCATION - TEACHING
H.S. SENIORS WHO HAVE LIVED IN PA AT LEAST 1 YEAR & ARE IN THE TOP 10% OF THEIR CLASS. FOR UNDERGRAD STUDY IN PA IN AN ACCREDITED PROGRAM LEADING TO CREDENTIALS TO TEACH AT PRE-SCHOOL; ELEMENTARY OR SECONDARY LEVEL.
US CITIZEN OR LEGAL RESIDENT. RECIPIENTS ARE REQUIRED TO TEACH IN ANY STATE FOR 2 YEARS FOR EACH YEAR OF FUNDING OR 1/2 THAT TIME IF THEY TEACH IN A CRITICAL TEACHER SHORTAGE AREA. WRITE FOR COMPLETE INFORMATION.

109

PHI DELTA KAPPA INC (SCHOLARSHIP GRANTS FOR PROSPECTIVE TEACHERS)
PO BOX 789; 8TH & UNION AVE
BLOOMINGTON IN 47402
812/339-1156
AMOUNT: $1000 - $2000
DEADLINE(S): JAN 31
FIELD(S): TEACHING
OPEN TO HIGH SCHOOL SENIORS IN UPPER 1/3 OF THEIR CLASS WHO PLAN TO PURSUE CAREER AS TEACHER OR EDUCATOR. BASED ON SCHOLASTIC ACHIEVEMENT; SCHOOL-COMMUNITY ACTIVITIES; RECOMMENDATIONS & AN ESSAY. USA OR CANADIAN CITIZEN OR LEGAL RESIDENT.
43 SCHOLARSHIPS PER YEAR. WRITE TO THE ATTN OF SCHOLARSHIP GRANTS FOR COMPLETE INFORMATION.

110

RHODE ISLAND HIGHER EDUCATION ASSISTANCE AUTHORITY (PAUL DOUGLAS TEACHER SCHOLARSHIP PROGRAM)
560 JEFFERSON BLVD
WARWICK RI 02886
401/277-2050
AMOUNT: $5000 PER YEAR FOR UP TO 4 YEARS
DEADLINE(S): MAR 1

FIELD(S): EDUCATION - TEACHING
FEDERALLY FUNDED PROGRAM TO ENCOURAGE OUTSTANDING UNDERGRADUATE STUDENTS TO PURSUE TEACHING CAREERS AT PRE-SCHOOL; ELEMENTARY & SECONDARY LEVELS. FOR STUDY AT ELIGIBLE INSTITUTIONS. US CITIZEN OR LEGAL RESIDENT.
RECIPIENTS ARE REQUIRED TO TEACH IN ANY STATE FOR 2 YEARS FOR EACH YEAR OF FUNDING OR 1/2 THAT FOR TEACHING IN A CRITICAL TEACHER SHORTAGE AREA. WRITE FOR COMPLETE INFORMATION.

111

TECHNOLOGY STUDENT ASSOCIATION (SCHOLARSHIPS)
1914 ASSOCIATION DR
RESTON VA 22091
703/860-9000
AMOUNT: $250 - $500
DEADLINE(S): MAY 1
FIELD(S): TECHNOLOGY EDUCATION
OPEN TO STUDENT MEMBERS OF THE TECHNOLOGY STUDENT ASSOCIATION WHO CAN DEMONSTRATE FINANCIAL NEED. GRADE POINT AVERAGE IS NOT A CONSIDERATION BUT APPLICANTS MUST BE ACCEPTED TO A 4-YEAR COLLEGE OR UNIVERSITY.
FUNDS ARE SENT TO AND ADMINISTERED BY THE RECIPIENT'S COLLEGE OR UNIVERSITY. WRITE FOR COMPLETE INFORMATION.

112

UNITED COMMERCIAL TRAVELERS OF AMERICA (GRADUATE SCHOLARSHIP PROGRAM)
632 NORTH PARK STREET
COLUMBUS OH 43215
614/228-3276
AMOUNT: $750 PER YEAR
DEADLINE(S): NONE
FIELD(S): SPECIAL EDUCATION
OPEN TO UNDERGRADUATE JUNIORS & SENIORS; GRADUATE STUDENTS; TEACHERS & PERSONS WHO PLAN TO TEACH THE MENTALLY RETARDED. AWARDS TENABLE AT ACCREDITED INSTITUTIONS. USA OR CANADIAN CITIZEN.
APPROX 500 AWARDS PER YEAR. PREFERENCE TO (BUT NOT LIMITED TO) UCT MEMBERS. WRITE FOR COMPLETE INFORMATION.

113

UTAH STATE OFFICE OF EDUCATION (CAREER TEACHING SCHOLARSHIPS)
250 E 500 SO
SALT LAKE CITY UT 84111
801/538-7741
AMOUNT: FULL TUITION AND FEES
DEADLINE(S): MAR 30
FIELD(S): EDUCATION-TEACHER
AWARDS TO OUTSTANDING UTAH HIGH SCHOOL GRADUATES OR COLLEGE FRESHMEN. AT UNDERGRAD SOPH/JUNIOR/OR SENIOR LEVEL AWARDS OPEN TO ANY STUDENT (RESIDENT OR NON-RESIDENT) STUDYING IN A UTAH STATE COLLEGE OR UNIVERSITY TO BE A TEACHER.
APPROX 150 SCHOLARSHIPS PER YEAR. MUST DEMONSTRATE FINANCIAL NEED. WRITE FOR COMPLETE INFORMATION.

114

VIRGINIA STATE COUNCIL OF HIGHER EDUCATION (PAUL DOUGLAS TEACHER SCHOLARSHIP PROGRAM)
101 N 14TH ST; JAMES MONROE BLDG
RICHMOND VA 23219
804-225-2141
AMOUNT: UP TO $5000 PER YEAR
DEADLINE(S): VARIES
FIELD(S): EDUCATION
FEDERAL PROGRAM OPEN TO VIRGINIA RESIDENTS IN TOP 10% OF HIGH SCHOOL CLASS & ACCEPTED TO OR ENROLLED IN FULL-TIME UNDERGRADUATE TEACHER EDUCATION PROGRAM. SCHOLARSHIPS ARE RENEWABLE FOR UP TO 4 YEARS. USA CITIZEN OR LEGAL RESIDENT.
RECIPIENTS AGREE TO TEACH IN A DESIGNATED TEACHER SHORTAGE AREA FOR EACH YEAR OF FUNDING RECEIVED. OTHERWISE THE SCHOLARSHIP BECOMES A LOAN & MUST BE REPAID. WRITE FOR COMPLETE INFORMATION.

115

WISCONSIN CONGRESS OF PARENTS AND TEACHERS INC (BROOKMIRE-HASTINGS SCHOLARSHIPS)
4797 HAYES RD; SUITE 2
MADISON WI 53704-3256
608/244-1455
AMOUNT: $1000
DEADLINE(S): FEB 15

FIELD(S): EDUCATION - TEACHING
WISCONSIN RESIDENT. OPEN TO SENIORS IN PUBLIC HIGH SCHOOLS. AWARDED TO OUTSTANDING HIGH SCHOOL GRADUATES WHO INTEND TO PURSUE A CAREER IN THE FIELD OF CHILD CARE/EDUCATION.
WRITE FOR COMPLETE INFORMATION.

116

WORLD LEISURE & RECREATION ASSN (TOM & RUTH RIVERS SCHOLARSHIP PROGRAM)
PO BOX 309
SHARBOT LAKE ONTARIO K0H 2P0 CANADA
613/279-3173
AMOUNT: VARIES
DEADLINE(S): JAN 1
FIELD(S): RECREATION; LEISURE STUDIES; RESOURCES EDUCATION
SCHOLARSHIPS INTENDED TO ALLOW COLLEGE SENIORS OR GRADUATE STUDENTS IN RECREATION OR LEISURE SERVICES PROGRAMS TO ATTEND INTERNATIONAL MEETINGS/CONFERENCES OR CONVENTIONS THEREBY GAINING A BROADER PERSPECTIVE OF WORLD LEISURE & RECREATION.
WRITE FOR COMPLETE INFORMATION.

117

Y'S MEN INTERNATIONAL (U.S. AREA - ALEXANDER SCHOLARSHIP-LOAN FUND)
BILL WARD; AREA SERVICE DIRECTOR; 17909 MANHATTAN PL.
TORRANCE CA 90504
WRITTEN INQUIRY ONLY
AMOUNT: UP TO $1500 PER YEAR
DEADLINE(S): MAY 1; OCT 1
FIELD(S): BUSINESS ADMINISTRATION; YOUTH LEADERSHIP
OPEN TO UNDERGRADUATES. REPAYMENT IS WAIVED FOR THOSE WHO AGREE TO WORK FOR YMCA AFTER GRADUATION FOR AT LEAST A YEAR FOR EACH YEAR OF FUNDING. HISTORY OF PREVIOUS YMCA PARTICIPATION IS HELPFUL. USA CITIZEN OR LEGAL RESIDENT.
12 TO 16 SCHOLARSHIPS PER YEAR. RENEWABLE. WRITE FOR COMPLETE INFORMATION.

SCHOOL OF ENGINEERING

118

ALEXANDER GRAHAM BELL ASSOCIATION FOR THE DEAF (ROBERT H WEITBRECHT SCHOLARSHIP AWARD)
3417 VOLTA PLACE
WASHINGTON DC 20007
202/337-5220
AMOUNT: $750
DEADLINE(S): APR 15
FIELD(S): ENGINEERING/SCIENCE
OPEN TO ORAL DEAF STUDENTS WHO WERE BORN WITH A PROFOUND HEARING IMPAIRMENT OR WHO SUFFERED SUCH A LOSS BEFORE ACQUIRING LANGUAGE. MUST BE ACCEPTED INTO A FULL-TIME ACADEMIC PROGRAM FOR HEARING STUDENTS. NORTH AMERICAN CITIZEN.
WRITE FOR COMPLETE INFORMATION.

119

AMERICAN CONSULTING ENGINEERS COUNCIL (SCHOLARSHIP PROGRAM)
1015 15TH STREET NW; #802
WASHINGTON DC 20005
202/347-7474
AMOUNT: $1000 - $5000
DEADLINE(S): MAR 15
FIELD(S): ENGINEERING
OPEN TO UNDERGRADUATE JUNIORS AND SENIORS AND 5TH YEAR STUDENTS IN A 5-YEAR PROGRAM WHO ARE IN THE TOP 1/2 OF THEIR CLASS AND ATTENDING A USA COLLEGE OR UNIVERSITY ACCREDITED BY THE A.B.E.T. USA CITIZEN.
15 TO 20 AWARDS PER YEAR. WRITE FOR COMPLETE INFORMATION.

120

AMERICAN INDIAN SCIENCE & ENGINEERING SOCIETY (SANTA FE PACIFIC FOUNDATION SCHOLARSHIPS)
1630 30TH ST; SUITE 301
BOULDER CO 80301
303/492-8658
AMOUNT: UP TO $2500 PER YEAR FOR 4 YEARS
DEADLINE(S): MAR 15
FIELD(S): BUSINESS; ENGINEERING; SCIENCE; HEALTH ADMINISTRATION

OPEN TO GRADUATING HIGH SCHOOL SENIORS WITH 1/4 DEGREE OR MORE INDIAN BLOOD. MUST RESIDE IN KS; OK; CO; AZ; NM OR SAN BERNARDINO COUNTY CA (AT&SF RAILWAY SERVICE AREA). 2 OF THE 5 SCHOLARSHIPS ARE DESIGNATED FOR NAVAJO TRIBE MEMBERS.

MUST PLAN TO ATTEND A 4 YEAR POST-SECONDARY ACCREDITED EDUCATIONAL INSTITUTION. WRITE FOR COMPLETE INFORMATION.

121

AMERICAN SOCIETY FOR ENGINEERING EDUCATION (WASHINGTON INTERNSHIPS FOR STUDENTS OF ENGINEERING)

ELEVEN DUPONT CIRCLE; #200
WASHINGTON DC 20036
202/745-3616

AMOUNT: $2700 STIPEND + TRAVEL ALLOWANCE

DEADLINE(S): DEC 10

FIELD(S): ENGINEERING-PUBLIC POLICY

FOR TOP 3RD-YEAR ENGINEERING STUDENTS. 10-WEEK SUMMER INTERNSHIP IN WASHINGTON DC TO LEARN HOW ENGINEERS CONTRIBUTE TO PUBLIC POLICY DECISIONS ON COMPLEX TECHNOLOGICAL MATTERS. STUDENTS RECEIVE 5 QUARTER CREDITS FROM UNIV OF WASHINGTON.

17 INTERNSHIPS PER SUMMER. WRITE FOR COMPLETE INFORMATION.

122

ARGONNE NATIONAL LABORATORY (STUDENT RESEARCH PARTICIPATION PROGRAM; THESIS RESEARCH)

DIV OF EDUCATIONAL PROGRAMS; 9700 SOUTH CASS AVE
ARGONNE IL 60439
312/972-3366

AMOUNT: $200 PER WEEK STIPEND

DEADLINE(S): FEB 1; MAY 15; OCT 15

FIELD(S): PHYSICAL SCIENCES; LIFE SCIENCES; EARTH SCIENCES; MATHEMATICS; COMPUTER SCIENCES; ENGINEERING; FUSION & FISSION ENERGY

1-SEMESTER ACCREDITED INTERNSHIP PROGRAM TO PERMIT STUDENTS TO WORK IN ABOVE AREAS IN RELATION TO ENERGY DEVELOPMENT. OPEN TO FULL-TIME UNDERGRAD JUNIORS; SENIORS & 1ST YEAR GRAD STUDENTS. USA CITIZEN OR LEGAL RESIDENT.

THESIS RESEARCH AWARDS OPEN TO DOCTORAL CANDIDATES WORKING ON THEIR DISSERTATION. WRITE FOR COMPLETE INFORMATION.

123

ARTHUR & DOREEN PARRETT SCHOLARSHIP TRUST FUND (SCHOLARSHIPS)

C/O US BANK OF WASHINGTON; PO BOX 720; TRUST DEPT - 4TH FLOOR
SEATTLE WA 98111
206/344-3691

AMOUNT: UP TO $1000

DEADLINE(S): JUL 31

FIELD(S): ENGINEERING; SCIENCE; MEDICINE; DENTISTRY

WASHINGTON STATE RESIDENT. UNDERGRADUATE SCHOLARSHIPS OPEN TO STUDENTS WHO ARE ENROLLED IN ABOVE SCHOOLS. AWARDS TENABLE AT ANY ACCREDITED UNDERGRADUATE COLLEGE OR UNIVERSITY. USA CITIZEN OR LEGAL RESIDENT.

APPROXIMATELY 15 AWARDS PER YEAR. WRITE FOR COMPLETE INFORMATION.

124

BOYS & GIRLS CLUBS OF SAN DIEGO (SPENCE REESE SCHOLARSHIP FUND)

3760 FOURTH AVE; SUITE 1
SAN DIEGO CA 92103
619/298-3520

AMOUNT: $2000 PER YEAR FOR 4 YEARS

DEADLINE(S): MAY 15

FIELD(S): MEDICINE; LAW; ENGINEERING; POLITICAL SCIENCE

OPEN TO MALE HIGH SCHOOL SENIORS PLANNING A CAREER IN ABOVE FIELDS. PREFERENCE TO STUDENTS WITHIN A 250 MILE RADIUS OF SAN DIEGO. BOYS CLUB AFFILIATION IS NOT REQUIRED.

APPLICATIONS ARE AVAILABLE IN JANUARY. MUST ENCLOSE A SELF-ADDRESSED STAMPED ENVELOPE TO RECEIVE APPLICATION. A $10 PROCESSING FEE IS REQUIRED WITH COMPLETED APPLICATION. WRITE FOR COMPLETE INFORMATION.

125

BUSINESS AND PROFESSIONAL WOMEN'S FOUNDATION (BPW LOANS FOR WOMEN IN ENGINEERING STUDIES)
2012 MASSACHUSETTS AVE NW
WASHINGTON DC 20036
202/293-1200
AMOUNT: UP TO $5000 PER YEAR
DEADLINE(S): APR 15 POSTMARK (APPLICATIONS AVAILABLE ONLY OCT 1 - APR 1)
FIELD(S): ENGINEERING
OPEN TO WOMEN WHO ARE ACCEPTED FOR UNDERGRADUATE OR GRADUATE LEVEL STUDY IN A PROGRAM ACCREDITED BY THE ACCREDITATION BOARD FOR ENGINEERING AND TECHNOLOGY. FOR LAST 2 YEARS OF STUDY. USA CITIZEN.
MUST DEMONSTRATE FINANCIAL NEED. APPLICATIONS AVAILABLE ONLY BETWEEN OCT 1 AND APR 1. SEND SELF-ADDRESSED STAMPED ($.52) #10 ENVELOPE FOR APPLICATION & COMPLETE INFORMATION.

126

BUSINESS AND PROFESSIONAL WOMEN'S FOUNDATION (CAREER ADVANCEMENT SCHOLARSHIPS)
2012 MASSACHUSETTS AVE NW
WASHINGTON DC 20036
202/293-1200
AMOUNT: $500 - $1000
DEADLINE(S): APR 15 POSTMARK (APPS AVAILABLE ONLY OCT 1 - APR 1)
FIELD(S): COMPUTER SCIENCE; EDUCATION; PARALEGAL; ENGINEERING; SCIENCE (EXCEPT HEALTH CARE)
OPEN TO WOMEN (30 OR OLDER) WITHIN 12-24 MONTHS OF COMPLETING UNDERGRAD OR GRAD STUDY IN USA (INCLUDING PUERTO RICO & THE VIRGIN ISLANDS). SHOULD LEAD TO ENTRY OR REENTRY INTO THE WORK FORCE OR IMPROVE CAREER ADVANCEMENT CHANCES.
MUST SHOW FINANCIAL NEED. SEND SELF-ADDRESSED STAMPED ($.52) #10 ENVELOPE FOR APPLICATION & COMPLETE INFORMATION. NOT FOR STUDY AT DOCTORAL LEVEL.

127

CAPE CANAVERAL CHAPTER RETIRED OFFICERS ASSOC (SCHOLARSHIPS)
PO BOX 4186
PATRICK AFB FL 32925
WRITTEN INQUIRY
AMOUNT: APPROX $1500 PER YEAR
DEADLINE(S): MAY 31
FIELD(S): SCIENCE; MATHEMATICS; ENGINEERING; LIBERAL ARTS; CHEMISTRY
OPEN ONLY TO BREVARD COUNTY FLORIDA RESIDENTS WHO ARE UNDERGRADUATE JUNIORS OR SENIORS AT ANY 4-YEAR COLLEGE IN THE USA & THE SON OR DAUGHTER OF ACTIVE DUTY OR RETIRED MILITARY PERSONNEL. USA CITIZEN.
AWARDS RENEWABLE FOR ONE YEAR. WRITE TO THE SCHOLARSHIP PROGRAM COMMITTEE; ADDRESS ABOVE; FOR COMPLETE INFORMATION.

128

CIVIL AIR PATROL (CAP UNDERGRADUATE SCHOLARSHIPS)
NATIONAL HEADQUARTERS
MAXWELL AFB AL 36112
205/293-5332
AMOUNT: $750
DEADLINE(S): MAR 15
FIELD(S): HUMANITIES; SCIENCE; ENGINEERING; EDUCATION
OPEN TO CAP MEMBERS WHO HAVE RECEIVED THE BILLY MITCHELL AWARD OR THE SENIOR RATING IN LEVEL II OF THE SENIOR TRAINING PROGRAM. FOR UNDERGRADUATE STUDY IN THE ABOVE AREAS.
WRITE FOR COMPLETE INFORMATION.

129

COMMITTEE ON INSTITUTIONAL COOPERATION (CIC PRE-DOCTORAL FELLOWSHIPS)
KIRKWOOD HALL RM 111; INDIANA UNIV.
BLOOMINGTON IN 47405
812/855-0822
AMOUNT: $9500 + TUITION (5 YEARS)
DEADLINE(S): JAN 2
FIELD(S): HUMANITIES; SOCIAL SCIENCES; NATURAL SCIENCES; MATHEMATICS; ENGINEERING
PRE-DOCTORAL FELLOWSHIPS FOR USA CITIZENS OF AFRICAN AMERICAN; AMERICAN

INDIAN; MEXICAN AMERICAN OR PUERTO RICAN HERITAGE. MUST HOLD OR EXPECT TO RECEIVE BACHELOR'S DEGREE BY LATE SUMMER FROM A REGIONALLY ACCREDITED COLLEGE OR UNIVERSITY.

AWARDS FOR SPECIFIED UNIVERSITIES IN IL; IN; IA; MI; MN; OH; WI; PA. WRITE FOR DETAILS.

130

CONSULTING ENGINEERS COUNCIL OF NEW JERSEY (LOUIS GOLDBERG SCHOLARSHIP FUND)

66 MORRIS AVE
SPRINGFIELD NJ 07081
201/379-1100

AMOUNT: $1000

DEADLINE(S): JAN 27

FIELD(S): ENGINEERING

OPEN TO UNDERGRADUATE STUDENTS WHO HAVE COMPLETED AT LEAST 2 YEARS OF STUDY AT AN ABET ACCREDITED COLLEGE OR UNIVERSITY IN NEW JERSEY; IN TOP 1/2 OF THEIR CLASS & ARE CONSIDERING A CAREER AS A CONSULTING ENGINEER. USA CITIZEN.

RECIPIENTS WILL BE ELIGIBLE FOR AMERICAN CONSULTING ENGINEERS COUNCIL NATIONAL SCHOLARSHIPS OF $2000 - $5000. WRITE FOR COMPLETE INFORMATION.

131

GENERAL LEARNING CORPORATION (DUPONT & GLC SCIENCE ESSAY AWARDS PROGRAM)

60 REVERE DR
NORTHBROOK IL 60062
800/323-5471; IN ILLINOIS 708/205-3000

AMOUNT: UP TO $1500

DEADLINE(S): JAN 15

FIELD(S): SCIENCES

ANNUAL ESSAY COMPETITION OPEN TO STUDENTS IN GRADES 7-12 IN USA & CANADA. CASH AWARDS FOR 1ST; 2ND; 3RD & HON MENTION. 1ST-PLACE ESSAYISTS; THEIR SCIENCE TEACHER & 1 PARENT RECEIVE TRIP TO NAT'L SCIENCE TEACHERS CONFERENCE IN BOSTON.

CONTACT YOUR SCIENCE TEACHER OR ADDRESS ABOVE FOR COMPLETE INFORMATION.

132

H. FLETCHER BROWN FUND (SCHOLARSHIPS)

C/O BANK OF DELAWARE; TRUST DEPT; PO BOX 791
WILMINGTON DE 19899
302/429-2827

AMOUNT: VARIES

DEADLINE(S): APR 15

FIELD(S): MEDICINE; DENTISTRY; LAW; ENGINEERING; CHEMISTRY

OPEN TO STUDENTS BORN IN DELAWARE; GRADUATED FROM A DELAWARE HIGH SCHOOL & STILL RESIDING IN DELAWARE. FOR FOUR YEARS OF STUDY (UNDERGRAD OR GRAD) LEADING TO A DEGREE THAT ENABLES APPLICANT TO PRACTICE IN CHOSEN FIELD.

SCHOLARSHIPS ARE BASED ON NEED; SCHOLASTIC ACHIEVEMENT; GOOD MORAL CHARACTER. RENEWABLE. WRITE FOR COMPLETE INFORMATION.

133

ILLUMINATING ENGINEERING SOCIETY OF NORTH AMERICA (ROBERT THUNEN MEMORIAL EDUCATION FUND-SCHOLARSHIPS)

345 EAST 47TH STREET
NEW YORK NY 10017
212-705-7915

AMOUNT: VARIES

DEADLINE(S): NONE SPECIFIED

FIELD(S): ARCHITECTURE; ARCHITECTURAL ENGINEERING; ELECTRICAL ENGINEERING; INTERIOR DESIGN; THEATRE

SCHOLARSHIPS FOR STUDENTS IN THE ABOVE FIELDS WHO ARE INTERESTED IN STUDYING LIGHTING. OPEN TO 3RD & 4TH YEAR UNDERGRADUATE STUDENTS AT ACCREDITED INSTITUTIONS IN NORTHERN CALIFORNIA; OREGON; WASHINGTON & NORTHERN NEVADA.

SUPPORT MAY ALSO BE PROVIDED TO GRADUATE STUDENTS (WITHIN THE GEOGRAPHICAL AREA NOTED ABOVE) WHO HAVE SPECIFIC LIGHTING PROJECTS AS PART OF THEIR COURSE WORK. WRITE FOR COMPLETE INFORMATION.

134

INTERNATIONAL ASSOCIATION OF FIRE CHIEFS FOUNDATION (SCHOLARSHIP PROGRAM)

1329 18TH STREET NW
WASHINGTON DC 20036
202-833-3420

AMOUNT: $250

DEADLINE(S): AUG 15
FIELD(S): BUSINESS & URBAN ADMINISTRATION; ENGINEERING; FIRE SCIENCE
OPEN TO MEMBERS OF A FIRE SERVICE OF A STATE; COUNTY; PROVINCIAL; MUNICIPAL; COMMUNITY; INDUSTRIAL OR FEDERAL FIRE DEPARTMENT.
18 SCHOLARSHIPS PER YEAR. RENEWABLE. WRITE FOR COMPLETE DETAILS.

135

JOSEPH BLAZEK FOUNDATION (SCHOLARSHIPS)
8 SOUTH MICHIGAN AVE
CHICAGO IL 60603
312/372-3880
AMOUNT: $750 PER YEAR FOR 4 YEARS
DEADLINE(S): FEB 1
FIELD(S): SCIENCE; CHEMISTRY; ENGINEERING; MATHEMATICS; PHYSICS
OPEN TO RESIDENTS OF COOK COUNTY (ILLINOIS) WHO ARE HIGH SCHOOL SENIORS PLANNING TO STUDY IN THE ABOVE FIELDS AT A FOUR YEAR COLLEGE OR UNIVERSITY.
20 SCHOLARSHIPS PER YEAR. RENEWABLE. WRITE FOR COMPLETE INFORMATION.

136

NAACP NATIONAL HEADQUARTERS (NAACP WILLEMS SCHOLARSHIP)
4805 MOUNT HOPE DR
BALTIMORE MD 21215
301/358-8900
AMOUNT: $2000 - $3000
DEADLINE(S): APR 30
FIELD(S): ENGINEERING; CHEMISTRY; PHYSICS; COMPUTER SCIENCE; MATHEMATICS
OPEN TO NAACP MEMBERS MAJORING IN ONE OF THE ABOVE AREAS AND POSSESS A CUMULATIVE GPA OF 3.0 OR BETTER. UNDERGRADS RECEIVE MAXIMUM OF $8000 IN ANNUAL INSTALLMENTS OF $2000. GRADUATES ARE AWARDED A $3000 SCHOLARSHIP WHICH CAN BE RENEWED.
WRITE FOR COMPLETE INFORMATION.

137

NATIONAL ACTION COUNCIL FOR MINORITIES IN ENGINEERING-NACME INC. (INCENTIVE GRANTS PROGRAM)
3 WEST 35TH ST; 3RD FLOOR
NEW YORK NY 10001
212/279-2626; FAX 212/629-5178
AMOUNT: $500 - $3000
DEADLINE(S): SET BY COLLEGES
FIELD(S): ENGINEERING
OPEN TO AMERICAN INDIAN; AFRICAN AMERICAN; MEXICAN-AMERICAN; OR PUERTO RICAN. DEMONSTRATE NEED OR BE DESIGNATED TO RECEIVE A MERIT AWARD. FOR FULL-TIME ENROLLMENT IN ONE OF THE PARTICIPATING COLLEGES. US CITIZEN OR PERMANENT RESIDENT.
MUST BE AN ENTERING FRESHMAN OR TRANSFER STUDENT FOR THE INITIAL AWARD. WRITE FOR COMPLETE INFORMATION & LIST OF PARTICIPATING COLLEGES.

138

NATIONAL DEFENSE TRANSPORTATION ASSOCIATION - SAN FRANCISCO BAY AREA CHAPTER (NDTA SCHOLARSHIP)
PO BOX 24676
OAKLAND CA 94623
WRITTEN INQUIRY
AMOUNT: $1000
DEADLINE(S): MAY 1
FIELD(S): TRANSPORTATION
OPEN TO USA CITIZENS STUDYING IN THE FIELD OF BUSINESS; ENGINEERING; PLANNING OR ENVIRONMENT IN PREPARATION FOR A CAREER RELATED TO TRANSPORTATION. FINANCIAL NEED WILL BE CONSIDERED.
WRITE FOR COMPLETE INFORMATION.

139

NATIONAL ITALIAN AMERICAN FOUNDATION (RAYTHEON ENGINEERING SCHOLARSHIP)
DR. M.LOMBARDO; EDUCATION DIRECTOR; 666 11TH ST NW; SUITE 800
WASHINGTON DC 20001
202/638-2137
AMOUNT: $1000
DEADLINE(S): MAY 31
FIELD(S): ENGINEERING
OPEN TO UNDERGRADUATE AND GRADUATE STUDENTS OF ITALIAN HERITAGE WHO ARE MAJORING IN ENGINEERING. APPLICATION REQUIRES EVIDENCE OF FINANCIAL NEED AND AN ESSAY (1 TYPED PAGE MAXIMUM) DESCRIBING STUDENT'S ITALIAN BACKGROUND.
WRITE FOR COMPLETE INFORMATION.

140

NATIONAL SOCIETY OF PROFESSIONAL ENGINEERS EDUCATIONAL FOUNDATION (SCHOLARSHIPS AND GRANTS)
1420 KING STREET
ALEXANDRIA VA 22314
703/684-2830
AMOUNT: $1000 - $4000 + SOME FULL SCHOLARSHIPS
DEADLINE(S): NOV 15
FIELD(S): ENGINEERING
SCHOLARSHIPS OPEN TO HIGH SCHOOL SENIORS WHO ARE IN TOP 25% OF THEIR CLASS. AWARDS TENABLE AT ACCREDITED COLLEGES & UNIVERSITIES IN USA. USA CITIZEN.
APPROX 150 AWARDS PER YEAR. APPLICATIONS AVAILABLE IN AUG; SEP & OCT OF YEAR PRECEDING COLLEGE ENTRY. SPECIAL SCHOLARSHIPS FOR MINORITIES & FEMALES ALSO. WRITE FOR COMPLETE INFORMATION.

141

NATIONAL URBAN LEAGUE INC (NUL-KRAFT SCHOLARSHIP/INTERN PROGRAM FOR MINORITY STUDENTS)
500 EAST 62ND ST; 10TH FLOOR; DIRECTOR OF EDUCATION
NEW YORK NY 10021
212-310-9000
AMOUNT: $1000-5000 PER YEAR
DEADLINE(S): MAR 28
FIELD(S): ENGINEERING/SALES/MARKETING/ MANUFACTURING OPERATIONS/FINANCE/ BUSINESS ADMINISTRATION
OPEN TO MINORITY UNDERGRADUATE STUDENTS AT ACCREDITED INSTITUTIONS WHO ARE IN TOP 25% OF THEIR CLASS & WILL BE ENTERING THEIR 3RD OR JUNIOR YEAR AT THE TIME THE AWARD COMMENCES. US CITIZEN OR LEGAL RESIDENT.
10 AWARDS PER YEAR. WRITE FOR COMPLETE INFORMATION.

142

NELLIE MARTIN CARMAN SCHOLARSHIP TRUST (SCHOLARSHIPS)
1121 244TH ST SW; #65
BOTHELL WA 98021
206/486-6575
AMOUNT: UP TO $1000
DEADLINE(S): MAR 15
FIELD(S): ALL FIELDS OF STUDY EXCEPT THOSE NOTED BELOW
OPEN TO SENIORS IN KING; PIERCE & SNOHOMISH COUNTY (WA) HIGH SCHOOLS WHO HAVE LIVED IN WASHINGTON AT LEAST 5 YRS. FOR UNDERGRADUATE STUDY IN WASHINGTON IN ALL FIELDS EXCEPT MUSIC; SCULPTURE; DRAWING; INTERIOR DESIGN & HOME ECONOMICS.
APPLICATIONS AVAILABLE ONLY THROUGH HIGH SCHOOLS. NOMINATION BY HS COUNSELOR IS REQUIRED. AWARDS ARE RENEWABLE. USA CITIZEN.

143

NEW YORK CITY TRANSIT AUTHORITY (TRANSIT CORPS OF ENGINEERS PROGRAM)
ENGINEERING DEPT; 370 JAY ST
BROOKLYN NY 11201
718/330-8699
AMOUNT: TUITION
DEADLINE(S): JAN 1
FIELD(S): ENGINEERING; ENGINEERING TECHNOLOGY
OPEN TO UPPER DIVISION OR GRADUATE STUDENTS ENROLLED IN AN ENGINEERING PROGRAM OR NYC TRANSIT AUTHORITY EMPLOYEES. MUST AGREE TO WORK FOR NYC TRANSIT UNTIL AMOUNTS EXPENDED ARE AMORTIZED OVER 4-YEAR PERIOD.
PROGRAM OF STUDY SHOULD BE IN NEW YORK AND BE ACCREDITED BY ABET. WRITE FOR COMPLETE INFORMATION.

144

NEW YORK TELEPHONE (SCHOLARSHIP PROGRAM FOR BLACK AND HISPANIC STUDENTS)
COTE; PO BOX 2810
CHERRY HILL NJ 08034
609/573-9400
AMOUNT: $2000
DEADLINE(S): APR 30
FIELD(S): ENGINEERING; SCIENCE; COMPUTER SCIENCE; NURSING
OPEN TO BLACK OR HISPANIC STUDENTS WHO RESIDE IN NEW YORK AND ATTEND ACCREDITED NEW YORK STATE SCHOOLS. FOR FULL TIME STUDENTS ENROLLED AS A SECOND SEMESTER SOPHOMORES IN A 4 YEAR UNDERGRADUATE PROGRAM LEADING TO A BACHELOR DEGREE.
FINANCIAL NEED IS A CONSIDERATION. RENEWABLE. WRITE FOR COMPLETE INFORMATION.

145

NORTH CAROLINA OFFICE OF BUDGET AND MANAGEMENT (NC HEALTH; SCIENCES & MATH SCHOLARSHIP-LOAN PROGRAM)
116 WEST JONES ST; #2054
RALEIGH NC 27611
919-733-2164
AMOUNT: $2500 - $7500 PER YEAR
DEADLINE(S): JAN 8 - MAY 5
FIELD(S): HEALTH PROFESSIONS; SCIENCES; ENGINEERING

LOW-INTEREST SCHOLARSHIP LOANS OPEN TO NORTH CAROLINA RESIDENTS OF AT LEAST 1 YEAR WHO ARE PURSUING AN ASSOCIATES; UNDERGRADUATE OR GRADUATE DEGREE IN THE ABOVE AREAS AT AN ACCREDITED INSTITUTION IN THE USA.

LOANS MAY BE RETIRED AFTER GRADUATION BY WORKING (1 YEAR FOR EACH YEAR FUNDED) AT DESIGNATED INSTITUTIONS. WRITE FOR COMPLETE DETAILS.

146

PACIFIC GAS & ELECTRIC CO. (SCHOLARSHIPS FOR HIGH SCHOOL SENIORS)
77 BEALE ST; ROOM 2837
SAN FRANCISCO CA 94106
415/973-1338
AMOUNT: $1000 - $4000
DEADLINE(S): NOV 15
FIELD(S): ENGINEERING; COMPUTER SCIENCE; MATHEMATICS; MARKETING; BUSINESS; ECONOMICS

HIGH SCHOOL SENIORS IN GOOD ACADEMIC STANDING WHO RESIDE IN OR ATTEND HIGH SCHOOL IN AREAS SERVED BY PG&E ARE ELIGIBLE TO COMPETE FOR SCHOLARSHIPS AWARDED ON A REGIONAL BASIS. NOT OPEN TO CHILDREN OF PG&E EMPLOYEES.

36 AWARDS PER YEAR. APPLICATIONS & BROCHURES ARE AVAILABLE IN ALL HIGH SCHOOLS WITHIN PG&E'S SERVICE AREA AND AT PG&E OFFICES.

147

ROBERT SCHRECK MEMORIAL FUND (GRANTS)
C/O TEXAS COMMERCE BANK-TRUST DEPT; PO DRAWER 140
EL PASO TX 79980
915/546-6515
AMOUNT: $500 - $1500
DEADLINE(S): JUL 15; NOV 15
FIELD(S): MEDICINE; VETERINARY MEDICINE; PHYSICS; CHEMISTRY; ARCHITECTURE; ENGINEERING; EPISCOPAL CLERGY

GRANTS TO UNDERGRADUATE JUNIORS OR SENIORS OR GRADUATE STUDENTS WHO HAVE BEEN RESIDENTS OF EL PASO COUNTY FOR AT LEAST TWO YEARS. MUST BE USA CITIZEN OR LEGAL RESIDENT AND HAVE A HIGH GRADE POINT AVERAGE. FINANCIAL NEED IS A CONSIDERATION.

WRITE FOR COMPLETE INFORMATION.

148

SCIENCE SERVICE (WESTINGHOUSE SCIENCE SCHOLARSHIPS AND AWARDS)
1719 'N' STREET NW
WASHINGTON DC 20036
202/785-2255
AMOUNT: $1000 - $10000 PER YEAR FOR 4 YEARS
DEADLINE(S): DEC 1
FIELD(S): ENGINEERING; SCIENCE; MATHEMATICS

OPEN TO HIGH SCHOOL SENIORS WHO EXPECT TO COMPLETE COLLEGE ENTRANCE QUALIFICATIONS BEFORE OCT 1. NO AGE LIMIT. ONE OF THE REQUIREMENTS WILL BE A WRITTEN REPORT ON AN INDEPENDENT SCIENTIFIC RESEARCH PROJECT. USA CITIZEN OR LEGAL RESIDENT.

40 AWARDS PER YEAR WHICH ARE RENEWED FOR THREE SUBSEQUENT YEARS. WRITE FOR COMPLETE INFORMATION.

149

SOCIETY OF AUTOMOTIVE ENGINEERS (SAE SCHOLARSHIPS)
400 COMMONWEALTH DR
WARRENDALE PA 15096
412/776-4841
AMOUNT: $500 - $6000
DEADLINE(S): JAN 1
FIELD(S): ENGINEERING

OPEN TO HIGH SCHOOL JUNIORS AND SENIORS WHO INTEND TO PURSUE AN ENGINEERING PROGRAM ACCREDITED BY EAC/ABET; HAVE AT LEAST A 3.5 GPA AND RANK IN THE 90TH PERCENTILE IN BOTH MATH AND VERBAL SAT OR ACT SCORES.

A NUMBER OF SCHOLARSHIPS AVAILABLE WITH VARYING REQUIREMENTS. WRITE FOR COMPLETE INFORMATION.

150

SOCIETY OF HISPANIC PROFESSIONAL ENGINEERS FOUNDATION (SHPE SCHOLARSHIPS)
5400 E OLYMPIC BLVD; SUITE 306
LOS ANGELES CA 90022
213/888-2080
AMOUNT: $500 - $3000
DEADLINE(S): APR 15
FIELD(S): ENGINEERING & SCIENCE
OPEN TO DESERVING STUDENTS OF HISPANIC DESCENT WHO ARE SEEKING CAREERS IN ENGINEERING AND SCIENCE. FOR FULL TIME UNDERGRADUATE OR GRADUATE STUDY AT A COLLEGE OR UNIVERSITY. ACADEMIC ACHIEVEMENT AND FINANCIAL NEED ARE CONSIDERATIONS.
WRITE FOR COMPLETE INFORMATION.

151

SOCIETY OF WOMEN ENGINEERS (ADMIRAL GRACE MURRAY HOPPER SCHOLARSHIP)
345 EAST 47TH ST; ROOM 305
NEW YORK NY 10017
212/705-7855
AMOUNT: $1000
DEADLINE(S): MAY 15
FIELD(S): ENGINEERING; COMPUTER SCIENCE
OPEN TO WOMEN WHO ARE USA CITIZENS AND ARE ENTERING A FOUR YEAR PROGRAM FOR THE STUDY OF ENGINEERING OR COMPUTER SCIENCE AS FRESHMEN. APPLICATIONS AVAILABLE FROM MARCH THROUGH MAY ONLY.
WRITE FOR COMPLETE INFORMATION. ENCLOSE SELF ADDRESSED STAMPED ENVELOPE.

152

SOCIETY OF WOMEN ENGINEERS (GENERAL ELECTRIC FOUNDATION SCHOLARSHIPS; WESTINGHOUSE BERTHA LAMME SCHOLARSHIPS; TRW SCHOLARSHIPS)
345 EAST 47TH ST; ROOM 305
NEW YORK NY 10017
212/705-7855
AMOUNT: $1000 GE & WESTINGHOUSE; $2500 TRW
DEADLINE(S): MAY 15
FIELD(S): ENGINEERING
OPEN TO WOMEN WHO ARE USA CITIZENS AND ARE ENTERING AN ABET ACCREDITED SCHOOL AS FRESHMEN AND AS ENGINEERING MAJORS. APPLICATIONS AVAILABLE FROM MARCH THROUGH MAY ONLY.
G.E. SCHOLARSHIPS ARE RENEWABLE UP TO THREE YEARS. WRITE FOR COMPLETE INFORMATION. ENCLOSE SELF-ADDRESSED STAMPED ENVELOPE.

153

SOCIETY OF WOMEN ENGINEERS (MASWE MEMORIAL; LILLIAN M. GILBRETH; IVY PARKER MEMORIAL; DAVID SARNOFF RESEARCH CENTER SCHOLARSHIPS)
345 EAST 47TH STREET
NEW YORK NY 10017
212/705-7855
AMOUNT: $1000 - $3000
DEADLINE(S): FEB 1
FIELD(S): ENGINEERING
FOR WOMEN WHO ARE MAJORING IN ENGINEERING AT ACCREDITED COLLEGES AND UNIVERSITIES IN USA ENTERING THEIR JUNIOR OR SENIOR YEAR. APPLICANTS FOR PARKER AND MASWE AWARDS MUST DEMONSTRATE FINANCIAL NEED.
APPLICATIONS AVAILABLE OCT THROUGH JAN ONLY. SEND SELF-ADDRESSED STAMPED ENVELOPE FOR COMPLETE INFORMATION.

154

SOCIETY OF WOMEN ENGINEERS (OLIVE LYNN SALEMBIER REENTRY SCHOLARSHIPS)
345 EAST 47TH STREET
NEW YORK NY 10017
212/705-7855
AMOUNT: $2000
DEADLINE(S): MAY 15
FIELD(S): ENGINEERING
OPEN TO WOMEN WHO HAVE BEEN OUT OF THE ENGINEERING JOB MARKET FOR A MINIMUM OF TWO YEARS. AWARD IS TO ENABLE RECIPIENT TO OBTAIN THE CREDENTIALS NECESSARY TO REENTER THE JOB MARKET AS AN ENGINEER. FOR ANY YEAR OF UNDERGRAD OR GRAD STUDY.
APPLICATIONS AVAILABLE MARCH THROUGH MAY ONLY. WRITE FOR COMPLETE INFORMATION. ENCLOSE SELF-ADDRESSED STAMPED ENVELOPE.

155

SOCIETY OF WOMEN ENGINEERS (UNITED TECHNOLOGIES CORPORATION SCHOLARSHIP/NORTHROP CORP./DIGITAL EQUIPMENT CORP. SCHOLARSHIP

345 E 47TH STREET
NEW YORK NY 10017
212/705-7855

AMOUNT: $1000
DEADLINE(S): FEB 1
FIELD(S): ENGINEERING

FOR SOPHOMORE WOMEN WHO ARE MAJORING IN ENGINEERING AT ACCREDITED COLLEGES AND PURSUING AN ENGINEERING DEGREE. NORTHROP & DIGITAL SCHOLARSHIPS REQUIRE RECIPIENTS TO BE STUDENT SWE MEMBERS.

DIGITAL REQUIRES ATTENDANCE AT A NY OR NEW ENGLAND COLLEGE. UNITED TECHNOLOGIES AWARD IS RENEWABLE FOR TWO YEARS. APPLICATIONS AVAILABLE OCTOBER THROUGH JANUARY ONLY. SEND SELF ADDRESSED STAMPED ENVELOPE FOR COMPLETE INFORMATION.

156

THOMAS ALVA EDISON FOUNDATION (EDISON/MCGRAW SCHOLARSHIP PROGRAM)

3000 BOOK BUILDING
DETROIT MI 48226
313/965-1149

AMOUNT: $5000 SCHOLARSHIPS (2); $1000 SCHOLARSHIPS (10)
DEADLINE(S): DEC 1
FIELD(S): SCIENCE; ENGINEERING & TECHNOLOGY

OUTSTANDING HIGH SCHOOL STUDENTS. NO FORMAL APPLICATION. SUBMIT A PROPOSAL NOT TO EXCEED 1000 WORDS ON A COMPLETED EXPERIMENT OR A PROJECT IDEA WHICH WOULD HAVE 'PRACTICAL APPLICATION' IN FIELDS OF SCIENCE AND/OR ENGINEERING.

INCLUDE LETTER OF RECOMMENDATION FROM A TEACHER OR SPONSOR WHICH DESCRIBES HOW YOU EXEMPLIFY CREATIVITY & INGENUITY DEMONSTRATED BY LIFE & WORK OF THOMAS EDISON & MAX MCGRAW. MAIL ENTRY TO DR.R.A.DEAN; BOX 2800; LA JOLLA CA 92038-2800.

157

TYSON FOUNDATION INC. (SCHOLARSHIP PROGRAM)

2210 OAKLAWN
SPRINGDALE AR 72764
501/756-4955

AMOUNT: UP TO $1000/SEMESTER
DEADLINE(S): JUN 21
FIELD(S): BUSINESS; AGRICULTURE; ENGINEERING; COMPUTER SCIENCE; NURSING

OPEN TO USA CITIZENS WHO LIVE IN THE VICINITY OF TYSON FOOD FACILITIES AND MAINTAIN A 2.5 GPA. MUST WORK AND CARRY AT LEAST 12 SEMESTER HOURS OR EQUIVALENT. FOR UNDERGRADUATE STUDY AT SCHOOLS IN USA.

RECIPIENTS SIGN A PLEDGE EITHER TO REPAY THE SCHOLARSHIP MONEY OR HELP ANOTHER DESERVING STUDENT NOT RELATED BY BLOOD OR MARRIAGE TO ATTEND COLLEGE. WRITE FOR COMPLETE INFORMATION.

158

U.S. DEPT. OF EDUCATION (INDIAN FELLOWSHIP PROGRAM)

400 MARYLAND AVENUE SW; RM 2177; MAIL STOP 6335
WASHINGTON DC 20202
202/401-1902

AMOUNT: $1000 - $34000 (AVERAGE $13000)
DEADLINE(S): FEB 7
FIELD(S): BUSINESS ADMIN; ENGINEERING; NATURAL RESOURCES & RELATED AREAS

FELLOWSHIPS FOR AMERICAN INDIANS OR ALASKAN NATIVES WHO ARE US CITIZENS AND SEEKING UNDERGRADUATE OR GRADUATE DEGREES IN THE ABOVE FIELDS AT ACCREDITED INSTITUTIONS IN USA.

APPROXIMATELY 90 CONTINUATION AND 35 NEW AWARDS PER YEAR. WRITE FOR COMPLETE INFORMATION.

AERONAUTICS

159

AIR TRAFFIC CONTROL ASSOCIATION INC (SCHOLARSHIP AWARDS PROGRAM)

2300 CLARENDON BLVD; #711
ARLINGTON VA 22201
703/522-5717

AMOUNT: $1500 - $2500
DEADLINE(S): AUG 1
FIELD(S): AERONAUTICS; AVIATION; RELATED AREAS
SCHOLARSHIPS OPEN TO PROMISING MEN & WOMEN WHO ARE FULL-TIME UNDERGRADUATE OR GRADUATE STUDENTS IN THE ABOVE AREAS. SCHOLARSHIPS OF UP TO $600 ALSO AVAILABLE FOR PART-TIME STUDENTS. USA CITIZEN.
FINANCIAL NEED IS A CONSIDERATION BUT NOT DETERMINATIVE. WRITE FOR COMPLETE INFORMATION.

160

AMERICAN GEOLOGICAL INSTITUTE (MINORITY PARTICIPATION PROGRAM SCHOLARSHIPS)
4220 KING ST
ALEXANDRIA VA 22302
703/379-2480
AMOUNT: UP TO $10000 PER YEAR UNDERGRAD; $4000 PER YEAR GRAD
DEADLINE(S): FEB 1
FIELD(S): EARTH SCIENCES; SPACE SCIENCES; MARINE SCIENCES
FOR FULL TIME UNDERGRADUATE OR GRADUATE STUDY IN THE ABOVE FIELDS. OPEN TO AMERICAN BLACKS; NATIVE AMERICANS & HISPANIC AMERICANS. MUST BE USA CITIZEN AND DEMONSTRATE FINANCIAL NEED.
APPROX 80 AWARDS PER YEAR. RENEWALS POSSIBLE WITH REAPPLICATION. WRITE FOR COMPLETE INFORMATION.

161

AMERICAN INSTITUTE OF AERONAUTICS AND ASTRONAUTICS - STUDENT PROGRAMS DEPARTMENT
370 L'ENFANT PROMENADE SW
WASHINGTON DC 20024
202/646-7458
AMOUNT: $1000
DEADLINE(S): JAN 31
FIELD(S): AERONAUTICS; AERONAUTICAL ENGINEERING
SCHOLARSHIPS OPEN TO UNDERGRADUATE STUDENTS ENROLLED AT AN ACCREDITED COLLEGE OR UNIVERSITY WHO HAVE COMPLETED AT LEAST ONE SEMESTER & HAVE AT LEAST A 3.0 GPA. USA CITIZEN OR LEGAL RESIDENT.
20-30 AWARDS PER YEAR. APPLICANT SHOULD BE PLANNING ENTRY INTO AN AEROSPACE ENGINEERING TECHNOLOGY FIELD. WRITE FOR COMPLETE INFORMATION.

162

AOPA AIR SAFETY FOUNDATION (MCALLISTER & BURNSIDE SCHOLARSHIPS)
421 AVIATION WAY
FREDERICK MD 21701
301/695-2170
AMOUNT: $1000 (MCALLISTER); $1200 (BURNSIDE)
DEADLINE(S): MAR 31
FIELD(S): AVIATION
SCHOLARSHIPS OPEN TO UNDERGRADUATE JUNIORS & SENIORS WHO ARE ENROLLED IN AN ACCREDITED AVIATION DEGREE PROGRAM WITH AN ACADEMIC PROFICIENCY OF 3.0 OR BETTER (ON A 4.0 SYSTEM). USA CITIZEN.
WRITE FOR COMPLETE INFORMATION.

163

AVIATION DISTRIBUTORS AND MANUFACTURERS ASSOCIATION INTERNATIONAL (ADMA INTERNATIONAL SCHOLARSHIP FUND)
1900 ARCH STREET
PHILADELPHIA PA 19103
215/564-3484
AMOUNT: $1000
DEADLINE(S): APR 10
FIELD(S): AVIATION MANAGEMENT; PROFESSIONAL PILOT
OPEN TO STUDENTS SEEKING A CAREER IN AVIATION MANAGEMENT OR AS PROFESSIONAL PILOTS. EMPHASIS MAY BE IN GENERAL AVIATION; AIRWAY SCIENCE MANAGEMENT; AVIATION MAINTENANCE; FLIGHT ENGINEER OR AIRWAY A/C SYSTEMS MANAGEMENT.
APPLICANTS MUST BE STUDYING IN THE AVIATION FIELD IN A FOUR-YEAR SCHOOL HAVING AN AVIATION PROGRAM AND MUST HAVE COMPLETED AT LEAST TWO YEARS OF THEIR PROGRAM. WRITE FOR COMPLETE INFORMATION.

164

EAA AVIATION FOUNDATION (SCHOLARSHIP PROGRAM)

WHITMAN REGIONAL AIRPORT; PO BOX 3065
OSHKOSH WI 54903
414/426-4888

AMOUNT: $200 TO $1500

DEADLINE(S): APR 1

FIELD(S): AVIATION

TEN DIFFERENT SCHOLARSHIP PROGRAMS OPEN TO WELL ROUNDED INDIVIDUALS INVOLVED IN SCHOOL AND COMMUNITY ACTIVITIES AS WELL AS AVIATION. APPLICANTS' ACADEMIC RECORDS SHOULD VERIFY THEIR ABILITY TO COMPLETE THEIR EDUCATIONAL PROGRAM.

FINANCIAL NEED IS A CONSIDERATION. WRITE FOR COMPLETE INFORMATION.

165

EASTERN NEW ENGLAND NINETY-NINES INC. (MARJOURIE VAN VLIET AVIATION MEMORIAL SCHOLARSHIP)

207 SANDY POND RD
LINCOLN MA 01773
617/259-0222

AMOUNT: $2000

DEADLINE(S): JAN 31

FIELD(S): AERONAUTICS; AVIATION MAINTENANCE; FLIGHT TRAINING

OPEN TO HIGH SCHOOL SENIORS OR BEYOND WHO LIVE IN ONE OF THE NEW ENGLAND STATES; PLAN A CAREER IN AVIATION AND HAVE APPLIED TO AN AVIATION RELATED EDUCATION OR TRAINING PROGRAM. SHOW FINANCIAL NEED.

CAN USE FOR TUITION AND/OR FLIGHT TRAINING. WRITE FOR COMPLETE INFORMATION.

166

ELECTRONIC INDUSTRIES FOUNDATION (SCHOLARSHIP FUND)

919 18TH ST; SUITE 900
WASHINGTON DC 20006
202/955-5814

AMOUNT: $2000

DEADLINE(S): FEB 1

FIELD(S): AERONAUTICS; COMPUTER SCIENCE; ELECTRICAL ENGINEERING; ENGINEERING TECHNOLOGY; APPLIED MATHEMATICS; MICROBIOLOGY

OPEN TO DISABLED STUDENTS WHO ARE PURSUING CAREERS IN HIGH-TECH AREAS THROUGH ACADEMIC OR TECHNICAL TRAINING. AWARDS TENABLE AT RECOGNIZED UNDERGRADUATE & GRADUATE COLLEGES & UNIVERSITIES. USA CITIZEN. FINANCIAL NEED IS A CONSIDERATION.

6 AWARDS PER YEAR. RENEWABLE. WRITE FOR COMPLETE INFORMATION.

167

HUGHES AIRCRAFT COMPANY (BACHELOR OF SCIENCE SCHOLARSHIP)

PO BOX 80028 (C1/B168) TECH. ED. CENTER
LOS ANGELES CA 90080
310-568-6711

AMOUNT: ALL EDUCATIONAL EXPENSES + SALARY & RELOCATION EXPENSES

DEADLINE(S): APPLY BETWEEN OCT & MAR PRIOR TO JUNE COMPLETION OF SOPHOMORE YEAR.

FIELD(S): ELECTRICAL MECHANICAL OR AEROSPACE ENGINEERING OR COMPUTER SCIENCE; MATHEMATICS; OR PHYSICS

OPEN TO STUDENTS WITH UPPER DIVISION STANDING OR AA DEGREE & AT LEAST A 3.0 GPA WHO HAVE BEEN ADMITTED WITHOUT CONDITION TO A UNIVERSITY ACCREDITED BY THE ACCREDITATION BOARD FOR ENGINEERING & TECHNOLOGY (ABET).

WORK STUDY OR FULL STUDY PROGRAMS. USA CITIZEN. MOST AWARDS ARE FOR WORK-STUDY NEAR HUGHES PLANTS. WRITE FOR COMPLETE INFORMATION.

168

INTERNATIONAL SOCIETY OF WOMEN AIRLINE PILOTS (ISA INTERNATIONAL CAREER SCHOLARSHIP/FIORENZA DE BERNARDI MERIT AWARD)

PO BOX 66268
CHICAGO IL 60666
WRITTEN INQUIRY

AMOUNT: $500 - $1500

DEADLINE(S): APR 1

FIELD(S): PURSUIT OF AIRLINE PILOT CAREER

OPEN TO WOMEN THROUGHOUT THE WORLD WHO ARE PURSUING A CAREER AS AN AIRLINE PILOT AND HAVE AT LEAST 350 HRS OF FLIGHT EXPERIENCE. SELECTION BASED ON NEED; DEMONSTRATED DEDICATION TO

CAREER GOAL; WORK EXPERIENCE AND HISTORY; RECOMMENDATIONS.
PERSONAL INTERVIEW IS REQUIRED. WRITE FOR COMPLETE INFORMATION.

169

MOONEY AIRCRAFT PILOTS ASSOCIATION SAFETY FOUNDATION (AL AND ART MOONEY SCHOLARSHIP PROGRAM)
MARK BUNZEL; AVTEX CORP; 2105 S. BASCOM AVE; #290
CAMPBELL CA 95008
408/245-2374
AMOUNT: $1000
DEADLINE(S): JUL 1
FIELD(S): AVIATION (FLIGHT SAFETY)
OPEN TO STUDENTS HAVING A CAREER OBJECTIVE WHICH WOULD PROMOTE FLIGHT SAFETY WHO HAVE COMPLETED HALF OF THEIR COURSE OF STUDY. MUST BE A MEMBER OF MAPA OR BE SPONSORED BY A MEMBER. ESSAY ON HOW CAREER WILL PROMOTE FLIGHT SAFETY IS REQUIRED
CANDIDATES SHOULD HAVE 3.0 OR BETTER GPA. CONTACT DENNIS MCGUIRE AT ABOVE ADDRESS FOR APPLICATION FORM AND COMPLETE INFORMATION.

170

NATIONAL BUSINESS AIRCRAFT ASSOCIATION (SCHOLARSHIPS)
1200 18TH ST NW
WASHINGTON DC 20036
202/783-9000; FAX 202/331-8364
AMOUNT: $500
DEADLINE(S): OCT 31
FIELD(S): AVIATION
OPEN TO COLLEGE SOPHOMORES; JUNIORS OR SENIORS WHO WILL BE CONTINUING IN SCHOOL THE FOLLOWING ACADEMIC YEAR IN AN AVIATION RELATED BACCALAUREATE OR GRADUATE PROGRAM. MUST BE USA CITIZEN AND HAVE 3.0 OR BETTER GPA.
10 AWARDS PER YEAR. WRITE FOR COMPLETE INFORMATION.

171

NATIONAL SPACE CLUB (DR. ROBERT H. GODDARD SPACE SCIENCE AND ENGINEERING SCHOLARSHIP)
655 15TH ST NW; #300
WASHINGTON DC 20005
202/639-4210
AMOUNT: $7500
DEADLINE(S): JAN 4
FIELD(S): AERONAUTICS
OPEN TO UNDERGRADUATE JUNIORS & SENIORS WHO HAVE SCHOLASTIC PLANS LEADING TO FUTURE PARTICIPATION IN THE AEROSPACE SCIENCES AND TECHNOLOGY. USA CITIZEN.
WRITE FOR COMPLETE INFORMATION.

172

SPACE FOUNDATION (SPACE DEVELOPMENT STRATEGIES AWARD)
DR. DAVID J. NORTON; EDUCATIONAL GRANT PROGRAM; 4800 RESEARCH FOREST DR.
THE WOODLANDS TX 77381
713/363-7944; FAX 713/363-7914
AMOUNT: $1000
DEADLINE(S): OCT 1
FIELD(S): PRIVATE SECTOR INVOLVEMENT IN SPACE SCIENCE
AWARD'S PURPOSE IS TO STIMULATE STRATEGIC THINKING ON THE ROLE OF THE PRIVATE SECTOR IN SPACE. COMPETITION IS FOR THE BEST PAPER IN THE AREA OF SPACE POLICY FOR SPACE DEVELOPMENT EMPHASIZING ROLES FOR THE PRIVATE SECTOR.
PAPER SHOULD RUN 2500 - 4000 WORDS. WRITE FOR COMPLETE INFORMATION.

173

U.S. AIR FORCE ROTC (4-YEAR SCHOLARSHIP PROGRAM)
AFROTC/RROO; RECRUITING OPERATIONS BRANCH
MAXWELL AFB AL 36112
205/953-2091
AMOUNT: TUITION + FEES & BOOKS + $100 PER MONTH STIPEND
DEADLINE(S): DEC 1
FIELD(S): AERONAUTICAL ENGINEERING; CIVIL ENGINEERING; MECHANICAL ENGINEERING; MATHEMATICS; PHYSICS; NURSING & SOME LIBERAL ARTS
OPEN TO USA CITIZENS WHO ARE AT LEAST 17 AND WILL GRADUATE FROM COLLEGE BEFORE AGE 25. MUST COMPLETE APPLICATION; FURNISH SAT/ACT SCORES; HIGH SCHOOL TRANSCRIPTS AND RECORD OF EXTRACURRICULAR ACTIVITIES.

MUST QUALIFY ON AIR FORCE MEDICAL EXAMINATION. ABOUT 1600 SCHOLARSHIPS AWARDED EACH YEAR AT CAMPUSES WHICH OFFER AIR FORCE ROTC.

174

VERTICAL FLIGHT FOUNDATION (UNDERGRADUATE/GRADUATE SCHOLARSHIPS)
217 N WASHINGTON ST
ALEXANDRIA VA 22314
703/684-6777
AMOUNT: UP TO $2000
DEADLINE(S): FEB 1
FIELD(S): MECHANICAL ENGINEERING; ELECTRICAL ENGINEERING; AEROSPACE ENGINEERING
ANNUAL SCHOLARSHIPS OPEN TO UNDERGRADUATE & GRADUATE STUDENTS IN THE ABOVE AREAS WHO ARE INTERESTED IN PURSUING CAREERS IN SOME ASPECT OF HELICOPTER OR VERTICAL FLIGHT. FOR FULL TIME STUDY AT ACCREDITED SCHOOL OF ENGINEERING.
WRITE FOR COMPLETE INFORMATION.

175

VIRGINIA AIRPORT OPERATORS COUNCIL (VAOC AVIATION SCHOLARSHIP AWARD)
HAMPTON UNIVERSITY; AIRWAY SCIENCE PROGRAM
HAMPTON VA 23668
804/727-5417
AMOUNT: $2000
DEADLINE(S): APR 30
FIELD(S): AVIATION
OPEN TO VIRGINIA HIGH SCHOOL SENIORS WHO HAVE BEEN ACCEPTED INTO AN ACCREDITED POST-SECONDARY AVIATION EDUCATION PROGRAM. APPLICANTS NEED A 3.0 OR BETTER GPA AND SHOULD BE PLANNING A CAREER IN AVIATION.
WRITE FOR COMPLETE INFORMATION.

ARCHITECTURE

176

AMERICAN ARCHITECTURAL FOUNDATION (AIA/AIAF SCHOLARSHIP PROGRAM)
1735 NEW YORK AVENUE NW
WASHINGTON DC 20006
202/626-7511
AMOUNT: $500 - $2500
DEADLINE(S): FEB 3
FIELD(S): ARCHITECTURE
OPEN TO UNDERGRADUATE STUDENTS IN THEIR FINAL 2 YEARS & GRADUATE STUDENTS PURSUING THEIR MASTER'S DEGREE. AWARDS TENABLE AT ACCREDITED INSTITUTIONS IN THE USA & CANADA.
APPLICATIONS AVAILABLE ONLY THROUGH THE OFFICE OF THE DEAN OR DEPARTMENT HEAD AT AN NAAB OR RAIC SCHOOL OF ARCHITECTURE.

177

AMERICAN ARCHITECTURAL FOUNDATION (MINORITY/DISADVANTAGED SCHOLARSHIP PROGRAM)
1735 NEW YORK AVENUE NW
WASHINGTON DC 20006
202/626-7511
AMOUNT: VARIES
DEADLINE(S): DEC 4 FOR NOMINATION; JAN 15 FOR APPLICATION
FIELD(S): ARCHITECTURE
OPEN TO MINORITY &/OR DISADVANTAGED STUDENTS WHO ARE TRANSFERRING TO AN NAAB SCHOOL OF ARCHITECTURE OR COLLEGE FRESHMEN ENTERING A PROGRAM LEADING TO A PROFESSIONAL DEGREE (BACHELOR OR MASTER OF ARCHITECTURE.)
NOMINATION BY AN INDIVIDUAL FAMILIAR WITH STUDENT'S INTEREST AND POTENTIAL TO BE AN ARCHITECT IS REQUIRED. 20 SCHOLARSHIPS PER YEAR. WRITE FOR COMPLETE INFORMATION.

178

ARTS INTERNATIONAL; INSTITUTE OF INTERNATIONAL EDUCATION (CINTAS FELLOWSHIP PROGRAM)
809 UNITED NATIONS PLAZA
NEW YORK NY 10017
212/984-5370
AMOUNT: $10000
DEADLINE(S): MAR 1
FIELD(S): ARCHITECTURE; PAINTING; PHOTOGRAPHY; SCULPTURE; PRINTMAKING; MUSIC COMPOSITION; CREATIVE WRITING
FELLOWSHIPS OPEN TO ARTISTS WHO ARE OF CUBAN ANCESTRY OR CUBAN CITIZENS LIVING OUTSIDE OF CUBA. THEY ARE

INTENDED TO FOSTER & ENCOURAGE THE PROFESSIONAL DEVELOPMENT & RECOGNITION OF TALENTED CREATIVE ARTISTS IN THE ABOVE AREAS.
FELLOWSHIPS ARE NOT AWARDED FOR FURTHERANCE OF ACADEMIC STUDY. 5-10 AWARDS PER YEAR. WRITE FOR COMPLETE INFORMATION.

179

LANDSCAPE ARCHITECTURE FOUNDATION (CLASS FUND SCHOLARSHIPS)
4401 CONNECTICUT AVE NW; SUITE 500
WASHINGTON DC 20008
202/686-0068
AMOUNT: $500 - $2000
DEADLINE(S): APR 3
FIELD(S): LANDSCAPE ARCHITECTURE
OPEN TO SOUTHERN CALIFORNIA STUDENTS ENROLLED AT CALIFORNIA POLYTECHNIC INSTITUTE (POMONA OR SAN LUIS OBISPO); USC; UCLA & UC-IRVINE WHO SHOW PROMISE & A COMMITMENT TO LANDSCAPE ARCHITECTURE AS A PROFESSION.
WRITE FOR COMPLETE INFORMATION.

180

LANDSCAPE ARCHITECTURE FOUNDATION (GRACE & ROBERT FRASER LANDSCAPE AWARD)
4401 CONNECTICUT AVE NW; SUITE 500
WASHINGTON DC 20008
202/686-0068
AMOUNT: $500
DEADLINE(S): MAY 4
FIELD(S): LANDSCAPE ARCHITECTURE
AWARD TO RECOGNIZE INNOVATIVE HORTICULTURAL RESEARCH OR DESIGN AS IT RELATES TO THE PROFESSION OF LANDSCAPE ARCHITECTURE. OPEN TO GRADUATE AND UNDERGRADUATE STUDENTS.
WRITE FOR COMPLETE INFORMATION.

181

LANDSCAPE ARCHITECTURE FOUNDATION (HARRIETT BARNHART WIMMER SCHOLARSHIP)
4401 CONNECTICUT AVE NW; SUITE 500
WASHINGTON DC 20008
202/686-0068
AMOUNT: $500
DEADLINE(S): MAY 4
FIELD(S): LANDSCAPE ARCHITECTURE
OPEN TO WOMEN GOING INTO THEIR FINAL YEAR OF UNDERGRADUATE STUDY AT A USA OR CANADIAN UNIVERSITY WHO HAVE DEMONSTRATED EXCELLENCE IN THEIR DESIGN ABILITY & SENSITIVITY TO THE ENVIRONMENT.
WRITE FOR COMPLETE INFORMATION.

182

LANDSCAPE ARCHITECTURE FOUNDATION (LANDCADD INC SCHOLARSHIP FUND)
4401 CONNECTICUT AVE NW; SUITE 500
WASHINGTON DC 20008
202/686-0068
AMOUNT: $500
DEADLINE(S): MAY 4
FIELD(S): LANDSCAPE ARCHITECTURE
SCHOLARSHIPS OPEN TO UNDERGRADUATE & GRADUATE STUDENTS WHO WISH TO UTILIZE TECHNOLOGICAL ADVANCEMENTS SUCH AS COMPUTER-AIDED DESIGN; VIDEO IMAGING AND/OR TELECOMMUNICATIONS IN THEIR CAREER.
WRITE FOR COMPLETE INFORMATION.

183

LANDSCAPE ARCHITECTURE FOUNDATION (LESTER WALLS III ENDOWMENT SCHOLARSHIP)
4401 CONNECTICUT AVE NW; SUITE 500
WASHINGTON DC 20008
202/686-0068
AMOUNT: $500
DEADLINE(S): MAY 4
FIELD(S): LANDSCAPE ARCHITECTURE
SCHOLARSHIP OPEN TO HANDICAPPED STUDENTS PURSUING A DEGREE IN LANDSCAPE ARCHITECTURE OR FOR RESEARCH ON BARRIER-FREE DESIGN FOR THE DISABLED.
WRITE FOR COMPLETE INFORMATION.

184

LANDSCAPE ARCHITECTURE FOUNDATION (RAYMOND E. PAGE SCHOLARSHIP FUND)
4401 CONNECTICUT AVE NW; SUITE 500
WASHINGTON DC 20008
202/686-0068
AMOUNT: $500
DEADLINE(S): MAY 4
FIELD(S): LANDSCAPE ARCHITECTURE

SCHOLARSHIPS OPEN TO ANY UNDERGRADUATE OR GRADUATE STUDENT WHO IS IN NEED OF FINANCIAL ASSISTANCE.
WRITE FOR COMPLETE INFORMATION.

185

LANDSCAPE ARCHITECTURE FOUNDATION (STUDENT RESEARCH GRANTS)
4401 CONNECTICUT AVE NW; SUITE 500
WASHINGTON DC 20008
202/686-0068
AMOUNT: $1000
DEADLINE(S): MAY 4
FIELD(S): LANDSCAPE ARCHITECTURE
RESEARCH GRANTS TO ENCOURAGE STUDENT EFFORTS IN PRACTICAL RESEARCH & EXPAND THE KNOWLEDGE BASE OF THE PROFESSION. OPEN TO UNDERGRADUATE & GRADUATE STUDENTS.
WRITE FOR COMPLETE INFORMATION.

186

LANDSCAPE ARCHITECTURE FOUNDATION (THE COXE GROUP SCHOLARSHIP)
4401 CONNECTICUT AVE NW; SUITE 500
WASHINGTON DC 20008
202/686-0068
AMOUNT: $1000
DEADLINE(S): MAY 4
FIELD(S): LANDSCAPE ARCHITECTURE
SCHOLARSHIP OPEN TO 4TH; 5TH & 6TH YEAR LANDSCAPE ARCHITECTURE STUDENTS WHO HAVE DEMONSTRATED ABILITY & NEED.
WRITE FOR COMPLETE INFORMATION.

187

LANDSCAPE ARCHITECTURE FOUNDATION (THE EDITH H. HENDERSON SCHOLARSHIP)
4401 CONNECTICUT AVE NW; SUITE 500
WASHINGTON DC 20008
202/686-0068
AMOUNT: $500
DEADLINE(S): MAY 4
FIELD(S): LANDSCAPE ARCHITECTURE
SCHOLARSHIP OPEN TO FEMALE STUDENTS AT THE UNIVERSITY OF GEORGIA WHO ARE ENTERING THEIR FINAL YEAR OF UNDERGRADUATE STUDY OR ANY YEAR OF GRADUATE STUDY.
WRITE FOR COMPLETE INFORMATION.

188

LANDSCAPE ARCHITECTURE FOUNDATION (THE RAINBIRD COMPANY SCHOLARSHIP)
4401 CONNECTICUT AVE NW; SUITE 500
WASHINGTON DC 20008
202/686-0068
AMOUNT: $1000
DEADLINE(S): MAY 4
FIELD(S): LANDSCAPE ARCHITECTURE
OPEN TO LANDSCAPE ARCHITECTURE STUDENTS IN THEIR FINAL 2 YEARS OF UNDERGRADUATE STUDY WHO HAVE DEMONSTRATED COMMITMENT TO THE PROFESSION THROUGH PARTICIPATION IN EXTRACURRICULAR ACTIVITIES & EXEMPLARY SCHOLASTIC ACHIEVEMENTS.
WRITE FOR COMPLETE INFORMATION.

189

LANDSCAPE ARCHITECTURE FOUNDATION (WILLIAM LOCKLIN SCHOLARSHIP)
4401 CONNECTICUT AVE NW; SUITE 500
WASHINGTON DC 20008
202/686-0068
AMOUNT: $500
DEADLINE(S): MAY 4
FIELD(S): LANDSCAPE ARCHITECTURE
SCHOLARSHIPS OPEN TO UNDERGRADUATE & GRADUATE STUDENTS WHO ARE PURSUING A PROGRAM IN LIGHTING DESIGN. PURPOSE IS TO STRESS THE IMPORTANCE OF 24-HOUR LIGHTING IN LANDSCAPE DESIGNS.
WRITE FOR COMPLETE INFORMATION.

190

NATIONAL ASSOCIATION OF WOMEN IN CONSTRUCTION (EL CAMINO REAL CHAPTER #158 SCHOLARSHIP)
MARIE REVERE; PO BOX 7131
SAN JOSE CA 95150
408/452-4644
AMOUNT: $1000
DEADLINE(S): MAY 1
FIELD(S): CIVIL ENGINEERING; CONSTRUCTION; ARCHITECTURE; ARCHITECTURAL ENGINEERING
OPEN TO MEN OR WOMEN UNDERGRADUATES WHO ARE GOING INTO THEIR JUNIOR YEAR AT AN ACCREDITED 4-YEAR CALIFORNIA COLLEGE. USA CITIZEN.
WRITE FOR COMPLETE INFORMATION.

191

NATIONAL ASSOCIATION OF WOMEN IN CONSTRUCTION (FOUNDERS' SCHOLARSHIP FOUNDATION AWARDS)
327 S ADAMS
FT WORTH TX 76104
817/877-5551
AMOUNT: NOT SPECIFIED
DEADLINE(S): FEB 15
FIELD(S): FIELDS RELATED TO A CAREER IN CONSTRUCTION
OPEN TO FULL TIME STUDENTS ENROLLED IN A CONSTRUCTION RELATED PROGRAM LEADING TO AN ASSOCIATE OR BACHELOR DEGREE. APPLICANTS SHOULD BE IN AT LEAST THEIR FIRST YEAR OF COLLEGE AND HAVE AT LEAST ONE YEAR REMAINING.
AWARDS COMMITTEE CONSIDERS GRADES; INTEREST IN CONSTRUCTION; EXTRACURRICULAR ACTIVITIES; EMPLOYMENT EXPERIENCE; FINANCIAL NEED & EVALUATION BY ACADEMIC ADVISOR. WRITE FOR COMPLETE INFORMATION.

192

NATIONAL DEFENSE TRANSPORTATION ASSOCIATION - SAN FRANCISCO BAY AREA CHAPTER (NDTA SCHOLARSHIP)
PO BOX 24676
OAKLAND CA 94623
WRITTEN INQUIRY
AMOUNT: $1000
DEADLINE(S): MAY 1
FIELD(S): TRANSPORTATION
OPEN TO USA CITIZENS STUDYING IN THE FIELD OF BUSINESS; ENGINEERING; PLANNING OR ENVIRONMENT IN PREPARATION FOR A CAREER RELATED TO TRANSPORTATION. FINANCIAL NEED WILL BE CONSIDERED.
WRITE FOR COMPLETE INFORMATION.

193

NATIONAL INSTITUTE FOR ARCHITECTURAL EDUCATION (J. DINKELOO TRAVELING FELLOWSHIPS TO ROME)
30 WEST 22ND ST
NEW YORK NY 10010
212/924-7000
AMOUNT: $5000
DEADLINE(S): MAY 15
FIELD(S): ARCHITECTURAL DESIGN & TECHNOLOGY
TRAVELING FELLOWSHIPS TENABLE AT THE AMERICAN ACADEMY IN ROME ITALY. OPEN TO USA CITIZENS WHO HAVE OR ANTICIPATE RECEIVING THEIR FIRST PROFESSIONAL DEGREE IN ARCHITECTURE BETWEEN JUNE OF THE COMPETITION YEAR & JUNE 3 YEARS PRIOR.
WRITE FOR COMPLETE INFORMATION.

194

NATIONAL INSTITUTE FOR ARCHITECTURAL EDUCATION (LLOYD WARREN FELLOWSHIPS)
30 WEST 22ND ST
NEW YORK NY 10010
212/924-7000
AMOUNT: UP TO $6000
DEADLINE(S): FEB 28
FIELD(S): ARCHITECTURE
ARCHITECTURAL DESIGN COMPETITION OPEN TO STUDENTS WHO HAVE RECEIVED OR ANTICIPATE RECEIVING THEIR FIRST PROFESSIONAL DEGREE IN ARCHITECTURE FROM A USA SCHOOL BETWEEN JUNE OF COMPETITION YEAR & JUNE 3 YEARS PRIOR.
AWARDS ARE TO SUPPORT TRAVEL/STUDY TRIPS ABROAD. TRAVEL MUST COMMENCE WITHIN ONE YEAR OF AWARD. WRITE FOR COMPLETE INFORMATION.

195

NATIONAL INSTITUTE FOR ARCHITECTURAL EDUCATION (WILLIAM VAN ALEN ARCHITECT MEMORIAL FELLOWSHIP)
30 WEST 22ND STREET
NEW YORK NY 10010
212-924-7000
AMOUNT: UP TO $5000
DEADLINE(S): MAY 8
FIELD(S): ARCHITECTURE; CIVIL ENGINEERING
DESIGN COMPETITION OPEN TO UNDERGRADUATE & MASTER'S STUDENTS ENROLLED IN AN ACCREDITED ARCHITECTURAL OR ENGINEERING PROGRAM IN THE USA OR CANADA.
WINNERS WILL RECEIVE AWARDS FOR TRAVEL & STUDY ABROAD. CONTACT ADDRESS ABOVE FOR COMPLETE DETAILS.

196

NATIONAL ROOFING FOUNDATION (NRF SCHOLARSHIP AWARDS PROGRAM)
O'HARE INTERNATIONAL CENTER; 10255 W. HIGGINS RD; SUITE 600
ROSEMONT IL 60018
708/299-9070
AMOUNT: $2000
DEADLINE(S): JAN 15
FIELD(S): ARCHITECTURE; CONSTRUCTION
OPEN TO HIGH SCHOOL SENIORS; UNDERGRADUATE AND GRADUATE ARCHITECTURAL STUDENTS OR STUDENTS OF ANOTHER CURRICULUM RELATED TO THE ROOFING INDUSTRY. APPLICANTS MUST BE USA CITIZENS.
FOR FULL TIME STUDY AT AN ACCREDITED 4 YEAR COLLEGE OR UNIVERSITY. SEND A SELF-ADDRESSED STAMPED ENVELOPE (#10) TO RECEIVE AN APPLICATION.

197

NATIONAL STONE ASSN./AMERICAN SOCIETY OF LANDSCAPE ARCHITECTS (STUDENT COMPETITION)
1415 ELLIOT PLACE NW
WASHINGTON DC 20007
202/342-1100
AMOUNT: $1000; $500; $300
DEADLINE(S): MAY 1
FIELD(S): LANDSCAPE ARCHITECTURE
CONTEST IN WHICH UNDERGRADUATE LANDSCAPE ARCHITECTURE STUDENTS WORK WITH A LOCAL ROCK QUARRY TO PRODUCE A RECLAMATION PROPOSAL.
WRITE FOR COMPLETE INFORMATION.

198

NEW JERSEY SOCIETY OF ARCHITECTS (AIA/NJ SCHOLARSHIP PROGRAM)
900 ROUTE NINE; 2ND FLOOR
WOODBRIDGE NJ 07095
908/636-5680
AMOUNT: $250 - $1500
DEADLINE(S): APR 16
FIELD(S): ARCHITECTURE
OPEN TO NEW JERSEY RESIDENTS WHO ARE ENROLLED IN OR ACCEPTED TO AN ACCREDITED SCHOOL OF ARCHITECTURE AND HAVE COMPLETED ONE YEAR OF STUDY TOWARD THE FIRST PROFESSIONAL ARCHITECTURAL DEGREE. MUST DEMONSTRATE TALENT AND FINANCIAL NEED.
MUST BE USA CITIZEN AND INTEND TO PURSUE ARCHITECTURAL CAREER IN NEW JERSEY. 20 AWARDS PER YEAR. WRITE FOR COMPLETE INFORMATION.

199

NEW YORK CITY DEPT. OF PERSONNEL (GOVERNMENT SCHOLARS INTERNSHIP PROGRAM)
2 WASHINGTON ST; 15TH FLOOR
NEW YORK NY 10004
212/487-5698
AMOUNT: $2500
DEADLINE(S): JAN 27
FIELD(S): PUBLIC ADMINISTRATION; URBAN PLANNING; GOVERNMENT; PUBLIC SERVICE; URBAN AFFAIRS
10-WEEK SUMMER INTERN PROGRAM OPEN TO UNDERGRADUATE SOPHOMORES; JUNIORS & SENIORS. PROGRAM PROVIDES STUDENTS WITH UNIQUE OPPORTUNITY TO LEARN ABOUT NY CITY GOVERNMENT. INTERNSHIPS AVAILABLE IN VIRTUALLY EVERY CITY AGENCY & MAYORAL OFFICE.
WRITE FOR COMPLETE INFORMATION.

200

NEW YORK CITY DEPT. OF PERSONNEL (URBAN FELLOWS PROGRAM)
2 WASHINGTON ST; 15TH FLOOR
NEW YORK NY 10004
212/487-5698
AMOUNT: $17000 STIPEND
DEADLINE(S): JAN 26
FIELD(S): PUBLIC ADMINISTRATION; URBAN PLANNING; GOVERNMENT; PUBLIC SERVICE; URBAN AFFAIRS
FELLOWSHIP PROGRAM PROVIDES ONE ACADEMIC YEAR (9 MONTHS) OF FULL-TIME WORK EXPERIENCE IN URBAN GOVERNMENT. OPEN TO GRADUATING COLLEGE SENIORS AND RECENT COLLEGE GRADUATES. USA CITIZEN.
WRITE FOR COMPLETE INFORMATION.

201

NEW YORK FOUNDATION FOR THE ARTS (ARTIST'S FELLOWSHIPS & SERVICES)
155 AVE OF THE AMERICAS; 14TH FLOOR
NEW YORK NY 10013

212/366-6900; FAX 212/366-1778
AMOUNT: $7000
DEADLINE(S): SEP 30
FIELD(S): VISUAL ARTS; LITERATURE; ARCHITECTURE; MUSIC AND MEDIA
FELLOWSHIPS & SERVICES OPEN TO ORIGINATING ARTISTS OVER 18 WHO HAVE BEEN NY STATE RESIDENTS FOR 2 YEARS PREVIOUS TO APPLICATION DATE & ARE NOT ENROLLED IN A DEGREE AWARDING COURSE OF STUDY. AWARDS ARE TO ASSIST IN CREATION OF ONGOING WORK.
APPLICATIONS AVAILABLE IN SPRINT OF EACH YEAR. ABOUT 120 FELLOWSHIPS PER YEAR; MANY OTHER SERVICES ARE AVAILABLE. NOT FOR ACADEMIC STUDY. WRITE FOR COMPLETE INFORMATION.

202

ROBERT SCHRECK MEMORIAL FUND (GRANTS)
C/O TEXAS COMMERCE BANK-TRUST DEPT; PO DRAWER 140
EL PASO TX 79980
915/546-6515
AMOUNT: $500 - $1500
DEADLINE(S): JUL 15; NOV 15
FIELD(S): MEDICINE; VETERINARY MEDICINE; PHYSICS; CHEMISTRY; ARCHITECTURE; ENGINEERING; EPISCOPAL CLERGY
GRANTS TO UNDERGRADUATE JUNIORS OR SENIORS OR GRADUATE STUDENTS WHO HAVE BEEN RESIDENTS OF EL PASO COUNTY FOR AT LEAST TWO YEARS. MUST BE USA CITIZEN OR LEGAL RESIDENT AND HAVE A HIGH GRADE POINT AVERAGE. FINANCIAL NEED IS A CONSIDERATION.
WRITE FOR COMPLETE INFORMATION.

203

SAN FRANCISCO BAY AREA CHAPTER - NATIONAL DEFENSE TRANSPORTATION ASSN (NDTA MERIT SCHOLARSHIP)
BOX 24676
OAKLAND CA 94623
WRITTEN INQUIRY
AMOUNT: $2000
DEADLINE(S): MAR 31
FIELD(S): BUSINESS; ENGINEERING; PLANNING; ENVIRONMENT (AS RELATED TO TRANSPORTATION)
OPEN TO USA CITIZENS ENROLLED IN AN ACCREDITED UNDERGRADUATE DEGREE OR VOCATIONAL PROGRAM IN ABOVE FIELDS WHO PLAN TO PURSUE A CAREER RELATED TO TRANSPORTATION. FINANCIAL NEED WILL BE CONSIDERED.
WRITE FOR COMPLETE INFORMATION.

204

SKIDMORE OWINGS & MERRILL FOUNDATION (TRAVELLING FELLOWSHIP PROGRAM)
224 S MICHIGAN AVE; SUITE 1000
CHICAGO IL 60604
312/554-9090
AMOUNT: $10000 - $25000
DEADLINE(S): NONE SPECIFIED
FIELD(S): ARCHITECTURE
OPEN TO UNDERGRADUATE AND GRADUATE ARCHITECTURE STUDENTS. CANDIDATES MUST BE USA CITIZENS WHO ARE ATTENDING OR RECENTLY GRADUATED FROM AN ACCREDITED ARCHITECTURE SCHOOL.
WRITE FOR COMPLETE INFORMATION.

205

SMITHSONIAN INSTITUTION (COOPER-HEWITT MUSEUM OF DESIGN SUMMER INTERNSHIPS)
COOPER-HEWITT MUSEUM; 2 EAST 91ST ST
NEW YORK NY 10128
212/860-6868; FAX 212/860-6909
AMOUNT: VARIES
DEADLINE(S): MAR 31
FIELD(S): ART; DESIGN; ARCHITECTURE; MUSEUM STUDIES
10-WEEK SUMMER INTERNSHIPS AT THE COOPER-HEWITT MUSEUM OPEN TO UNDERGRADUATE AND GRADUATE STUDENTS.
WRITE FOR COMPLETE INFORMATION.

206

SMITHSONIAN INSTITUTION (MINORITY UNDERGRADUATE & GRADUATE INTERNSHIP)
OFFICE OF FELLOWSHIPS & GRANTS; 955 L'ENFANT PLAZA; SUITE 7300
WASHINGTON DC 20560
202/287-3271
AMOUNT: $250 - $300 PER WEEK STIPEND + TRAVEL
DEADLINE(S): FEB 15; JUN 15; OCT 15
FIELD(S): DESIGN; ARCHITECTURE; ART; MUSEUM STUDIES

INTERNSHIPS OPEN TO MINORITY STUDENTS FOR RESEARCH & STUDY AT THE SMITHSONIAN OR THE COOPER-HEWITT MUSEUM OF DESIGN IN NEW YORK CITY. THE MUSEUM'S COLLECTION SPANS 3000 YEARS OF DESIGN FROM ANCIENT POTTERY TO MODERN FASHION & ADVERTISING.

UNDERGRADUATES RECEIVE $250 PER WEEK STIPEND & GRADUATE STUDENTS RECEIVE $300 PER WEEK STIPEND. WRITE FOR COMPLETE INFORMATION.

207

UNIVERSITY OF ILLINOIS AT URBANA-CHAMPAIGN (LYDIA E. PARKER BATES SCHOLARSHIP)

STUDENT SERVICES BLDG; 610 EAST JOHN STREET

CHAMPAIGN IL 61820

217/333-0100

AMOUNT: VARIES

DEADLINE(S): MAR 15

FIELD(S): ART; ARCHITECTURE; LANDSCAPE ARCHITECTURE; URBAN PLANNING; DANCE; THEATER

OPEN TO UNDERGRADUATE STUDENTS IN THE COLLEGE OF FINE & APPLIED ARTS WHO ARE ATTENDING THE UNIVERSITY OF ILLINOIS AT URBANA-CHAMPAIGN. MUST DEMONSTRATE FINANCIAL NEED AND HAVE 3.85 GPA (5.0 = A SCALE).

175 AWARDS PER YEAR. RECIPIENTS MUST CARRY AT LEAST 14 CREDIT HOURS PER SEMESTER. CONTACT OFFICE OF STUDENT FINANCIAL AID.

208

VIRGINIA MUSEUM OF FINE ARTS (UNDERGRAD/GRADUATE & PROFESSIONAL FELLOWSHIPS)

2800 GROVE AVE

RICHMOND VA 23221

804/367-0824

AMOUNT: UP TO $4000 UNDERGRADS; $5000 GRADS; $8000 PROFESSIONALS

DEADLINE(S): MAR 1

FIELD(S): ART; FINE ARTS; ART HISTORY (GRADUATE ONLY); ARCHITECTURE; PHOTOGRAPHY; FILM; VIDEO

VIRGINIA RESIDENT FOR 1 YEAR PRIOR TO DEADLINE. US CITIZEN OR LEGAL RESIDENT. PROFESSIONAL ARTIST FELLOWSHIPS ALSO AVAILABLE. NEED IS CONSIDERED.

ART; FINE ARTS & ART HISTORY FOR GRADUATE STUDENTS ONLY. 9-12 AWARDS PER YEAR. WRITE FOR COMPLETE INFORMATION.

209

WAVERLY COMMUNITY HOUSE INC (F. LAMMONT BELIN ARTS SCHOLARSHIPS)

SCHOLARSHIPS SELECTION COMMITTEE

WAVERLY PA 18471

717/586-8191

AMOUNT: $9000

DEADLINE(S): DEC 15

FIELD(S): PAINTING; SCULPTURE; MUSIC; DRAMA; DANCE; LITERATURE; ARCHITECTURE; PHOTOGRAPHY

APPLICANTS MUST RESIDE IN THE ABINGTONS OR POCONO REGIONS OF NORTHEASTERN PENNSYLVANIA. THEY MUST FURNISH PROOF OF EXCEPTIONAL ABILITY IN THEIR CHOSEN FIELD BUT NEED NO FORMAL TRAINING IN ANY ACADEMIC OR PROFESSIONAL PROGRAM.

USA CITIZENSHIP REQUIRED. FINALISTS MUST APPEAR IN PERSON BEFORE THE SELECTION COMMITTEE. WRITE FOR COMPLETE INFORMATION.

210

WEBB INSTITUTE OF NAVAL ARCHITECTURE (ADMISSIONS SCHOLARSHIPS)

CRESCENT BEACH RD

GLEN COVE NY 11542

516/671-2213

AMOUNT: FULL TUITION FOR 4 YEARS

DEADLINE(S): FEB 15

FIELD(S): NAVAL ARCHITECTURE; MARINE ENGINEERING

OPEN TO H.S. STUDENTS AGED 16-24 WHO ARE IN TOP 10% OF THEIR CLASS & HAVE AT LEAST 3.2 GPA ON 4.0 SCALE. SELECTION BASED ON COLLEGE BOARDS; SAT'S; DEMONSTRATED INTEREST IN ABOVE AREAS & INTERVIEW. USA CITIZEN.

20 TO 25 FOUR YEAR FULL TUITION UNDERGRAD SCHOLARSHIPS PER YEAR TO WEBB INSTITUTE. WRITE FOR COMPLETE INFORMATION.

211

WEST VIRGINIA SOCIETY OF ARCHITECTS/AIA (SCHOLARSHIP)

PO BOX 813; 405 CAPITOL ST; SUITE I

CHARLESTON WV 25323

304/344-9872
AMOUNT: $2000
DEADLINE(S): MAY 30
FIELD(S): ARCHITECTURE
OPEN TO WEST VIRGINIA RESIDENTS ENROLLED IN AT LEAST THEIR SECOND YEAR OF AN ACCREDITED ARCHITECTURAL PROGRAM. CANDIDATES MUST SUBMIT LETTER STATING NEED; QUALIFICATIONS AND DESIRE.
WRITE FOR COMPLETE INFORMATION.

CIVIL ENG

212

AMERICAN SOCIETY OF CIVIL ENGINEERS (ACSE CONSTRUCTION ENGINEERING SCHOLARSHIP AND STUDENT PRIZES)
345 EAST 47TH ST
NEW YORK NY 10017
800/548-2723 OUTSIDE NY; 800/628-0041 INSIDE NY
AMOUNT: $1000
DEADLINE(S): APR 1
FIELD(S): CONSTRUCTION ENGINEERING
OPEN TO COLLEGE FRESHMEN; SOPHOMORES OR JUNIORS WHO ARE MEMBERS IN GOOD STANDING OF AN ASCE STUDENT CHAPTER OR CLUB AND WHO WRITE A PAPER ON TOPICS RELATING IN A SIGNIFICANT WAY TO CONSTRUCTION.
ONE PAPER WILL BE CHOSEN AS A SEMI-FINALIST FROM EACH OF THE FOUR SOCIETY ZONES. ONE AWARD PER YEAR. WRITE FOR COMPLETE INFORMATION.

213

AMERICAN SOCIETY OF CIVIL ENGINEERS (B. CHARLES TINEY MEMORIAL ASCE STUDENT CHAPTER SCHOLARSHIP)
345 EAST 47TH ST
NEW YORK NY 10017
800/548-2723 OUTSIDE NY; 800/628-0041 INSIDE NY
AMOUNT: $2000 MAXIMUM
DEADLINE(S): FEB 1
FIELD(S): CIVIL ENGINEERING
OPEN TO FRESHMEN; SOPHOMORES OR JUNIORS WHO ARE STUDENT MEMBERS OF ASCE IN GOOD STANDING. AWARDS TENABLE AT ABET ACCREDITED COLLEGES & UNIVERSITIES. MUST DEMONSTRATE FINANCIAL NEED.
WRITE FOR COMPLETE INFORMATION.

214

AMERICAN SOCIETY OF CIVIL ENGINEERS (SAMUEL FLETCHER TAPMAN SCHOLARSHIPS)
345 EAST 47TH ST
NEW YORK NY 10017
800/548-ACSE
AMOUNT: $1500
DEADLINE(S): FEB 15
FIELD(S): CIVIL ENGINEERING
OPEN TO UNDERGRADUATE FRESHMEN; SOPHOMORES & JUNIORS WHO ARE ACSE STUDENT MEMBERS IN GOOD STANDING. AWARDS TENABLE AT ABET ACCREDITED COLLEGES & UNIVERSITIES.
WRITE FOR COMPLETE INFORMATION.

215

AMERICAN SOCIETY OF CIVIL ENGINEERS (THE FREEMAN FELLOWSHIP)
345 EAST 47TH ST
NEW YORK NY 10017
800/548-2723 OUTSIDE NY; 800/628-0041 INSIDE NY
AMOUNT: VARIES
DEADLINE(S): FEB 1
FIELD(S): CIVIL ENGINEERING
FELLOWSHIPS TO ENCOURAGE RESEARCH IN CIVIL ENGINEERING. OPEN TO YOUNG ENGINEERS (UNDER 45) WHO ARE MEMBERS OF ASCE. GRANTS ARE MADE TOWARD EXPENSES FOR EXPERIMENTS; OBSERVATIONS & COMPILATIONS TO DISCOVER NEW & ACCURATE DATA.
WRITE FOR COMPLETE INFORMATION.

216

ASSOCIATED GENERAL CONTRACTORS EDUCATION AND RESEARCH FOUNDATION (UNDERGRADUATE SCHOLARSHIP PROGRAM)
1957 'E' ST NW
WASHINGTON DC 20006
202/393-2040
AMOUNT: $1500 PER YEAR FOR UP TO 4 YEARS
DEADLINE(S): NOV 15
FIELD(S): CONSTRUCTION; CIVIL ENGINEERING
OPEN TO HIGH SCHOOL SENIORS; COLLEGE FRESHMEN; SOPHOMORES AND JUNIORS ENROLLED IN OR PLANNING TO ENROLL IN A 4-YEAR DEGREE PROGRAM IN CONSTRUCTION AND/OR CIVIL ENGINEERING. JUNIORS MUST

HAVE ONE FULL YEAR OF COURSE WORK REMAINING.
MUST BE USA CITIZEN OR LEGAL RESIDENT AND DESIRE A CAREER IN THE CONSTRUCTION INDUSTRY. WRITE FOR COMPLETE INFORMATION.

217

ASSOCIATED GENERAL CONTRACTORS EDUCATION AND RESEARCH FOUNDATION (JAMES L ALLHANDS ESSAY COMPETITION)
1957 'E' ST NW
WASHINGTON DC 20006
202/393-2040
AMOUNT: $1000; $500; $300
DEADLINE(S): DEC 1
FIELD(S): CONSTRUCTION
ANNUAL ESSAY COMPETITION OPEN TO FULL-TIME UNDERGRAD SENIORS IN ACCREDITED 4-YR PROGRAM. ESSAY SHOULD RELATE TO CONSTRUCTION AND/OR GENERAL CONTRACTING & BE GENERAL MANAGEMENT RELATED RATHER THAN TECHNICAL. USA CITIZEN OR LEGAL RESIDENT.
ESSAY THEME CHANGES YEAR TO YEAR. WINNERS WILL ALSO RECEIVE TRIP TO AGC'S ANNUAL 5-DAY CONVENTION IN NEW ORLEANS. WRITE FOR COMPLETE INFORMATION.

218

CONSTRUCTION EDUCATION FOUNDATION (ASSOCIATED BUILDERS & CONTRACTORS SCHOLARSHIP PROGRAM)
729 15TH STREET NW
WASHINGTON DC 20005
202/637-8800
AMOUNT: $500 - $2000
DEADLINE(S): DEC 15
FIELD(S): CONSTRUCTION
OPEN TO UNDERGRADUATE STUDENTS WHO ARE ENROLLED IN AN ACCREDITED 4-YEAR DEGREE PROGRAM; HAVE COMPLETED THEIR 1ST YEAR OF STUDY & INTEND TO PURSUE A CAREER IN THE CONSTRUCTION INDUSTRY.
APPROXIMATELY 20 SCHOLARSHIPS PER YEAR. APPLICATIONS AVAILABLE OCT 1 EACH YEAR. WRITE FOR COMPLETE INFORMATION.

219

FOUNDATION OF THE WALL & CEILING INDUSTRY (SCHOLARSHIP PROGRAM)
1600 CAMERON ST; 2ND FL
ALEXANDRIA VA 22314
703/684-2924
AMOUNT: $500
DEADLINE(S): DEC 1
FIELD(S): CONSTRUCTION
OPEN TO UNDERGRADUATE STUDENTS WHO ARE ENROLLED IN A 2-YEAR OR 4-YEAR COURSE OF STUDY (AS A SOPHOMORE; JUNIOR OR SENIOR) AT AN ACCREDITED INSTITUTION IN THE USA.
15 AWARDS PER YEAR. RENEWABLE. WRITE FOR COMPLETE INFORMATION.

220

NATIONAL ASSOCIATION OF PLUMBING-HEATING-COOLING CONTRACTORS EDUCATIONAL FOUNDATION (NAPHCC SCHOLARSHIP PROGRAM)
PO BOX 6808
FALLS CHURCH VA 22046
703/237-8100
AMOUNT: $2500
DEADLINE(S): APR 1
FIELD(S): PLUMBING; HEATING; COOLING; CONSTRUCTION; BUSINESS ADMINISTRATION
SCHOLARSHIPS ARE AVAILABLE TO HIGH SCHOOL SENIORS AND INCOMING FRESHMEN WHO ARE ENROLLED IN BA PROGRAMS. STUDENTS MUST HAVE A SPONSOR WHO HAS BEEN A MEMBER IN GOOD STANDING IN THE NAPHCC FOR AT LEAST TWO YEARS. USA CITIZEN.
SCHOLARSHIPS RENEWABLE. WRITE FOR COMPLETE INFORMATION.

221

NATIONAL ASSOCIATION OF WATER COMPANIES - NEW JERSEY CHAPTER (SCHOLARSHIP)
C/O NJ-AMERICAN WATER CO - EASTERN DIV 661 SHREWSBURY AVE
SHREWSBURY NJ 07702
908/842-6900; FAX 908/842-7541
AMOUNT: $2500
DEADLINE(S): APR 1 (POSTMARK)
FIELD(S): BUSINESS ADMINISTRATION; BIOLOGY; CHEMISTRY; ENGINEERING

OPEN TO USA CITIZENS WHO HAVE LIVED IN NJ AT LEAST 5 YEARS AND PLAN A CAREER IN THE INVESTOR-OWNED WATER UTILITY INDUSTRY IN DISCIPLINES SUCH AS THOSE ABOVE. MUST BE UNDERGRAD OR GRADUATE STUDENT IN A 2 OR 4 YEAR NJ COLLEGE OR UNIVERSITY.

GPA OF 3.0 OR BETTER REQUIRED. WRITE FOR COMPLETE INFORMATION.

222

NATIONAL ASSOCIATION OF WOMEN IN CONSTRUCTION (EL CAMINO REAL CHAPTER #158 SCHOLARSHIP)

MARIE REVERE; PO BOX 7131
SAN JOSE CA 95150
408/452-4644

AMOUNT: $1000

DEADLINE(S): MAY 1

FIELD(S): CIVIL ENGINEERING; CONSTRUCTION; ARCHITECTURE; ARCHITECTURAL ENGINEERING

OPEN TO MEN OR WOMEN UNDERGRADUATES WHO ARE GOING INTO THEIR JUNIOR YEAR AT AN ACCREDITED 4-YEAR CALIFORNIA COLLEGE. USA CITIZEN.

WRITE FOR COMPLETE INFORMATION.

223

NATIONAL ASSOCIATION OF WOMEN IN CONSTRUCTION (FOUNDERS' SCHOLARSHIP FOUNDATION AWARDS)

327 S ADAMS
FT WORTH TX 76104
817/877-5551

AMOUNT: NOT SPECIFIED

DEADLINE(S): FEB 15

FIELD(S): FIELDS RELATED TO A CAREER IN CONSTRUCTION

OPEN TO FULL TIME STUDENTS ENROLLED IN A CONSTRUCTION RELATED PROGRAM LEADING TO AN ASSOCIATE OR BACHELOR DEGREE. APPLICANTS SHOULD BE IN AT LEAST THEIR FIRST YEAR OF COLLEGE AND HAVE AT LEAST ONE YEAR REMAINING.

AWARDS COMMITTEE CONSIDERS GRADES; INTEREST IN CONSTRUCTION; EXTRACURRICULAR ACTIVITIES; EMPLOYMENT EXPERIENCE; FINANCIAL NEED & EVALUATION BY ACADEMIC ADVISOR. WRITE FOR COMPLETE INFORMATION.

224

NATIONAL ROOFING FOUNDATION (NRF SCHOLARSHIP AWARDS PROGRAM)

O'HARE INTERNATIONAL CENTER; 10255 W. HIGGINS RD; SUITE 600
ROSEMONT IL 60018
708/299-9070

AMOUNT: $2000

DEADLINE(S): JAN 15

FIELD(S): ARCHITECTURE; CONSTRUCTION

OPEN TO HIGH SCHOOL SENIORS; UNDERGRADUATE AND GRADUATE ARCHITECTURAL STUDENTS OR STUDENTS OF ANOTHER CURRICULUM RELATED TO THE ROOFING INDUSTRY. APPLICANTS MUST BE USA CITIZENS.

FOR FULL TIME STUDY AT AN ACCREDITED 4 YEAR COLLEGE OR UNIVERSITY. SEND A SELF-ADDRESSED STAMPED ENVELOPE (#10) TO RECEIVE AN APPLICATION.

225

NORTH DAKOTA DEPARTMENT OF TRANSPORTATION (GRANTS)

HUMAN RESOURCES DIVISION; 608 EAST BLVD AVE
BISMARCK ND 58505
701/224-2574

AMOUNT: $1000 PER YEAR

DEADLINE(S): FEB 15

FIELD(S): CIVIL ENGINEERING

FINANCIAL AID GRANTS OPEN TO UNDERGRADUATE STUDENTS AT RECOGNIZED COLLEGES & UNIVERSITIES IN NORTH DAKOTA WHO HAVE COMPLETED AT LEAST 1 YEAR OF STUDIES IN CIVIL ENGINEERING OR CIVIL ENGINEERING TECHNOLOGY.

2-4 GRANTS PER YEAR. RENEWABLE. WRITE FOR COMPLETE INFORMATION.

226

PACIFIC GAS & ELECTRIC CO. (SCHOLARSHIPS FOR HIGH SCHOOL SENIORS)

77 BEALE ST; ROOM 2837
SAN FRANCISCO CA 94106
415/973-1338

AMOUNT: $1000 - $4000

DEADLINE(S): NOV 15

FIELD(S): ENGINEERING; COMPUTER SCIENCE; MATHEMATICS; MARKETING; BUSINESS; ECONOMICS

HIGH SCHOOL SENIORS IN GOOD ACADEMIC STANDING WHO RESIDE IN OR ATTEND HIGH SCHOOL IN AREAS SERVED BY PG&E ARE ELIGIBLE TO COMPETE FOR SCHOLARSHIPS AWARDED ON A REGIONAL BASIS. NOT OPEN TO CHILDREN OF PG&E EMPLOYEES.

36 AWARDS PER YEAR. APPLICATIONS & BROCHURES ARE AVAILABLE IN ALL HIGH SCHOOLS WITHIN PG&E'S SERVICE AREA AND AT PG&E OFFICES.

227

SAN FRANCISCO BAY AREA CHAPTER - NATIONAL DEFENSE TRANSPORTATION ASSN (NDTA MERIT SCHOLARSHIP)

BOX 24676

OAKLAND CA 94623

WRITTEN INQUIRY

AMOUNT: $2000

DEADLINE(S): MAR 31

FIELD(S): BUSINESS; ENGINEERING; PLANNING; ENVIRONMENT (AS RELATED TO TRANSPORTATION)

OPEN TO USA CITIZENS ENROLLED IN AN ACCREDITED UNDERGRADUATE DEGREE OR VOCATIONAL PROGRAM IN ABOVE FIELDS WHO PLAN TO PURSUE A CAREER RELATED TO TRANSPORTATION. FINANCIAL NEED WILL BE CONSIDERED.

WRITE FOR COMPLETE INFORMATION.

228

U.S. AIR FORCE ROTC (4-YEAR SCHOLARSHIP PROGRAM)

AFROTC/RROO; RECRUITING OPERATIONS BRANCH

MAXWELL AFB AL 36112

205/953-2091

AMOUNT: TUITION + FEES & BOOKS + $100 PER MONTH STIPEND

DEADLINE(S): DEC 1

FIELD(S): AERONAUTICAL ENGINEERING; CIVIL ENGINEERING; MECHANICAL ENGINEERING; MATHEMATICS; PHYSICS; NURSING & SOME LIBERAL ARTS

OPEN TO USA CITIZENS WHO ARE AT LEAST 17 AND WILL GRADUATE FROM COLLEGE BEFORE AGE 25. MUST COMPLETE APPLICATION; FURNISH SAT/ACT SCORES; HIGH SCHOOL TRANSCRIPTS AND RECORD OF EXTRACURRICULAR ACTIVITIES.

MUST QUALIFY ON AIR FORCE MEDICAL EXAMINATION. ABOUT 1600 SCHOLARSHIPS AWARDED EACH YEAR AT CAMPUSES WHICH OFFER AIR FORCE ROTC.

COMPUTER SCIENCE

229

ARGONNE NATIONAL LABORATORY (STUDENT RESEARCH PARTICIPATION PROGRAM; THESIS RESEARCH)

DIV OF EDUCATIONAL PROGRAMS; 9700 SOUTH CASS AVE

ARGONNE IL 60439

312/972-3366

AMOUNT: $200 PER WEEK STIPEND

DEADLINE(S): FEB 1; MAY 15; OCT 15

FIELD(S): PHYSICAL SCIENCES; LIFE SCIENCES; EARTH SCIENCES; MATHEMATICS; COMPUTER SCIENCES; ENGINEERING; FUSION & FISSION ENERGY

1-SEMESTER ACCREDITED INTERNSHIP PROGRAM TO PERMIT STUDENTS TO WORK IN ABOVE AREAS IN RELATION TO ENERGY DEVELOPMENT. OPEN TO FULL-TIME UNDERGRAD JUNIORS; SENIORS & 1ST YEAR GRAD STUDENTS. USA CITIZEN OR LEGAL RESIDENT.

THESIS RESEARCH AWARDS OPEN TO DOCTORAL CANDIDATES WORKING ON THEIR DISSERTATION. WRITE FOR COMPLETE INFORMATION.

230

AT&T BELL LABORATORIES (ENGINEERING SCHOLARSHIP PROGRAM)

CRAWFORDS CORNER ROAD; ROOM 1E-213

HOLMDEL NJ 07733

201/949-4300

AMOUNT: FULL-TUITION & FEES + MONTHLY STIPEND

DEADLINE(S): JAN 15

FIELD(S): ELECTRICAL ENGINEERING; MECHANICAL ENGINEERING; COMPUTER SCIENCE; SYSTEMS ENGINEERING; COMPUTER ENGINEERING

UNDERGRADUATE SCHOLARSHIPS TO ENCOURAGE MINORITIES AND WOMEN TO ENTER ENGINEERING PROFESSION. SUMMER EMPLOYMENT AT BELL LABS INCLUDED. MUST MAINTAIN 3.0 OR BETTER GPA AND

SATISFACTORY JOB PERFORMANCE. USA CITIZEN OR PERMANENT RESIDENT.

SCHOLARSHIPS ARE RENEWABLE UNTIL COMPLETION OF BS DEGREE. WRITE FOR COMPLETE INFORMATION.

231

AT&T BELL LABORATORIES (SUMMER RESEARCH PROGRAM FOR MINORITIES & WOMEN)

101 CRAWFORDS CORNER RD; RM 1B-209
HOLMDEL NJ 07733
908/949-3728

AMOUNT: SALARY + TRAVEL & LIVING EXPENSES FOR SUMMER

DEADLINE(S): DEC 1

FIELD(S): ENGINEERING; MATH; SCIENCES; COMPUTER SCIENCE

PROGRAM OFFERS MINORITY STUDENTS & WOMEN STUDENTS TECHNICAL EMPLOYMENT EXPERIENCE AT BELL LABORATORIES. STUDENTS SHOULD HAVE COMPLETED THEIR THIRD YEAR OF STUDY AT AN ACCREDITED COLLEGE OR UNIVERSITY. USA CITIZEN OR PERMANENT RESIDENT.

SELECTION IS BASED PARTIALLY ON ACADEMIC ACHIEVEMENT AND PERSONAL MOTIVATION. WRITE SPECIAL PROGRAMS MANAGER - SRP FOR COMPLETE INFORMATION.

232

BUSINESS AND PROFESSIONAL WOMEN'S FOUNDATION (CAREER ADVANCEMENT SCHOLARSHIPS)

2012 MASSACHUSETTS AVE NW
WASHINGTON DC 20036
202/293-1200

AMOUNT: $500 - $1000

DEADLINE(S): APR 15 POSTMARK (APPS AVAILABLE ONLY OCT 1 - APR 1)

FIELD(S): COMPUTER SCIENCE; EDUCATION; PARALEGAL; ENGINEERING; SCIENCE (EXCEPT HEALTH CARE)

OPEN TO WOMEN (30 OR OLDER) WITHIN 12-24 MONTHS OF COMPLETING UNDERGRAD OR GRAD STUDY IN USA (INCLUDING PUERTO RICO & THE VIRGIN ISLANDS). SHOULD LEAD TO ENTRY OR REENTRY INTO THE WORK FORCE OR IMPROVE CAREER ADVANCEMENT CHANCES.

MUST SHOW FINANCIAL NEED. SEND SELF-ADDRESSED STAMPED ($.52) #10 ENVELOPE FOR APPLICATION & COMPLETE INFORMATION. NOT FOR STUDY AT DOCTORAL LEVEL.

233

DEVRY INC (SCHOLARSHIP PROGRAM)

ONE TOWER LANE
OAKBROOK TERRACE IL 60181
708/571-7700; 800/323-4256

AMOUNT: FULL TUITION (40); 1/2 TUITION (80)

DEADLINE(S): MAR 22

FIELD(S): ELECTRONICS ENGINEERING TECHNOLOGY; COMPUTER INFORMATION SYSTEMS; BUSINESS OPERATIONS; TELECOMMUNICATIONS MANAGEMENT; ACCOUNTING

40 FULL-TUITION & 80 1/2 TUITION UNDERGRADUATE SCHOLARSHIPS. OPEN TO USA HIGH SCHOOL GRADUATES WHO WISH TO ENROLL IN A FULLY ACCREDITED BACHELOR OF SCIENCE DEGREE PROGRAM AT ONE OF THE DEVRY INSTITUTES LOCATED THROUGHOUT NORTH AMERICA.

AWARDS RENEWABLE PROVIDED 2.5 GPA IS MAINTAINED. CONTACT YOUR GUIDANCE COUNSELOR; NEAREST DEVRY INSTITUTE OR ADDRESS ABOVE FOR COMPLETE INFORMATION.

234

ELECTRONIC INDUSTRIES FOUNDATION (SCHOLARSHIP FUND)

919 18TH ST; SUITE 900
WASHINGTON DC 20006
202/955-5814

AMOUNT: $2000

DEADLINE(S): FEB 1

FIELD(S): AERONAUTICS; COMPUTER SCIENCE; ELECTRICAL ENGINEERING; ENGINEERING TECHNOLOGY; APPLIED MATHEMATICS; MICROBIOLOGY

OPEN TO DISABLED STUDENTS WHO ARE PURSUING CAREERS IN HIGH-TECH AREAS THROUGH ACADEMIC OR TECHNICAL TRAINING. AWARDS TENABLE AT RECOGNIZED UNDERGRADUATE & GRADUATE COLLEGES & UNIVERSITIES. USA CITIZEN. FINANCIAL NEED IS A CONSIDERATION.

6 AWARDS PER YEAR. RENEWABLE. WRITE FOR COMPLETE INFORMATION.

235

HUGHES AIRCRAFT COMPANY (BACHELOR OF SCIENCE SCHOLARSHIP)
PO BOX 80028 (C1/B168) TECH. ED. CENTER
LOS ANGELES CA 90080
310-568-6711
AMOUNT: ALL EDUCATIONAL EXPENSES + SALARY & RELOCATION EXPENSES
DEADLINE(S): APPLY BETWEEN OCT & MAR PRIOR TO JUNE COMPLETION OF SOPHOMORE YEAR.
FIELD(S): ELECTRICAL MECHANICAL OR AEROSPACE ENGINEERING OR COMPUTER SCIENCE; MATHEMATICS; OR PHYSICS
OPEN TO STUDENTS WITH UPPER DIVISION STANDING OR AA DEGREE & AT LEAST A 3.0 GPA WHO HAVE BEEN ADMITTED WITHOUT CONDITION TO A UNIVERSITY ACCREDITED BY THE ACCREDITATION BOARD FOR ENGINEERING & TECHNOLOGY (ABET).
WORK STUDY OR FULL STUDY PROGRAMS. USA CITIZEN. MOST AWARDS ARE FOR WORK-STUDY NEAR HUGHES PLANTS. WRITE FOR COMPLETE INFORMATION.

236

INSTITUTE OF ELECTRICAL AND ELECTRONICS ENGINEERS (COMPUTER SOCIETY RICHARD E. MERWIN SCHOLARSHIP)
1730 MASSACHUSETTS AVE NW
WASHINGTON DC 20036
202/371-0101
AMOUNT: $3000
DEADLINE(S): MAY 15
FIELD(S): COMPUTER SCIENCE
OPEN TO GRADUATE; JUNIOR AND SENIOR STUDENTS IN COMPUTER RELATED ENGINEERING FIELDS WHO ARE ACTIVE IN THEIR IEEE COMPUTER BRANCH CHAPTER.
WRITE FOR COMPLETE INFORMATION.

237

NAACP NATIONAL HEADQUARTERS (NAACP WILLEMS SCHOLARSHIP)
4805 MOUNT HOPE DR
BALTIMORE MD 21215
301/358-8900
AMOUNT: $2000 - $3000
DEADLINE(S): APR 30
FIELD(S): ENGINEERING; CHEMISTRY; PHYSICS; COMPUTER SCIENCE; MATHEMATICS
OPEN TO NAACP MEMBERS MAJORING IN ONE OF THE ABOVE AREAS AND POSSESS A CUMULATIVE GPA OF 3.0 OR BETTER. UNDERGRADS RECEIVE MAXIMUM OF $8000 IN ANNUAL INSTALLMENTS OF $2000. GRADUATES ARE AWARDED A $3000 SCHOLARSHIP WHICH CAN BE RENEWED.
WRITE FOR COMPLETE INFORMATION.

238

NATIONAL RADIO ASTRONOMY OBSERVATORY (SUMMER RESEARCH ASSISTANTSHIPS)
EDGEMONT ROAD
CHARLOTTESVILLE VA 22903
804/296-0211
AMOUNT: $1000 - $1300 PER MONTH + TRAVEL EXPENSES
DEADLINE(S): FEB 1
FIELD(S): ASTRONOMY; PHYSICS; COMPUTER SCIENCE; ELECTRICAL ENGINEERING
SUMMER RESEARCH ASSISTANTSHIPS OPEN TO UNDERGRADUATES WHO HAVE COMPLETED AT LEAST 3 YEARS OF STUDY AND TO GRADUATE STUDENTS WHO HAVE COMPLETED NO MORE THAN 2 YEARS. TENABLE AT NRAO SITES.
APPROXIMATELY 20 AWARDS PER YEAR. WRITE FOR COMPLETE INFORMATION.

239

NEW YORK TELEPHONE (SCHOLARSHIP PROGRAM FOR BLACK AND HISPANIC STUDENTS)
COTE; PO BOX 2810
CHERRY HILL NJ 08034
609/573-9400
AMOUNT: $2000
DEADLINE(S): APR 30
FIELD(S): ENGINEERING; SCIENCE; COMPUTER SCIENCE; NURSING
OPEN TO BLACK OR HISPANIC STUDENTS WHO RESIDE IN NEW YORK AND ATTEND ACCREDITED NEW YORK STATE SCHOOLS. FOR FULL TIME STUDENTS ENROLLED AS SECOND SEMESTER SOPHOMORES IN A 4 YEAR UNDERGRADUATE PROGRAM LEADING TO A BACHELORS DEGREE.
FINANCIAL NEED IS A CONSIDERATION. RENEWABLE. WRITE FOR COMPLETE INFORMATION.

240

PACIFIC GAS & ELECTRIC CO. (SCHOLARSHIPS FOR HIGH SCHOOL SENIORS)
77 BEALE ST; ROOM 2837
SAN FRANCISCO CA 94106
415/973-1338
AMOUNT: $1000 - $4000
DEADLINE(S): NOV 15
FIELD(S): ENGINEERING; COMPUTER SCIENCE; MATHEMATICS; MARKETING; BUSINESS; ECONOMICS

HIGH SCHOOL SENIORS IN GOOD ACADEMIC STANDING WHO RESIDE IN OR ATTEND HIGH SCHOOL IN AREAS SERVED BY PG&E ARE ELIGIBLE TO COMPETE FOR SCHOLARSHIPS AWARDED ON A REGIONAL BASIS. NOT OPEN TO CHILDREN OF PG&E EMPLOYEES.

36 AWARDS PER YEAR. APPLICATIONS & BROCHURES ARE AVAILABLE IN ALL HIGH SCHOOLS WITHIN PG&E'S SERVICE AREA AND AT PG&E OFFICES.

241

SOCIETY OF WOMEN ENGINEERS (ADMIRAL GRACE MURRAY HOPPER SCHOLARSHIP)
345 EAST 47TH ST; ROOM 305
NEW YORK NY 10017
212/705-7855
AMOUNT: $1000
DEADLINE(S): MAY 15
FIELD(S): ENGINEERING; COMPUTER SCIENCE

OPEN TO WOMEN WHO ARE USA CITIZENS AND ARE ENTERING A FOUR YEAR PROGRAM FOR THE STUDY OF ENGINEERING OR COMPUTER SCIENCE AS FRESHMEN. APPLICATIONS AVAILABLE FROM MARCH THROUGH MAY ONLY.

WRITE FOR COMPLETE INFORMATION. ENCLOSE SELF-ADDRESSED STAMPED ENVELOPE.

242

STATE FARM COMPANIES FOUNDATION (EXCEPTIONAL STUDENT FELLOWSHIP)
1 STATE FARM PLAZA
BLOOMINGTON IL 61710
WRITTEN INQUIRY
AMOUNT: $3000
DEADLINE(S): FEB 28
FIELD(S): ACCOUNTING; BUSINESS ADMINISTRATION; ACTUARIAL SCIENCE; COMPUTER SCIENCE; ECONOMICS; FINANCE; INSURANCE; INVESTMENTS; MARKETING; MATHEMATICS; STATISTICS

OPEN TO CURRENT FULL TIME COLLEGE JUNIORS AND SENIORS MAJORING IN ANY OF THE FIELDS ABOVE. ONLY STUDENTS NOMINATED BY THE COLLEGE DEAN OR A DEPARTMENT HEAD QUALIFY AS CANDIDATES. APPLICATIONS WITHOUT NOMINATIONS WILL NOT BE CONSIDERED.

USA CITIZEN. GPA OF 3.4 OR BETTER (4.0 SCALE) IS REQUIRED. 50 FELLOWSHIPS PER YEAR. WRITE FOR COMPLETE INFORMATION.

243

STATE FARM COMPANIES FOUNDATION (EXCEPTIONAL STUDENT FELLOWSHIP AWARDS)
ONE STATE FARM PLAZA; SC-3
BLOOMINGTON IL 61710
309/766-2039
AMOUNT: $3000
DEADLINE(S): FEB 15
FIELD(S): BUSINESS RELATED FIELDS; COMPUTER SCIENCE; PRELAW; MATHEMATICS

OPEN TO EXCEPTIONAL CURRENT JUNIOR OR SENIOR UNDERGRADUATES IN THE ABOVE FIELDS. MUST BE NOMINATED BY DEAN OR DEPARTMENT HEAD. US CITIZEN. MUST BE COLLEGE JUNIOR OR SENIOR AT TIME OF APPLICATION.

50 FELLOWSHIPS PER ACADEMIC YEAR. APPLICATIONS AND NOMINATIONS AVAILABLE NOV 1. WRITE FOR COMPLETE INFORMATION.

244

TANDY TECHNOLOGY SCHOLARS (STUDENT SCHOLARSHIPS; TEACHER AWARDS)
TCU STATION; BOX 32897
FORT WORTH TX 76129
817/924-4087
AMOUNT: $1000 STUDENTS; $2500 TEACHERS
DEADLINE(S): OCT 16
FIELD(S): MATHEMATICS; SCIENCE; COMPUTER SCIENCE

PROGRAM RECOGNIZES ACADEMIC PERFORMANCE AND OUTSTANDING ACHIEVEMENTS BY MATHEMATICS; SCIENCE AND COMPUTER SCIENCE STUDENTS AND TEACHERS. STUDENTS RECEIVE SCHOLARSHIP FOR UNDERGRADUATE STUDY; TEACHERS GET CASH.

MUST BE A SENIOR IN AN ENROLLED HIGH SCHOOL LOCATED IN ONE OF THE 50 STATES. 100 STUDENT & 100 TEACHER AWARDS PER YEAR. WRITE FOR COMPLETE INFORMATION.

245

TYSON FOUNDATION INC. (SCHOLARSHIP PROGRAM)
2210 OAKLAWN
SPRINGDALE AR 72764
501/756-4955
AMOUNT: UP TO $1000/SEMESTER
DEADLINE(S): JUN 21
FIELD(S): BUSINESS; AGRICULTURE; ENGINEERING; COMPUTER SCIENCE; NURSING

OPEN TO USA CITIZENS WHO LIVE IN THE VICINITY OF TYSON FOOD FACILITIES AND MAINTAIN A 2.5 GPA. MUST WORK AND CARRY AT LEAST 12 SEMESTER HOURS OR EQUIVALENT. FOR UNDERGRADUATE STUDY AT SCHOOLS IN USA.

RECIPIENTS SIGN A PLEDGE EITHER TO REPAY THE SCHOLARSHIP MONEY OR HELP ANOTHER DESERVING STUDENT NOT RELATED BY BLOOD OR MARRIAGE TO ATTEND COLLEGE. WRITE FOR COMPLETE INFORMATION.

ELECTRICAL ENG

246

AMERICAN RADIO RELAY LEAGUE FOUNDATION (DR. JAMES L. LAWSON MEMORIAL SCHOLARSHIP)
225 MAIN ST
NEWINGTON CT 06111
203/666-1541
AMOUNT: $500
DEADLINE(S): FEB 15
FIELD(S): ELECTRONICS; COMMUNICATIONS

OPEN TO RADIO AMATEURS HOLDING AT LEAST A GENERAL LICENSE AND RESIDING IN CT; MA; ME; NH; RI; VT; OR NY AND ATTENDING A SCHOOL IN ONE OF THOSE STATES.

WRITE FOR COMPLETE INFORMATION.

247

AMERICAN RADIO RELAY LEAGUE FOUNDATION (EDMUND A METZGER SCHOLARSHIP FUND)
225 MAIN ST
NEWINGTON CT 06111
203/666-1541
AMOUNT: $500
DEADLINE(S): FEB 15
FIELD(S): ELECTRICAL ENGINEERING

OPEN TO ARRL MEMBERS WHO ARE RESIDENTS OF ARRL CENTRAL DIV (ILLINOIS; INDIANA; WISCONSIN); ATTEND A 4-YEAR UNIVERSITY IN ARRL CENTRAL DIV & ARE CURRENTLY LICENSED RADIO AMATEURS.

WRITE FOR COMPLETE INFORMATION.

248

AMERICAN RADIO RELAY LEAGUE FOUNDATION (IRVING W. COOK WAOCGS SCHOLARSHIP)
225 MAIN ST
NEWINGTON CT 06111
203/666-1541
AMOUNT: $500
DEADLINE(S): FEB 15
FIELD(S): ELECTRONICS; COMMUNICATIONS

OPEN TO RESIDENTS OF KANSAS WHO HOLD ANY CLASS OF RADIO AMATEUR LICENSE AND ARE SEEKING A BACCALAUREATE OR HIGHER DEGREE. FOR STUDY IN ANY USA COLLEGE OR UNIVERSITY.

WRITE FOR COMPLETE INFORMATION.

249

AMERICAN RADIO RELAY LEAGUE FOUNDATION (L PHILIP & ALICE J WICKER SCHOLARSHIP FUND)
225 MAIN ST
NEWINGTON CT 06111
203/666-1541
AMOUNT: $1000
DEADLINE(S): FEB 15
FIELD(S): ELECTRICAL ENGINEERING; COMMUNICATIONS

OPEN TO STUDENTS WHO ARE RESIDENTS OF ARRL ROANOKE DIV (N.CAROLINA; S.CAROLINA; VIRGINIA; W.VIRGINIA); ATTEND A SCHOOL IN THE ROANOKE DIV AS AN UNDERGRADUATE OR GRADUATE STUDENT & ARE AT LEAST GENERAL CLASS LICENSED RADIO AMATEURS.

WRITE FOR COMPLETE INFORMATION.

250

AMERICAN RADIO RELAY LEAGUE FOUNDATION (PAUL & HELEN L GRAUER SCHOLARSHIP FUND)
225 MAIN ST
NEWINGTON CT 06111
203/666-1541
AMOUNT: $1000
DEADLINE(S): FEB 15
FIELD(S): ELECTRICAL ENGINEERING; COMMUNICATIONS
OPEN TO ARRL MIDWEST DIV RESIDENTS (IOWA; KANSAS; MISSOURI; NEBRASKA) WHO ARE LICENSED RADIO AMATEURS & ENROLLED FULL TIME AS AN UNDERGRADUATE OR GRADUATE STUDENT AT AN ACCREDITED INSTITUTION IN THE ARRL MIDWEST DIV.
WRITE FOR COMPLETE INFORMATION.

251

AMERICAN RADIO RELAY LEAGUE FOUNDATION (PERRY F HADLOCK MEMORIAL SCHOLARSHIP FUND)
225 MAIN ST
NEWINGTON CT 06111
203/666-1541
AMOUNT: $1000
DEADLINE(S): FEB 15
FIELD(S): ELECTRICAL ENGINEERING
OPEN TO STUDENTS WHO ARE GENERAL CLASS LICENSED RADIO AMATEURS; HAVE DEMONSTRATED ENTHUSIASM IN PROMOTING AMATEUR RADIO & ARE ENROLLED FULL TIME AS AN UNDERGRADUATE OR GRADUATE STUDENT AT AN ACCREDITED INSTITUTION.
WRITE FOR COMPLETE INFORMATION.

252

AMERICAN RADIO RELAY LEAGUE FOUNDATION (SENATOR BARRY GOLDWATER (#K7UGA) SCHOLARSHIP FUND)
225 MAIN ST
NEWINGTON CT 06111
203/666-1541
AMOUNT: $5000
DEADLINE(S): FEB 15
FIELD(S): COMMUNICATIONS
OPEN TO STUDENTS WHO ARE LICENSED RADIO AMATEURS & ENROLLED FULL TIME AS AN UNDERGRADUATE OR GRADUATE STUDENT AT AN ACCREDITED INSTITUTION IN A FIELD RELATED TO COMMUNICATIONS.
WRITE FOR COMPLETE INFORMATION.

253

AT&T BELL LABORATORIES (ENGINEERING SCHOLARSHIP PROGRAM)
CRAWFORDS CORNER ROAD; ROOM 1E-213
HOLMDEL NJ 07733
201/949-4300
AMOUNT: FULL-TUITION & FEES + MONTHLY STIPEND
DEADLINE(S): JAN 15
FIELD(S): ELECTRICAL ENGINEERING; MECHANICAL ENGINEERING; COMPUTER SCIENCE; SYSTEMS ENGINEERING; COMPUTER ENGINEERING
UNDERGRADUATE SCHOLARSHIPS TO ENCOURAGE MINORITIES AND WOMEN TO ENTER ENGINEERING PROFESSION. SUMMER EMPLOYMENT AT BELL LABS INCLUDED. MUST MAINTAIN 3.0 OR BETTER GPA AND SATISFACTORY JOB PERFORMANCE. USA CITIZEN OR PERMANENT RESIDENT.
SCHOLARSHIPS ARE RENEWABLE UNTIL COMPLETION OF BS DEGREE. WRITE FOR COMPLETE INFORMATION.

254

AT&T BELL LABORATORIES (SUMMER RESEARCH PROGRAM FOR MINORITIES & WOMEN)
101 CRAWFORDS CORNER RD; RM 1B-209
HOLMDEL NJ 07733
908/949-3728
AMOUNT: SALARY + TRAVEL & LIVING EXPENSES FOR SUMMER
DEADLINE(S): DEC 1
FIELD(S): ENGINEERING; MATH; SCIENCES; COMPUTER SCIENCE
PROGRAM OFFERS MINORITY STUDENTS & WOMEN STUDENTS TECHNICAL EMPLOYMENT EXPERIENCE AT BELL LABORATORIES. STUDENTS SHOULD HAVE COMPLETED THEIR THIRD YEAR OF STUDY AT AN ACCREDITED COLLEGE OR UNIVERSITY. USA CITIZEN OR PERMANENT RESIDENT.
SELECTION IS BASED PARTIALLY ON ACADEMIC ACHIEVEMENT AND PERSONAL MOTIVATION. WRITE SPECIAL PROGRAMS MANAGER - SRP FOR COMPLETE INFORMATION.

255

DEVRY INC (SCHOLARSHIP PROGRAM)
ONE TOWER LANE
OAKBROOK TERRACE IL 60181
708/571-7700; 800/323-4256

AMOUNT: FULL TUITION (40); 1/2 TUITION (80)
DEADLINE(S): MAR 22
FIELD(S): ELECTRONICS ENGINEERING TECHNOLOGY; COMPUTER INFORMATION SYSTEMS; BUSINESS OPERATIONS; TELECOMMUNICATIONS MANAGEMENT; ACCOUNTING

40 FULL-TUITION & 80 1/2 TUITION UNDERGRADUATE SCHOLARSHIPS. OPEN TO USA HIGH SCHOOL GRADUATES WHO WISH TO ENROLL IN A FULLY ACCREDITED BACHELOR OF SCIENCE DEGREE PROGRAM AT ONE OF THE DEVRY INSTITUTES LOCATED THROUGHOUT NORTH AMERICA.

AWARDS RENEWABLE PROVIDED 2.5 GPA IS MAINTAINED. CONTACT YOUR GUIDANCE COUNSELOR; NEAREST DEVRY INSTITUTE OR ADDRESS ABOVE FOR COMPLETE INFORMATION.

256 ——————————

ELECTRONIC INDUSTRIES FOUNDATION (SCHOLARSHIP FUND)
919 18TH ST; SUITE 900
WASHINGTON DC 20006
202/955-5814
AMOUNT: $2000
DEADLINE(S): FEB 1
FIELD(S): AERONAUTICS; COMPUTER SCIENCE; ELECTRICAL ENGINEERING; ENGINEERING TECHNOLOGY; APPLIED MATHEMATICS; MICROBIOLOGY

OPEN TO DISABLED STUDENTS WHO ARE PURSUING CAREERS IN HIGH-TECH AREAS THROUGH ACADEMIC OR TECHNICAL TRAINING. AWARDS TENABLE AT RECOGNIZED UNDERGRADUATE & GRADUATE COLLEGES & UNIVERSITIES. USA CITIZEN. FINANCIAL NEED IS A CONSIDERATION.

6 AWARDS PER YEAR. RENEWABLE. WRITE FOR COMPLETE INFORMATION.

257 ——————————

HUGHES AIRCRAFT COMPANY (BACHELOR OF SCIENCE SCHOLARSHIP)
PO BOX 80028 (C1/B168) TECH. ED. CENTER
LOS ANGELES CA 90080
310-568-6711
AMOUNT: ALL EDUCATIONAL EXPENSES + SALARY & RELOCATION EXPENSES
DEADLINE(S): APPLY BETWEEN OCT & MAR PRIOR TO JUNE COMPLETION OF SOPHOMORE YEAR.
FIELD(S): ELECTRICAL MECHANICAL OR AEROSPACE ENGINEERING OR COMPUTER SCIENCE; MATHEMATICS; OR PHYSICS

OPEN TO STUDENTS WITH UPPER DIVISION STANDING OR AA DEGREE & AT LEAST A 3.0 GPA WHO HAVE BEEN ADMITTED WITHOUT CONDITION TO A UNIVERSITY ACCREDITED BY THE ACCREDITATION BOARD FOR ENGINEERING & TECHNOLOGY (ABET).

WORK STUDY OR FULL STUDY PROGRAMS. USA CITIZEN. MOST AWARDS ARE FOR WORK-STUDY NEAR HUGHES PLANTS. WRITE FOR COMPLETE INFORMATION.

258 ——————————

NATIONAL ASSOCIATION OF WOMEN IN CONSTRUCTION (FOUNDERS' SCHOLARSHIP FOUNDATION AWARDS)
327 S ADAMS
FT WORTH TX 76104
817/877-5551
AMOUNT: NOT SPECIFIED
DEADLINE(S): FEB 15
FIELD(S): FIELDS RELATED TO A CAREER IN CONSTRUCTION

OPEN TO FULL TIME STUDENTS ENROLLED IN A CONSTRUCTION RELATED PROGRAM LEADING TO AN ASSOCIATE OR BACHELOR DEGREE. APPLICANTS SHOULD BE IN AT LEAST THEIR FIRST YEAR OF COLLEGE AND HAVE AT LEAST ONE YEAR REMAINING.

AWARDS COMMITTEE CONSIDERS GRADES; INTEREST IN CONSTRUCTION; EXTRACURRICULAR ACTIVITIES; EMPLOYMENT EXPERIENCE; FINANCIAL NEED & EVALUATION BY ACADEMIC ADVISOR. WRITE FOR COMPLETE INFORMATION.

259 ——————————

NATIONAL RADIO ASTRONOMY OBSERVATORY (SUMMER RESEARCH ASSISTANTSHIPS)
EDGEMONT ROAD
CHARLOTTESVILLE VA 22903
804/296-0211
AMOUNT: $1000 - $1300 PER MONTH + TRAVEL EXPENSES
DEADLINE(S): FEB 1

FIELD(S): ASTRONOMY; PHYSICS; COMPUTER SCIENCE; ELECTRICAL ENGINEERING

SUMMER RESEARCH ASSISTANTSHIPS OPEN TO UNDERGRADUATES WHO HAVE COMPLETED AT LEAST 3 YEARS OF STUDY AND TO GRADUATE STUDENTS WHO HAVE COMPLETED NO MORE THAN 2 YEARS. TENABLE AT NRAO SITES.

APPROXIMATELY 20 AWARDS PER YEAR. WRITE FOR COMPLETE INFORMATION.

260

PACIFIC GAS & ELECTRIC CO. (SCHOLARSHIPS FOR HIGH SCHOOL SENIORS)

77 BEALE ST; ROOM 2837
SAN FRANCISCO CA 94106
415/973-1338

AMOUNT: $1000 - $4000

DEADLINE(S): NOV 15

FIELD(S): ENGINEERING; COMPUTER SCIENCE; MATHEMATICS; MARKETING; BUSINESS; ECONOMICS

HIGH SCHOOL SENIORS IN GOOD ACADEMIC STANDING WHO RESIDE IN OR ATTEND HIGH SCHOOL IN AREAS SERVED BY PG&E ARE ELIGIBLE TO COMPETE FOR SCHOLARSHIPS AWARDED ON A REGIONAL BASIS. NOT OPEN TO CHILDREN OF PG&E EMPLOYEES.

36 AWARDS PER YEAR. APPLICATIONS & BROCHURES ARE AVAILABLE IN ALL HIGH SCHOOLS WITHIN PG&E'S SERVICE AREA AND AT PG&E OFFICES.

261

RADIO FREE EUROPE/RADIO LIBERTY (ENGINEERING INTERN PROGRAM)

PERSONNEL DIVISION; 1201 CONNECTICUT AVE NW
WASHINGTON DC 20036
202/457-6936

AMOUNT: DAILY STIPEND OF 55 GERMAN MARKS + ACCOMMODATIONS

DEADLINE(S): FEB 22

FIELD(S): ELECTRICAL ENGINEERING

INTERNSHIP IN GERMANY OPEN TO GRADUATE OR EXCEPTIONALLY QUALIFIED UNDERGRAD ELECTRICAL ENGINEERING STUDENTS. PREFERENCE TO THOSE WHO HAVE COMPLETED COURSES IN SUBJECTS RELATED TO THE TECHNICAL ASPECTS OF INTERNATIONAL BROADCASTING.

AT LEAST BASIC ABILITY TO SPEAK GERMAN IS HIGHLY DESIRABLE. WRITE FOR COMPLETE INFORMATION.

262

VERTICAL FLIGHT FOUNDATION (UNDERGRADUATE/GRADUATE SCHOLARSHIPS)

217 N WASHINGTON ST
ALEXANDRIA VA 22314
703/684-6777

AMOUNT: UP TO $2000

DEADLINE(S): FEB 1

FIELD(S): MECHANICAL ENGINEERING; ELECTRICAL ENGINEERING; AEROSPACE ENGINEERING

ANNUAL SCHOLARSHIPS OPEN TO UNDERGRADUATE & GRADUATE STUDENTS IN THE ABOVE AREAS WHO ARE INTERESTED IN PURSUING CAREERS IN SOME ASPECT OF HELICOPTER OR VERTICAL FLIGHT. FOR FULL TIME STUDY AT ACCREDITED SCHOOL OF ENGINEERING.

WRITE FOR COMPLETE INFORMATION.

ENGINEERING TECH

263

AMERICAN CERAMIC SOCIETY (JOHN & EDITH WACHTMAN SCHOLARSHIP IN CERAMICS)

725 CERAMIC PLACE
WESTERVILLE OH 43081
614/890-4700

AMOUNT: $5000

DEADLINE(S): FEB 1

FIELD(S): CERAMIC SCIENCE & ENGINEERING

OPEN TO HIGH SCHOOL SENIORS WHO DECLARE THEIR INTENTION TO PURSUE A DEGREE IN CERAMICS. SELECTION BASED ON STUDENT'S CAPABILITY; PREVIOUS RECORD; CHARACTER AND PERSONAL RESOLVE. MUST BE USA CITIZEN.

FINANCIAL NEED IS A CONSIDERATION. ENROLLMENT IN A COLLEGE OR UNIVERSITY OFFERING A DEGREE IN CERAMIC SCIENCE OR ENGINEERING IS REQUIRED. WRITE FOR COMPLETE INFORMATION.

264

AMERICAN NUCLEAR SOCIETY (JOHN & MURIEL LANDIS SCHOLARSHIPS)
555 NORTH KENSINGTON AVE
LA GRANGE PARK IL 60525
312/352-6611
AMOUNT: $3500
DEADLINE(S): MAR 1
FIELD(S): NUCLEAR ENGINEERING
OPEN TO ANY UNDERGRADUATE OR GRADUATE STUDENT THAT HAS GREATER THAN AVERAGE FINANCIAL NEED & IS PLANNING A CAREER IN NUCLEAR ENGINEERING OR A NUCLEAR RELATED FIELD. AWARDS TENABLE AT ACCREDITED INSTITUTIONS IN THE USA.
MUST BE USA CITIZEN OR HAVE A PERMANENT RESIDENT VISA. 8 AWARDS PER YEAR. WRITE FOR COMPLETE INFORMATION.

265

AMERICAN NUCLEAR SOCIETY (UNDERGRADUATE SCHOLARSHIPS)
555 NORTH KENSINGTON AVE
LA GRANGE PARK IL 60525
312/352-6611
AMOUNT: $1000 - $3000
DEADLINE(S): MAR 1
FIELD(S): NUCLEAR ENGINEERING
SCHOLARSHIPS OPEN TO UNDERGRADUATE STUDENTS WHO HAVE COMPLETED AT LEAST 1 YEAR OF STUDY IN AN ACCREDITED NUCLEAR ENGINEERING (OR NUCLEAR RELATED AREA) PROGRAM AT A COLLEGE OR UNIVERSITY IN THE USA. USA CITIZEN OR LEGAL RESIDENT.
15 AWARDS PER YEAR. WRITE FOR COMPLETE INFORMATION.

266

AMERICAN SOCIETY OF HEATING; REFRIGERATING & AIR-CONDITIONING ENGINEERS (ASHRAE SCHOLARSHIP FUND)
1791 TULLIE CIRCLE NE
ATLANTA GA 30329
404/636-8400
AMOUNT: $2000 - $5000
DEADLINE(S): DEC 15
FIELD(S): HEATING; REFRIGERATION & AIR-CONDITIONING; VENTILATION
OPEN TO UNDERGRADUATE STUDENTS WHO PLAN A CAREER IN THE ABOVE FIELDS. MUST HAVE AT LEAST 1 FULL YEAR OF UNDERGRADUATE STUDY REMAINING. MINIMUM 3.0 GPA (4.0 SCALE). AWARDS TENABLE AT ACCREDITED INSTITUTIONS IN THE USA & CANADA.
AWARDS RENEWABLE. FINANCIAL NEED IS CONSIDERED. WRITE FOR COMPLETE INFORMATION.

267

AMERICAN SOCIETY OF MECHANICAL ENGINEERS (STUDENT ASSISTANCE LOAN PROGRAM)
345 E 47TH ST
NEW YORK NY 10017
212/705-7375
AMOUNT: UP TO $2500
DEADLINE(S): APR 1; NOV 1
FIELD(S): MECHANICAL ENGINEERING; ENGINEERING TECHNOLOGY (STUDENT ASSISTANCE LOAN PROGRAM)
LOANS TO STUDENT MEMBERS OF ASME WHO ARE UNDERGRADUATE OR GRADUATE STUDENTS ENROLLED IN SCHOOLS WITH ACCREDITED MECHANICAL ENGINEERING OR ENGINEERING TECHNOLOGY CURRICULA. MINIMUM 2.0 GPA ON 4.0 SCALE. USA CITIZEN.
FIRST PREFERENCE GIVEN TO UNDERGRADUATE JUNIORS AND SENIORS. WRITE FOR COMPLETE INFORMATION.

268

AMERICAN WELDING SOCIETY (SCHOLARSHIP PROGRAM)
550 NW LEJEUNE RD; PO BOX 351040
MIAMI FL 33135
305/443-9353
AMOUNT: VARIES
DEADLINE(S): JUN 1
FIELD(S): WELDING TECHNOLOGY
OPEN TO USA CITIZENS WHO RESIDE IN THE USA & ARE ENROLLED IN AN ACCREDITED MATERIAL JOINING OR SIMILAR PROGRAM. AWARDS ARE TENABLE AT JUNIOR COLLEGES; COLLEGES; UNIVERSITIES & INSTITUTIONS IN THE USA.
WRITE FOR COMPLETE INFORMATION.

269

ASSOCIATION OF OFFICIAL ANALYTICAL CHEMISTS (HARVEY W. WILEY SCHOLARSHIP AWARD)
2200 WILSON BLVD; SUITE 400
ARLINGTON VA 22201
703-522-3032
AMOUNT: $500 PER YEAR FOR 2 YEARS
DEADLINE(S): MAY 1 OF SOPHOMORE YEAR
FIELD(S): CHEMISTRY; MICROBIOLOGY & RELATED SCIENCES
OPEN TO UNDERGRADUATE SOPHOMORES WHO HAVE MAINTAINED AT LEAST 'B' AVERAGE. AWARDS ARE FOR JUNIOR & SENIOR YEAR IN ABOVE AREAS. MEDICAL; DENTAL; NURSING; ETC MAJORS NOT ELIGIBLE.
WRITE FOR COMPLETE INFORMATION.

270

AT&T BELL LABORATORIES (SUMMER RESEARCH PROGRAM FOR MINORITIES & WOMEN)
101 CRAWFORDS CORNER RD; RM 1B-209
HOLMDEL NJ 07733
908/949-3728
AMOUNT: SALARY + TRAVEL & LIVING EXPENSES FOR SUMMER
DEADLINE(S): DEC 1
FIELD(S): ENGINEERING; MATH; SCIENCES; COMPUTER SCIENCE
PROGRAM OFFERS MINORITY STUDENTS & WOMEN STUDENTS TECHNICAL EMPLOYMENT EXPERIENCE AT BELL LABORATORIES. STUDENTS SHOULD HAVE COMPLETED THEIR THIRD YEAR OF STUDY AT AN ACCREDITED COLLEGE OR UNIVERSITY. USA CITIZEN OR PERMANENT RESIDENT.
SELECTION IS BASED PARTIALLY ON ACADEMIC ACHIEVEMENT AND PERSONAL MOTIVATION. WRITE SPECIAL PROGRAMS MANAGER - SRP FOR COMPLETE INFORMATION.

271

CHEMICAL MANUFACTURERS ASSOCIATION (TEACHER AWARDS)
2501 M STREET NW
WASHINGTON DC 20037
202/887-1223
AMOUNT: $2500 REGIONAL AWARD; $5000 NATIONAL
DEADLINE(S): JAN 29
FIELD(S): SCIENCE ; CHEMISTRY; CHEMICAL ENGINEERING
SIX NATIONAL AND EIGHT REGIONAL AWARDS WILL BE OFFERED TO COLLEGE AND HIGH SCHOOL CHEMISTRY OR CHEMICAL ENGINEERING TEACHERS IN THE USA OR CANADA. CRITERIA ARE EXCELLENCE IN TEACHING; DEDICATION & MOTIVATION OF STUDENTS TO SCIENCE CAREERS.
FOR TEACHERS OF GENERAL SCIENCE; CHEMISTRY AND CHEMICAL ENGINEERING ONLY. WRITE FOR COMPLETE INFORMATION.

272

DEVRY INC (SCHOLARSHIP PROGRAM)
ONE TOWER LANE
OAKBROOK TERRACE IL 60181
708/571-7700; 800/323-4256
AMOUNT: FULL TUITION (40); 1/2 TUITION (80)
DEADLINE(S): MAR 22
FIELD(S): ELECTRONICS ENGINEERING TECHNOLOGY; COMPUTER INFORMATION SYSTEMS; BUSINESS OPERATIONS; TELECOMMUNICATIONS MANAGEMENT; ACCOUNTING
40 FULL-TUITION & 80 1/2 TUITION UNDERGRADUATE SCHOLARSHIPS. OPEN TO USA HIGH SCHOOL GRADUATES WHO WISH TO ENROLL IN A FULLY ACCREDITED BACHELOR OF SCIENCE DEGREE PROGRAM AT ONE OF THE DEVRY INSTITUTES LOCATED THROUGHOUT NORTH AMERICA.
AWARDS RENEWABLE PROVIDED 2.5 GPA IS MAINTAINED. CONTACT YOUR GUIDANCE COUNSELOR; NEAREST DEVRY INSTITUTE OR ADDRESS ABOVE FOR COMPLETE INFORMATION.

273

ELECTRONIC INDUSTRIES FOUNDATION (SCHOLARSHIP FUND)
919 18TH ST; SUITE 900
WASHINGTON DC 20006
202/955-5814
AMOUNT: $2000
DEADLINE(S): FEB 1
FIELD(S): AERONAUTICS; COMPUTER SCIENCE; ELECTRICAL ENGINEERING; ENGINEERING TECHNOLOGY; APPLIED MATHEMATICS; MICROBIOLOGY
OPEN TO DISABLED STUDENTS WHO ARE PURSUING CAREERS IN HIGH-TECH AREAS

THROUGH ACADEMIC OR TECHNICAL TRAINING. AWARDS TENABLE AT RECOGNIZED UNDERGRADUATE & GRADUATE COLLEGES & UNIVERSITIES. USA CITIZEN. FINANCIAL NEED IS A CONSIDERATION.

6 AWARDS PER YEAR. RENEWABLE. WRITE FOR COMPLETE INFORMATION.

274

INSTITUTE OF INDUSTRIAL ENGINEERS (IIE SCHOLARSHIPS)
25 TECHNOLOGY PARK/ATLANTA
NORCROSS GA 30092
404/449-0460
AMOUNT: VARIES
DEADLINE(S): NOV 15 (NOMINATIONS); FEB 15 (APPLICATIONS)
FIELD(S): INDUSTRIAL ENGINEERING

UNDERGRADUATE & GRADUATE SCHOLARSHIPS OPEN TO ACTIVE IIE MEMBERS WITH AT LEAST 1 FULL YEAR OF STUDY REMAINING AT AN ACCREDITED COLLEGE OR UNIVERSITY IN NORTH AMERICA. A GPA OF 3.4 OR BETTER IS REQUIRED.

APPLICATIONS WILL BE MAILED ONLY TO STUDENTS NOMINATED BY THEIR DEPARTMENT HEAD. WRITE FOR NOMINATION FORMS & COMPLETE INFORMATION.

275

INTERNATIONAL SOCIETY FOR OPTICAL ENGINEERING (SCHOLARSHIPS & GRANTS)
PO BOX 10
BELLINGHAM WA 98227
206/676-3290
AMOUNT: $500 - $5000
DEADLINE(S): APR 3
FIELD(S): OPTICAL ENGINEERING

SCHOLARSHIP AWARDS ARE FOR EDUCATIONAL PURPOSES WITH FINAL SELECTIONS BASED UPON AN ASSESSMENT OF THE STUDENT'S POTENTIAL CONTRIBUTION TO OPTICS OR OPTICAL ENGINEERING.

30 TO 35 AWARDS PER YEAR. APPLICATIONS MAY BE OBTAINED BY WRITING TO MR. WARREN J. SMITH; CHAIRMAN; SPIE EDUCATION COMMITTEE; ADDRESS ABOVE.

276

INTERNATIONAL SOCIETY FOR OPTICAL ENGINEERING (OPTICAL RADIATION CORP. LIGHT SOURCE SCHOLARSHIP)
PO BOX 10
BELLINGHAM WA 98227
206/676-3290; FAX 206/647-1445
AMOUNT: $1500
DEADLINE(S): APR 3
FIELD(S): OPTICAL ENGINEERING (LIGHT SOURCE)

OPEN TO UNDERGRADUATE OR GRADUATE STUDENT IN A QUALIFIED INSTITUTION INVOLVED IN ANY STUDY OR USE OF LIGHT. STUDY MUST TAKE ADVANTAGE OF NON-NATURAL LIGHT FOR ILLUMINATION REQUIRING AN ELECTRICAL DISCHARGE (EXCLUDING A LASER SOURCE).

ACTIVITY SHOULD BE CENTERED AROUIND THE PROPAGATION, GENERATION AND MANIPULATION OF LIGHT OR THE INTERACTION OF LIGHT WITH MATTER. WRITE FOR COMPLETE INFORMATION.

277

JAMES F. LINCOLN ARC WELDING FOUNDATION (AWARDS PROGRAM)
PO BOX 17035
CLEVELAND OH 44117
216/481-4300
AMOUNT: UP TO $2000
DEADLINE(S): JUN 15
FIELD(S): ARC WELDING TECHNOLOGY

OPEN TO UNDERGRADUATE & GRADUATE ENGINEERING & TECHNOLOGY STUDENTS WHO SOLVE DESIGN ENGINEERING OR FABRICATION PROBLEMS INVOLVING THE KNOWLEDGE OR APPLICATION OF ARC WELDING.

TOTAL OF 29 AWARDS; 17 FOR UNDERGRADUATE AND 12 FOR GRADUATE STUDENTS. WRITE FOR COMPLETE INFORMATION.

278

NATIONAL ACADEMY FOR NUCLEAR TRAINING (SCHOLARSHIPS)
SCHOLARSHIP REVIEW COMMITTEE; PO BOX 6302
PRINCETON NJ 08541
215/750-8323
AMOUNT: $2250 PER YEAR
DEADLINE(S): FEB 1
FIELD(S): NUCLEAR ENGINEERING

OPEN TO FULL TIME UNDERGRADS STUDYING NUCLEAR ENGINEERING WHO HAVE AT LEAST ONE AND AT MOST THREE FULL ACADEMIC YEARS REMAINING BEFORE GRADUATION. MUST BE USA CITIZEN AND HAVE A 3.0 OR BETTER GPA.

275 AWARDS ANNUALLY; RENEWABLE UP TO THREE YEARS. WRITE FOR COMPLETE INFORMATION.

279 ---

NATIONAL ASSOCIATION OF PLUMBING-HEATING-COOLING CONTRACTORS EDUCATIONAL FOUNDATION (NAPHCC SCHOLARSHIP PROGRAM)

PO BOX 6808
FALLS CHURCH VA 22046
703/237-8100

AMOUNT: $2500

DEADLINE(S): APR 1

FIELD(S): PLUMBING; HEATING; COOLING; CONSTRUCTION; BUSINESS ADMINISTRATION

SCHOLARSHIPS ARE AVAILABLE TO HIGH SCHOOL SENIORS AND INCOMING FRESHMEN WHO ARE ENROLLED IN BA PROGRAMS. STUDENTS MUST HAVE A SPONSOR WHO HAS BEEN A MEMBER IN GOOD STANDING IN THE NAPHCC FOR AT LEAST TWO YEARS. USA CITIZEN.

SCHOLARSHIPS RENEWABLE. WRITE FOR COMPLETE INFORMATION.

280 ---

NATIONAL ASSOCIATION OF WATER COMPANIES - NEW JERSEY CHAPTER (SCHOLARSHIP)

C/O NJ-AMERICAN WATER CO - EASTERN DIV 661 SHREWSBURY AVE
SHREWSBURY NJ 07702
908/842-6900; FAX 908/842-7541

AMOUNT: $2500

DEADLINE(S): APR 1 (POSTMARK)

FIELD(S): BUSINESS ADMINISTRATION; BIOLOGY; CHEMISTRY; ENGINEERING

OPEN TO USA CITIZENS WHO HAVE LIVED IN NJ AT LEAST 5 YEARS AND PLAN A CAREER IN THE INVESTOR-OWNED WATER UTILITY INDUSTRY IN DISCIPLINES SUCH AS THOSE ABOVE. MUST BE UNDERGRAD OR GRADUATE STUDENT IN A 2 OR 4 YEAR NJ COLLEGE OR UNIVERSITY.

GPA OF 3.0 OR BETTER REQUIRED. WRITE FOR COMPLETE INFORMATION.

281 ---

NCSU PULP & PAPER FOUNDATION (SCHOLARSHIPS)

PO BOX 8005
RALEIGH NC 27695
919/515-5660

AMOUNT: $1200 - $3700

DEADLINE(S): JAN 15

FIELD(S): PULP & PAPER SCIENCE & TECHNOLOGY

OPEN TO UNDERGRADUATE STUDENTS ACCEPTED TO OR ENROLLED IN NORTH CAROLINA STATE UNIV. & MAJORING IN PULP & PAPER SCIENCE TECHNOLOGY. USA CITIZEN.

N.C. RESIDENTS RECEIVE $1200; OUT-OF-STATE STUDENTS RECEIVE $3700. AWARDS RENEWABLE ANNUALLY. WRITE FOR COMPLETE INFORMATION.

282 ---

NORTH AMERICAN DIE CASTING ASSOCIATION (DAVID LAINE MEMORIAL SCHOLARSHIPS)

2000 NORTH FIFTH AVE
RIVER GROVE IL 60171
312/452-0700

AMOUNT: VARIES

DEADLINE(S): MAY 1

FIELD(S): DIE CASTING TECHNOLOGY

OPEN TO STUDENTS ENROLLED AT AN ENGINEERING COLLEGE AFFILIATED WITH THE FOUNDRY EDUCATIONAL FOUNDATION (FEF) & REGISTERED WITH FEF FOR THE CURRENT YEAR. USA CITIZEN.

FOR UNDERGRADUATE OR GRADUATE STUDY. WRITE FOR COMPLETE INFORMATION.

283 ---

SAN FRANCISCO BAY AREA CHAPTER - NATIONAL DEFENSE TRANSPORTATION ASSN (NDTA MERIT SCHOLARSHIP)

BOX 24676
OAKLAND CA 94623
WRITTEN INQUIRY

AMOUNT: $2000

DEADLINE(S): MAR 31

FIELD(S): BUSINESS; ENGINEERING; PLANNING; ENVIRONMENT (AS RELATED TO TRANSPORTATION)

OPEN TO USA CITIZENS ENROLLED IN AN ACCREDITED UNDERGRADUATE DEGREE OR

VOCATIONAL PROGRAM IN ABOVE FIELDS WHO PLAN TO PURSUE A CAREER RELATED TO TRANSPORTATION. FINANCIAL NEED WILL BE CONSIDERED.
WRITE FOR COMPLETE INFORMATION.

284

SOCIETY OF MANUFACTURING ENGINEERING EDUCATION FOUNDATION (WILLIAM E WEISEL SCHOLARSHIP FUND)
ONE SME DRIVE; PO BOX 930
DEARBORN MI 48121
313/271-1500 EXT 512
AMOUNT: $1000
DEADLINE(S): MAR 1
FIELD(S): MANUFACTURING ENGINEERING; ENGINEERING TECHNOLOGY
OPEN TO FULL-TIME UNDERGRADUATE STUDENTS AT ACCREDITED SCHOOLS WHO ARE SEEKING A CAREER IN MANUFACTURING/ROBOTICS/AUTOMATED SYSTEMS; HAVE COMPLETED 30 CREDIT HOURS IN THIS AREA & HAVE AT LEAST 2.75 GPA (4.0 SCALE). USA OR CANADIAN CITIZEN.
WRITE FOR COMPLETE INFORMATION.

285

SOCIETY OF WOMEN ENGINEERS (AIR PRODUCTS & CHEMICALS INC SCHOLARSHIP)
345 E 47TH ST; ROOM 305
NEW YORK NY 10017
212-705-7855
AMOUNT: $1000
DEADLINE(S): FEB 1
FIELD(S): CHEMICAL ENGINEERING
OPEN TO WOMEN WHO ARE ENTERING THEIR SOPHOMORE OR JUNIOR YEARS AT A COLLEGE OR UNIVERSITY WITH AN ACCREDITED ENGINEERING PROGRAM AND ARE MAJORING IN CHEMICAL ENGINEERING. MUST BE USA CITIZEN. PREFERENCE TO MEMBERS OF ETHNIC MINORITIES.
APPLICATIONS AVAILABLE OCT THROUGH JAN ONLY. SEND STAMPED SELF-ADDRESSED ENVELOPE FOR COMPLETE INFORMATION.

286

TECHNOLOGY STUDENT ASSOCIATION (SCHOLARSHIPS)
1914 ASSOCIATION DR
RESTON VA 22091
703/860-9000
AMOUNT: $250 - $500
DEADLINE(S): MAY 1
FIELD(S): TECHNOLOGY EDUCATION
OPEN TO STUDENT MEMBERS OF THE TECHNOLOGY STUDENT ASSOCIATION WHO CAN DEMONSTRATE FINANCIAL NEED. GRADE POINT AVERAGE IS NOT A CONSIDERATION BUT APPLICANTS MUST BE ACCEPTED TO A 4-YEAR COLLEGE OR UNIVERSITY.
FUNDS ARE SENT TO AND ADMINISTERED BY THE RECIPIENT'S COLLEGE OR UNIVERSITY. WRITE FOR COMPLETE INFORMATION.

287

U.S. AIR FORCE ROTC (4-YEAR SCHOLARSHIP PROGRAM)
AFROTC/RROO; RECRUITING OPERATIONS BRANCH
MAXWELL AFB AL 36112
205/953-2091
AMOUNT: TUITION + FEES & BOOKS + $100 PER MONTH STIPEND
DEADLINE(S): DEC 1
FIELD(S): AERONAUTICAL ENGINEERING; CIVIL ENGINEERING; MECHANICAL ENGINEERING; MATHEMATICS; PHYSICS; NURSING & SOME LIBERAL ARTS
OPEN TO USA CITIZENS WHO ARE AT LEAST 17 AND WILL GRADUATE FROM COLLEGE BEFORE AGE 25. MUST COMPLETE APPLICATION; FURNISH SAT/ACT SCORES; HIGH SCHOOL TRANSCRIPTS AND RECORD OF EXTRACURRICULAR ACTIVITIES.
MUST QUALIFY ON AIR FORCE MEDICAL EXAMINATION. ABOUT 1600 SCHOLARSHIPS AWARDED EACH YEAR AT CAMPUSES WHICH OFFER AIR FORCE ROTC.

288

UNIVERSITY OF MAINE PULP & PAPER FOUNDATION (SCHOLARSHIPS)
5737 JENNESS HALL
ORONO ME 04469
207-581-2296
AMOUNT: $1000; TUITION
DEADLINE(S): FEB 15
FIELD(S): ENGINEERING
OPEN TO UNDERGRADUATE STUDENTS ACCEPTED TO OR ENROLLED IN THE UNIVERSITY OF MAINE AT ORONO WHO HAVE

DEMONSTRATED AN INTEREST IN A PAPER RELATED CAREER. USA OR CANADIAN CITIZEN.

25 $1000 SCHOLARSHIPS AWARDED TO 1ST YEAR STUDENTS & 100 TUITION SCHOLARSHIPS (EQUAL TO MAINE RESIDENT TUITION). WRITE FOR COMPLETE INFORMATION.

289

WASHINGTON PULP & PAPER FOUNDATION (SCHOLARSHIP PROGRAM)
C/O UNIV. OF WASHINGTON (AR-10)
SEATTLE WA 98195
206/543-2763
AMOUNT: $2000 - $6000
DEADLINE(S): MAR 1
FIELD(S): PULP & PAPER TECHNOLOGY

AWARDS ARE FULL TUITION UNDERGRADUATE SCHOLARSHIPS AT THE UNIV. OF WASHINGTON. OPEN TO STUDENTS WHO ARE ACCEPTED TO OR ENROLLED IN THE PULP & PAPER SCIENCE CURRICULUM AT THE UNIV. USA CITIZEN OR LEGAL RESIDENT.

APPROX 50 AWARDS PER YEAR. RENEWABLE. WRITE FOR COMPLETE INFORMATION.

MECHANICAL ENG

290

AMERICAN GEOLOGICAL INSTITUTE (MINORITY PARTICIPATION PROGRAM SCHOLARSHIPS)
4220 KING ST
ALEXANDRIA VA 22302
703/379-2480
AMOUNT: UP TO $10000 PER YEAR UNDERGRAD; $4000 PER YEAR GRAD
DEADLINE(S): FEB 1
FIELD(S): EARTH SCIENCES; SPACE SCIENCES; MARINE SCIENCES

FOR FULL TIME UNDERGRADUATE OR GRADUATE STUDY IN THE ABOVE FIELDS. OPEN TO AMERICAN BLACKS; NATIVE AMERICANS & HISPANIC AMERICANS. MUST BE USA CITIZEN AND DEMONSTRATE FINANCIAL NEED.

APPROX 80 AWARDS PER YEAR. RENEWALS POSSIBLE WITH REAPPLICATION. WRITE FOR COMPLETE INFORMATION.

291

AMERICAN SOCIETY OF MECHANICAL ENGINEERS (STUDENT ASSISTANCE LOAN PROGRAM)
345 E 47TH ST
NEW YORK NY 10017
212/705-7375
AMOUNT: UP TO $2500
DEADLINE(S): APR 1; NOV 1
FIELD(S): MECHANICAL ENGINEERING; ENGINEERING TECHNOLOGY (STUDENT ASSISTANCE LOAN PROGRAM)

LOANS TO STUDENT MEMBERS OF ASME WHO ARE UNDERGRADUATE OR GRADUATE STUDENTS ENROLLED IN SCHOOLS WITH ACCREDITED MECHANICAL ENGINEERING OR ENGINEERING TECHNOLOGY CURRICULA. MINIMUM 2.0 GPA ON 4.0 SCALE. USA CITIZEN.

FIRST PREFERENCE GIVEN TO UNDERGRADUATE JUNIORS AND SENIORS. WRITE FOR COMPLETE INFORMATION.

292

AMERICAN SOCIETY OF MECHANICAL ENGINEERS AUXILIARY INC (SYLVIA W FARNY SCHOLARSHIP)
345 E 47TH ST
NEW YORK NY 10017
212/705-7746
AMOUNT: $1000
DEADLINE(S): FEB 1
FIELD(S): MECHANICAL ENGINEERING

US CITIZEN ENROLLED IN JUNIOR YEAR OF UNDERGRADUATE STUDY IN SCHOOL WITH ACCREDITED MECHANICAL ENGINEERING CURRICULA IN USA. AWARD IS FOR SENIOR YEAR OF STUDY. MUST BE STUDENT MEMBER OF ASME.

4-6 SCHOLARSHIPS PER YEAR. SEND INQUIRIES TO MRS. E.H. MOSS JR; RT 1 BOX 212; LEDBETTER TX 78946 OR TO ADDRESS ABOVE. REQUESTS FOR APPLICATIONS MUST BE RECEIVED BY CHAIRMAN BY FEB 1.

293

AMERICAN SOCIETY OF MECHANICAL ENGINEERS NATIONAL OFFICE (STUDENT ASSISTANCE LOAN PROGRAM)
345 EAST 47TH STREET
NEW YORK NY 10017
212-705-7375
AMOUNT: $2500 MAX

DEADLINE(S): JAN 1 - APR 1
FIELD(S): MECHANICAL ENGINEERING
US CITIZEN. UNDERGRAD FRESHMAN/SOPHOMORE/OR JUNIOR. STUDENT MEMBER OF ASME & FULL-TIME STUDENT IN AN ABET ACCREDITED PROGRAM IN USA. DEMONSTRATE NEED.
ABOUT 60 LOANS PER YEAR. WRITE FOR COMPLETE DETAILS.

294

ASM FOUNDATION FOR EDUCATION & RESEARCH (SCHOLARSHIP PROGRAM)
STUDENT OUTREACH PROGRAM
MATERIALS PARK OH 44073
216/338-5151
AMOUNT: 34 $500 AWARDS; 3 $2000 AWARDS; 1 FULL TUITION AWARD
DEADLINE(S): JUN 15
FIELD(S): METALLURGY; MATERIALS SCIENCE
OPEN TO UNDERGRADUATE STUDENTS WHO ARE MAJORING IN METALLURGY/MATERIALS AND HAVE COMPLETED AT LEAST 1 YEAR OF STUDY. FOR CITIZENS OF USA; CANADA OR MEXICO WHO ARE ENROLLED IN A RECOGNIZED COLLEGE OR UNIVERSITY IN THE USA; CANADA OR MEXICO.
MUST BE IN JUNIOR OR SENIOR YEAR AND DEMONSTRATE FINANCIAL NEED FOR FULL TUITION AWARD. WRITE FOR COMPLETE INFORMATION.

295

AT&T BELL LABORATORIES (ENGINEERING SCHOLARSHIP PROGRAM)
CRAWFORDS CORNER ROAD; ROOM 1E-213
HOLMDEL NJ 07733
201/949-4300
AMOUNT: FULL-TUITION & FEES + MONTHLY STIPEND
DEADLINE(S): JAN 15
FIELD(S): ELECTRICAL ENGINEERING; MECHANICAL ENGINEERING; COMPUTER SCIENCE; SYSTEMS ENGINEERING; COMPUTER ENGINEERING
UNDERGRADUATE SCHOLARSHIPS TO ENCOURAGE MINORITIES AND WOMEN TO ENTER ENGINEERING PROFESSION. SUMMER EMPLOYMENT AT BELL LABS INCLUDED. MUST MAINTAIN 3.0 OR BETTER GPA AND SATISFACTORY JOB PERFORMANCE. USA CITIZEN OR PERMANENT RESIDENT.
SCHOLARSHIPS ARE RENEWABLE UNTIL COMPLETION OF BS DEGREE. WRITE FOR COMPLETE INFORMATION.

296

AT&T BELL LABORATORIES (SUMMER RESEARCH PROGRAM FOR MINORITIES & WOMEN)
101 CRAWFORDS CORNER RD; RM 1B-209
HOLMDEL NJ 07733
908/949-3728
AMOUNT: SALARY + TRAVEL & LIVING EXPENSES FOR SUMMER
DEADLINE(S): DEC 1
FIELD(S): ENGINEERING; MATH; SCIENCES; COMPUTER SCIENCE
PROGRAM OFFERS MINORITY STUDENTS & WOMEN STUDENTS TECHNICAL EMPLOYMENT EXPERIENCE AT BELL LABORATORIES. STUDENTS SHOULD HAVE COMPLETED THEIR THIRD YEAR OF STUDY AT AN ACCREDITED COLLEGE OR UNIVERSITY. USA CITIZEN OR PERMANENT RESIDENT.
SELECTION IS BASED PARTIALLY ON ACADEMIC ACHIEVEMENT AND PERSONAL MOTIVATION. WRITE SPECIAL PROGRAMS MANAGER - SRP FOR COMPLETE INFORMATION.

297

HUGHES AIRCRAFT COMPANY (BACHELOR OF SCIENCE SCHOLARSHIP)
PO BOX 80028 (C1/B168) TECH. ED. CENTER
LOS ANGELES CA 90080
310-568-6711
AMOUNT: ALL EDUCATIONAL EXPENSES + SALARY & RELOCATION EXPENSES
DEADLINE(S): APPLY BETWEEN OCT & MAR PRIOR TO JUNE COMPLETION OF SOPHOMORE YEAR.
FIELD(S): ELECTRICAL MECHANICAL OR AEROSPACE ENGINEERING OR COMPUTER SCIENCE; MATHEMATICS; OR PHYSICS
OPEN TO STUDENTS WITH UPPER DIVISION STANDING OR AA DEGREE & AT LEAST A 3.0 GPA WHO HAVE BEEN ADMITTED WITHOUT CONDITION TO A UNIVERSITY ACCREDITED BY THE ACCREDITATION BOARD FOR ENGINEERING & TECHNOLOGY (ABET).
WORK STUDY OR FULL STUDY PROGRAMS. USA CITIZEN. MOST AWARDS ARE FOR WORK STUDY NEAR HUGHES PLANTS. WRITE FOR COMPLETE INFORMATION.

298

NATIONAL ASSOCIATION OF WATER COMPANIES - NEW JERSEY CHAPTER (SCHOLARSHIP)
C/O NJ-AMERICAN WATER CO - EASTERN DIV 661 SHREWSBURY AVE
SHREWSBURY NJ 07702
908/842-6900; FAX 908/842-7541
AMOUNT: $2500
DEADLINE(S): APR 1 (POSTMARK)
FIELD(S): BUSINESS ADMINISTRATION; BIOLOGY; CHEMISTRY; ENGINEERING
OPEN TO USA CITIZENS WHO HAVE LIVED IN NJ AT LEAST 5 YEARS AND PLAN A CAREER IN THE INVESTOR-OWNED WATER UTILITY INDUSTRY IN DISCIPLINES SUCH AS THOSE ABOVE. MUST BE UNDERGRAD OR GRADUATE STUDENT IN A 2 OR 4 YEAR NJ COLLEGE OR UNIVERSITY.
GPA OF 3.0 OR BETTER REQUIRED. WRITE FOR COMPLETE INFORMATION.

299

NATIONAL STONE ASSOCIATION (NSA QUARRY ENGINEERING SCHOLARSHIPS)
1415 ELLIOT PLACE NW
WASHINGTON DC 20007
202/342-1100
AMOUNT: $2000
DEADLINE(S): MAY 1
FIELD(S): QUARRY ENGINEERING
OPEN TO STUDENTS INTENDING TO PURSUE A CAREER IN THE CRUSHED STONE INDUSTRY AND WHO ARE ENROLLED IN AN UNDERGRADUATE PROGRAM WORKING TOWARD THIS OBJECTIVE. FINANCIAL NEED IS A CONSIDERATION BUT NOT A REQUIREMENT.
FIVE AWARDS PER YEAR. RENEWAL POSSIBLE. WRITE FOR COMPLETE INFORMATION.

300

NATIONAL STONE ASSOCIATION (SAMUEL C. KRAUS JR. MEMORIAL SCHOLARSHIP)
1415 ELLIOT PL NW
WASHINGTON DC 20007
202/342-1100
AMOUNT: $2000
DEADLINE(S): MAY 1
FIELD(S): MINING ENGINEERING OR GEOLOGY
OPEN TO PROMISING MINING ENGINEERING OR GEOLOGY MAJORS AT THE UNIVERSITY OF MISSOURI AT ROLLA WHO INTEND TO PURSUE A CAREER IN THE CRUSHED STONE INDUSTRY. FINANCIAL NEED IS A CONSIDERATION BUT NOT A REQUIREMENT.
WRITE FOR COMPLETE INFORMATION.

301

SOCIETY OF MINING ENGINEERS (COAL DIVISION SCHOLARSHIPS)
PO BOX 625002; 8307 SHAFFER PKWY
LITTLETON CO 80162
303-973-9550
AMOUNT: UP TO $1000
DEADLINE(S): VARIES WITH SCHOOL
FIELD(S): MINING ENGINEERING
OPEN TO SME MEMBERS WHO HAVE CHOSEN AS A CAREER PATH THE FIELD OF MINING ENGINEERING WITH AN EMPHASIS ON COAL. AWARDS ARE TENABLE ONLY AT COLLEGES & UNIVERSITIES IN THE USA THAT ARE ABET ACCREDITED & ENGAGED IN COAL-RELATED ACTIVITIES.
SCHOLARSHIPS ARE AWARDED BY THE SCHOOLS; CONTACT THE DEPT HEAD OF MINING ENGINEERING AT INSTITUTION(S) OF INTEREST.

302

SOCIETY OF MINING ENGINEERS (EUGENE P. PFLEIDER MEMORIAL SCHOLARSHIP)
PO BOX 625002; 8307 SHAFFER PKWY
LITTLETON CO 80162
303-973-9550
AMOUNT: UP TO $1000
DEADLINE(S): NOV 30
FIELD(S): MINING ENGINEERING
OPEN TO UNDERGRADUATE SOPHOMORES WHO ARE PURSUING A CAREER IN MINING ENGINEERING. AWARDS TENABLE AT ANY USA COLLEGE OR UNIV. THAT OFFERS AN ACCREDITED BA DEGREE IN MINING ENGINEERING. USA CITIZEN.
WRITE FOR COMPLETE DETAILS.

303

SOCIETY OF MINING ENGINEERS (INDUSTRIAL MINERALS DIVISION SCHOLARSHIPS)
PO BOX 625002; 8307 SHAFFER PKWY
LITTLETON CO 80162
303-973-9550
AMOUNT: UP TO $2000
DEADLINE(S): NOV 30

FIELD(S): MINING ENGINEERING; GEOLOGY; MINERALS ECONOMICS

OPEN TO SME MEMBERS WHO ARE JUNIORS; SENIORS OR GRAD STUDENTS & DESIRE TO DEVELOP THEIR SKILLS IN INDUSTRIAL MINERALS. AWARDS TENABLE AT ANY USA COLLEGE OR UNIV. THAT OFFERS AN ACCREDITED BA; MASTERS OR PHD DEGREE IN THE ABOVE AREAS.

WRITE FOR COMPLETE DETAILS.

304

SOCIETY OF MINING ENGINEERS (MINING & EXPLORATION DIVISION SCHOLARSHIPS)

PO BOX 625002; 8307 SHAFFER PKWY

LITTLETON CO 80162

303-973-9550

AMOUNT: VARIES

DEADLINE(S): NOV 30

FIELD(S): MAT'LS SCIENCE/METALLURGY; MINING ENGINEERING; GEOLOGY; RELATED AREAS

OPEN TO UNDERGRADUATE STUDENTS WHO ARE PURSUING A CAREER IN THE MINERALS INDUSTRY. AWARDS TENABLE AT ANY USA COLLEGE OR UNIV. THAT OFFERS AN ABET ACCREDITED DEGREE IN THE ABOVE AREAS. USA CITIZEN OR LEGAL RESIDENT.

WRITE FOR COMPLETE DETAILS.

305

SOCIETY OF MINING ENGINEERS (MINERAL & METALLURGICAL DIVISION SCHOLARSHIPS)

PO BOX 625002; 8307 SHAFFER PKWY

LITTLETON CO 80162

303-973-9550

AMOUNT: $1000 - $2000

DEADLINE(S): OCT 1

FIELD(S): MAT'LS SCIENCE/METALLURGY

OPEN TO SME MEMBERS WHO ARE FULL-TIME UNDERGRADUATE JUNIORS OR SENIORS & ARE PURSUING A CAREER IN THE MINERALS INDUSTRY. AWARDS ARE TENABLE AT USA COLLEGES & UNIVERSITIES THAT ARE ABET ACCREDITED. MINIMUM 2.5 GPA ON 4.0 SCALE. USA CITIZEN.

6 AWARDS PER YEAR. WRITE FOR COMPLETE DETAILS.

306

U.S. AIR FORCE ROTC (4-YEAR SCHOLARSHIP PROGRAM)

AFROTC/RROO; RECRUITING OPERATIONS BRANCH

MAXWELL AFB AL 36112

205/953-2091

AMOUNT: TUITION + FEES & BOOKS + $100 PER MONTH STIPEND

DEADLINE(S): DEC 1

FIELD(S): AERONAUTICAL ENGINEERING; CIVIL ENGINEERING; MECHANICAL ENGINEERING; MATHEMATICS; PHYSICS; NURSING & SOME LIBERAL ARTS

OPEN TO USA CITIZENS WHO ARE AT LEAST 17 AND WILL GRADUATE FROM COLLEGE BEFORE AGE 25. MUST COMPLETE APPLICATION; FURNISH SAT/ACT SCORES; HIGH SCHOOL TRANSCRIPTS AND RECORD OF EXTRACURRICULAR ACTIVITIES.

MUST QUALIFY ON AIR FORCE MEDICAL EXAMINATION. ABOUT 1600 SCHOLARSHIPS AWARDED EACH YEAR AT CAMPUSES WHICH OFFER AIR FORCE ROTC.

307

VALPARAISO UNIVERSITY (MECHANICAL ENGINEERING SCHOLARSHIPS)

MECHANICAL ENGINEERING DEPT

VALPARAISO IN 46383

219/464-5054

AMOUNT: $500

DEADLINE(S): APR 1

FIELD(S): MECHANICAL ENGINEERING

SCHOLARSHIPS OPEN TO OUTSTANDING STUDENTS (MINIMUM 3.8 GPA) FOR THEIR 3RD OR 4TH YEAR OF UNDERGRADUATE STUDY. AWARDS ARE FOR FULL-TIME STUDY AT VALPARAISO UNIVERSITY.

4 AWARDS PER YEAR. RENEWABLE. WRITE TO THE MECHANICAL ENGINEERING DEPARTMENT CHAIRMAN FOR COMPLETE INFORMATION.

308

VERTICAL FLIGHT FOUNDATION (UNDERGRADUATE/GRADUATE SCHOLARSHIPS)

217 N.WASHINGTON ST

ALEXANDRIA VA 22314

703/684-6777

AMOUNT: UP TO $2000

DEADLINE(S): FEB 1
FIELD(S): MECHANICAL ENGINEERING; ELECTRICAL ENGINEERING; AEROSPACE ENGINEERING
ANNUAL SCHOLARSHIPS OPEN TO UNDERGRADUATE & GRADUATE STUDENTS IN THE ABOVE AREAS WHO ARE INTERESTED IN PURSUING CAREERS IN SOME ASPECT OF HELICOPTER OR VERTICAL FLIGHT. FOR FULL TIME STUDY AT ACCREDITED SCHOOL OF ENGINEERING.
WRITE FOR COMPLETE INFORMATION.

309

WEBB INSTITUTE OF NAVAL ARCHITECTURE (ADMISSIONS SCHOLARSHIPS)
CRESCENT BEACH RD
GLEN COVE NY 11542
516/671-2213
AMOUNT: FULL TUITION FOR 4 YEARS
DEADLINE(S): FEB 15
FIELD(S): NAVAL ARCHITECTURE; MARINE ENGINEERING
OPEN TO H.S. STUDENTS AGED 16-24 WHO ARE IN TOP 10% OF THEIR CLASS & HAVE AT LEAST 3.2 GPA ON 4.0 SCALE. SELECTION BASED ON COLLEGE BOARDS; SAT'S; DEMONSTRATED INTEREST IN ABOVE AREAS & INTERVIEW. USA CITIZEN.
20 TO 25 FOUR YEAR FULL TUITION UNDERGRAD SCHOLARSHIPS PER YEAR TO WEBB INSTITUTE. WRITE FOR COMPLETE INFORMATION.

310

WOMAN'S AUXILIARY TO THE AMERICAN INSTITUTE OF MINING METALLURGICAL & PETROLEUM ENGINEERS (WAAIME SCHOLARSHIP LOAN FUND)
345 E 47TH ST; 14TH FLOOR
NEW YORK NY 10017
WRITTEN INQUIRY ONLY
AMOUNT: VARIES
DEADLINE(S): MAR 15
FIELD(S): EARTH SCIENCES; MINING ENGINEERING; PETROLEUM ENGINEERING
OPEN TO UNDERGRADUATE JUNIORS & SENIORS AND GRADUATE STUDENTS. ELIGIBLE APPLICANTS RECEIVE A SCHOLARSHIP LOAN FOR ALL OR PART OF THEIR EDUCATION. RECIPIENTS REPAY ONLY 50% WITH NO INTEREST CHARGES.
REPAYMENT TO BEGIN BY 6 MONTHS AFTER GRADUATION AND BE COMPLETED WITHIN 6 YEARS. WRITE TO WAAIME SCHOLARSHIP LOAN FUND; ADDRESS ABOVE; FOR COMPLETE INFORMATION.

SCHOOL OF HUMANITIES

311

ALPHA DELTA KAPPA (1995 ADK FINE ARTS GRANTS)
1615 WEST 92ND STREET
KANSAS CITY MO 64114
816/363-5525
AMOUNT: $5000 FIRST PLACE; $3000 SECOND
DEADLINE(S): JUN 1 1994
FIELD(S): INSTRUMENTAL MUSIC (STRINGS); VISUAL ARTS (FINE ARTS ORIGINAL CRAFTS)
OPEN TO ALL QUALIFIED UNDERGRADS; GRADS & POST GRADS. CATEGORIES CHANGE EVERY 2 YRS. CATEGORIES FOR 1995 ARE INSTRUMENTAL MUSIC (STRINGS) AND IN VISUAL ARTS (FINE ARTS ORIGINAL CRAFTS).
GRANTS ARE PAID OVER A TWO YEAR PERIOD. REQUEST APPLICATIONS AFTER JUL 1 1993 FROM KAREN LOONEY; ADK GRANTS COORDINATOR; ADDRESS ABOVE. YOU MUST SPECIFY CATEGORY.

312

ASSOCIATION FOR EDUCATION IN JOURNALISM & MASS COMMUNICATION (CORRESPONDENTS FUND SCHOLARSHIPS)
UNIV OF SOUTH CAROLINA COLLEGE OF JOURNALISM
COLUMBIA SC 29208
803/777-2005
AMOUNT: UP TO $2000
DEADLINE(S): APR 30
FIELD(S): JOURNALISM; MASS COMMUNICATIONS; LIBERAL ARTS
OPEN TO CHILDREN OF PRINT OR BROADCAST JOURNALISTS WHO ARE FOREIGN CORRESPONDENTS FOR A USA NEWS MEDIUM. FOR UNDERGRADUATE; GRADUATE OR POST-GRADUATE STUDY AT ANY ACCREDITED COLLEGE OR UNIVERSITY IN THE USA.
PREFERENCE TO JOURNALISM OR COMMUNICATIONS MAJORS. 8-15 RENEWABLE AWARDS PER YEAR. WRITE FOR COMPLETE INFORMATION.

313

CAPE CANAVERAL CHAPTER RETIRED OFFICERS ASSOC (SCHOLARSHIPS)
PO BOX 4186
PATRICK AFB FL 32925
WRITTEN INQUIRY
AMOUNT: APPROX $1500 PER YEAR
DEADLINE(S): MAY 31
FIELD(S): SCIENCE; MATHEMATICS; ENGINEERING; LIBERAL ARTS; CHEMISTRY
OPEN ONLY TO BREVARD COUNTY FLORIDA RESIDENTS WHO ARE UNDERGRADUATE JUNIORS OR SENIORS AT ANY 4-YEAR COLLEGE IN THE USA & THE SON OR DAUGHTER OF ACTIVE DUTY OR RETIRED MILITARY PERSONNEL. USA CITIZEN.
AWARDS RENEWABLE FOR ONE YEAR. WRITE TO THE SCHOLARSHIP PROGRAM COMMITTEE; ADDRESS ABOVE; FOR COMPLETE INFORMATION.

314

CHAUTAUQUA INSTITUTION (SCHOLARSHIPS)
SCHOOLS OFFICE; BOX 1098; DEPT. 6
CHAUTAUQUA NY 14722
716/357-6233
AMOUNT: VARIES
DEADLINE(S): APR 1
FIELD(S): ART; MUSIC; DANCE; THEATER
SCHOLARSHIPS FOR SUMMER SCHOOL ONLY. AWARDS ARE BASED ON AUDITIONS (PORTFOLIO IN ART) INDICATING PROFICIENCY; FINANCIAL NEED IS A CONSIDERATION.
SOME AUDITIONS ARE REQUIRED IN PERSON BUT TAPED AUDITIONS ALSO ARE ACCEPTABLE. 250 AWARDS PER YEAR. WRITE OR CALL FOR COMPLETE INFORMATION.

315

CIVIL AIR PATROL (CAP UNDERGRADUATE SCHOLARSHIPS)
NATIONAL HEADQUARTERS
MAXWELL AFB AL 36112
205/293-5332
AMOUNT: $750
DEADLINE(S): MAR 15
FIELD(S): HUMANITIES; SCIENCE; ENGINEERING; EDUCATION
OPEN TO CAP MEMBERS WHO HAVE RECEIVED THE BILLY MITCHELL AWARD OR THE SENIOR RATING IN LEVEL II OF THE SENIOR TRAINING PROGRAM. FOR UNDERGRADUATE STUDY IN THE ABOVE AREAS.
WRITE FOR COMPLETE INFORMATION.

316

FLORIDA DEPT. OF EDUCATION (CHALLENGER ASTRONAUTS MEMORIAL SCHOLARSHIP PROGRAM)
OFFICE OF STUDENT FINANCIAL ASSISTANCE; KNOTT BLDG
TALLAHASSEE FL 32399
904/488-4095
AMOUNT: $4000 PER YEAR
DEADLINE(S): MAR 1
FIELD(S): LIBERAL ARTS; EDUCATION
FLORIDA RESIDENT FOR AT LEAST 1 YEAR FOR PURPOSES OTHER THAN EDUCATION. OPEN TO FLORIDA HIGH SCHOOL SENIORS WHO PLAN TO COMPLETE AN UNDERGRADUATE DEGREE IN LIBERAL ARTS OR PURSUE A TEACHING CAREER.
MUST BE NOMINATED BY DISTRICT SCHOOL BOARD BASED ON ACTIVITIES; RECOMMENDATIONS AND ESSAY ON 'THE CHALLENGE OF SPACE.' WRITE FOR COMPLETE INFORMATION.

317

INSTITUTE FOR HUMANE STUDIES (CLAUDE R. LAMBE FELLOWSHIPS)
GEORGE MASON UNIVERSITY; 4400 UNIVERSITY DRIVE
FAIRFAX VA 22030
703/323-1055
AMOUNT: $17500
DEADLINE(S): JAN 15
FIELD(S): SOCIAL SCIENCES; LAW; HUMANITIES
OPEN TO GRADUATE STUDENTS AND UNDERGRADS WHO WILL HAVE JUNIOR OR SENIOR STANDING AT ACCREDITED COLLEGES AND UNIVERSITIES THE NEXT ACADEMIC YEAR. AWARD IS TO SUPPORT STUDENTS WITH A DEMONSTRATED INTEREST IN THE CLASSICAL LIBERAL TRADITION.
RECIPIENT WILL BE INTENT ON PURSUING AN INTELLECTUAL/SCHOLARLY CAREER IN ONE OF THE ABOVE AREAS. WRITE FOR COMPLETE INFORMATION.

318

NATIONAL ENDOWMENT FOR THE HUMANITIES (YOUNGER SCHOLARS AWARDS)
1100 PENNSYLVANIA AVE NW; #316
WASHINGTON DC 20506
202/786-0463
AMOUNT: $2000 - $2400 STIPEND
DEADLINE(S): NOV 1
FIELD(S): HUMANITIES DISCIPLINES
PROGRAM PROVIDES OUTSTANDING STUDENTS WITH A UNIQUE OPPORTUNITY TO CONDUCT AN INDEPENDENT RESEARCH AND WRITING PROJECT FOR 9 WEEKS DURING THE SUMMER UNDER SUPERVISION OF A HUMANITIES SCHOLAR.
OPEN TO HIGH SCHOOL STUDENTS & COLLEGE FRESHMEN; SOPHOMORES & JUNIORS. USA CITIZEN OR LEGAL RESIDENT. 160 AWARDS PER YEAR. WRITE FOR COMPLETE INFORMATION.

319

NATIONAL FOUNDATION OF THE BLIND (HUMANITIES SCHOLARSHIP)
815 4TH AVE; #200
GRINNELL IA 50112
515-236-3366
AMOUNT: $2500
DEADLINE(S): MAR 31
FIELD(S): HUMANITIES (ART; ENGLISH; FOREIGN LANGUAGES; HISTORY; PHILOSOPHY; RELIGION)
OPEN TO LEGALLY BLIND STUDENTS PURSUING OR PLANNING TO PURSUE A POST-SECONDARY EDUCATION IN THE ABOVE AREAS. SCHOLARSHIPS ARE AWARDED ON BASIS OF ACADEMIC EXCELLENCE; COMMUNITY SERVICE AND FINANCIAL NEED.
WRITE FOR COMPLETE INFORMATION.

320

NATIONAL LEAGUE OF AMERICAN PEN WOMEN INC. (SCHOLARSHIP GRANTS FOR MATURE WOMEN)
1300 SEVENTEENTH ST. N.W.
WASHINGTON DC 20036
202/785-1997
AMOUNT: $1000
DEADLINE(S): JAN
FIELD(S): ART; MUSIC; CREATIVE WRITING
THE NATIONAL LEAGUE OF AMERICAN PEN WOMEN GIVES THREE $1000 GRANTS IN EVEN NUMBERED YEARS TO WOMEN AGE 35 AND OVER. SHOULD SUBMIT SLIDES; MANUSCRIPTS OR MUSICAL COMPOSITIONS SUITED TO THE CRITERIA FOR THAT YEAR.
WRITE FOR COMPLETE INFORMATION.

321

UNITARIAN UNIVERSALIST ASSN (SCHOLARSHIPS AND AWARDS)
25 BEACON STREET
BOSTON MA 02108
617-742-2100
AMOUNT: $100 - $700
DEADLINE(S): MAR 15
FIELD(S): ART; POETRY; MUSIC
FOR GRADUATE OR UNDERGRADUATE STUDY. APPLICANTS MUST BE MEMBERS OF THE UNITARIAN CHURCH OR BE SPONSORED BY A UNITARIAN UNIVERSALIST SOCIETY.
SEND A SELF-ADDRESSED STAMPED ENVELOPE TO ABOVE ADDRESS FOR COMPLETE INFORMATION.

AREA STUDIES

322

AMERICAN ASSOCIATION OF TEACHERS OF FRENCH (NATIONAL FRENCH CONTEST)
SIDNEY L. TEITELBAUM; BOX 1178
LONG BEACH NY 11561
516/897-8119; FAX 516/938-2273
AMOUNT: VARIES
DEADLINE(S): FEB 1
FIELD(S): FRENCH LANGUAGE; FRENCH STUDIES
NATIONAL FRENCH CONTEST IS AN EXAMINATION TAKEN THROUGHOUT THE COUNTRY. STUDENTS ARE RANKED REGIONALLY AND NATIONALLY AND ARE ELIGIBLE FOR BOTH REGIONAL AND NATIONAL AWARDS.
NOT A SCHOLARSHIP. WINNERS RECEIVE TRIPS; MEDALS AND BOOKS. WRITE FOR COMPLETE INFORMATION.

323

AMERICAN ASSOCIATION OF TEACHERS OF ITALIAN (COLLEGE ESSAY IN ITALIAN)
CAL STATE UNIV CHICO - FOREIGN LANGUAGE DEPT
CHICO CA 95929
WRITTEN INQUIRIES
AMOUNT: $300 - $100

DEADLINE(S): JUN 15
FIELD(S): ITALIAN LANGUAGE; ITALIAN STUDIES
CONTEST OPEN TO UNDERGRADUATE STUDENTS AT ACCREDITED COLLEGES & UNIVERSITIES IN NORTH AMERICA. ESSAY IN ITALIAN LANGUAGE ON TOPIC PERTAINING TO LITERATURE OR CULTURE.
WRITE TO PROF EUGENIO FRONGIA AT ADDRESS ABOVE FOR COMPLETE INFORMATION.

324

COMMITTEE ON INSTITUTIONAL COOPERATION (CIC PREDOCTORAL FELLOWSHIPS)
KIRKWOOD HALL RM 111; INDIANA UNIV.
BLOOMINGTON IN 47405
812/855-0822
AMOUNT: $9500 + TUITION (5 YEARS)
DEADLINE(S): JAN 2
FIELD(S): HUMANITIES; SOCIAL SCIENCES; NATURAL SCIENCES; MATHEMATICS; ENGINEERING
PREDOCTORAL FELLOWSHIPS FOR USA CITIZENS OF AFRICAN AMERICAN; AMERICAN INDIAN; MEXICAN AMERICAN OR PUERTO RICAN HERITAGE. MUST HOLD OR EXPECT TO RECEIVE BACHELOR'S DEGREE BY LATE SUMMER FROM A REGIONALLY ACCREDITED COLLEGE OR UNIVERSITY.
AWARDS FOR SPECIFIED UNIVERSITIES IN IL; IN; IA; MI; MN; OH; WI; PA. WRITE FOR DETAILS.

325

CREOLE-AMERICAN GENEALOGICAL SOCIETY INC. (CREOLE SCHOLARSHIPS)
PO BOX 2666; CHURCH STREET STATION
NEW YORK NY 10008
WRITTEN INQUIRY ONLY
AMOUNT: $1500
DEADLINE(S): APPLY BETWEEN JAN 1 AND APR 30
FIELD(S): GENEALOGY OR LANGUAGE OR CREOLE CULTURE
AWARDS IN THE ABOVE AREAS OPEN TO INDIVIDUALS OF MIXED RACIAL ANCESTRY WHO SUBMIT A FOUR-GENERATION GENEAOLOGICAL CHART ATTESTING TO CREOLE ANCESTRY AND/OR INTERRACIAL PARENTAGE. FOR UNDERGRADUATE OR GRADUATE STUDY/RESEARCH.
FOR SCHOLARSHIP/AWARD INFORMATION SEND $2 MONEY ORDER AND SELF-ADDRESSED STAMPED ENVELOPE TO ADDRESS ABOVE. CASH AND PERSONAL CHECKS ARE NOT ACCEPTED. LETTERS WITHOUT SASE AND HANDLING CHARGE WILL NOT BE ANSWERED.

326

DUMBARTON OAKS (THE BLISS PRIZE FELLOWSHIP IN BYZANTINE STUDIES)
1703 32ND ST NW
WASHINGTON DC 20007
202/342-3232
AMOUNT: UP TO $28000
DEADLINE(S): NOV 1
FIELD(S): BYZANTINE STUDIES
OPEN TO OUTSTANDING COLLEGE SENIORS WHO PLAN TO ENTER THE FIELD OF BYZANTINE STUDIES. MUST BE IN LAST YEAR OF STUDIES OR ALREADY HOLD BA AND HAVE COMPLETED AT LEAST ONE YEAR OF GREEK BY THE END OF THE SENIOR YEAR.
STUDENTS MUST BE NOMINATED BY THEIR ADVISORS BY OCT 15 AND ATTEND GRADUATE SCHOOL IN THE USA OR CANADA. WRITE FOR COMPLETE INFORMATION.

327

INSTITUTE FOR HUMANE STUDIES (CLAUDE R. LAMBE FELLOWSHIPS)
GEORGE MASON UNIVERSITY; 4400 UNIVERSITY DRIVE
FAIRFAX VA 22030
703/323-1055
AMOUNT: $17500
DEADLINE(S): JAN 15
FIELD(S): SOCIAL SCIENCES; LAW; HUMANITIES
OPEN TO GRADUATE STUDENTS AND UNDERGRADS WHO WILL HAVE JUNIOR OR SENIOR STANDING AT ACCREDITED COLLEGES AND UNIVERSITIES THE NEXT ACADEMIC YEAR. AWARD IS TO SUPPORT STUDENTS WITH A DEMONSTRATED INTEREST IN THE CLASSICAL LIBERAL TRADITION.
RECIPIENT WILL BE INTENT ON PURSUING AN INTELLECTUAL/SCHOLARLY CAREER IN ONE OF THE ABOVE AREAS. WRITE FOR COMPLETE INFORMATION.

328

IRISH AMERICAN CULTURAL INSTITUTE (IRISH WAY SCHOLARSHIPS)
PO BOX 5026; 2115 SUMMIT AVE
ST PAUL MN 55105
612/647-5678
AMOUNT: $250 - $1000
DEADLINE(S): APRIL
FIELD(S): IRISH STUDIES
A SUMMER STUDY & RECREATION PROGRAM IN THE REPUBLIC OF IRELAND. OPEN TO 9TH-12TH GRADE HIGH SCHOOL STUDENTS WHO HAVE AN INTEREST IN IRISH CULTURE & ARE USA CITIZENS.
30-40 AWARDS PER YEAR. WRITE FOR COMPLETE INFORMATION.

329

MEMORIAL FOUNDATION FOR JEWISH CULTURE (INTERNATIONAL SCHOLARSHIP PROGRAM FOR COMMUNITY SERVICE)
15 EAST 26TH ST; ROOM 1903
NEW YORK NY 10010
212/679-4074
AMOUNT: VARIES
DEADLINE(S): NOV 30
FIELD(S): JEWISH STUDIES
OPEN TO ANY INDIVIDUAL REGARDLESS OF COUNTRY OF ORIGIN FOR UNDERGRAD STUDY THAT LEADS TO CAREERS IN THE RABBINATE; JEWISH EDUCATION; SOCIAL WORK OR AS RELIGIOUS FUNCTIONARIES IN DIASPORA JEWISH COMMUNITIES OUTSIDE THE USA; ISRAEL & CANADA.
MUST COMMIT TO SERVE IN A COMMUNITY OF NEED FOR 2 OR 3 YEARS. THOSE PLANNING TO SERVE IN THE USA; CANADA OR ISRAEL ARE EXCLUDED FROM THIS PROGRAM. WRITE FOR COMPLETE INFORMATION.

330

MEMORIAL FOUNDATION FOR JEWISH CULTURE (SOVIET JEWRY COMMUNITY SERVICE SCHOLARSHIP PROGRAM)
15 EAST 26TH ST; ROOM 1901
NEW YORK NY 10010
212/679-4074
AMOUNT: NOT SPECIFIED
DEADLINE(S): NOV 30
FIELD(S): JEWISH STUDIES
OPEN TO SOVIET JEWS ENROLLED OR PLANNING TO ENROLL IN RECOGNIZED INSTITUTIONS OF HIGHER JEWISH LEARNING. MUST AGREE TO SERVE A COMMUNITY OF SOVIET JEWS ANYWHERE IN THE WORLD FOR A MINIMUM OF THREE YEARS.
GRANTS ARE TO HELP PREPARE WELL QUALIFIED SOVIET JEWS TO SERVE IN THE USSR OR WHEREVER THE FOUNDATION DEEMS NECESSARY. WRITE FOR COMPLETE INFORMATION.

331

MIDWAY COLLEGE (INSTITUTIONAL AID PROGRAM-SCHOLARSHIPS AND GRANTS)
FINANCIAL AID OFFICE
MIDWAY KY 40347
606-846-4421
AMOUNT: VARIES
DEADLINE(S): MAR 15
FIELD(S): NURSING; PARALEGAL; BILINGUAL BUSINESS; FRENCH STUDIES; SPANISH STUDIES; EQUINE STUDIES
SCHOLARSHIPS & GRANTS OPEN TO WOMEN WHO ARE ACCEPTED FOR ENROLLMENT AT MIDWAY COLLEGE. AWARDS SUPPORT UNDERGRADUATE STUDY IN THE ABOVE AREAS.
APPROX 200 AWARDS PER YEAR. CONTACT ADDRESS ABOVE FOR COMPLETE DETAILS.

332

MINISTRY OF EDUCATION OF THE REPUBLIC OF CHINA (SCHOLARSHIPS FOR FOREIGN STUDENTS)
5 SOUTH CHUNG-SHAN ROAD
TAIPEI TAIWAN R.O.C.
321-6375; 321-7644
AMOUNT: NT$8000
DEADLINE(S): BETWEEN FEB 1 AND APR 30
FIELD(S): CHINESE STUDIES
UNDERGRADUATE & GRADUATE SCHOLARSHIPS ARE AVAILABLE TO FOREIGN STUDENTS WISHING TO STUDY IN TAIWAN R.O.C. MUST STUDY FULL TIME.
SCHOLARSHIPS ARE RENEWABLE. 300 AWARDS PER YEAR. WRITE FOR COMPLETE INFORMATION.

333

MONGOLIA SOCIETY (DR. GOMBOJAB HANGIN MEMORIAL SCHOLARSHIP)
321-322 GOODBODY HALL; INDIANA UNIV.
BLOOMINGTON IN 47405

812/855-4078
AMOUNT: $3000 - $3500
DEADLINE(S): JAN 1
FIELD(S): MONGOLIAN STUDIES
OPEN TO STUDENTS OF MONGOLIAN NATIONALITY (PERMANENT RESIDENT OF MONGOLIA; CHINA OR THE FORMER SOVIET UNION) TO PURSUE MONGOLIAN STUDIES IN THE USA. RECIPIENT WILL RECEIVE MONEY IN ONE LUMP SUM UPON ARRIVAL IN THE USA.
REPORT ON RECIPIENT'S ACTIVITIES IS DUE AT CONCLUSION OF THE AWARD YEAR. WRITE FOR COMPLETE INFORMATION.

334

NATIONAL ITALIAN AMERICAN FOUNDATION (ROSE BASILE GREEN SCHOLARSHIP)
DR. M.LOMBARDO; EDUCATION DIRECTOR; 666 11TH ST NW; SUITE 800
WASHINGTON DC 20001
202/638-2137
AMOUNT: $1000
DEADLINE(S): MAY 31
FIELD(S): ITALIAN-AMERICAN STUDIES
OPEN TO UNDERGRADUATES OF ITALIAN HERITAGE WHOSE EMPHASIS IS ON ITALIAN-AMERICAN STUDIES. EVIDENCE OF FINANCIAL NEED AND AN ESSAY (1 TYPED PAGE MAXIMUM) DESCRIBING ITALIAN HERITAGE ARE REQUIRED.
WRITE FOR COMPLETE INFORMATION.

335

NELLIE MARTIN CARMAN SCHOLARSHIP TRUST (SCHOLARSHIPS)
1121 244TH ST SW; #65
BOTHELL WA 98021
206/486-6575
AMOUNT: UP TO $1000
DEADLINE(S): MAR 15
FIELD(S): ALL FIELDS OF STUDY EXCEPT THOSE NOTED BELOW
OPEN TO SENIORS IN KING; PIERCE & SNOHOMISH COUNTY (WA) HIGH SCHOOLS WHO HAVE LIVED IN WASHINGTON AT LEAST 5 YRS. FOR UNDERGRADUATE STUDY IN WASHINGTON IN ALL FIELDS EXCEPT MUSIC; SCULPTURE; DRAWING; INTERIOR DESIGN & HOME ECONOMICS.
APPLICATIONS AVAILABLE ONLY THROUGH HIGH SCHOOLS. NOMINATION BY HS COUNSELOR IS REQUIRED. AWARDS ARE RENEWABLE. USA CITIZEN.

336

PEN AMERICAN CENTER (RENATO POGGIOLI TRANSLATION PRIZE)
568 BROADWAY; SUITE 401
NEW YORK NY 10012
212/334-1660
AMOUNT: $3000
DEADLINE(S): JAN 15
FIELD(S): ITALIAN LITERATURE & TRANSLATION
THIS AWARD IS GIVEN TO A YOUNG OR DEVELOPING TRANSLATOR WHO HAS IN PROGRESS A BOOK-LENGTH TRANSLATION OF A WORK OF ITALIAN LITERATURE. APPLICANTS WHO PLAN A RESEARCH TRIP TO ITALY ARE FAVORED. USA CITIZEN.
WRITE FOR COMPLETE INFORMATION.

337

RADIO FREE EUROPE/RADIO LIBERTY (MEDIA & OPINION RESEARCH ON EASTERN EUROPE & THE FORMER SOVIET UNION)
PERSONNEL DIVISION; 1201 CONNECTICUT AVE NW
WASHINGTON DC 20036
WRITTEN INQUIRY
AMOUNT: DAILY STIPEND OF 48 GERMAN MARKS PLUS ACCOMMODATIONS
DEADLINE(S): FEB 22
FIELD(S): COMMUNICATIONS; MARKET RESEARCH; STATISTICS; SOCIOLOGY; SOCIAL PSYCHOLOGY; EAST EUROPEAN STUDIES
INTERNSHIP OPEN TO GRADUATE STUDENT OR EXCEPTIONALLY QUALIFIED UNDERGRADUATE IN THE ABOVE AREAS WHO CAN DEMONSTRATE KNOWLEDGE OF QUANTITATIVE RESEARCH METHODS; COMPUTER APPLICATIONS AND PUBLIC OPINION SURVEY TECHNIQUES.
EAST EUROPEAN LANGUAGE SKILLS WOULD BE AN ADVANTAGE. WRITE FOR COMPLETE INFORMATION.

338

SOIL AND WATER CONSERVATION SOCIETY (SCHOLARSHIPS IN CONSERVATION)
7515 NE ANKENY ROAD
ANKENY IA 50021
515/289-2331; FAX 515/289-1227
AMOUNT: $1000
DEADLINE(S): APR 1

FIELD(S): CONSERVATION; EARTH SCIENCES; AGRICULTURE; RELATED AREAS

OPEN TO UNDERGRADUATES ENROLLED IN AN AGRICULTURAL OR NATURAL RESOURCE RELATED CURRICULUM WHO HAVE COMPLETED TWO YEARS OF STUDY IN AN ACCREDITED COLLEGE AND HAVE A 2.5 OR BETTER GPA. MUST BE WORKING TOWARD A BS DEGREE.

WRITE FOR COMPLETE INFORMATION.

339

SONS OF NORWAY FOUNDATION (KING OLAV V NORWEGIAN-AMERICAN HERITAGE FUND)

1455 WEST LAKE STREET
MINNEAPOLIS MN 55408
612/827-3611

AMOUNT: $250 - $3000

DEADLINE(S): MAR 1

FIELD(S): NORWEGIAN STUDIES

OPEN TO USA CITIZENS 18 OR OLDER WHO HAVE DEMONSTRATED A KEEN AND SINCERE INTEREST IN THE NORWEGIAN HERITAGE. THE STUDENT MUST BE ENROLLED IN A RECOGNIZED EDUCATIONAL INSTITUTION AND BE STUDYING A SUBJECT RELATED TO THE NORWEGIAN HERITAGE.

FINANCIAL NEED IS A CONSIDERATION BUT IT IS SECONDARY TO SCHOLARSHIP. 12 AWARDS PER YEAR. WRITE FOR COMPLETE INFORMATION.

ART

340

ACADEMY OF MOTION PICTURE ARTS AND SCIENCES (STUDENT ACADEMY AWARDS COMPETITION)

8949 WILSHIRE BLVD
BEVERLY HILLS CA 90211
310/278-8990

AMOUNT: $2000; $1500; $1000

DEADLINE(S): APR 1

FIELD(S): FILMMAKING

STUDENT ACADEMY AWARDS COMPETITION IS OPEN TO STUDENT FILMMAKERS WHO HAVE NO PROFESSIONAL EXPERIENCE AND ARE ENROLLED IN ACCREDITED COLLEGES AND UNIVERSITIES. AWARDS ARE FOR COMPLETED FILM PROJECTS ONLY.

WRITE FOR COMPLETE INFORMATION.

341

ALASKA STATE COUNCIL ON THE ARTS (INDIVIDUAL ARTIST FELLOWSHIPS & GRANTS)

411 W 4TH AVE; SUITE 1E
ANCHORAGE AK 99501
907/279-1558

AMOUNT: $5000

DEADLINE(S): OCT 1

FIELD(S): VISUAL ARTS; CRAFTS; PHOTOGRAPHY - ODD NUMBERED YEARS. MUSIC COMPOSITION; CHOREOGRAPHY; MEDIA ARTS; LITERATURE - EVEN NUMBERED YEARS.

OPEN TO ALASKA RESIDENTS WHO ARE ENGAGED IN THE CREATION OF NEW WORKS. FULL TIME STUDENTS ARE NOT ELIGIBLE.

WRITE FOR COMPLETE INFORMATION.

342

AMERICAN COLLEGE FOR THE APPLIED ARTS (EMILIO PUCCI SCHOLARSHIPS)

3330 PEACHTREE RD NE; ADMISSIONS OFFICE
ATLANTA GA 30326
404/231-9000

AMOUNT: $1000 (DISTRIBUTED OVER 6 QTRS)

DEADLINE(S): MAY 1

FIELD(S): FASHION DESIGN; MERCHANDISING; INTERIOR DESIGN; COMMERCIAL ART; BUSINESS ADMINISTRATION

SCHOLARSHIPS ARE FOR HIGH SCHOOL STUDENTS WHO ARE INTERESTED IN EITHER A 2-YEAR OR 4-YEAR PROGRAM AT ONE OF THE AMERICAN COLLEGES FOR THE APPLIED ARTS IN ATLANTA; LOS ANGELES OR LONDON. SCHOLARSHIP IS APPLIED TOWARD TUITION.

WRITE FOR APPLICATIONS AND COMPLETE INFORMATION.

343

AMERICAN SOCIETY OF INTERIOR DESIGNERS EDUCATIONAL FOUNDATION (YALE R. BURGE SCHOLARSHIP COMPETITION)

608 MASSACHUSETTS AVE NE
WASHINGTON DC 20002
202/546-3480; FAX 202/546-3240

AMOUNT: $250 - $500

DEADLINE(S): FEB 1 FOR REGISTRATION; APR 1 FOR ENTRIES

FIELD(S): INTERIOR DESIGN

COMPETITION DESIGNED TO ENCOURAGE STUDENTS TO SERIOUSLY PLAN THEIR PORTFOLIOS. OPEN TO STUDENTS IN THEIR FINAL YEAR OF UNDERGRAD STUDY WHO ARE ENROLLED IN AT LEAST A 3 YEAR PROGRAM OF INTERIOR DESIGN.

A $10 ENTRY FEE IS REQUIRED WITH REGISTRATION. SEND SELF-ADDRESSED STAMPED ENVELOPE FOR COMPLETE INFORMATION.

344

AMERICAN WOMEN IN RADIO & TELEVISION (HOUSTON INTERNSHIP PROGRAM)

APRILLE MEEK; AWRT-HOUSTON; PO BOX 980908
HOUSTON TX 77098
WRITTEN INQUIRY

AMOUNT: $500 PER YEAR

DEADLINE(S): MAR 1

FIELD(S): RADIO; TELEVISION; FILM & VIDEO; ADVERTISING; MARKETING

INTERNSHIPS OPEN TO STUDENTS WHO ARE JUNIORS; SENIORS OR GRADUATE STUDENTS AT GREATER HOUSTON AREA COLLEGES & UNIVERSITIES.

WRITE FOR COMPLETE INFORMATION.

345

ARTS INTERNATIONAL; INSTITUTE OF INTERNATIONAL EDUCATION (CINTAS FELLOWSHIP PROGRAM)

809 UNITED NATIONS PLAZA
NEW YORK NY 10017
212/984-5370

AMOUNT: $10000

DEADLINE(S): MAR 1

FIELD(S): ARCHITECTURE; PAINTING; PHOTOGRAPHY; SCULPTURE; PRINTMAKING; MUSIC COMPOSITION; CREATIVE WRITING

FELLOWSHIPS OPEN TO ARTISTS WHO ARE OF CUBAN ANCESTRY OR CUBAN CITIZENS LIVING OUTSIDE OF CUBA. THEY ARE INTENDED TO FOSTER & ENCOURAGE THE PROFESSIONAL DEVELOPMENT & RECOGNITION OF TALENTED CREATIVE ARTISTS IN THE ABOVE AREAS.

FELLOWSHIPS ARE NOT AWARDED FOR FURTHERANCE OF ACADEMIC STUDY. 5-10 AWARDS PER YEAR. WRITE FOR COMPLETE INFORMATION.

346

BLACK AMERICAN CINEMA SOCIETY (FILMMAKERS GRANTS PROGRAM)

3617 MONTCLAIR STREET
LOS ANGELES CA 90018
213/737-3292; FAX 213/737-2842

AMOUNT: UP TO $3000

DEADLINE(S): FEB 22

FIELD(S): FILMMAKING

OPEN TO BLACK FILMMAKERS. APPLICATIONS ACCEPTED ONLY FROM THE INDIVIDUAL(S) WHO HAVE PRIMARY CREATIVE RESPONSIBILITY FOR THE FILM. PROJECT (1 PER GRANT CYCLE) MAY BE SUBMITTED IN 16MM FILM OR 3/4" VIDEO. USA CITIZEN OR LEGAL RESIDENT.

PROJECTS MUST BE MADE IN THE USA. CONTACT ADDRESS ABOVE FOR COMPLETE INFORMATION.

347

BUSH FOUNDATION (BUSH ARTIST FELLOWSHIPS)

E900 FIRST NATIONAL BANK BLDG; 322 MINNESOTA ST.
ST PAUL MN 55101
612/227-5222

AMOUNT: UP TO $26000 STIPEND + $7000 EXPENSES

DEADLINE(S): LATE OCT; EARLY NOV

FIELD(S): LITERATURE; MUSIC COMPOSITION; CHOREOGRAPHY; VISUAL ARTS; SCRIPTWORKS

OPEN TO WRITERS; VISUAL ARTISTS; COMPOSERS & CHOREOGRAPHERS WHO ARE RESIDENTS OF MN; ND; SD OR WESTERN WI & AT LEAST 25 YRS OLD. AWARDS ARE TO HELP ARTISTS WORK FULL-TIME IN THEIR CHOSEN FIELD; NOT FOR ACADEMIC STUDY.

15 FELLOWSHIPS PER YEAR; 6-18 MONTHS IN DURATION. WRITE FOR COMPLETE INFORMATION.

348

CALIFORNIA COLLEGE OF ARTS & CRAFTS (UNDERGRADUATE AND GRADUATE SCHOLARSHIPS)

5212 BROADWAY
OAKLAND CA 94618
510/653-8118

AMOUNT: VARIES

DEADLINE(S): MAR 1

FIELD(S): ART

OPEN TO UNDERGRADUATE AND GRADUATE STUDENTS ACCEPTED TO OR ENROLLED IN A DEGREE PROGRAM AT THE CALIFORNIA COLLEGE OF ARTS AND CRAFTS. MUST BE A USA CITIZEN OR LEGAL RESIDENT AND DEMONSTRATE FINANCIAL NEED.

APPROX 600 AWARDS PER YEAR. RENEWABLE. CONTACT OFFICE OF ENROLLMENT SERVICES FOR COMPLETE INFORMATION.

349

DISTRICT OF COLUMBIA COMMISSION ON THE ARTS & HUMANITIES (GRANTS)

410 EIGHTH ST NW; 5TH FLOOR
WASHINGTON DC 20004
202/724-5613; TDD 202/727-318; FAX 202/727-4135

AMOUNT: $5000

DEADLINE(S): FEB 15

FIELD(S): ARTS; PERFORMING ARTS; LITERATURE

APPLICANTS FOR GRANTS MUST BE PROFESSIONAL ARTISTS AND RESIDENTS OF WASHINGTON D.C. FOR AT LEAST ONE YEAR PRIOR TO SUBMITTING APPLICATION. AWARDS INTENDED TO GENERATE ARTS ENDEAVORS WITHIN THE WASHINGTON D.C. COMMUNITY.

OPEN ALSO TO ARTS ORGANIZATIONS THAT TRAIN; EXHIBIT OR PERFORM WITHIN D.C. 150 GRANTS PER YEAR. WRITE FOR COMPLETE INFORMATION.

350

FLORIDA ARTS COUNCIL (INDIVIDUAL ARTISTS FELLOWSHIPS)

FLA DEPT OF STATE; DIV OF CULTURAL AFFAIRS; STATE CAPITOL
TALLAHASSEE FL 32399
904/487-2980

AMOUNT: UP TO $5000

DEADLINE(S): FEB 15 (APR 15 FOR VISUAL ARTS)

FIELD(S): VISUAL ARTS; DANCE; FOLK ARTS; MEDIA; MUSIC; THEATER; LITERARY ARTS

FELLOWSHIPS AWARDED TO INDIVIDUAL ARTISTS IN THE ABOVE AREAS. MUST BE FLORIDA RESIDENTS; USA CITIZENS AND OVER 18 YEARS OLD. MAY NOT BE A DEGREE SEEKING STUDENT; FUNDING IS FOR SUPPORT OF ARTISTIC ENDEAVORS ONLY.

FORTY AWARDS PER YEAR. WRITE FOR COMPLETE INFORMATION.

351

FOUNDATION OF FLEXOGRAPHIC TECHNICAL ASSN (FLEXOGRAPHY SCHOLARSHIPS)

900 MARCONI AVE
RONKONKOMA NY 11779
516/737-6026

AMOUNT: $500

DEADLINE(S): MAR 20

FIELD(S): GRAPHIC ARTS

OPEN TO HIGH SCHOOL GRADUATES WHO ARE ACCEPTED TO OR ENROLLED AS A SOPHOMORE OR JUNIOR AT A COLLEGE OFFERING A COURSE OF STUDY IN FLEXOGRAPHY. STUDENTS AT 2 YEAR JUNIOR COLLEGES ALSO MAY APPLY. GPA OF 3.0 OR BETTER IS REQUIRED.

APPROX 13 RENEWABLE SCHOLARSHIPS PER YEAR. WRITE FOR COMPLETE INFORMATION.

352

FRANCES HOOK SCHOLARSHIP FUND (2 DIMENSIONAL ART CONTEST)

430B W COUNTY ROAD D
NEW BRIGHTON MN 55112
612/636-6436

AMOUNT: VARIES

DEADLINE(S): MAR 1

FIELD(S): ART

OPEN TO FULL TIME UNDERGRADUATE ART STUDENTS AGE 24 OR YOUNGER. AWARDS ARE INTENDED TO PAY FOR ART SUPPLIES AND/OR TUITION.

TOTAL PRIZE MONEY IS $55000. 74 AWARDS PER YEAR. WRITE FOR COMPLETE INFORMATION.

353

GEORGIA COUNCIL FOR THE ARTS (INDIVIDUAL ARTIST GRANTS)

530 MEANS ST NW; SUITE 115
ATLANTA GA 30318
404/651-7920

AMOUNT: UP TO $5000

DEADLINE(S): APR 20

FIELD(S): THE ARTS

GRANTS TO SUPPORT ARTISTIC PROJECTS BY PROFESSIONAL ARTISTS WHO HAVE BEEN GEORGIA RESIDENTS AT LEAST ONE YEAR PRIOR TO APPLICATION. SELECTION IS BASED ON PROJECT'S ARTISTIC MERIT AND ITS POTENTIAL FOR CAREER DEVELOPMENT.

GRANTS DO NOT SUPPORT ACADEMIC STUDY. WRITE FOR COMPLETE INFORMATION.

354

GRAPHIC ARTS TECHNICAL FOUNDATION (SCHOLARSHIP TRUST FUND SCHOLARSHIPS)
4615 FORBES AVE
PITTSBURGH PA 15213
412/621-6941
AMOUNT: $500 - $1000
DEADLINE(S): JAN 15 - STUDENTS NOT IN COLLEGE; MAR 15 - STUDENTS ALREADY ENROLLED
FIELD(S): GRAPHIC ARTS; PRINTING; PRINTMAKING

OPEN TO HIGH SCHOOL SENIORS & UNDERGRADUATE FRESHMEN; SOPHOMORES & JUNIORS AT RECOGNIZED 2-YEAR & 4-YEAR COLLEGES & UNIVERSITIES IN THE USA. AWARDS SUPPORT FULL TIME STUDY IN THE ABOVE AREAS. USA CITIZEN.

APPROX 100 AWARDS PER YEAR. RENEWABLE FOR UP TO FOUR YEARS PROVIDED YOU MAINTAIN YOUR ELIGIBILITY. WRITE FOR COMPLETE INFORMATION.

355

HAYSTACK MOUNTAIN SCHOOL OF CRAFTS (SCHOLARSHIP PROGRAM)
ADMISSIONS OFFICE; PO BOX 518
DEER ISLE ME 04627
207/348-2306
AMOUNT: $400
DEADLINE(S): MAR 25
FIELD(S): CRAFTS; GRAPHIC ARTS

SCHOLARSHIPS ARE FOR STUDY IN GRAPHICS; CERAMICS; WEAVING; JEWELRY; GLASS; BLACKSMITHING; FABRIC & WOOD. LIMITED WORK SCHOLARSHIPS ALSO ARE AVAILABLE.

SCHOLARSHIPS ARE TENABLE AT THE SCHOOL OF CRAFTS FOR THE SIX SUMMER SESSIONS. EACH SESSION IS ONE; TWO OR THREE WEEKS LONG. WRITE FOR COMPLETE INFORMATION.

356

HOME FASHION PRODUCTS ASSN (DESIGN COMPETITION)
355 LEXINGTON AVE
NEW YORK NY 10017
212/661-4261
AMOUNT: $1000
DEADLINE(S): JUN 30
FIELD(S): INTERIOR DESIGN; FASHION DESIGN

ANNUAL TEXTILE OR HOME FURNISHINGS DESIGN COMPETITION OPEN TO ANY UNDERGRADUATE STUDENT WHO IS ENROLLED IN AN ACCREDITED 2-YEAR OR 4-YEAR SCHOOL OF ART OR DESIGN.

APPLICATIONS ACCEPTED FROM DEPARTMENT CHAIRMEN ONLY NOT INDIVIDUALS. WRITE FOR COMPLETE INFORMATION.

357

ILLINOIS ARTS COUNCIL (ARTISTS FELLOWSHIP AWARDS)
100 W RANDOLPH; SUITE 10-500
CHICAGO IL 60601
312/814-6750
AMOUNT: $500 - $15000
DEADLINE(S): NOV 1
FIELD(S): CHOREOGRAPHY; VISUAL ARTS; LITERATURE; FILM; VIDEO; PLAYWRITING; MUSIC COMPOSITION; CRAFTS; ETHNIC & FOLK ARTS; PERFORMANCE ART; PHOTOGRAPHY

OPEN TO PROFESSIONAL ARTISTS WHO ARE ILLINOIS RESIDENTS. AWARDS ARE IN RECOGNITION OF WORK IN THE ABOVE AREAS; THEY ARE NOT FOR CONTINUING STUDY. STUDENTS ARE NOT ELIGIBLE.

WRITE TO ADDRESS ABOVE FOR APPLICATION FORM.

358

INSTITUTE FOR HUMANE STUDIES (CLAUDE R. LAMBE FELLOWSHIPS)
GEORGE MASON UNIVERSITY; 4400 UNIVERSITY DRIVE
FAIRFAX VA 22030
703/323-1055
AMOUNT: $17500
DEADLINE(S): JAN 15
FIELD(S): SOCIAL SCIENCES; LAW; HUMANITIES

OPEN TO GRADUATE STUDENTS AND UNDERGRADS WHO WILL HAVE JUNIOR OR SENIOR STANDING AT ACCREDITED COLLEGES AND UNIVERSITIES THE NEXT ACADEMIC YEAR. AWARD IS TO SUPPORT STUDENTS WITH A DEMONSTRATED INTEREST IN THE CLASSICAL LIBERAL TRADITION.

RECIPIENT WILL BE INTENT ON PURSUING AN INTELLECTUAL/SCHOLARLY CAREER IN ONE OF THE ABOVE AREAS. WRITE FOR COMPLETE INFORMATION.

359

INTERNATIONAL FURNISHINGS & DESIGN ASSOCIATION (IFDA STUDENT DESIGN COMPETITION)
107 WORLD TRADE CENTER; PO BOX 58045
DALLAS TX 75258
214/747-2406
AMOUNT: $2000 - $3500
DEADLINE(S): MAR 1
FIELD(S): STUDENT DESIGN COMPETITION
DESIGN COMPETITION OPEN TO GRADUATE STUDENTS; 2ND; 3RD OR 4TH YEAR UNDERGRAD STUDENTS ENROLLED IN AN ACCREDITED UNIVERSITY OR COLLEGE WITH SCHOOLS OF DESIGN; CRAFTS OR ARTS; AND 2ND YEAR STUDENTS IN A 2-YEAR SCHOOL OF DESIGN.
NATIONAL AND REGIONAL PRIZES. WRITE FOR COMPLETE INFORMATION.

360

JAPANESE AMERICAN CITIZENS LEAGUE (HENRY & CHIYO KUWAHARA CREATIVE ARTS SCHOLARSHIP)
1765 SUTTER ST
SAN FRANCISCO CA 94115
415/921-5225
AMOUNT: VARIES
DEADLINE(S): APR 1
FIELD(S): CREATIVE ARTS
OPEN TO JACL MEMBERS OR THEIR CHILDREN OR ANY AMERICAN OF JAPANESE ANCESTRY. APPLICANTS MUST SUBMIT A KUWAHARA CREATIVE ARTS SCHOLARSHIP APPLICATION. AWARD IS TO ENCOURAGE CREATIVE PROJECTS THAT REFLECT THE JAPANESE EXPERIENCE AND CULTURE.
SEND STAMPED SELF-ADDRESSED ENVELOPE FOR COMPLETE INFORMATION.

361

LADIES AUXILIARY TO THE VETERANS OF FOREIGN WARS OF THE UNITED STATES (YOUNG AMERICAN PATRIOTIC ART AWARD)
ATTN BRENDA H. HAMPTON; 406 W 34TH ST
KANSAS CITY MO 64111
816/561-8655
AMOUNT: $300 - $2500
DEADLINE(S): APR 15
FIELD(S): ART COMPETITION
THIS PROGRAM GIVES HIGH SCHOOL STUDENTS AN OPPORTUNITY TO DISPLAY THEIR ARTISTIC TALENTS AND THEIR IDEAS ON AMERICA AND AT THE SAME TIME BE ELIGIBLE FOR FUNDS TO FURTHER THEIR ART EDUCATION. USA CITIZEN.
CONTACT LOCAL VFW AUXILIARY OFFICE OR ADDRESS ABOVE FOR COMPLETE INFORMATION.

362

MEMPHIS COLLEGE OF ART (PORTFOLIO AWARDS)
OVERTON PARK; 1930 POPLAR AVE
MEMPHIS TN 38104
WRITTEN INQUIRY
AMOUNT: $200 - $4275 (HALF TUITION) PER YEAR
DEADLINE(S): NOV 15 - JUN 15
FIELD(S): VISUAL ARTS
AWARDS ARE GIVEN TO EXCELLENT VISUAL ART PORTFOLIOS SUBMITTED BY EITHER HIGH SCHOOL STUDENTS OR TRANSFER STUDENTS. AWARDS TO BE USED FOR FULL TIME ENROLLMENT AT MEMPHIS COLLEGE OF ART. INTERNATIONAL STUDENTS ARE WELCOME.
AWARDS ARE RENEWABLE FOR FOUR YEARS. WRITE FOR COMPLETE INFORMATION.

363

METROPOLITAN MUSEUM OF ART (INTERNSHIPS)
1000 FIFTH AVENUE
NEW YORK NY 10028
212/570-3710
AMOUNT: $2200; $2500; $8000; $12000 (DEPENDING ON INTERNSHIP)
DEADLINE(S): FEB 1
FIELD(S): ART CONSERVATION
INTERNSHIPS OPEN TO UNDERGRADUATE AND GRADUATE STUDENTS WHO INTEND TO PURSUE CAREERS IN ART MUSEUMS. THERE ARE PROGRAMS FOR GRAD AND UNDERGRAD STUDENTS; MINORITIES AND DISADVANTAGED INDIVIDUALS.
TYPED APPLICATION SHOULD INCLUDE NAME; HOME & SCHOOL ADDRESSES & TELEPHONE NUMBERS; EDUCATION & EMPLOYMENT RESUME; TWO ACADEMIC RECOMMENDATIONS; UNDERGRAD & GRADUATE TRANSCRIPTS; ESSAY. WRITE FOR COMPLETE INFORMATION.

364

MILLAY COLONY FOR THE ARTS (RESIDENCIES)
STEEPLETOP; PO BOX 3
AUSTERLITZ NY 12017
518/392-3103
AMOUNT: RESIDENCY
DEADLINE(S): SEP 1; FEB 1; MA[illegible]
FIELD(S): CREATIVE WRIT[illegible] ARTS; MUSIC COMPOSITIO[illegible], GRAPHIC ARTS; POETRY

CANCELLED

THE COLONY [illegible] RESIDENCIES PER YEAR [illegible] ONALS IN THE ABOVE FI[illegible] S NO APPLICATION FEE AND N[illegible] COLONY RESIDENCY.
RESID[illegible] IES ARE FOR ONE MONTH AND USUALLY COVER A PERIOD FROM THE FIRST TO THE 28TH OF EACH MONTH. WRITE FOR COMPLETE INFORMATION.

365

MINNESOTA STATE ARTS BOARD (GRANTS PROGRAM)
432 SUMMIT AVE
ST PAUL MN 55102
612/297-2603
AMOUNT: FELLOWSHIPS $6000; CAREER OPPORTUNITY GRANTS $100 - $1000 OR SPECIAL RESIDENCY STIPEND.
DEADLINE(S): SEP - VISUAL ARTS; OCT - MUSIC & DANCE; DEC - LITERATURE & THEATER
FIELD(S): LITERATURE; MUSIC; THEATER; DANCE; VISUAL ARTS
CAREER ADVANCEMENT GRANTS OPEN TO PROFESSIONAL ARTISTS WHO ARE RESIDENTS OF MINNESOTA. GRANTS ARE NOT INTENDED FOR SUPPORT OF TUITION OR WORK TOWARD ANY DEGREE.
CAREER OPPORTUNITY GRANTS AND FELLOWSHIPS ARE AVAILABLE. ARTISTS ALSO ARE ELIGIBLE FOR A SPECIAL RESIDENCE AT HEADLANDS CENTER FOR THE ARTS NEAR SAN FRANCISCO. WRITE FOR COMPLETE INFORMATION.

366

NATIONAL ENDOWMENT FOR THE ARTS (VISUAL ARTISTS FELLOWSHIPS)
1100 PENNSYLVANIA AVE NW
WASHINGTON DC 20506
202/682-5448
AMOUNT: $15000 - $20000
DEADLINE(S): VARIOUS IN JAN; FEB & MAR
FIELD(S): VISUAL ARTS
FELLOWSHIPS OPEN TO PRACTICING PROFESSIONAL ARTISTS OF EXCEPTIONAL TALENT IN ALL AREAS OF THE VISUAL ARTS. AWARDS ARE TO ASSIST CREATIVE DEVELOPMENT. THEY WILL NOT SUPPORT ACADEMIC STUDY. USA CITIZEN OR LEGAL RESIDENT.
STUDENTS ARE NOT ELIGIBLE TO APPLY. WRITE FOR COMPLETE INFORMATION.

367

NATIONAL FEDERATION OF THE BLIND (ORACLE CORPORATION SCHOLARSHIP)
814 4TH AVE; #200
GRINNELL IA 50112
515/236-3366
AMOUNT: $2500
DEADLINE(S): MAR 31
FIELD(S): HUMANITIES (ART; ENGLISH; FOREIGN LANGUAGES; HISTORY; PHILOSOPHY; RELIGION)
OPEN TO LEGALLY BLIND STUDENTS PURSUING OR PLANNING TO PURSUE A FULL TIME POST SECONDARY COURSE OF STUDY IN THE TRADITIONAL HUMANITIES. AWARDS BASED ON ACADEMIC EXCELLENCE; COMMUNITY SERVICE; FINANCIAL NEED.
WRITE FOR COMPLETE INFORMATION.

368

NATIONAL FOUNDATION FOR ADVANCEMENT IN THE ARTS (ARTS RECOGNITION AND TALENT SEARCH)
300 NE SECOND AVE
MIAMI FL 33132
305/237-3416
AMOUNT: $100 - $3000
DEADLINE(S): OCT 1
FIELD(S): CREATIVE ARTS; PERFORMING ARTS
OPEN TO HIGH SCHOOL SENIORS WITH TALENT IN SUCH ARTS AS THE DANCE; MUSIC; MUSIC/JAZZ; THEATER; VISUAL ARTS; FILM; VIDEO; WRITING. AWARDS CAN BE USED ANYWHERE FOR ANY PURPOSE. FOR US CITIZENS OR RESIDENTS.
UP TO 100 AWARDS PER YEAR. WRITE FOR COMPLETE INFORMATION.

369

NATIONAL FOUNDATION OF THE BLIND (HUMANITIES SCHOLARSHIP)
815 4TH AVE; #200
GRINNELL IA 50112
515-236-3366
AMOUNT: $2500
DEADLINE(S): MAR 31
FIELD(S): HUMANITIES (ART; ENGLISH; FOREIGN LANGUAGES; HISTORY; PHILOSOPHY; RELIGION)
OPEN TO LEGALLY BLIND STUDENTS PURSUING OR PLANNING TO PURSUE A POST-SECONDARY EDUCATION IN THE ABOVE AREAS. SCHOLARSHIPS ARE AWARDED ON BASIS OF ACADEMIC EXCELLENCE; COMMUNITY SERVICE AND FINANCIAL NEED.
WRITE FOR COMPLETE INFORMATION.

370

NATIONAL PARENT-TEACHER ASSOCIATION (REFLECTIONS SCHOLARSHIP PROGRAM)
700 NORTH RUSH ST
CHICAGO IL 60611
312/787-0977
AMOUNT: $750
DEADLINE(S): NOV 30 TO REQUEST PACKET; JAN 29 FOR COMPLETED APPLICATIONS
FIELD(S): VISUAL ARTS; LITERATURE; MUSIC; PHOTOGRAPHY
OPEN TO HIGH SCHOOL SENIORS WHO ATTEND A SCHOOL WITH A PTA OR PTSA AFFILIATED WITH THE NATIONAL PTA AND WHO ENTER THE REFLECTIONS PROGRAM. FOR UNDERGRADUATE STUDY IN ANY OF THE ABOVE FIELDS.
WRITE FOR COMPLETE INFORMATION.

371

NATIONAL SCULPTURE SOCIETY (ALEX J. ETTL GRANT)
15 EAST 26TH ST
NEW YORK NY 10010
212/889-6960
AMOUNT: $5000
DEADLINE(S): OCT 31
FIELD(S): SCULPTURE
OPEN TO USA CITIZENS OR RESIDENTS WHO ARE REALIST OR FIGURATIVE SCULPTORS AND HAVE DEMONSTRATED A COMMITMENT TO SCULPTING AND OUTSTANDING ABILITY. APPLICANTS SUBMIT AT LEAST 10 8X10 INCH PHOTOS OF HIS/HER WORK AND A BRIEF BIOGRAPHY.
APPLICANTS MAY NOT BE SCULPTOR MEMBERS OF THE NATIONAL SCULPTURE SOCIETY. WRITE FOR COMPLETE INFORMATION.

372

NATIONAL SCULPTURE SOCIETY (YOUNG SCULPTOR AWARDS COMPETITION)
15 EAST 26TH STREET
NEW YORK NY 10010
212/889-6960
AMOUNT: $1000; $750; $500; $250
DEADLINE(S): MAY 15
FIELD(S): SCULPTURE
COMPETITION IS OPEN TO SCULPTORS UNDER AGE 36 WHO ARE RESIDENTS OF THE USA. A JURY OF PROFESSIONAL SCULPTORS WILL MAKE THEIR SELECTIONS BASED UPON 5-10 BLACK & WHITE 8 X 10 PHOTOS OF EACH ENTRANT'S WORKS.
IN ADDITION TO CASH AWARDS & PRIZES PHOTOS OF WINNERS' WORKS WILL BE PUBLISHED IN SCULPTURE REVIEW MAGAZINE. WRITE FOR COMPLETE INFORMATION ON OTHER PRIZES AND EXHIBITIONS.

373

NEW YORK FOUNDATION FOR THE ARTS (ARTIST'S FELLOWSHIPS & SERVICES)
155 AVE OF THE AMERICAS; 14TH FLOOR
NEW YORK NY 10013
212/366-6900; FAX 212/366-1778
AMOUNT: $7000
DEADLINE(S): SEP 30
FIELD(S): VISUAL ARTS; LITERATURE; ARCHITECTURE; MUSIC AND MEDIA
FELLOWSHIPS & SERVICES OPEN TO ORIGINATING ARTISTS OVER 18 WHO HAVE BEEN NY STATE RESIDENTS FOR 2 YEARS PREVIOUS TO APPLICATION DATE & ARE NOT ENROLLED IN A DEGREE AWARDING COURSE OF STUDY. AWARDS ARE TO ASSIST IN CREATION OF ONGOING WORK.
APPLICATIONS AVAILABLE IN SPRING OF EACH YEAR. ABOUT 120 FELLOWSHIPS PER YEAR; MANY OTHER SERVICES ARE AVAILABLE. NOT FOR ACADEMIC STUDY. WRITE FOR COMPLETE INFORMATION.

374

OHIO ARTS COUNCIL (OAC SCHOLARSHIP PROGRAM)
727 E MAIN ST
COLUMBUS OH 43205
614/466-2613
AMOUNT: $1000
DEADLINE(S): APR 15 (SENIOR YEAR OF HIGH SCHOOL)
FIELD(S): DANCE; MUSIC; THEATRE ARTS; VISUAL ARTS; WRITING
OHIO RESIDENTS. OPEN TO HIGH SCHOOL SENIORS WHO WISH TO CONTINUE THEIR ARTS TRAINING AND EDUCATION AT AN ACCREDITED COLLEGE OR UNIVERSITY IN THE STATE OF OHIO.
WRITE FOR COMPLETE INFORMATION.

375

PASTEL SOCIETY OF AMERICA (PSA SCHOLARSHIPS)
15 GRAMERCY PARK SOUTH
NEW YORK NY 10003
212/533-6931
AMOUNT: TUITION ONLY (NO CASH AWARDS)
DEADLINE(S): MAY 30 (FOR SUBMISSION OF SLIDES)
FIELD(S): PAINTING (PASTELS ONLY)
OPEN TO TALENTED PASTEL ARTISTS AT ALL LEVELS OF STUDY. AWARDS ARE FOR THE STUDY OF PASTEL ARTS AT THE ART STUDENTS LEAGUE; PSA STUDIO OR WITH A PRIVATE PSA TEACHER. DURATION RANGES FROM 1 WEEK TO 1 CLASS PER WEEK FOR 1 YEAR.
20 AWARDS PER YEAR. WRITE FOR COMPLETE INFORMATION.

376

PRINCESS GRACE FOUNDATION-USA (SCHOLARSHIPS FOR UNDERGRADUATE AND GRADUATE THESIS FILM PRODUCTIONS)
725 PARK AVE
NEW YORK NY 10021
212/744-3221
AMOUNT: $3500 UNDERGRAD SENIORS; $7500 GRADUATE THESIS (MAXIMUMS)
DEADLINE(S): JUN 1
FIELD(S): FILM
SCHOLARSHIPS FOR UNDERGRAD SENIORS AND GRADUATE STUDENTS FOR THESIS FILM PRODUCTIONS. MUST BE NOMINATED BY DEANS OR DEPT CHAIRMEN OF ESTABLISHED USA COLLEGES & UNIVERSITIES THAT HAVE BEEN INVITED TO APPLY.
NOMINEES MUST HAVE COMPLETED ONE FILM AND BE USA CITIZENS OR PERMANENT RESIDENTS. WRITE FOR COMPLETE INFORMATION.

377

SAN FRANCISCO FOUNDATION (JAMES D PHELAN ART AWARDS)
685 MARKET ST; SUITE 910
SAN FRANCISCO CA 94105
415/543-0223 EXT 22
AMOUNT: $2500
DEADLINE(S): EARLY FALL
FIELD(S): PRINTMAKING; PHOTOGRAPHY; FILM & VIDEO
OPEN TO CALIFORNIA-BORN ARTISTS IN ABOVE AREAS. PRINTMAKING & PHOTOGRAPHY AWARDS IN ODD-NUMBERED YEARS AND FILM & VIDEO AWARDS IN EVEN NUMBERED YEARS. USA CITIZEN.
AWARDS WILL BE PRESENTED AT A PUBLIC RECEPTION AND SCREENING OF WINNERS' WORKS. WRITE FOR COMPLETE INFORMATION.

378

SCHOLASTIC INC (SCHOLASTIC ART AWARDS)
730 BROADWAY
NEW YORK NY 10003
212/505-3566
AMOUNT: TUITION
DEADLINE(S): APPLY SEP 15 - JAN 1
FIELD(S): ART; PHOTOGRAPHY
OPEN TO STUDENTS IN GRADES 7-12. FINALISTS IN REGIONAL COMPETITIONS GO ON TO THE NATIONAL LEVEL.
MORE THAN 100 UNDERGRADUATE SCHOLARSHIPS ARE OFFERED PER YEAR. SEND REQUESTS FOR INFORMATION BETWEEN SEP 15 AND JAN 1.

379

SCRIPPS HOWARD FOUNDATION (CHARLES M. SCHULZ AWARD)
312 WALNUT ST; 28TH FLOOR
CINCINNATI OH 45201
513/977-3035
AMOUNT: $2000
DEADLINE(S): JAN 14

FIELD(S): COLLEGE CARTOONIST

AWARD TO HONOR OUTSTANDING COLLEGE CARTOONISTS & TO ENCOURAGE THEM TO LAUNCH POST-GRADUATE PROFESSIONAL CAREERS. OPEN TO ANY STUDENT CARTOONIST AT A COLLEGE NEWSPAPER OR MAGAZINE IN THE USA & ITS TERRITORIES.

APPLICATIONS AVAILABLE DURING THE FALL MONTHS. WRITE FOR COMPLETE INFORMATION.

380

SCRIPPS HOWARD FOUNDATION (ROBERT P SCRIPPS GRAPHIC ARTS GRANTS)

312 WALNUT ST; 28TH FLOOR
CINCINNATI OH 45201
513/977-3035

AMOUNT: UP TO $3000

DEADLINE(S): DEC 20 FOR AN APPLICATION; FEB 25 FOR MAILING IN APPLICATION

FIELD(S): GRAPHIC ARTS (NEWSPAPER INDUSTRY)

PREFERENCE TO UNDERGRAD JUNIORS; SENIORS OR GRAD STUDENTS MAJORING IN GRAPHIC ARTS AS APPLIED TO NEWSPAPERS WHO HAVE POTENTIAL (IN COLLEGE AUTHORITIES' OPINION) OF BECOMING NEWSPAPER PRODUCTION ADMINISTRATORS. US CITIZEN OR LEGAL RESIDENT.

RENEWABLE WITH REAPPLICATION. QUALIFIED STUDENTS SHOULD SUBMIT A LETTER (BEFORE DEC 20) REQUESTING AN APPLICATION AND STATING COLLEGE MAJOR AND CAREER GOAL.

381

SMITHSONIAN INSTITUTION (COOPER-HEWITT MUSEUM OF DESIGN SUMMER INTERNSHIPS)

COOPER-HEWITT MUSEUM; 2 EAST 91ST ST
NEW YORK NY 10128
212/860-6868; FAX 212/860-6909

AMOUNT: VARIES

DEADLINE(S): MAR 31

FIELD(S): ART; DESIGN; ARCHITECTURE; MUSEUM STUDIES

10-WEEK SUMMER INTERNSHIPS AT THE COOPER-HEWITT MUSEUM OPEN TO UNDERGRADUATE AND GRADUATE STUDENTS.

WRITE FOR COMPLETE INFORMATION.

382

SMITHSONIAN INSTITUTION (MINORITY UNDERGRADUATE & GRADUATE INTERNSHIP)

OFFICE OF FELLOWSHIPS & GRANTS; 955 L'ENFANT PLAZA; SUITE 7300
WASHINGTON DC 20560
202/287-3271

AMOUNT: $250 - $300 PER WEEK STIPEND + TRAVEL

DEADLINE(S): FEB 15; JUN 15; OCT 15

FIELD(S): DESIGN; ARCHITECTURE; ART; MUSEUM STUDIES

INTERNSHIPS OPEN TO MINORITY STUDENTS FOR RESEARCH & STUDY AT THE SMITHSONIAN OR THE COOPER-HEWITT MUSEUM OF DESIGN IN NEW YORK CITY. THE MUSEUM'S COLLECTION SPANS 3000 YEARS OF DESIGN FROM ANCIENT POTTERY TO MODERN FASHION & ADVERTISING.

UNDERGRADUATES RECEIVE $250 PER WEEK STIPEND & GRADUATE STUDENTS RECEIVE $300 PER WEEK STIPEND. WRITE FOR COMPLETE INFORMATION.

383

SMITHSONIAN INSTITUTION (PETER KRUEGER SUMMER INTERNSHIP PROGRAM)

COOPER-HEWETT MUSEUM; 2 EAST 91ST ST
NEW YORK NY 10128
212/860-6868; FAX 212/860-6909

AMOUNT: $2500

DEADLINE(S): MAR 31

FIELD(S): ART HISTORY; ARCHITECTURAL HISTORY; DESIGN

TEN WEEK SUMMER INTERNSHIPS OPEN TO GRADUATE AND UNDERGRADUATE STUDENTS CONSIDERING A CAREER IN THE MUSEUM PROFESSION. INTERNS WILL ASSIST ON SPECIAL RESEARCH OR EXHIBITION PROJECTS AND PARTICIPATE IN DAILY MUSEUM ACTIVITIES.

INTERNSHIP COMMENCES IN JUNE AND ENDS IN AUGUST. HOUSING IS NOT PROVIDED. WRITE FOR COMPLETE INFORMATION.

384

SOCIETY FOR IMAGING SCIENCE AND TECHNOLOGY (RAYMOND DAVIS SCHOLARSHIP)

7003 KILWORTH LANE
SPRINGFIELD VA 22151

703/642-9090; FAX 703/642-9094
AMOUNT: $1000
DEADLINE(S): DEC 15
FIELD(S): PHOTOGRAPHIC SCIENCE OR ENGINEERING
SCHOLARSHIPS FOR UNDERGRADUATE JUNIORS OR SENIORS OR GRADUATE STUDENTS FOR FULL TIME CONTINUING STUDIES IN THE THEORY OR PRACTICE OF PHOTOGRAPHIC SCIENCE INCLUDING ANY KIND OF IMAGE FORMATION INITIATED BY RADIANT ENERGY.
WRITE FOR COMPLETE INFORMATION.

385

SOCIETY OF ILLUSTRATORS (ANNUAL STUDENT SCHOLARSHIP SHOW)
128 EAST 63RD STREET
NEW YORK NY 10021
WRITTEN INQUIRIES
AMOUNT: $300 - $2500
DEADLINE(S): NONE
FIELD(S): ILLUSTRATION; GRAPHIC ARTS
THE ANNUAL STUDENT SCHOLARSHIP SHOW IS A JUDGED ART COMPETITION & IS OPEN TO STUDENTS WHO ARE ENROLLED IN UNIVERSITY LEVEL ILLUSTRATION & GRAPHIC ARTS PROGRAMS.
30 AWARDS PER YEAR. HAVE YOUR INSTRUCTOR CONTACT ADDRESS ABOVE FOR COMPLETE INFORMATION.

386

SOLOMON R. GUGGENHEIM MUSEUM (FELLOWSHIP AND VOLUNTARY INTERNSHIP PROGRAMS)
1071 FIFTH AVE
NEW YORK NY 10128
212/423-3600
AMOUNT: STIPENDS VARY (SOME POSITIONS NON-PAID)
DEADLINE(S): AUG 15; DEC 15; MAR 15
FIELD(S): ARTS ADMINISTRATION; ART HISTORY
TEN WEEK INTERNSHIP OPEN TO STUDENTS IN THE ABOVE FIELDS WHO HAVE COMPLETED AT LEAST TWO YEARS OF UNDERGRADUATE STUDY; FELLOWSHIPS OPEN TO GRADUATE STUDENTS HOLDING BA OR MA IN ART HISTORY.
DIRECT INQUIRIES TO ADDRESS ABOVE; ATTN INTERNSHIP PROGRAM.

387

TENNESSEE ARTS COMMISSION (INDIVIDUAL ARTISTS' FELLOWSHIPS)
320 SIXTH AVE NORTH; #100
NASHVILLE TN 37243
615/741-1701
AMOUNT: $2500 - $5000
DEADLINE(S): JAN 11
FIELD(S): VISUAL ARTS; PERFORMING ARTS; CREATIVE ARTS
GRANTS OPEN TO ARTISTS WHO ARE RESIDENTS OF THE STATE OF TENNESSEE. DURATION OF AWARD IS ONE YEAR. APPLICANTS MUST BE PROFESSIONAL ARTISTS. FULL TIME STUDENTS ARE NOT ELIGIBLE.
WRITE FOR COMPLETE INFORMATION.

388

UNIVERSITY FILM AND VIDEO ASSN (GRANTS)
J. STEPHEN HANK; DEPT OF DRAMA & COMMUNICATIONS; UNIVERSITY OF NEW ORLEANS; LAKEFRONT
NEW ORLEANS LA 70148
WRITTEN INQUIRY ONLY
AMOUNT: VARIES
DEADLINE(S): JAN 1
FIELD(S): FILM & VIDEO
OPEN TO UNDERGRADUATE & GRADUATE STUDENTS WHO ARE SPONSORED BY A FACULTY MEMBER WHO IS ACTIVE IN THE FILM AND VIDEO ASSOCIATION. GRANTS FOR STUDENT FILM OR VIDEO PRODUCTIONS OR RESEARCH PROJECTS.
RESEARCH PROJECTS MAY BE IN HISTORICAL; CRITICAL; THEORETICAL OR EXPERIMENTAL STUDIES OF FILM OR VIDEO. WRITE FOR COMPLETE INFORMATION.

389

UNIVERSITY OF ILLINOIS AT URBANA-CHAMPAIGN (LYDIA E. PARKER BATES SCHOLARSHIP)
STUDENT SERVICES BLDG; 610 EAST JOHN STREET
CHAMPAIGN IL 61820
217/333-0100
AMOUNT: VARIES
DEADLINE(S): MAR 15
FIELD(S): ART; ARCHITECTURE; LANDSCAPE ARCHITECTURE; URBAN PLANNING; DANCE; THEATER

OPEN TO UNDERGRADUATE STUDENTS IN THE COLLEGE OF FINE & APPLIED ARTS WHO ARE ATTENDING THE UNIVERSITY OF ILLINOIS AT URBANA-CHAMPAIGN. MUST DEMONSTRATE FINANCIAL NEED AND HAVE 3.85 GPA (5.0 = A SCALE).

175 AWARDS PER YEAR. RECIPIENTS MUST CARRY AT LEAST 14 CREDIT HOURS PER SEMESTER. CONTACT OFFICE OF STUDENT FINANCIAL AID.

390

VIRGINIA MUSEUM OF FINE ARTS (UNDERGRAD/GRADUATE & PROFESSIONAL FELLOWSHIPS)
2800 GROVE AVE
RICHMOND VA 23221
804/367-0824
AMOUNT: UP TO $4000 UNDERGRADS; $5000 GRADS; $8000 PROFESSIONALS
DEADLINE(S): MAR 1
FIELD(S): ART; FINE ARTS; ART HISTORY (GRADUATE ONLY); ARCHITECTURE; PHOTOGRAPHY; FILM; VIDEO

VIRGINIA RESIDENT FOR 1 YEAR PRIOR TO DEADLINE. US CITIZEN OR LEGAL RESIDENT. PROFESSIONAL ARTIST FELLOWSHIPS ALSO AVAILABLE. NEED IS CONSIDERED.

ART; FINE ARTS & ART HISTORY FOR GRADUATE STUDENTS ONLY. 9-12 AWARDS PER YEAR. WRITE FOR COMPLETE INFORMATION.

391

WAVERLY COMMUNITY HOUSE INC (F. LAMMONT BELIN ARTS SCHOLARSHIPS)
SCHOLARSHIPS SELECTION COMMITTEE
WAVERLY PA 18471
717/586-8191
AMOUNT: $9000
DEADLINE(S): DEC 15
FIELD(S): PAINTING; SCULPTURE; MUSIC; DRAMA; DANCE; LITERATURE; ARCHITECTURE; PHOTOGRAPHY

APPLICANTS MUST RESIDE IN THE ABINGTONS OR POCONO REGIONS OF NORTHEASTERN PENNSYLVANIA. THEY MUST FURNISH PROOF OF EXCEPTIONAL ABILITY IN THEIR CHOSEN FIELD BUT NEED NO FORMAL TRAINING IN ANY ACADEMIC OR PROFESSIONAL PROGRAM.

USA CITIZENSHIP REQUIRED. FINALISTS MUST APPEAR IN PERSON BEFORE THE SELECTION COMMITTEE. WRITE FOR COMPLETE INFORMATION.

392

WELLESLEY COLLEGE (HARRIET A SHAW FELLOWSHIPS)
OFFICE OF FINANCIAL AID; BOX GR; SECRETARY GRADUATE FELLOWSHIPS
WELLESLEY MA 02181
617-235-0320
AMOUNT: UP TO $3000 STIPEND PER YEAR
DEADLINE(S): DEC 15
FIELD(S): MUSIC; ART HISTORY

OPEN TO WOMEN WHO ARE BA DEGREE GRADUATES OF WELLESLEY COLLEGE. AWARD IS FOR GRADUATE STUDY OR RESEARCH IN THE ABOVE AREAS AT AN ACCREDITED INSTITUTION OF YOUR CHOICE IN THE USA OR ABROAD.

APPLICATIONS AVAILABLE UP TO NOV 24 FROM ADDRESS ABOVE.

ENGLISH LANG / LIT

393

ACADEMY OF MOTION PICTURE ARTS AND SCIENCES (DON & GEE NICHOLL FELLOWSHIPS IN SCREENWRITING)
8949 WILSHIRE BLVD
BEVERLY HILLS CA 90211
310/247-3059
AMOUNT: $20000
DEADLINE(S): JUN 1
FIELD(S): SCREENWRITING

FELLOWSHIPS OPEN TO ANY ENGLISH LANGUAGE WRITER WHO IS PREPARING FOR A CAREER AS A SCREENWRITER BUT HAS NOT AS YET BEEN PAID TO WRITE A SCREENPLAY OR TELEPLAY. AWARD MAY NOT BE USED TO CONTINUE OR COMPLETE FORMAL EDUCATION.

5 AWARDS PER YEAR. SEND SELF-ADDRESSED STAMPED ENVELOPE FOR COMPLETE INFORMATION.

394

ALASKA STATE COUNCIL ON THE ARTS (INDIVIDUAL ARTIST FELLOWSHIPS & GRANTS)
411 W 4TH AVE; SUITE 1E
ANCHORAGE AK 99501
907/279-1558
AMOUNT: $5000
DEADLINE(S): OCT 1

FIELD(S): VISUAL ARTS; CRAFTS; PHOTOGRAPHY - ODD NUMBERED YEARS. MUSIC COMPOSITION; CHOREOGRAPHY; MEDIA ARTS; LITERATURE - EVEN NUMBERED YEARS.

OPEN TO ALASKA RESIDENTS WHO ARE ENGAGED IN THE CREATION OF NEW WORKS. FULL TIME STUDENTS ARE NOT ELIGIBLE.

WRITE FOR COMPLETE INFORMATION.

395

ALPHA MU GAMMA NATIONAL OFFICE (GODDARD; INDOVINA; AND KRAKOWSKI SCHOLARSHIPS)

C/0 LOS ANGELES CITY COLLEGE; 855 N VERMONT AVE
LOS ANGELES CA 90029
213/953-4434

AMOUNT: $500

DEADLINE(S): JAN 4

FIELD(S): LANGUAGE & LITERATURE; LINGUISTICS

UNDERGRADUATE SCHOLARSHIPS OPEN TO STUDENT MEMBERS IN COLLEGES HAVING ALPHA MU GAMMA CHAPTERS. STUDENT MEMBERS MUST HAVE COMPLETED AT LEAST ONE AND ONE-HALF SEMESTERS OF COLLEGE WORK AND HAVE 'A' GRADES IN A FOREIGN LANGUAGE.

RENEWABLE. WRITE FOR COMPLETE INFORMATION.

396

AMERICAN COLLEGE THEATRE FESTIVAL (COLUMBIA PICTURES TELEVISION AWARD FOR COMEDY PLAYWRITING)

JFK CENTER FOR THE PERFORMING ARTS
WASHINGTON DC 20566
202-416-8850

AMOUNT: $10940

DEADLINE(S): DEC 20

FIELD(S): COMEDY PLAYWRITING

UNDERGRADUATE OR GRADUATE STUDENT. AWARD IS PRESENTED TO WRITER OF BEST COMEDY PLAY ENTERED IN STUDENT PLAYWRITING AWARDS PROGRAM. IT CONSISTS OF AN ASSIGNMENT TO WRITE A TELEPLAY FOR ONE OF THE EMBASSY COMMUNICATIONS TELEVISION SERIES.

WRITE FOR COMPLETE INFORMATION. US CITIZEN. SCHOOL MUST BE PARTICIPATING IN ACTF.

397

AMERICAN COLLEGE THEATRE FESTIVAL (MICHAEL KANIN PLAYWRITING AWARDS PROGRAM/IRENE RYAN ACTING SCHOLARSHIPS)

JFK CENTER FOR THE PERFORMING ARTS
WASHINGTON DC 20566
202-416-8850

AMOUNT: $500 - $10940

DEADLINE(S): DEC 10

FIELD(S): PLAYWRITING COMPETITION (DRAMA/COMEDY/MUSICAL); THEATRE; DRAMA

UNDERGRAD OR GRADUATE STUDENT. 10 PLAYWRITING AWARD PROGRAMS ARRANGED BY MICHAEL KANIN. MAJOR AWARDS GO TO STUDENT WRITERS WHOSE PLAYS ARE PRODUCED AS PART OF FESTIVAL. MANY OTHER AWARDS/FELLOWSHIPS/PROFESSIONAL ASSIGNMENTS INCLUDED.

ACTORS IN THE REGIONAL & NATIONAL PRODUCTIONS ARE ELIGIBLE FOR THE IRENE RYAN ACTING SCHOLARSHIPS WHICH RANGE FROM $250-2500. WRITE FOR COMPLETE DETAILS ON BOTH PROGRAMS.

398

AMERICAN FOUNDATION FOR THE BLIND (R.L. GILLETTE SCHOLARSHIP FUND)

15 WEST 16TH ST
NEW YORK NY 10011
212/620-2000; TDD 212/620-2158

AMOUNT: $1000

DEADLINE(S): APR 1

FIELD(S): CREATIVE WRITING; LITERATURE; MUSIC PERFORMANCE

OPEN TO LEGALLY BLIND WOMEN WHO ARE ENROLLED IN A 4-YEAR BACHELOR'S DEGREE PROGRAM IN THE ABOVE AREAS AT A RECOGNIZED COLLEGE OR UNIVERSITY. CREATIVE WRITING SAMPLE OR MUSIC PERFORMANCE TAPE WILL BE REQUIRED. USA CITIZEN.

WRITE FOR COMPLETE INFORMATION.

399

AMERICAN LEGION (NATIONAL HIGH SCHOOL ORATORICAL CONTEST)

PO BOX 1055
INDIANAPOLIS IN 46206
317/635-8411

AMOUNT: $12000 - $18000 (NATIONAL); $3000 (SECTIONAL); $1000 (REGIONAL)
DEADLINE(S): SEP - OCT (BY STATE)
FIELD(S): ORATORY
COMPETITION OPEN TO HIGH SCHOOL STUDENTS. UNDERGRADUATE SCHOLARSHIPS GO TO THE TOP FOUR WINNING CONTESTANTS OF THE COMPETITION. PARTICIPANTS AT THE REGIONAL LEVEL ALL RECEIVE $1000 SCHOLARSHIPS. USA CITIZEN.
WRITE TO THE AMERICAN LEGION HEADQUARTERS IN YOUR STATE OF RESIDENCE FOR CONTEST PROCEDURES.

400

AMERICAN PHILOLOGICAL ASSOCIATION (LIONEL PEARSON FELLOWSHIP)
PROFESSOR F. CARTER PHILIPS; BOX 1646; STATION B; VANDERBILT UNIVERSITY
NASHVILLE TN 37235
WRITTEN INQUIRY
AMOUNT: LIVING STIPEND; ACADEMIC FEES; AIRFARE & TRAVEL EXPENSES
DEADLINE(S): SEP 27 FOR NOMINATIONS; OCT 31 FOR COMPLETED APPLICATIONS
FIELD(S): PHILOLOGY (GREEK; LATIN)
OPEN TO APPLICANTS IN THEIR FINAL YEAR OF UNDERGRAD STUDY AT USA/CANADIAN UNIVERSITIES. FOR ONE YEAR OF STUDY AT AN ENGLISH OR SCOTTISH UNIVERSITY BY GREEK; LATIN OR CLASSICS MAJORS.
CANDIDATES MUST BE NOMINATED BY A FACULTY MEMBER AT THEIR UNDERGRAD INSTITUTION. WRITE FOR COMPLETE INFORMATION.

401

ARTS INTERNATIONAL; INSTITUTE OF INTERNATIONAL EDUCATION (CINTAS FELLOWSHIP PROGRAM)
809 UNITED NATIONS PLAZA
NEW YORK NY 10017
212/984-5370
AMOUNT: $10000
DEADLINE(S): MAR 1
FIELD(S): ARCHITECTURE; PAINTING; PHOTOGRAPHY; SCULPTURE; PRINTMAKING; MUSIC COMPOSITION; CREATIVE WRITING
FELLOWSHIPS OPEN TO ARTISTS WHO ARE OF CUBAN ANCESTRY OR CUBAN CITIZENS LIVING OUTSIDE OF CUBA. THEY ARE INTENDED TO FOSTER & ENCOURAGE THE PROFESSIONAL DEVELOPMENT & RECOGNITION OF TALENTED CREATIVE ARTISTS IN THE ABOVE AREAS.
FELLOWSHIPS ARE NOT AWARDED FOR FURTHERANCE OF ACADEMIC STUDY. 5-10 AWARDS PER YEAR. WRITE FOR COMPLETE INFORMATION.

402

ASSOCIATION FOR INFORMATION AND IMAGE MANAGEMENT (JOHN P. EAGER SCHOLARSHIP PROGRAM)
1100 WAYNE AVE; #1100
SILVER SPRING MD 20910
301/587-8202
AMOUNT: $5000
DEADLINE(S): DEC 30
FIELD(S): LIBRARY SCIENCE
OPEN TO ANY STUDENT WITH 3.0 GRADE AVG OR HIGHER WHO IS ENROLLED IN AN ACCREDITED UNDERGRADUATE OR GRADUATE PROGRAM OF STUDY IN INFORMATION AND IMAGE MANAGEMENT.
WRITE FOR COMPLETE INFORMATION.

403

BEVERLY HILLS THEATRE GUILD (JULIE HARRIS PLAYWRIGHT AWARD COMPETITION)
2815 N BEACHWOOD DR
LOS ANGELES CA 90068
213/465-2703
AMOUNT: $1000; $2000; $5000
DEADLINE(S): NOV 1 (ENTRIES ACCEPTED AUG 1 - NOV 1)
FIELD(S): PLAYWRITING COMPETITION
ANNUAL COMPETITION OF FULL-LENGTH (90 MINUTES) UNPRODUCED & UNPUBLISHED PLAYS WRITTEN FOR THE THEATRE. MUSICALS; 1-ACT PLAYS; ADAPTATIONS; TRANSLATIONS & PLAYS ENTERED IN OTHER COMPETITIONS NOT ELIGIBLE. OPEN TO ANY USA CITIZEN.
CO-AUTHORSHIPS ARE PERMISSIBLE. $5000 FOR 1ST; $2000 FOR 2ND & $1000 FOR 3RD. SEND SELF-ADDRESSED STAMPED ENVELOPE FOR COMPLETE INFORMATION.

404

BUSH FOUNDATION (BUSH ARTIST FELLOWSHIPS)
E900 FIRST NATIONAL BANK BLDG; 322 MINNESOTA ST
ST PAUL MN 55101
612/227-5222

AMOUNT: UP TO $26000 STIPEND + $7000 EXPENSES
DEADLINE(S): LATE OCT; EARLY NOV
FIELD(S): LITERATURE; MUSIC COMPOSITION; CHOREOGRAPHY; VISUAL ARTS; SCRIPTWORKS

OPEN TO WRITERS; VISUAL ARTISTS; COMPOSERS & CHOREOGRAPHERS WHO ARE RESIDENTS OF MN; ND; SD OR WESTERN WI & AT LEAST 25 YRS OLD. AWARDS ARE TO HELP ARTISTS WORK FULL-TIME IN THEIR CHOSEN FIELD; NOT FOR ACADEMIC STUDY.

15 FELLOWSHIPS PER YEAR; 6-18 MONTHS IN DURATION. WRITE FOR COMPLETE INFORMATION.

405 ———

CALIFORNIA LIBRARY ASSOCIATION (REFERENCE SERVICE PRESS FELLOWSHIP)
717 K ST; SUITE 300
SACRAMENTO CA 95814
916/447-8541
AMOUNT: $2000
DEADLINE(S): MAY 31
FIELD(S): LIBRARY SCIENCE (MASTER'S)

OPEN TO COLLEGE SENIORS OR GRADUATES WHO HAVE BEEN ACCEPTED IN AN ACCREDITED MLS PROGRAM. FOR RESIDENTS OF CA ATTENDING LIBRARY SCHOOL IN ANY STATE OR RESIDENT OF ANY STATE ATTENDING A CA LIBRARY SCHOOL.

STUDENTS PURSUING AN MLS ON A PART TIME OR FULL TIME BASIS ARE EQUALLY ELIGIBLE. WRITE FOR COMPLETE INFORMATION.

406 ———

CATHOLIC LIBRARY ASSOCIATION (GRANT)
461 WEST LANCASTER AVENUE
HAVERFORD PA 19041
215/649-5251
AMOUNT: $1500
DEADLINE(S): FEB 1
FIELD(S): LIBRARY SCIENCE

OPEN TO MEMBERS OF NATIONAL CATHOLIC LIBRARY ASSOCIATION. PURPOSE OF AWARD IS TO ADD EXPERTISE IN THE FIELD OF CHILDREN'S OR SCHOOL LIBRARIANSHIP.

WRITE FOR COMPLETE INFORMATION.

407 ———

CONNECTICUT LIBRARY ASSOCIATION (PROGRAM FOR EDUCATION GRANTS)
638 PROSPECT AVE
HARTFORD CT 06105
203/232-4825
AMOUNT: VARIES
DEADLINE(S): NONE
FIELD(S): LIBRARIANSHIP

CONTINUING EDUCATION GRANTS FOR LIBRARY EMPLOYEES; VOLUNTEER TRUSTEES OR FRIENDS OF THE LIBRARY IN THE STATE OF CONNECTICUT. MUST JOIN CLA TO BE ELIGIBLE. TUITION COST IS NOT COVERED.

4-5 GRANTS PER YEAR. WRITE FOR COMPLETE INFORMATION.

408 ———

CREOLE-AMERICAN GENEALOGICAL SOCIETY INC. (CREOLE SCHOLARSHIPS)
PO BOX 2666; CHURCH STREET STATION
NEW YORK NY 10008
WRITTEN INQUIRY ONLY
AMOUNT: $1500
DEADLINE(S): APPLY BETWEEN JAN 1 AND APR 30
FIELD(S): GENEALOGY OR LANGUAGE OR CREOLE CULTURE

AWARDS IN THE ABOVE AREAS OPEN TO INDIVIDUALS OF MIXED RACIAL ANCESTRY WHO SUBMIT A FOUR-GENERATION GENEAOLOGICAL CHART ATTESTING TO CREOLE ANCESTRY AND/OR INTERRACIAL PARENTAGE. FOR UNDERGRADUATE OR GRADUATE STUDY/RESEARCH.

FOR SCHOLARSHIP/AWARD INFORMATION SEND $2 MONEY ORDER AND SELF ADDRESSED STAMPED ENVELOPE TO ADDRESS ABOVE. CASH AND PERSONAL CHECKS ARE NOT ACCEPTED. LETTERS WITHOUT SASE AND HANDLING CHARGE WILL NOT BE ANSWERED.

409 ———

DISTRICT OF COLUMBIA COMMISSION ON THE ARTS & HUMANITIES (GRANTS)
410 EIGHTH ST NW; 5TH FLOOR
WASHINGTON DC 20004
202/724-5613; TDD 202/727-318; FAX 202/727-4135
AMOUNT: $5000
DEADLINE(S): FEB 15
FIELD(S): ARTS; PERFORMING ARTS; LITERATURE

AMOUNT: $2500
DEADLINE(S): MAR 31
FIELD(S): HUMANITIES (ART; ENGLISH; FOREIGN LANGUAGES; HISTORY; PHILOSOPHY; RELIGION)
OPEN TO LEGALLY BLIND STUDENTS PURSUING OR PLANNING TO PURSUE A FULL TIME POST SECONDARY COURSE OF STUDY IN THE TRADITIONAL HUMANITIES. AWARDS BASED ON ACADEMIC EXCELLENCE; COMMUNITY SERVICE; FINANCIAL NEED.
WRITE FOR COMPLETE INFORMATION.

420 ———

NATIONAL FOUNDATION FOR ADVANCEMENT IN THE ARTS (ARTS RECOGNITION AND TALENT SEARCH)
300 NE SECOND AVE
MIAMI FL 33132
305/237-3416
AMOUNT: $100 - $3000
DEADLINE(S): OCT 1
FIELD(S): CREATIVE ARTS; PERFORMING ARTS
OPEN TO HIGH SCHOOL SENIORS WITH TALENT IN SUCH ARTS AS THE DANCE; MUSIC; MUSIC/JAZZ; THEATER; VISUAL ARTS; FILM; VIDEO; WRITING. AWARDS CAN BE USED ANYWHERE FOR ANY PURPOSE. FOR US CITIZENS OR RESIDENTS.
UP TO 100 AWARDS PER YEAR. WRITE FOR COMPLETE INFORMATION.

421 ———

NATIONAL FOUNDATION OF THE BLIND (HUMANITIES SCHOLARSHIP)
815 4TH AVE; #200
GRINNELL IA 50112
515-236-3366
AMOUNT: $2500
DEADLINE(S): MAR 31
FIELD(S): HUMANITIES (ART; ENGLISH; FOREIGN LANGUAGES; HISTORY; PHILOSOPHY; RELIGION)
OPEN TO LEGALLY BLIND STUDENTS PURSUING OR PLANNING TO PURSUE A POST-SECONDARY EDUCATION IN THE ABOVE AREAS. SCHOLARSHIPS ARE AWARDED ON BASIS OF ACADEMIC EXCELLENCE; COMMUNITY SERVICE AND FINANCIAL NEED.
WRITE FOR COMPLETE INFORMATION.

422 ———

NATIONAL JUNIOR CLASSICAL LEAGUE (SCHOLARSHIPS)
MIAMI UNIVERSITY
OXFORD OH 45056
513/529-7741
AMOUNT: $500 - $1000
DEADLINE(S): MAY 1
FIELD(S): CLASSICS
OPEN TO NJCL MEMBERS WHO ARE HIGH SCHOOL SENIORS AND PLAN TO STUDY CLASSICS (THOUGH CLASSICS MAJOR IS NOT REQUIRED). PREFERENCE WILL BE GIVEN TO A STUDENT WHO PLANS TO PURSUE A TEACHING CAREER IN THE CLASSICS (ALSO NOT A REQUIREMENT).
MUST BE A MEMBER OF A NATIONAL JUNIOR CLASSICAL LEAGUE CLUB. WRITE FOR COMPLETE INFORMATION.

423 ———

NATIONAL PARENT-TEACHER ASSOCIATION (REFLECTIONS SCHOLARSHIP PROGRAM)
700 NORTH RUSH ST
CHICAGO IL 60611
312/787-0977
AMOUNT: $750
DEADLINE(S): NOV 30 TO REQUEST PACKET; JAN 29 FOR COMPLETED APPLICATIONS
FIELD(S): VISUAL ARTS; LITERATURE; MUSIC; PHOTOGRAPHY
OPEN TO HIGH SCHOOL SENIORS WHO ATTEND A SCHOOL WITH A PTA OR PTSA AFFILIATED WITH THE NATIONAL PTA AND WHO ENTER THE REFLECTIONS PROGRAM. FOR UNDERGRADUATE STUDY IN ANY OF THE ABOVE FIELDS.
WRITE FOR COMPLETE INFORMATION.

424 ———

NATIONAL SPEAKERS ASSOCIATION (NSA SCHOLARSHIP)
1500 S PRIEST DR
TEMPE AZ 85281
602/968-2552; FAX 602/968-0911
AMOUNT: $2000
DEADLINE(S): JUN 1
FIELD(S): ORAL COMMUNICATIONS
OPEN TO COLLEGE JUNIORS; SENIORS OR GRADUATE STUDENTS WHO ARE MAJORING OR MINORING IN SPEECH OR A DIRECTLY RELATED FIELD. MUST BE FULL TIME

STUDENT IN AN ACCREDITED COLLEGE OR UNIVERSITY. NEED AT LEAST 3.0 GPA.

FOUR AWARDS PER YEAR TO WELL ROUNDED STUDENTS CAPABLE OF LEADERSHIP AND HAVING POTENTIAL TO MAKE AN IMPACT BY USING ORAL COMMUNICATIONS.

425

NATIONAL URBAN LEAGUE INC (ANNUAL NUL/GRANDMET ESSAY CONTEST)

500 EAST 62ND ST; 10TH FLOOR; DIRECTOR OF EDUCATION
NEW YORK NY 10021
212-310-9000

AMOUNT: $1000
DEADLINE(S): MAR 28
FIELD(S): CREATIVE WRITING

ESSAY CONTEST OPEN TO RESIDENTS OF USA WHO ARE UNDERGRADUATE STUDENTS AT AN ACCREDITED INSTITUTION. ENTRIES MUST ADDRESS THE ANNUAL THEME IN 500-1000 WORDS.

15 AWARDS PER YEAR. WRITE FOR CURRENT THEME AND COMPLETE INFORMATION.

426

NELLIE MARTIN CARMAN SCHOLARSHIP TRUST (SCHOLARSHPS)

1121 244TH ST SW; #65
BOTHELL WA 98021
206/486-6575

AMOUNT: UP TO $1000
DEADLINE(S): MAR 15
FIELD(S): ALL FIELDS OF STUDY EXCEPT THOSE NOTED BELOW

OPEN TO SENIORS IN KING; PIERCE & SNOHOMISH COUNTY (WA) HIGH SCHOOLS WHO HAVE LIVED IN WASHINGTON AT LEAST 5 YRS. FOR UNDERGRADUATE STUDY IN WASHINGTON IN ALL FIELDS EXCEPT MUSIC; SCULPTURE; DRAWING; INTERIOR DESIGN & HOME ECONOMICS.

APPLICATIONS AVAILABLE ONLY THROUGH HIGH SCHOOLS. NOMINATION BY HS COUNSELOR IS REQUIRED. AWARDS ARE RENEWABLE. USA CITIZEN.

427

NEW YORK FOUNDATION FOR THE ARTS (ARTIST'S FELLOWSHIPS & SERVICES)

155 AVE OF THE AMERICAS; 14TH FLOOR
NEW YORK NY 10013
212/366-6900; FAX 212/366-1778

AMOUNT: $7000
DEADLINE(S): SEP 30
FIELD(S): VISUAL ARTS; LITERATURE; ARCHITECTURE; MUSIC AND MEDIA

FELLOWSHIPS & SERVICES OPEN TO ORIGINATING ARTISTS OVER 18 WHO HAVE BEEN NY STATE RESIDENTS FOR 2 YEARS PREVIOUS TO APPLICATION DATE & ARE NOT ENROLLED IN A DEGREE AWARDING COURSE OF STUDY. AWARDS ARE TO ASSIST IN CREATION OF ONGOING WORK.

APPLICATIONS AVAILABLE IN SPRING OF EACH YEAR. ABOUT 120 FELLOWSHIPS PER YEAR; MANY OTHER SERVICES ARE AVAILABLE. NOT FOR ACADEMIC STUDY. WRITE FOR COMPLETE INFORMATION.

428

OHIO ARTS COUNCIL (OAC SCHOLARSHIP PROGRAM)

727 E MAIN ST
COLUMBUS OH 43205
614/466-2613

AMOUNT: $1000
DEADLINE(S): APR 15 (SENIOR YEAR OF HIGH SCHOOL)
FIELD(S): DANCE; MUSIC; THEATRE ARTS; VISUAL ARTS; WRITING

OHIO RESIDENTS. OPEN TO HIGH SCHOOL SENIORS WHO WISH TO CONTINUE THEIR ARTS TRAINING AND EDUCATION AT AN ACCREDITED COLLEGE OR UNIVERSITY IN THE STATE OF OHIO.

WRITE FOR COMPLETE INFORMATION.

429

PARAMOUNT PICTURES - EDDIE MURPHY PRODUCTIONS (WRITING FELLOWSHIP)

5555 MELROSE AVE
HOLLYWOOD CA 90038
WRITTEN INQUIRY

AMOUNT: APPROX $25000
DEADLINE(S): FEB 1
FIELD(S): SCREENWRITING

POST-GRADUATE FILM & TV WRITING INTERNSHIPS AT PARAMOUNT PICTURES. OPEN TO RECENT BACHELOR'S DEGREE GRADUATES OF HAMPTON UNIVERSITY & HOWARD UNIVERSITY.

RENEWABLE. WRITE FOR COMPLETE INFORMATION.

430

PLAYWRIGHTS' CENTER (MCKNIGHT ADVANCEMENT GRANT)
2301 FRANKLIN AVENUE EAST
MINNEAPOLIS MN 55406
612/332-7481; FAX 612/332-6037
AMOUNT: $8500
DEADLINE(S): JAN 6
FIELD(S): PLAYWRITING

OPEN TO PLAYWRIGHTS WHOSE WORK DEMONSTRATES EXCEPTIONAL ARTISTIC MERIT & POTENTIAL & WHOSE PRIMARY RESIDENCE IS IN MINNESOTA. TWO WORKS BY APPLICANT MUST HAVE BEEN FULLY PRODUCED BY PROFESSIONAL THEATERS.

RECIPIENTS MUST DESIGNATE TWO MONTHS OF THE GRANT YEAR IN WHICH THEY WILL ACTIVELY PARTICIPATE IN CENTER PROGRAMS. APPLICATIONS AVAILABLE NOV 2. WRITE FOR COMPLETE INFORMATION.

431

PLAYWRIGHTS' CENTER (MIDWEST PLAYLABS)
2301 FRANKLIN AVENUE EAST
MINNEAPOLIS MN 55406
612/332-7481; FAX 612/332-6037
AMOUNT: HONORARIA; TRAVEL EXPENSES; ROOM AND BOARD
DEADLINE(S): DEC 1
FIELD(S): PLAYWRITING

TWO WEEK WORKSHOP OPEN TO USA CITIZENS WHO ARE AUTHORS OF UNPRODUCED; UNPUBLISHED FULL LENGTH PLAYS (NO ONE-ACTS). EACH PLAY RECEIVES A PUBLIC READING FOLLOWED BY AUDIENCE DISCUSSION OF THE WORK.

FOUR TO SIX PLAYWRIGHTS CHOSEN BY OPEN SCRIPT COMPETITION. CONFERENCE IS INTENDED TO ALLOW PLAYWRIGHTS TO TAKE RISKS FREE OF ARTISTIC RESTRAINT. APPLICATIONS AVAILABLE BY OCT 1. SEND SASE FOR COMPLETE INFORMATION.

432

POETRY SOCIETY OF AMERICA (CASH AWARDS)
15 GRAMERCY PARK
NEW YORK NY 10003
212-254-9628
AMOUNT: $100
DEADLINE(S): DEC 31
FIELD(S): POETRY

THE POETRY SOCIETY'S EXTENSIVE ANNUAL AWARDS COMPETITION IS AIMED AT ADVANCING EXCELLENCE IN POETRY & ENCOURAGING SKILL IN TRADITIONAL FORMS AS WELL AS EXPERIMENTATION IN CONTEMPORARY FORMS. THESE ARE CASH AWARDS NOT SCHOLARSHIPS.

SEND STAMPED SELF-ADDRESSED ENVELOPE FOR CONTEST RULES AND BROCHURE.

433

POETRY SOCIETY OF AMERICA (CONTESTS OPEN TO PSA MEMBERS)
15 GRAMERCY PARK
NEW YORK NY 10003
WRITTEN INQUIRY
AMOUNT: VARIES WITH AWARD
DEADLINE(S): OCT 1 - DEC 31
FIELD(S): POETRY

VARIOUS CONTESTS OPEN TO PSA MEMBERS. ONLY 1 SUBMISSION MAY BE SENT FOR EACH CONTEST. ALL SUBMISSIONS MUST BE UNPUBLISHED ON DATE OF ENTRY & NOT SCHEDULED FOR PUBLICATION BY THE DATE OF THE PSA AWARDS CEREMONY HELD IN THE SPRING.

SEND SELF-ADDRESSED STAMPED ENVELOPE FOR CONTEST RULES BROCHURE.

434

RIPON COLLEGE (MUSIC & DEBATE-FORENSICS SCHOLARSHIPS)
PO BOX 248; 300 SEWARD ST; ADMISSIONS OFFICE
RIPON WI 54971
414/748-8102
AMOUNT: $1500
DEADLINE(S): MAR 1
FIELD(S): MUSIC; DEBATE-FORENSICS

SCHOLARSHIPS RECOGNIZE & ENCOURAGE ACADEMIC POTENTIAL & ACCOMPLISHMENT IN ABOVE FIELDS. RENEWABLE UP TO 3 YRS PROVIDED RECIPIENT MAINTAINS 2.7 GPA FIRST YEAR AND 3.0 IN THE FOLLOWING YEARS.

20 AWARDS PER YEAR. MUST APPLY AND BE ACCEPTED FOR ADMISSION TO RIPON COLLEGE. WRITE FOR COMPLETE INFORMATION.

435

ROTARY FOUNDATION OF ROTARY INTERNATIONAL (CULTURAL AMBASSADORIAL SCHOLARSHIPS)
1 ROTARY CENTER; 1560 SHERMAN AV
EVANSTON IL 60201
313/866-3000
AMOUNT: TUITION; FEES; LIVING EXPENSES; TRAVEL
DEADLINE(S): CONTACT LOCAL ROTARY CLUB
FIELD(S): LANGUAGES (ENGLISH; FRENCH; GERMAN; ITALIAN; JAPANESE; POLISH; PORTUGUESE; RUSSIAN; SPANISH; SWAHILI)
SCHOLARSHIPS OF 3 TO 6 MONTHS FOR STUDY ABROAD OF LANGUAGES IN WHICH APPLICANT MAY BE SOMEWHAT COMPETENT. STUDY LOCATIONS ARE ASSIGNED BY ROTARY. AT LEAST 1 YEAR OF TRAINING IN PREFERRED LANGUAGE REQUIRED.
APPLICATION DEADLINES ARE SET BY LOCAL CLUBS AND MAY BE AS EARLY AS MARCH OR AS LATE AS JUL 15. CONTACT LOCAL ROTARY CLUB FOR COMPLETE INFORMATION.

436

SAN FRANCISCO FOUNDATION (JAMES D. PHELAN LITERARY AWARD)
685 MARKET ST; SUITE 910
SAN FRANCISCO CA 94105
415/543-0223 EXT 22
AMOUNT: $2000
DEADLINE(S): JAN 15
FIELD(S): LITERATURE
OPEN TO CALIFORNIA-BORN AUTHORS OF AN UNPUBLISHED WORK-IN-PROGRESS (FICTION; NON-FICTION OR POETRY) WHO ARE BETWEEN 20-35 YEARS OF AGE AND ARE USA CITIZENS.
WRITERS OF NON-FICTION ARE ALSO ELIGIBLE FOR THE $1000 JOSEPH HENRY JACKSON HONORABLE MENTION AWARD. WRITE FOR COMPLETE INFORMATION.

437

SAN FRANCISCO FOUNDATION (JOSEPH HENRY JACKSON LITERARY AWARD)
685 MARKET ST; SUITE 910
SAN FRANCISCO CA 94105
415/543-0223 EXT 22
AMOUNT: $2000
DEADLINE(S): JAN 15
FIELD(S): LITERATURE
OPEN TO N. CALIFORNIA OR NEVADA RESIDENTS (FOR 3 CONSECUTIVE YEARS IMMEDIATELY PRIOR TO CLOSING DATE OF THE COMPETITION) WHO ARE AUTHORS OF UNPUBLISHED WORK-IN-PROGRESS (FICTION; NON-FICTION OR POETRY) & BETWEEN 20-35 YEARS OF AGE.
WRITERS OF NON-FICTION ARE ALSO ELIGIBLE FOR THE $1000 JOSEPH HENRY JACKSON HONORABLE MENTION AWARD. WRITE FOR COMPLETE INFORMATION.

438

SCHOLASTIC INC (SCHOLASTIC WRITING AWARDS SCHOLARSHIPS)
730 BROADWAY
NEW YORK NY 10003
212/505-3566
AMOUNT: NOT SPECIFIED
DEADLINE(S): APPLY SEP 15 - JAN 1
FIELD(S): WRITING
WRITING COMPETITION OPEN TO STUDENTS IN GRADES 7-12.
WRITE BETWEEN SEP 15 AND JAN 1 FOR COMPETITION DETAILS.

439

SONS OF THE AMERICAN REVOLUTION (DOUGLASS G. HIGH HISTORICAL ORATION CONTEST)
1000 SOUTH 4TH ST
LOUISVILLE KY 40203
WRITTEN INQUIRY
AMOUNT: $1000-1ST PRIZE; $600-2ND PRIZE; $400-3RD PRIZE
DEADLINE(S): STATE DEADLINE FEB 1
FIELD(S): ORATORY
COMPETITION OPEN TO HIGH SCHOOL SOPHOMORES; JUNIORS & SENIORS WHO SUBMIT AN ORIGINAL 5 TO 6 MINUTE ORATION ON A PERSONALITY; EVENT OR DOCUMENT OF THE AMERICAN REVOLUTIONARY WAR & HOW IT RELATES TO AMERICA TODAY.
ORATION MUST BE DELIVERED FROM MEMORY WITHOUT PROPS OR CHARTS. WRITE FOR COMPLETE INFORMATION.

440

STANLEY DRAMA AWARD (PLAYWRITING AWARDS COMPETITION)
C/O WAGNER COLLEGE DRAMA DEPT; HOWARD AVE & CAMPUS RD
STATEN ISLAND NY 10301
718/390-3256
AMOUNT: $2000
DEADLINE(S): SEP 1
FIELD(S): PLAYWRITING COMPETITION
ANNUAL AWARD FOR THE BEST PLAY OR MUSICAL SUBMITTED TO THE COMPETITION. SCRIPT MUST NOT HAVE BEEN COMMERCIALLY PRODUCED OR PUBLISHED AND SHOULD BE RECOMMENDED BY A THEATRE PROFESSIONAL.
APPLICATION MUST BE SUBMITTED WITH SCRIPT. PREVIOUS WINNERS ARE NOT ELIGIBLE. WRITE FOR COMPLETE INFORMATION.

441

TENNESSEE ARTS COMMISSION (INDIVIDUAL ARTISTS' FELLOWSHIPS)
320 SIXTH AVE NORTH; #100
NASHVILLE TN 37243
615/741-1701
AMOUNT: $2500 - $5000
DEADLINE(S): JAN 11
FIELD(S): VISUAL ARTS; PERFORMING ARTS; CREATIVE ARTS
GRANTS OPEN TO ARTISTS WHO ARE RESIDENTS OF THE STATE OF TENNESSEE. DURATION OF AWARD IS ONE YEAR. APPLICANTS MUST BE PROFESSIONAL ARTISTS. FULL TIME STUDENTS ARE NOT ELIGIBLE.
WRITE FOR COMPLETE INFORMATION.

442

U.S. MARINE CORPS HISTORICAL CENTER (COLLEGE INTERNSHIPS)
BUILDING 58; WASHINGTON NAVY YARD
WASHINGTON DC 20374
202/433-3839
AMOUNT: APPROX $500 FOR DAILY EXPENSES
DEADLINE(S): NONE SPECIFIED
FIELD(S): U.S. MILITARY HISTORY; HISTORIAN; LIBRARY SCIENCE; MUSEUM STUDIES
OPEN TO UNDERGRADUATE STUDENTS AT A COLLEGE OR UNIVERSITY WHICH WILL GRANT ACADEMIC CREDIT FOR WORK EXPERIENCE AS INTERNS AT THE ADDRESS ABOVE OR AT THE MARINE CORPS AIRGROUND MUSEUM IN QUANTICO VIRGINIA.
ALL INTERNSHIPS ARE REGARDED AS BEGINNING PROFESSIONAL-LEVEL HISTORIAN; CURATOR; LIBRARIAN OR ARCHIVIST POSITIONS. WRITE FOR COMPLETE INFORMATION.

443

VETERANS OF FOREIGN WARS OF THE UNITED STATES (VOICE OF DEMOCRACY BROADCAST SCRIPTWRITING CONTEST)
VFW BLDG; 406 W 34TH ST
KANSAS CITY MO 64111
816/756-3390
AMOUNT: $1000 - $20000
DEADLINE(S): NOV 15
FIELD(S): CREATIVE WRITING
OPEN TO SOPHOMORES; JUNIORS & SENIORS IN PUBLIC; PRIVATE & PAROCHIAL HIGH SCHOOLS. CONTESTANTS WILL BE JUDGED ON THEIR INTERPRETATION OF AN ANNUAL THEME. THEY MAY NOT REFER TO THEIR RACE OR NATIONAL ORIGIN AS A MEANS OF IDENTIFICATION.
USA CITIZEN. 29 AWARDS PER YEAR. CONTACT LOCAL VFW POST OR HIGH SCHOOL FOR DETAILS.

444

WAVERLY COMMUNITY HOUSE INC (F. LAMMONT BELIN ARTS SCHOLARSHIPS)
SCHOLARSHIPS SELECTION COMMITTEE
WAVERLY PA 18471
717/586-8191
AMOUNT: $9000
DEADLINE(S): DEC 15
FIELD(S): PAINTING; SCULPTURE; MUSIC; DRAMA; DANCE; LITERATURE; ARCHITECTURE; PHOTOGRAPHY
APPLICANTS MUST RESIDE IN THE ABINGTONS OR POCONO REGIONS OF NORTHEASTERN PENNSYLVANIA. THEY MUST FURNISH PROOF OF EXCEPTIONAL ABILITY IN THEIR CHOSEN FIELD BUT NEED NO FORMAL TRAINING IN ANY ACADEMIC OR PROFESSIONAL PROGRAM.
USA CITIZENSHIP REQUIRED. FINALISTS MUST APPEAR IN PERSON BEFORE THE SELECTION COMMITTEE. WRITE FOR COMPLETE INFORMATION.

FOREIGN LANGUAGE

445

AMERICAN ASSOCIATION OF TEACHERS OF FRENCH (NATIONAL FRENCH CONTEST)
SIDNEY L. TEITELBAUM; BOX 1178
LONG BEACH NY 11561
516/897-8119; FAX 516/938-2273
AMOUNT: VARIES
DEADLINE(S): FEB 1
FIELD(S): FRENCH LANGUAGE; FRENCH STUDIES
NATIONAL FRENCH CONTEST IS AN EXAMINATION TAKEN THROUGHOUT THE COUNTRY. STUDENTS ARE RANKED REGIONALLY AND NATIONALLY AND ARE ELIGIBLE FOR BOTH REGIONAL AND NATIONAL AWARDS.
NOT A SCHOLARSHIP. WINNERS RECEIVE TRIPS; MEDALS AND BOOKS. WRITE FOR COMPLETE INFORMATION.

446

AMERICAN ASSOCIATION OF TEACHERS OF GERMAN (NATIONAL AATG/PAD AWARDS)
112 HADDONTOWNE CT; #104
CHERRY HILL NJ 08034
609/795-5553
AMOUNT: COSTS OF TRAVEL & STUDY
DEADLINE(S): DEC 1
FIELD(S): GERMAN LANGUAGE
THIS IS A TESTING PROGRAM FOR HIGH SCHOOL STUDENTS STUDYING GERMAN. STUDENTS SCORING IN THE 90TH PERCENTILE OR ABOVE ARE ELIGIBLE FOR AN ALL-EXPENSE-PAID STUDY-TRIP TO GERMANY. USA CITIZEN.
UP TO 70 TRAVEL-STUDY AWARDS PER YEAR. WRITE FOR COMPLETE INFORMATION.

447

AMERICAN ASSOCIATION OF TEACHERS OF ITALIAN (COLLEGE ESSAY IN ITALIAN)
CAL STATE UNIV CHICO; FOREIGN LANGUAGE DEPT
CHICO CA 95929
WRITTEN INQUIRIES
AMOUNT: $300 - $100
DEADLINE(S): JUN 15
FIELD(S): ITALIAN LANGUAGE; ITALIAN STUDIES
CONTEST OPEN TO UNDERGRADUATE STUDENTS AT ACCREDITED COLLEGES & UNIVERSITIES IN NORTH AMERICA. ESSAY IN ITALIAN LANGUAGE ON TOPIC PERTAINING TO LITERATURE OR CULTURE.
WRITE TO PROF EUGENIO FRONGIA AT ADDRESS ABOVE FOR COMPLETE INFORMATION.

448

AMERICAN COUNCIL OF LEARNED SOCIETIES (EAST EUROPEAN LANGUAGE TRAINING GRANTS)
OFFICE OF FELLOWSHIPS & GRANTS; 228 E 45TH ST
NEW YORK NY 10017
WRITTEN INQUIRY
AMOUNT: $2000 - $2500
DEADLINE(S): MAR 1
FIELD(S): EAST EUROPEAN LANGUAGES
GRANTS OF $2000 EACH OFFERED FOR THE FIRST OR SECOND YEAR STUDY OF ANY EAST EUROPEAN LANGUAGE (EXCEPT RUSSIAN) IN THE USA. $2500 GRANTS OFFERED FOR INTERMEDIATE OR ADVANCED TRAINING IN THESE LANGUAGES IN EASTERN EUROPE.
USA CITIZEN OR LEGAL RESIDENT. FOR ADVANCED UNDERGRAD; GRAD OR POSTGRAD STUDY. WRITE FOR COMPLETE INFORMATION.

449

AMERICAN INSTITUTE OF INDIAN STUDIES (AIIS 9-MONTH LANGUAGE PROGRAM)
C/O UNIV OF CHICAGO; FOSTER HALL; 1130 E 59TH ST
CHICAGO IL 60637
312/702-8638
AMOUNT: $3000 PLUS TRAVEL
DEADLINE(S): JAN 31
FIELD(S): LANGUAGES OF INDIA
FELLOWSHIPS HELD IN INDIA OPEN TO GRADUATE STUDENTS WHO HAVE A MINIMUM OF 2 YEARS OR 240 HOURS OF CLASSROOM INSTRUCTION IN A LANGUAGE OF INDIA. USA CITIZEN.
10 FELLOWSHIPS PER YEAR. WRITE FOR COMPLETE INFORMATION.

450

AUSTRIAN CULTURAL INSTITUTE (GRANTS FOR AMERICAN STUDENTS TO STUDY GERMAN IN AUSTRIA)
11 EAST 52ND ST
NEW YORK NY 10022
212/759-5165; FAX 212/319-9636
AMOUNT: AS 10.000 (APPROX $830) + TUITION ALLOWANCE
DEADLINE(S): JAN 31
FIELD(S): GERMAN LANGUAGE
OPEN TO USA CITIZENS BETWEEN 20 AND 35; WHO HAVE COMPLETED AT LEAST TWO YEARS OF COLLEGE AND HAVE STUDIED GERMAN FOR AT LEAST TWO YEARS. GRANTS ALSO MAY BE USED FOR RESEARCH AT AN AUSTRIAN LIBRARY OR RESEARCH INSTITUTION ARCHIVE.
THREE ONE-MONTH GRANTS AVAILABLE FOR USE BETWEEN JUL 1 AND SEP 30. WRITE FOR COMPLETE INFORMATION.

451

INSTITUTE FOR HUMANE STUDIES (CLAUDE R. LAMBE FELLOWSHIPS)
GEORGE MASON UNIVERSITY; 4400 UNIVERSITY DRIVE
FAIRFAX VA 22030
703/323-1055
AMOUNT: $17500
DEADLINE(S): JAN 15
FIELD(S): SOCIAL SCIENCES; LAW; HUMANITIES
OPEN TO GRADUATE STUDENTS AND UNDERGRADS WHO WILL HAVE JUNIOR OR SENIOR STANDING AT ACCREDITED COLLEGES OR UNIVERSITIES THE NEXT ACADEMIC YEAR. AWARD IS TO SUPPORT STUDENTS WITH A DEMONSTRATED INTEREST IN THE CLASSICAL LIBERAL TRADITION.
RECIPIENT WILL BE INTENT ON PURSUING AN INTELLECTUAL/SCHOLARLY CAREER IN ONE OF THE ABOVE AREAS. WRITE FOR COMPLETE INFORMATION.

452

LUSO-AMERICAN EDUCATION FOUNDATION (GENERAL SCHOLARSHIPS)
PO BOX 1768
OAKLAND CA 94604
510/452-4465
AMOUNT: VARIES
DEADLINE(S): MAR 1
FIELD(S): PORTUGUESE LANGUAGE/OR ALL FIELDS FOR PORTUGUESE DESCENT
CALIFORNIA RESIDENT UNDER 21. HS SENIOR WHO WILL ENROLL FULL TIME IN 4-YR PROGRAM & WILL TAKE PORTUGUESE LANGUAGE CLASSES/OR IS OF PORTUGUESE DESCENT/OR MEMBER OF ORGANIZATION WHOSE SCHOLARSHIPS ARE ADMIN. BY LUSO-AMER FOUND. 3.0 GPA.
WRITE FOR COMPLETE INFORMATION.

453

NATIONAL FEDERATION OF THE BLIND (ORACLE CORPORATION SCHOLARSHIP)
814 4TH AVE; #200
GRINNELL IA 50112
515/236-3366
AMOUNT: $2500
DEADLINE(S): MAR 31
FIELD(S): HUMANITIES (ART; ENGLISH; FOREIGN LANGUAGES; HISTORY; PHILOSOPHY; RELIGION)
OPEN TO LEGALLY BLIND STUDENTS PURSUING OR PLANNING TO PURSUE A FULL TIME POST SECONDARY COURSE OF STUDY IN THE TRADITIONAL HUMANITIES. AWARDS BASED ON ACADEMIC EXCELLENCE; COMMUNITY SERVICE; FINANCIAL NEED.
WRITE FOR COMPLETE INFORMATION.

454

NATIONAL FOUNDATION OF THE BLIND (HUMANITIES SCHOLARSHIP)
815 4TH AVE; #200
GRINNELL IA 50112
515-236-3366
AMOUNT: $2500
DEADLINE(S): MAR 31
FIELD(S): HUMANITIES (ART; ENGLISH; FOREIGN LANGUAGES; HISTORY; PHILOSOPHY; RELIGION)
OPEN TO LEGALLY BLIND STUDENTS PURSUING OR PLANNING TO PURSUE A POST-SECONDARY EDUCATION IN THE ABOVE AREAS. SCHOLARSHIPS ARE AWARDED ON BASIS OF ACADEMIC EXCELLENCE; COMMUNITY SERVICE AND FINANCIAL NEED.
WRITE FOR COMPLETE INFORMATION.

455

NATIONAL ITALIAN AMERICAN FOUNDATION (FRANCES M. RELLO SCHOLARSHIP)

DR. M. LOMBARDO; EDUCATION DIRECTOR; 666 11TH ST NW; SUITE 800
WASHINGTON DC 20001
202/638-2137

AMOUNT: $1000

DEADLINE(S): MAY 31

FIELD(S): ITALIAN LANGUAGE (TEACHER)

OPEN TO UNDERGRADUATE AND GRADUATE ITALIAN-AMERICAN WOMEN WITH AN ITALIAN LANGUAGE MAJOR WHO ARE PLANNING TO TEACH ITALIAN IN THE SECONDARY SCHOOLS. EVIDENCE OF FINANCIAL NEED AND ESSAY ON APPLICANT'S ITALIAN HERITAGE ARE REQUIRED.

WRITE FOR COMPLETE INFORMATION.

456

NELLIE MARTIN CARMAN SCHOLARSHIP TRUST (SCHOLARSHIPS)

1121 244TH ST SW; #65
BOTHELL WA 98021
206/486-6575

AMOUNT: UP TO $1000

DEADLINE(S): MAR 15

FIELD(S): ALL FIELDS OF STUDY EXCEPT THOSE NOTED BELOW

OPEN TO SENIORS IN KING; PIERCE & SNOHOMISH COUNTY (WA) HIGH SCHOOLS WHO HAVE LIVED IN WASHINGTON AT LEAST 5 YRS. FOR UNDERGRADUATE STUDY IN WASHINGTON IN ALL FIELDS EXCEPT MUSIC; SCULPTURE; DRAWING; INTERIOR DESIGN & HOME ECONOMICS.

APPLICATIONS AVAILABLE ONLY THROUGH HIGH SCHOOLS. NOMINATION BY HS COUNSELOR IS REQUIRED. AWARDS ARE RENEWABLE. USA CITIZEN.

457

NORWICH JUBILEE ESPERANTO FOUNDATION (TRAVEL GRANTS)

37 GRANVILLE COURT
OXFORD 0X3 0HS ENGLAND
0865-245509

AMOUNT: UP TO 1000 POUNDS STERLING

DEADLINE(S): NONE

FIELD(S): ESPERANTO-THE INTERNATIONAL LANGUAGE

TRAVEL GRANTS OPEN TO THOSE WHO SPEAK ESPERANTO AND WISH TO IMPROVE THEIR USE OF THE LANGUAGE THROUGH TRAVEL IN THE UNITED KINGDOM. CANDIDATES MUST BE UNDER AGE 26 AND ABLE TO LECTURE IN ESPERANTO.

INQUIRIES WITHOUT INDICATION OF FLUENCY AND INTEREST IN ESPERANTO WILL NOT BE ACKNOWLEDGED. UP TO 25 AWARDS PER YEAR. RENEWABLE. WRITE FOR COMPLETE INFORMATION.

458

PHI SIGMA IOTA-OFFICE OF THE PRESIDENT (SCHOLARSHIP PROGRAM)

UNIV OF NEVADA LAS VEGAS; FOREIGN LANGUAGE DEPT
LAS VEGAS NV 89154
702/739-3431; FAX 702/739-3850

AMOUNT: $500

DEADLINE(S): MAR 1

FIELD(S): FOREIGN LANGUAGES; LITERATURES; CULTURE

OPEN ONLY TO ACTIVE MEMBERS OF PHI SIGMA IOTA (FOREIGN LANGUAGES HONOR SOCIETY) WHO MEET STANDARDS OF EXCELLENCE IN SCHOLARSHIP IN ANY OF THE FOREIGN LANGUAGES. MAINTAIN 'B' OR BETTER GRADE AVERAGE.

WRITE FOR COMPLETE INFORMATION.

459

ROTARY FOUNDATION OF ROTARY INTERNATIONAL (CULTURAL AMBASSADORIAL SCHOLARSHIPS)

1 ROTARY CENTER; 1560 SHERMAN AV
EVANSTON IL 60201
313/866-3000

AMOUNT: TUITION; FEES; LIVING EXPENSES; TRAVEL

DEADLINE(S): CONTACT LOCAL ROTARY CLUB

FIELD(S): LANGUAGES (ENGLISH; FRENCH; GERMAN; ITALIAN; JAPANESE; POLISH; PORTUGUESE; RUSSIAN; SPANISH; SWAHILI)

SCHOLARSHIPS OF 3 TO 6 MONTHS FOR STUDY ABROAD OF LANGUAGES IN WHICH APPLICANT MAY BE SOMEWHAT COMPETENT. STUDY LOCATIONS ARE ASSIGNED BY ROTARY. AT LEAST 1 YEAR OF TRAINING IN PREFERRED LANGUAGE REQUIRED.

APPLICATION DEADLINES ARE SET BY LOCAL CLUBS AND MAY BE AS EARLY AS MARCH OR AS LATE AS JUL 15. CONTACT LOCAL ROTARY CLUB FOR COMPLETE INFORMATION.

PERFORMING ARTS

460

AFFILIATE ARTISTS INC. (RESIDENCIES)
37 WEST 65TH ST
NEW YORK NY 10023
212-580-2000
AMOUNT: $1000 FOR EACH 5-DAY RESIDENCY
DEADLINE(S): VARIES
FIELD(S): PERFORMING ARTS
ONE TO SIX WEEK RESIDENCIES FOR PROFESSIONALLY EXPERIENCED PERFORMING ARTISTS WHO HAVE UNDERGONE RIGOROUS AUDITIONS WITH AAI. AAI DOES NOT OFFER EDUCATIONAL SUPPORT IN ANY FORM.
WRITE FOR COMPLETE INFORMATION.

461

ALASKA STATE COUNCIL ON THE ARTS (INDIVIDUAL ARTIST FELLOWSHIPS & GRANTS)
411 W 4TH AVE; SUITE 1E
ANCHORAGE AK 99501
907/279-1558
AMOUNT: $5000
DEADLINE(S): OCT 1
FIELD(S): VISUAL ARTS; CRAFTS; PHOTOGRAPHY - ODD NUMBERED YEARS. MUSIC COMPOSITION; CHOREOGRAPHY; MEDIA ARTS; LITERATURE - EVEN NUMBERED YEARS.
OPEN TO ALASKA RESIDENTS WHO ARE ENGAGED IN THE CREATION OF NEW WORKS. FULL TIME STUDENTS ARE NOT ELIGIBLE.
WRITE FOR COMPLETE INFORMATION.

462

AMERICAN ACCORDION MUSICOLOGICAL SOCIETY (CONTEST)
334 SOUTH BROADWAY
PITMAN NJ 08071
609/854-6628
AMOUNT: $100 - $250
DEADLINE(S): SEP 10
FIELD(S): MUSIC COMPOSITION
ANNUAL COMPETITION OPEN TO AMATEUR OR PROFESSIONAL MUSIC COMPOSERS WHO WRITE A SERIOUS PIECE MUSIC (OF SIX MINUTES OR MORE) FOR THE ACCORDION.
WRITE FOR COMPLETE INFORMATION.

463

AMERICAN COLLEGE THEATRE FESTIVAL (MICHAEL KANIN PLAYWRITING AWARDS PROGRAM/IRENE RYAN ACTING SCHOLARSHIPS)
JFK CENTER FOR THE PERFORMING ARTS
WASHINGTON DC 20566
202-416-8850
AMOUNT: $500 - $10940
DEADLINE(S): DEC 10
FIELD(S): PLAYWRITING COMPETITION (DRAMA/COMEDY/MUSICAL); THEATRE; DRAMA
UNDERGRAD OR GRADUATE STUDENT. 10 PLAYWRITING AWARD PROGRAMS ARRANGED BY MICHAEL KANIN. MAJOR AWARDS GO TO STUDENT WRITERS WHOSE PLAYS ARE PRODUCED AS PART OF FESTIVAL. MANY OTHER AWARDS/FELLOWSHIPS/PROFESSIONAL ASSIGNMENTS INCLUDED.
ACTORS IN THE REGIONAL & NATIONAL PRODUCTIONS ARE ELIGIBLE FOR THE IRENE RYAN ACTING SCHOLARSHIPS WHICH RANGE FROM $250-2500. WRITE FOR COMPLETE DETAILS ON BOTH PROGRAMS.

464

AMERICAN FOUNDATION FOR THE BLIND (GLADYS C. ANDERSON MEMORIAL SCHOLARSHIP)
15 WEST 16TH ST
NEW YORK NY 10011
212/620-2000; TDD 212/620-2158
AMOUNT: $1000
DEADLINE(S): APR 1
FIELD(S): MUSIC PERFORMANCE; SINGING
UNDERGRADUATE SCHOLARSHIPS OPEN TO LEGALLY BLIND WOMEN STUDYING RELIGIOUS OR CLASSICAL MUSIC AT THE COLLEGE LEVEL. SAMPLE PERFORMANCE TAPE OF VOICE OR INSTRUMENTAL SELECTION WILL BE REQUIRED. USA CITIZEN.
WRITE FOR COMPLETE INFORMATION.

465

AMERICAN FOUNDATION FOR THE BLIND (R.L. GILLETTE SCHOLARSHIP FUND)
15 WEST 16TH ST
NEW YORK NY 10011
212/620-2000; TDD 212/620-2158
AMOUNT: $1000
DEADLINE(S): APR 1

FIELD(S): CREATIVE WRITING; LITERATURE; MUSIC PERFORMANCE

OPEN TO LEGALLY BLIND WOMEN WHO ARE ENROLLED IN A 4-YEAR BACHELOR'S DEGREE PROGRAM IN THE ABOVE AREAS AT A RECOGNIZED COLLEGE OR UNIVERSITY. CREATIVE WRITING SAMPLE OR MUSIC PERFORMANCE TAPE WILL BE REQUIRED. USA CITIZEN.

WRITE FOR COMPLETE INFORMATION.

466

ARTS INTERNATIONAL; INSTITUTE OF INTERNATIONAL EDUCATION (CINTAS FELLOWSHIP PROGRAM)

809 UNITED NATIONS PLAZA
NEW YORK NY 10017
212/984-5370

AMOUNT: $10000

DEADLINE(S): MAR 1

FIELD(S): ARCHITECTURE; PAINTING; PHOTOGRAPHY; SCULPTURE; PRINTMAKING; MUSIC COMPOSITION; CREATIVE WRITING

FELLOWSHIPS OPEN TO ARTISTS WHO ARE OF CUBAN ANCESTRY OR CUBAN CITIZENS LIVING OUTSIDE OF CUBA. THEY ARE INTENDED TO FOSTER & ENCOURAGE THE PROFESSIONAL DEVELOPMENT & RECOGNITION OF TALENTED CREATIVE ARTISTS IN THE ABOVE AREAS.

FELLOWSHIPS ARE NOT AWARDED FOR FURTHERANCE OF ACADEMIC STUDY. 5-10 AWARDS PER YEAR. WRITE FOR COMPLETE INFORMATION.

467

ASCAP FOUNDATION (THE) - (MUSIC COMPOSITION AWARDS PROGRAM)

ASCAP BUILDING; 1 LINCOLN PLAZA
NEW YORK NY 10023
212/621-6219

AMOUNT: $250 - $1500

DEADLINE(S): MAR 15

FIELD(S): MUSIC COMPOSITION COMPETITION

COMPETITION IS OPEN TO YOUNG COMPOSERS WHO ARE UNDER 30 YEARS OF AGE AS OF MARCH 15 OF THE YEAR OF APPLICATION. WINNING COMPOSITIONS SELECTED BY PANEL OF JUDGES.

AWARDS HELP YOUNG COMPOSERS CONTINUE THEIR STUDIES AND DEVELOP THEIR SKILLS. 15 AWARDS PER YEAR. WRITE FOR COMPLETE INFORMATION.

468

ASSOCIATED MALE CHORUSES OF AMERICA (SCHOLARSHIP FUND)

FORBES H. MARTINSON; PO BOX 771
BRAINERD MN 56401
218/568-4067

AMOUNT: $500 PER YEAR

DEADLINE(S): FEB 1

FIELD(S): SINGING

UNDERGRADUATE SCHOLARSHIPS TO DESERVING MALE VOCAL STUDENTS TO FURTHER THEIR TRAINING WHILE THEY ARE IN COLLEGE.

6 SCHOLARSHIPS PER YEAR. WRITE FOR COMPLETE INFORMATION.

469

BALTIMORE OPERA COMPANY (VOCAL COMPETITION FOR AMERICAN OPERATIC ARTISTS)

101 W READ ST; SUITE 605
BALTIMORE MD 21201
301/727-0592

AMOUNT: $1000 - $12000

DEADLINE(S): MAY 15

FIELD(S): SINGING

ANNUAL CONTEST FOR OPERATIC SINGERS BETWEEN 20 AND 35 YEARS OF AGE WHO ARE USA CITIZENS AND CAN PRESENT 2 LETTERS OF RECOMMENDATION FROM RECOGNIZED MUSICAL AUTHORITIES.

EIGHT AWARDS ANNUALLY; RENEWABLE BY COMPETITION. THERE IS A $35 APPLICATION FEE. WRITE FOR COMPLETE INFORMATION.

470

BARNUM FESTIVAL (JENNY LIND CONTEST)

1070 MAIN ST
BRIDGEPORT CT 06604
WRITTEN INQUIRY

AMOUNT: $1000 SCHOLARSHIP & TICKET TO SWEDEN

DEADLINE(S): COMPETITION HELD MAY 30

FIELD(S): MUSIC (VOICE) CONTEST

OPEN TO WOMEN BETWEEN 18 AND 25 WHO HAVE HAD FORMAL TRAINING IN OPERATIC OR CONCERT SINGING BUT HAVE NOT REACHED PROFESSIONAL STATUS. ONLY RESIDENTS OR STUDENTS FROM THE STATE OF CONNECTICUT MAY APPLY.

APPLICATION FORMS; COPIES OF THE INFORMATION MEMO AND OTHER

MATERIALS ON THE JENNY LIND CONTEST MAY BE OBTAINED FROM THE BARNUM FESTIVAL OFFICE.

471

BOSTON SAFE DEPOSIT & TRUST COMPANY (MADELINE H. SOREN TRUST; SUSAN GLOVER HITCHCOCK MUSIC SCHOLARSHIP)
ONE BOSTON PLACE
BOSTON MA 02108
617-722-7340
AMOUNT: $500 - $2000
DEADLINE(S): MAY 1
FIELD(S): MUSIC
OPEN TO WOMEN WHO ARE MASSACHUSETTS RESIDENTS AND ARE GRADUATES OF MASSACHUSETTS HIGH SCHOOLS FOR UNDERGRADUATE STUDY AT MASSACHUSETTS COLLEGES OR UNIVERSITIES.
RECOMMENDATION OF MUSIC DEPARTMENT AND FINANCIAL AID OFFICE OF A BOSTON AREA UNIVERSITY OR COLLEGE IS REQUIRED. WRITE FOR COMPLETE INFORMATION.

472

BROADCAST MUSIC INC (BMI AWARDS TO STUDENT COMPOSERS)
320 W 57TH ST
NEW YORK NY 10019
212/586-2000
AMOUNT: $500 - $2500
DEADLINE(S): FEB 8
FIELD(S): MUSIC COMPOSITION AWARDS
CITIZENS OR PERMANENT RESIDENTS OF WESTERN HEMISPHERE; ENROLLED IN ACCREDITED SECONDARY SCHOOLS; COLLEGES OR CONSERVATORIES OF MUSIC; OR ENGAGED IN PRIVATE STUDY OF MUSIC WITH A RECOGNIZED ESTABLISHED TEACHER. MUST BE UNDER 26.
15 AWARDS PER YEAR. WRITE FOR COMPLETE INFORMATION.

473

BRYAN INTERNATIONAL STRING COMPETITION (MUSIC PERFORMANCE AWARDS)
NORTH CAROLINA SYMPHONY; PO BOX 28026
RALEIGH NC 27611
919/733-2750
AMOUNT: $12000 1ST PRIZE; $6000 2ND PRIZE; $3000 3RD PRIZE
DEADLINE(S): JAN 2, 1996, AND EVERY FOR YEARS THEREAFTER
FIELD(S): MUSIC PERFORMANCE COMPETITION (VIOLIN; VIOLA; CELLO)
AUDITIONS FOR COMPETITION OPEN TO VIOLINISTS; VIOLISTS; CELLISTS BETWEEN THE AGES OF 18 AND 30. COMPETITION IS OPEN TO ALL NATIONALITIES AND IS HELD EVERY FOUR YEARS. NEXT COMPETITION WILL BE IN 1996.
WRITE FOR COMPLETE INFORMATION.

474

BUSH FOUNDATION (BUSH ARTIST FELLOWSHIPS)
E900 FIRST NATIONAL BANK BLDG; 322 MINNESOTA ST
ST PAUL MN 55101
612/227-5222
AMOUNT: UP TO $26000 STIPEND + $7000 EXPENSES
DEADLINE(S): LATE OCT; EARLY NOV
FIELD(S): LITERATURE; MUSIC COMPOSITION; CHOREOGRAPHY; VISUAL ARTS; SCRIPTWORKS
OPEN TO WRITERS; VISUAL ARTISTS; COMPOSERS & CHOREOGRAPHERS WHO ARE RESIDENTS OF MN; ND; SD OR WESTERN WI & AT LEAST 25 YRS OLD. AWARDS ARE TO HELP ARTISTS WORK FULL-TIME IN THEIR CHOSEN FIELD; NOT FOR ACADEMIC STUDY.
15 FELLOWSHIPS PER YEAR; 6-18 MONTHS IN DURATION. WRITE FOR COMPLETE INFORMATION.

475

CHATHAM COLLEGE (MINNA KAUFMANN RUUD FUND)
WOODLAND RD; OFFICE OF ADMISSIONS
PITTSBURGH PA 15232
412/365-1290
AMOUNT: $3500 PER YEAR (AVG) + FEES & PRIVATE ACCOMPANIST
DEADLINE(S): MAR 1
FIELD(S): VOCAL MUSIC; INSTRUMENTAL MUSIC
WOMEN ONLY. AWARDS FOR FULL-TIME UNDERGRADUATE STUDY AT CHATHAM COLLEGE. SCHOLARSHIPS OPEN TO PROMISING YOUNG FEMALE VOCALISTS OR

INSTRUMENTALISTS WHO ARE ACCEPTED FOR ADMISSION & PASS AN AUDITION.
AWARDS RENEWABLE. WRITE FOR COMPLETE INFORMATION.

476

COLUMBIA UNIVERSITY (JOSEPH H. BEARNS PRIZE IN MUSIC)
DEPT OF MUSIC; 703 DODGE HALL
NEW YORK NY 10027
212-854-3825
AMOUNT: $3000; $2000
DEADLINE(S): FEB 1 (OF ODD-NUMBERED YEARS)
FIELD(S): MUSIC COMPOSITION
COMPETITION OPEN TO YOUNG COMPOSERS AGED 18-25. THERE ARE TWO CATEGORIES FOR MUSIC COMPOSITION. ONE AWARD OF $3000 FOR LARGER FORMS & ONE AWARD OF $2000 FOR SMALLER FORMS. NO MORE THAN ONE ENTRY SHOULD BE SENT. USA CITIZEN.
WRITE TO ATTN OF BEARNS PRIZE COMMITTEE AT ADDRESS ABOVE FOR COMPLETE DETAILS.

477

CURTIS INSTITUTE OF MUSIC (TUITION SCHOLARSHIPS)
ADMISSIONS OFFICE; 1726 LOCUST ST
PHILADELPHIA PA 19103
215/893-5252
AMOUNT: FULL TUITION
DEADLINE(S): JAN 15
FIELD(S): MUSIC; VOICE; OPERA; ACCOMPANYING
FULL-TUITION SCHOLARSHIPS OPEN TO STUDENTS IN THE ABOVE AREAS WHO ARE ACCEPTED FOR FULL-TIME STUDY AT THE CURTIS INSTITUTE OF MUSIC. (OPERA AND ACCOMPANYING ARE FOR MASTER OF MUSIC CANDIDATES ONLY.)
APPROX 50 AWARDS PER YEAR. SCHOLARSHIPS ARE RENEWABLE. WRITE FOR COMPLETE INFORMATION.

478

DELTA OMICRON INTERNATIONAL MUSIC FRATERNITY (COMPOSITION COMPETITION-TRIENNIAL)
12297 W TENNESSEE PL
LAKEWOOD CO 80228
606/266-1215
AMOUNT: $500 AND PREMIERE
DEADLINE(S): MAR 30 EVERY SECOND YEAR AFTER TRIENNIUM
FIELD(S): MUSIC COMPOSITION
CONTEST OPEN TO MUSIC COMPOSERS OF COLLEGE AGE OR ABOVE FOR A WORK OF 10 TO 15 MINUTES IN DURATION IN THE CATEGORY SELECTED FOR THE PARTICULAR COMPETITION. (FOR 1993 - AN INSTRUMENTAL TRIO.)
CONTACT JUDITH EIDSON AT ADDRESS ABOVE FOR COMPLETE INFORMATION.

479

DISTRICT OF COLUMBIA COMMISSION ON THE ARTS & HUMANITIES (GRANTS)
410 EIGHTH ST NW; 5TH FLOOR
WASHINGTON DC 20004
202/724-5613; TDD 202/727-318; FAX 202/727-4135
AMOUNT: $5000
DEADLINE(S): FEB 15
FIELD(S): ARTS; PERFORMING ARTS; LITERATURE
APPLICANTS FOR GRANTS MUST BE PROFESSIONAL ARTISTS AND RESIDENTS OF WASHINGTON DC FOR AT LEAST ONE YEAR PRIOR TO SUBMITTING APPLICATION. AWARDS INTENDED TO GENERATE ARTS ENDEAVORS WITHIN THE WASHINGTON DC COMMUNITY.
OPEN ALSO TO ARTS ORGANIZATIONS THAT TRAIN; EXHIBIT OR PERFORM WITHIN DC 150 GRANTS PER YEAR. WRITE FOR COMPLETE INFORMATION.

480

ETUDE MUSIC CLUB OF SANTA ROSA (MUSIC COMPETITION FOR INSTRUMENTALISTS)
PO BOX 823
SANTA ROSA CA 95402
707/538-5325
AMOUNT: $600 FIRST (5); $300 SECOND (5)
DEADLINE(S): DEC 25
FIELD(S): CLASSICAL INSTRUMENTAL MUSIC
COMPETITION IS OPEN TO ANY HIGH SCHOOL STUDENT (GRADES 9-12) WHO IS A RESIDENT OF SONOMA; NAPA OR MENDOCINO COUNTIES & IS STUDYING MUSIC WITH A PRIVATE TEACHER OF MUSIC OR IS RECOMMENDED BY HIS/HER SCHOOL'S MUSIC DEPT.
WRITE FOR COMPLETE INFORMATION.

481

ETUDE MUSIC CLUB OF SANTA ROSA (MUSIC COMPETITION FOR VOCALISTS)
PO BOX 823
SANTA ROSA CA 95402
707/538-5325
AMOUNT: $600 FIRST (5); $300 SECOND (5)
DEADLINE(S): DEC 25
FIELD(S): CLASSICAL VOCALISTS
COMPETITION IS OPEN TO VOCALISTS BETWEEN THE AGES OF 16 & 20 WHO ARE RESIDENTS OF SONOMA; NAPA OR MENDOCINO COUNTIES & ARE STUDYING MUSIC WITH A PRIVATE TEACHER OF MUSIC OR ARE RECOMMENDED BY THEIR SCHOOL'S MUSIC DEPARTMENT.
WRITE FOR COMPLETE INFORMATION.

482

FARGO-MOORHEAD SYMPHONY ORCHESTRAL ASSOCIATION (SIGWALD THOMPSON COMPOSITION AWARD COMPETITION)
PO BOX 1753
FARGO ND 58107
218/233-8397
AMOUNT: $2500
DEADLINE(S): SEP 30 (EVEN NUMBERED YEARS)
FIELD(S): MUSIC COMPOSITION
THIS AWARD WAS ESTABLISHED TO BIENNIALLY SELECT AMERICAN COMPOSERS FOR THE COMMISSIONING OF A WORK TO BE PREMIERED BY THE FARGO-MOORHEAD SYMPHONY ORCHESTRA DURING ITS CONCERT SEASON. USA CITIZEN.
PROGRAM IS UNDER REVIEW. PROGRAM'S FUTURE DIRECTION WILL BE ANNOUNCED AT END OF 1992-93 SEASON.

483

FELLOWSHIP OF UNITED METHODISTS IN WORSHIP; MUSIC & OTHER ARTS (MEMORIAL FUND SCHOLARSHIPS)
G.L. SMITH; 802 INGLESIDE PL.
EVANSTON IL 60201
708-864-2768
AMOUNT: $1000
DEADLINE(S): JUN 1
FIELD(S): MUSIC; WORSHIP; PERFORMING ARTS RELATED TO WORSHIP
OPEN TO UNDERGRADUATES WHO ARE PLANNING A CAREER (IN THE ABOVE FIELDS) IN THE METHODIST CHURCH. MUST HAVE BEEN A UNITED METHODIST CHURCH MEMBER FOR AT LEAST ONE YEAR PRIOR TO APPLICATION. DEMONSTRATE FINANCIAL NEED.
WRITE TO DR. GERALD L. SMITH - CHAIRPERSON; ABOVE ADDRESS FOR COMPLETE DETAILS. INQUIRE ONLY IF YOU ARE DEDICATING YOUR CAREER TO THE CHURCH.

484

FLORIDA ARTS COUNCIL (INDIVIDUAL ARTISTS FELLOWSHIPS)
FLA DEPT OF STATE; DIV OF CULTURAL AFFAIRS; STATE CAPITOL
TALLAHASSEE FL 32399
904/487-2980
AMOUNT: UP TO $5000
DEADLINE(S): FEB 15 (APR 15 FOR VISUAL ARTS)
FIELD(S): VISUAL ARTS; DANCE; FOLK ARTS; MEDIA; MUSIC; THEATER; LITERARY ARTS
FELLOWSHIPS AWARDED TO INDIVIDUAL ARTISTS IN THE ABOVE AREAS. MUST BE FLORIDA RESIDENTS; USA CITIZENS AND OVER 18 YEARS OLD. MAY NOT BE A DEGREE SEEKING STUDENT; FUNDING IS FOR SUPPORT OF ARTISTIC ENDEAVORS ONLY.
FORTY AWARDS PER YEAR. WRITE FOR COMPLETE INFORMATION.

485

GEORGIA COUNCIL FOR THE ARTS (INDIVIDUAL ARTIST GRANTS)
530 MEANS ST NW; SUITE 115
ATLANTA GA 30318
404/651-7920
AMOUNT: UP TO $5000
DEADLINE(S): APR 20
FIELD(S): THE ARTS
GRANTS TO SUPPORT ARTISTIC PROJECTS BY PROFESSIONAL ARTISTS WHO HAVE BEEN GEORGIA RESIDENTS AT LEAST ONE YEAR PRIOR TO APPLICATION. SELECTION IS BASED ON PROJECT'S ARTISTIC MERIT AND ITS POTENTIAL FOR CAREER DEVELOPMENT.
GRANTS DO NOT SUPPORT ACADEMIC STUDY. WRITE FOR COMPLETE INFORMATION.

486

GLENN MILLER BIRTHPLACE SOCIETY (SCHOLARSHIP COMPETITION)
711 N 14TH ST
CLARINDA IA 51632
712-542-4439
AMOUNT: $750 VOCAL; $1250 INSTRUMENTAL

DEADLINE(S): APR 2
FIELD(S): MUSIC PERFORMANCE
INSTRUMENTAL & VOCAL MUSIC COMPETITIONS OPEN TO HIGH SCHOOL SENIORS & UNDERGRADUATE FRESHMEN AT RECOGNIZED COLLEGES & MUSIC SCHOOLS. AUDITION TAPE REQUIRED WITH APPLICATION. WINNERS PERFORM AT CLARINDA'S GLENN MILLER FESTIVAL IN JUNE.
ALL FACETS OF COMPETITION ARE REVIEWED AFTER EACH COMPETITION. EARLY INQUIRY IS RECOMMENDED. WRITE FOR COMPLETE INFORMATION.

487

HONOLULU SYMPHONY ASSOCIATES (ORCHESTRA SCHOLARSHIPS)
1441 KAPIOLANI BLVD; SUITE 1515
HONOLULU HI 96814
808/942-2200
AMOUNT: $288 (36 LESSONS
DEADLINE(S): AUDITIONS DURING SPRING SCHOOL BREAK
FIELD(S): ORCHESTRA/HAWAII RESIDENTS
OPEN TO RESIDENTS OF HAWAII WHO ARE IN THE 7TH THROUGH 12TH GRADES. SCHOLARSHIPS ARE FOR PARTIAL PAYMENT FOR MUSIC LESSONS WITH A MEMBER OF THE HAWAII SYMPHONY ORCHESTRA. AWARDS ARE BASED ON STUDENT'S TALENT AND PROGRESS.
22 AWARDS PER YEAR. RENEWABLE FOR 4 YEARS. CONTACT MARILYN TRANKLE; VOLUNTEER COORDINATOR; FOR COMPLETE INFORMATION.

488

HOWARD UNIVERSITY (DEBBIE ALLEN & PHYLICIA RASHAD'S DR. ANDREW ALLEN CREATIVE ARTS SCHOLARSHIP)
COLLEGE OF FINE ARTS; DEPT THEATRE ARTS; 6TH & FAIRMONT NW
WASHINGTON DC 20059
202/806-7050
AMOUNT: $5000
DEADLINE(S): APR 1
FIELD(S): DRAMA; SINGING; DANCING
SCHOLARSHIP OPEN TO ALL UNDERGRADUATE JUNIORS & SENIORS AT HOWARD UNIVERSITY WHO DISPLAY EXCELLENCE & VERSATILITY IN ALL 3 AREAS OF THEATRE - ACTING; SINGING & DANCING.
WRITE FOR COMPLETE INFORMATION.

489

ILLINOIS ARTS COUNCIL (ARTISTS FELLOWSHIP AWARDS)
100 W RANDOLPH; SUITE 10-500
CHICAGO IL 60601
312/814-6750
AMOUNT: $500 - $15000
DEADLINE(S): NOV 1
FIELD(S): CHOREOGRAPHY; VISUAL ARTS; LITERATURE; FILM; VIDEO; PLAYWRITING; MUSIC COMPOSITION; CRAFTS; ETHNIC & FOLK ARTS; PERFORMANCE ART; PHOTOGRAPHY
OPEN TO PROFESSIONAL ARTISTS WHO ARE ILLINOIS RESIDENTS. AWARDS ARE IN RECOGNITION OF WORK IN THE ABOVE AREAS; THEY ARE NOT FOR CONTINUING STUDY. STUDENTS ARE NOT ELIGIBLE.
WRITE TO ADDRESS ABOVE FOR APPLICATION FORM.

490

INSTITUTE FOR HUMANE STUDIES (CLAUDE R. LAMBE FELLOWSHIPS)
GEORGE MASON UNIVERSITY; 4400 UNIVERSITY DRIVE
FAIRFAX VA 22030
703/323-1055
AMOUNT: $17500
DEADLINE(S): JAN 15
FIELD(S): SOCIAL SCIENCES; LAW; HUMANITIES
OPEN TO GRADUATE STUDENTS AND UNDERGRADS WHO WILL HAVE JUNIOR OR SENIOR STANDING AT ACCREDITED COLLEGES AND UNIVERSITIES THE NEXT ACADEMIC YEAR. AWARD IS TO SUPPORT STUDENTS WITH A DEMONSTRATED INTEREST IN THE CLASSICAL LIBERAL TRADITION.
RECIPIENT WILL BE INTENT ON PURSUING AN INTELLECTUAL/SCHOLARLY CAREER IN ONE OF THE ABOVE AREAS. WRITE FOR COMPLETE INFORMATION.

491

INTERNATIONAL COMPETITION FOR SYMPHONIC COMPOSITION (PREMIO CITTA DI TRIESTE)
PIAZZA DELL'UNITA D'ITALIA 4 - PALAZZO MUNICIPALE
34121 TRIESTE ITALY
040-6751-68844

AMOUNT: 5 MIL. LIRA-1ST; 2.5 MIL. LIRA-2ND; 1.5 MIL. LIRA-3RD
DEADLINE(S): AUG 31
FIELD(S): MUSIC COMPOSITION
OPEN TO ANYONE WHO SUBMITS AN ORIGINAL COMPOSITION FOR FULL ORCHESTRA (NORMAL SYMPHONIC INSTRUMENTATION). COMPOSITION MAY HAVE BEEN PERFORMED AND PUBLISHED BUT NOT BEFORE JAN 1 1988.
PREVIOUS FIRST PRIZE WINNERS ARE EXCLUDED FROM COMPETITION. WRITE TO SECRETARIAT OF THE MUSIC AWARD AT ADDRESS ABOVE FOR COMPLETE INFORMATION.

492

INTERNATIONAL VOCAL COMPETITION 'S-HERTOGENBOSCH
PO BOX 1225
5200 BG 'S-HERTOGENBOSCH THE NETHERLANDS
0/73-136569
AMOUNT: $20000 TOTAL PRIZES
DEADLINE(S): JUL 1
FIELD(S): SINGING COMPETITION
ANNUAL VOCAL COMPETITION TO REWARD EXCEPTIONAL SINGING TALENT OF ALL NATIONALITIES (UP TO 32 YEARS OLD). PRIZES FOR OPERA; ORATORIO AND LIED CATEGORIES; VARIOUS OTHER PRIZES. ENTRY FEE OF 175 DUTCH GUILDERS IS REQUIRED.
WRITE FOR COMPLETE INFORMATION.

493

JAPANESE AMERICAN CITIZENS LEAGUE (AIKO SUSANNA TASHIRO HIRATSUKA MEMORIAL SCHOLARSHIP)
1765 SUTTER ST
SAN FRANCISCO CA 94115
415/921-5225
AMOUNT: VARIES
DEADLINE(S): APR 1
FIELD(S): CREATIVE ARTS
OPEN TO JACL MEMBERS OR THEIR CHILDREN OR ANY AMERICAN OF JAPANESE ANCESTRY. SCHOLARSHIP IS AWARDED TO A FRESHMAN OR UNDERGRADUATE STUDYING IN THE PERFORMING ARTS. SUBMIT PERFORMANCE REVIEWS AND/OR INSTRUCTOR EVALUATIONS.
SEND STAMPED SELF-ADDRESSED ENVELOPE FOR COMPLETE INFORMATION.

494

LIEDERKRANZ FOUNDATION (SCHOLARSHIP AWARDS)
6 EAST 87TH STREET
NEW YORK NY 10128
212/534-0880
AMOUNT: $1000 - $4000
DEADLINE(S): DEC 1
FIELD(S): VOCAL MUSIC
12-15 SCHOLARSHIPS AWARDED BY COMPETITION EACH YEAR. AWARDS CAN BE USED ANYWHERE. THERE IS A $25 APPLICATION FEE AND A LOWER AGE LIMIT OF 20.
CONTACT COMPETITION DIRECTOR JOHN BALME AT ADDRESS ABOVE FOR APPLICATION REGULATIONS; AUDITION SCHEDULES AND OTHER DETAILS.

495

LOREN L. ZACHARY SOCIETY FOR THE PERFORMING ARTS (ANNUAL NATIONAL VOCAL COMPETITION FOR YOUNG OPERA SINGERS)
2250 GLOAMING WAY
BEVERLY HILLS CA 90210
310/276-2731
AMOUNT: $1000 - $3000 + ROUND-TRIP AIR TRANSPORTATION FOR AUDITIONS IN EUROPE
DEADLINE(S): FEB 7 (NY); MAR 16 (LA); MAY (FINAL COMPETITION)
FIELD(S): SINGING-OPERA
ANNUAL VOCAL COMPETITION OPEN TO YOUNG (AGED 21-33 FEMALES; 21-35 MALES) OPERA SINGERS. THE COMPETITION IS GEARED TOWARD FINDING EMPLOYMENT FOR THEM IN EUROPEAN OPERA HOUSES.
APPROX 10 AWARDS PER YEAR. APPLICATIONS AVAILABLE IN NOVEMBER. SEND SELF-ADDRESSED STAMPED ENVELOPE TO ADDRESS ABOVE FOR APPLICATION & COMPLETE INFORMATION.

496

MERCYHURST COLLEGE (D'ANGELO SCHOOL OF MUSIC SCHOLARSHIPS)
GLENWOOD HILLS
ERIE PA 16546
814/825-0363
AMOUNT: VARIES
DEADLINE(S): APR
FIELD(S): MUSIC

MUSIC SCHOLARSHIPS AT THE D'ANGELO SCHOOL OF MUSIC OF MERCYHURST COLLEGE ARE AWARDED TO TALENTED YOUNG MUSICIANS WHO ARE READY TO START THEIR COLLEGE EDUCATION. AWARDS ARE FOR FULL-TIME UNDERGRADUATE STUDY.

35 AWARDS PER YEAR. RENEWABLE. WRITE FOR COMPLETE INFORMATION.

497

MERCYHURST COLLEGE (D'ANGELO YOUNG ARTIST COMPETITION)

GLENWOOD HILLS
ERIE PA 16546
814/825-0363

AMOUNT: $10000; $5000; $3000

DEADLINE(S): JAN 15

FIELD(S): VOICE; STRINGS; PIANO

FOR MUSICIANS AGED 18-30. ROTATING CYCLE OF AREAS (VOICE 1993; STRINGS 1994; PIANO 1995). DOLLAR AWARDS & PERFORMANCE CONTRACTS. WRITE FOR APPLICATION & REPERTOIRE REQUIREMENTS IN THE FALL OF THE YEAR PRECEDING YEAR OF COMPETITION.

WRITE FOR COMPLETE INFORMATION.

498

MILLAY COLONY FOR THE ARTS (RESIDENCIES)

STEEPLETOP; PO BOX 3
AUSTERLITZ NY 12017
518/392-3103

AMOUNT: RESIDENCY

DEADLINE(S): SEP 1; FEB 1; [illegible]

FIELD(S): CREATIVE WR[illegible]UAL ARTS; MUSIC COMPOSIT[illegible]TURE; GRAPHIC ARTS; POETR[illegible]

CANCELLED

THE COLON[illegible]S 60 RESIDENCIES PER YEA[illegible]ESSIONALS IN THE ABOVE FIEL[illegible]ERE IS NO APPLICATION FEE AND NO FEE FOR COLONY RESIDENCY.

RESIDENCIES ARE FOR ONE MONTH AND USUALLY COVER A PERIOD FROM THE FIRST TO THE 28TH OF EACH MONTH. WRITE FOR COMPLETE INFORMATION.

499

MILWAUKEE MUSIC SCHOLARSHIP FOUNDATION (MUSIC SCHOLARSHIPS)

LISA SIVANICH; FIRSTAR TRUST CO; PO BOX 2054
MILWAUKEE WI 53201
414/765-5668

AMOUNT: $300 TO $1000

DEADLINE(S): FEB 1

FIELD(S): MUSIC

OPEN TO WISCONSIN RESIDENTS AGE 16 TO 26 FOR UNDERGRADUATE STUDY. APPLICANTS COMPETE IN RECITALS FOR AWARDS.

WRITE FOR COMPLETE INFORMATION.

500

MINNESOTA STATE ARTS BOARD (GRANTS PROGRAM)

432 SUMMIT AVE
ST PAUL MN 55102
612/297-2603

AMOUNT: FELLOWSHIPS $6000; CAREER OPPORTUNITY GRANTS $100 - $1000 OR SPECIAL RESIDENCY STIPEND.

DEADLINE(S): SEP - VISUAL ARTS; OCT - MUSIC & DANCE; DEC - LITERATURE & THEATER

FIELD(S): LITERATURE; MUSIC; THEATER; DANCE; VISUAL ARTS

CAREER ADVANCEMENT GRANTS OPEN TO PROFESSIONAL ARTISTS WHO ARE RESIDENTS OF MINNESOTA. GRANTS ARE NOT INTENDED FOR SUPPORT OF TUITION OR WORK TOWARD ANY DEGREE.

CAREER OPPORTUNITY GRANTS AND FELLOWSHIPS ARE AVAILABLE. ARTISTS ALSO ARE ELIGIBLE FOR A SPECIAL RESIDENCE AT HEADLANDS CENTER FOR THE ARTS NEAR SAN FRANCISCO. WRITE FOR COMPLETE INFORMATION.

501

NAPA VALLEY SYMPHONY ASSOCIATION (ROBERT MONDAVI MUSIC ACHIEVEMENT AWARDS)

ELLE WHEELER; 2407 CALIFORNIA BLVD
NAPA CA 94558
707/226-6872

AMOUNT: $2000 AND $1000 CASH PRIZES

DEADLINE(S): FEB 12

FIELD(S): MUSIC PERFORMANCE

CONTEST HELD IN ODD-NUMBERED YEARS FOR MUSICIANS AGE 18 TO 25. COMPETITION IS IN THE FOLLOWING SEQUENCE OF INSTRUMENTS—1993 PIANO; 1995 WOODWINDS; 1997 CELLO AND BASS; 1999 BRASS; 2001 VIOLINS AND VIOLAS.

APPLICANTS SUBMIT AUDITION CASETTE RECORDING AND A NON-REFUNDABLE $25 ENTRANCE FEE WITH THE APPLICATION. WRITE FOR COMPLETE INFORMATION.

502

NATIONAL ASSOCIATION OF TEACHERS OF SINGING (ARTIST AWARDS COMPETITION)
2800 UNIVERSITY BLVD NORTH
JACKSONVILLE FL 32211
904/744-9022
AMOUNT: $2500 TO $5000
DEADLINE(S): VARIES
FIELD(S): SINGING
PURPOSE OF THE PROGRAM IS TO SELECT YOUNG SINGERS WHO ARE READY FOR PROFESSIONAL CAREERS AND TO ENCOURAGE THEM TO CARRY ON THE TRADITION OF FINE SINGING.
APPLICANTS SHOULD BE BETWEEN 21 AND 35 YEARS OLD AND HAVE STUDIED WITH A NATS TEACHER FOR AT LEAST ONE ACADEMIC YEAR. 6 AWARDS EVERY 18 MONTHS. WRITE FOR COMPLETE INFORMATION.

503

NATIONAL FEDERATION OF MUSIC CLUBS SCHOLARSHIP AND AWARDS PROGRAM (STUDENT AWARDS)
1336 N DELAWARE ST
INDIANAPOLIS IN 46202
317/638-4003
AMOUNT: $100 - $5000
DEADLINE(S): VARIOUS
FIELD(S): MUSIC PERFORMANCE; MUSIC COMPOSITION
NUMEROUS SCHOLARSHIP & AWARD PROGRAMS OPEN TO YOUNG MUSICIANS AGED 16-35 WHO ARE EITHER GROUP OR INDIVIDUAL MEMBERS OF THE NAT'L FED OF MUSIC CLUBS. THE PROGRAMS PROVIDE OPPORTUNITIES FOR STUDENTS INTERESTED IN PROFESSIONAL MUSIC CAREERS.
REQUEST SCHOLARSHIP & AWARDS CHART FROM THE ADDRESS ABOVE. INCLUDE SELF-ADDRESSED BUSINESS SIZE ENVELOPE WITH 52 CENTS POSTAGE.

504

NATIONAL FOUNDATION FOR ADVANCEMENT IN THE ARTS (ARTS RECOGNITION AND TALENT SEARCH)
300 NE SECOND AVE
MIAMI FL 33132
305/237-3416
AMOUNT: $100 - $3000
DEADLINE(S): OCT 1
FIELD(S): CREATIVE ARTS; PERFORMING ARTS
OPEN TO HIGH SCHOOL SENIORS WITH TALENT IN SUCH ARTS AS THE DANCE; MUSIC; MUSIC/JAZZ; THEATER; VISUAL ARTS; FILM; VIDEO; WRITING. AWARDS CAN BE USED ANYWHERE FOR ANY PURPOSE. FOR US CITIZENS OR RESIDENTS.
UP TO 100 AWARDS PER YEAR. WRITE FOR COMPLETE INFORMATION.

505

NATIONAL GUILD OF COMMUNITY SCHOOLS OF THE ARTS (YOUNG COMPOSERS AWARDS)
40 NORTH VAN BRUNT ST; SUITE 32
ENGLEWOOD NJ 07631
201/871-3337
AMOUNT: $1000; $750; $500; $250
DEADLINE(S): APR 1
FIELD(S): MUSIC COMPOSITION
COMPETITION OPEN TO STUDENTS AGED 13-18 (AS OF JUN 30 OF AWARD YEAR) WHO ARE ENROLLED IN A PUBLIC OR PRIVATE SECONDARY SCHOOL; RECOGNIZED MUSICAL SCHOOL OR ENGAGED IN PRIVATE STUDY OF MUSIC WITH AN ESTABLISHED TEACHER IN THE USA OR CANADA.
USA OR CANADIAN CITIZEN OR LEGAL RESIDENT. WRITE FOR COMPLETE INFORMATION.

506

NATIONAL ITALIAN AMERICAN FOUNDATION (NIAF - PAVAROTTI SCHOLARSHIP)
DR. M.LOMBARDO; EDUCATION DIRECTOR; 666 11TH ST NW; SUITE 800
WASHINGTON DC 20001
202/638-2137
AMOUNT: $1000
DEADLINE(S): MAY 31
FIELD(S): MUSIC
OPEN TO UNDERGRADUATE OR GRADUATE MUSIC STUDENTS OF ITALIAN HERITAGE FROM SOUTHERN CALIFORNIA. APPLICANTS SUBMIT EVIDENCE OF FINANCIAL NEED AND AN ESSAY DESCRIBING THEIR ITALIAN BACKGROUND.
WRITE FOR COMPLETE INFORMATION.

507

NATIONAL ITALIAN AMERICAN FOUNDATION (SERGIO FRANCHI MUSIC SCHOLARSHIP IN VOICE PERFORMANCE)

DR. M. LOMBARDO; EDUCATION DIRECTOR; 666 11TH ST NW; SUITE 800
WASHINGTON DC 20001
202/638-2137

AMOUNT: $2000
DEADLINE(S): MAY 31
FIELD(S): VOCAL MUSIC

OPEN TO UNDERGRADUATE OR GRADUATE VOCAL MUSIC STUDENTS OF ITALIAN HERITAGE WHO SATISFY THE ADMISSION REQUIREMENTS OF THE CATHOLIC UNIVERSITY OF AMERICA'S BENJAMIN T. ROME SCHOOL OF MUSIC. ESSAY AND EVIDENCE OF FINANCIAL NEED ARE REQUIRED.

WRITE FOR COMPLETE INFORMATION.

508

NATIONAL PARENT-TEACHER ASSOCIATION (REFLECTIONS SCHOLARSHIP PROGRAM)

700 NORTH RUSH ST.
CHICAGO IL 60611
312/787-0977

AMOUNT: $750
DEADLINE(S): NOV 30 TO REQUEST PACKET; JAN 29 FOR COMPLETED APPLICATIONS
FIELD(S): VISUAL ARTS; LITERATURE; MUSIC; PHOTOGRAPHY

OPEN TO HIGH SCHOOL SENIORS WHO ATTEND A SCHOOL WITH A PTA OR PTSA AFFILIATED WITH THE NATIONAL PTA AND WHO ENTER THE REFLECTIONS PROGRAM. FOR UNDERGRADUATE STUDY IN ANY OF THE ABOVE FIELDS.

WRITE FOR COMPLETE INFORMATION.

509

NEW JERSEY STATE OPERA (CASH AWARDS)

1020 BROAD STREET
NEWARK NJ 07102
201/623-5757

AMOUNT: AWARDS TOTAL $10000
DEADLINE(S): VARIES EACH YEAR
FIELD(S): OPERA

PROFESSIONAL SINGERS BETWEEN THE AGES OF 22 AND 34 CAN APPLY FOR THIS COMPETITION. SINGERS COMPETING SHOULD HAVE BEEN REPRESENTED BY AN ARTISTS' MANAGEMENT FIRM FOR NO MORE THAN ONE YEAR. MANAGEMENT REPRESENTATION NOT REQUIRED FOR ENTRY.

CONTACT ADDRESS ABOVE FOR COMPLETE INFORMATION.

510

NEW YORK CITY OPERA (JULIUS RUDEL AWARD)

NEW YORK STATE THEATER; 20 LINCOLN CENTER
NEW YORK NY 10023
212/870-5600

AMOUNT: $12000
DEADLINE(S): NONE
FIELD(S): OPERA & MUSIC MANAGEMENT (CAREER SUPPORT)

APPLICANTS SHOULD PRESENT EVIDENCE OF ARTISTIC ACCOMPLISHMENTS ALONG WITH A RESUME AND LETTERS OF RECOMMENDATION; ALSO A STATEMENT OUTLINING HOW AFFILIATION WITH THE NYC OPERA WILL FURTHER APPLICANT'S ARTISTIC AND CAREER GOALS.

AWARD RECIPIENT PERFORMS ADMINISTRATIVE TASKS FOR NYC OPERA BUT RECIPIENT IS ENCOURAGED TO CONTINUE OUTSIDE ARTISTIC WORK. WRITE FOR COMPLETE INFORMATION.

511

NEW YORK FOUNDATION FOR THE ARTS (ARTIST'S FELLOWSHIPS & SERVICES)

155 AVE OF THE AMERICAS; 14TH FLOOR
NEW YORK NY 10013
212/366-6900; FAX 212/366-1778

AMOUNT: $7000
DEADLINE(S): SEP 30
FIELD(S): VISUAL ARTS; LITERATURE; ARCHITECTURE; MUSIC AND MEDIA

FELLOWSHIPS & SERVICES OPEN TO ORIGINATING ARTISTS OVER 18 WHO HAVE BEEN NY STATE RESIDENTS FOR 2 YEARS PREVIOUS TO APPLICATION DATE & ARE NOT ENROLLED IN A DEGREE AWARDING COURSE OF STUDY. AWARDS ARE TO ASSIST IN CREATION OF ONGOING WORK.

APPLICATIONS AVAILABLE IN SPRING OF EACH YEAR. ABOUT 120 FELLOWSHIPS PER YEAR; MANY OTHER SERVICES ARE AVAILABLE. NOT FOR ACADEMIC STUDY. WRITE FOR COMPLETE INFORMATION.

512

NEW YORK PHILHARMONIC (MUSIC ASSISTANCE FUND SCHOLARSHIPS)
AVERY FISCHER HALL; BROADWAY AT 65TH ST
NEW YORK NY 10023
212/580-8700
AMOUNT: UP TO $2500
DEADLINE(S): JAN 15
FIELD(S): ORCHESTRAL MUSIC STUDY
OPEN TO USA CITIZENS OF AFRICAN DESCENT WHO ARE PURSUING DEGREES AT CONSERVATORIES AND UNIVERSITY SCHOOLS OF MUSIC. FOR ORCHESTRAL INSTRUMENTS ONLY; PIANO NOT INCLUDED.
AWARDS ARE RENEWABLE AND BASED ON RECOMMENDATIONS; PERSONAL AUDITIONS AND FINANCIAL NEED. WRITE FOR COMPLETE INFORMATION.

513

OHIO ARTS COUNCIL (OAC SCHOLARSHIP PROGRAM)
727 E MAIN ST
COLUMBUS OH 43205
614/466-2613
AMOUNT: $1000
DEADLINE(S): APR 15 (SENIOR YEAR OF HIGH SCHOOL)
FIELD(S): DANCE; MUSIC; THEATRE ARTS; VISUAL ARTS; WRITING
OHIO RESIDENTS. OPEN TO HIGH SCHOOL SENIORS WHO WISH TO CONTINUE THEIR ARTS TRAINING AND EDUCATION AT AN ACCREDITED COLLEGE OR UNIVERSITY IN THE STATE OF OHIO.
WRITE FOR COMPLETE INFORMATION.

514

OHIO BAPTIST EDUCATION SOCIETY (SCHOLARSHIPS)
PO BOX 288
GRANVILLE OH 43023
614/587-1531
AMOUNT: VARIES
DEADLINE(S): APR 1
FIELD(S): PULPIT MINISTRY; CHRISTIAN LEADERSHIP EDUCATION; CHURCH MUSIC
OHIO RESIDENT. MEMBER OF AN AMERICAN BAPTIST CHURCH IN OHIO. SHOULD BE COMPLETING SECOND YEAR OF UNDERGRADUATE STUDY AT AN ACCREDITED INSTITUTION. US CITIZEN OR LEGAL RESIDENT.
MUST DEMONSTRATE FINANCIAL NEED. NUMBER OF AWARDS DEPENDS ON THE INCOME FROM THE SMALL ENDOWMENT OF THE SOCIETY. WRITE FOR COMPLETE INFORMATION.

515

PITTSBURGH NEW MUSIC ENSEMBLE (HARVEY GAUL BI-ANNUAL COMPOSITION CONTEST)
600 FORBES AVE
PITTSBURGH PA 15219
412/261-0554
AMOUNT: $1500
DEADLINE(S): APR 15
FIELD(S): MUSIC COMPOSITION
OPEN TO USA CITIZENS. PRIZES ARE GIVEN FOR NEW WORKS SCORED FOR SIX TO FIFTEEN INSTRUMENTS. AN ENTRY FEE OF $10 MUST ACCOMPANY EACH COMPOSITION SUBMITTED. COMPOSERS MAY ENTER MORE THAN ONE COMPOSITION.
WRITE FOR COMPLETE INFORMATION.

516

PRINCESS GRACE FOUNDATION-USA (THEATER SCHOLARSHIPS)
725 PARK AVE
NEW YORK NY 10021
212/744-3221
AMOUNT: $3500 - $15000
DEADLINE(S): MAR 31
FIELD(S): THEATER; DANCE; FILM
OPEN TO UNDERGRADUATE SENIORS OR GRADUATE STUDENTS IN THEIR LAST YEAR OF PROFESSIONAL TRAINING AT A NON PROFIT SCHOOL IN THE USA. MUST BE NOMINATED BY THE DEAN OR DEPARTMENT CHAIRMAN OF A PROFESSIONAL SCHOOL IN THEATER.
USA CITIZEN OR LEGAL RESIDENT. WRITE FOR COMPLETE INFORMATION.

517

QUEEN MARIE JOSE (MUSICAL PRIZE CONTEST)
CASE POSTALE; 1252 MEINIER
GENEVA SWITZERLAND
WRITTEN INQUIRY
AMOUNT: 10000 SWISS FRANCS
DEADLINE(S): MAY 31

FIELD(S): MUSIC COMPOSITION COMPETITION
THIS CONTEST IS OPEN TO COMPOSERS OF ALL NATIONALITIES WITHOUT AGE LIMIT. MUSICAL SCORES PREFERABLY WRITTEN IN INK TOGETHER WITH A TAPE RECORDING OF THE WORK WILL BE REQUIRED.
WRITE FOR COMPLETE INFORMATION.

518

QUEEN SONJA INTERNATIONAL MUSIC COMPETITION (PIANO/VOICE COMPETITION)
PO BOX 1568 VIKA
N-0116 OSLO 1 NORWAY
+47 2 46 40 55
AMOUNT: APPROX $40000 TOTAL PRIZE MONEY
DEADLINE(S): FEB 1 - EVERY 3 YEARS
FIELD(S): PIANO; VOICE
THE NEXT COMPETITION WILL BE FOR SINGERS IN 1995. IN ADDITION TO CASH AWARDS FOR THE 4 FINALISTS (PLACES 1-4) THE BOARD OF DIRECTORS WILL ENDEAVOUR TO PROVIDE THEM WITH SOLO ENGAGEMENTS IN VARIOUS NORDIC CITIES.
WRITE FOR COMPLETE INFORMATION.

519

RIPON COLLEGE (MUSIC & DEBATE-FORENSICS SCHOLARSHIPS)
PO BOX 248; 300 SEWARD ST; ADMISSIONS OFFICE
RIPON WI 54971
414/748-8102
AMOUNT: $1500
DEADLINE(S): MAR 1
FIELD(S): MUSIC; DEBATE-FORENSICS
SCHOLARSHIPS RECOGNIZE & ENCOURAGE ACADEMIC POTENTIAL & ACCOMPLISHMENT IN ABOVE FIELDS. RENEWABLE UP TO 3 YRS PROVIDED RECIPIENT MAINTAINS 2.7 GPA FIRST YEAR AND 3.0 IN THE FOLLOWING YEARS.
20 AWARDS PER YEAR. MUST APPLY AND BE ACCEPTED FOR ADMISSION TO RIPON COLLEGE. WRITE FOR COMPLETE INFORMATION.

520

SANTA BARBARA FOUNDATION (MARY & EDITH PILLSBURY FOUNDATION SCHOLARSHIPS)
15 E CARRILLO ST
SANTA BARBARA CA 93101
805/963-1873
AMOUNT: VARIES
DEADLINE(S): MAY 15
FIELD(S): MUSIC PERFORMANCE; MUSIC COMPOSITION
OPEN TO TALENTED MUSIC STUDENTS WHO ARE SANTA BARBARA COUNTY RESIDENTS OR HAVE STRONG SANTA BARBARA TIES. AWARDS MAY BE USED FOR MUSIC LESSONS; CAMPS OR COLLEGE TUITION. USA CITIZEN. FINANCIAL NEED IS A CONSIDERATION.
APPROXIMATELY 30 SCHOLARSHIPS PER YEAR; RENEWABLE. WRITE FOR COMPLETE INFORMATION.

521

TENNESSEE ARTS COMMISSION (INDIVIDUAL ARTISTS' FELLOWSHIPS)
320 SIXTH AVE NORTH; #100
NASHVILLE TN 37243
615/741-1701
AMOUNT: $2500 - $5000
DEADLINE(S): JAN 11
FIELD(S): VISUAL ARTS; PERFORMING ARTS; CREATIVE ARTS
GRANTS OPEN TO ARTISTS WHO ARE RESIDENTS OF THE STATE OF TENNESSEE. DURATION OF AWARD IS ONE YEAR. APPLICANTS MUST BE PROFESSIONAL ARTISTS. FULL TIME STUDENTS ARE NOT ELIGIBLE.
WRITE FOR COMPLETE INFORMATION.

522

UNIVERSITY OF ALABAMA AT BIRMINGHAM (THEATRE & DANCE SCHOLARSHIPS)
UAB STATION; SCHOOL OF ARTS & HUMANITIES; DEPT OF THEATRE & DANCE
BIRMINGHAM AL 35294
205/934-3236
AMOUNT: $1000
DEADLINE(S): SPRING
FIELD(S): THEATRE; DANCE
SCHOLARSHIPS OPEN TO HIGH SCHOOL SENIORS WITH ABOVE AVERAGE GPA & THEATRE/DANCE TALENT. FOR UNDERGRADUATE STUDY AT THE UNIVERSITY OF ALABAMA/BIRMINGHAM. WINNERS WILL APPEAR IN VARIOUS SHOWS & TOURING GROUPS.
APPROXIMATELY 30 AWARDS PER YEAR. RENEWABLE. WRITE TO THE DEPARTMENT CHAIRMAN FOR COMPLETE INFORMATION.

523

UNIVERSITY OF ILLINOIS AT URBANA-CHAMPAIGN (LYDIA E. PARKER BATES SCHOLARSHIP)
STUDENT SERVICES BLDG; 610 EAST JOHN STREET
CHAMPAIGN IL 61820
217/333-0100
AMOUNT: VARIES
DEADLINE(S): MAR 15
FIELD(S): ART; ARCHITECTURE; LANDSCAPE ARCHITECTURE; URBAN PLANNING; DANCE; THEATER

OPEN TO UNDERGRADUATE STUDENTS IN THE COLLEGE OF FINE & APPLIED ARTS WHO ARE ATTENDING THE UNIVERSITY OF ILLINOIS AT URBANA-CHAMPAIGN. MUST DEMONSTRATE FINANCIAL NEED AND HAVE 3.85 GPA (5.0 = A SCALE).

175 AWARDS PER YEAR. RECIPIENTS MUST CARRY AT LEAST 14 CREDIT HOURS PER SEMESTER. CONTACT OFFICE OF STUDENT FINANCIAL AID.

524

VIRGIN ISLANDS BOARD OF EDUCATION (MUSIC SCHOLARSHIPS)
PO BOX 11900
ST THOMAS VI 00801
809/774-4546
AMOUNT: $2000
DEADLINE(S): MAR 31
FIELD(S): MUSIC

OPEN TO BONAFIDE RESIDENTS OF THE VIRGIN ISLANDS WHO ARE ENROLLED IN AN ACCREDITED MUSIC PROGRAM AT AN INSTITUTION OF HIGHER LEARNING.

THIS SCHOLARSHIP IS GRANTED FOR THE DURATION OF THE COURSE PROVIDED THE RECIPIENTS MAINTAIN AT LEAST A 'C' AVERAGE. WRITE FOR COMPLETE INFORMATION.

525

WAMSO (YOUNG ARTIST COMPETITION)
1111 NICOLLET MALL
MINNEAPOLIS MN 55403
612/371-5654
AMOUNT: $2500 1ST PRIZE PLUS PERFORMANCE WITH MN ORCHESTRA
DEADLINE(S): NOV 1 (COMPETITION USUALLY HELD IN JAN)
FIELD(S): PIANO & ORCHESTRAL INSTRUMENTS

COMPETITION OFFERS 4 PRIZES & POSSIBLE SCHOLARSHIPS TO H.S & COLLEGE STUDENTS IN SCHOOLS IN IA; MN; MO; NE; ND; SD; WI & THE CANADIAN PROVINCES OF MANITOBA & ONTARIO. ENTRANTS MAY NOT HAVE PASSED THEIR 26TH BIRTHDAY ON DATE OF COMPETITION.

FOR LIST OF REPERTOIRES & COMPLETE INFORMATION SPECIFY YOUR INSTRUMENT & WRITE TO ADDRESS ABOVE.

526

WAVERLY COMMUNITY HOUSE INC (F. LAMMONT BELIN ARTS SCHOLARSHIPS)
SCHOLARSHIPS SELECTION COMMITTEE
WAVERLY PA 18471
717/586-8191
AMOUNT: $9000
DEADLINE(S): DEC 15
FIELD(S): PAINTING; SCULPTURE; MUSIC; DRAMA; DANCE; LITERATURE; ARCHITECTURE; PHOTOGRAPHY

APPLICANTS MUST RESIDE IN THE ABINGTONS OR POCONO REGIONS OF NORTHEASTERN PENNSYLVANIA. THEY MUST FURNISH PROOF OF EXCEPTIONAL ABILITY IN THEIR CHOSEN FIELD BUT NEED NO FORMAL TRAINING IN ANY ACADEMIC OR PROFESSIONAL PROGRAM.

USA CITIZENSHIP REQUIRED. FINALISTS MUST APPEAR IN PERSON BEFORE THE SELECTION COMMITTEE. WRITE FOR COMPLETE INFORMATION.

527

WELLESLEY COLLEGE (HARRIET A. SHAW FELLOWSHIPS)
OFFICE OF FINANCIAL AID; BOX GR; SECRETARY GRADUATE FELLOWSHIPS
WELLESLEY MA 02181
617-235-0320
AMOUNT: UP TO $3000 STIPEND PER YEAR
DEADLINE(S): DEC 15
FIELD(S): MUSIC; ART HISTORY

OPEN TO WOMEN WHO ARE BA DEGREE GRADUATES OF WELLESLEY COLLEGE. AWARD IS FOR GRADUATE STUDY OR RESEARCH IN THE ABOVE AREAS AT AN ACCREDITED INSTITUTION OF YOUR CHOICE IN THE USA OR ABROAD.

APPLICATIONS AVAILABLE UP TO NOV 24 FROM ADDRESS ABOVE.

528

WORLD MODELING ASSOCIATION (SCHOLARSHIP)
4401 SAN PEDRO DR NE; #801
ALBUQUERQUE NM 87109
505/883-2823
AMOUNT: $500 - $2000
DEADLINE(S): FEB 1
FIELD(S): FASHION MODELING; PERFORMING ARTS
CAREER SUPPORT FOR STUDENTS WHO ARE AT LEAST 16 YEARS OLD AND HAVE THE PHYSICAL REQUIREMENTS TO SUCCEED IN MODELING OR THE PERFORMING ARTS. MOTIVATION; SKILLS; POSTURE; GROOMING AND COMMUNICATION ABILITY ARE CONSIDERATIONS.
WRITE FOR COMPLETE INFORMATION.

PHILOSOPHY

529

AMERICAN CATHOLIC HISTORICAL ASSOCIATION (THE JOHN GILMARY SHEA PRIZE)
C/O CATHOLIC UNIVERSITY OF AMERICA
WASHINGTON DC 20064
201/635-5079
AMOUNT: $300
DEADLINE(S): OCT 1
FIELD(S): CREATIVE WRITING - CATHOLIC CHURCH
PRIZE FOR THE BOOK PUBLISHED WITHIN LAST YEAR JUDGED TO HAVE MADE THE MOST SIGNIFICANT CONTRIBUTION TO THE HISTORY OF THE CATHOLIC CHURCH. MUST BE CITIZEN OR PERMANENT RESIDENT OF USA OR CANADA.
PUBLISHERS OR AUTHORS SHOULD SEND 3 COPIES OF THE WORK TO THE JUDGES AT THE ADDRESS ABOVE.

530

AMERICAN SOCIETY OF CHURCH HISTORY (ALBERT C. OUTLER PRIZE IN ECUMENICAL CHURCH HISTORY)
328 DELAND AVENUE
INDIALANTIC FL 32903
WRITTEN INQUIRY
AMOUNT: $1000 - $3000
DEADLINE(S): JUN 1
FIELD(S): CREATIVE WRITING - THEOLOGY
AWARD OF $1000 TO THE AUTHOR OF A BOOK-LENGTH MANUSCRIPT ON ECUMENICAL CHURCH HISTORY & A POSSIBLE GRANT OF UP TO $3000 FOR PUBLICATION. SHOULD BE CHIEFLY CONCERNED WITH THE PROBLEMS OF CHRISTIAN UNITY & DISUNITY IN ANY PERIOD.
WRITE FOR COMPLETE INFORMATION.

531

AMERICAN SOCIETY OF CHURCH HISTORY (BREWER PRIZE)
328 DELAND AVENUE
INDIALANTIC FL 32903
WRITTEN INQUIRY
AMOUNT: $1000
DEADLINE(S): NOV 1
FIELD(S): CREATIVE WRITING - THEOLOGY
AWARD FOR BEST BOOK LENGTH MANUSCRIPT OR ESSAY WRITTEN ON TOPICS DEALING WITH CHURCH HISTORY. PRIZE IS FOR THE PURPOSE OF PUBLISHING WORK.
NO MANUSCRIPT PREVIOUSLY SUBMITTED WILL BE CONSIDERED. WRITE FOR COMPLETE INFORMATION.

532

AMERICAN SOCIETY OF CHURCH HISTORY (JANE DEMPSEY DOUGLASS PRIZE)
DR. S.J. STEIN; 1420 E MAXWELL LN
BLOOMINGTON IN 47401
WRITTEN INQUIRY
AMOUNT: $250
DEADLINE(S): AUG 1
FIELD(S): CREATIVE WRITING - THEOLOGY
PRIZE FOR THE BEST UNPUBLISHED ESSAY ON SOME ASPECT OF THE ROLE OF WOMEN IN THE HISTORY OF CHRISTIANITY. THE MANUSCRIPT WILL BE PUBLISHED IN CHURCH HISTORY.
WRITE FOR COMPLETE INFORMATION.

533

AMERICAN SOCIETY OF CHURCH HISTORY (PHILIP SCHAFF PRIZE)
328 DELAND AVENUE
INDIALANTIC FL 32903
WRITTEN INQUIRY
AMOUNT: $1000
DEADLINE(S): MAR 1 1993 FOR BOOKS PUBLISHED DURING 1991 OR 1992

FIELD(S): CREATIVE WRITING - THEOLOGY
PRIZE FOR BEST PUBLISHED BOOK WRITTEN WITHIN NORTHERN AMERICAN SCHOLARLY COMMUNITY. WORK MUST PRESENT ORIGINAL RESEARCH ON HISTORY OF CHRISTIANITY.
BOOKS MUST HAVE BEEN PUBLISHED WITHIN 2 YEARS OF AWARD YEAR.

534 ---

CHRISTIAN CHURCH (DISCIPLES OF CHRIST - BLACK 'STAR SUPPORTER' SCHOLARSHIP FUND)
PO BOX 1986
INDIANAPOLIS IN 46206
317/353-1491
AMOUNT: VARIES
DEADLINE(S): APR 15
FIELD(S): THEOLOGY
OPEN TO CHRISTIAN CHURCH (DISCIPLES OF CHRIST) MEMBERS WHO ARE BLACK OR AFRO AMERICAN AND ARE ENROLLED IN AN ACCREDITED BACHELORS DEGREE OR GRADUATE PROGRAM IN PREPARATION FOR THE MINISTRY. ABOVE AVERAGE GPA; FINANCIAL NEED.
RENEWABLE. WRITE FOR COMPLETE INFORMATION.

535 ---

CIVIL AIR PATROL (CASSADAY-ELMORE MINISTERIAL SCHOLARSHIP)
NATIONAL HEADQUARTERS/TT
MAXWELL AFB; AL 36112
205/293-5332
AMOUNT: $750
DEADLINE(S): MAR 15
FIELD(S): MINISTRY
OPEN TO A CAP CADET WHO PLANS TO ENTER THE MINISTRY AND HAS BEEN ACCEPTED INTO AN ACCREDITED COLLEGE. ONE YEAR SCHOLARSHIP FOR UNDERGRADUATE STUDY.
WRITE FOR COMPLETE INFORMATION.

536 ---

CLEM JAUNICH EDUCATION TRUST (SCHOLARSHIPS)
5353 GAMBLE DR; SUITE 110
MINNEAPOLIS MN 55416
612/546-1555
AMOUNT: $750 - $3000
DEADLINE(S): JUL 15
FIELD(S): THEOLOGY; MEDICINE
OPEN TO STUDENTS WHO HAVE ATTENDED PUBLIC OR PAROCHIAL SCHOOL IN THE DELANO (MN) SCHOOL DISTRICT OR CURRENTLY RESIDE WITHIN 7 MILES OF THE CITY OF DELANO MN. AWARDS SUPPORT UNDERGRADUATE OR GRADUATE STUDY IN THEOLOGY OR MEDICINE.
4-6 SCHOLARSHIPS PER YEAR. WRITE FOR COMPLETE INFORMATION.

537 ---

FITZGERALD MEMORIAL FUND (SCHOLARSHIPS)
FIRST OF AMERICA TRUST COMPANY; 301 SW ADAMS ST
PEORIA IL 61652
309/655-5000
AMOUNT: VARIES
DEADLINE(S): NONE SPECIFIED
FIELD(S): THEOLOGY
UNDERGRADUATE SCHOLARSHIPS AVAILABLE FOR STUDENTS PREPARING FOR PRIESTHOOD AT A CATHOLIC UNIVERSITY OR COLLEGE.
WRITE FOR COMPLETE INFORMATION.

538 ---

INSTITUTE FOR HUMANE STUDIES (CLAUDE R. LAMBE FELLOWSHIPS)
GEORGE MASON UNIVERSITY; 4400 UNIVERSITY DRIVE
FAIRFAX VA 22030
703/323-1055
AMOUNT: $17500
DEADLINE(S): JAN 15
FIELD(S): SOCIAL SCIENCES; LAW; HUMANITIES
OPEN TO GRADUATE STUDENTS AND UNDERGRADS WHO WILL HAVE JUNIOR OR SENIOR STANDING AT ACCREDITED COLLEGES AND UNIVERSITIES THE NEXT ACADEMIC YEAR. AWARD IS TO SUPPORT STUDENTS WITH A DEMONSTRATED INTEREST IN THE CLASSICAL LIBERAL TRADITION.
RECIPIENT WILL BE INTENT ON PURSUING AN INTELLECTUAL/SCHOLARLY CAREER IN ONE OF THE ABOVE AREAS. WRITE FOR COMPLETE INFORMATION.

539

J. HUGH AND EARLE W. FELLOWS MEMORIAL FUND (SCHOLARSHIP LOANS)

PENSACOLA JUNIOR COLLEGE EXEC VP; 1000 COLLEGE BLVD
PENSACOLA FL 32504
904/484-1706

AMOUNT: EACH IS NEGOTIATED INDIVIDUALLY
DEADLINE(S): NONE
FIELD(S): MEDICINE; NURSING; MEDICAL TECHNOLOGY; THEOLOGY

OPEN TO BONAFIDE RESIDENTS OF THE FLORIDA COUNTIES OF ESCAMBIA; SANTA ROSA; OKALOOSA OR WALTON. FOR UNDERGRADUATE STUDY IN THE FIELDS LISTED ABOVE. USA CITIZEN.

LOANS ARE INTEREST-FREE UNTIL GRADUATION. WRITE FOR COMPLETE INFORMATION.

540

JIMMIE ULLERY CHARITABLE TRUST (SCHOLARSHIP GRANT)

SCHOLARSHIP COMMITTEE; CHRISTIAN EDUCATION DEPT; 1ST PRESBYTERIAN CHURCH; 709 S BOSTON
TULSA OK 74193
918/586-5845

AMOUNT: $1000 - $1200
DEADLINE(S): JUN 1
FIELD(S): THEOLOGY

OPEN TO PRESBYTERIAN STUDENTS IN FULL-TIME CHRISTIAN SERVICE. SCHOLARSHIPS ARE USUALLY (BUT NOT ALWAYS) AWARDED FOR STUDY AT PRESBYTERIAN THEOLOGICAL SEMINARIES. USA CITIZEN OR LEGAL RESIDENT.

6-8 SCHOLARSHIPS PER YEAR. WRITE FOR COMPLETE INFORMATION.

541

NATIONAL FEDERATION OF THE BLIND (ORACLE CORPORATION SCHOLARSHIP)

814 4TH AVE; #200
GRINNELL IA 50112
515/236-3366

AMOUNT: $2500
DEADLINE(S): MAR 31
FIELD(S): HUMANITIES (ART; ENGLISH; FOREIGN LANGUAGES; HISTORY; PHILOSOPHY; RELIGION)

OPEN TO LEGALLY BLIND STUDENTS PURSUING OR PLANNING TO PURSUE A FULL TIME POST SECONDARY COURSE OF STUDY IN THE TRADITIONAL HUMANITIES. AWARDS BASED ON ACADEMIC EXCELLENCE; COMMUNITY SERVICE; FINANCIAL NEED.

WRITE FOR COMPLETE INFORMATION.

542

NATIONAL FOUNDATION OF THE BLIND (HUMANITIES SCHOLARSHIP)

815 4TH AVE; #200
GRINNELL IA 50112
515-236-3366

AMOUNT: $2500
DEADLINE(S): MAR 31
FIELD(S): HUMANITIES (ART; ENGLISH; FOREIGN LANGUAGES; HISTORY; PHILOSOPHY; RELIGION)

OPEN TO LEGALLY BLIND STUDENTS PURSUING OR PLANNING TO PURSUE A POST-SECONDARY EDUCATION IN THE ABOVE AREAS. SCHOLARSHIPS ARE AWARDED ON BASIS OF ACADEMIC EXCELLENCE; COMMUNITY SERVICE AND FINANCIAL NEED.

WRITE FOR COMPLETE INFORMATION.

543

NELLIE MARTIN CARMAN SCHOLARSHIP TRUST (SCHOLARSHIPS)

1121 244TH ST SW; #65
BOTHELL WA 98021
206/486-6575

AMOUNT: UP TO $1000
DEADLINE(S): MAR 15
FIELD(S): ALL FIELDS OF STUDY EXCEPT THOSE NOTED BELOW

OPEN TO SENIORS IN KING; PIERCE & SNOHOMISH COUNTY (WA) HIGH SCHOOLS WHO HAVE LIVED IN WASHINGTON AT LEAST 5 YRS. FOR UNDERGRADUATE STUDY IN WASHINGTON IN ALL FIELDS EXCEPT MUSIC; SCULPTURE; DRAWING; INTERIOR DESIGN & HOME ECONOMICS.

APPLICATIONS AVAILABLE ONLY THROUGH HIGH SCHOOLS. NOMINATION BY HS COUNSELOR IS REQUIRED. AWARDS ARE RENEWABLE. USA CITIZEN.

544

NORTH AMERICAN BAPTIST SEMINARY (FINANCIAL AID GRANTS)
1321 WEST 22ND STREET
SIOUX FALLS SD 57105
605/336-6588
AMOUNT: UP TO $1900
DEADLINE(S): NONE
FIELD(S): THEOLOGY
FINANCIAL AID GRANTS ARE OPEN TO STUDENTS WHO ARE ENROLLED FULL TIME AT NORTH AMERICAN BAPTIST SEMINARY. FINANCIAL NEED IS A CONSIDERATION.
APPROX 70 AWARDS PER YEAR. WRITE FOR COMPLETE INFORMATION.

545

OHIO BAPTIST EDUCATION SOCIETY (SCHOLARSHIPS)
PO BOX 288
GRANVILLE OH 43023
614/587-1531
AMOUNT: VARIES
DEADLINE(S): APR 1
FIELD(S): PULPIT MINISTRY; CHRISTIAN LEADERSHIP EDUCATION; CHURCH MUSIC
OHIO RESIDENT. MEMBER OF AN AMERICAN BAPTIST CHURCH IN OHIO. SHOULD BE COMPLETING SECOND YEAR OF UNDERGRADUATE STUDY AT AN ACCREDITED INSTITUTION. US CITIZEN OR LEGAL RESIDENT.
MUST DEMONSTRATE FINANCIAL NEED. NUMBER OF AWARDS DEPENDS ON THE INCOME FROM THE SMALL ENDOWMENT OF THE SOCIETY. WRITE FOR COMPLETE INFORMATION.

546

ROBERT SCHRECK MEMORIAL FUND (GRANTS)
C/O TEXAS COMMERCE BANK-TRUST DEPT; PO DRAWER 140
EL PASO TX 79980
915/546-6515
AMOUNT: $500 - $1500
DEADLINE(S): JUL 15; NOV 15
FIELD(S): MEDICINE; VETERINARY MEDICINE; PHYSICS; CHEMISTRY; ARCHITECTURE; ENGINEERING; EPISCOPAL CLERGY
GRANTS TO UNDERGRADUATE JUNIORS OR SENIORS OR GRADUATE STUDENTS WHO HAVE BEEN RESIDENTS OF EL PASO COUNTY FOR AT LEAST TWO YEARS. MUST BE USA CITIZEN OR LEGAL RESIDENT AND HAVE A HIGH GRADE POINT AVERAGE. FINANCIAL NEED IS A CONSIDERATION.
WRITE FOR COMPLETE INFORMATION.

547

SANDEE THOMPSON MEMORIAL SCHOLARSHIP FOUNDATION (SCHOLARSHIPS)
1211 NAPOLEON MANOR NE
LAWRENCEVILLE GA 30243
WRITTEN INQUIRY ONLY
AMOUNT: $500
DEADLINE(S): MAR 15
FIELD(S): MEDICINE; NURSING; PHYSICAL THERAPY; RELIGION
OPEN TO UNDERGRADUATE AND GRADUATE STUDENTS HAVING AN INTEREST IN SERVING HUMANITY AND RELIEVING HUMAN SUFFERING. MUST HAVE MEDICAL OR RELIGIOUS ORIENTED CAREER GOAL WITH PHYSICAL THERAPY A HIGH PREFERENCE.
STUDENTS SHOULD BE ENTERING AT LEAST JUNIOR YEAR AT AN ACCREDITED COLEGE OR UNIVERSITY. FINANCIAL INFORMATION REQUIRED. SEND STAMPED SELF-ADDRESSED ENVELOPE FOR COMPLETE INFORMATION.

548

SOUTHEASTERN COLLEGE OF THE ASSEMBLIES OF GOD (NATIONAL JEWISH COMMITTEE SCHOLARSHIP)
1000 LONGFELLOW BLVD
LAKELAND FL 33801
813/665-4404
AMOUNT: $500 PER YEAR
DEADLINE(S): FEB 1
FIELD(S): THEOLOGY
OPEN TO A JEWISH STUDENT WHO HAS CONVERTED TO CHRISTIANITY AND IS PREPARING FOR A FUTURE MINISTRY WITH THE ASSEMBLIES OF GOD DIVISION OF HOME MISSIONS. TENABLE AT ANY ASSEMBLY OF GOD COLLEGE. MUST DEMONSTRATE FINANCIAL NEED.
APPLICANTS MUST BE IN THEIR JUNIOR OR SENIOR YEAR OF COLLEGE. WRITE FOR COMPLETE INFORMATION.

549

UNITED METHODIST CHURCH (YOUTH MINISTRY - DAVID W. SELF & RICHARD S. SMITH SCHOLARSHIPS)

PO BOX 840
NASHVILLE TN 37202
615/340-7184

AMOUNT: $1000
DEADLINE(S): JUN 1
FIELD(S): CHURCH VOCATION

OPEN TO UNITED METHODIST CHURCH YOUTH WHO HAS AT LEAST A 2.0 HIGH SCHOOL GPA; HAS BEEN ACTIVE IN HIS OR HER LOCAL CHURCH AT LEAST 1 YEAR; IS ENTERING COLLEGE AS A FRESHMAN IN PURSUIT OF A CHURCH CAREER; & CAN DEMONSTRATE FINANCIAL NEED.

OBTAIN APPLICATION BETWEEN NOV 1 & MAY 15. WRITE FOR COMPLETE INFORMATION.

550

VIRGINIA BAPTIST GENERAL BOARD (VIRGINIA BAPTIST MINISTERIAL UNDERGRADUATE STUDENT AID)

PO BOX 8568
RICHMOND VA 23226
WRITTEN INQUIRY

AMOUNT: VARIES
DEADLINE(S): AUG 1
FIELD(S): THEOLOGY

OPEN TO RESIDENTS OF VIRGINIA WHO ARE ENROLLED AS AN UNDERGRADUATE STUDENT AT A SOUTHERN BAPTIST CONVENTION SCHOOL; STUDYING TO BECOME A SOUTHERN BAPTIST MINISTER & A MEMBER OF A CHURCH ASSOCIATED WITH BAPTIST GENERAL ASSOCIATION OF VA.

50 AWARDS PER YEAR. LOANS ARE NON-REPAYABLE IF RECIPIENT WORKS FOR A CHRISTIAN RELATED SERVICE FOR 2 YEARS. WRITE FOR COMPLETE INFORMATION.

551

WOMAN'S NATIONAL AUXILIARY CONVENTION (MEMORIAL STUDENT LOAN FUND)

PO BOX 1088
NASHVILLE TN 37202
615/361-1010

AMOUNT: VARIES
DEADLINE(S): NONE
FIELD(S): BIBLE

LOANS AT 7% INTEREST OPEN TO STUDENTS IN THE SECOND AND FOLLOWING YEARS AT FREE WILL BAPTIST BIBLE COLLEGE. INTEREST PAYMENTS BEGIN 1 YEAR FROM DATE OF LOAN AND PAYMENTS ON PRINCIPAL 3 MONTHS AFTER GRADUATION OR WITHDRAWAL FROM COLLEGE.

WRITE TO EXECUTIVE SECRETARY-TREASURER MARY R. WISEHART AT ADDRESS ABOVE FOR COMPLETE INFORMATION.

SCHOOL OF NATURAL RESOURCES

552

EXPLORERS CLUB (YOUTH ACTIVITY FUND)

46 EAST 70TH ST
NEW YORK NY 10021
212/628-8383; FAX 212/288-4449

AMOUNT: $200 - $1000
DEADLINE(S): APR 15
FIELD(S): NATURAL SCIENCES

OPEN TO HIGH SCHOOL AND UNDERGRADUATE COLLEGE STUDENTS TO HELP THEM PARTICIPATE IN FIELD RESEARCH IN THE NATURAL SCIENCES ANYWHERE IN THE WORLD. GRANTS ARE TO HELP WITH TRAVEL COSTS & EXPENSES; JOINT FUNDING IS STRONGLY RECOMMENDED.

USA CITIZEN OR LEGAL RESIDENT. APPLICATIONS AVAILABLE IN FEBRUARY BEFORE APRIL DEADLINE. WRITE FOR COMPLETE INFORMATION.

553

GENERAL LEARNING CORPORATION (DUPONT & GLC SCIENCE ESSAY AWARDS PROGRAM)

60 REVERE DR
NORTHBROOK IL 60062
800/323-5471; IN ILLINOIS 708/205-3000

AMOUNT: UP TO $1500
DEADLINE(S): JAN 15
FIELD(S): SCIENCES

ANNUAL ESSAY COMPETITION OPEN TO STUDENTS IN GRADES 7-12 IN USA & CANADA. CASH AWARDS FOR 1ST; 2ND; 3RD & HON MENTION. 1ST-PLACE ESSAYISTS; THEIR SCIENCE TEACHER & 1 PARENT RECEIVE TRIP TO NAT'L SCIENCE TEACHERS CONFERENCE IN BOSTON.

CONTACT YOUR SCIENCE TEACHER OR ADDRESS ABOVE FOR COMPLETE INFORMATION.

554

NATIONAL FEDERATION OF THE BLIND (HOWARD BROWN RICKARD SCHOLARSHIP)
814 4TH AVE; #200
GRINNELL IA 50112
515/236-3366
AMOUNT: $2500
DEADLINE(S): MAR 31
FIELD(S): NATURAL SCIENCES; ARCHITECTURE; ENGINEERING; MEDICINE; LAW
SCHOLARSHIPS FOR UNDERGRADUATE OR GRADUATE STUDY IN THE ABOVE AREAS. OPEN TO LEGALLY BLIND STUDENTS ENROLLED FULL TIME AT ACCREDITED POST SECONDARY INSTITUTIONS.
AWARDS BASED ON ACADEMIC EXCELLENCE; SERVICE TO THE COMMUNITY AND FINANCIAL NEED. WRITE FOR COMPLETE INFORMATION.

555

NELLIE MARTIN CARMAN SCHOLARSHIP TRUST (SCHOLARSHIPS)
1121 244TH ST SW; #65
BOTHELL WA 98021
206/486-6575
AMOUNT: UP TO $1000
DEADLINE(S): MAR 15
FIELD(S): ALL FIELDS OF STUDY EXCEPT THOSE NOTED BELOW
OPEN TO SENIORS IN KING; PIERCE & SNOHOMISH COUNTY (WA) HIGH SCHOOLS WHO HAVE LIVED IN WASHINGTON AT LEAST 5 YRS. FOR UNDERGRADUATE STUDY IN WASHINGTON IN ALL FIELDS EXCEPT MUSIC; SCULPTURE; DRAWING; INTERIOR DESIGN & HOME ECONOMICS.
APPLICATIONS AVAILABLE ONLY THROUGH HIGH SCHOOLS. NOMINATION BY HS COUNSELOR IS REQUIRED. AWARDS ARE RENEWABLE. USA CITIZEN.

556

SLOCUM-LUNZ FOUNDATION (SCHOLARSHIPS & GRANTS)
PO BOX 12559; 205 FORT JOHNSON
CHARLESTON SC 29422
803/762-5052
AMOUNT: UP TO $2000
DEADLINE(S): APR 1
FIELD(S): NATURAL SCIENCES; MARINE SCIENCES
OPEN TO BEGINNING GRADUATE STUDENTS & PHD CANDIDATES ENROLLED AT INSTITUTIONS LOCATED IN SOUTH CAROLINA. AWARDS SUPPORT RESEARCH STUDIES IN THE ABOVE AREAS.
ACADEMIC WORK MUST BE PERFORMED IN SOUTH CAROLINA. WRITE FOR COMPLETE INFORMATION.

557

U.S. DEPT OF EDUCATION (INDIAN FELLOWSHIP PROGRAM)
400 MARYLAND AVENUE SW; RM 2177; MAIL STOP 6335
WASHINGTON DC 20202
202/401-1902
AMOUNT: $1000 - $34000 (AVERAGE $13000)
DEADLINE(S): FEB 7
FIELD(S): BUSINESS ADMIN; ENGINEERING; NATURAL RESOURCES & RELATED AREAS
FELLOWSHIPS FOR AMERICAN INDIANS OR ALASKAN NATIVES WHO ARE US CITIZENS AND SEEKING UNDERGRADUATE OR GRADUATE DEGREES IN THE ABOVE FIELDS AT ACCREDITED INSTITUTIONS IN USA.
APPROXIMATELY 90 CONTINUATION AND 35 NEW AWARDS PER YEAR. WRITE FOR COMPLETE INFORMATION.

AGRICULTURE

558

ABBIE SARGENT MEMORIAL SCHOLARSHIP INC (SCHOLARSHIPS)
295 SHEEP DAVIS ROAD
CONCORD NH 03301
603/224-1934
AMOUNT: $200
DEADLINE(S): MAR 15
FIELD(S): AGRICULTURE; VETERINARY MEDICINE; HOME ECONOMICS
OPEN TO NEW HAMPSHIRE RESIDENT WHO IS HIGH SCHOOL GRADUATE WITH GOOD GRADES AND CHARACTER. FOR UNDERGRADUATE OR GRADUATE STUDY. USA LEGAL RESIDENT. DEMONSTRATE FINANCIAL NEED.
RENEWABLE WITH REAPPLICATION. WRITE FOR COMPLETE INFORMATION.

559

AMERICAN JUNIOR BRAHMAN ASSOCIATION (LADIES OF THE ABBA SCHOLARSHIP)
1313 LA CONCHA LANE
HOUSTON TX 77054
WRITTEN INQUIRY
AMOUNT: $500 - $1000
DEADLINE(S): APR 30
FIELD(S): AGRICULTURE
OPEN TO GRADUATING HIGH SCHOOL SENIORS WHO ARE MEMBERS OF THE JUNIOR BRAHMAN ASSOCIATION. FOR FULL TIME UNDERGRADUATE STUDY.
1-4 AWARDS PER YEAR. WRITE FOR COMPLETE INFORMATION.

560

BEDDING PLANTS FOUNDATION INC (CARL DIETZ MEMORIAL SCHOLARSHIP)
PO BOX 27241
LANSING MI 48909
517/694-8537
AMOUNT: $1000
DEADLINE(S): APR 1
FIELD(S): HORTICULTURE
OPEN TO UNDERGRADUATE STUDENTS IN HORTICULTURE WITH A SPECIFIC INTEREST IN BEDDING PLANTS. AWARDS ARE TENABLE AT ACCREDITED COLLEGES & UNIVERSITIES IN THE USA & CANADA.
RENEWABLE. FINANCIAL NEED IS A CONSIDERATION. WRITE FOR COMPLETE INFORMATION.

561

BEDDING PLANTS FOUNDATION INC (EARL J. SMALL GROWERS INC SCHOLARSHIPS)
PO BOX 27241
LANSING MI 48909
517/694-8537
AMOUNT: $2000
DEADLINE(S): APR 1
FIELD(S): HORTICULTURE
OPEN TO USA & CANADIAN CITIZENS ATTENDING ACCREDITED 4-YEAR COLLEGES OR UNIVERSITIES IN THE USA OR CANADA. AWARDS SUPPORT UNDERGRADUATE STUDY.
RENEWABLE. FINANCIAL NEED IS A CONSIDERATION. WRITE FOR COMPLETE INFORMATION.

562

BEDDING PLANTS FOUNDATION INC (HAROLD BETTINGER MEMORIAL SCHOLARSHIP)
PO BOX 27241
LANSING MI 48909
517/694-8537
AMOUNT: $1000
DEADLINE(S): APR 1
FIELD(S): HORTICULTURE
OPEN TO UNDERGRADUATE & GRADUATE HORTICULTURE MAJORS WITH BUSINESS AND/OR MARKETING EMPHASIS OR BUSINESS AND/OR MARKETING MAJORS WITH HORTICULTURE EMPHASIS. AWARDS TENABLE AT ACCREDITED 4-YEAR COLLEGES & UNIVERSITIES IN THE USA OR CANADA.
RENEWABLE. FINANCIAL NEED IS A CONSIDERATION. WRITE FOR COMPLETE INFORMATION.

563

BEDDING PLANTS FOUNDATION INC (JAMES K. RATHMELL JR. MEMORIAL SCHOLARSHIP)
PO BOX 27241
LANSING MI 48909
517/694-8537
AMOUNT: UP TO $2000
DEADLINE(S): APR 1
FIELD(S): HORTICULTURE
OPEN TO SERIOUS UNDERGRADUATE OR GRADUATE COLLEGE STUDENTS FOR WORK/STUDY PROGRAMS OUTSIDE THE USA OR CANADA IN THE FIELD OF FLORICULTURE OR HORTICULTURE. PREFERENCE TO THOSE PLANNING PROGRAMS OF SIX MONTHS OR MORE.
USA CITIZEN. FINANCIAL NEED IS A CONSIDERATION. WRITE FOR COMPLETE INFORMATION.

564

CALIFORNIA FARM BUREAU SCHOLARSHIP FOUNDATION (SCHOLARSHIPS)
1601 EXPOSITION BLVD
SACRAMENTO CA 95815
916/924-4052
AMOUNT: $1250 - $1750
DEADLINE(S): MAR 1
FIELD(S): AGRICULTURE
OPEN TO ANY STUDENT ENTERING OR ATTENDING AN ACCREDITED 4-YEAR COLLEGE OR UNIVERSITY IN CALIFORNIA &

MAJORING IN AN AGRICULTURE RELATED FIELD. MEMBERSHIP IN A COUNTY FARM BUREAU IS NOT REQUIRED.
RENEWABLE. WRITE FOR COMPLETE INFORMATION.

565

COMMITTEE ON INSTITUTIONAL COOPERATION (CIC PREDOCTORAL FELLOWSHIPS)
KIRKWOOD HALL RM 111; INDIANA UNIV
BLOOMINGTON IN 47405
812/855-0822
AMOUNT: $9500 + TUITION (5 YEARS)
DEADLINE(S): JAN 2
FIELD(S): HUMANITIES; SOCIAL SCIENCES; NATURAL SCIENCES; MATHEMATICS; ENGINEERING
PREDOCTORAL FELLOWSHIPS FOR USA CITIZENS OF AFRICAN AMERICAN; AMERICAN INDIAN; MEXICAN AMERICAN OR PUERTO RICAN HERITAGE. MUST HOLD OR EXPECT TO RECEIVE BACHELOR'S DEGREE BY LATE SUMMER FROM A REGIONALLY ACCREDITED COLLEGE OR UNIVERSITY.
AWARDS FOR SPECIFIED UNIVERSITIES IN IL; IN; IA; MI; MN; OH; WI; PA. WRITE FOR DETAILS.

566

DAIRY RECOGNITION EDUCATION FOUNDATION (LOW INTEREST LOANS)
6245 EXECUTIVE BLVD
ROCKVILLE MD 20852
301/984-1444
AMOUNT: UP TO $1500
DEADLINE(S): NONE
FIELD(S): DAIRY SCIENCE; FOOD SCIENCE
LOW-INTEREST LOANS (CURRENTLY 4%) FOR CITIZENS OF THE USA & CANADA WHO ARE IN GOOD ACADEMIC STANDING IN THE ABOVE AREAS. AWARDS SUPPORT UNDERGRADUATE STUDY. PREFERENCE GIVEN TO STUDENTS WHO HAVE COMPLETED AT LEAST ONE YEAR OF COLLEGE.
10-20 AWARDS PER YEAR. WRITE FOR COMPLETE INFORMATION.

567

DAIRY SHRINE (DAIRY STUDENT RECOGNITION PROGRAM SCHOLARSHIP AWARDS)
LIZ A HENRY; PO BOX 459; 6908 RIVER RD
DEFOREST WI 53532
608/846-3721
AMOUNT: $200 - $1000
DEADLINE(S): APR 1
FIELD(S): DAIRY SCIENCE
SCHOLARSHIPS FOR COLLEGE JUNIORS AND SENIORS MAJORING IN DAIRY SCIENCE AND RELATED FIELDS WHO PLAN TO WORK WITH DAIRY CATTLE AND/OR WITHIN THE DAIRY INDUSTRY AFTER GRADUATION. MUST BE NOMINATED BY COLLEGE DAIRY SCIENCE DEPARTMENT.
10 AWARDS PER YEAR. CONTACT YOUR DAIRY SCIENCE DEPARTMENT OR WRITE FOR COMPLETE INFORMATION.

568

DOG WRITERS' EDUCATIONAL TRUST (SCHOLARSHIPS)
BERTA I. PICKETT; PO BOX 2220
PAYSON AZ 85547
602/474-8867
AMOUNT: $1000
DEADLINE(S): DEC 31
FIELD(S): VETERINARY MEDICINE; ANIMAL BEHAVIOR; JOURNALISM
OPEN TO APPLICANTS WHOSE PARENTS; GRANDPARENTS OR OTHER CLOSE RELATIVES (OR THE APPLICANT) ARE OR HAVE BEEN INVOLVED IN THE WORLD OF DOGS AS EXHIBITORS; BREEDERS; HANDLERS; JUDGES; CLUB OFFICERS OR OTHER ACTIVITIES.
SCHOLARSHIPS SUPPORT UNDERGRADUATE OR GRADUATE STUDY. 10 AWARDS PER YEAR. SEND SELF-ADDRESSED STAMPED ENVELOPE FOR COMPLETE INFORMATION AND APPLICATION.

569

GOLF COURSE SUPERINTENDENTS ASSOCIATION OF AMERICA (GCSAA SCHOLARSHIPS)
1421 RESEARCH PARK DRIVE
LAWRENCE KS 66049
913/841-224O
AMOUNT: $1000 - $5000
DEADLINE(S): OCT 1
FIELD(S): TURFGRASS MANAGEMENT
OPEN TO APPLICANTS WHO HAVE COMPLETED THE 1ST YEAR OF A 2-YEAR PROGRAM; THE 2ND YEAR OF A 4-YEAR PROGRAM OR ARE ENROLLED IN A GRADUATE PROGRAM. USA CITIZEN OR LEGAL RESIDENT.
5-10 SCHOLARSHIPS PER YEAR. RENEWABLE. WRITE FOR COMPLETE INFORMATION.

570

MIDWAY COLLEGE (INSTITUTIONAL AID PROGRAM-SCHOLARSHIPS AND GRANTS)
FINANCIAL AID OFFICE
MIDWAY KY 40347
606-846-4421
AMOUNT: VARIES
DEADLINE(S): MAR 15
FIELD(S): NURSING; PARALEGAL; BILINGUAL BUSINESS; FRENCH STUDIES; SPANISH STUDIES; EQUINE STUDIES
SCHOLARSHIPS & GRANTS OPEN TO WOMEN WHO ARE ACCEPTED FOR ENROLLMENT AT MIDWAY COLLEGE. AWARDS SUPPORT UNDERGRADUATE STUDY IN THE ABOVE AREAS.
APPROX 200 AWARDS PER YEAR. CONTACT ADDRESS ABOVE FOR COMPLETE DETAILS.

571

MOORMAN COMPANY FUND (SCHOLARSHIPS IN AGRICULTURE)
1000 N 30TH ST
QUINCY IL 62301
217/222-7100
AMOUNT: VARIES
DEADLINE(S): VARIES
FIELD(S): AGRICULTURE
MOORMAN SCHOLARSHIPS OPEN TO UNDERGRADUATE STUDENTS AT 38 LAND GRANT COLLEGES OF AGRICULTURE IN THE USA. AWARDS BASED ON SCHOLASTIC RECORD; LEADERSHIP QUALITIES & GENUINE INTEREST IN THE AG FIELD.
RECIPIENTS SHOULD RESIDE IN THE SAME STATE AS THE UNIVERSITY AWARDING THE SCHOLARSHIP. CONTACT THE DEAN OF YOUR UNIVERSITY'S COLLEGE OF AGRICULTURE FOR FURTHER INFORMATION.

572

NATIONAL ASSOCIATION OF ANIMAL BREEDERS (COORDINATED RESEARCH PROGRAM)
TECHNICAL DIRECTOR; PO BOX 1033
COLUMBIA MO 65205
314/445-4406; FAX 314/446-2279
AMOUNT: UP TO $10000 PER ANNUM
DEADLINE(S): FEB 1
FIELD(S): ANIMAL BREEDING AND REPRODUCTIVE PHYSIOLOGY WITH EMPHASIS ON ARTIFICIAL INSEMINATION.
OPEN TO RESEARCHERS IN THE AREAS OF REPRODUCTIVE PHYSIOLOGY; GENETICS & ANIMAL HEALTH RELATED TO BOVINE ARTIFICIAL INSEMINATION. GENERAL AREAS OF RESEARCH CONSIDERED INCLUDE FERTILITY; SIRE HEALTH RESEARCH; GENETIC & MARKET RESEARCH.
WRITE FOR COMPLETE INFORMATION.

573

NATIONAL ASSOCIATION OF COUNTY AGRICULTURE AGENTS (SCHOLARSHIP FUND)
PO BOX 367
CONWAY NH 03818
WRITTEN INQUIRY
AMOUNT: $1000
DEADLINE(S): NONE
FIELD(S): AGRICULTURE
UNDERGRADUATE SCHOLARSHIPS OPEN ONLY TO MEMBERS OF THE NATIONAL ASSN OF COUNTY AGRICULTURAL AGENTS. SCHOLARSHIPS ARE AWARDED BASED UPON A WRITTEN APPLICATION. USA CITIZEN OR LEGAL RESIDENT.
APPROX 180 AWARDS PER YEAR. WRITE FOR COMPLETE INFORMATION.

574

NATIONAL COUNCIL OF FARMER COOPERATIVES (UNDERGRADUATE AWARDS)
50 F STREET NW; #900
WASHINGTON DC 20001
202/626-8700
AMOUNT: $200
DEADLINE(S): JUN 15
FIELD(S): AGRICULTURE
THE COUNCIL AWARDS $200 TO EACH OF 5 UNDERGRADUATES WHO WRITE OUTSTANDING TERM PAPERS ON TOPICS CONCERNED WITH AGRICULTURAL COOPERATIVES. MUST BE ENROLLED IN JUNIOR OR SENIOR YEAR AT A COLLEGE OR UNIVERSITY.
EACH ENTRY MUST BE ACCOMPANIED BY A REGISTRATION FORM WHICH IS AVAILABLE FROM NCFC AND MUST BE POSTMARKED BY JUNE 15. WRITE FOR COMPLETE INFORMATION.

575

NATIONAL FEED INGREDIENTS ASSOCIATION (SCHOLARSHIP PROGRAM)
1 CORPORATE PL; 1501 42ND ST; #375
WEST DES MOINES IA 50265
515/225-9611
AMOUNT: $1000
DEADLINE(S): MAR 15
FIELD(S): ANIMAL SCIENCE; AGRICULTURE; AGRI-BUSINESS

OPEN TO UNDERGRADUATE AND GRADUATE AGRICULTURE AND ANIMAL SCIENCE STUDENTS. ACADEMIC EXCELLENCE; PARTICIPATION IN ASSOCIATED STUDENT ACTIVITIES AND FINANCIAL NEED ARE CONSIDERATIONS.

VARIOUS SPONSORS ESTABLISH INDIVIDUAL CRITERIA. MOST REQUIRE USA CITIZENSHIP OR LEGAL RESIDENCY. WRITE FOR COMPLETE INFORMATION.

576

NATIONAL FFA FOUNDATION (COLLEGE & VOC/TECH SCHOOL SCHOLARSHIP PROGRAM)
PO BOX 15160
ALEXANDRIA VA 22309
WRITTEN INQUIRY
AMOUNT: $500 - $5000 (VARIES WITH SPONSOR)
DEADLINE(S): FEB 15 (POSTMARK)
FIELD(S): AGRICULTURE

AGRICULTURE SCHOLARSHIPS OFFERED TO FFA AND NON FFA MEMBERS BY OVER 150 SPONSORING ORGANIZATIONS. SOME ARE LIMITED TO SPECIFIC STATES AND/OR COLLEGES OR HAVE OTHER REQUIREMENTS.

WRITE FOR SCHOLARSHIP GUIDE WHICH CONTAINS APPLICATION FORM AND DETAILS OF THE AWARDS. EARLY SUBMISSION OF APPLICATIONS IS ENCOURAGED.

577

NATIONAL JUNIOR HORTICULTURAL ASSOCIATION (SCOTTISH GARDENING SCHOLARSHIP)
401 N 4TH
DURANT OK 74701
WRITTEN INQUIRY
AMOUNT: TRANSPORTATION; STIPEND; FOOD AND LODGING
DEADLINE(S): OCT 1
FIELD(S): HORTICULTURE

PROGRAM PROVIDES A 1-YEAR HORTICULTURAL STUDY & WORK EXPERIENCE PROGRAM IN SCOTLAND AT THE THREAVE SCHOOL OF PRACTICAL GARDENING. PREVIOUS WORK IN HORTICULTURE IS ESSENTIAL. MUST BE BETWEEN 18 AND 21 AND A USA CITIZEN.

WRITE FOR PROGRAM OUTLINE AND COMPLETE INFORMATION.

578

PROFESSIONAL GROUNDS MANAGEMENT SOCIETY (SCHOLARSHIPS)
10402 RIDGELAND ROAD; SUITE 4
COCKEYSVILLE MD 21030
410/667-1833
AMOUNT: UP TO $1000
DEADLINE(S): JUL 1
FIELD(S): GROUNDS MANAGEMENT OR A CLOSELY RELATED FIELD

OPEN TO UNDERGRADUATE OR GRADUATE STUDENTS INTERESTED IN THE GREENS INDUSTRY; GROUNDS MANAGEMENT OR A CLOSELY RELATED FIELD. SOCIETY MEMBERSHIP IS NOT REQUIRED. USA OR CANADIAN CITIZEN.

WRITE FOR COMPLETE INFORMATION.

579

SAFEWAY STORES INC (GRAND NATIONAL JUNIOR LIVESTOCK EXPOSITION SCHOLARSHIPS)
C/O COW PALACE; PO BOX 34206
SAN FRANCISCO CA 94134
415/469-6000
AMOUNT: $800
DEADLINE(S): FEB 1
FIELD(S): ANIMAL SCIENCE

OPEN TO CALIF HIGH SCHOOL SENIORS WHO ARE 4-H OR FFA MEMBERS; 'PARTICIPATE' IN THE JUNIOR GRAND NATIONAL & PLAN TO ENROLL IN ANY ACCREDITED 2 OR 4-YEAR AGRICULTURAL PROGRAM OF STUDY IN THE USA.

WRITE FOR COMPLETE INFORMATION.

580

SAN DIEGO COUNTY COW-BELLES (MEMORIAL SCHOLARSHIP)
PO BOX 331
DULZURA CA 92017
619-468-3687
AMOUNT: $700

DEADLINE(S): JUL 31
FIELD(S): ANIMAL SCIENCE
OPEN TO STUDENTS WITH A BEEF INDUSTRY RELATED CAREER GOAL WHO HAVE COMPLETED 1 YEAR OF A 4-YEAR COLLEGE OR HAVE BEEN ACCEPTED BY A 4-YEAR COLLEGE AFTER 2 YEARS IN A COMMUNITY COLLEGE. MUST LIVE IN SAN DIEGO COUNTY & SHOW FINANCIAL NEED.
NEED 3.0 OR BETTER GPA. WRITE FOR COMPLETE DETAILS.

581

SAN MATEO COUNTY FARM BUREAU (SCHOLARSHIP)
765 MAIN STREET
HALF MOON BAY CA 94019
415/726-4485
AMOUNT: VARIES
DEADLINE(S): APR 1
FIELD(S): ALL AREAS OF STUDY
OPEN TO ENTERING COLLEGE FRESHMEN AND CONTINUING STUDENTS WHO ARE MEMBERS OF THE SAN MATEO COUNTY FARM BUREAU OR THE DEPENDENT CHILD OF A MEMBER.
WRITE FOR COMPLETE INFORMATION.

582

SOIL AND WATER CONSERVATION SOCIETY (SCHOLARSHIPS IN CONSERVATION)
7515 NE ANKENY ROAD
ANKENY IA 50021
515/289-2331; FAX 515/289-1227
AMOUNT: $1000
DEADLINE(S): APR 1
FIELD(S): CONSERVATION; EARTH SCIENCES; AGRICULTURE; RELATED AREAS
OPEN TO UNDERGRADUATES ENROLLED IN AN AGRICULTURAL OR NATURAL RESOURCE RELATED CURRICULUM WHO HAVE COMPLETED TWO YEARS OF STUDY IN AN ACCREDITED COLLEGE AND HAVE A 2.5 OR BETTER GPA. MUST BE WORKING TOWARD A BS DEGREE.
WRITE FOR COMPLETE INFORMATION.

583

THERESA CORTI FAMILY AGRICULTURAL TRUST (SCHOLARSHIP PROGRAM)
WELLS FARGO BANK TRUST DEPT; 2222 W SHAW AVE; SUITE 11
FRESNO CA 93711
209/445-7732
AMOUNT: VARIES
DEADLINE(S): FEB 28
FIELD(S): AGRICULTURE
OPEN TO STUDENTS WHO ARE AGRICULTURE MAJORS AND GRADUATES OF KERN COUNTY HIGH SCHOOLS. FOR UNDERGRADUATE STUDY AT ACCREDITED COLLEGES AND UNIVERSITIES. MUST CARRY AT LEAST 12 UNITS AND HAVE A 2.0 OR BETTER GPA.
FINANCIAL NEED IS A CONSIDERATION. WRITE FOR COMPLETE INFORMATION.

584

TYSON FOUNDATION INC. (SCHOLARSHIP PROGRAM)
2210 OAKLAWN
SPRINGDALE AR 72764
501/756-4955
AMOUNT: UP TO $1000/SEMESTER
DEADLINE(S): JUN 21
FIELD(S): BUSINESS; AGRICULTURE; ENGINEERING; COMPUTER SCIENCE; NURSING
OPEN TO USA CITIZENS WHO LIVE IN THE VICINITY OF TYSON FOOD FACILITIES AND MAINTAIN A 2.5 GPA. MUST WORK AND CARRY AT LEAST 12 SEMESTER HOURS OR EQUIVALENT. FOR UNDERGRADUATE STUDY AT SCHOOLS IN USA.
RECIPIENTS SIGN A PLEDGE EITHER TO REPAY THE SCHOLARSHIP MONEY OR HELP ANOTHER DESERVING STUDENT NOT RELATED BY BLOOD OR MARRIAGE TO ATTEND COLLEGE. WRITE FOR COMPLETE INFORMATION.

585

UNITED AGRIBUSINESS LEAGUE (UAL SCHOLARSHIP PROGRAM)
54 CORPORATE PARK
IRVINE CA 92714
714/975-1424
AMOUNT: $2000 - $3500
DEADLINE(S): MAR 31
FIELD(S): AGRICULTURE; AGRIBUSINESS
OPEN TO UAL MEMBER EMPLOYEES & THEIR DEPENDENT CHILDREN. AWARDS SUPPORT UNDERGRADUATE OR GRADUATE STUDY IN THE ABOVE AREAS AT RECOGNIZED COLLEGES & UNIVERSITIES.
AWARDS RENEWABLE. WRITE FOR COMPLETE INFORMATION.

586

UNITED DAIRY INDUSTRY ASSOCIATION (DAIRY SHRINE-UDIA MILK MARKETING SCHOLARSHIPS)
10255 W HIGGINS RD; #900
ROSEMONT IL 60018
708/803-2000
AMOUNT: VARIES
DEADLINE(S): APR 1
FIELD(S): DAIRY MARKETING
OPEN TO UNDERGRADUATE SOPHOMORES; JUNIORS & SENIORS ENROLLED IN AN ACCREDITED AGRICULTURAL PROGRAM IN THE USA. AT LEAST 2.5 GPA ON 4.0 SCALE. PURPOSE IS TO ENCOURAGE QUALIFIED APPLICANTS TO PURSUE A CAREER IN DAIRY MARKETING.
WRITE FOR COMPLETE INFORMATION.

587

WELLS FARGO BANK (GRAND NATIONAL STOCK SHOW SCHOLARSHIPS)
C/O COW PALACE; PO BOX 34206
SAN FRANCISCO CA 94134
415/469-6000
AMOUNT: $1000
DEADLINE(S): VARIES
FIELD(S): ANIMAL SCIENCE
OPEN TO CALIF HIGH SCHOOL SENIORS WHO ARE 4-H OR FFA MEMBERS; 'PARTICIPATE' IN THE GRAND NATIONAL & PLAN TO ENROLL IN ANY ACCREDITED 2 OR 4-YEAR AGRICULTURAL PROGRAM IN THE USA.
WRITE FOR COMPLETE INFORMATION.

588

WORCESTER COUNTY HORTICULTURAL SOCIETY (SCHOLARSHIP PROGRAM)
TOWER HILL BOTANIC GARDEN
BOYLSTON MA 01505
508/869-6111
AMOUNT: $500 - $2000
DEADLINE(S): MAY 1
FIELD(S): HORTICULTURE
OPEN TO UNDERGRADUATES IN THEIR JUNIOR OR SENIOR YEAR AND TO GRADUATE STUDENTS WHO RESIDE IN NEW ENGLAND OR ATTEND A NEW ENGLAND COLLEGE OR UNIVERSITY AND ARE MAJORING IN HORTICULTURE OR A HORTICULTURE RELATED FIELD.
SELECTIONS BASED ON INTEREST IN HORTICULTURE; SINCERITY OF PURPOSE; ACADEMIC PERFORMANCE; FINANCIAL NEED. WRITE FOR COMPLETE INFORMATION.

EARTH SCIENCE

589

AMERICAN GEOLOGICAL INSTITUTE (MINORITY PARTICIPATION PROGRAM SCHOLARSHIPS)
4220 KING ST
ALEXANDRIA VA 22302
703/379-2480
AMOUNT: UP TO $10000 PER YEAR UNDERGRAD; $4000 PER YEAR GRAD
DEADLINE(S): FEB 1
FIELD(S): EARTH SCIENCES; SPACE SCIENCES; MARINE SCIENCES
FOR FULL TIME UNDERGRADUATE OR GRADUATE STUDY IN THE ABOVE FIELDS. OPEN TO AMERICAN BLACKS; NATIVE AMERICANS & HISPANIC AMERICANS. MUST BE USA CITIZEN AND DEMONSTRATE FINANCIAL NEED.
APPROX 80 AWARDS PER YEAR. RENEWALS POSSIBLE WITH REAPPLICATION. WRITE FOR COMPLETE INFORMATION.

590

AMERICAN METEOROLOGICAL SOCIETY (FATHER JAMES B. MACELWANE ANNUAL AWARDS)
45 BEACON STREET
BOSTON MA 02108
617-227-2425
AMOUNT: $300 1ST; $200 2ND; $100 3RD
DEADLINE(S): JUN 15
FIELD(S): METEOROLOGY
AWARDS ARE FOR ORIGINAL PAPERS ON METEOROLOGY. OPEN TO ALL UNDERGRADUATE STUDENTS ENROLLED IN COLLEGES & UNIVERSITIES IN THE AMERICAS AT THE TIME PAPER IS WRITTEN. PURPOSE IS TO STIMULATE INTEREST IN METEOROLOGY AMONG COLLEGE STUDENTS.
WRITE FOR COMPLETE INFORMATION.

591

AMERICAN METEOROLOGICAL SOCIETY (HOWARD H. HANKS JR & HOWARD T. ORVILLE SCHOLARSHIPS IN METEOROLOGY)

45 BEACON STREET
BOSTON MA 02108
617-227-2425

AMOUNT: $700 (HANKS SCHOLARSHIP); $2000 (ORVILLE SCHOLARSHIP)

DEADLINE(S): JUN 15

FIELD(S): METEOROLOGY; ATMOSPHERIC SCIENCE

OPEN TO UNDERGRADUATE JUNIORS MAJORING IN METEOROLOGY OR SOME OTHER ASPECT OF ATMOSPHERIC SCIENCE. AWARDS ARE FOR THE FINAL YEAR OF UNDERGRADUATE STUDY AND BASED ON ACADEMIC EXCELLENCE.

WRITE FOR COMPLETE INFORMATION.

592

ARGONNE NATIONAL LABORATORY (STUDENT RESEARCH PARTICIPATION PROGRAM; THESIS RESEARCH)

DIV OF EDUCATIONAL PROGRAMS; 9700 SOUTH CASS AVE
ARGONNE IL 60439
312/972-3366

AMOUNT: $200 PER WEEK STIPEND

DEADLINE(S): FEB 1; MAY 15; OCT 15

FIELD(S): PHYSICAL SCIENCES; LIFE SCIENCES; EARTH SCIENCES; MATHEMATICS; COMPUTER SCIENCES; ENGINEERING; FUSION & FISSION ENERGY

1-SEMESTER ACCREDITED INTERNSHIP PROGRAM TO PERMIT STUDENTS TO WORK IN ABOVE AREAS IN RELATION TO ENERGY DEVELOPMENT. OPEN TO FULL-TIME UNDERGRAD JUNIORS; SENIORS & 1ST YEAR GRAD STUDENTS. USA CITIZEN OR LEGAL RESIDENT.

THESIS RESEARCH AWARDS OPEN TO DOCTORAL CANDIDATES WORKING ON THEIR DISSERTATION. WRITE FOR COMPLETE INFORMATION.

593

ARTHUR & DOREEN PARRETT SCHOLARSHIP TRUST FUND (SCHOLARSHIPS)

C/O U.S. BANK OF WASHINGTON; PO BOX 720; TRUST DEPT; 4TH FLOOR
SEATTLE WA 98111
206/344-3691

AMOUNT: UP TO $1000

DEADLINE(S): JUL 31

FIELD(S): ENGINEERING; SCIENCE; MEDICINE; DENTISTRY

WASHINGTON STATE RESIDENT. UNDERGRADUATE SCHOLARSHIPS OPEN TO STUDENTS WHO ARE ENROLLED IN ABOVE SCHOOLS. AWARDS TENABLE AT ANY ACCREDITED UNDERGRADUATE COLLEGE OR UNIVERSITY. USA CITIZEN OR LEGAL RESIDENT.

APPROXIMATELY 15 AWARDS PER YEAR. WRITE FOR COMPLETE INFORMATION.

594

NATIONAL CAMPERS AND HIKERS ASSOCIATION (NCHA MEMBER SCHOLARSHIPS)

BARBARA HARPER; SCHOLARSHIP DIRECTOR; 74 W GENESEE ST
SKANEATELES NY 13152
315/658-5223

AMOUNT: $500 - $2000

DEADLINE(S): APR 15

FIELD(S): CONSERVATION; ECOLOGY; WILDLIFE MANAGEMENT; FORESTRY

FOR UNDERGRADUATE STUDENTS MAJORING IN FIELDS RELATED TO CONSERVATION; ECOLOGY OR OUTDOOR ACTIVITIES. FAMILY MUST HOLD MEMBERSHIP IN NCHA & APPLICANT MUST BE IN TOP 2/5 OF CLASS.

SCHOLARSHIPS ARE RENEWABLE UP TO 4 YEARS. WRITE FOR COMPLETE INFORMATION.

595

NATIONAL RADIO ASTRONOMY OBSERVATORY (SUMMER RESEARCH ASSISTANTSHIPS)

EDGEMONT ROAD
CHARLOTTESVILLE VA 22903
804/296-0211

AMOUNT: $1000 - $1300 PER MONTH + TRAVEL EXPENSES

DEADLINE(S): FEB 1

FIELD(S): ASTRONOMY; PHYSICS; COMPUTER SCIENCE; ELECTRICAL ENGINEERING

SUMMER RESEARCH ASSISTANTSHIPS OPEN TO UNDERGRADUATES WHO HAVE COMPLETED AT LEAST 3 YEARS OF STUDY AND TO GRADUATE STUDENTS WHO HAVE

COMPLETED NO MORE THAN 2 YEARS. TENABLE AT NRAO SITES.

APPROXIMATELY 20 AWARDS PER YEAR. WRITE FOR COMPLETE INFORMATION.

596

NATIONAL STONE ASSOCIATION (SAMUEL C. KRAUS JR. MEMORIAL SCHOLARSHIP)

1415 ELLIOT PL NW

WASHINGTON DC 20007

202/342-1100

AMOUNT: $2000

DEADLINE(S): MAY 1

FIELD(S): MINING ENGINEERING OR GEOLOGY

OPEN TO PROMISING MINING ENGINEERING OR GEOLOGY MAJORS AT THE UNIVERSITY OF MISSOURI AT ROLLA WHO INTEND TO PURSUE A CAREER IN THE CRUSHED STONE INDUSTRY. FINANCIAL NEED IS A CONSIDERATION BUT NOT A REQUIREMENT.

WRITE FOR COMPLETE INFORMATION.

597

NORTHEASTERN LOGGERS' ASSOCIATION (SCHOLARSHIP PROGRAM)

PO BOX 69

OLD FORGE NY 13420

315/369-3078

AMOUNT: $1000 - $2000

DEADLINE(S): JAN 15

FIELD(S): FORESTRY

OPEN TO UNDERGRADUATE JUNIORS IN 4-YEAR PROGRAMS & 2ND-YEAR STUDENTS IN 2-YEAR FORESTRY OR WOOD SCIENCE PROGRAMS. MUST BE ENROLLED IN SCHOOLS IN THE 25-STATE AREA DESIGNATED BY THE US FOREST SERVICE AS COMPRISING THE 'NORTHEASTERN REGION.'

A WRITTEN PAPER ON ANNOUNCED TOPIC IS REQUIRED. WRITE FOR COMPLETE INFORMATION.

598

PENN STATE UNIVERSITY - COLLEGE OF EARTH & MINERAL SCIENCES (SCHOLARSHIPS)

COMMITTEE ON SCHOLARSHIPS & AWARDS; 116 DEIKE BLDG

UNIVERSITY PARK PA 16802

814/865-6546

AMOUNT: $500 - $2500

DEADLINE(S): NONE

FIELD(S): GEOSCIENCES; METEOROLOGY; MINERAL ECONOMICS; MATERIALS SCIENCE; MINERAL ENGINEERING

SCHOLARSHIP PROGRAM OPEN TO OUTSTANDING UNDERGRADUATE STUDENTS ACCEPTED TO OR ENROLLED IN PENN STATE'S COLLEGE OF EARTH & MINERAL SCIENCES. MINIMUM GPA OF 3.15 ON 4.0 SCALE.

290 AWARDS PER YEAR. RENEWABLE. CONTACT DEAN'S OFFICE FOR COMPLETE INFORMATION.

599

PLANETARY SOCIETY (COLLEGE FELLOWSHIP & NEW MILLENNIUM)

65 N CATALINA AVE

PASADENA CA 91106

818/793-5100

AMOUNT: VARIES

DEADLINE(S): JUN 30

FIELD(S): PLANETARY SCIENCES

OPEN TO USA AND CANADIAN HIGH SCHOOL SENIORS AND UNDERGRADUATE STUDENTS ENROLLED IN AN ACCREDITED PLANETARY SCIENCE PROGRAM. AWARDS BASED ON GPA; WRITTEN ESSAY; CAREER PLANS.

WRITE FOR COMPLETE INFORMATION.

600

SOCIETY OF EXPLORATION GEOPHYSICISTS EDUCATION FOUNDATION (SCHOLARSHIP PROGRAM)

PO BOX 702740

TULSA OK 74170

918/493-3516

AMOUNT: $500 - $3000

DEADLINE(S): MAR 1

FIELD(S): GEOPHYSICS & RELATED EARTH SCIENCES

UNDERGRADUATE & GRADUATE SCHOLARSHIPS OPEN TO STUDENTS WHO ARE ACCEPTED TO OR ENROLLED IN AN ACCREDITED PROGRAM IN THE USA OR ITS POSSESSIONS & INTEND TO PURSUE A CAREER IN EXPLORATION GEOPHYSICS.

60-100 AWARDS PER YEAR. RENEWABLE. INTEREST IN AND APTITUDE FOR PHYSICS; MATHEMATICS AND GEOLOGY REQUIRED. WRITE FOR COMPLETE INFORMATION.

601

SOCIETY OF MINING ENGINEERS (INDUSTRIAL MINERALS DIVISION SCHOLARSHIPS)
PO BOX 625002; 8307 SHAFFER PKWY
LITTLETON CO 80162
303-973-9550
AMOUNT: UP TO $2000
DEADLINE(S): NOV 30
FIELD(S): MINING ENGINEERING; GEOLOGY; MINERALS ECONOMICS
OPEN TO SME MEMBERS WHO ARE JUNIORS; SENIORS OR GRAD STUDENTS & DESIRE TO DEVELOP THEIR SKILLS IN INDUSTRIAL MINERALS. AWARDS TENABLE AT ANY USA COLLEGE OR UNIV. THAT OFFERS AN ACCREDITED BA; MASTERS OR PHD DEGREE IN THE ABOVE AREAS.
WRITE FOR COMPLETE DETAILS.

602

SOCIETY OF MINING ENGINEERS (MINING & EXPLORATION DIVISION SCHOLARSHIPS)
PO BOX 625002; 8307 SHAFFER PKWY
LITTLETON CO 80162
303-973-9550
AMOUNT: VARIES
DEADLINE(S): NOV 30
FIELD(S): MAT'LS SCIENCE/METALLURGY; MINING ENGINEERING; GEOLOGY; RELATED AREAS
OPEN TO UNDERGRADUATE STUDENTS WHO ARE PURSUING A CAREER IN THE MINERALS INDUSTRY. AWARDS TENABLE AT ANY USA COLLEGE OR UNIV. THAT OFFERS AN ABET ACCREDITED DEGREE IN THE ABOVE AREAS. USA CITIZEN OR LEGAL RESIDENT.
WRITE FOR COMPLETE DETAILS.

603

SOIL AND WATER CONSERVATION SOCIETY (SCHOLARSHIPS IN CONSERVATION)
7515 NE ANKENY ROAD
ANKENY IA 50021
515/289-2331; FAX 515/289-1227
AMOUNT: $1000
DEADLINE(S): APR 1
FIELD(S): CONSERVATION; EARTH SCIENCES; AGRICULTURE; RELATED AREAS
OPEN TO UNDERGRADUATES ENROLLED IN AN AGRICULTURAL OR NATURAL RESOURCE RELATED CURRICULUM WHO HAVE COMPLETED TWO YEARS OF STUDY IN AN ACCREDITED COLLEGE AND HAVE A 2.5 OR BETTER GPA. MUST BE WORKING TOWARD A BS DEGREE.
WRITE FOR COMPLETE INFORMATION.

604

U.S. AIR FORCE ROTC (4-YEAR SCHOLARSHIP PROGRAM)
AFROTC/RROO; RECRUITING OPERATIONS BRANCH
MAXWELL AFB AL 36112
205/953-2091
AMOUNT: TUITION + FEES & BOOKS + $100 PER MONTH STIPEND
DEADLINE(S): DEC 1
FIELD(S): AERONAUTICAL ENGINEERING; CIVIL ENGINEERING; MECHANICAL ENGINEERING; MATHEMATICS; PHYSICS; NURSING & SOME LIBERAL ARTS
OPEN TO USA CITIZENS WHO ARE AT LEAST 17 AND WILL GRADUATE FROM COLLEGE BEFORE AGE 25. MUST COMPLETE APPLICATION; FURNISH SAT/ACT SCORES; HIGH SCHOOL TRANSCRIPTS AND RECORD OF EXTRACURRICULAR ACTIVITIES.
MUST QUALIFY ON AIR FORCE MEDICAL EXAMINATION. ABOUT 1600 SCHOLARSHIPS AWARDED EACH YEAR AT CAMPUSES WHICH OFFER AIR FORCE ROTC.

605

WOMAN'S AUXILIARY TO THE AMERICAN INSTITUTE OF MINING METALLURGICAL & PETROLEUM ENGINEERS (WAAIME SCHOLARSHIP LOAN FUND)
345 E 47TH ST; 14TH FLOOR
NEW YORK NY 10017
WRITTEN INQUIRY ONLY
AMOUNT: VARIES
DEADLINE(S): MAR 15
FIELD(S): EARTH SCIENCES; MINING ENGINEERING; PETROLEUM ENGINEERING
OPEN TO UNDERGRADUATE JUNIORS & SENIORS AND GRADUATE STUDENTS. ELIGIBLE APPLICANTS RECEIVE A SCHOLARSHIP LOAN FOR ALL OR PART OF THEIR EDUCATION. RECIPIENTS REPAY ONLY 50% WITH NO INTEREST CHARGES.
REPAYMENT TO BEGIN BY 6 MONTHS AFTER GRADUATION AND BE COMPLETED WITHIN 6 YEARS. WRITE TO WAAIME SCHOLARSHIP LOAN FUND; ADDRESS ABOVE; FOR COMPLETE INFORMATION.

ENVIRO STUDIES

606

ARGONNE NATIONAL LABORATORY (STUDENT RESEARCH PARTICIPATION PROGRAM; THESIS RESEARCH)

DIV OF EDUCATIONAL PROGRAMS; 9700 SOUTH CASS AVE

ARGONNE IL 60439

312/972-3366

AMOUNT: $200 PER WEEK STIPEND

DEADLINE(S): FEB 1; MAY 15; OCT 15

FIELD(S): PHYSICAL SCIENCES; LIFE SCIENCES; EARTH SCIENCES; MATHEMATICS; COMPUTER SCIENCES; ENGINEERING; FUSION & FISSION ENERGY

1-SEMESTER ACCREDITED INTERNSHIP PROGRAM TO PERMIT STUDENTS TO WORK IN ABOVE AREAS IN RELATION TO ENERGY DEVELOPMENT. OPEN TO FULL-TIME UNDERGRAD JUNIORS; SENIORS & 1ST YEAR GRAD STUDENTS. USA CITIZEN OR LEGAL RESIDENT.

THESIS RESEARCH AWARDS OPEN TO DOCTORAL CANDIDATES WORKING ON THEIR DISSERTATION. WRITE FOR COMPLETE INFORMATION.

607

EARTHWATCH EXPEDITIONS INC. (EARTHWATCH SCHOLARSHIP AND FELLOWSHIP PROGRAM)

PO BOX 403; 680 MOUNT AUBURN ST

WATERTOWN MA 02172

617/926-8200 OR 800/776-0188 EXT 203

AMOUNT: $100 - $2000

DEADLINE(S): FEB 15

FIELD(S): ARCHAEOLOGY; ANTHROPOLOGY; ENVIRONMENTAL STUDIES; BIOLOGY; MARINE SCIENCE

NATIONAL COMPETITION. WINNERS ARE GIVEN AN OPPORTUNITY TO WORK IN THE FIELD FOR 2-3 WEEKS WITH A PROFESSIONAL SCIENTIST ON A RESEARCH EXPEDITION. AWARDS ARE FOR HIGH SCHOOL STUDENTS AND TEACHERS ONLY.

250 AWARDS PER YEAR. WRITE FOR COMPLETE INFORMATION.

608

EDMUND NILES HUYCK PRESERVE (GRADUATE AND POST-GRADUATE RESEARCH GRANTS)

MAIN ST

RENSSELAERVILLE NY 12147

518/797-3440

AMOUNT: UP TO $3500

DEADLINE(S): FEB 1

FIELD(S): ECOLOGY; BEHAVIOR; EVOLUTION; NATURAL HISTORY

GRANTS TO SUPPORT GRADUATE AND POST GRADUATE SCIENTISTS CONDUCTING RESEARCH ON THE NATURAL RESOURCES OF THE HUYCK PRESERVE. FUNDS ARE NOT AVAILABLE TO HELP STUDENTS DEFRAY COLLEGE EXPENSES.

HOUSING AND LAB SPACE ARE PROVIDED AT THE PRESERVE. WRITE FOR COMPLETE INFORMATION.

609

GARDEN CLUB OF AMERICA (CLARA CARTER HIGGINS SCHOLARSHIP)

598 MADISON AVE

NEW YORK NY 10022

212/753-8287

AMOUNT: $1000 TO $1500 (VARIES YEARLY)

DEADLINE(S): FEB 15

FIELD(S): ENVIRONMENTAL STUDIES

ANNUAL SCHOLARSHIP FOR A SUMMER COURSE IN ENVIRONMENTAL STUDIES. AWARD TENABLE AT ANY ACCREDITED COLLEGE OR UNIVERSITY IN USA. OPEN TO UNDERGRADUATE OR GRADUATE STUDENTS WHO ARE USA CITIZENS OR LEGAL RESIDENTS.

CONTACT CONSERVATION CHAIRMAN AT ADDRESS ABOVE.

610

GLENN CARRINGTON FOUNDATION (ALASKA SCHOLARSHIP TO BENEFIT NATIVE ALASKANS)

927 LARKSPUR RD

OAKLAND CA 94610

510/763-9762

AMOUNT: UP TO $2000

DEADLINE(S): MAR 1

FIELD(S): BUSINESS; EDUCATION; ENVIRONMENT; POLITICAL SCIENCE; COMMUNICATIONS

OPEN TO ALASKA RESIDENTS COMMITTED TO HELPING NATIVE ALASKANS GOVERN;

EDUCATE; DEVELOP BUSINESSES AND IMPROVE THEIR MANAGEMENT ABILITIES. MUST DEMONSTRATE PERSONAL AND FAMILY FINANCIAL NEED.
WRITE FOR COMPLETE INFORMATION.

611

NATIONAL CAMPERS AND HIKERS ASSOCIATION (NCHA MEMBER SCHOLARSHIPS)
BARBARA HARPER; SCHOLARSHIP DIRECTOR; 74 W GENESEE ST
SKANEATELES NY 13152
315/658-5223
AMOUNT: $500 - $2000
DEADLINE(S): APR 15
FIELD(S): CONSERVATION; ECOLOGY; WILDLIFE MANAGEMENT; FORESTRY
FOR UNDERGRADUATE STUDENTS MAJORING IN FIELDS RELATED TO CONSERVATION; ECOLOGY OR OUTDOOR ACTIVITIES. FAMILY MUST HOLD MEMBERSHIP IN NCHA & APPLICANT MUST BE IN TOP 2/5 OF CLASS.
SCHOLARSHIPS ARE RENEWABLE UP TO 4 YEARS. WRITE FOR COMPLETE INFORMATION.

612

NATIONAL DEFENSE TRANSPORTATION ASSOCIATION - SAN FRANCISCO BAY AREA CHAPTER (NDTA SCHOLARSHIP)
PO BOX 24676
OAKLAND CA 94623
WRITTEN INQUIRY
AMOUNT: $1000
DEADLINE(S): MAY 1
FIELD(S): TRANSPORTATION
OPEN TO USA CITIZENS STUDYING IN THE FIELD OF BUSINESS; ENGINEERING; PLANNING OR ENVIRONMENT IN PREPARATION FOR A CAREER RELATED TO TRANSPORTATION. FINANCIAL NEED WILL BE CONSIDERED.
WRITE FOR COMPLETE INFORMATION.

613

NATIONAL ENVIRONMENTAL HEALTH ASSN (NEHA SCHOLARSHIP AWARDS)
VICKI POTTER; MEMBER LIAISON; 720 S COLORADO BLVD; #970; S TOWER
DENVER CO 80222
303/756-9090
AMOUNT: $850
DEADLINE(S): FEB 1
FIELD(S): ENVIRONMENTAL HEALTH
UNDERGRADUATE SCHOLARSHIPS TO BE USED TOWARD TUITION AND FEES OF A COLLEGE SOPHOMORE OR JUNIOR ENROLLED IN AN ENVIRONMENTAL HEALTH CURRICULUM AT AN APPROVED USA COLLEGE OR UNIVERSITY.
SCHOLARSHIPS RENEWABLE. WRITE FOR COMPLETE INFORMATION.

614

SAN FRANCISCO BAY AREA CHAPTER - NATIONAL DEFENSE TRANSPORTATION ASSN (NDTA MERIT SCHOLARSHIP)
BOX 24676
OAKLAND CA 94623
WRITTEN INQUIRY
AMOUNT: $2000
DEADLINE(S): MAR 31
FIELD(S): BUSINESS; ENGINEERING; PLANNING; ENVIRONMENT (AS RELATED TO TRANSPORTATION)
OPEN TO USA CITIZENS ENROLLED IN AN ACCREDITED UNDERGRADUATE DEGREE OR VOCATIONAL PROGRAM IN ABOVE FIELDS WHO PLAN TO PURSUE A CAREER RELATED TO TRANSPORTATION. FINANCIAL NEED WILL BE CONSIDERED.
WRITE FOR COMPLETE INFORMATION.

615

SIGURD OLSON ENVIRONMENTAL INSTITUTE - LOONWATCH (SIGURD T. OLSON RESEARCH FUND)
NORTHLAND COLLEGE
ASHLAND WI 54806
715/682-4531
AMOUNT: UP TO $1000
DEADLINE(S): JAN 6
FIELD(S): RESEARCH ON THE COMMON LOON (GAVIA IMMER)
OPEN TO STUDENTS AT ALL LEVELS FOR STUDY OF LOON POPULATIONS IN THE UPPER GREAT LAKES.
RENEWABLE. WRITE FOR COMPLETE INFORMATION.

616

SMITHSONIAN INSTITUTION ENVIRONMENTAL RESEARCH CENTER (WORK/LEARN PROGRAM)
PO BOX 28
EDGEWATER MD 21037
301/798-4424; 202/287-3321

AMOUNT: STIPEND
DEADLINE(S): MAR 1; JUL 1; DEC 1
FIELD(S): ENVIRONMENTAL STUDIES
WORK/LEARN INTERNSHIPS AT THE CENTER OPEN TO UNDERGRADUATE & GRADUATE STUDENTS. COMPETITIVE PROGRAM WHICH OFFERS UNIQUE OPPORTUNITY TO GAIN EXPOSURE TO & EXPERIENCE IN ENVIRONMENTAL RESEARCH.
PROJECTS GENERALLY COINCIDE WITH ACADEMIC SEMESTERS & SUMMER SESSIONS AND ARE NORMALLY 12 - 15 WEEKS. WRITE FOR COMPLETE INFORMATION.

617

SOCIETY FOR RANGE MANAGEMENT (MASONIC-RANGE SCIENCE SCHOLARSHIP)
1839 YORK ST
DENVER CO 80206
303/355-7070
AMOUNT: NOT SPECIFIED
DEADLINE(S): JAN 15
FIELD(S): RANGE MANAGEMENT
OPEN TO HIGH SCHOOL SENIORS PLANNING TO MAJOR IN RANGE SCIENCE OR A COLLEGE FRESHMAN MAJORING IN RANGE SCIENCE. MUST BE SPONSORED BY SOCIETY FOR RANGE MGMT; NATL ASSN OF CONSERVATION DISTRICTS OR THE SOIL & WATER CONSERVATION SOCIETY.
WRITE FOR COMPLETE INFORMATION.

618

SOIL AND WATER CONSERVATION SOCIETY (SCHOLARSHIPS IN CONSERVATION)
7515 NE ANKENY ROAD
ANKENY IA 50021
515/289-2331; FAX 515/289-1227
AMOUNT: $1000
DEADLINE(S): APR 1
FIELD(S): CONSERVATION; EARTH SCIENCES; AGRICULTURE; RELATED AREAS
OPEN TO UNDERGRADUATES ENROLLED IN AN AGRICULTURAL OR NATURAL RESOURCE RELATED CURRICULUM WHO HAVE COMPLETED TWO YEARS OF STUDY IN AN ACCREDITED COLLEGE AND HAVE A 2.5 OR BETTER GPA. MUST BE WORKING TOWARD A BS DEGREE.
WRITE FOR COMPLETE INFORMATION.

619

WATER ENVIRONMENT FEDERATION (STUDENT PAPER COMPETITION)
SUSAN PHILLIPS; 601 WYTHE ST
ALEXANDRIA VA 22314
703/684-2407
AMOUNT: $1000 FIRST PRIZE; $500 SECOND; $250 THIRD IN EACH OF 4 CATEGORIES
DEADLINE(S): JAN 1
FIELD(S): WATER POLLUTION
AWARDS FOR 500 TO 1000 WORD ABSTRACTS DEALING WITH WATER POLLUTION CONTROL; WATER QUALITY PROBLEMS; WATER RELATED CONCERNS OR HAZARDOUS WASTES. OPEN TO OPERATIONS STUDENTS (AA DEGREE CANDIDATES) AS WELL AS UNDERGRAD AND GRAD STUDENTS.
ALSO OPEN TO RECENTLY GRADUATED STUDENTS (WITHIN 1 CALENDAR YEAR OF JAN 1 DEADLINE). WRITE FOR COMPLETE INFORMATION.

MARINE SCIENCE

620

AMERICAN GEOLOGICAL INSTITUTE (MINORITY PARTICIPATION PROGRAM SCHOLARSHIPS)
4220 KING ST
ALEXANDRIA VA 22302
703/379-2480
AMOUNT: UP TO $10000 PER YEAR UNDERGRAD; $4000 PER YEAR GRAD
DEADLINE(S): FEB 1
FIELD(S): EARTH SCIENCES; SPACE SCIENCES; MARINE SCIENCES
FOR FULL TIME UNDERGRADUATE OR GRADUATE STUDY IN THE ABOVE FIELDS. OPEN TO AMERICAN BLACKS; NATIVE AMERICANS & HISPANIC AMERICANS. MUST BE USA CITIZEN AND DEMONSTRATE FINANCIAL NEED.
APPROX 80 AWARDS PER YEAR. RENEWALS POSSIBLE WITH REAPPLICATION. WRITE FOR COMPLETE INFORMATION.

621

EARTHWATCH EXPEDITIONS INC. (EARTHWATCH SCHOLARSHIP AND FELLOWSHIP PROGRAM)
PO BOX 403; 680 MOUNT AUBURN ST
WATERTOWN MA 02172

617/926-8200 OR 800/776-0188 EXT 203
AMOUNT: $100 - $2000
DEADLINE(S): FEB 15
FIELD(S): ARCHAEOLOGY; ANTHROPOLOGY; ENVIRONMENTAL STUDIES; BIOLOGY; MARINE SCIENCE

NATIONAL COMPETITION. WINNERS ARE GIVEN AN OPPORTUNITY TO WORK IN THE FIELD FOR 2-3 WEEKS WITH A PROFESSIONAL SCIENTIST ON A RESEARCH EXPEDITION. AWARDS ARE FOR HIGH SCHOOL STUDENTS AND TEACHERS ONLY.

250 AWARDS PER YEAR. WRITE FOR COMPLETE INFORMATION.

622 ---

HOUSTON UNDERWATER CLUB (SEASPACE SCHOLARSHIPS)
PO BOX 3753
HOUSTON TX 77253
713/467-6675
AMOUNT: $1000 (AVERAGE)
DEADLINE(S): MAR 15
FIELD(S): MARINE SCIENCES; MARINE BIOLOGY OR GEOLOGY; NAUTICAL ARCHAEOLOGY; BIOLOGICAL OCEANOGRAPHY; OCEAN & FISHERY SCIENCES; NAVAL/MARINE ENGINEERING; NAVAL SCIENCE

OPEN TO COLLEGE JUNIORS; SENIORS AND GRADUATE STUDENTS WHO ASPIRE TO A CAREER IN THE MARINE SCIENCES AND ATTEND A USA SCHOOL. UNDERGRADS SHOULD HAVE AT LEAST A 3.5 GPA; GRADUATES AT LEAST 3.0. MUST DEMONSTRATE FINANCIAL NEED.

AVERAGE OF 9 AWARDS PER YEAR. APPLICATIONS MUST BE RECEIVED BY MAR 15 DEADLINE TO BE CONSIDERED. WRITE FOR COMPLETE INFORMATION.

623 ---

WOMAN'S SEAMAN'S FRIEND SOCIETY OF CONNECTICUT INC. (SCHOLARSHIP PROGRAM)
74 FORBES AVE
NEW HAVEN CT 06512
203-467-3887
AMOUNT: VARIES
DEADLINE(S): APR 1 FOR SUMMER STUDIES; MAY 15 FOR FALL AND SPRING
FIELD(S): MARINE SCIENCES

OPEN TO CONNECTICUT RESIDENTS WHO ARE ENROLLED IN A MARINE SCIENCES PROGRAM AT ANY COLLEGE OR ANY STATE MARITIME ACADEMY. ALSO OPEN TO RESIDENTS OF OTHER STATES WHO ARE MAJORING IN MARINE SCIENCES AT AN APPROVED CONNECTICUT INSTITUTION.

AWARDS RENEWABLE WITH REAPPLICATION. WRITE FOR COMPLETE INFORMATION.

624 ---

WOODS HOLE OCEANOGRAPHIC INSTITUTION (SUMMER STUDENT FELLOWSHIP)
FELLOWSHIPS COORDINATOR
WOODS HOLE MA 02543
508/548-1400; EXT 2200
AMOUNT: $3660 STIPEND FOR 12-WEEK PROGRAM + POSSIBLE TRAVEL ALLOWANCE
DEADLINE(S): MAR 1
FIELD(S): OCEANOGRAPHY

SUMMER FELLOWSHIPS TO STUDY OCEANOGRAPHY AT THE WOODS HOLE OCEANOGRAPHIC INSTITUTION. OPEN TO UNDERGRADUATES WHO HAVE COMPLETED THEIR JUNIOR YEAR AND BEGINNING GRADUATE STUDENTS.

APPLICANTS MUST BE STUDYING IN ANY FIELDS OF SCIENCE OR ENGINEERING AND HAVE AT LEAST A TENTATIVE INTEREST IN OCEANOGRAPHY. WRITE FOR COMPLETE INFORMATION.

NATURAL HISTORY

625 ---

COMMITTEE ON INSTITUTIONAL COOPERATION (CIC PREDOCTORAL FELLOWSHIPS)
KIRKWOOD HALL RM 111; INDIANA UNIV
BLOOMINGTON IN 47405
812/855-0822
AMOUNT: $9500 + TUITION (5 YEARS)
DEADLINE(S): JAN 2
FIELD(S): HUMANITIES; SOCIAL SCIENCES; NATURAL SCIENCES; MATHEMATICS; ENGINEERING

PREDOCTORAL FELLOWSHIPS FOR USA CITIZENS OF AFRICAN AMERICAN; AMERICAN INDIAN; MEXICAN AMERICAN OR PUERTO RICAN HERITAGE. MUST HOLD OR EXPECT TO RECEIVE BACHELOR'S DEGREE BY LATE

SUMMER FROM A REGIONALLY ACCREDITED COLLEGE OR UNIVERSITY.
AWARDS FOR SPECIFIED UNIVERSITIES IN IL; IN; IA; MI; MN; OH; WI; PA. WRITE FOR DETAILS.

626

CREOLE-AMERICAN GENEALOGICAL SOCIETY INC (CREOLE SCHOLARSHIPS)
PO BOX 2666; CHURCH STREET STATION
NEW YORK NY 10008
WRITTEN INQUIRY ONLY
AMOUNT: $1500
DEADLINE(S): APPLY BETWEEN JAN 1 AND APR 30
FIELD(S): GENEALOGY OR LANGUAGE OR CREOLE CULTURE
AWARDS IN THE ABOVE AREAS OPEN TO INDIVIDUALS OF MIXED RACIAL ANCESTRY WHO SUBMIT A FOUR-GENERATION GENEAOLOGICAL CHART ATTESTING TO CREOLE ANCESTRY AND/OR INTERRACIAL PARENTAGE. FOR UNDERGRADUATE OR GRADUATE STUDY/RESEARCH.
FOR SCHOLARSHIP/AWARD INFORMATION SEND $2 MONEY ORDER AND SELF-ADDRESSED STAMPED ENVELOPE TO ADDRESS ABOVE. CASH AND PERSONAL CHECKS ARE NOT ACCEPTED. LETTERS WITHOUT SASE AND HANDLING CHARGE WILL NOT BE ANSWERED.

627

EARTHWATCH EXPEDITIONS INC (EARTHWATCH SCHOLARSHIP AND FELLOWSHIP PROGRAM)
PO BOX 403; 680 MOUNT AUBURN ST
WATERTOWN MA 02172
617/926-8200 OR 800/776-0188 EXT 203
AMOUNT: $100 - $2000
DEADLINE(S): FEB 15
FIELD(S): ARCHAEOLOGY; ANTHROPOLOGY; ENVIRONMENTAL STUDIES; BIOLOGY; MARINE SCIENCE
NATIONAL COMPETITION. WINNERS ARE GIVEN AN OPPORTUNITY TO WORK IN THE FIELD FOR 2-3 WEEKS WITH A PROFESSIONAL SCIENTIST ON A RESEARCH EXPEDITION. AWARDS ARE FOR HIGH SCHOOL STUDENTS AND TEACHERS ONLY.
250 AWARDS PER YEAR. WRITE FOR COMPLETE INFORMATION.

628

EDMUND NILES HUYCK PRESERVE (GRADUATE AND POST-GRADUATE RESEARCH GRANTS)
MAIN ST
RENSSELAERVILLE NY 12147
518/797-3440
AMOUNT: UP TO $3500
DEADLINE(S): FEB 1
FIELD(S): ECOLOGY; BEHAVIOR; EVOLUTION; NATURAL HISTORY
GRANTS TO SUPPORT GRADUATE AND POST-GRADUATE SCIENTISTS CONDUCTING RESEARCH ON THE NATURAL RESOURCES OF THE HUYCK PRESERVE. FUNDS ARE NOT AVAILABLE TO HELP STUDENTS DEFRAY COLLEGE EXPENSES.
HOUSING AND LAB SPACE ARE PROVIDED AT THE PRESERVE. WRITE FOR COMPLETE INFORMATION.

629

SMITHSONIAN INSTITUTION (COOPER-HEWITT MUSEUM OF DESIGN SUMMER INTERNSHIPS)
COOPER-HEWITT MUSEUM; 2 EAST 91ST ST
NEW YORK NY 10128
212/860-6868; FAX 212/860-6909
AMOUNT: VARIES
DEADLINE(S): MAR 31
FIELD(S): ART; DESIGN; ARCHITECTURE; MUSEUM STUDIES
10-WEEK SUMMER INTERNSHIPS AT THE COOPER-HEWITT MUSEUM OPEN TO UNDERGRADUATE AND GRADUATE STUDENTS.
WRITE FOR COMPLETE INFORMATION.

630

SMITHSONIAN INSTITUTION (MINORITY UNDERGRADUATE & GRADUATE INTERNSHIP)
OFFICE OF FELLOWSHIPS & GRANTS; 955 L'ENFANT PLAZA; SUITE 7300
WASHINGTON DC 20560
202/287-3271
AMOUNT: $250 - $300 PER WEEK STIPEND + TRAVEL
DEADLINE(S): FEB 15; JUN 15; OCT 15
FIELD(S): DESIGN; ARCHITECTURE; ART; MUSEUM STUDIES
INTERNSHIPS OPEN TO MINORITY STUDENTS FOR RESEARCH & STUDY AT THE

SMITHSONIAN OR THE COOPER-HEWITT MUSEUM OF DESIGN IN NEW YORK CITY. THE MUSEUM'S COLLECTION SPANS 3000 YEARS OF DESIGN FROM ANCIENT POTTERY TO MODERN FASHION & ADVERTISING.

UNDERGRADUATES RECEIVE $250 PER WEEK STIPEND & GRADUATE STUDENTS RECEIVE $300 PER WEEK STIPEND. WRITE FOR COMPLETE INFORMATION.

631

SMITHSONIAN INSTITUTION (PETER KRUEGER SUMMER INTERNSHIP PROGRAM)

COOPER-HEWETT MUSEUM; 2 EAST 91ST ST
NEW YORK NY 10128
212/860-6868; FAX 212/860-6909

AMOUNT: $2500

DEADLINE(S): MAR 31

FIELD(S): ART HISTORY; ARCHITECTURAL HISTORY; DESIGN

TEN WEEK SUMMER INTERNSHIPS OPEN TO GRADUATE AND UNDERGRADUATE STUDENTS CONSIDERING A CAREER IN THE MUSEUM PROFESSION. INTERNS WILL ASSIST ON SPECIAL RESEARCH OR EXHIBITION PROJECTS AND PARTICIPATE IN DAILY MUSEUM ACTIVITIES.

INTERNSHIP COMMENCES IN JUNE AND ENDS IN AUGUST. HOUSING IS NOT PROVIDED. WRITE FOR COMPLETE INFORMATION.

632

U.S. MARINE CORPS HISTORICAL CENTER (COLLEGE INTERNSHIPS)

BUILDING 58; WASHINGTON NAVY YARD
WASHINGTON DC 20374
202/433-3839

AMOUNT: APPROX $500 FOR DAILY EXPENSES

DEADLINE(S): NONE SPECIFIED

FIELD(S): U.S. MILITARY HISTORY; HISTORIAN; LIBRARY SCIENCE; MUSEUM STUDIES

OPEN TO UNDERGRADUATE STUDENTS AT A COLLEGE OR UNIVERSITY WHICH WILL GRANT ACADEMIC CREDIT FOR WORK EXPERIENCE AS INTERNS AT THE ADDRESS ABOVE OR AT THE MARINE CORPS AIRGROUND MUSEUM IN QUANTICO VIRGINIA.

ALL INTERNSHIPS ARE REGARDED AS BEGINNING PROFESSIONAL-LEVEL HISTORIAN; CURATOR; LIBRARIAN OR ARCHIVIST POSITIONS. WRITE FOR COMPLETE INFORMATION.

SCHOOL OF SCIENCE

633

ALEXANDER GRAHAM BELL ASSOCIATION FOR THE DEAF (ROBERT H. WEITBRECHT SCHOLARSHIP AWARD)

3417 VOLTA PLACE
WASHINGTON DC 20007
202/337-5220

AMOUNT: $750

DEADLINE(S): APR 15

FIELD(S): ENGINEERING/SCIENCE

OPEN TO ORAL DEAF STUDENTS WHO WERE BORN WITH A PROFOUND HEARING IMPAIRMENT OR WHO SUFFERED SUCH A LOSS BEFORE ACQUIRING LANGUAGE. MUST BE ACCEPTED INTO A FULL-TIME ACADEMIC PROGRAM FOR HEARING STUDENTS. NORTH AMERICA CITIZEN.

WRITE FOR COMPLETE INFORMATION.

634

AMERICAN INDIAN SCIENCE & ENGINEERING SOCIETY (SANTA FE PACIFIC FOUNDATION SCHOLARSHIPS)

1630 30TH ST; SUITE 301
BOULDER CO 80301
303/492-8658

AMOUNT: UP TO $2500 PER YEAR FOR 4 YEARS

DEADLINE(S): MAR 15

FIELD(S): BUSINESS; ENGINEERING; SCIENCE; HEALTH ADMINISTRATION

OPEN TO GRADUATING HIGH SCHOOL SENIORS WITH 1/4 DEGREE OR MORE INDIAN BLOOD. MUST RESIDE IN KS; OK; CO; AZ; NM OR SAN BERNARDINO COUNTY CA (AT&SF RAILWAY SERVICE AREA). 2 OF THE 5 SCHOLARSHIPS ARE DESIGNATED FOR NAVAJO TRIBE MEMBERS.

MUST PLAN TO ATTEND A 4 YEAR POST-SECONDARY ACCREDITED EDUCATIONAL INSTITUTION. WRITE FOR COMPLETE INFORMATION.

635

CAPE CANAVERAL CHAPTER RETIRED OFFICERS ASSOC (SCHOLARSHIPS)

PO BOX 4186
PATRICK AFB FL 32925
WRITTEN INQUIRY

AMOUNT: APPROX $1500 PER YEAR

DEADLINE(S): MAY 31
FIELD(S): SCIENCE; MATHEMATICS; ENGINEERING; LIBERAL ARTS; CHEMISTRY
OPEN ONLY TO BREVARD COUNTY FLORIDA RESIDENTS WHO ARE UNDERGRADUATE JUNIORS OR SENIORS AT ANY 4-YEAR COLLEGE IN THE USA & THE SON OR DAUGHTER OF ACTIVE DUTY OR RETIRED MILITARY PERSONNEL. USA CITIZEN.
AWARDS RENEWABLE FOR ONE YEAR. WRITE TO THE SCHOLARSHIP PROGRAM COMMITTEE; ADDRESS ABOVE; FOR COMPLETE INFORMATION.

636

CHEMICAL MANUFACTURERS ASSOCIATION (TEACHER AWARDS)
2501 M STREET NW
WASHINGTON DC 20037
202/887-1223
AMOUNT: $2500 REGIONAL AWARD; $5000 NATIONAL
DEADLINE(S): JAN 29
FIELD(S): SCIENCE ; CHEMISTRY; CHEMICAL ENGINEERING
SIX NATIONAL AND EIGHT REGIONAL AWARDS WILL BE OFFERED TO COLLEGE AND HIGH SCHOOL CHEMISTRY OR CHEMICAL ENGINEERING TEACHERS IN THE USA OR CANADA. CRITERIA ARE EXCELLENCE IN TEACHING; DEDICATION & MOTIVATION OF STUDENTS TO SCIENCE CAREERS.
FOR TEACHERS OF GENERAL SCIENCE; CHEMISTRY AND CHEMICAL ENGINEERING ONLY. WRITE FOR COMPLETE INFORMATION.

637

CIVIL AIR PATROL (CAP UNDERGRADUATE SCHOLARSHIPS)
NATIONAL HEADQUARTERS
MAXWELL AFB AL 36112
205/293-5332
AMOUNT: $750
DEADLINE(S): MAR 15
FIELD(S): HUMANITIES; SCIENCE; ENGINEERING; EDUCATION
OPEN TO CAP MEMBERS WHO HAVE RECEIVED THE BILLY MITCHELL AWARD OR THE SENIOR RATING IN LEVEL II OF THE SENIOR TRAINING PROGRAM. FOR UNDERGRADUATE STUDY IN THE ABOVE AREAS.
WRITE FOR COMPLETE INFORMATION.

638

GENERAL LEARNING CORPORATION (DUPONT & GLC SCIENCE ESSAY AWARDS PROGRAM)
60 REVERE DR
NORTHBROOK IL 60062
800/323-5471; IN ILLINOIS 708/205-3000
AMOUNT: UP TO $1500
DEADLINE(S): JAN 15
FIELD(S): SCIENCES
ANNUAL ESSAY COMPETITION OPEN TO STUDENTS IN GRADES 7-12 IN USA & CANADA. CASH AWARDS FOR 1ST; 2ND; 3RD & HON MENTION. 1ST-PLACE ESSAYISTS; THEIR SCIENCE TEACHER & 1 PARENT RECEIVE TRIP TO NAT'L SCIENCE TEACHERS CONFERENCE IN BOSTON.
CONTACT YOUR SCIENCE TEACHER OR ADDRESS ABOVE FOR COMPLETE INFORMATION.

639

JOSEPH BLAZEK FOUNDATION (SCHOLARSHIPS)
8 SOUTH MICHIGAN AVE.
CHICAGO IL 60603
312/372-3880
AMOUNT: $750 PER YEAR FOR 4 YEARS
DEADLINE(S): FEB 1
FIELD(S): SCIENCE; CHEMISTRY; ENGINEERING; MATHEMATICS; PHYSICS
OPEN TO RESIDENTS OF COOK COUNTY (ILLINOIS) WHO ARE HIGH SCHOOL SENIORS PLANNING TO STUDY IN THE ABOVE FIELDS AT A FOUR YEAR COLLEGE OR UNIVERSITY.
20 SCHOLARSHIPS PER YEAR. RENEWABLE. WRITE FOR COMPLETE INFORMATION.

640

NATIONAL FEDERATION OF THE BLIND (HOWARD BROWN RICKARD SCHOLARSHIP)
814 4TH AVE; #200
GRINNELL IA 50112
515/236-3366
AMOUNT: $2500
DEADLINE(S): MAR 31
FIELD(S): NATURAL SCIENCES; ARCHITECTURE; ENGINEERING; MEDICINE; LAW
SCHOLARSHIPS FOR UNDERGRADUATE OR GRADUATE STUDY IN THE ABOVE AREAS. OPEN TO LEGALLY BLIND STUDENTS ENROLLED FULL TIME AT ACCREDITED POST SECONDARY INSTITUTIONS.

AWARDS BASED ON ACADEMIC EXCELLENCE; SERVICE TO THE COMMUNITY AND FINANCIAL NEED. WRITE FOR COMPLETE INFORMATION.

641

NEW YORK TELEPHONE (SCHOLARSHIP PROGRAM FOR BLACK AND HISPANIC STUDENTS)
COTE; PO BOX 2810
CHERRY HILL NJ 08034
609/573-9400
AMOUNT: $2000
DEADLINE(S): APR 30
FIELD(S): ENGINEERING; SCIENCE; COMPUTER SCIENCE; NURSING

OPEN TO BLACK OR HISPANIC STUDENTS WHO RESIDE IN NEW YORK AND ATTEND ACCREDITED NEW YORK STATE SCHOOLS. FOR FULL TIME STUDENTS ENROLLED AS A SECOND SEMESTER SOPHOMORE IN A 4 YEAR UNDERGRADUATE PROGRAM LEADING TO A BACHELOR DEGREE.

FINANCIAL NEED IS A CONSIDERATION. RENEWABLE. WRITE FOR COMPLETE INFORMATION.

642

NORTH CAROLINA OFFICE OF BUDGET AND MANAGEMENT (NC HEALTH; SCIENCES & MATH SCHOLARSHIP-LOAN PROGRAM)
116 WEST JONES ST; #2054
RALEIGH NC 27611
919-733-2164
AMOUNT: $2500 - $7500 PER YEAR
DEADLINE(S): JAN 8 - MAY 5
FIELD(S): HEALTH PROFESSIONS; SCIENCES; ENGINEERING

LOW-INTEREST SCHOLARSHIP LOANS OPEN TO NORTH CAROLINA RESIDENTS OF AT LEAST 1 YEAR WHO ARE PURSUING AN ASSOCIATES; UNDERGRADUATE OR GRADUATE DEGREE IN THE ABOVE AREAS AT AN ACCREDITED INSTITUTION IN THE USA.

LOANS MAY BE RETIRED AFTER GRADUATION BY WORKING (1 YEAR FOR EACH YEAR FUNDED) AT DESIGNATED INSTITUTIONS. WRITE FOR COMPLETE DETAILS.

643

SALES ASSOCIATION OF THE CHEMICAL INDUSTRY (FOUR-YEAR SCHOLARSHIP)
1 GAIL COURT
PISCATAWAY NJ 08854
908/463-1540
AMOUNT: $500 PER YEAR FOR 4 YEARS
DEADLINE(S): MAY 30
FIELD(S): CHEMICAL/SCIENCE RELATED STUDIES

OPEN TO HIGH SCHOOL SENIORS WHO LIVE IN NY; DE; NJ; CT; DE OR PA. OR WHO ARE RELATED TO A MEMBER OF SACI. FOR STUDY AT ANY ACCREDITED COLLEGE OR UNIVERSITY. CRITERIA ARE ACADEMIC ACHIEVEMENT AND EXTRACURRICULAR ACTIVITIES.

SEND SELF-ADDRESSED STAMPED ENVELOPE (BUSINESS SIZE) FOR COMPLETE INFORMATION.

644

SCIENCE SERVICE (WESTINGHOUSE SCIENCE SCHOLARSHIPS AND AWARDS)
1719 'N' STREET NW
WASHINGTON DC 20036
202/785-2255
AMOUNT: $1000 - $10000 PER YEAR FOR 4 YEARS
DEADLINE(S): DEC 1
FIELD(S): ENGINEERING; SCIENCE; MATHEMATICS

OPEN TO HIGH SCHOOL SENIORS WHO EXPECT TO COMPLETE COLLEGE ENTRANCE QUALIFICATIONS BEFORE OCT 1. NO AGE LIMIT. ONE OF THE REQUIREMENTS WILL BE A WRITTEN REPORT ON AN INDEPENDENT SCIENTIFIC RESEARCH PROJECT. USA CITIZEN OR LEGAL RESIDENT.

40 AWARDS PER YEAR WHICH ARE RENEWED FOR THREE SUBSEQUENT YEARS. WRITE FOR COMPLETE INFORMATION.

645

SOCIETY OF HISPANIC PROFESSIONAL ENGINEERS FOUNDATION (SHPE SCHOLARSHIPS)
5400 E OLYMPIC BLVD; SUITE 306
LOS ANGELES CA 90022
213/888-2080
AMOUNT: $500 - $3000
DEADLINE(S): APR 15
FIELD(S): ENGINEERING & SCIENCE

OPEN TO DESERVING STUDENTS OF HISPANIC DESCENT WHO ARE SEEKING CAREERS IN ENGINEERING AND SCIENCE. FOR FULL TIME UNDERGRADUATE OR GRADUATE STUDY AT A COLLEGE OR UNIVERSITY. ACADEMIC ACHIEVEMENT AND FINANCIAL NEED ARE CONSIDERATIONS.

WRITE FOR COMPLETE INFORMATION.

646

TANDY TECHNOLOGY SCHOLARS (STUDENT SCHOLARSHIPS; TEACHER AWARDS)

TCU STATION; BOX 32897
FORT WORTH TX 76129
817/924-4087

AMOUNT: $1000 STUDENTS; $2500 TEACHERS

DEADLINE(S): OCT 16

FIELD(S): MATHEMATICS; SCIENCE; COMPUTER SCIENCE

PROGRAM RECOGNIZES ACADEMIC PERFORMANCE AND OUTSTANDING ACHIEVEMENTS BY MATHEMATICS; SCIENCE AND COMPUTER SCIENCE STUDENTS AND TEACHERS. STUDENTS RECEIVE SCHOLARSHIP FOR UNDERGRADUATE STUDY; TEACHERS GET CASH.

MUST BE A SENIOR IN AN ENROLLED HIGH SCHOOL LOCATED IN ONE OF THE 50 STATES. 100 STUDENT & 100 TEACHER AWARDS PER YEAR. WRITE FOR COMPLETE INFORMATION.

647

THOMAS ALVA EDISON FOUNDATION (EDISON/MCGRAW SCHOLARSHIP PROGRAM)

3000 BOOK BUILDING
DETROIT MI 48226
313/965-1149

AMOUNT: $5000 SCHOLARSHIPS (2); $1000 SCHOLARSHIPS (10)

DEADLINE(S): DEC 1

FIELD(S): SCIENCE; ENGINEERING & TECHNOLOGY

OUTSTANDING HIGH SCHOOL STUDENTS. NO FORMAL APPLICATION. SUBMIT A PROPOSAL NOT TO EXCEED 1000 WORDS ON A COMPLETED EXPERIMENT OR A PROJECT IDEA WHICH WOULD HAVE 'PRACTICAL APPLICATION' IN FIELDS OF SCIENCE AND/OR ENGINEERING.

INCLUDE LETTER OF RECOMMENDATION FROM A TEACHER OR SPONSOR WHICH DESCRIBES HOW YOU EXEMPLIFY CREATIVITY & INGENUITY DEMONSTRATED BY LIFE & WORK OF THOMAS EDISON & MAX MCGRAW. MAIL ENTRY TO DR. R.A.DEAN; BOX 2800; LA JOLLA CA 92038-2800.

648

WILLIAM M. GRUPE FOUNDATION INC (SCHOLARSHIPS)

PO BOX 775
LIVINGSTON NJ 07039
201/661-9387

AMOUNT: $500 - $2000

DEADLINE(S): MAR 1

FIELD(S): MEDICINE; NURSING

FOR RESIDENTS OF BERGEN; ESSEX OR HUDSON COUNTY NJ. ANNUAL SCHOLARSHIP AID TO GOOD STUDENTS IN NEED OF FINANCIAL SUPPORT IN THE ABOVE FIELDS. USA CITIZEN.

50-100 AWARDS PER YEAR. STUDENTS MAY APPLY EVERY YEAR. WRITE FOR COMPLETE INFORMATION.

BIOLOGY

649

AMERICAN SOCIETY FOR ENOLOGY AND VITICULTURE (SCHOLARSHIP)

PO BOX 1855
DAVIS CA 95617
916/753-3142

AMOUNT: NO PREDETERMINED AMOUNTS

DEADLINE(S): MAR 1

FIELD(S): ENOLOGY (WINE MAKING); VITICULTURE (GRAPE GROWING)

FOR COLLEGE JUNIORS; SENIORS OR GRAD STUDENTS ENROLLED IN AN ACCREDITED NORTH AMERICAN COLLEGE OR UNIVERSITY IN A SCIENCE CURRICULUM BASIC TO THE WINE AND GRAPE INDUSTRY. NORTH AMERICAN RESIDENT.

UNDERGRADS NEED 3.0 OR BETTER OVERALL GPA; GRADS 3.2 OR BETTER OVERALL GPA. SCHOLARSHIPS ARE RENEWABLE; FINANCIAL NEED IS CONSIDERED. WRITE FOR COMPLETE INFORMATION.

650

AMERICAN SOCIETY OF ZOOLOGISTS (LIBBIE H. HYMAN SCHOLARSHIP FUND)

104 SIRIUS CIRCLE
THOUSAND OAKS CA 91360

WRITTEN INQUIRY ONLY
AMOUNT: VARIES
DEADLINE(S): MAR 30
FIELD(S): ZOOLOGY - SUMMER RESEARCH
OPEN TO COLLEGE SENIORS AND BEGINNING GRADUATE STUDENTS. MODEST GRANTS IN AID INTENDED TO PARTIALLY SUPPORT SUMMER FIELD STATION RESEARCH.
REQUEST APPLICATIONS FROM DR. JOSEPH L. SIMON; DEPT. OF BIOLOGY; UNIV. OF SOUTH FLA; TAMPA FL 33620

651

ARTHUR & DOREEN PARRETT SCHOLARSHIP TRUST FUND (SCHOLARSHIPS)
C/O U.S. BANK OF WASHINGTON; PO BOX 720; TRUST DEPT; 4TH FLOOR
SEATTLE WA 98111
206/344-3691
AMOUNT: UP TO $1000
DEADLINE(S): JUL 31
FIELD(S): ENGINEERING; SCIENCE; MEDICINE; DENTISTRY
WASHINGTON STATE RESIDENT. UNDERGRADUATE SCHOLARSHIPS OPEN TO STUDENTS WHO ARE ENROLLED IN ABOVE SCHOOLS. AWARDS TENABLE AT ANY ACCREDITED UNDERGRADUATE COLLEGE OR UNIVERSITY. USA CITIZEN OR LEGAL RESIDENT.
APPROXIMATELY 15 AWARDS PER YEAR. WRITE FOR COMPLETE INFORMATION.

652

ASSOCIATION OF OFFICIAL ANALYTICAL CHEMISTS (HARVEY W. WILEY SCHOLARSHIP AWARD)
2200 WILSON BLVD; SUITE 400
ARLINGTON VA 22201
703-522-3032
AMOUNT: $500 PER YEAR FOR 2 YEARS
DEADLINE(S): MAY 1 OF SOPHOMORE YEAR
FIELD(S): CHEMISTRY; MICROBIOLOGY & RELATED SCIENCES
OPEN TO UNDERGRADUATE SOPHOMORES WHO HAVE MAINTAINED AT LEAST 'B' AVERAGE. AWARDS ARE FOR JUNIOR & SENIOR YEAR IN ABOVE AREAS. MEDICAL; DENTAL; NURSING; ETC MAJORS NOT ELIGIBLE.
WRITE FOR COMPLETE INFORMATION.

653

BUSINESS AND PROFESSIONAL WOMEN'S FOUNDATION (CAREER ADVANCEMENT SCHOLARSHIPS)
2012 MASSACHUSETTS AVE NW
WASHINGTON DC 20036
202/293-1200
AMOUNT: $500 - $1000
DEADLINE(S): APR 15 POSTMARK (APPS AVAILABLE ONLY OCT 1 - APR 1)
FIELD(S): COMPUTER SCIENCE; EDUCATION; PARALEGAL; ENGINEERING; SCIENCE (EXCEPT HEALTH CARE)
OPEN TO WOMEN (30 OR OLDER) WITHIN 12-24 MONTHS OF COMPLETING UNDERGRAD OR GRAD STUDY IN USA (INCLUDING PUERTO RICO & THE VIRGIN ISLANDS). SHOULD LEAD TO ENTRY OR REENTRY INTO THE WORK FORCE OR IMPROVE CAREER ADVANCEMENT CHANCES.
MUST SHOW FINANCIAL NEED. SEND SELF-ADDRESSED STAMPED ($.52) #10 ENVELOPE FOR APPLICATION & COMPLETE INFORMATION. NOT FOR STUDY AT DOCTORAL LEVEL.

654

COMMITTEE ON INSTITUTIONAL COOPERATION (CIC PREDOCTORAL FELLOWSHIPS)
KIRKWOOD HALL RM 111; INDIANA UNIV
BLOOMINGTON IN 47405
812/855-0822
AMOUNT: $9500 + TUITION (5 YEARS)
DEADLINE(S): JAN 2
FIELD(S): HUMANITIES; SOCIAL SCIENCES; NATURAL SCIENCES; MATHEMATICS; ENGINEERING
PREDOCTORAL FELLOWSHIPS FOR USA CITIZENS OF AFRICAN AMERICAN; AMERICAN INDIAN; MEXICAN AMERICAN OR PUERTO RICAN HERITAGE. MUST HOLD OR EXPECT TO RECEIVE BACHELOR'S DEGREE BY LATE SUMMER FROM A REGIONALLY ACCREDITED COLLEGE OR UNIVERSITY.
AWARDS FOR SPECIFIED UNIVERSITIES IN IL; IN; IA; MI; MN; OH; WI; PA. WRITE FOR DETAILS.

655

EARTHWATCH EXPEDITIONS INC. (EARTHWATCH SCHOLARSHIP AND FELLOWSHIP PROGRAM)
PO BOX 403; 680 MOUNT AUBURN ST
WATERTOWN MA 02172
617/926-8200 OR 800/776-0188 EXT 203
AMOUNT: $100 - $2000
DEADLINE(S): FEB 15
FIELD(S): ARCHAEOLOGY; ANTHROPOLOGY; ENVIRONMENTAL STUDIES; BIOLOGY; MARINE SCIENCE
NATIONAL COMPETITION. WINNERS ARE GIVEN AN OPPORTUNITY TO WORK IN THE FIELD FOR 2-3 WEEKS WITH A PROFESSIONAL SCIENTIST ON A RESEARCH EXPEDITION. AWARDS ARE FOR HIGH SCHOOL STUDENTS AND TEACHERS ONLY.
250 AWARDS PER YEAR. WRITE FOR COMPLETE INFORMATION.

656

ELECTRONIC INDUSTRIES FOUNDATION (SCHOLARSHIP FUND)
919 18TH ST; SUITE 900
WASHINGTON DC 20006
202/955-5814
AMOUNT: $2000
DEADLINE(S): FEB 1
FIELD(S): AERONAUTICS; COMPUTER SCIENCE; ELECTRICAL ENGINEERING; ENGINEERING TECHNOLOGY; APPLIED MATHEMATICS; MICROBIOLOGY
OPEN TO DISABLED STUDENTS WHO ARE PURSUING CAREERS IN HIGH-TECH AREAS THROUGH ACADEMIC OR TECHNICAL TRAINING. AWARDS TENABLE AT RECOGNIZED UNDERGRADUATE & GRADUATE COLLEGES & UNIVERSITIES. USA CITIZEN. FINANCIAL NEED IS A CONSIDERATION.
6 AWARDS PER YEAR. RENEWABLE. WRITE FOR COMPLETE INFORMATION.

657

ENTOMOLOGICAL SOCIETY OF AMERICA (SCHOLARSHIP PROGRAM)
9301 ANNAPOLIS ROAD; SUITE 300
LANHAM MD 20706
301/731-4535
AMOUNT: $500; $1500
DEADLINE(S): MAY 31
FIELD(S): ENTOMOLOGY; BIOLOGY OR RELATED SCIENCE
FOR UNDERGRADUATE STUDY IN THE ABOVE FIELDS. MUST BE A CITIZEN OF AND ENROLLED IN A RECOGNIZED COLLEGE OR UNIVERSITY IN THE USA; CANADA OR MEXICO. APPLICANTS MUST HAVE ACCUMULATED AT LEAST 30 SEMESTER HOURS BY THE TIME AWARD IS PRESENTED.
WRITE FOR COMPLETE INFORMATION.

658

NATIONAL ASSOCIATION OF WATER COMPANIES - NEW JERSEY CHAPTER (SCHOLARSHIP)
C/O NJ-AMERICAN WATER CO; EASTERN DIV 661 SHREWSBURY AVE
SHREWSBURY NJ 07702
908/842-6900; FAX 908/842-7541
AMOUNT: $2500
DEADLINE(S): APR 1 (POSTMARK)
FIELD(S): BUSINESS ADMINISTRATION; BIOLOGY; CHEMISTRY; ENGINEERING
OPEN TO USA CITIZENS WHO HAVE LIVED IN NJ AT LEAST 5 YEARS AND PLAN A CAREER IN THE INVESTOR-OWNED WATER UTILITY INDUSTRY IN DISCIPLINES SUCH AS THOSE ABOVE. MUST BE UNDERGRAD OR GRADUATE STUDENT IN A 2 OR 4 YEAR NJ COLLEGE OR UNIVERSITY.
GPA OF 3.0 OR BETTER REQUIRED. WRITE FOR COMPLETE INFORMATION.

659

NATIONAL RESEARCH COUNCIL (HOWARD HUGHES MEDICAL INSTITUTE PREDOCTORAL FELLOWSHIPS IN BIOLOGICAL SCIENCES)
FELLOWSHIP OFFC; 2101 CONSTITUTION AV NW
WASHINGTON DC 20418
202/334-2872
AMOUNT: $14000 ANNUAL STIPEND + $11700 COST OF EDUCATION ALLOWANCE
DEADLINE(S): NOV 1
FIELD(S): BIOLOGICAL SCIENCES
OPEN TO COLLEGE SENIORS OR GRADUATES AT OR NEAR THE BEGINNING OF THEIR STUDY TOWARD A PHD OR SCD IN BIOLOGICAL SCIENCES. USA CITIZENS MAY STUDY IN THE USA OR ABROAD; FOREIGN NATIONALS MAY STUDY ONLY IN THE USA.
WRITE FOR COMPLETE INFORMATION.

660

NELLIE MARTIN CARMAN SCHOLARSHIP TRUST (SCHOLARSHIPS)
1121 244TH ST SW; #65
BOTHELL WA 98021
206/486-6575
AMOUNT: UP TO $1000
DEADLINE(S): MAR 15
FIELD(S): ALL FIELDS OF STUDY EXCEPT THOSE NOTED BELOW
OPEN TO SENIORS IN KING; PIERCE & SNOHOMISH COUNTY (WA) HIGH SCHOOLS WHO HAVE LIVED IN WASHINGTON AT LEAST 5 YRS. FOR UNDERGRADUATE STUDY IN WASHINGTON IN ALL FIELDS EXCEPT MUSIC; SCULPTURE; DRAWING; INTERIOR DESIGN & HOME ECONOMICS.
APPLICATIONS AVAILABLE ONLY THROUGH HIGH SCHOOLS. NOMINATION BY HS COUNSELOR IS REQUIRED. AWARDS ARE RENEWABLE. USA CITIZEN.

661

TERATOLOGY SOCIETY (STUDENT TRAVEL GRANTS)
9650 ROCKVILLE PIKE
BETHESDA MD 20814
301/571-1841
AMOUNT: $250
DEADLINE(S): MAY 1
FIELD(S): TERATOLOGY
TRAVEL ASSISTANCE GRANTS OPEN TO UNDERGRADUATES; GRADUATES & POST-GRADUATES FOR ATTENDANCE AT THE TERATOLOGY SOCIETY'S ANNUAL MEETING FOR ABSTRACT PRESENTATION. PURPOSE IS TO PROMOTE INTEREST IN & ADVANCE STUDY OF BIOLOGICAL ABNORMALITIES.
10 AWARDS PER YEAR. WRITE FOR COMPLETE INFORMATION.

662

WILSON ORNITHOLOGICAL SOCIETY (FUERTES; NICE & STEWART GRANTS)
C/O MUSEUM OF ZOOLOGY; UNIV OF MICHIGAN
ANN ARBOR MI 48109
WRITTEN INQUIRY ONLY
AMOUNT: $200
DEADLINE(S): JAN 15
FIELD(S): ORNITHOLOGY
GRANTS TO SUPPORT AVIAN RESEARCH. OPEN TO ANYONE PRESENTING A SUITABLE RESEARCH PROBLEM IN ORNITHOLOGY. RESEARCH PROPOSAL REQUIRED.
5-6 GRANTS PER YEAR. NOT RENEWABLE. WRITE FOR COMPLETE INFORMATION.

CHEMISTRY

663

ARTHUR & DOREEN PARRETT SCHOLARSHIP TRUST FUND (SCHOLARSHIPS)
C/O U.S. BANK OF WASHINGTON; PO BOX 720; TRUST DEPT; 4TH FLOOR
SEATTLE WA 98111
206/344-3691
AMOUNT: UP TO $1000
DEADLINE(S): JUL 31
FIELD(S): ENGINEERING; SCIENCE; MEDICINE; DENTISTRY
WASHINGTON STATE RESIDENT. UNDERGRADUATE SCHOLARSHIPS OPEN TO STUDENTS WHO ARE ENROLLED IN ABOVE FIELDS. AWARDS TENABLE AT ANY ACCREDITED UNDERGRADUATE COLLEGE OR UNIVERSITY. USA CITIZEN OR LEGAL RESIDENT.
APPROXIMATELY 15 AWARDS PER YEAR. WRITE FOR COMPLETE INFORMATION.

664

ASSOCIATION OF OFFICIAL ANALYTICAL CHEMISTS (HARVEY W. WILEY SCHOLARSHIP AWARD)
2200 WILSON BLVD; SUITE 400
ARLINGTON VA 22201
703-522-3032
AMOUNT: $500 PER YEAR FOR 2 YEARS
DEADLINE(S): MAY 1 OF SOPHOMORE YEAR
FIELD(S): CHEMISTRY; MICROBIOLOGY & RELATED SCIENCES
OPEN TO UNDERGRADUATE SOPHOMORES WHO HAVE MAINTAINED AT LEAST 'B' AVERAGE. AWARDS ARE FOR JUNIOR & SENIOR YEAR IN ABOVE AREAS. MEDICAL; DENTAL; NURSING; ETC MAJORS NOT ELIGIBLE.
WRITE FOR COMPLETE INFORMATION.

665

AT&T BELL LABORATORIES (SUMMER RESEARCH PROGRAM FOR MINORITIES & WOMEN)
101 CRAWFORDS CORNER RD; RM 1B-209
HOLMDEL NJ 07733
908/949-3728

AMOUNT: SALARY + TRAVEL & LIVING EXPENSES FOR SUMMER
DEADLINE(S): DEC 1
FIELD(S): ENGINEERING; MATH; SCIENCES; COMPUTER SCIENCE
PROGRAM OFFERS MINORITY STUDENTS & WOMEN STUDENTS TECHNICAL EMPLOYMENT EXPERIENCE AT BELL LABORATORIES. STUDENTS SHOULD HAVE COMPLETED THEIR THIRD YEAR OF STUDY AT AN ACCREDITED COLLEGE OR UNIVERSITY. USA CITIZEN OR PERMANENT RESIDENT.
SELECTION IS BASED PARTIALLY ON ACADEMIC ACHIEVEMENT AND PERSONAL MOTIVATION. WRITE SPECIAL PROGRAMS MANAGER - SRP FOR COMPLETE INFORMATION.

666

BUSINESS AND PROFESSIONAL WOMEN'S FOUNDATION (CAREER ADVANCEMENT SCHOLARSHIPS)
2012 MASSACHUSETTS AVE NW
WASHINGTON DC 20036
202/293-1200
AMOUNT: $500 - $1000
DEADLINE(S): APR 15 POSTMARK (APPS AVAILABLE ONLY OCT 1 - APR 1)
FIELD(S): COMPUTER SCIENCE; EDUCATION; PARALEGAL; ENGINEERING; SCIENCE (EXCEPT HEALTH CARE)
OPEN TO WOMEN (30 OR OLDER) WITHIN 12-24 MONTHS OF COMPLETING UNDERGRAD OR GRAD STUDY IN USA (INCLUDING PUERTO RICO & THE VIRGIN ISLANDS). SHOULD LEAD TO ENTRY OR REENTRY INTO THE WORK FORCE OR IMPROVE CAREER ADVANCEMENT CHANCES.
MUST SHOW FINANCIAL NEED. SEND SELF-ADDRESSED STAMPED ($.52) #10 ENVELOPE FOR APPLICATION & COMPLETE INFORMATION. NOT FOR STUDY AT DOCTORAL LEVEL.

667

CAPE CANAVERAL CHAPTER RETIRED OFFICERS ASSOC (SCHOLARSHIPS)
PO BOX 4186
PATRICK AFB FL 32925
WRITTEN INQUIRY
AMOUNT: APPROX $1500 PER YEAR
DEADLINE(S): MAY 31
FIELD(S): SCIENCE; MATHEMATICS; ENGINEERING; LIBERAL ARTS; CHEMISTRY
OPEN ONLY TO BREVARD COUNTY FLORIDA RESIDENTS WHO ARE UNDERGRADUATE JUNIORS OR SENIORS AT ANY 4-YEAR COLLEGE IN THE USA & THE SON OR DAUGHTER OF ACTIVE DUTY OR RETIRED MILITARY PERSONNEL. USA CITIZEN.
AWARDS RENEWABLE FOR ONE YEAR. WRITE TO THE SCHOLARSHIP PROGRAM COMMITTEE; ADDRESS ABOVE; FOR COMPLETE INFORMATION.

668

CHEMICAL MANUFACTURERS ASSOCIATION (TEACHER AWARDS)
2501 M STREET NW
WASHINGTON DC 20037
202/887-1223
AMOUNT: $2500 REGIONAL AWARD; $5000 NATIONAL
DEADLINE(S): JAN 29
FIELD(S): SCIENCE ; CHEMISTRY; CHEMICAL ENGINEERING
SIX NATIONAL AND EIGHT REGIONAL AWARDS WILL BE OFFERED TO COLLEGE AND HIGH SCHOOL CHEMISTRY OR CHEMICAL ENGINEERING TEACHERS IN THE USA OR CANADA. CRITERIA ARE EXCELLENCE IN TEACHING; DEDICATION & MOTIVATION OF STUDENTS TO SCIENCE CAREERS.
FOR TEACHERS OF GENERAL SCIENCE; CHEMISTRY AND CHEMICAL ENGINEERING ONLY. WRITE FOR COMPLETE INFORMATION.

669

H. FLETCHER BROWN FUND (SCHOLARSHIPS)
C/O BANK OF DELAWARE; TRUST DEPT; PO BOX 791
WILMINGTON DE 19899
302/429-2827
AMOUNT: VARIES
DEADLINE(S): APR 15
FIELD(S): MEDICINE; DENTISTRY; LAW; ENGINEERING; CHEMISTRY
OPEN TO STUDENTS BORN IN DELAWARE; GRADUATED FROM A DELAWARE HIGH SCHOOL & STILL RESIDING IN DELAWARE. FOR FOUR YEARS OF STUDY (UNDERGRAD OR GRAD) LEADING TO A DEGREE THAT ENABLES APPLICANT TO PRACTICE IN CHOSEN FIELD.

SCHOLARSHIPS ARE BASED ON NEED; SCHOLASTIC ACHIEVEMENT; GOOD MORAL CHARACTER. RENEWABLE. WRITE FOR COMPLETE INFORMATION.

670

INTERNATIONAL ORDER OF THE KING'S DAUGHTERS AND SONS (HEALTH CAREERS SCHOLARSHIPS)

PO BOX 1017
CHAUTAUQUA NY 14722
716/357-4951

AMOUNT: UP TO $1000
DEADLINE(S): APR 1
FIELD(S): MEDICINE; DENTISTRY; NURSING; PHYSICAL THERAPY; OCCUPATIONAL THERAPY; MEDICAL TECHNOLOGIES; PHARMACY

OPEN TO STUDENTS ACCEPTED TO/ENROLLED IN AN ACCREDITED USA OR CANADIAN 4-YR OR GRADUATE SCHOOL. RN CANDIDATES MUST HAVE COMPLETED 1ST YEAR; BA CANDIDATES IN AT LEAST 3RD YEAR. PRE MED STUDENTS NOT ELIGIBLE.

USA OR CANADIAN CITIZEN. THOSE SEEKING MD OR DDS DEGREES MUST BE IN 2ND YR OF MED OR DENTAL SCHOOL. FOR APPLICATIONS AND COMPLETE INFO SEND SASE TO MRS. MERLE RABER; 6024 E CHICAGO RD; JONESVILLE MI 49250.

671

NAACP NATIONAL HEADQUARTERS (NAACP WILLEMS SCHOLARSHIP)

4805 MOUNT HOPE DR
BALTIMORE MD 21215
301/358-8900

AMOUNT: $2000 - $3000
DEADLINE(S): APR 30
FIELD(S): ENGINEERING; CHEMISTRY; PHYSICS; COMPUTER SCIENCE; MATHEMATICS

OPEN TO NAACP MEMBERS MAJORING IN ONE OF THE ABOVE AREAS AND POSSESS A CUMULATIVE GPA OF 3.0 OR BETTER. UNDERGRADS RECEIVE MAXIMUM OF $8000 IN ANNUAL INSTALLMENTS OF $2000. GRADUATES ARE AWARDED A $3000 SCHOLARSHIP WHICH CAN BE RENEWED.

WRITE FOR COMPLETE INFORMATION.

672

NATIONAL ASSOCIATION OF WATER COMPANIES - NEW JERSEY CHAPTER (SCHOLARSHIP)

C/O NJ-AMERICAN WATER CO; EASTERN DIV 661 SHREWSBURY AVE
SHREWSBURY NJ 07702
908/842-6900; FAX 908/842-7541

AMOUNT: $2500
DEADLINE(S): APR 1 (POSTMARK)
FIELD(S): BUSINESS ADMINISTRATION; BIOLOGY; CHEMISTRY; ENGINEERING

OPEN TO USA CITIZENS WHO HAVE LIVED IN NJ AT LEAST 5 YEARS AND PLAN A CAREER IN THE INVESTOR-OWNED WATER UTILITY INDUSTRY IN DISCIPLINES SUCH AS THOSE ABOVE. MUST BE UNDERGRAD OR GRADUATE STUDENT IN A 2 OR 4 YEAR NJ COLLEGE OR UNIVERSITY.

GPA OF 3.0 OR BETTER REQUIRED. WRITE FOR COMPLETE INFORMATION.

673

NELLIE MARTIN CARMAN SCHOLARSHIP TRUST (SCHOLARSHIPS)

1121 244TH ST SW; #65
BOTHELL WA 98021
206/486-6575

AMOUNT: UP TO $1000
DEADLINE(S): MAR 15
FIELD(S): ALL FIELDS OF STUDY EXCEPT THOSE NOTED BELOW

OPEN TO SENIORS IN KING; PIERCE & SNOHOMISH COUNTY (WA) HIGH SCHOOLS WHO HAVE LIVED IN WASHINGTON AT LEAST 5 YRS. FOR UNDERGRADUATE STUDY IN WASHINGTON IN ALL FIELDS EXCEPT MUSIC; SCULPTURE; DRAWING; INTERIOR DESIGN & HOME ECONOMICS.

APPLICATIONS AVAILABLE ONLY THROUGH HIGH SCHOOLS. NOMINATION BY HS COUNSELOR IS REQUIRED. AWARDS ARE RENEWABLE. USA CITIZEN.

674

ROBERT SCHRECK MEMORIAL FUND (GRANTS)

C/O TEXAS COMMERCE BANK-TRUST DEPT; PO DRAWER 140
EL PASO TX 79980
915/546-6515

AMOUNT: $500 - $1500
DEADLINE(S): JUL 15; NOV 15

FIELD(S): MEDICINE; VETERINARY MEDICINE; PHYSICS; CHEMISTRY; ARCHITECTURE; ENGINEERING; EPISCOPAL CLERGY

GRANTS TO UNDERGRADUATE JUNIORS OR SENIORS OR GRADUATE STUDENTS WHO HAVE BEEN RESIDENTS OF EL PASO COUNTY FOR AT LEAST TWO YEARS. MUST BE USA CITIZEN OR LEGAL RESIDENT AND HAVE A HIGH GRADE POINT AVERAGE. FINANCIAL NEED IS A CONSIDERATION.

WRITE FOR COMPLETE INFORMATION.

675

SALES ASSOCIATION OF THE CHEMICAL INDUSTRY (FOUR-YEAR SCHOLARSHIP)

1 GAIL COURT
PISCATAWAY NJ 08854
908/463-1540

AMOUNT: $500 PER YEAR FOR 4 YEARS
DEADLINE(S): MAY 30
FIELD(S): CHEMICAL/SCIENCE RELATED STUDIES

OPEN TO HIGH SCHOOL SENIORS WHO LIVE IN NY; DE; NJ; CT; DE OR PA. OR WHO ARE RELATED TO A MEMBER OF SACI. FOR STUDY AT ANY ACCREDITED COLLEGE OR UNIVERSITY. CRITERIA ARE ACADEMIC ACHIEVEMENT AND EXTRACURRICULAR ACTIVITIES.

SEND SELF-ADDRESSED STAMPED ENVELOPE (BUSINESS SIZE) FOR COMPLETE INFORMATION.

676

SALES ASSOCIATION OF THE CHEMICAL INDUSTRY (ONE-YEAR SCHOLARSHIP)

ONE GAIL COURT
PISCATAWAY NJ 08854
908/463-1540

AMOUNT: $500
DEADLINE(S): MAY 30
FIELD(S): CHEMISTRY

OPEN TO RESIDENTS OF CT; NY; NJ; PA OR DE OR TO THOSE WHO ARE RELATED TO A SACI MEMBER. FOR UNDERGRADUATE OR GRADUATE STUDY AT ACCREDITED COLLEGES OR UNIVERSITIES. USA CITIZEN OR LEGAL RESIDENT.

CRITERIA ARE ACADEMIC ACHIEVEMENT AND EXTRACURRICULAR ACTIVITIES. SEND SELF-ADDRESSED STAMPED ENVELOPE (BUSINESS SIZE) FOR COMPLETE INFORMATION.

MATHEMATICS

677

AMERICAN PHYSICAL SOCIETY (SCHOLARSHIPS FOR MINORITY UNDERGRADUATE STUDENTS IN PHYSICS)

335 EAST 45TH STREET
NEW YORK NY 10017
212/682-7341

AMOUNT: $2000
DEADLINE(S): FEB 25
FIELD(S): PHYSICS

OPEN TO ANY BLACK; HISPANIC OR AMERICAN INDIAN USA CITIZEN WHO IS MAJORING OR PLANS TO MAJOR IN PHYSICS AND IS A HIGH SCHOOL SENIOR OR COLLEGE FRESHMAN OR SOPHOMORE.

EACH SCHOLARSHIP IS SPONSORED BY A CORPORATION. WRITE FOR COMPLETE INFORMATION.

678

ARGONNE NATIONAL LABORATORY (STUDENT RESEARCH PARTICIPATION PROGRAM; THESIS RESEARCH)

DIV OF EDUCATIONAL PROGRAMS; 9700 SOUTH CASS AVE
ARGONNE IL 60439
312/972-3366

AMOUNT: $200 PER WEEK STIPEND
DEADLINE(S): FEB 1; MAY 15; OCT 15
FIELD(S): PHYSICAL SCIENCES; LIFE SCIENCES; EARTH SCIENCES; MATHEMATICS; COMPUTER SCIENCES; ENGINEERING; FUSION & FISSION ENERGY

1-SEMESTER ACCREDITED INTERNSHIP PROGRAM TO PERMIT STUDENTS TO WORK IN ABOVE AREAS IN RELATION TO ENERGY DEVELOPMENT. OPEN TO FULL-TIME UNDERGRAD JUNIORS; SENIORS & 1ST YEAR GRAD STUDENTS. USA CITIZEN OR LEGAL RESIDENT.

THESIS RESEARCH AWARDS OPEN TO DOCTORAL CANDIDATES WORKING ON THEIR DISSERTATION. WRITE FOR COMPLETE INFORMATION.

679

ARTHUR & DOREEN PARRETT SCHOLARSHIP TRUST FUND (SCHOLARSHIPS)

C/O U.S. BANK OF WASHINGTON; PO BOX 720; TRUST DEPT; 4TH FLOOR
SEATTLE WA 98111

206/344-3691
AMOUNT: UP TO $1000
DEADLINE(S): JUL 31
FIELD(S): ENGINEERING; SCIENCE; MEDICINE; DENTISTRY
WASHINGTON STATE RESIDENT. UNDERGRADUATE SCHOLARSHIPS OPEN TO STUDENTS WHO ARE ENROLLED IN ABOVE SCHOOLS. AWARDS TENABLE AT ANY ACCREDITED UNDERGRADUATE COLLEGE OR UNIVERSITY. USA CITIZEN OR LEGAL RESIDENT.
APPROXIMATELY 15 AWARDS PER YEAR. WRITE FOR COMPLETE INFORMATION.

680 ---

AT&T BELL LABORATORIES (SUMMER RESEARCH PROGRAM FOR MINORITIES & WOMEN)
101 CRAWFORDS CORNER RD; RM 1B-209
HOLMDEL NJ 07733
908/949-3728
AMOUNT: SALARY + TRAVEL & LIVING EXPENSES FOR SUMMER
DEADLINE(S): DEC 1
FIELD(S): ENGINEERING; MATH; SCIENCES; COMPUTER SCIENCE
PROGRAM OFFERS MINORITY STUDENTS & WOMEN STUDENTS TECHNICAL EMPLOYMENT EXPERIENCE AT BELL LABORATORIES. STUDENTS SHOULD HAVE COMPLETED THEIR THIRD YEAR OF STUDY AT AN ACCREDITED COLLEGE OR UNIVERSITY. USA CITIZEN OR PERMANENT RESIDENT.
SELECTION IS BASED PARTIALLY ON ACADEMIC ACHIEVEMENT AND PERSONAL MOTIVATION. WRITE SPECIAL PROGRAMS MANAGER - SRP FOR COMPLETE INFORMATION.

681 ---

BUSINESS AND PROFESSIONAL WOMEN'S FOUNDATION (CAREER ADVANCEMENT SCHOLARSHIPS)
2012 MASSACHUSETTS AVE NW
WASHINGTON DC 20036
202/293-1200
AMOUNT: $500 - $1000
DEADLINE(S): APR 15 POSTMARK (APPS AVAILABLE ONLY OCT 1 - APR 1)
FIELD(S): COMPUTER SCIENCE; EDUCATION; PARALEGAL; ENGINEERING; SCIENCE (EXCEPT HEALTH CARE)
OPEN TO WOMEN (30 OR OLDER) WITHIN 12-24 MONTHS OF COMPLETING UNDERGRAD OR GRAD STUDY IN USA (INCLUDING PUERTO RICO & THE VIRGIN ISLANDS). SHOULD LEAD TO ENTRY OR REENTRY INTO THE WORK FORCE OR IMPROVE CAREER ADVANCEMENT CHANCES.
MUST SHOW FINANCIAL NEED. SEND SELF-ADDRESSED STAMPED ($.52) #10 ENVELOPE FOR APPLICATION & COMPLETE INFORMATION. NOT FOR STUDY AT DOCTORAL LEVEL.

682 ---

CAPE CANAVERAL CHAPTER RETIRED OFFICERS ASSOC (SCHOLARSHIPS)
PO BOX 4186
PATRICK AFB FL 32925
WRITTEN INQUIRY
AMOUNT: APPROX $1500 PER YEAR
DEADLINE(S): MAY 31
FIELD(S): SCIENCE; MATHEMATICS; ENGINEERING; LIBERAL ARTS; CHEMISTRY
OPEN ONLY TO BREVARD COUNTY FLORIDA RESIDENTS WHO ARE UNDERGRADUATE JUNIORS OR SENIORS AT ANY 4-YEAR COLLEGE IN THE USA & THE SON OR DAUGHTER OF ACTIVE DUTY OR RETIRED MILITARY PERSONNEL. USA CITIZEN.
AWARDS RENEWABLE FOR ONE YEAR. WRITE TO THE SCHOLARSHIP PROGRAM COMMITTEE; ADDRESS ABOVE; FOR COMPLETE INFORMATION.

683 ---

COMMITTEE ON INSTITUTIONAL COOPERATION (CIC PREDOCTORAL FELLOWSHIPS)
KIRKWOOD HALL RM 111; INDIANA UNIV
BLOOMINGTON IN 47405
812/855-0822
AMOUNT: $9500 + TUITION (5 YEARS)
DEADLINE(S): JAN 2
FIELD(S): HUMANITIES; SOCIAL SCIENCES; NATURAL SCIENCES; MATHEMATICS; ENGINEERING
PREDOCTORAL FELLOWSHIPS FOR USA CITIZENS OF AFRICAN AMERICAN; AMERICAN INDIAN; MEXICAN AMERICAN OR PUERTO RICAN HERITAGE. MUST HOLD OR EXPECT TO RECEIVE BACHELOR'S DEGREE BY LATE

SUMMER FROM A REGIONALLY ACCREDITED COLLEGE OR UNIVERSITY.
AWARDS FOR SPECIFIED UNIVERSITIES IN IL; IN; IA; MI; MN; OH; WI; PA. WRITE FOR DETAILS.

684

ELECTRONIC INDUSTRIES FOUNDATION (SCHOLARSHIP FUND)
919 18TH ST; SUITE 900
WASHINGTON DC 20006
202/955-5814
AMOUNT: $2000
DEADLINE(S): FEB 1
FIELD(S): AERONAUTICS; COMPUTER SCIENCE; ELECTRICAL ENGINEERING; ENGINEERING TECHNOLOGY; APPLIED MATHEMATICS; MICROBIOLOGY
OPEN TO DISABLED STUDENTS WHO ARE PURSUING CAREERS IN HIGH-TECH AREAS THROUGH ACADEMIC OR TECHNICAL TRAINING. AWARDS TENABLE AT RECOGNIZED UNDERGRADUATE & GRADUATE COLLEGES & UNIVERSITIES. USA CITIZEN. FINANCIAL NEED IS A CONSIDERATION.
6 AWARDS PER YEAR. RENEWABLE. WRITE FOR COMPLETE INFORMATION.

685

HUGHES AIRCRAFT COMPANY (BACHELOR OF SCIENCE SCHOLARSHIP)
PO BOX 80028 (C1/B168) TECH. ED. CENTER
LOS ANGELES CA 90080
310-568-6711
AMOUNT: ALL EDUCATIONAL EXPENSES + SALARY & RELOCATION EXPENSES
DEADLINE(S): APPLY BETWEEN OCT & MAR PRIOR TO JUNE COMPLETION OF SOPHOMORE YEAR.
FIELD(S): ELECTRICAL MECHANICAL OR AEROSPACE ENGINEERING OR COMPUTER SCIENCE; MATHEMATICS; OR PHYSICS
OPEN TO STUDENTS WITH UPPER DIVISION STANDING OR AA DEGREE & AT LEAST A 3.0 GPA WHO HAVE BEEN ADMITTED WITHOUT CONDITION TO A UNIVERSITY ACCREDITED BY THE ACCREDITATION BOARD FOR ENGINEERING & TECHNOLOGY (ABET).
WORK STUDY OR FULL STUDY PROGRAMS. USA CITIZEN. MOST AWARDS ARE FOR WORK-STUDY NEAR HUGHES PLANTS. WRITE FOR COMPLETE INFORMATION.

686

NAACP NATIONAL HEADQUARTERS (NAACP WILLEMS SCHOLARSHIP)
4805 MOUNT HOPE DR
BALTIMORE MD 21215
301/358-8900
AMOUNT: $2000 - $3000
DEADLINE(S): APR 30
FIELD(S): ENGINEERING; CHEMISTRY; PHYSICS; COMPUTER SCIENCE; MATHEMATICS
OPEN TO NAACP MEMBERS MAJORING IN ONE OF THE ABOVE AREAS AND POSSESS A CUMULATIVE GPA OF 3.0 OR BETTER. UNDERGRADS RECEIVE MAXIMUM OF $8000 IN ANNUAL INSTALLMENTS OF $2000. GRADUATES ARE AWARDED A $3000 SCHOLARSHIP WHICH CAN BE RENEWED.
WRITE FOR COMPLETE INFORMATION.

687

NATIONAL RADIO ASTRONOMY OBSERVATORY (SUMMER RESEARCH ASSISTANTSHIPS)
EDGEMONT ROAD
CHARLOTTESVILLE VA 22903
804/296-0211
AMOUNT: $1000 - $1300 PER MONTH + TRAVEL EXPENSES
DEADLINE(S): FEB 1
FIELD(S): ASTRONOMY; PHYSICS; COMPUTER SCIENCE; ELECTRICAL ENGINEERING
SUMMER RESEARCH ASSISTANTSHIPS OPEN TO UNDERGRADUATES WHO HAVE COMPLETED AT LEAST 3 YEARS OF STUDY AND TO GRADUATE STUDENTS WHO HAVE COMPLETED NO MORE THAN 2 YEARS. TENABLE AT NRAO SITES.
APPROXIMATELY 20 AWARDS PER YEAR. WRITE FOR COMPLETE INFORMATION.

688

NELLIE MARTIN CARMAN SCHOLARSHIP TRUST (SCHOLARSHIPS)
1121 244TH ST SW; #65
BOTHELL WA 98021
206/486-6575
AMOUNT: UP TO $1000
DEADLINE(S): MAR 15
FIELD(S): ALL FIELDS OF STUDY EXCEPT THOSE NOTED BELOW
OPEN TO SENIORS IN KING; PIERCE & SNOHOMISH COUNTY (WA) HIGH SCHOOLS

WHO HAVE LIVED IN WASHINGTON AT LEAST 5 YRS. FOR UNDERGRADUATE STUDY IN WASHINGTON IN ALL FIELDS EXCEPT MUSIC; SCULPTURE; DRAWING; INTERIOR DESIGN & HOME ECONOMICS.

APPLICATIONS AVAILABLE ONLY THROUGH HIGH SCHOOLS. NOMINATION BY HS COUNSELOR IS REQUIRED. AWARDS ARE RENEWABLE. USA CITIZEN.

689

PACIFIC GAS & ELECTRIC CO. (SCHOLARSHIPS FOR HIGH SCHOOL SENIORS)

77 BEALE ST; ROOM 2837

SAN FRANCISCO CA 94106

415/973-1338

AMOUNT: $1000 - $4000

DEADLINE(S): NOV 15

FIELD(S): ENGINEERING; COMPUTER SCIENCE; MATHEMATICS; MARKETING; BUSINESS; ECONOMICS

HIGH SCHOOL SENIORS IN GOOD ACADEMIC STANDING WHO RESIDE IN OR ATTEND HIGH SCHOOL IN AREAS SERVED BY PG&E ARE ELIGIBLE TO COMPETE FOR SCHOLARSHIPS AWARDED ON A REGIONAL BASIS. NOT OPEN TO CHILDREN OF PG&E EMPLOYEES.

36 AWARDS PER YEAR. APPLICATIONS & BROCHURES ARE AVAILABLE IN ALL HIGH SCHOOLS WITHIN PG&E'S SERVICE AREA AND AT PG&E OFFICES.

690

RADIO FREE EUROPE/RADIO LIBERTY (MEDIA & OPINION RESEARCH ON EASTERN EUROPE & THE FORMER SOVIET UNION)

PERSONNEL DIVISION; 1201 CONNECTICUT AVE NW

WASHINGTON DC 20036

WRITTEN INQUIRY

AMOUNT: DAILY STIPEND OF 48 GERMAN MARKS PLUS ACCOMMODATIONS

DEADLINE(S): FEB 22

FIELD(S): COMMUNICATIONS; MARKET RESEARCH; STATISTICS; SOCIOLOGY; SOCIAL PSYCHOLOGY; EAST EUROPEAN STUDIES

INTERNSHIP OPEN TO GRADUATE STUDENT OR EXCEPTIONALLY QUALIFIED UNDERGRADUATE IN THE ABOVE AREAS WHO CAN DEMONSTRATE KNOWLEDGE OF QUANTITATIVE RESEARCH METHODS; COMPUTER APPLICATIONS AND PUBLIC OPINION SURVEY TECHNIQUES.

EAST EUROPEAN LANGUAGE SKILLS WOULD BE AN ADVANTAGE. WRITE FOR COMPLETE INFORMATION.

691

SCIENCE SERVICE (WESTINGHOUSE SCIENCE SCHOLARSHIPS AND AWARDS)

1719 'N' STREET NW

WASHINGTON DC 20036

202/785-2255

AMOUNT: $1000 - $10000 PER YEAR FOR 4 YEARS

DEADLINE(S): DEC 1

FIELD(S): ENGINEERING; SCIENCE; MATHEMATICS

OPEN TO HIGH SCHOOL SENIORS WHO EXPECT TO COMPLETE COLLEGE ENTRANCE QUALIFICATIONS BEFORE OCT 1. NO AGE LIMIT. ONE OF THE REQUIREMENTS WILL BE A WRITTEN REPORT ON AN INDEPENDENT SCIENTIFIC RESEARCH PROJECT. USA CITIZEN OR LEGAL RESIDENT.

40 AWARDS PER YEAR WHICH ARE RENEWED FOR THREE SUBSEQUENT YEARS. WRITE FOR COMPLETE INFORMATION.

692

SOCIETY OF PHYSICS STUDENTS (SPS SCHOLARSHIPS)

1825 CONNECTICUT AVE NW; #213

WASHINGTON DC 20009

202/232-6688

AMOUNT: $1000

DEADLINE(S): JAN 31

FIELD(S): PHYSICS

SPS MEMBERS. FOR FINAL YEAR OF FULL-TIME STUDY LEADING TO A BS DEGREE IN PHYSICS. CONSIDERATION GIVEN TO (1) HIGH SCHOLASTIC PERFORMANCE (2) POTENTIAL FOR CONTINUED SCHOLASTIC DEVELOPMENT IN PHYSICS AND (3) ACTIVE SPS PARTICIPATION.

NONRENEWABLE. 10 SCHOLARSHIPS PER YEAR. WRITE FOR COMPLETE INFORMATION.

693

STATE FARM COMPANIES FOUNDATION (EXCEPTIONAL STUDENT FELLOWSHIP)

1 STATE FARM PLAZA

BLOOMINGTON IL 61710

WRITTEN INQUIRY

AMOUNT: $3000

DEADLINE(S): FEB 28

FIELD(S): ACCOUNTING; BUSINESS ADMINISTRATION; ACTUARIAL SCIENCE; COMPUTER SCIENCE; ECONOMICS; FINANCE; INSURANCE; INVESTMENTS; MARKETING; MATHEMATICS; STATISTICS

OPEN TO CURRENT FULL TIME COLLEGE JUNIORS AND SENIORS MAJORING IN ANY OF THE FIELDS ABOVE. ONLY STUDENTS NOMINATED BY THE COLLEGE DEAN OR A DEPARTMENT HEAD QUALIFY AS CANDIDATES. APPLICATIONS WITHOUT NOMINATIONS WILL NOT BE CONSIDERED.

USA CITIZEN. GPA OF 3.4 OR BETTER (4.0 SCALE) IS REQUIRED. 50 FELLOWSHIPS PER YEAR. WRITE FOR COMPLETE INFORMATION.

694

STATE FARM COMPANIES FOUNDATION (EXCEPTIONAL STUDENT FELLOWSHIP AWARDS)

ONE STATE FARM PLAZA; SC-3
BLOOMINGTON IL 61710
309/766-2039

AMOUNT: $3000

DEADLINE(S): FEB 15

FIELD(S): BUSINESS RELATED FIELDS; COMPUTER SCIENCE; PRELAW; MATHEMATICS

OPEN TO EXCEPTIONAL CURRENT JUNIOR OR SENIOR UNDERGRADUATES IN THE ABOVE FIELDS. MUST BE NOMINATED BY DEAN OR DEPARTMENT HEAD. US CITIZEN. MUST BE COLLEGE JUNIOR OR SENIOR AT TIME OF APPLICATION.

50 FELLOWSHIPS PER ACADEMIC YEAR. APPLICATIONS AND NOMINATIONS AVAILABLE NOV 1. WRITE FOR COMPLETE INFORMATION.

695

TANDY TECHNOLOGY SCHOLARS (STUDENT SCHOLARSHIPS; TEACHER AWARDS)

TCU STATION; BOX 32897
FORT WORTH TX 76129
817/924-4087

AMOUNT: $1000 STUDENTS; $2500 TEACHERS

DEADLINE(S): OCT 16

FIELD(S): MATHEMATICS; SCIENCE; COMPUTER SCIENCE

PROGRAM RECOGNIZES ACADEMIC PERFORMANCE AND OUTSTANDING ACHIEVEMENTS BY MATHEMATICS; SCIENCE AND COMPUTER SCIENCE STUDENTS AND TEACHERS. STUDENTS RECEIVE SCHOLARSHIP FOR UNDERGRADUATE STUDY; TEACHERS GET CASH.

MUST BE A SENIOR IN AN ENROLLED HIGH SCHOOL LOCATED IN ONE OF THE 50 STATES. 100 STUDENT & 100 TEACHER AWARDS PER YEAR. WRITE FOR COMPLETE INFORMATION.

696

U.S. AIR FORCE ROTC (4-YEAR SCHOLARSHIP PROGRAM)

AFROTC/RROO; RECRUITING OPERATIONS BRANCH
MAXWELL AFB AL 36112
205/953-2091

AMOUNT: TUITION + FEES & BOOKS + $100 PER MONTH STIPEND

DEADLINE(S): DEC 1

FIELD(S): AERONAUTICAL ENGINEERING; CIVIL ENGINEERING; MECHANICAL ENGINEERING; MATHEMATICS; PHYSICS; NURSING & SOME LIBERAL ARTS

OPEN TO USA CITIZENS WHO ARE AT LEAST 17 AND WILL GRADUATE FROM COLLEGE BEFORE AGE 25. MUST COMPLETE APPLICATION; FURNISH SAT/ACT SCORES; HIGH SCHOOL TRANSCRIPTS AND RECORD OF EXTRACURRICULAR ACTIVITIES.

MUST QUALIFY ON AIR FORCE MEDICAL EXAMINATION. ABOUT 1600 SCHOLARSHIPS AWARDED EACH YEAR AT CAMPUSES WHICH OFFER AIR FORCE ROTC.

MEDICAL DOCTOR

697

AMERICAN INDIAN SCIENCE & ENGINEERING SOCIETY (SANTA FE PACIFIC FOUNDATION SCHOLARSHIPS)

1630 30TH ST; SUITE 301
BOULDER CO 80301
303/492-8658

AMOUNT: UP TO $2500 PER YEAR FOR 4 YEARS

DEADLINE(S): MAR 15

FIELD(S): BUSINESS; ENGINEERING; SCIENCE; HEALTH ADMINISTRATION

OPEN TO GRADUATING HIGH SCHOOL SENIORS WITH 1/4 DEGREE OR MORE INDIAN BLOOD. MUST RESIDE IN KS; OK; CO; AZ; NM OR SAN BERNARDINO COUNTY CA (AT&SF RAILWAY SERVICE AREA). 2 OF THE 5 SCHOLARSHIPS

ARE DESIGNATED FOR NAVAJO TRIBE MEMBERS.
MUST PLAN TO ATTEND A 4 YEAR POST-SECONDARY ACCREDITED EDUCATIONAL INSTITUTION. WRITE FOR COMPLETE INFORMATION.

698

AMERICAN MEDICAL ASSOCIATION (ROCK SLEYSTER MEMORIAL SCHOLARSHIP)
DIV OF UNDERGRADUATE MEDICAL EDUCATION; 515 N STATE ST
CHICAGO IL 60610
312/645-4691
AMOUNT: $2500
DEADLINE(S): MAY 1
FIELD(S): PSYCHIATRY
OPEN TO USA CITIZENS ENROLLED IN USA OR CANADIAN MEDICAL SCHOOLS THAT GRANT THE MD DEGREE WHO ASPIRE TO SPECIALIZE IN PSYCHIATRY. CANDIDATES MUST BE NOMINATED BY THEIR MEDICAL SCHOOL. NOMINEES MUST BE RISING SENIORS.
APPROX 20 SCHOLARSHIPS PER YEAR BASED ON DEMONSTRATED INTEREST IN PSYCHIATRY; SCHOLARSHIP & FINANCIAL NEED. WRITE FOR COMPLETE INFORMATION.

699

AMERICAN OSTEOPATHIC ASSOCIATION AUXILIARY (SCHOLARSHIP PROGRAM)
SCHOLARSHIP CHAIRMAN; 142 E ONTARIO ST
CHICAGO IL 60611
312/280-5819
AMOUNT: $3000 MAXIMUM
DEADLINE(S): JUN 1
FIELD(S): OSTEOPATHIC MEDICINE
OPEN TO CITIZENS OF USA OR CANADA WHO ARE ENTERING SOPHOMORE YEAR IN APPROVED COLLEGE OF OSTEOPATHIC MEDICINE. MUST BE IN TOP 20% OR HAVE HONORS FROM 1ST YEAR AND SHOW EVIDENCE OF FINANCIAL NEED AND MOTIVATION TOWARDS OSTEOPATHIC MEDICINE.
UNSPECIFIED NUMBER OF SCHOLARSHIPS PER YEAR. WRITE FOR COMPLETE INFORMATION.

700

ARTHUR & DOREEN PARRETT SCHOLARSHIP TRUST FUND (SCHOLARSHIPS)
C/O U.S. BANK OF WASHINGTON; PO BOX 720; TRUST DEPT; 4TH FLOOR
SEATTLE WA 98111
206/344-3691
AMOUNT: UP TO $1000
DEADLINE(S): JUL 31
FIELD(S): ENGINEERING; SCIENCE; MEDICINE; DENTISTRY
WASHINGTON STATE RESIDENT. UNDERGRADUATE SCHOLARSHIPS OPEN TO STUDENTS WHO ARE ENROLLED IN ABOVE SCHOOLS. AWARDS TENABLE AT ANY ACCREDITED UNDERGRADUATE COLLEGE OR UNIVERSITY. USA CITIZEN OR LEGAL RESIDENT.
APPROXIMATELY 15 AWARDS PER YEAR. WRITE FOR COMPLETE INFORMATION.

701

ASSOCIATION FOR THE CARE OF CHILDREN'S HEALTH (EMMA PLANK SCHOLARSHIP)
7910 WOODMONT AVE; SUITE 300
BETHESDA MD 20815
301/654-4549
AMOUNT: $500
DEADLINE(S): APR 1
FIELD(S): CHILD HEALTH
OPEN TO STUDENTS AT THE UNDERGRADUATE OR GRADUATE LEVEL STUDYING IN HEALTH RELATED AREAS THAT IMPACT ON CHILDREN.
WRITE FOR COMPLETE INFORMATION.

702

BOYS & GIRLS CLUBS OF SAN DIEGO (SPENCE REESE SCHOLARSHIP FUND)
3760 FOURTH AVE; SUITE 1
SAN DIEGO CA 92103
619/298-3520
AMOUNT: $2000 PER YEAR FOR 4 YEARS
DEADLINE(S): MAY 15
FIELD(S): MEDICINE; LAW; ENGINEERING; POLITICAL SCIENCE
OPEN TO MALE HIGH SCHOOL SENIORS PLANNING CAREER IN ABOVE FIELDS. PREFERENCE TO STUDENTS WITHIN A 250 MILE RADIUS OF SAN DIEGO. BOYS CLUB AFFILIATION IS NOT REQUIRED.
APPLICATIONS ARE AVAILABLE IN JANUARY. MUST ENCLOSE A SELF-ADDRESSED STAMPED

ENVELOPE TO RECEIVE APPLICATION. A $10 PROCESSING FEE IS REQUIRED WITH COMPLETED APPLICATION. WRITE FOR COMPLETE INFORMATION.

703

BUSINESS AND PROFESSIONAL WOMEN'S FOUNDATION (NEW YORK LIFE FOUNDATION SCHOLARSHIPS FOR WOMEN IN THE HEALTH PROFESSIONS)
2012 MASSACHUSETTS AVE NW
WASHINGTON DC 20036
202/293-1200
AMOUNT: $500 - $1000
DEADLINE(S): APR 15 POSTMARK (APPS. AVAILABLE ONLY OCT 1 - APR 1)
FIELD(S): HEALTH RELATED PROFESSIONS
OPEN TO WOMEN (25 OR OLDER) WHO ARE WITHIN 12-24 MONTHS OF COMPLETING THEIR UNDERGRADUATE PROGRAM OF STUDY IN USA. SHOULD LEAD TO ENTRY OR REENTRY INTO THE WORK FORCE OR IMPROVE CHANCES FOR CAREER ADVANCEMENT. USA CITIZEN.
MUST BE ACCEPTED INTO AN ACCREDITED PROGRAM AND DEMONSTRATE FINANCIAL NEED. SEND SELF-ADDRESSED STAMPED ENVELOPE (52 CENTS) #10 ENVELOPE FOR APPLICATION AND COMPLETE INFORMATION.

704

CHARLES E. SAAK TRUST (EDUCATIONAL GRANTS)
C/O WELLS FARGO BANK TRUST DEPT; 2222 W SHAW; #11
FRESNO CA 93711
WRITTEN INQUIRY ONLY
AMOUNT: VARIES
DEADLINE(S): MAR 31
FIELD(S): EDUCATION; MEDICINE
UNDERGRADUATE GRANTS FOR RESIDENTS OF THE PORTERVILLE-POPLAR AREA OF TULARE COUNTY CALIF. MUST CARRY A MINIMUM OF 12 UNITS; HAVE AT LEAST A 2.0 GPA; BE UNDER AGE 21 AND DEMONSTRATE FINANCIAL NEED.
APPROXIMATELY 100 AWARDS PER YEAR; RENEWABLE WITH REAPPLICATION. WRITE FOR COMPLETE INFORMATION.

705

CLEM JAUNICH EDUCATION TRUST (SCHOLARSHIPS)
5353 GAMBLE DR; SUITE 110
MINNEAPOLIS MN 55416
612/546-1555
AMOUNT: $750 - $3000
DEADLINE(S): JUL 15
FIELD(S): THEOLOGY; MEDICINE
OPEN TO STUDENTS WHO HAVE ATTENDED PUBLIC OR PAROCHIAL SCHOOL IN THE DELANO (MN) SCHOOL DISTRICT OR CURRENTLY RESIDE WITHIN 7 MILES OF THE CITY OF DELANO MN. AWARDS SUPPORT UNDERGRADUATE OR GRADUATE STUDY IN THEOLOGY OR MEDICINE.
4-6 SCHOLARSHIPS PER YEAR. WRITE FOR COMPLETE INFORMATION.

706

COMMUNITY FOUNDATION OF GREATER LORAIN COUNTY (A.C. SIDDALL EDUCATIONAL TRUST FUND SCHOLARSHIP)
1865 N RIDGE ROAD E; SUITE A
LORAIN OH 44055
216/277-0142 OR 216/323-4445
AMOUNT: $1000
DEADLINE(S): MAY 1
FIELD(S): HEALTH CARE
OPEN TO THOSE WHO WISH TO PURSUE OR FURTHER THEIR EDUCATION IN HEALTH CARE WHO HAVE BEEN OR ARE NOW EMPLOYED AND RESIDE IN OR WORK FOR A HEALTH CARE FACILITY WITHIN THE ALLEN MEMORIAL HOSPITAL DISTRICT IN LORAIN COUNTY.
MUST HAVE WORK EXPERIENCE AND DEMONSTRATE FINANCIAL NEED. APPLICATIONS AVAILABLE BEGINNING JAN 30 FROM ADMINISTRATOR; ALLEN MEMORIAL HOSPITAL; 200 W. LORAIN ST; OBERLIN OH 44074.

707

CUYAHOGA COUNTY MEDICAL FOUNDATION (SCHOLARSHIP GRANT PROGRAM)
11001 CEDAR AVE
CLEVELAND OH 44106
216/229-2200
AMOUNT: $500 - $1500
DEADLINE(S): JUN 1

FIELD(S): MEDICINE; DENTISTRY; PHARMACY; NURSING; OSTEOPATHY

GRANTS OPEN TO RESIDENTS OF CUYAHOGA COUNTY WHO ARE ACCEPTED TO OR ENROLLED IN AN ACCREDITED PROFESSIONAL SCHOOL IN ONE OF THE ABOVE AREAS. USA CITIZEN.

APPROX 40 AWARDS PER YEAR. WRITE FOR COMPLETE INFORMATION.

708

DUPAGE MEDICAL SOCIETY FOUNDATION (SCHOLARSHIP PROGRAM)

800 ROOSEVELT BLD B; #300
GLEN ELLYN IL 60137
312-858-9603

AMOUNT: $1000

DEADLINE(S): DEC - MAR

FIELD(S): MEDICINE; DENTISTRY; NURSING; MEDICAL TECHNOLOGY; PHARMACY

AWARDS FOR RESIDENTS OF DUPAGE COUNTY; ILLINOIS. OPEN TO THOSE SEEKING HEALTH CARE CAREER WHO ARE ENROLLED IN OR ATTENDING QUALIFIED SCHOOL. ELIGIBILITY BASED ON SCHOLASTIC ABILITY; COLLEGE ACCEPTANCE; FINANCIAL NEED; FAMILY CIRCUMSTANCES.

7 TO 13 SCHOLARSHIPS PER YEAR. RENEWABLE.

709

EDWARD BANGS AND ELZA KELLEY FOUNDATION (SCHOLARSHIP PROGRAM)

243 SOUTH ST
HYANNIS MA 02601
508/775-3117

AMOUNT: UP TO $4000

DEADLINE(S): APR 30

FIELD(S): MEDICINE; NURSING; HEALTH SCIENCES; RELATED AREAS

OPEN TO RESIDENTS OF BARNSTABLE COUNTY; MASS. SCHOLARSHIPS ARE INTENDED TO BENEFIT HEALTH & WELFARE OF BARNSTABLE COUNTY RESIDENTS. AWARDS SUPPORT STUDY AT RECOGNIZED UNDERGRADUATE; GRADUATE & PROFESSIONAL INSTITUTIONS.

FINANCIAL NEED IS A CONSIDERATION. WRITE FOR COMPLETE INFORMATION.

710

FAIRFAX COUNTY MEDICAL SOCIETY FOUNDATION (SCHOLARSHIPS)

8100 OAK STREET
DUNN LORING VA 22027
703/560-4855

AMOUNT: $1500

DEADLINE(S): MAY 25

FIELD(S): MEDICAL DOCTOR; MEDICAL RELATED DISCIPLINES; MEDICAL TECHNOLOGIES; NURSING

OPEN TO UNDERGRADUATE AND GRADUATE STUDENTS WHO ARE USA CITIZENS AND ARE RESIDENTS OF FAIRFAX COUNTY; VA. FOR STUDIES RELATED TO HUMAN HEALTH. MUST DEMONSTRATE FINANCIAL NEED.

11 AWARDS PER YEAR; RENEWABLE. WRITE FOR COMPLETE INFORMATION.

711

H. FLETCHER BROWN FUND (SCHOLARSHIPS)

C/O BANK OF DELAWARE; TRUST DEPT; PO BOX 791
WILMINGTON DE 19899
302/429-2827

AMOUNT: VARIES

DEADLINE(S): APR 15

FIELD(S): MEDICINE; DENTISTRY; LAW; ENGINEERING; CHEMISTRY

OPEN TO STUDENTS BORN IN DELAWARE; GRADUATED FROM A DELAWARE HIGH SCHOOL & STILL RESIDING IN DELAWARE. FOR FOUR YEARS OF STUDY (UNDERGRAD OR GRAD) LEADING TO A DEGREE THAT ENABLES APPLICANT TO PRACTICE IN CHOSEN FIELD.

SCHOLARSHIPS ARE BASED ON NEED; SCHOLASTIC ACHIEVEMENT; GOOD MORAL CHARACTER. RENEWABLE. WRITE FOR COMPLETE INFORMATION.

712

INTERNATIONAL ORDER OF THE KING'S DAUGHTERS AND SONS (HEALTH CAREERS SCHOLARSHIPS)

PO BOX 1017
CHAUTAUQUA NY 14722
716/357-4951

AMOUNT: UP TO $1000

DEADLINE(S): APR 1

FIELD(S): MEDICINE; DENTISTRY; NURSING; PHYSICAL THERAPY; OCCUPATIONAL THERAPY; MEDICAL TECHNOLOGIES; PHARMACY

OPEN TO STUDENTS ACCEPTED TO/ENROLLED IN AN ACCREDITED USA OR CANADIAN 4-YR OR GRADUATE SCHOOL. RN CANDIDATES MUST HAVE COMPLETED 1ST YEAR; BA CANDIDATES IN AT LEAST 3RD YEAR. PRE MED STUDENTS NOT ELIGIBLE.

USA OR CANADIAN CITIZEN. THOSE SEEKING MD OR DDS DEGREES MUST BE IN 2ND YR OF MED OR DENTAL SCHOOL. FOR APPLICATIONS AND COMPLETE INFO SEND SASE TO MRS. MERLE RABER; 6024 E. CHICAGO RD; JONESVILLE MI 49250.

713

J. HUGH AND EARLE W. FELLOWS MEMORIAL FUND (SCHOLARSHIP LOANS)

PENSACOLA JUNIOR COLLEGE EXEC VP; 1000 COLLEGE BLVD

PENSACOLA FL 32504

904/484-1706

AMOUNT: EACH IS NEGOTIATED INDIVIDUALLY

DEADLINE(S): NONE

FIELD(S): MEDICINE; NURSING; MEDICAL TECHNOLOGY; THEOLOGY

OPEN TO BONAFIDE RESIDENTS OF THE FLORIDA COUNTIES OF ESCAMBIA; SANTA ROSA; OKALOOSA OR WALTON. FOR UNDERGRADUATE STUDY IN THE FIELDS LISTED ABOVE. USA CITIZEN.

LOANS ARE INTEREST-FREE UNTIL GRADUATION. WRITE FOR COMPLETE INFORMATION.

714

JEWISH VOCATIONAL SERVICE (MARCUS & THERESA LEVIE EDUCATIONAL FUND SCHOLARSHIPS)

1 SOUTH FRANKLIN STREET

CHICAGO IL 60606

312/346-6700 EXT 2214

AMOUNT: $5000

DEADLINE(S): MAR 1

FIELD(S): SOCIAL WORK; MEDICINE; DENTISTRY; NURSING & OTHER RELATED PROFESSIONS & VOCATIONS

OPEN TO COOK COUNTY RESIDENTS OF THE JEWISH FAITH WHO PLAN CAREERS IN THE HELPING PROFESSIONS. MUST SHOW FINANCIAL NEED. FOR UNDERGRADUATE; GRADUATE OR VOCATIONAL STUDY. APPLICATIONS AVAILABLE BEGINNING DEC 1 FROM SCHOLARSHIP SECRETARY.

85-100 AWARDS PER YEAR. RENEWAL POSSIBLE WITH REAPPLICATION. WRITE FOR COMPLETE INFORMATION.

715

MARYLAND HIGHER EDUCATION COMMISSION (PROFESSIONAL SCHOOL SCHOLARSHIPS)

STATE SCHOLARSHIP ADMINISTRATION; 16 FRANCIS ST

ANNAPOLIS MD 21401

410/974-5370

AMOUNT: $200 - $1000

DEADLINE(S): MAR 1

FIELD(S): DENTISTRY; PHARMACY; MEDICINE; LAW; NURSING

OPEN TO MARYLAND RESIDENTS WHO HAVE BEEN ADMITTED AS FULL-TIME STUDENTS AT A PARTICIPATING GRADUATE INSTITUTION OF HIGHER LEARNING IN MARYLAND OR AN UNDERGRADUATE NURSING PROGRAM.

RENEWABLE UP TO 4 YEARS. WRITE FOR COMPLETE INFORMATION AND A LIST OF PARTICIPATING MARYLAND INSTITUTIONS.

716

MINNESOTA HEART ASSOCIATION (HELEN N. AND HAROLD B. SHAPIRA SCHOLARSHIP)

4701 WEST 77TH STREET

MINNEAPOLIS MN 55435

612/835-3300

AMOUNT: $1000

DEADLINE(S): MAY 1

FIELD(S): MEDICINE

OPEN TO PRE-MED UNDERGRADUATE STUDENTS & MEDICAL STUDENTS WHO ARE ACCEPTED TO OR ENROLLED IN AN ACCREDITED MINNESOTA COLLEGE OR UNIVERSITY. MEDICAL STUDENTS SHOULD BE IN A CURRICULUM THAT IS RELATED TO THE HEART AND CIRCULATORY SYSTEM.

MAY BE RENEWED ONCE. USA CITIZEN OR LEGAL RESIDENT. WRITE FOR COMPLETE INFORMATION.

717

NATIONS BANK TRUST DEPT (MINNIE L. MAFFETT SCHOLARSHIP TRUST)

PO BOX 831515

DALLAS TX 75283

214/559-6476

AMOUNT: $300 - $1000

DEADLINE(S): APR 1

FIELD(S): PRE MED; MEDICAL

OPEN TO USA CITIZENS WHO GRADUATED FROM LIMESTONE COUNTY TEXAS HIGH SCHOOLS. SCHOLARSHIPS FOR FULL TIME STUDY AT AN ACCREDITED TEXAS INSTITUTION.

30 SCHOLARSHIPS PER YEAR. WRITE TO DEBRA HITZELBERGER; VICE PRESIDENT AND TRUST OFFICER; ADDRESS ABOVE; FOR COMPLETE INFORMATION.

718

NELLIE MARTIN CARMAN SCHOLARSHIP TRUST (SCHOLARSHIPS)

1121 244TH ST SW; #65

BOTHELL WA 98021

206/486-6575

AMOUNT: UP TO $1000

DEADLINE(S): MAR 15

FIELD(S): ALL FIELDS OF STUDY EXCEPT THOSE NOTED BELOW

OPEN TO SENIORS IN KING; PIERCE & SNOHOMISH COUNTY (WA) HIGH SCHOOLS WHO HAVE LIVED IN WASHINGTON AT LEAST 5 YRS FOR UNDERGRADUATE STUDY IN WASHINGTON IN ALL FIELDS EXCEPT MUSIC; SCULPTURE; DRAWING; INTERIOR DESIGN & HOME ECONOMICS.

APPLICATIONS AVAILABLE ONLY THROUGH HIGH SCHOOLS. NOMINATION BY HS COUNSELOR IS REQUIRED. AWARDS ARE RENEWABLE. USA CITIZEN.

719

PENNSYLVANIA MEDICAL SOCIETY - EDUCATIONAL AND SCIENTIFIC TRUST (LOAN PROGRAM)

777 EAST PARK DRIVE; PO BOX 8820

HARRISBURG PA 17105

717/558-7750 EXT 424

AMOUNT: $1500 - $3000

DEADLINE(S): APR 1 TO JUL 1

FIELD(S): MEDICINE AND ALLIED HEALTH FIELDS

OPEN TO PENNSYLVANIA RESIDENTS WITH DEMONSTRATED FINANCIAL NEED WHO ARE SEEKING A MEDICAL DEGREE OR ARE ENROLLED IN 4-YEAR OR 2-YEAR PROGRAMS IN THE HEALTH FIELD. FOR STUDY IN USA.

APPROX 300 LOANS PER YEAR. WRITE FOR COMPLETE INFORMATION.

720

ROBERT SCHRECK MEMORIAL FUND (GRANTS)

C/O TEXAS COMMERCE BANK-TRUST DEPT; PO DRAWER 140

EL PASO TX 79980

915/546-6515

AMOUNT: $500 - $1500

DEADLINE(S): JUL 15; NOV 15

FIELD(S): MEDICINE; VETERINARY MEDICINE; PHYSICS; CHEMISTRY; ARCHITECTURE; ENGINEERING; EPISCOPAL CLERGY

GRANTS TO UNDERGRADUATE JUNIORS OR SENIORS OR GRADUATE STUDENTS WHO HAVE BEEN RESIDENTS OF EL PASO COUNTY FOR AT LEAST TWO YEARS. MUST BE USA CITIZEN OR LEGAL RESIDENT AND HAVE A HIGH GRADE POINT AVERAGE. FINANCIAL NEED IS A CONSIDERATION.

WRITE FOR COMPLETE INFORMATION.

721

SANDEE THOMPSON MEMORIAL SCHOLARSHIP FOUNDATION (SCHOLARSHIPS)

1211 NAPOLEON MANOR NE

LAWRENCEVILLE GA 30243

WRITTEN INQUIRY ONLY

AMOUNT: $500

DEADLINE(S): MAR 15

FIELD(S): MEDICINE; NURSING; PHYSICAL THERAPY; RELIGION

OPEN TO UNDERGRADUATE AND GRADUATE STUDENTS HAVING AN INTEREST IN SERVING HUMANITY AND RELIEVING HUMAN SUFFERING. MUST HAVE MEDICAL OR RELIGIOUS ORIENTED CAREER GOAL WITH PHYSICAL THERAPY A HIGH PREFERENCE.

STUDENTS SHOULD BE ENTERING AT LEAST JUNIOR YEAR AT AN ACCREDITED COLEGE OR UNIVERSITY. FINANCIAL INFORMATION REQUIRED. SEND STAMPED; SELF-ADDRESSED ENVELOPE FOR COMPLETE INFORMATION.

722

SOCIETY OF BIOLOGICAL PSYCHIATRY (ZISKIND-SOMERFIELD RESEARCH AWARD)

C/O A. JOHN RUSH MD; UT SOUTHWESTERN MEDICAL CENTER; 5323 HARRY HINES BLVD

DALLAS TX 75235

214/688-8766

AMOUNT: $2500

DEADLINE(S): MAR 31

FIELD(S): BIOLOGICAL PSYCHIATRY
OPEN TO SENIOR INVESTIGATORS WHO ARE MEMBERS OF THE SOCIETY OF BIOLOGICAL PSYCHIATRY. AWARD IS FOR BASIC OR CLINICAL RESEARCH BY SENIOR INVESTIGATORS 35 OR OLDER.
CANDIDATES MUST BE MEMBERS IN GOOD STANDING OF THE SOCIETY OF BIOLOGICAL PSYCHIATRY. WRITE FOR COMPLETE INFORMATION.

723

U.S. DEPT. OF HEALTH AND HUMAN SERVICES (INDIAN HEALTH SERVICE'S HEALTH SCHOLARSHIP PROGRAM; PUBLIC LAW 94-437)
TWINBROOK METRO PLAZA; SUITE 100; 12300 TWINBROOK PKWY
ROCKVILLE MD 20852
301/443-6197
AMOUNT: TUITION + FEES & MONTHLY STIPEND
DEADLINE(S): APR 15
FIELD(S): HEALTH PROFESSIONS
OPEN TO AMERICAN INDIAN OR ALASKA NATIVES WHO ENROLL IN COURSES THAT WILL LEAD TO A BACCALAUREATE DEGREE AND WILL PREPARE THEM FOR ACCEPTANCE INTO HEALTH PROFESSIONS SCHOOLS. RENEWABLE ANNUALLY WITH REAPPLICATION.
SCHOLARSHIP RECIPIENTS MUST INTEND TO SERVE THE INDIAN PEOPLE AS A HEALTH CARE PROVIDER. THEY INCUR A 1 YEAR SERVICE OBLIGATION TO THE INDIAN HEALTH SERVICE FOR EACH YEAR OF SUPPORT. WRITE FOR COMPLETE INFORMATION.

724

VASA ORDER OF AMERICA (THE ELLIS F. HILLNER AWARD)
E.G. JOHNSON; VICE GRAND MASTER; 4406 SALMON POINT
STOCKTON CA 95219
209/478-7498
AMOUNT: $1000
DEADLINE(S): JAN 15
FIELD(S): MEDICINE
OPEN TO STUDENTS ATTENDING OR PLANNING TO ATTEND AN ACCREDITED INSTITUTION FULL TIME FOR STUDIES IN THE MEDICAL FIELD. MUST HAVE BEEN A VASA MEMBER FOR AT LEAST ONE YEAR AND DEMONSTRATE FINANCIAL NEED.
WRITE FOR COMPLETE INFORMATION.

725

VIRGIN ISLANDS BOARD OF EDUCATION (NURSING & OTHER HEALTH SCHOLARSHIPS)
PO BOX 11900
ST THOMAS VI 00801
809/774-4546
AMOUNT: UP TO $1800
DEADLINE(S): MAR 31
FIELD(S): NURSING; MEDICINE; HEALTH RELATED AREAS
OPEN TO BONAFIDE RESIDENTS OF THE VIRGIN ISLANDS WHO ARE ACCEPTED BY AN ACCREDITED SCHOOL OF NURSING OR AN ACCREDITED INSTITUTION OFFERING COURSES IN ONE OF THE HEALTH RELATED FIELDS.
THIS SCHOLARSHIP IS GRANTED FOR THE DURATION OF THE COURSE PROVIDED THE RECIPIENTS MAINTAIN AT LEAST A 'C' AVERAGE. CONTACT ADDRESS ABOVE FOR COMPLETE INFORMATION.

MEDICAL RELATED DISCIPLINES

726

ABBIE SARGENT MEMORIAL SCHOLARSHIP INC (SCHOLARSHIPS)
295 SHEEP DAVIS ROAD
CONCORD NH 03301
603/224-1934
AMOUNT: $200
DEADLINE(S): MAR 15
FIELD(S): AGRICULTURE; VETERINARY MEDICINE; HOME ECONOMICS
OPEN TO NEW HAMPSHIRE RESIDENT WHO IS HIGH SCHOOL GRADUATE WITH GOOD GRADES AND CHARACTER. FOR UNDERGRADUATE OR GRADUATE STUDY. USA LEGAL RESIDENT. DEMONSTRATE FINANCIAL NEED.
RENEWABLE WITH REAPPLICATION. WRITE FOR COMPLETE INFORMATION.

727

AMERICAN ASSOCIATION OF WOMEN DENTISTS (GILLETTE HAYDEN MEMORIAL FOUNDATION)
95 WEST BROADWAY
SALEM NJ 08079
609/935-0467
AMOUNT: $2000
DEADLINE(S): AUG 1
FIELD(S): DENTISTRY
LOANS AVAILABLE TO WOMEN WHO ARE 3RD & 4TH YEAR PRE-DENTAL STUDENTS OR ARE GRADUATE DEGREE CANDIDATES. SCHOLARSHIP; NEED FOR ASSISTANCE AND AMOUNT OF DEBT CURRENTLY ACCUMULATED ARE MAIN POINTS CONSIDERED.
WRITE FOR COMPLETE INFORMATION.

728

AMERICAN COLLEGE OF MEDICAL GROUP ADMINISTRATORS (SCHOLARSHIPS)
104 INVERNESS TERRACE EAST
ENGLEWOOD CO 80112
303/799-1111
AMOUNT: $500 - $1000
DEADLINE(S): JUN 30
FIELD(S): AMBULATORY CARE/MEDICAL GROUP MANAGEMENT
OPEN TO UNDERGRADUATE OR GRADUATE STUDENTS WHO ARE PURSUING A FULL TIME COURSE OF STUDY THAT WILL LEAD TO A CAREER IN AMBULATORY CARE/MEDICAL GROUP MANAGEMENT. NEED FOR SCHOLARSHIP SUPPORT IS A CONSIDERATION IN MAKING AWARDS.
WRITE FOR COMPLETE INFORMATION.

729

AMERICAN FOUNDATION FOR PHARMACEUTICAL EDUCATION (GATEWAY SCHOLARSHIP PROGRAM)
618 SOMERSET ST; PO BOX 7126
NORTH PLAINFIELD NJ 07060
908/561-8077
AMOUNT: $9250
DEADLINE(S): OCT 1
FIELD(S): PHARMACY
OPEN TO UNDERGRADUATES IN THE LAST THREE YEARS OF A BACHELOR'S PROGRAM IN A COLLEGE OF PHARMACY. USA CITIZEN OR PERMANENT RESIDENT. $4250 IS AWARDED FOR AN UNDERGRAD RESEARCH PROJECT; THEN $5000 WHEN STUDENT ENROLLS IN A GRADUATE PROGRAM.
PURPOSE IS TO ENCOURAGE UNDERGRADUATES TO PURSUE THE PHD IN A PHARMACY COLLEGE GRADUATE PROGRAM. WRITE FOR COMPLETE INFORMATION.

730

AMERICAN FOUNDATION FOR VISION AWARENESS (EDUCATION/RESEARCH GRANTS)
243 NORTH LINDBERGH BLVD
ST LOUIS MO 63141
314/991-4100
AMOUNT: $1000 SCHOLARSHIPS; $5000 - $10000 RESEARCH GRANTS
DEADLINE(S): FEB 1
FIELD(S): OPTOMETRY
SCHOLARSHIPS OPEN TO OPTOMETRY STUDENTS. RESEARCH GRANTS OPEN TO SCIENTISTS DOING RESEARCH IN THE FIELD OF VISION.
WRITE FOR COMPLETE INFORMATION.

731

AMERICAN INDIAN SCIENCE & ENGINEERING SOCIETY (SANTA FE PACIFIC FOUNDATION SCHOLARSHIPS)
1630 30TH ST; SUITE 301
BOULDER CO 80301
303/492-8658
AMOUNT: UP TO $2500 PER YEAR FOR 4 YEARS
DEADLINE(S): MAR 15
FIELD(S): BUSINESS; ENGINEERING; SCIENCE; HEALTH ADMINISTRATION
OPEN TO GRADUATING HIGH SCHOOL SENIORS WITH 1/4 DEGREE OR MORE INDIAN BLOOD. MUST RESIDE IN KS; OK; CO; AZ; NM OR SAN BERNARDINO COUNTY CA (AT&SF RAILWAY SERVICE AREA). 2 OF THE 5 SCHOLARSHIPS ARE DESIGNATED FOR NAVAJO TRIBE MEMBERS.
MUST PLAN TO ATTEND A 4 YEAR POST-SECONDARY ACCREDITED EDUCATIONAL INSTITUTION. WRITE FOR COMPLETE INFORMATION.

732

AMERICAN PODIATRIC MEDICAL ASSN (SCHOLARSHIPS AND LOANS)
9312 OLD GEORGETOWN RD
BETHESDA MD 20814
301/571-9200

AMOUNT: $7500
DEADLINE(S): APR 3O
FIELD(S): PODIATRIC MEDICINE
SCHOLARSHIPS AND LOANS OPEN TO FOURTH-YEAR PODIATRY STUDENTS OR GRADUATE STUDENTS WHO WISH TO CONTINUE THEIR STUDIES FULL TIME. RECIPIENT MUST TAKE AT LEAST 12 CREDITS PER SEMESTER.
SELECTION IS BASED ON LEADERSHIP QUALITIES; PROFESSIONAL ATTITUDES & CHARACTER. AVAILABLE ONLY THROUGH SCHOOL'S FINANCIAL AID OFFICE.

733

AMERICAN SOCIETY FOR MEDICAL TECHNOLOGY (EDUCATION & RESEARCH FUND-JOHN C. LANG MEMORIAL AWARD)
2021 'L' STREET NW; SUITE 400
WASHINGTON DC 20036
202-785-3311
AMOUNT: $250
DEADLINE(S): FEB 1
FIELD(S): HEALTH CARE ADMINISTRATION
AWARD TO RECOGNIZE OUTSTANDING PERFORMANCE IN ADMINISTRATION & LABORATORY MANAGEMENT & TO ENCOURAGE INDIVIDUALS TO DESSIMATE THEIR KNOWLEDGE TO THE PROFESSION. ANYONE IN THE PROFESSION MAY APPLY OR BE NOMINATED.
WRITE TO EXECUTIVE DIRECTOR AT ADDRESS ABOVE FOR COMPLETE INFORMATION. ENCLOSE STAMPED SELF-ADDRESSED BUSINESS SIZE ENVELOPE.

734

AMERICAN VETERINARY MEDICAL ASSOCIATION FOUNDATION (AMVA AUXILIARY STUDENT LOAN FUND)
1931 N MEACHAM RD; SUITE 100
SCHAUMBURG IL 60173
708/925-8070 EXT 208
AMOUNT: UP TO $4000
DEADLINE(S): CONTINUAL
FIELD(S): VETERINARY MEDICINE
LOANS AVAILABLE TO WORTHY STUDENTS IN AMVA-ACCREDITED COLLEGES OF VETERINARY MEDICINE WHO NEED FINANCIAL AID TO COMPLETE THEIR SCHOOLING. PREFERENCE TO SENIORS BUT SOPHOMORES AND JUNIORS MAY BE CONSIDERED. USA CITIZEN.
APPLICANTS MUST BE MEMBERS OF AVMA STUDENT CHAPTER. WRITE FOR COMPLETE INFORMATION.

735

ARTHUR & DOREEN PARRETT SCHOLARSHIP TRUST FUND (SCHOLARSHIPS)
C/O U.S. BANK OF WASHINGTON; PO BOX 720; TRUST DEPT; 4TH FLOOR
SEATTLE WA 98111
206/344-3691
AMOUNT: UP TO $1000
DEADLINE(S): JUL 31
FIELD(S): ENGINEERING; SCIENCE; MEDICINE; DENTISTRY
WASHINGTON STATE RESIDENT. UNDERGRADUATE SCHOLARSHIPS OPEN TO STUDENTS WHO ARE ENROLLED IN ABOVE SCHOOLS. AWARDS TENABLE AT ANY ACCREDITED UNDERGRADUATE COLLEGE OR UNIVERSITY. USA CITIZEN OR LEGAL RESIDENT.
APPROXIMATELY 15 AWARDS PER YEAR. WRITE FOR COMPLETE INFORMATION.

736

ASSOCIATION OF OFFICIAL ANALYTICAL CHEMISTS (HARVEY W. WILEY SCHOLARSHIP AWARD)
2200 WILSON BLVD; SUITE 400
ARLINGTON VA 22201
703-522-3032
AMOUNT: $500 PER YEAR FOR 2 YEARS
DEADLINE(S): MAY 1 OF SOPHOMORE YEAR
FIELD(S): CHEMISTRY; MICROBIOLOGY & RELATED SCIENCES
OPEN TO UNDERGRADUATE SOPHOMORES WHO HAVE MAINTAINED AT LEAST 'B' AVERAGE. AWARDS ARE FOR JUNIOR & SENIOR YEAR IN ABOVE AREAS. MEDICAL; DENTAL; NURSING; ETC MAJORS NOT ELIGIBLE.
WRITE FOR COMPLETE INFORMATION.

737

AUXILIARY TO THE MICHIGAN OPTOMETRIC ASSOCIATION (SCHOLARSHIP PROGRAM)
511 ASHMUN; SUITE 201
SAULT STE. MARIE MI 49783
906/635-0861
AMOUNT: $400 - $1000

DEADLINE(S): MAR 1
FIELD(S): OPTOMETRY
MICHIGAN RESIDENT & STUDENT MEMBER OF MICHIGAN OPTOMETRIC ASSN APPLY IN 3RD YEAR OF STUDY AT A RECOGNIZED SCHOOL OF OPTOMETRY. MAINTAIN 'B' AVERAGE. US CITIZEN.
2-5 SCHOLARSHIPS PER YEAR. APPLICATIONS AVAILABLE IN NOVEMBER AT ALL OPTOMETRIC COLLEGES. WRITE FOR COMPLETE INFORMATION.

738

BUSINESS AND PROFESSIONAL WOMEN'S FOUNDATION (NEW YORK LIFE FOUNDATION SCHOLARSHIPS FOR WOMEN IN THE HEALTH PROFESSIONS)
2012 MASSACHUSETTS AVE NW
WASHINGTON DC 20036
202/293-1200
AMOUNT: $500 - $1000
DEADLINE(S): APR 15 POSTMARK (APPS. AVAILABLE ONLY OCT 1 - APR 1)
FIELD(S): HEALTH RELATED PROFESSIONS
OPEN TO WOMEN (25 OR OLDER) WHO ARE WITHIN 12-24 MONTHS OF COMPLETING THEIR UNDERGRADUATE PROGRAM OF STUDY IN USA. SHOULD LEAD TO ENTRY OR REENTRY INTO THE WORK FORCE OR IMPROVE CHANCES FOR CAREER ADVANCEMENT. USA CITIZEN.
MUST BE ACCEPTED INTO AN ACCREDITED PROGRAM AND DEMONSTRATE FINANCIAL NEED. SEND SELF-ADDRESSED STAMPED ENVELOPE (52 CENTS) #10 ENVELOPE FOR APPLICATION AND COMPLETE INFORMATION.

739

CHARLES E. SAAK TRUST (EDUCATIONAL GRANTS)
C/O WELLS FARGO BANK TRUST DEPT; 2222 W SHAW; #11
FRESNO CA 93711
WRITTEN INQUIRY ONLY
AMOUNT: VARIES
DEADLINE(S): MAR 31
FIELD(S): EDUCATION; MEDICINE
UNDERGRADUATE GRANTS FOR RESIDENTS OF THE PORTERVILLE-POPLAR AREA OF TULARE COUNTY CALIF. MUST CARRY A MINIMUM OF 12 UNITS; HAVE AT LEAST A 2.0 GPA; BE UNDER AGE 21 AND DEMONSTRATE FINANCIAL NEED.
APPROXIMATELY 100 AWARDS PER YEAR; RENEWABLE WITH REAPPLICATION. WRITE FOR COMPLETE INFORMATION.

740

COMMUNITY FOUNDATION OF GREATER LORAIN COUNTY (A.C. SIDDALL EDUCATIONAL TRUST FUND SCHOLARSHIP)
1865 N RIDGE ROAD E; SUITE A
LORAIN OH 44055
216/277-0142 OR 216/323-4445
AMOUNT: $1000
DEADLINE(S): MAY 1
FIELD(S): HEALTH CARE
OPEN TO THOSE WHO WISH TO PURSUE OR FURTHER THEIR EDUCATION IN HEALTH CARE WHO HAVE BEEN OR ARE NOW EMPLOYED AND RESIDE IN OR WORK FOR A HEALTH CARE FACILITY WITHIN THE ALLEN MEMORIAL HOSPITAL DISTRICT IN LORAIN COUNTY.
MUST HAVE WORK EXPERIENCE AND DEMONSTRATE FINANCIAL NEED. APPLICATIONS AVAILABLE BEGINNING JAN 30 FROM ADMINISTRATOR; ALLEN MEMORIAL HOSPITAL; 200 W LORAIN ST; OBERLIN OH 44074.

741

CUYAHOGA COUNTY MEDICAL FOUNDATION (SCHOLARSHIP GRANT PROGRAM)
11001 CEDAR AVE
CLEVELAND OH 44106
216/229-2200
AMOUNT: $500 - $1500
DEADLINE(S): JUN 1
FIELD(S): MEDICINE; DENTISTRY; PHARMACY; NURSING; OSTEOPATHY
GRANTS OPEN TO RESIDENTS OF CUYAHOGA COUNTY WHO ARE ACCEPTED TO OR ENROLLED IN AN ACCREDITED PROFESSIONAL SCHOOL IN ONE OF THE ABOVE AREAS. USA CITIZEN.
APPROX 40 AWARDS PER YEAR. WRITE FOR COMPLETE INFORMATION.

742

DOG WRITERS' EDUCATIONAL TRUST (SCHOLARSHIPS)
BERTA I. PICKETT; PO BOX 2220
PAYSON AZ 85547
602/474-8867

AMOUNT: $1000
DEADLINE(S): DEC 31
FIELD(S): VETERINARY MEDICINE; ANIMAL BEHAVIOR; JOURNALISM

OPEN TO APPLICANTS WHOSE PARENTS; GRANDPARENTS OR OTHER CLOSE RELATIVES (OR THE APPLICANT) ARE OR HAVE BEEN INVOLVED IN THE WORLD OF DOGS AS EXHIBITORS; BREEDERS; HANDLERS; JUDGES; CLUB OFFICERS OR OTHER ACTIVITIES.

SCHOLARSHIPS SUPPORT UNDERGRADUATE OR GRADUATE STUDY. 10 AWARDS PER YEAR. SEND SELF-ADDRESSED STAMPED ENVELOPE FOR COMPLETE INFORMATION AND APPLICATION.

743

DUPAGE MEDICAL SOCIETY FOUNDATION (SCHOLARSHIP PROGRAM)
800 ROOSEVELT BLD B; #300
GLEN ELLYN IL 60137
312-858-9603
AMOUNT: $1000
DEADLINE(S): DEC - MAR
FIELD(S): MEDICINE; DENTISTRY; NURSING; MEDICAL TECHNOLOGY; PHARMACY

AWARDS FOR RESIDENTS OF DUPAGE COUNTY; ILLINOIS. OPEN TO THOSE SEEKING HEALTH CARE CAREER WHO ARE ENROLLED IN OR ATTENDING QUALIFIED SCHOOL. ELIGIBILITY BASED ON SCHOLASTIC ABILITY; COLLEGE ACCEPTANCE; FINANCIAL NEED; FAMILY CIRCUMSTANCES.

7 TO 13 SCHOLARSHIPS PER YEAR. RENEWABLE.

744

EDWARD BANGS AND ELZA KELLEY FOUNDATION (SCHOLARSHIP PROGRAM)
243 SOUTH ST
HYANNIS MA 02601
508/775-3117
AMOUNT: UP TO $4000
DEADLINE(S): APR 30
FIELD(S): MEDICINE; NURSING; HEALTH SCIENCES; RELATED AREAS

OPEN TO RESIDENTS OF BARNSTABLE COUNTY MASS. SCHOLARSHIPS ARE INTENDED TO BENEFIT HEALTH & WELFARE OF BARNSTABLE COUNTY RESIDENTS. AWARDS SUPPORT STUDY AT RECOGNIZED UNDERGRADUATE; GRADUATE & PROFESSIONAL INSTITUTIONS.

FINANCIAL NEED IS A CONSIDERATION. WRITE FOR COMPLETE INFORMATION.

745

FAIRFAX COUNTY MEDICAL SOCIETY FOUNDATION (SCHOLARSHIPS)
8100 OAK STREET
DUNN LORING VA 22027
703/560-4855
AMOUNT: $1500
DEADLINE(S): MAY 25
FIELD(S): MEDICAL DOCTOR; MEDICAL RELATED DISCIPLINES; MEDICAL TECHNOLOGIES; NURSING

OPEN TO UNDERGRADUATE AND GRADUATE STUDENTS WHO ARE USA CITIZENS AND ARE RESIDENTS OF FAIRFAX COUNTY; VA. FOR STUDIES RELATED TO HUMAN HEALTH. MUST DEMONSTRATE FINANCIAL NEED.

11 AWARDS PER YEAR; RENEWABLE. WRITE FOR COMPLETE INFORMATION.

746

H. FLETCHER BROWN FUND (SCHOLARSHIPS)
C/O BANK OF DELAWARE; TRUST DEPT; PO BOX 791
WILMINGTON DE 19899
302/429-2827
AMOUNT: VARIES
DEADLINE(S): APR 15
FIELD(S): MEDICINE; DENTISTRY; LAW; ENGINEERING; CHEMISTRY

OPEN TO STUDENTS BORN IN DELAWARE; GRADUATED FROM A DELAWARE HIGH SCHOOL & STILL RESIDING IN DELAWARE. FOR FOUR YEARS OF STUDY (UNDERGRAD OR GRAD) LEADING TO A DEGREE THAT ENABLES APPLICANT TO PRACTICE IN CHOSEN FIELD.

SCHOLARSHIPS ARE BASED ON NEED; SCHOLASTIC ACHIEVEMENT; GOOD MORAL CHARACTER. RENEWABLE. WRITE FOR COMPLETE INFORMATION.

747

INDIANA DENTAL ASSOCIATION (LOAN PROGRAM)
INB NATIONAL BANK; ONE VIRGINIA AVE
INDIANAPOLIS IN 46204
317/266-5263
AMOUNT: UP TO $3000

DEADLINE(S): NONE SPECIFIED
FIELD(S): DENTISTRY
LOANS ARE MADE TO DENTAL STUDENTS (UNDERGRADUATE AND GRADUATE) WHO ARE RESIDENTS OF INDIANA ARE ENROLLED IN THE INDIANA UNIVERSITY SCHOOL OF DENTISTRY AND HAVE DEMONSTRATED A NEED FOR FINANCIAL ASSISTANCE.
CONTACT ROBERT D. GODFREY - BRANCH OFFICER - AT ADDRESS ABOVE FOR COMPLETE INFORMATION.

748

INTERNATIONAL CHIROPRACTORS ASSOCIATION (KING KOIL SPINAL GUARD/STUDENT (SICA); AUXILIARY (AICA) SCHOLARSHIPS)
1110 N GLEBE RD; STE 1000
ARLINGTON VA 22201
703/528-5000
AMOUNT: $100 - $1000
DEADLINE(S): SPRING
FIELD(S): CHIROPRACTIC
OPEN TO STUDENT MEMBERS OF ICA BASED ON ACADEMIC ACHIEVEMENT & SERVICE. AWARDS ARE TENABLE AT SCHOOLS WITH ICA CHAPTERS. AWARDS ARE NOT AVAILABLE FOR FRESHMAN YEAR OF STUDY.
CONTACT YOUR ICA CHAPTER OR ADDRESS ABOVE FOR COMPLETE INFORMATION.

749

INTERNATIONAL ORDER OF THE KING'S DAUGHTERS AND SONS (HEALTH CAREERS SCHOLARSHIPS)
PO BOX 1017
CHAUTAUQUA NY 14722
716/357-4951
AMOUNT: UP TO $1000
DEADLINE(S): APR 1
FIELD(S): MEDICINE; DENTISTRY; NURSING; PHYSICAL THERAPY; OCCUPATIONAL THERAPY; MEDICAL TECHNOLOGIES; PHARMACY
OPEN TO STUDENTS ACCEPTED TO/ENROLLED IN AN ACCREDITED USA OR CANADIAN 4-YR OR GRADUATE SCHOOL. RN CANDIDATES MUST HAVE COMPLETED 1ST YEAR; BA CANDIDATES IN AT LEAST 3RD YEAR. PRE MED STUDENTS NOT ELIGIBLE.
USA OR CANADIAN CITIZEN. THOSE SEEKING MD OR DDS DEGREES MUST BE IN 2ND YR OF MED OR DENTAL SCHOOL. FOR APPLICATIONS AND COMPLETE INFO SEND SASE TO MRS. MERLE RABER; 6024 E. CHICAGO RD; JONESVILLE MI 49250.

750

JEWISH VOCATIONAL SERVICE (MARCUS & THERESA LEVIE EDUCATIONAL FUND SCHOLARSHIPS)
1 SOUTH FRANKLIN STREET
CHICAGO IL 60606
312/346-6700 EXT 2214
AMOUNT: $5000
DEADLINE(S): MAR 1
FIELD(S): SOCIAL WORK; MEDICINE; DENTISTRY; NURSING & OTHER RELATED PROFESSIONS & VOCATIONS
OPEN TO COOK COUNTY RESIDENTS OF THE JEWISH FAITH WHO PLAN CAREERS IN THE HELPING PROFESSIONS. MUST SHOW FINANCIAL NEED. FOR UNDERGRADUATE; GRADUATE OR VOCATIONAL STUDY. APPLICATIONS AVAILABLE BEGINNING DEC 1 FROM SCHOLARSHIP SECRETARY.
85-100 AWARDS PER YEAR. RENEWAL POSSIBLE WITH REAPPLICATION. WRITE FOR COMPLETE INFORMATION.

751

MARYLAND HIGHER EDUCATION COMMISSION (PROFESSIONAL SCHOOL SCHOLARSHIPS)
STATE SCHOLARSHIP ADMINISTRATION; 16 FRANCIS ST
ANNAPOLIS MD 21401
410/974-5370
AMOUNT: $200 - $1000
DEADLINE(S): MAR 1
FIELD(S): DENTISTRY; PHARMACY; MEDICINE; LAW; NURSING
OPEN TO MARYLAND RESIDENTS WHO HAVE BEEN ADMITTED AS FULL-TIME STUDENTS AT A PARTICIPATING GRADUATE INSTITUTION OF HIGHER LEARNING IN MARYLAND OR AN UNDERGRADUATE NURSING PROGRAM.
RENEWABLE UP TO 4 YEARS. WRITE FOR COMPLETE INFORMATION AND A LIST OF PARTICIPATING MARYLAND INSTITUTIONS.

752

NATIONAL STRENGTH & CONDITIONING ASSN (CHALLENGE SCHOLARSHIPS)
PO BOX 81410
LINCOLN NE 68501
402/472-3000
AMOUNT: $1000
DEADLINE(S): APR 17
FIELD(S): FIELDS RELATED TO STRENGTH & CONDITIONING
OPEN TO NATIONAL STRENGTH & CONDITIONING ASSN MEMBERS. AWARDS ARE FOR UNDERGRADUATE OR GRADUATE STUDY.
WRITE FOR COMPLETE INFORMATION.

753

NELLIE MARTIN CARMAN SCHOLARSHIP TRUST (SCHOLARSHIPS)
1121 244TH ST SW; #65
BOTHELL WA 98021
206/486-6575
AMOUNT: UP TO $1000
DEADLINE(S): MAR 15
FIELD(S): ALL FIELDS OF STUDY EXCEPT THOSE NOTED BELOW
OPEN TO SENIORS IN KING; PIERCE & SNOHOMISH COUNTY (WA) HIGH SCHOOLS WHO HAVE LIVED IN WASHINGTON AT LEAST 5 YRS. FOR UNDERGRADUATE STUDY IN WASHINGTON IN ALL FIELDS EXCEPT MUSIC; SCULPTURE; DRAWING; INTERIOR DESIGN & HOME ECONOMICS.
APPLICATIONS AVAILABLE ONLY THROUGH HIGH SCHOOLS. NOMINATION BY HS COUNSELOR IS REQUIRED. AWARDS ARE RENEWABLE. USA CITIZEN.

754

ROBERT SCHRECK MEMORIAL FUND (GRANTS)
C/O TEXAS COMMERCE BANK-TRUST DEPT; PO DRAWER 140
EL PASO TX 79980
915/546-6515
AMOUNT: $500 - $1500
DEADLINE(S): JUL 15; NOV 15
FIELD(S): MEDICINE; VETERINARY MEDICINE; PHYSICS; CHEMISTRY; ARCHITECTURE; ENGINEERING; EPISCOPAL CLERGY
GRANTS TO UNDERGRADUATE JUNIORS OR SENIORS OR GRADUATE STUDENTS WHO HAVE BEEN RESIDENTS OF EL PASO COUNTY FOR AT LEAST TWO YEARS. MUST BE USA CITIZEN OR LEGAL RESIDENT AND HAVE A HIGH GRADE POINT AVERAGE. FINANCIAL NEED IS A CONSIDERATION.
WRITE FOR COMPLETE INFORMATION.

755

SANDEE THOMPSON MEMORIAL SCHOLARSHIP FOUNDATION (SCHOLARSHIPS)
1211 NAPOLEON MANOR NE
LAWRENCEVILLE GA 30243
WRITTEN INQUIRY ONLY
AMOUNT: $500
DEADLINE(S): MAR 15
FIELD(S): MEDICINE; NURSING; PHYSICAL THERAPY; RELIGION
OPEN TO UNDERGRADUATE AND GRADUATE STUDENTS HAVING AN INTEREST IN SERVING HUMANITY AND RELIEVING HUMAN SUFFERING. MUST HAVE MEDICAL OR RELIGIOUS ORIENTED CAREER GOAL WITH PHYSICAL THERAPY A HIGH PREFERENCE.
STUDENTS SHOULD BE ENTERING AT LEAST JUNIOR YEAR AT AN ACCREDITED COLEGE OR UNIVERSITY. FINANCIAL INFORMATION REQUIRED. SEND STAMPED; SELF-ADDRESSED ENVELOPE FOR COMPLETE INFORMATION.

756

U.S. DEPT. OF HEALTH AND HUMAN SERVICES (INDIAN HEALTH SERVICE'S HEALTH SCHOLARSHIP PROGRAM; PUBLIC LAW 94-437)
TWINBROOK METRO PLAZA; SUITE 100; 12300 TWINBROOK PKWY
ROCKVILLE MD 20852
301/443-6197
AMOUNT: TUITION + FEES & MONTHLY STIPEND
DEADLINE(S): APR 15
FIELD(S): HEALTH PROFESSIONS
OPEN TO AMERICAN INDIAN OR ALASKA NATIVES WHO ENROLL IN COURSES THAT WILL LEAD TO A BACCALAUREATE DEGREE AND WILL PREPARE THEM FOR ACCEPTANCE INTO HEALTH PROFESSIONS SCHOOLS. RENEWABLE ANNUALLY WITH REAPPLICATION.
SCHOLARSHIP RECIPIENTS MUST INTEND TO SERVE THE INDIAN PEOPLE AS A HEALTH CARE PROVIDER. THEY INCUR A 1 YEAR SERVICE OBLIGATION TO THE INDIAN

HEALTH SERVICE FOR EACH YEAR OF SUPPORT. WRITE FOR COMPLETE INFORMATION.

757

VASA ORDER OF AMERICA (THE ELLIS F. HILLNER AWARD)
E.G. JOHNSON; VICE GRAND MASTER; 4406 SALMON POINT
STOCKTON CA 95219
209/478-7498
AMOUNT: $1000
DEADLINE(S): JAN 15
FIELD(S): MEDICINE
OPEN TO STUDENTS ATTENDING OR PLANNING TO ATTEND AN ACCREDITED INSTITUTION FULL TIME FOR STUDIES IN THE MEDICAL FIELD. MUST HAVE BEEN A VASA MEMBER FOR AT LEAST ONE YEAR AND DEMONSTRATE FINANCIAL NEED.
WRITE FOR COMPLETE INFORMATION.

MEDICAL RESEARCH

758

ASSOCIATION FOR THE CARE OF CHILDREN'S HEALTH (EMMA PLANK SCHOLARSHIP)
7910 WOODMONT AVE; SUITE 300
BETHESDA MD 20815
301/654-4549
AMOUNT: $500
DEADLINE(S): APR 1
FIELD(S): CHILD HEALTH
OPEN TO STUDENTS AT THE UNDERGRADUATE OR GRADUATE LEVEL STUDYING IN HEALTH RELATED AREAS THAT IMPACT ON CHILDREN.
WRITE FOR COMPLETE INFORMATION.

759

ASSOCIATION OF OFFICIAL ANALYTICAL CHEMISTS (HARVEY W. WILEY SCHOLARSHIP AWARD)
2200 WILSON BLVD; SUITE 400
ARLINGTON VA 22201
703-522-3032
AMOUNT: $500 PER YEAR FOR 2 YEARS
DEADLINE(S): MAY 1 OF SOPHOMORE YEAR
FIELD(S): CHEMISTRY; MICROBIOLOGY & RELATED SCIENCES
OPEN TO UNDERGRADUATE SOPHOMORES WHO HAVE MAINTAINED AT LEAST 'B' AVERAGE. AWARDS ARE FOR JUNIOR & SENIOR YEAR IN ABOVE AREAS. MEDICAL; DENTAL; NURSING; ETC MAJORS NOT ELIGIBLE.
WRITE FOR COMPLETE INFORMATION.

760

BUSINESS AND PROFESSIONAL WOMEN'S FOUNDATION (NEW YORK LIFE FOUNDATION SCHOLARSHIPS FOR WOMEN IN THE HEALTH PROFESSIONS)
2012 MASSACHUSETTS AVE NW
WASHINGTON DC 20036
202/293-1200
AMOUNT: $500 - $1000
DEADLINE(S): APR 15 POSTMARK (APPS. AVAILABLE ONLY OCT 1 - APR 1)
FIELD(S): HEALTH RELATED PROFESSIONS
OPEN TO WOMEN (25 OR OLDER) WHO ARE WITHIN 12-24 MONTHS OF COMPLETING THEIR UNDERGRADUATE PROGRAM OF STUDY IN USA. SHOULD LEAD TO ENTRY OR REENTRY INTO THE WORK FORCE OR IMPROVE CHANCES FOR CAREER ADVANCEMENT. USA CITIZEN.
MUST BE ACCEPTED INTO AN ACCREDITED PROGRAM AND DEMONSTRATE FINANCIAL NEED. SEND SELF-ADDRESSED STAMPED ENVELOPE (52 CENTS) #10 ENVELOPE FOR APPLICATION AND COMPLETE INFORMATION.

761

CHARLES E. SAAK TRUST (EDUCATIONAL GRANTS)
C/O WELLS FARGO BANK TRUST DEPT; 2222 W SHAW; #11
FRESNO CA 93711
WRITTEN INQUIRY ONLY
AMOUNT: VARIES
DEADLINE(S): MAR 31
FIELD(S): EDUCATION; MEDICINE
UNDERGRADUATE GRANTS FOR RESIDENTS OF THE PORTERVILLE-POPLAR AREA OF TULARE COUNTY CALIF. MUST CARRY A MINIMUM OF 12 UNITS; HAVE AT LEAST A 2.0 GPA; BE UNDER AGE 21 AND DEMONSTRATE FINANCIAL NEED.
APPROXIMATELY 100 AWARDS PER YEAR; RENEWABLE WITH REAPPLICATION. WRITE FOR COMPLETE INFORMATION.

762

COMMUNITY FOUNDATION OF GREATER LORAIN COUNTY (A.C. SIDDALL EDUCATIONAL TRUST FUND SCHOLARSHIP)
1865 N RIDGE ROAD E; SUITE A
LORAIN OH 44055
216/277-0142 OR 216/323-4445
AMOUNT: $1000
DEADLINE(S): MAY 1
FIELD(S): HEALTH CARE
OPEN TO THOSE WHO WISH TO PURSUE OR FURTHER THEIR EDUCATION IN HEALTH CARE WHO HAVE BEEN OR ARE NOW EMPLOYED AND RESIDE IN OR WORK FOR A HEALTH CARE FACILITY WITHIN THE ALLEN MEMORIAL HOSPITAL DISTRICT IN LORAIN COUNTY.
MUST HAVE WORK EXPERIENCE AND DEMONSTRATE FINANCIAL NEED. APPLICATIONS AVAILABLE BEGINNING JAN 30 FROM ADMINISTRATOR; ALLEN MEMORIAL HOSPITAL; 200 W LORAIN ST; OBERLIN OH 44074.

763

EPILEPSY FOUNDATION OF AMERICA (BEHAVORIAL SCIENCES STUDENT FELLOWSHIPS)
4351 GARDEN CITY DR; SUITE 406
LANDOVER MD 20785
301/459-3700
AMOUNT: $1500
DEADLINE(S): MAR 2
FIELD(S): EPILEPSY RELATED STUDY OR TRAINING PROJECTS.
OPEN TO UNDERGRAD AND GRAD STUDENTS IN NURSING; PSYCHOLOGY AND RELATED AREAS WHO PROPOSE A 3-MONTH EPILEPSY-RELATED PROJECT TO BE CARRIED OUT IN A USA INSTITUTION AT WHICH THERE ARE ONGOING EPILEPSY RESEARCH; SERVICE OR TRAINING PROGRAMS.
FELLOWSHIP MUST BE UNDERTAKEN DURING A FREE PERIOD IN THE STUDENT'S YEAR. WRITE FOR COMPLETE INFORMATION.

764

INTERMURAL RESEARCH TRAINING AWARD (SUMMER INTERN PROGRAM)
OFFICE OF EDUCATION; BLDG 10; RM 1C-129
BETHESDA MD 20892
301/496-2427
AMOUNT: STIPEND
DEADLINE(S): FEB 1
FIELD(S): RESEARCH TRAINING (BIOMEDICAL RESEARCH)
SUMMER INTERN PROGRAM IS DESIGNED TO PROVIDE 'ACADEMICALLY TALENTED' UNDERGRADUATE; GRADUATE OR MEDICAL STUDENTS A UNIQUE OPPORTUNITY TO ACQUIRE VALUABLE HANDS-ON RESEARCH TRAINING AND EXPERIENCE IN THE NEUROSCIENCES.
WRITE FOR COMPLETE INFORMATION.

765

LUPUS FOUNDATION OF AMERICA (STUDENT SUMMER FELLOWSHIP PROGRAM)
4 RESEARCH PLACE; SUITE 180
ROCKVILLE MD 20850
301/670-9292
AMOUNT: $2000
DEADLINE(S): FEB 1
FIELD(S): LUPUS ERYTHEMATOSUS RESEARCH
SUMMER FELLOWSHIPS OPEN TO UNDERGRADS; GRADS & POST-GRADS BUT APPLICANTS ALREADY HAVING COLLEGE DEGREE ARE PREFERRED. APPLICATIONS ARE EVALUATED NIH-STYLE. PURPOSE IS TO ENCOURAGE STUDENTS TO PURSUE RESEARCH CAREERS IN ABOVE AREAS.
RESEARCH MAY BE CONDUCTED AT ANY RECOGNIZED INSTITUTION IN THE USA. APPLICATION MATERIALS AVAILABLE IN DECEMBER. 10 AWARDS PER YEAR. WRITE FOR COMPLETE INFORMATION.

766

NATIONAL INSTITUTES OF HEALTH - NATIONAL CENTER FOR RESEARCH RESOURCES (MINORITY HIGH SCHOOL RESEARCH APPRENTICE PROGRAM)
WESTWOOD BLDG RM 10A11; 5333 WESTBARD AVE
BETHESDA MD 20892
301/496-6743
AMOUNT: $2000
DEADLINE(S): DEC 1
FIELD(S): HEALTH SCIENCES RESEARCH
SUMMER PROGRAM DESIGNED TO OFFER MINORITY HIGH SCHOOL STUDENTS A MEANINGFUL EXPERIENCE IN VARIOUS ASPECTS OF HEALTH RELATED RESEARCH. ITS AIM IS TO STIMULATE STUDENTS'

INTEREST IN SCIENCE. TEACHERS ALSO MAY APPLY. USA CITIZENSHIP REQUIRED.
NIH SUPPORTS THIS PROGRAM AT OVER 391 RESEARCH INSTITUTIONS. STUDENTS MUST APPLY THROUGH PROGRAM DIRECTOR AT THE INSTITUTION. NOT A SCHOLARSHIP.

767

NATIONAL SOCIETY TO PREVENT BLINDNESS (STUDENT RESEARCH FELLOWSHIP)
500 EAST REMINGTON RD
SCHAUMBURG IL 60173
708/843-2020
AMOUNT: $1500 MAXIMUM ($500/MONTH)
DEADLINE(S): MAR 1
FIELD(S): OPHTHALMOLOGY AND VISUAL SCIENCES
STIPEND OPEN TO UNDERGRADUATES; MEDICAL STUDENTS OR GRADUATE STUDENTS FOR FULL TIME EXTRACURRICULAR EYE-RELATED RESEARCH DURING THE SUMMER MONTHS.
WRITE ADMINISTRATOR FOR BROCHURE AND APPLICATION.

768

SANDEE THOMPSON MEMORIAL SCHOLARSHIP FOUNDATION (SCHOLARSHIPS)
1211 NAPOLEON MANOR NE
LAWRENCEVILLE GA 30243
WRITTEN INQUIRY ONLY
AMOUNT: $500
DEADLINE(S): MAR 15
FIELD(S): MEDICINE; NURSING; PHYSICAL THERAPY; RELIGION
OPEN TO UNDERGRADUATE AND GRADUATE STUDENTS HAVING AN INTEREST IN SERVING HUMANITY AND RELIEVING HUMAN SUFFERING. MUST HAVE MEDICAL OR RELIGIOUS ORIENTED CAREER GOAL WITH PHYSICAL THERAPY A HIGH PREFERENCE.
STUDENTS SHOULD BE ENTERING AT LEAST JUNIOR YEAR AT AN ACCREDITED COLEGE OR UNIVERSITY. FINANCIAL INFORMATION REQUIRED. SEND STAMPED; SELF ADDRESSED ENVELOPE FOR COMPLETE INFORMATION.

769

VASA ORDER OF AMERICA (THE ELLIS F. HILLNER AWARD)
E.G. JOHNSON; VICE GRAND MASTER; 4406 SALMON POINT
STOCKTON CA 95219
209/478-7498
AMOUNT: $1000
DEADLINE(S): JAN 15
FIELD(S): MEDICINE
OPEN TO STUDENTS ATTENDING OR PLANNING TO ATTEND AN ACCREDITED INSTITUTION FULL TIME FOR STUDIES IN THE MEDICAL FIELD. MUST HAVE BEEN A VASA MEMBER FOR AT LEAST ONE YEAR AND DEMONSTRATE FINANCIAL NEED.
WRITE FOR COMPLETE INFORMATION.

MEDICAL TECHNOLOGIES

770

AMERICAN ART THERAPY ASSOCIATION (CAY DRACHNIK MINORITIES FUND)
1202 ALLANSON RD
MUNDELEIN IL 60060
708/949-6064
AMOUNT: NOT SPECIFIED
DEADLINE(S): SEP 15
FIELD(S): ART THERAPY
OPEN TO MINORITY GROUP MEMBERS ENROLLED IN AN AATA APPROVED PROGRAM. FUND IS SPECIFICALLY FOR THE PURCHASE OF BOOKS. MUST DEMONSTRATE FINANCIAL NEED THROUGH LETTERS OF REFERENCE; COPIES OF FINANCIAL AID FORMS; ETC.
WRITE FOR COMPLETE INFORMATION.

771

AMERICAN ART THERAPY ASSOCIATION (GLADYS AGELL AWARD FOR EXCELLENCE IN RESEARCH)
1202 ALLANSON ROAD
MUNDELEIN IL 60060
708/949-6064
AMOUNT: NOT SPECIFIED
DEADLINE(S): SEP 15
FIELD(S): ART THERAPY
OPEN TO AATA STUDENT MEMBERS. AWARD IS DESIGNED TO ENCOURAGE STUDENT RESEARCH AND GOES TO THE MOST

OUTSTANDING PROJECT COMPLETED WITHIN THE PAST YEAR IN THE AREA OF APPLIED ART THERAPY.

US CITIZEN. WRITE FOR COMPLETE INFORMATION.

772

AMERICAN ASSOCIATION OF MEDICAL ASSISTANTS ENDOWMENT (MAXINE WILLIAMS SCHOLARSHIP FUND)

20 N WACKER DR; #1575
CHICAGO IL 60606
312/899-1500

AMOUNT: $500

DEADLINE(S): FEB 1; JUN 1

FIELD(S): MEDICAL ASSISTANT

UNDERGRADUATE SCHOLARSHIPS OPEN TO HIGH SCHOOL GRADUATES WHO SUBMIT A WRITTEN STATEMENT EXPRESSING INTEREST IN A CAREER AS A MEDICAL ASSISTANT.

3-7 SCHOLARSHIPS PER YEAR. RENEWABLE. WRITE FOR COMPLETE INFORMATION.

773

AMERICAN DENTAL ASSISTANTS ASSN (SOUTHARD SCHOLARSHIPS FOR DENTAL ASSISTANT TEACHER EDUCATION)

919 N MICHIGAN AVE; SUITE 3400
CHICAGO IL 60611
312/664-3327

AMOUNT: $100 - $1000

DEADLINE(S): JUL 15

FIELD(S): DENTAL ASSISTANT EDUCATION

OPEN TO APPLICANTS WHO ARE HIGH SCHOOL GRADUATES (OR HOLD EQUIVALENT CREDENTIALS) & ARE ENROLLED IN OR ACCEPTED TO DENTAL ASSISTANT TEACHER EDUCATION PROGRAM LEADING TO BACHELORS OR GRADUATE DEGREE. USA CITIZEN.

WRITE FOR COMPLETE INFORMATION.

774

AMERICAN DENTAL HYGIENISTS ASSN (CERTIFICATE SCHOLARSHIP PROGRAM; BACCALAUREATE SCHOLARSHIP PROGRAM; MINORITY SCHOLARSHIP FUND)

444 NORTH MICHIGAN AVE; SUITE 3400
CHICAGO IL 60611
312/440-8900

AMOUNT: $1500 MAXIMUM

DEADLINE(S): MAY 1

FIELD(S): DENTAL HYGIENE

OPEN TO STUDENTS ENTERING THEIR FINAL YEAR IN AN ASSOCIATES/CERTIFICATE PROGRAM OR WHO HAVE COMPLETED AT LEAST 1 YEAR IN A BACHELORS PROGRAM & WILL RECEIVE A DEGREE TO PRACTICE DENTAL HYGIENE IN THE CURRENT YEAR OR YEAR THE AWARD IS MADE.

20-25 AWARDS PER YEAR. MINIMUM GPA OF 3.0 (4.0 SCALE) IS REQUIRED. WRITE FOR COMPLETE INFORMATION.

775

AMERICAN FOUNDATION FOR THE BLIND (RUDOLPH DILLMAN MEMORIAL SCHOLARSHIP)

15 WEST 16TH ST
NEW YORK NY 10011
212/620-2000; TDD 212/620-2158

AMOUNT: $2500

DEADLINE(S): APR 1

FIELD(S): REHABILITATION; EDUCATION OF BLIND & VISUALLY IMPAIRED

OPEN TO LEGALLY BLIND UNDERGRADUATE OR GRADUATE STUDENTS ACCEPTED TO OR ENROLLED IN AN ACCREDITED PROGRAM WITHIN THE BROAD AREAS OF REHABILITATION AND/OR EDUCATION OF THE BLIND AND VISUALLY IMPAIRED. USA CITIZEN.

THREE AWARDS PER YEAR. WRITE FOR COMPLETE INFORMATION.

776

AMERICAN FOUNDATION FOR THE BLIND (TELESENSORY SCHOLARSHIP)

15 WEST 16TH ST
NEW YORK NY 10011
212/620-2000; TDD 212/620-2158

AMOUNT: $1000

DEADLINE(S): APR 1

FIELD(S): REHABILITATION; EDUCATION OF BLIND & VISUALLY IMPAIRED

OPEN TO LEGALLY BLIND UNDERGRADUATE & GRADUATE STUDENTS ACCEPTED TO OR ENROLLED IN AN ACCREDITED PROGRAM WITHIN THE BROAD AREAS OF REHABILITATION AND/OR EDUCATION OF THE BLIND AND VISUALLY IMPAIRED. USA CITIZEN.

WRITE FOR COMPLETE INFORMATION.

777

AMERICAN FUND FOR DENTAL HEALTH (DENTAL LABORATORY TECHNOLOGY SCHOLARSHIPS)
211 E CHICAGO AVE; SUITE 820
CHICAGO IL 60611
312/787-6270
AMOUNT: UP TO $500
DEADLINE(S): JUN 1
FIELD(S): DENTAL LAB TECHNOLOGY
OPEN TO HIGH SCHOOL GRADUATE ENROLLED OR PLANNING TO ENROLL IN ACCREDITED DENTAL LABORATORY TECHNOLOGY PROGRAM. BASIC CRITERIA ARE ACADEMIC RECORD; FINANCIAL NEED & LETTER OF ACCEPTANCE. FOR FIRST OR SECOND YEAR OF STUDY.
MUST BE USA CITIZEN. 10-12 SCHOLARSHIPS ANNUALLY. RENEWABLE UPON REAPPLICATION. WRITE FOR COMPLETE INFORMATION.

778

AMERICAN KINESIOTHERAPY ASSOCIATION (SCHOLARSHIP PROGRAM)
PO BOX 611; WRIGHT BROS STATION
DAYTON OH 45409
WRITTEN INQUIRY
AMOUNT: $500
DEADLINE(S): MAY 1
FIELD(S): KINESIOTHERAPY
OPEN TO STUDENTS WHO HOLD OR ARE IN THE PROCESS OF OBTAINING A DEGREE IN KINESIOTHERAPY; PLAN A CAREER IN KINESIOTHERAPY & ARE SPONSORED BY A CERTIFIED KINESIOTHERAPIST.
WRITE FOR COMPLETE INFORMATION.

779

AMERICAN MEDICAL RECORD ASSOCIATION (FOUNDATION OF RECORD EDUCATION UNDERGRAD SCHOLARSHIP)
919 N MICHIGAN AVE; SUITE 1400
CHICAGO IL 60611
312/787-2672
AMOUNT: $1500
DEADLINE(S): JUL 1
FIELD(S): MEDICAL RECORD ADMINISTRATION
OPEN TO UNDERGRADUATES IN THEIR FINAL YEAR OF A PROGRAM LEADING TO A MEDICAL RECORD ADMINISTRATION DEGREE. PROGRAM MUST BE APPROVED BY THE CAHEA AND APPLICANTS MUST BE USA CITIZENS. INDEPENDENT STUDY PROGRAM STUDENTS ARE NOT ELIGIBLE.
WRITE FOR COMPLETE INFORMATION.

780

AMERICAN MEDICAL RECORD ASSOCIATION (GRACE WHITING MYERS - MALCOLM T. MACEACHERN STUDENT LOAN FUND)
875 NORTH MICHIGAN AVENUE; SUITE 1850
CHICAGO IL 60611
312/787-2672
AMOUNT: $1000 - $2400
DEADLINE(S): JUN 15; OCT 15
FIELD(S): MEDICAL RECORDS
OPEN TO UNDERGRADUATE STUDENTS BEGINNING THEIR FINAL YEAR OF AN ACCREDITED MEDICAL RECORD ADMINISTRATION OR MEDICAL RECORD TECHNOLOGY PROGRAM AND TO GRADUATE STUDENTS WORKING TOWARD A MASTERS OR PHD IN THE MEDICAL RECORD FIELD.
APPLICANTS SHOULD BE FULL TIME STUDENTS AND USA CITIZENS.

781

AMERICAN MEDICAL TECHNOLOGISTS (AMT SCHOLARSHIPS)
710 HIGGINS ROAD
PARK RIDGE IL 60068
708/823-5169
AMOUNT: $250
DEADLINE(S): APR 1
FIELD(S): MEDICAL TECHNOLOGY; DENTAL ASSISTANT; MEDICAL ASSISTANT
OPEN TO HIGH SCHOOL GRADUATES OR HIGH SCHOOL SENIORS WHO PLAN TO ENROLL OR ARE ENROLLED IN AN ACCREDITED PROGRAM IN THE ABOVE AREAS IN THE USA.
WRITE FOR COMPLETE INFORMATION.

782

AMERICAN RESPIRATORY CARE FOUNDATION (STUDENT SCHOLARSHIP PROGRAMS)
11030 ABLES LANE
DALLAS TX 75229
214/243-2272
AMOUNT: $500; $1000; $1250
DEADLINE(S): JUN 1
FIELD(S): RESPIRATORY THERAPY
SCHOLARSHIPS FOR AMA-APPROVED RESPIRATORY THERAPY PROGRAMS. MUST

HAVE MEDICAL OR TECHNICAL DIRECTOR'S SPONSORSHIP; MAINTAIN A 3.0 OR BETTER GPA AND BE USA CITIZEN.

ELIGIBILITY REQUIREMENTS VARY. MINORITY SCHOLARSHIP OFFERED. WRITE FOR COMPLETE INFORMATION.

783

AMERICAN SOCIETY FOR MEDICAL TECHNOLOGY (EDUCATION & RESEARCH FUND - SKONIE UNDERGRADUATE SCHOLARSHIP)

2021 'L' ST NW; SUITE 400
WASHINGTON DC 20036
202/785-3311

AMOUNT: $1000

DEADLINE(S): FEB 1

FIELD(S): MEDICAL TECHNOLOGY

OPEN TO MEDICAL TECHNOLOGY STUDENTS WHO WILL ENTER THEIR SENIOR YEAR WITHIN 12 MONTHS AND ARE CITIZENS OR PERMANENT RESIDENTS OF THE USA. APPLICANTS MUST BE FULL TIME STUDENTS.

WRITE TO EXECUTIVE DIRECTOR AT ADDRESS ABOVE FOR COMPLETE INFORMATION. ENCLOSE STAMPED SELF-ADDRESSED BUSINESS SIZE ENVELOPE.

784

AMERICAN SOCIETY FOR MEDICAL TECHNOLOGY (EDUCATION & RESEARCH FUND - INSTRUMENTATION LABORATORY UNDERGRADUATE SCHOLARSHIP)

2021 'L' ST NW; SUITE 400
WASHINGTON DC 20036
202/785-3311

AMOUNT: $3000 (IN INSTALLMENTS THROUGHOUT JUNIOR & SENIOR YEARS OF STUDY)

DEADLINE(S): FEB 1

FIELD(S): MEDICAL TECHNOLOGY

OPEN TO MEDICAL TECHNOLOGY STUDENTS ENROLLED FULL TIME IN A DEGREE PROGRAM. APPLICANTS MUST BE ENROLLED FULL TIME IN A DEGREE PROGRAM; HAVE COMPLETED THEIR SOPHOMORE YEAR AND BE A PERMANENT USA RESIDENT.

WRITE TO EXECUTIVE DIRECTOR AT ADDRESS ABOVE FOR COMPLETE INFORMATION. ENCLOSE STAMPED SELF-ADDRESSED BUSINESS SIZE ENVELOPE.

785

AMERICAN SOCIETY OF CLINICAL PATHOLOGISTS (SCHOLARSHIP PROGRAM)

2100 W HARRISON ST
CHICAGO IL 60612
312/738-1336 EXT. 221

AMOUNT: $1000

DEADLINE(S): SEP 30

FIELD(S): CYTOTECHNOLOGY; HISTOLOGIC TECHNOLOGY; MEDICAL LABORATORY TECHNOLOGY; MEDICAL TECHNOLOGY

OPEN TO UNDERGRADUATES IN THEIR FINAL CLINICAL YEAR OF TRAINING IN A CAHEA (COMMITTEE ON ALLIED HEALTH EDUCATION AND ACCREDITATION) APPROVED PROGRAM IN THE ABOVE AREAS. APPLICANTS MUST SUPPLY A BRIEF SUMMARY OF ANNUAL INCOME AND EXPENSES.

USA CITIZEN OR LEGAL RESIDENT. WRITE FOR COMPLETE INFORMATION.

786

AMERICAN SPEECH-LANGUAGE-HEARING FOUNDATION (YOUNG SCHOLARS AWARD FOR MINORITY STUDENTS)

10801 ROCKVILLE PIKE
ROCKVILLE MD 20852
301/897-5700; FAX 301/571-0457

AMOUNT: $2000

DEADLINE(S): JUN 1

FIELD(S): SPEECH LANGUAGE PATHOLOGY; AUDIOLOGY

OPEN TO ETHNIC MINORITIES WHO ARE FULL TIME COLLEGE SENIORS PLANNING TO ENTER GRADUATE STUDY IN THE ABOVE AREAS. APPLICANTS MUST SUBMIT A FORMAL PAPER RELATED TO SPEECH/LANGUAGE PATHOLOGY OR AUDIOLOGY FOR CONSIDERATION.

PAPERS WILL BE JUDGED ON MERIT OF CONTENT AND TECHNICAL MERIT. WRITE FOR COMPLETE INFORMATION.

787

ASSOCIATION OF OFFICIAL ANALYTICAL CHEMISTS (HARVEY W. WILEY SCHOLARSHIP AWARD)

2200 WILSON BLVD; SUITE 400
ARLINGTON VA 22201
703-522-3032

AMOUNT: $500 PER YEAR FOR 2 YEARS

DEADLINE(S): MAY 1 OF SOPHOMORE YEAR

FIELD(S): CHEMISTRY; MICROBIOLOGY & RELATED SCIENCES

OPEN TO UNDERGRADUATE SOPHOMORES WHO HAVE MAINTAINED AT LEAST 'B' AVERAGE. AWARDS ARE FOR JUNIOR & SENIOR YEAR IN ABOVE AREAS. MEDICAL; DENTAL; NURSING; ETC MAJORS NOT ELIGIBLE.

WRITE FOR COMPLETE INFORMATION.

788

BUSINESS AND PROFESSIONAL WOMEN'S FOUNDATION (NEW YORK LIFE FOUNDATION SCHOLARSHIPS FOR WOMEN IN THE HEALTH PROFESSIONS)

2012 MASSACHUSETTS AVE NW
WASHINGTON DC 20036
202/293-1200

AMOUNT: $500 - $1000

DEADLINE(S): APR 15 POSTMARK (APPS. AVAILABLE ONLY OCT 1 - APR 1)

FIELD(S): HEALTH RELATED PROFESSIONS

OPEN TO WOMEN (25 OR OLDER) WHO ARE WITHIN 12-24 MONTHS OF COMPLETING THEIR UNDERGRADUATE PROGRAM OF STUDY IN USA. SHOULD LEAD TO ENTRY OR REENTRY INTO THE WORK FORCE OR IMPROVE CHANCES FOR CAREER ADVANCEMENT. USA CITIZEN.

MUST BE ACCEPTED INTO AN ACCREDITED PROGRAM AND DEMONSTRATE FINANCIAL NEED. SEND SELF-ADDRESSED STAMPED ENVELOPE (52 CENTS) #10 ENVELOPE FOR APPLICATION AND COMPLETE INFORMATION.

789

CHARLES E. SAAK TRUST (EDUCATIONAL GRANTS)

C/O WELLS FARGO BANK TRUST DEPT; 2222 W SHAW; #11
FRESNO CA 93711
WRITTEN INQUIRY ONLY

AMOUNT: VARIES

DEADLINE(S): MAR 31

FIELD(S): EDUCATION; MEDICINE

UNDERGRADUATE GRANTS FOR RESIDENTS OF THE PORTERVILLE-POPLAR AREA OF TULARE COUNTY CALIF. MUST CARRY A MINIMUM OF 12 UNITS; HAVE AT LEAST A 2.0 GPA; BE UNDER AGE 21 AND DEMONSTRATE FINANCIAL NEED.

APPROXIMATELY 100 AWARDS PER YEAR; RENEWABLE WITH REAPPLICATION. WRITE FOR COMPLETE INFORMATION.

790

COMMUNITY FOUNDATION OF GREATER LORAIN COUNTY (A.C. SIDDALL EDUCATIONAL TRUST FUND SCHOLARSHIP)

1865 N RIDGE ROAD E; SUITE A
LORAIN OH 44055
216/277-0142 OR 216/323-4445

AMOUNT: $1000

DEADLINE(S): MAY 1

FIELD(S): HEALTH CARE

OPEN TO THOSE WHO WISH TO PURSUE OR FURTHER THEIR EDUCATION IN HEALTH CARE WHO HAVE BEEN OR ARE NOW EMPLOYED AND RESIDE IN OR WORK FOR A HEALTH CARE FACILITY WITHIN THE ALLEN MEMORIAL HOSPITAL DISTRICT IN LORAIN COUNTY.

MUST HAVE WORK EXPERIENCE AND DEMONSTRATE FINANCIAL NEED. APPLICATIONS AVAILABLE BEGINNING JAN 30 FROM ADMINISTRATOR; ALLEN MEMORIAL HOSPITAL; 200 W LORAIN ST; OBERLIN OH 44074.

791

DAUGHTERS OF THE AMERICAN REVOLUTION (NSDAR OCCUPATIONAL THERAPY SCHOLARSHIPS)

1776 'D' ST NW
WASHINGTON DC 20006
202/879-3292

AMOUNT: $500 - $1000 (ONE TIME AWARD)

DEADLINE(S): FEB 15; AUG 15

FIELD(S): OCCUPATIONAL THERAPY; PHYSICAL THERAPY

OPEN TO GRADUATE AND UNDERGRAD STUDENTS ENROLLED IN AN ACCREDITED THERAPY PROGRAM IN THE USA. CANDIDATE MUST BE SPONSORED BY LOCAL DAR CHAPTER AND A USA CITIZEN. SCHOLARSHIP AWARDED BIANNUALLY BASED ON ACADEMIC EXCELLENCE; RECOMMENDATIONS.

WRITE FOR COMPLETE INFORMATION. SEND SELF-ADDRESSED STAMPED ENVELOPE.

792

DUPAGE MEDICAL SOCIETY FOUNDATION (SCHOLARSHIP PROGRAM)

800 ROOSEVELT BLD B; #300
GLEN ELLYN IL 60137
312-858-9603

AMOUNT: $1000

DEADLINE(S): DEC - MAR

FIELD(S): MEDICINE; DENTISTRY; NURSING; MEDICAL TECHNOLOGY; PHARMACY

AWARDS FOR RESIDENTS OF DUPAGE COUNTY; ILLINOIS. OPEN TO THOSE SEEKING HEALTH CARE CAREER WHO ARE ENROLLED IN OR ATTENDING QUALIFIED SCHOOL. ELIGIBILITY BASED ON SCHOLASTIC ABILITY; COLLEGE ACCEPTANCE; FINANCIAL NEED; FAMILY CIRCUMSTANCES.

7 TO 13 SCHOLARSHIPS PER YEAR. RENEWABLE.

793

EASTER SEAL SOCIETY OF IOWA (SCHOLARSHIPS & AWARDS)

PO BOX 4002
DES MOINES IA 50333
515/289-1933

AMOUNT: $400 - $600

DEADLINE(S): APR 15

FIELD(S): PHYSICAL REHABILITATION; MENTAL REHABILITATION; & RELATED AREAS

OPEN TO IOWA RESIDENTS WHO ARE FULL-TIME UNDERGRADUATE SOPHOMORES; JUNIORS; SENIORS OR GRADUATE STUDENTS AT ACCREDITED INSTITUTIONS; PLANNING A CAREER IN THE BROAD FIELD OF REHABILITATION; FINANCIALLY NEEDY & IN TOP 40% OF THEIR CLASS.

6 SCHOLARSHIPS PER YEAR. RENEWABLE. WRITE FOR COMPLETE INFORMATION.

794

EDWARD BANGS AND ELZA KELLEY FOUNDATION (SCHOLARSHIP PROGRAM)

243 SOUTH ST
HYANNIS MA 02601
508/775-3117

AMOUNT: UP TO $4000

DEADLINE(S): APR 30

FIELD(S): MEDICINE; NURSING; HEALTH SCIENCES; RELATED AREAS

OPEN TO RESIDENTS OF BARNSTABLE COUNTY MASS. SCHOLARSHIPS ARE INTENDED TO BENEFIT HEALTH & WELFARE OF BARNSTABLE COUNTY RESIDENTS. AWARDS SUPPORT STUDY AT RECOGNIZED UNDERGRADUATE; GRADUATE & PROFESSIONAL INSTITUTIONS.

FINANCIAL NEED IS A CONSIDERATION. WRITE FOR COMPLETE INFORMATION.

795

EMPIRE COLLEGE (DEAN'S SCHOLARSHIP)

3033 CLEVELAND
SANTA ROSA CA 95403
707/546-4000

AMOUNT: $250 - $1500

DEADLINE(S): APR 15

FIELD(S): COURT REPORTING; ACCOUNTING; SECRETARIAL; LEGAL; MEDICAL (CLINICAL & ADMINISTRATIVE); TRAVEL & TOURISM; GENERAL BUSINESS.

OPEN TO HIGH SCHOOL SENIORS WHO MEET ADMISSION REQUIREMENTS AND WANT TO ATTEND EMPIRE COLLEGE IN SANTA ROSA CALIF. USA CITIZENSHIP REQUIRED.

TEN SCHOLARSHIPS PER YEAR. CONTACT MS. MARLENE MARELLO - HIGH SCHOOL DIRECTOR - FOR COMPLETE INFORMATION.

796

FAIRFAX COUNTY MEDICAL SOCIETY FOUNDATION (SCHOLARSHIPS)

8100 OAK STREET
DUNN LORING VA 22027
703/560-4855

AMOUNT: $1500

DEADLINE(S): MAY 25

FIELD(S): MEDICAL DOCTOR; MEDICAL RELATED DISCIPLINES; MEDICAL TECHNOLOGIES; NURSING

OPEN TO UNDERGRADUATE AND GRADUATE STUDENTS WHO ARE USA CITIZENS AND ARE RESIDENTS OF FAIRFAX COUNTY; VA. FOR STUDIES RELATED TO HUMAN HEALTH. MUST DEMONSTRATE FINANCIAL NEED.

11 AWARDS PER YEAR; RENEWABLE. WRITE FOR COMPLETE INFORMATION.

797

FLORIDA DENTAL ASSOCIATION (DENTAL HYGIENE SCHOLARSHIP PROGRAM)

3021 SWANN AVE
TAMPA FL 33609
813/877-7597

AMOUNT: VARIES

DEADLINE(S): JUL 1; DEC 1; APR 1

FIELD(S): DENTAL HYGIENE

OPEN TO RESIDENTS OF FLORIDA WHO HAVE BEEN ACCEPTED FOR ENROLLMENT IN AN ACCREDITED DENTAL HYGIENE SCHOOL IN FLORIDA. PREFERENCE TO APPLICANTS FROM AREAS IN FLORIDA WITH DENTAL HYGIENIST SHORTAGES.

WRITE FOR COMPLETE INFORMATION.

798

GROUP HEALTH COOPERATIVE AUXILIARY (HEALTH CAREER SCHOLARSHIPS)

1730 MINOR AVE; #1520
SEATTLE WA 98101
206/287-4394

AMOUNT: $1000

DEADLINE(S): FEB 6

FIELD(S): DIRECT PATIENT HEALTH CARE

OPEN ONLY TO EMPLOYEES OF THE GROUP HEALTH CARE COOPERATIVE. FOR UNDERGRADUATE STUDY IN AREAS OF MEDICINE INVOLVING DIRECT PATIENT CARE (SUCH AS NURSING; PHYSICAL THERAPY; ETC.) MUST DEMONSTRATE FINANCIAL NEED.

WRITE FOR COMPLETE INFORMATION.

799

INTERNATIONAL ORDER OF THE KING'S DAUGHTERS AND SONS (HEALTH CAREERS SCHOLARSHIPS)

PO BOX 1017
CHAUTAUQUA NY 14722
716/357-4951

AMOUNT: UP TO $1000

DEADLINE(S): APR 1

FIELD(S): MEDICINE; DENTISTRY; NURSING; PHYSICAL THERAPY; OCCUPATIONAL THERAPY; MEDICAL TECHNOLOGIES; PHARMACY

OPEN TO STUDENTS ACCEPTED TO/ENROLLED IN AN ACCREDITED USA OR CANADIAN 4-YR OR GRADUATE SCHOOL. RN CANDIDATES MUST HAVE COMPLETED 1ST YEAR; BA CANDIDATES IN AT LEAST 3RD YEAR. PRE MED STUDENTS NOT ELIGIBLE.

USA OR CANADIAN CITIZEN. THOSE SEEKING MD OR DDS DEGREES MUST BE IN 2ND YR OF MED OR DENTAL SCHOOL. FOR APPLICATIONS AND COMPLETE INFO SEND SASE TO MRS. MERLE RABER; 6024 E CHICAGO RD; JONESVILLE MI 49250.

800

J. HUGH AND EARLE W. FELLOWS MEMORIAL FUND (SCHOLARSHIP LOANS)

PENSACOLA JUNIOR COLLEGE EXEC VP; 1000 COLLEGE BLVD
PENSACOLA FL 32504
904/484-1706

AMOUNT: EACH IS NEGOTIATED INDIVIDUALLY

DEADLINE(S): NONE

FIELD(S): MEDICINE; NURSING; MEDICAL TECHNOLOGY; THEOLOGY

OPEN TO BONAFIDE RESIDENTS OF THE FLORIDA COUNTIES OF ESCAMBIA; SANTA ROSA; OKALOOSA OR WALTON. FOR UNDERGRADUATE STUDY IN THE FIELDS LISTED ABOVE. USA CITIZEN.

LOANS ARE INTEREST-FREE UNTIL GRADUATION. WRITE FOR COMPLETE INFORMATION.

801

JEWISH VOCATIONAL SERVICE (MARCUS & THERESA LEVIE EDUCATIONAL FUND SCHOLARSHIPS)

1 SOUTH FRANKLIN STREET
CHICAGO IL 60606
312/346-6700 EXT 2214

AMOUNT: $5000

DEADLINE(S): MAR 1

FIELD(S): SOCIAL WORK; MEDICINE; DENTISTRY; NURSING & OTHER RELATED PROFESSIONS & VOCATIONS

OPEN TO COOK COUNTY RESIDENTS OF THE JEWISH FAITH WHO PLAN CAREERS IN THE HELPING PROFESSIONS. MUST SHOW FINANCIAL NEED. FOR UNDERGRADUATE; GRADUATE OR VOCATIONAL STUDY. APPLICATIONS AVAILABLE BEGINNING DEC 1 FROM SCHOLARSHIP SECRETARY.

85-100 AWARDS PER YEAR. RENEWAL POSSIBLE WITH REAPPLICATION. WRITE FOR COMPLETE INFORMATION.

802

MARYLAND HIGHER EDUCATION COMMISSION (PHYSICAL & OCCUPATIONAL THERAPISTS & ASSISTANTS SCHOLARSHIPS)

STATE SCHOLARSHIP ADMINISTRATION; 16 FRANCIS ST
ANNAPOLIS MD 21401
410/974-5370

AMOUNT: $2000

DEADLINE(S): JUL 1

FIELD(S): OCCUPATIONAL THERAPY; PHYSICAL THERAPY

OPEN TO MARYLAND RESIDENTS WHO ENROLL FULL TIME IN POSTSECONDARY INSTITUTIONS HAVING APPROVED OCCUPATIONAL OR PHYSICAL THERAPY PROGRAMS THAT LEAD TO MARYLAND LICENSING AS A THERAPIST OR ASSISTANT.

RECIPIENTS AGREE TO ONE YEAR OF SERVICE AT A PUBLIC SCHOOL; STATE HOSPITAL OR OTHER APPROVED SITE FOR EACH YEAR OF AWARD. WRITE FOR COMPLETE INFORMATION.

803

MARYLAND HIGHER EDUCATION COMMISSION (REIMBURSEMENT OF FIREFIGHTER & RESCUE SQUAD MEMBERS)

STATE SCHOLARSHIP ADMINISTRATION; 16 FRANCIS ST.

ANNAPOLIS MD 21401

410/974-5370

AMOUNT: TUITION REIMBURSEMENT UP TO $2300

DEADLINE(S): JUL 1

FIELD(S): FIRE SERVICE OR EMERGENCY MEDICAL TECHNOLOGY

OPEN TO MARYLAND RESIDENTS AFFILIATED WITH AN ORGANIZED FIRE DEPARTMENT OR RESCUE SQUAD IN MARYLAND. FOR FULL OR PART TIME STUDY AT A MARYLAND INSTITUTION. REIMBURSEMENT MADE ONE YEAR AFTER SUCCESSFUL COMPLETION OF COURSE(S).

FOR UNDERGRADUATE OR GRADUATE STUDY IN MARYLAND. RENEWABLE. WRITE FOR COMPLETE INFORMATION.

804

NATIONAL ASSOCIATION OF AMERICAN BUSINESS CLUBS (SCHOLARSHIPS)

PO BOX 5127

HIGH POINT NC 27262

919/869-2166

AMOUNT: $500 - $1500

DEADLINE(S): APR 15

FIELD(S): PHYSICAL THERAPY; MUSIC THERAPY; OCCUPATIONAL THERAPY; SPEECH-LANGUAGE PATHOLOGY; HEARING-AUDIOLOGY; THERAPEUTIC RECREATION.

OPEN TO UNDERGRADUATE JUNIORS; SENIORS & GRADUATE STUDENTS WHO HAVE GOOD SCHOLASTIC STANDING & PLAN TO ENTER PRACTICE IN HIS OR HER FIELD IN THE USA. GPA OF 3.0 OR BETTER (4.0 SCALE) AND USA CITIZENSHIP REQUIRED.

400-500 SCHOLARSHIPS PER YEAR. RENEWABLE WITH REAPPLICATION. WRITE FOR COMPLETE INFORMATION.

805

NATIONAL ATHLETIC TRAINERS ASSOCIATION (NATA UNDERGRADUATE & GRADUATE SCHOLARSHIP PROGRAM)

2952 STEMMONS

DALLAS TX 75247

214/637-6282

AMOUNT: $1500

DEADLINE(S): FEB 1

FIELD(S): ATHLETIC TRAINER

SCHOLARSHIP PROGRAM OPEN TO STUDENT MEMBERS OF NATA WHO HAVE EXCELLENT ACADEMIC RECORD; HAVE EXCELLED AS STUDENT ATHLETIC TRAINER & HAVE COMPLETED AT LEAST THEIR FRESHMAN YEAR OF STUDY AT AN ACCREDITED COLLEGE OR UNIVERSITY IN THE USA.

30 AWARDS PER YEAR. WRITE TO NATA GRANTS & SCHOLARSHIPS COMMITTEE (ADDRESS ABOVE) FOR COMPLETE INFORMATION.

806

NATIONAL STRENGTH & CONDITIONING ASSN (CHALLENGE SCHOLARSHIPS)

PO BOX 81410

LINCOLN NE 68501

402/472-3000

AMOUNT: $1000

DEADLINE(S): APR 17

FIELD(S): FIELDS RELATED TO STRENGTH & CONDITIONING

OPEN TO NATIONAL STRENGTH & CONDITIONING ASSN MEMBERS. AWARDS ARE FOR UNDERGRADUATE OR GRADUATE STUDY.

WRITE FOR COMPLETE INFORMATION.

807

NELLIE MARTIN CARMAN SCHOLARSHIP TRUST (SCHOLARSHIPS)

1121 244TH ST SW; #65

BOTHELL WA 98021

206/486-6575

AMOUNT: UP TO $1000

DEADLINE(S): MAR 15

FIELD(S): ALL FIELDS OF STUDY EXCEPT THOSE NOTED BELOW

OPEN TO SENIORS IN KING; PIERCE & SNOHOMISH COUNTY (WA) HIGH SCHOOLS WHO HAVE LIVED IN WASHINGTON AT LEAST 5 YRS. FOR UNDERGRADUATE STUDY IN WASHINGTON IN ALL FIELDS EXCEPT MUSIC;

SCULPTURE; DRAWING; INTERIOR DESIGN & HOME ECONOMICS.

APPLICATIONS AVAILABLE ONLY THROUGH HIGH SCHOOLS. NOMINATION BY HS COUNSELOR IS REQUIRED. AWARDS ARE RENEWABLE. USA CITIZEN.

808

NORTH CAROLINA SOCIETY FOR MEDICAL TECHNOLOGY (SCHOLARSHIP AWARD)

PO BOX 62262
DURHAM NC 27715
WRITTEN INQUIRY

AMOUNT: APPROX $300 - $700 (AMOUNTS APPROVED ANNUALLY)

DEADLINE(S): JUN 1

FIELD(S): MEDICAL TECHNOLOGY/MEDICAL LABORATORY TECHNICIAN

OPEN TO NORTH CAROLINA RESIDENTS WHO HAVE BEEN ACCEPTED IN AN APPROVED CLINICAL LABORATORY SCIENCE PROGRAM. MUST MEET NORTH CAROLINA RESIDENCY REQUIREMENTS.

SCHOLARSHIPS ARE RENEWABLE. WRITE FOR COMPLETE INFORMATION.

809

SANDEE THOMPSON MEMORIAL SCHOLARSHIP FOUNDATION (SCHOLARSHIPS)

1211 NAPOLEON MANOR NE
LAWRENCEVILLE GA 30243
WRITTEN INQUIRY ONLY

AMOUNT: $500

DEADLINE(S): MAR 15

FIELD(S): MEDICINE; NURSING; PHYSICAL THERAPY; RELIGION

OPEN TO UNDERGRADUATE AND GRADUATE STUDENTS HAVING AN INTEREST IN SERVING HUMANITY AND RELIEVING HUMAN SUFFERING. MUST HAVE MEDICAL OR RELIGIOUS ORIENTED CAREER GOAL WITH PHYSICAL THERAPY A HIGH PREFERENCE.

STUDENTS SHOULD BE ENTERING AT LEAST JUNIOR YEAR AT AN ACCREDITED COLEGE OR UNIVERSITY. FINANCIAL INFORMATION REQUIRED. SEND STAMPED; SELF-ADDRESSED ENVELOPE FOR COMPLETE INFORMATION.

810

U.S. DEPT. OF HEALTH AND HUMAN SERVICES (NATIONAL HEALTH SERVICE CORPS SCHOLARSHIPS - PHYSICIAN ASSISTANTS)

US PUBLIC HEALTH RECRUITMENT; 8201 GREENSBORO DR; SUITE 600
MCLEAN VA 22102
703/734-6855 OR 800/221-9393

AMOUNT: TUITION; FEES; EXPENSES PLUS MONTHLY STIPEND

DEADLINE(S): NONE SPECIFIED

FIELD(S): PHYSICIAN ASSISTANT

OPEN TO USA CITIZENS ENROLLED OR ACCEPTED FOR ENROLLMENT IN A BACCALAUREATE OR POST BACCALAUREATE PROGRAM LEADING TO CERTIFICATION AS A PRIMARY CARE PHYSICIAN ASSISTANT.

RECIPIENTS ARE OBLIGATED TO SERVE IN A HEALTH PROFESSIONAL SHORTAGE AREA FOR ONE YEAR FOR EACH YEAR OF SUPPORT (MINIMUM OF TWO YEARS). WRITE OR CALL FOR INFORMATION ONE YEAR PRIOR TO APPLYING.

811

UNITED CEREBRAL PALSY ASSOCIATIONS OF NEW YORK STATE (PHYSICAL THERAPY SCHOLARSHIP)

330 W 34TH ST
NEW YORK NY 10001
212/947-5770; FAX 212/594-4538

AMOUNT: $5000

DEADLINE(S): DEC 1

FIELD(S): PHYSICAL THERAPY

OPEN TO QUALIFYING SENIOR PHYSICAL THERAPY STUDENTS. RECIPIENTS MUST AGREE TO ACCEPT EMPLOYMENT BY UCP OF NY FULL TIME FOR 18 CONSECUTIVE MONTHS. APPLICANTS ARE JUDGED ON ACADEMIC RECORD; REFERENCES; PERSONAL INTERVIEW.

APPLICANTS MUST BE ELIGIBLE TO SIT FOR NEW YORK STATE PHYSICAL THERAPY LICENSING EXAM UPON GRADUATION. WRITE FOR COMPLETE INFORMATION.

812

VASA ORDER OF AMERICA (THE ELLIS F. HILLNER AWARD)

E.G. JOHNSON; VICE GRAND MASTER; 4406 SALMON POINT
STOCKTON CA 95219

209/478-7498
AMOUNT: $1000
DEADLINE(S): JAN 15
FIELD(S): MEDICINE
OPEN TO STUDENTS ATTENDING OR PLANNING TO ATTEND AN ACCREDITED INSTITUTION FULL TIME FOR STUDIES IN THE MEDICAL FIELD. MUST HAVE BEEN A VASA MEMBER FOR AT LEAST ONE YEAR AND DEMONSTRATE FINANCIAL NEED.
WRITE FOR COMPLETE INFORMATION.

NURSING

813

ACADEMY OF MEDICINE OF CLEVELAND AUXILIARY (HEALTH CAREERS COMMITTEE-SCHOLARSHIPS)
11001 CEDAR AVE
CLEVELAND OH 44106
216-229-2200
AMOUNT: $400 TO $600
DEADLINE(S): APR 1
FIELD(S): NURSING
MUST BE RESIDENT OF CUYAHOGA COUNTY OH; ACCEPTED TO AN ACCREDITED UNDERGRAD PROGRAM FOR A SPECIFIC HEALTH CAREER IN A CUYAHOGA COUNTY SCHOOL OR HEALTH CARE FACILITY; DEMONSTRATE FINANCIAL NEED AND HAVE A GPA OF 2.0 OR BETTER (4.0 SCALE).
CONTACT MAURINE M. RUGGLES ADDRESS ABOVE FOR COMPLETE INFORMATION.

814

AMERICAN ASSOCIATION OF CRITICAL CARE NURSES (EDUCATIONAL ADVANCEMENT SCHOLARSHIP PROGRAM)
101 COLUMBIA
ALISO VIEJO CA 92656
714/362-2000 OR 800/899-2226 EXT 376
AMOUNT: $1500
DEADLINE(S): JAN 15 POSTMARK
FIELD(S): CRITICAL CARE NURSING
OPEN TO AACN MEMBERS WHO ARE RN'S AND ARE WORKING OR HAVE WORKED IN A CRITICAL CARE UNIT. FOR UNDERGRADUATE (JUNIOR OR SENIOR STATUS) OR GRADUATE STUDY. SHOULD HAVE WORKED CRITICAL CARE FOR 1 YR OF THE LAST 3 AND HAVE 3.0 OR BETTER GPA.
37 AWARDS FOR BACCALAUREATE STUDY AND 17 FOR GRADUATE STUDY PER YEAR. AT LEAST 20% OF THE AWARDS WILL GO TO ETHNIC MINORITIES. WRITE FOR COMPLETE INFORMATION.

815

AMERICAN ASSOCIATION OF NURSE ANESTHETISTS (EDUCATIONAL LOANS)
216 HIGGINS ROAD
PARK RIDGE IL 60068
708/692-7050
AMOUNT: $500 - $2500
DEADLINE(S): NONE
FIELD(S): NURSE ANESTHETIST
LOANS AVAILABLE TO AANA MEMBERS & ASSOCIATE MEMBERS ENROLLED IN A SCHOOL OF ANESTHESIA APPROVED BY THE COUNCIL ON ACCREDITATION OF NURSE ANESTHESIA EDUCATIONAL PROGRAMS. LOANS ARE INTENDED TO COVER UNEXPECTED EVENTS OF AN EMERGENCY NATURE.
CONTACT THE FINANCE DIRECTOR ADDRESS ABOVE FOR COMPLETE INFORMATION.

816

AMERICAN COLLEGE OF NURSE-MIDWIVES FOUNDATION (SCHOLARSHIPS PROGRAM)
1522 'K' STREET NW; #1000
WASHINGTON DC 20005
202/289-0171
AMOUNT: $1000
DEADLINE(S): MAR 1
FIELD(S): NURSE-MIDWIFERY
SCHOLARSHIPS OPEN TO STUDENTS ENROLLED IN ACNM ACCREDITED CERTIFICATE OR GRADUATE NURSE-MIDWIFERY PROGRAMS. STUDENT MEMBERSHIP IN ACNM & COMPLETION OF ONE CLINICAL MODULE OR SEMESTER ALSO REQUIRED.
5-10 AWARDS PER YEAR. APPLICATIONS & INFORMATION AVAILABLE FROM VIOLET BARKAUSKAS CNM; UNIV OF MICHIGAN SCHOOL OF OB NURSING; 400 N INGALLS; ANN ARBOR MI 48109-0604.

817

AMERICAN LEGION AUXILIARY (DEPARTMENT OF THE DISTRICT OF COLUMBIA NURSES SCHOLARSHIP)
DEPARTMENT SECRETARY; 1 SCOTT CIRCLE NW; #404
WASHINGTON DC 20336
WRITTEN INQUIRY ONLY
AMOUNT: NOT SPECIFIED

DEADLINE(S): NONE GIVEN
FIELD(S): NURSING
OPEN TO NURSING STUDENTS WHO HAVE COMPLETED THEIR FIRST YEAR OF COLLEGE. MUST BE THE DAUGHTER OF A VETERAN OF THE USA ARMED FORCES AND RESIDE IN THE WASHINGTON DC METROPOLITAN AREA.
WRITE FOR COMPLETE INFORMATION.

818 ———

AMERICAN LEGION AUXILIARY (PAST PRESIDENTS PARLEY NURSING SCHOLARSHIP)
STATE VETERANS SERVICE BUILDING
ST PAUL MN 55155
612/224-7634
AMOUNT: $500
DEADLINE(S): MAR 15
FIELD(S): NURSING
MINNESOTA RESIDENT WHO IS A MEMBER OF THE DEPT OF MINNESOTA AMERICAN LEGION AUXILIARY AND HAS A 2.0 OR BETTER GPA. TO HELP NEEDY & DESERVING STUDENTS OR ADULTS COMMENCE OR FURTHER THEIR EDUCATION IN NURSING AT A MINNESOTA SCHOOL.
WRITE FOR COMPLETE INFORMATION.

819 ———

ASSOCIATION FOR THE CARE OF CHILDREN'S HEALTH (EMMA PLANK SCHOLARSHIP)
7910 WOODMONT AVE; SUITE 300
BETHESDA MD 20815
301/654-4549
AMOUNT: $500
DEADLINE(S): APR 1
FIELD(S): CHILD HEALTH
OPEN TO STUDENTS AT THE UNDERGRADUATE OR GRADUATE LEVEL STUDYING IN HEALTH RELATED AREAS THAT IMPACT ON CHILDREN.
WRITE FOR COMPLETE INFORMATION.

820 ———

ASSOCIATION OF OPERATING ROOM NURSES (AORN SCHOLARSHIP PROGRAM)
SCHOLARSHIP BOARD; 2170 S PARKER RD; SUITE 300
DENVER CO 80231
303/755-6300
AMOUNT: TUITION & FEES
DEADLINE(S): MAY 1
FIELD(S): NURSING
OPEN TO ACTIVE OR ASSOCIATE AORN MEMBERS FOR AT LEAST 1 CONSECUTIVE YEAR PRIOR TO DEADLINE DATE. AWARDS SUPPORT PRE-NURSING; BA DEGREE; MASTER'S DEGREE & DOCTORAL DEGREE PROGRAMS ACCREDITED BY THE NLN OR OTHER ACCEPTABLE ACCREDITING BODY.
FOR FULL OR PART-TIME STUDY IN THE USA. MINIMUM 3.0 GPA ON 4.0 SCALE. RENEWABLE. WRITE FOR COMPLETE INFORMATION.

821 ———

BUSINESS AND PROFESSIONAL WOMEN'S FOUNDATION (NEW YORK LIFE FOUNDATION SCHOLARSHIPS FOR WOMEN IN THE HEALTH PROFESSIONS)
2012 MASSACHUSETTS AVE NW
WASHINGTON DC 20036
202/293-1200
AMOUNT: $500 - $1000
DEADLINE(S): APR 15 POSTMARK (APPS. AVAILABLE ONLY OCT 1 - APR 1)
FIELD(S): HEALTH RELATED PROFESSIONS
OPEN TO WOMEN (25 OR OLDER) WHO ARE WITHIN 12-24 MONTHS OF COMPLETING THEIR UNDERGRADUATE PROGRAM OF STUDY IN USA. SHOULD LEAD TO ENTRY OR REENTRY INTO THE WORK FORCE OR IMPROVE CHANCES FOR CAREER ADVANCEMENT. USA CITIZEN.
MUST BE ACCEPTED INTO AN ACCREDITED PROGRAM AND DEMONSTRATE FINANCIAL NEED. SEND SELF-ADDRESSED STAMPED ENVELOPE (52 CENTS) #10 ENVELOPE FOR APPLICATION AND COMPLETE INFORMATION.

822 ———

COMMUNITY FOUNDATION OF GREATER LORAIN COUNTY (A.C. SIDDALL EDUCATIONAL TRUST FUND SCHOLARSHIP)
1865 N RIDGE ROAD E; SUITE A
LORAIN OH 44055
216/277-0142 OR 216/323-4445
AMOUNT: $1000
DEADLINE(S): MAY 1
FIELD(S): HEALTH CARE
OPEN TO THOSE WHO WISH TO PURSUE OR FURTHER THEIR EDUCATION IN HEALTH CARE WHO HAVE BEEN OR ARE NOW EMPLOYED AND RESIDE IN OR WORK FOR A HEALTH CARE FACILITY WITHIN THE ALLEN MEMORIAL HOSPITAL DISTRICT IN LORAIN COUNTY.

MUST HAVE WORK EXPERIENCE AND DEMONSTRATE FINANCIAL NEED. APPLICATIONS AVAILABLE BEGINNING JAN 30 FROM ADMINISTRATOR; ALLEN MEMORIAL HOSPITAL; 200 W LORAIN ST; OBERLIN OH 44074.

823

CONNECTICUT LEAGUE FOR NURSING (SCHOLARSHIPS)
PO BOX 365
WALLINGFORD CT 06492
203/265-4248
AMOUNT: $500; $450; $300
DEADLINE(S): OCT 30
FIELD(S): NURSING
UNDERGRADUATE SCHOLARSHIPS OPEN TO CONNECTICUT RESIDENTS IN THEIR FINAL YEAR OF STUDY AT A CONNECTICUT SCHOOL OF NURSING. AWARDS ARE BASED ON MERIT AND FINANCIAL NEED. SCHOOL MUST BE AGENCY MEMBER OF THE CONNECTICUT LEAGUE FOR NURSING.
THREE AWARDS PER YEAR. CONTACT EXECUTIVE DIRECTOR JUDITH GILKES BENSON AT ABOVE ADDRESS FOR COMPLETE INFORMATION.

824

CUYAHOGA COUNTY MEDICAL FOUNDATION (SCHOLARSHIP GRANT PROGRAM)
11001 CEDAR AVE
CLEVELAND OH 44106
216/229-2200
AMOUNT: $500 - $1500
DEADLINE(S): JUN 1
FIELD(S): MEDICINE; DENTISTRY; PHARMACY; NURSING; OSTEOPATHY
GRANTS OPEN TO RESIDENTS OF CUYAHOGA COUNTY WHO ARE ACCEPTED TO OR ENROLLED IN AN ACCREDITED PROFESSIONAL SCHOOL IN ONE OF THE ABOVE AREAS. USA CITIZEN.
APPROX 40 AWARDS PER YEAR. WRITE FOR COMPLETE INFORMATION.

825

DAUGHTERS OF THE AMERICAN REVOLUTION (CAROLINE HOLT NURSING SCHOLARSHIPS)
1776 'D' ST NW
WASHINGTON DC 20006
202/879-3292
AMOUNT: $500 (ONE TIME AWARD)
DEADLINE(S): FEB 15; AUG 15
FIELD(S): NURSING
OPEN TO UNDERGRADUATE STUDENTS ENROLLED IN AN ACCREDITED NURSING PROGRAM IN THE USA. NO AFFILIATION OR RELATION TO DAR IS REQUIRED BUT APPLICANTS MUST BE SPONSORED BY A LOCAL DAR CHAPTER AND USA CITIZENS.
AWARDS ARE BASED ON ACADEMIC EXCELLENCE; FINANCIAL NEED AND RECOMMENDATIONS. WRITE FOR COMPLETE INFORMATION. SEND SELF-ADDRESSED STAMPED ENVELOPE.

826

DUPAGE MEDICAL SOCIETY FOUNDATION (SCHOLARSHIP PROGRAM)
800 ROOSEVELT BLD B; #300
GLEN ELLYN IL 60137
312-858-9603
AMOUNT: $1000
DEADLINE(S): DEC - MAR
FIELD(S): MEDICINE; DENTISTRY; NURSING; MEDICAL TECHNOLOGY; PHARMACY
AWARDS FOR RESIDENTS OF DUPAGE COUNTY; ILLINOIS. OPEN TO THOSE SEEKING HEALTH CARE CAREER WHO ARE ENROLLED IN OR ATTENDING QUALIFIED SCHOOL. ELIGIBILITY BASED ON SCHOLASTIC ABILITY; COLLEGE ACCEPTANCE; FINANCIAL NEED; FAMILY CIRCUMSTANCES.
7 TO 13 SCHOLARSHIPS PER YEAR. RENEWABLE.

827

EDWARD BANGS AND ELZA KELLEY FOUNDATION (SCHOLARSHIP PROGRAM)
243 SOUTH ST
HYANNIS MA 02601
508/775-3117
AMOUNT: UP TO $4000
DEADLINE(S): APR 30
FIELD(S): MEDICINE; NURSING; HEALTH SCIENCES; RELATED AREAS
OPEN TO RESIDENTS OF BARNSTABLE COUNTY MASS. SCHOLARSHIPS ARE INTENDED TO BENEFIT HEALTH & WELFARE OF BARNSTABLE COUNTY RESIDENTS. AWARDS SUPPORT STUDY AT RECOGNIZED UNDERGRADUATE; GRADUATE & PROFESSIONAL INSTITUTIONS.
FINANCIAL NEED IS A CONSIDERATION. WRITE FOR COMPLETE INFORMATION.

828

EPILEPSY FOUNDATION OF AMERICA (BEHAVIORAL SCIENCES STUDENT FELLOWSHIPS)

4351 GARDEN CITY DR; SUITE 406
LANDOVER MD 20785
301/459-3700

AMOUNT: $1500
DEADLINE(S): MAR 2
FIELD(S): EPILEPSY RELATED STUDY OR TRAINING PROJECTS

OPEN TO UNDERGRAD AND GRAD STUDENTS IN NURSING; PSYCHOLOGY AND RELATED AREAS WHO PROPOSE A 3-MONTH EPILEPSY-RELATED PROJECT TO BE CARRIED OUT IN A USA INSTITUTION AT WHICH THERE ARE ONGOING EPILEPSY RESEARCH; SERVICE OR TRAINING PROGRAMS.

FELLOWSHIP MUST BE UNDERTAKEN DURING A FREE PERIOD IN THE STUDENT'S YEAR. WRITE FOR COMPLETE INFORMATION.

829

FAIRFAX COUNTY MEDICAL SOCIETY FOUNDATION (SCHOLARSHIPS)

8100 OAK STREET
DUNN LORING VA 22027
703/560-4855

AMOUNT: $1500
DEADLINE(S): MAY 25
FIELD(S): MEDICAL DOCTOR; MEDICAL RELATED DISCIPLINES; MEDICAL TECHNOLOGIES; NURSING

OPEN TO UNDERGRADUATE AND GRADUATE STUDENTS WHO ARE USA CITIZENS AND ARE RESIDENTS OF FAIRFAX COUNTY; VA FOR STUDIES RELATED TO HUMAN HEALTH. MUST DEMONSTRATE FINANCIAL NEED.

11 AWARDS PER YEAR; RENEWABLE. WRITE FOR COMPLETE INFORMATION.

830

GENERAL HOSPITAL #2 NURSES ALUMNAE (SCHOLARSHIP FUND)

PO BOX 413657
KANSAS CITY MO 64141
WRITTEN INQUIRY

AMOUNT: $500
DEADLINE(S): MAR 31
FIELD(S): NURSING

OPEN TO ANY BLACK STUDENT ENROLLED IN A REGISTERED NURSING PROGRAM AT ANY ACCREDITED SCHOOL OF NURSING IN THE USA. MUST SHOW FINANCIAL NEED AND FURNISH COPY OF ACADEMIC RECORD.

APPLICANTS TO PROVIDE STATEMENT OF WHY FIELD OF NURSING WAS CHOSEN AND WHAT THE AWARD WOULD MEAN TO THEM. WRITE FOR COMPLETE INFORMATION.

831

GOOD SAMARITAN FOUNDATION (NURSING SCHOLARSHIPS)

5615 KIRBY DR; SUITE 308
HOUSTON TX 77005
713-529-4647

AMOUNT: VARIES
DEADLINE(S): NONE
FIELD(S): NURSING

OPEN TO ALL NURSING STUDENTS AT 'TEXAS' SCHOOLS WHO HAVE ATTAINED THE CLINICAL LEVEL OF THEIR NURSING EDUCATION. AWARDS SUPPORT FULL-TIME STUDY IN ALL ACCREDITED NURSING PROGRAMS (LVN; DIPLOMA; ADN; RN; BSN). USA CITIZEN OR LEGAL RESIDENT.

STUDENTS SHOULD TRY TO APPLY AT LEAST 6 MONTHS PRIOR TO THE START OF CLINICAL COURSES. APPROX 600 AWARDS PER YEAR. RENEWABLE. WRITE FOR COMPLETE DETAILS.

832

GROUP HEALTH COOPERATIVE AUXILIARY (HEALTH CAREER SCHOLARSHIPS)

1730 MINOR AVE; #1520
SEATTLE WA 98101
206/287-4394

AMOUNT: $1000
DEADLINE(S): FEB 6
FIELD(S): DIRECT PATIENT HEALTH CARE

OPEN ONLY TO EMPLOYEES OF THE GROUP HEALTH CARE COOPERATIVE. FOR UNDERGRADUATE STUDY IN AREAS OF MEDICINE INVOLVING DIRECT PATIENT CARE (SUCH AS NURSING; PHYSICAL THERAPY; ETC.) MUST DEMONSTRATE FINANCIAL NEED.

WRITE FOR COMPLETE INFORMATION.

833

HARVEY AND BERNICE JONES FOUNDATION

PO BOX 233
SPRINGDALE AR 72765
501/756-0611

AMOUNT: VARIES

DEADLINE(S): NONE SPECIFIED
FIELD(S): NURSING
SCHOLARSHIPS AVAILABLE TO RESIDENTS OF SPRINGDALE AR WHO WANT TO PURSUE A CAREER IN NURSING. MUST BE USA CITIZEN AND DEMONSTRATE FINANCIAL NEED.
NUMBER OF AWARDS PER YEAR VARIES. CONTACT ADDRESS ABOVE FOR COMPLETE INFORMATION.

834

INDIANA STATE STUDENT ASSISTANCE COMMISSION (NURSING SCHOLARSHIP FUND)
150 W MARKET ST; 5TH FLOOR
INDIANAPOLIS IN 46204
317/232-2350
AMOUNT: UP TO $5000
DEADLINE(S): VARIES WITH COLLEGE
FIELD(S): NURSING
OPEN TO INDIANA RESIDENTS ENROLLED IN AN UNDERGRADUATE NURSING PROGRAM AT AN INDIANA COLLEGE OR UNIVERSITY. APPLICANTS MUST HAVE A GPA OF 2.0 OR BETTER (4.0 SCALE).
MUST DEMONSTRATE FINANCIAL NEED. WRITE FOR COMPLETE INFORMATION.

835

INTERNATIONAL ORDER OF THE KING'S DAUGHTERS AND SONS (HEALTH CAREERS SCHOLARSHIPS)
PO BOX 1017
CHAUTAUQUA NY 14722
716/357-4951
AMOUNT: UP TO $1000
DEADLINE(S): APR 1
FIELD(S): MEDICINE; DENTISTRY; NURSING; PHYSICAL THERAPY; OCCUPATIONAL THERAPY; MEDICAL TECHNOLOGIES; PHARMACY
OPEN TO STUDENTS ACCEPTED TO/ENROLLED IN AN ACCREDITED USA OR CANADIAN 4-YR OR GRADUATE SCHOOL. RN CANDIDATES MUST HAVE COMPLETED 1ST YEAR; BA CANDIDATES IN AT LEAST 3RD YEAR. PRE MED STUDENTS NOT ELIGIBLE.
USA OR CANADIAN CITIZEN. THOSE SEEKING MD OR DDS DEGREES MUST BE IN 2ND YR OF MED OR DENTAL SCHOOL. FOR APPLICATIONS AND COMPLETE INFO SEND SASE TO MRS. MERLE RABER; 6024 E CHICAGO RD; JONESVILLE MI 49250.

836

J. HUGH AND EARLE W. FELLOWS MEMORIAL FUND (SCHOLARSHIP LOANS)
PENSACOLA JUNIOR COLLEGE EXEC VP; 1000 COLLEGE BLVD
PENSACOLA FL 32504
904/484-1706
AMOUNT: EACH IS NEGOTIATED INDIVIDUALLY
DEADLINE(S): NONE
FIELD(S): MEDICINE; NURSING; MEDICAL TECHNOLOGY; THEOLOGY
OPEN TO BONAFIDE RESIDENTS OF THE FLORIDA COUNTIES OF ESCAMBIA; SANTA ROSA; OKALOOSA OR WALTON. FOR UNDERGRADUATE STUDY IN THE FIELDS LISTED ABOVE. USA CITIZEN.
LOANS ARE INTEREST-FREE UNTIL GRADUATION. WRITE FOR COMPLETE INFORMATION.

837

JEWISH VOCATIONAL SERVICE (MARCUS & THERESA LEVIE EDUCATIONAL FUND SCHOLARSHIPS)
1 SOUTH FRANKLIN STREET
CHICAGO IL 60606
312/346-6700 EXT 2214
AMOUNT: $5000
DEADLINE(S): MAR 1
FIELD(S): SOCIAL WORK; MEDICINE; DENTISTRY; NURSING & OTHER RELATED PROFESSIONS & VOCATIONS
OPEN TO COOK COUNTY RESIDENTS OF THE JEWISH FAITH WHO PLAN CAREERS IN THE HELPING PROFESSIONS. MUST SHOW FINANCIAL NEED. FOR UNDERGRADUATE; GRADUATE OR VOCATIONAL STUDY. APPLICATIONS AVAILABLE BEGINNING DEC 1 FROM SCHOLARSHIP SECRETARY.
85-100 AWARDS PER YEAR. RENEWAL POSSIBLE WITH REAPPLICATION. WRITE FOR COMPLETE INFORMATION.

838

MARYLAND HIGHER EDUCATION COMMISSION (PROFESSIONAL SCHOOL SCHOLARSHIPS)
STATE SCHOLARSHIP ADMINISTRATION; 16 FRANCIS ST
ANNAPOLIS MD 21401
410/974-5370
AMOUNT: $200 - $1000
DEADLINE(S): MAR 1

FIELD(S): DENTISTRY; PHARMACY; MEDICINE; LAW; NURSING

OPEN TO MARYLAND RESIDENTS WHO HAVE BEEN ADMITTED AS FULL-TIME STUDENTS AT A PARTICIPATING GRADUATE INSTITUTION OF HIGHER LEARNING IN MARYLAND OR AN UNDERGRADUATE NURSING PROGRAM.

RENEWABLE UP TO 4 YEARS. WRITE FOR COMPLETE INFORMATION AND A LIST OF PARTICIPATING MARYLAND INSTITUTIONS.

839

MARYLAND HIGHER EDUCATION COMMISSION (STATE NURSING SCHOLARSHIP & LIVING GRANT)

STATE SCHOLARSHIP ADMINISTRATION; 16 FRANCIS ST

ANNAPOLIS MD 21401

410/974-5370

AMOUNT: SCHOLARSHIP $2400/YEAR; GRANT $2400/YEAR

DEADLINE(S): SCHOLARSHIP JUN 15; GRANT MAR 1

FIELD(S): NURSING

MD RESIDENT. FOR FULL OR PART TIME GRAD OR UNDERGRAD STUDY IN MD. MUST AGREE TO SERVE AS FULL TIME NURSE IN MD AFTER GRADUATION AND HAVE 3.0 OR BETTER GPA. MUST HOLD NURSING SCHOLARSHIP AND SHOW FINANCIAL NEED FOR LIVING EXPENSES GRANT.

RENEWABLE. WRITE FOR COMPLETE INFORMATION.

840

MATERNITY CENTER ASSOCIATION (HAZEL CORBIN ASSISTANCE FUND-STIPEND AWARDS)

48 EAST 92ND ST

NEW YORK NY 10128

212/369-7300

AMOUNT: MONTHLY STIPEND-AMOUNT VARIES

DEADLINE(S): VARIES

FIELD(S): NURSE-MIDWIFERY

MONTHLY STIPEND FOR NURSE-MIDWIFERY STUDENTS (THEY MUST BE NURSES ALREADY) WHO ARE ENROLLED IN AN ACCREDITED SCHOOL OF MIDWIFERY AND WHO PLAN TO PRACTICE NURSE-MIDWIFERY IN THE USA FOR AT LEAST 1 YEAR UPON CERTIFICATION.

WRITE FOR COMPLETE INFORMATION.

841

MCFARLAND CHARITABLE FOUNDATION TRUST (NURSING SCHOLARSHIPS)

L.M. BUTLER; VP; HAVANA NAT'L BANK; 112 S ORANGE; POB 489

HAVANA IL 62644

309/543-3361

AMOUNT: $3000 - $12000

DEADLINE(S): APR 1

FIELD(S): REGISTERED NURSING

ILLINOIS RESIDENT & USA CITIZEN. OPEN TO UNDERGRAD RN DEGREE CANDIDATES ENROLLED IN ACCREDITED INSTITUTIONS. RECIPIENTS MUST AGREE TO RETURN TO HAVANA IL AREA TO WORK AS RN FOR AN AGREED UPON NUMBER OF YEARS UPON COMPLETION OF EDUCATION.

WRITTEN CONTRACT WITH CO-SIGNERS IS REQUIRED. PENALTY FOR BREACH OF CONTRACT IS SEVERE. 6-10 AWARDS PER YEAR. WRITE FOR COMPLETE INFORMATION.

842

MIDWAY COLLEGE (INSTITUTIONAL AID PROGRAM-SCHOLARSHIPS AND GRANTS)

FINANCIAL AID OFFICE

MIDWAY KY 40347

606-846-4421

AMOUNT: VARIES

DEADLINE(S): MAR 15

FIELD(S): NURSING; PARALEGAL; BILINGUAL BUSINESS; FRENCH STUDIES; SPANISH STUDIES; EQUINE STUDIES

SCHOLARSHIPS & GRANTS OPEN TO WOMEN WHO ARE ACCEPTED FOR ENROLLMENT AT MIDWAY COLLEGE. AWARDS SUPPORT UNDERGRADUATE STUDY IN THE ABOVE AREAS.

APPROX 200 AWARDS PER YEAR. CONTACT ADDRESS ABOVE FOR COMPLETE DETAILS.

843

MISSISSIPPI BOARD OF TRUSTEES OF STATE INSTITUTIONS OF HIGHER LEARNING (NURSING EDUCATION SCHOLARSHIP GRANTS)

3825 RIDGEWOOD ROAD

JACKSON MS 39211

601/982-6570

AMOUNT: $50 - $3000

DEADLINE(S): NONE SPECIFIED

FIELD(S): NURSING

OPEN TO REGISTERED NURSES WHO HAVE LIVED IN MISSISSIPPI AT LEAST ONE YEAR AND ARE ENROLLED IN A NURSING PROGRAM AT AN ACCREDITED MISSISSIPPI INSTITUTION IN PURSUIT OF A BACHELOR OF SCIENCE OR GRADUATE DEGREE.

SCHOLARSHIPS ARE RENEWABLE. WRITE FOR COMPLETE INFORMATION.

844

MISSOURI LEAGUE FOR NURSING (SCHOLARSHIPS)

PO BOX 104476

JEFFERSON CITY MO 65110

314/635-5355

AMOUNT: $100 - $5000

DEADLINE(S): SEP 30

FIELD(S): NURSING

OPEN TO NURSING STUDENTS WHO RESIDE IN MISSOURI AND ARE ATTENDING AN NLN ACCREDITED SCHOOL IN MISSOURI. FOR COURSE WORK LEADING TO LICENSING AS AN LPN OR RN OR TO A BSN OR MSN DEGREE. MUST DEMONSTRATE FINANCIAL NEED.

APPLICATION MUST BE MADE THROUGH THE DIRECTOR OF NURSING AT THE STUDENT'S SCHOOL.

845

NAACOG - THE ORGANIZATION FOR OBSTETRIC; GYNECOLOGIC & NEONATAL NURSES (NAACOG FELLOWSHIPS)

409 12TH ST SW

WASHINGTON DC 20024

202-863-2434; 800-673-8499 EXT 2434

AMOUNT: $2000

DEADLINE(S): APR 1

FIELD(S): NURSING OBSTETRICS; GYNECOLOGY; NEONATOLOGY

OPEN TO MEMBERS AND ASSOCIATE MEMBERS OF NAACOG WHO ARE PURSUING OR ALREADY HAVE A NURSING DEGREE AT ANY LEVEL. SHOULD HAVE 2 YEARS EXPERIENCE IN THE ABOVE AREAS.

THREE AWARDS ANNUALLY. WRITE TO THE EDUCATION AND RESEARCH DEPARTMENT AT THE ADDRESS ABOVE FOR COMPLETE INFORMATION.

846

NATIONAL BLACK NURSES' ASSOCIATION INC. (DR. LAURANNE SAMS SCHOLARSHIP)

PO BOX 1823

WASHINGTON DC 20013

202/393-6870

AMOUNT: $1000

DEADLINE(S): APR 15

FIELD(S): NURSING

SCHOLARSHIPS FOR STUDENTS ENROLLED IN A NURSING PROGRAM (AD; DIPLOMA; BSN; LPN/LVN) WHO ARE IN GOOD SCHOLASTIC STANDING AND ARE MEMBERS OF THE ASSOCIATION.

WRITE FOR COMPLETE INFORMATION.

847

NATIONAL FOUNDATION FOR LONG-TERM HEALTH CARE (JAMES D. DURANTE NURSE SCHOLARSHIP PROGRAM)

1201 'L' STREET NW

WASHINGTON DC 20005

202/842-4444

AMOUNT: $500

DEADLINE(S): EARLY JUNE

FIELD(S): NURSING

OPEN TO LPN AND RN STUDENTS WHO SEEK TO CONTINUE OR FURTHER THEIR EDUCATION.

20 $500 SCHOLARSHIPS PER YEAR. SEND A STAMPED SELF-ADDRESSED LEGAL SIZE ENVELOPE WITH REQUEST FOR APPLICATION IN THE EARLY SPRING.

848

NATIONAL FOUNDATION FOR LONG TERM HEALTH CARE (REGISTERED NURSE EDUCATION AWARD)

AMERICAN HEALTH CARE ASSOCIATION; 1201 L ST NW

WASHINGTON DC 20005

202/842-4444

AMOUNT: $1000

DEADLINE(S): [illegible]

FIELD(S): [illegible]

AWARD[illegible]AL OR CONTINUING TRAIN[illegible]N A REGISTERED NURSE PROGRAM FOR PEOPLE WORKING IN LONG-TERM CARE FACILITIES ASSOCIATED WITH AMERICAN HEALTH CARE ASSOCIATION. FOR STUDY IN USA ONLY.

15-20 AWARDS PER YEAR. WRITE FOR COMPLETE INFORMATION.

849

NATIONAL STUDENT NURSES ASSN FOUNDATION (SCHOLARSHIP PROGRAM)
555 WEST 57TH STREET
NEW YORK NY 10019
212/581-2215
AMOUNT: $1000 TO $2500
DEADLINE(S): FEB 1
FIELD(S): NURSING
OPEN TO STUDENTS ENROLLED IN STATE APPROVED SCHOOLS OF NURSING OR PRE-NURSING IN ASSOCIATE DEGREE; BACCALAUREATE; DIPLOMA; GENERIC DOCTORATE OR GENERIC MASTER'S PROGRAMS. FINANCIAL NEED; GRADES; COMMUNITY ACTIVITIES ARE CONSIDERATIONS.
APPLICATIONS AVAILABLE SEPTEMBER THROUGH JAN 15. SEND SELF-ADDRESSED STAMPED (52 CENTS) LEGAL SIZE ENVELOPE FOR APPLICATION. APPLICATION MUST BE ACCOMPANIED BY $5 PROCESSING FEE.

850

NELLIE MARTIN CARMAN SCHOLARSHIP TRUST (SCHOLARSHIPS)
1121 244TH ST SW #65
BOTHELL WA 98021
206/486-6575
AMOUNT: UP TO $1000
DEADLINE(S): MAR 15
FIELD(S): ALL FIELDS OF STUDY EXCEPT THOSE NOTED BELOW
OPEN TO SENIORS IN KING; PIERCE & SNOHOMISH COUNTY (WA) HIGH SCHOOLS WHO HAVE LIVED IN WASHINGTON AT LEAST 5 YRS. FOR UNDERGRADUATE STUDY IN WASHINGTON IN ALL FIELDS EXCEPT MUSIC; SCULPTURE; DRAWING; INTERIOR DESIGN & HOME ECONOMICS.
APPLICATIONS AVAILABLE ONLY THROUGH HIGH SCHOOLS. NOMINATION BY HS COUNSELOR IS REQUIRED. AWARDS ARE RENEWABLE. USA CITIZEN.

851

NEW HAMPSHIRE POST-SECONDARY EDUCATION COMMISSION (NURSING EDUCATION ASSISTANCE GRANTS)
TWO INDUSTRIAL PARK DR
CONCORD NH 03301
603/271-2555
AMOUNT: $600 - $2000
DEADLINE(S): JUN 1; DEC 15
FIELD(S): NURSING
OPEN TO NEW HAMPSHIRE RESIDENTS WHO ARE ACCEPTED TO OR ENROLLED IN AN APPROVED NURSING PROGRAM IN THE STATE OF NEW HAMPSHIRE. USA CITIZEN OR LEGAL RESIDENT. MUST DEMONSTRATE FINANCIAL NEED.
APPROX 110 GRANTS PER YEAR. WRITE FOR COMPLETE INFORMATION.

852

NEW YORK TELEPHONE (SCHOLARSHIP PROGRAM FOR BLACK AND HISPANIC STUDENTS)
COTE; PO BOX 2810
CHERRY HILL NJ 08034
609/573-9400
AMOUNT: $2000
DEADLINE(S): APR 30
FIELD(S): ENGINEERING; SCIENCE; COMPUTER SCIENCE; NURSING
OPEN TO BLACK OR HISPANIC STUDENTS WHO RESIDE IN NEW YORK AND ATTEND ACCREDITED NEW YORK STATE SCHOOLS. FOR FULL TIME STUDENTS ENROLLED AS A SECOND SEMESTER SOPHOMORES IN A 4 YEAR UNDERGRADUATE PROGRAM LEADING TO A BACHELOR DEGREE.
FINANCIAL NEED IS A CONSIDERATION. RENEWABLE. WRITE FOR COMPLETE INFORMATION.

853

OHIO LEAGUE FOR NURSING (GRANTS AND LOANS)
STUDENT AID COMMITTEE; 2800 EUCLID AVE; SUITE 235
CLEVELAND OH 44115
216/781-7222
AMOUNT: VARIES
DEADLINE(S): FEB 1 - MAY 1
FIELD(S): NURSING
OPEN TO NURSING STUDENTS WHO ARE RESIDENTS OF GREATER CLEVELAND AREA (CUYAHOGA; GEAUGA; LAKE; LORAIN COUNTIES) & WILL AGREE TO WORK IN A HEALTH-CARE FACILITY IN THIS AREA FOR AT LEAST A YEAR AFTER GRADUATION. USA CITIZEN OR LEGAL RESIDENT.
40-45 AWARDS PER YEAR. WRITE FOR COMPLETE INFORMATION.

854

ONCOLOGY NURSING FOUNDATION (SCHOLARSHIPS)
501 HOLIDAY DRIVE
PITTSBURGH PA 15220
412/921-7373
AMOUNT: $1000 UNDERGRAD (10); $2500 GRADUATE (8); $2500 DOCTORAL (5)
DEADLINE(S): JAN 15
FIELD(S): NURSING
OPEN TO REGISTERED NURSES WHO ARE SEEKING A BACHELOR'S; MASTER'S OR DOCTORAL DEGREE IN AN NLN ACCREDITED NURSING PROGRAM & HAVE AN INTEREST IN ONCOLOGY NURSING.
WRITE FOR COMPLETE INFORMATION.

855

SANDEE THOMPSON MEMORIAL SCHOLARSHIP FOUNDATION (SCHOLARSHIPS)
1211 NAPOLEON MANOR NE
LAWRENCEVILLE GA 30243
WRITTEN INQUIRY ONLY
AMOUNT: $500
DEADLINE(S): MAR 15
FIELD(S): MEDICINE; NURSING; PHYSICAL THERAPY; RELIGION
OPEN TO UNDERGRADUATE AND GRADUATE STUDENTS HAVING AN INTEREST IN SERVING HUMANITY AND RELIEVING HUMAN SUFFERING. MUST HAVE MEDICAL OR RELIGIOUS ORIENTED CAREER GOAL WITH PHYSICAL THERAPY A HIGH PREFERENCE.
STUDENTS SHOULD BE ENTERING AT LEAST JUNIOR YEAR AT AN ACCREDITED COLEGE OR UNIVERSITY. FINANCIAL INFORMATION REQUIRED. SEND STAMPED; SELF-ADDRESSED ENVELOPE FOR COMPLETE INFORMATION.

856

TYSON FOUNDATION INC. (SCHOLARSHIP PROGRAM)
2210 OAKLAWN
SPRINGDALE AR 72764
501/756-4955
AMOUNT: UP TO $1000/SEMESTER
DEADLINE(S): JUN 21
FIELD(S): BUSINESS; AGRICULTURE; ENGINEERING; COMPUTER SCIENCE; NURSING
OPEN TO USA CITIZENS WHO LIVE IN THE VICINITY OF TYSON FOOD FACILITIES AND MAINTAIN A 2.5 GPA. MUST WORK AND CARRY AT LEAST 12 SEMESTER HOURS OR EQUIVALENT. FOR UNDERGRADUATE STUDY AT SCHOOLS IN USA.
RECIPIENTS SIGN A PLEDGE EITHER TO REPAY THE SCHOLARSHIP MONEY OR HELP ANOTHER DESERVING STUDENT NOT RELATED BY BLOOD OR MARRIAGE TO ATTEND COLLEGE. WRITE FOR COMPLETE INFORMATION.

857

U.S. AIR FORCE ROTC (4-YEAR SCHOLARSHIP PROGRAM)
AFROTC/RROO; RECRUITING OPERATIONS BRANCH
MAXWELL AFB AL 36112
205/953-2091
AMOUNT: TUITION + FEES & BOOKS + $100 PER MONTH STIPEND
DEADLINE(S): DEC 1
FIELD(S): AERONAUTICAL ENGINEERING; CIVIL ENGINEERING; MECHANICAL ENGINEERING; MATHEMATICS; PHYSICS; NURSING & SOME LIBERAL ARTS
OPEN TO USA CITIZENS WHO ARE AT LEAST 17 AND WILL GRADUATE FROM COLLEGE BEFORE AGE 25. MUST COMPLETE APPLICATION; FURNISH SAT/ACT SCORES; HIGH SCHOOL TRANSCRIPTS AND RECORD OF EXTRACURRICULAR ACTIVITIES.
MUST QUALIFY ON AIR FORCE MEDICAL EXAMINATION. ABOUT 1600 SCHOLARSHIPS AWARDED EACH YEAR AT CAMPUSES WHICH OFFER AIR FORCE ROTC.

858

U.S. DEPT. OF HEALTH AND HUMAN SERVICES (INDIAN HEALTH SERVICE'S HEALTH SCHOLARSHIP PROGRAM; PUBLIC LAW 94-437)
TWINBROOK METRO PLAZA; SUITE 100; 12300 TWINBROOK PKWY
ROCKVILLE MD 20852
301/443-6197
AMOUNT: TUITION + FEES & MONTHLY STIPEND
DEADLINE(S): APR 15
FIELD(S): HEALTH PROFESSIONS
OPEN TO AMERICAN INDIAN OR ALASKA NATIVES WHO ENROLL IN COURSES THAT WILL LEAD TO A BACCALAUREATE DEGREE AND WILL PREPARE THEM FOR ACCEPTANCE

INTO HEALTH PROFESSIONS SCHOOLS. RENEWABLE ANNUALLY WITH REAPPLICATION.

SCHOLARSHIP RECIPIENTS MUST INTEND TO SERVE THE INDIAN PEOPLE AS A HEALTH CARE PROVIDER. THEY INCUR A 1 YEAR SERVICE OBLIGATION TO THE INDIAN HEALTH SERVICE FOR EACH YEAR OF SUPPORT. WRITE FOR COMPLETE INFORMATION.

859

VASA ORDER OF AMERICA (THE ELLIS F. HILLNER AWARD)

E.G. JOHNSON; VICE GRAND MASTER; 4406 SALMON POINT

STOCKTON CA 95219

209/478-7498

AMOUNT: $1000

DEADLINE(S): JAN 15

FIELD(S): MEDICINE

OPEN TO STUDENTS ATTENDING OR PLANNING TO ATTEND AN ACCREDITED INSTITUTION FULL TIME FOR STUDIES IN THE MEDICAL FIELD. MUST HAVE BEEN A VASA MEMBER FOR AT LEAST ONE YEAR AND DEMONSTRATE FINANCIAL NEED.

WRITE FOR COMPLETE INFORMATION.

860

VIRGIN ISLANDS BOARD OF EDUCATION (NURSING & OTHER HEALTH SCHOLARSHIPS)

PO BOX 11900

ST THOMAS VI 00801

809/774-4546

AMOUNT: UP TO $1800

DEADLINE(S): MAR 31

FIELD(S): NURSING; MEDICINE; HEALTH RELATED AREAS

OPEN TO BONAFIDE RESIDENTS OF THE VIRGIN ISLANDS WHO ARE ACCEPTED BY AN ACCREDITED SCHOOL OF NURSING OR AN ACCREDITED INSTITUTION OFFERING COURSES IN ONE OF THE HEALTH RELATED FIELDS.

THIS SCHOLARSHIP IS GRANTED FOR THE DURATION OF THE COURSE PROVIDED THE RECIPIENTS MAINTAIN AT LEAST A ‘C’ AVERAGE. CONTACT ADDRESS ABOVE FOR COMPLETE INFORMATION.

861

VIRGINIA BAPTIST GENERAL BOARD (JULIAN A. HUDGENS TRUST FUND)

PO BOX 8568

RICHMOND VA 23226

WRITTEN INQUIRY

AMOUNT: VARIES

DEADLINE(S): AUG

FIELD(S): NURSING

OPEN TO RESIDENTS OF VIRGINIA WHO ARE PURSUING A CAREER AS A NURSING MISSIONARY & ARE A MEMBER OF A CHURCH ASSOCIATED WITH THE BAPTIST GENERAL ASSN OF VIRGINIA.

LOANS ARE NON-REPAYABLE IF RECIPIENT WORKS AS A MISSIONARY FOR 2 YEARS. WRITE FOR COMPLETE INFORMATION.

862

VIRGINIA DEPARTMENT OF HEALTH - PUBLIC HEALTH NURSING (VIRGINIA STATE NURSING SCHOLARSHIPS)

1500 E MAIN ST; PO BOX 2448

RICHMOND VA 23218

WRITTEN INQUIRY

AMOUNT: $150 - $2000

DEADLINE(S): APR 30 FOR ENROLLED STUDENTS; JUN 30 FOR ENTERING STUDENTS.

FIELD(S): NURSING

OPEN TO VIRGINIA RESIDENTS ENROLLED OR ACCEPTED IN A VIRGINIA SCHOOL OF NURSING. FOR FULL TIME STUDY LEADING TO AN UNDERGRADUATE OR GRADUATE NURSING DEGREE. MUST AGREE TO ENGAGE IN FULL TIME NURSING PRACTICE IN VIRGINIA UPON GRADUATION.

SCHOLARSHIPS ARE RENEWABLE. MUST DEMONSTRATE FINANCIAL NEED AND HAVE AT LEAST A 2.5 CUMULATIVE GRADE POINT AVERAGE. WRITE FOR COMPLETE INFORMATION.

863

WISCONSIN LEAGUE FOR NURSING INC (SCHOLARSHIP)

2121 EAST NEWPORT AVE

MILWAUKEE WI 53211

414/332-6271

AMOUNT: $500

DEADLINE(S): FEB 28

FIELD(S): NURSING

WISC RESIDENT ENROLLED IN NATIONAL LEAGUE FOR NURSING ACCREDITED PROGRAM IN WISC. CATEGORIES- RN SEEKING BSN/STUDENT SEEKING RN (ADN DIPLOMA OR BSN)/BSN-RN'S SEEKING MSN. GPA 3.0 OR BETTER. HALFWAY THROUGH ACADEMIC PROGRAM. US CITIZEN

MUST DEMONSTRATE FINANCIAL NEED AND BE RECOMMENDED BY DEAN OR DIRECTOR. WRITE FOR COMPLETE INFORMATION.

NUTRITION

864

ABBIE SARGENT MEMORIAL SCHOLARSHIP INC (SCHOLARSHIPS)
295 SHEEP DAVIS ROAD
CONCORD NH 03301
603/224-1934
AMOUNT: $200
DEADLINE(S): MAR 15
FIELD(S): AGRICULTURE; VETERINARY MEDICINE; HOME ECONOMICS

OPEN TO NEW HAMPSHIRE RESIDENT WHO IS HIGH SCHOOL GRADUATE WITH GOOD GRADES AND CHARACTER. FOR UNDERGRADUATE OR GRADUATE STUDY. USA LEGAL RESIDENT. DEMONSTRATE FINANCIAL NEED.

RENEWABLE WITH REAPPLICATION. WRITE FOR COMPLETE INFORMATION.

865

AMERICAN ASSOCIATION OF CEREAL CHEMISTS (UNDERGRADUATE SCHOLARSHIPS AND GRADUATE FELLOWSHIPS)
SCHOLARSHIP DEPT; 3340 PILOT KNOB RD
ST PAUL MN 55121
612/454-7250
AMOUNT: $1000 - $2000 UNDERGRAD; $2000 - $3000 GRAD
DEADLINE(S): APR 1
FIELD(S): FOOD SCIENCE

SCHOLARSHIPS AND FELLOWSHIPS OPEN TO STUDENTS MAJORING IN OR INTERESTED IN A CAREER IN CEREAL SCIENCE OR TECHNOLOGY; INCLUDING BAKING OR RELATED AREA. STRONG ACADEMIC RECORD AND CAREER INTEREST ARE THE IMPORTANT CRITERIA.

AACC MEMBERSHIP IS HELPFUL BUT NOT NECESSARY. WRITE FOR COMPLETE INFORMATION.

866

AMERICAN DIETETIC ASSOCIATION (DIETETIC TECHNICIAN)
216 W JACKSON BLVD; SUITE 800
CHICAGO IL 60606
800/877-1600 EXT 4876
AMOUNT: $250 - $1000
DEADLINE(S): FEB 13 (REQUEST APPLICATION BY JAN 15)
FIELD(S): DIETETIC TECHNICIAN

OPEN TO STUDENTS IN THEIR FIRST YEAR OF STUDY IN AN ADA-APPROVED DIETETIC TECHNICIAN PROGRAM. IF SELECTED STUDENT MAY USE THE SCHOLARSHIP FOR STUDY DURING SECOND YEAR. MUST BE USA CITIZEN AND SHOW EVIDENCE OF LEADERSHIP & ACADEMIC ABILITY.

FINANCIAL NEED; PROFESSIONAL POTENTIAL & SCHOLARSHIP ARE CONSIDERATIONS. WRITE FOR COMPLETE INFORMATION.

867

AMERICAN DIETETIC ASSOCIATION FOUNDATION (BACCALAUREATE OR COORDINATED PROGRAM)
216 W JACKSON BLVD; SUITE 800
CHICAGO IL 60606
800/877-1600 EXT 4876
AMOUNT: $250 - $1000
DEADLINE(S): FEB 13 (REQUEST APPLICATION BY JAN 15)
FIELD(S): DIETETICS

OPEN TO STUDENTS WHO HAVE COMPLETED THE ACADEMIC REQUIREMENTS IN AN ADA-ACCREDITED OR APPROVED COLLEGE OR UNIVERSITY PROGRAM FOR MINIMUM STANDING AS A JUNIOR. MUST BE USA CITIZEN AND SHOW PROMISE OF VALUE TO THE PROFESSION.

FINANCIAL NEED; PROFESSIONAL POTENTIAL & SCHOLARSHIP ARE CONSIDERATIONS. WRITE FOR COMPLETE INFORMATION.

868

AMERICAN DIETETIC ASSOCIATION FOUNDATION (DIETETIC INTERNSHIPS)
216 WEST JACKSON BLVD; SUITE 800
CHICAGO IL 60606
800/877-1600 EXT 4876
AMOUNT: $250 - $2500
DEADLINE(S): FEB 13 - REQUEST APPLICATION BY JAN 15

FIELD(S): DIETETIC INTERNSHIPS
OPEN TO STUDENTS WHO HAVE APPLIED TO AN ADA-ACCREDITED DIETETIC INTERNSHIP AND WHO SHOW PROMISE OF BEING A VALUABLE CONTRIBUTING MEMBER TO THE PROFESSION. USA CITIZENSHIP REQUIRED.
FINANCIAL NEED; PROFESSIONAL POTENTIAL & SCHOLARSHIP ARE CONSIDERATIONS. WRITE FOR COMPLETE INFORMATION.

869

AMERICAN DIETETIC ASSOCIATION FOUNDATION (KRAFT GENERAL FOODS FELLOWSHIP PROGRAM)
216 WEST JACKSON; SUITE 800
CHICAGO IL 60606
312/899-0040
AMOUNT: $10000 PER YEAR
DEADLINE(S): JUN 1
FIELD(S): NUTRITION
OPEN TO SENIOR UNDERGRADUATE & GRADUATE STUDENTS WHO PROPOSE TO PURSUE GRADUATE WORK RELATED TO NUTRITION RESEARCH OR NUTRITION EDUCATION & CONSUMER AWARENESS AT RECOGNIZED INSTITUTIONS IN THE USA. FOR CITIZENS OF USA; MEXICO & CANADA.
FELLOWSHIPS RENEWABLE FOR UP TO 3 YEARS. WRITE FOR COMPLETE INFORMATION.

870

AMERICAN DIETETIC ASSOCIATION FOUNDATION (PREPROFESSIONAL PRACTICE PROGRAM - AP4)
216 W JACKSON BLVD; SUITE 800
CHICAGO IL 60606
800/877-1600 EXT 4876
AMOUNT: $250 - $2500
DEADLINE(S): FEB 13 (REQUEST APPLICATION BY JAN 15)
FIELD(S): DIETETICS
OPEN TO UNDERGRADUATE AND GRADUATE STUDENTS WHO ARE ENROLLED OR PLAN TO ENROLL IN AN ADA-APPROVED PREPROFESSIONAL PRACTICE PROGRAM AND WHO SHOW PROMISE OF BEING A VALUABLE CONTRIBUTING MEMBER OF THE PROFESSION. USA CITIZENSHIP REQUIRED.
FINANCIAL NEED; PROFESSIONAL POTENTIAL & SCHOLARSHIP ARE CONSIDERATIONS. WRITE FOR COMPLETE INFORMATION.

871

ASSOCIATION FOR THE CARE OF CHILDREN'S HEALTH (EMMA PLANK SCHOLARSHIP)
7910 WOODMONT AVE; SUITE 300
BETHESDA MD 20815
301/654-4549
AMOUNT: $500
DEADLINE(S): APR 1
FIELD(S): CHILD HEALTH
OPEN TO STUDENTS AT THE UNDERGRADUATE OR GRADUATE LEVEL STUDYING IN HEALTH RELATED AREAS THAT IMPACT ON CHILDREN.
WRITE FOR COMPLETE INFORMATION.

872

BUSINESS AND PROFESSIONAL WOMEN'S FOUNDATION (NEW YORK LIFE FOUNDATION SCHOLARSHIPS FOR WOMEN IN THE HEALTH PROFESSIONS)
2012 MASSACHUSETTS AVE NW
WASHINGTON DC 20036
202/293-1200
AMOUNT: $500 - $1000
DEADLINE(S): APR 15 POSTMARK (APPS. AVAILABLE ONLY OCT 1 - APR 1)
FIELD(S): HEALTH RELATED PROFESSIONS
OPEN TO WOMEN (25 OR OLDER) WHO ARE WITHIN 12-24 MONTHS OF COMPLETING THEIR UNDERGRADUATE PROGRAM OF STUDY IN USA. SHOULD LEAD TO ENTRY OR REENTRY INTO THE WORK FORCE OR IMPROVE CHANCES FOR CAREER ADVANCEMENT. USA CITIZEN.
MUST BE ACCEPTED INTO AN ACCREDITED PROGRAM AND DEMONSTRATE FINANCIAL NEED. SEND SELF-ADDRESSED STAMPED ENVELOPE (52 CENTS) #10 ENVELOPE FOR APPLICATION AND COMPLETE INFORMATION.

873

COMMUNITY FOUNDATION OF GREATER LORAIN COUNTY (A.C. SIDDALL EDUCATIONAL TRUST FUND SCHOLARSHIP)
1865 N. RIDGE ROAD E; SUITE A
LORAIN OH 44055
216/277-0142 OR 216/323-4445
AMOUNT: $1000
DEADLINE(S): MAY 1
FIELD(S): HEALTH CARE
OPEN TO THOSE WHO WISH TO PURSUE OR FURTHER THEIR EDUCATION IN HEALTH CARE WHO HAVE BEEN OR ARE NOW

EMPLOYED AND RESIDE IN OR WORK FOR A HEALTH CARE FACILITY WITHIN THE ALLEN MEMORIAL HOSPITAL DISTRICT IN LORAIN COUNTY.

MUST HAVE WORK EXPERIENCE AND DEMONSTRATE FINANCIAL NEED. APPLICATIONS AVAILABLE BEGINNING JAN 30 FROM ADMINISTRATOR; ALLEN MEMORIAL HOSPITAL; 200 W LORAIN ST; OBERLIN OH 44074.

874

DAIRY RECOGNITION EDUCATION FOUNDATION (LOW INTEREST LOANS)

6245 EXECUTIVE BLVD
ROCKVILLE MD 20852
301/984-1444

AMOUNT: UP TO $1500
DEADLINE(S): NONE
FIELD(S): DAIRY SCIENCE; FOOD SCIENCE

LOW-INTEREST LOANS (CURRENTLY 4%) FOR CITIZENS OF THE USA & CANADA WHO ARE IN GOOD ACADEMIC STANDING IN THE ABOVE AREAS. AWARDS SUPPORT UNDERGRADUATE STUDY. PREFERENCE GIVEN TO STUDENTS WHO HAVE COMPLETED AT LEAST ONE YEAR OF COLLEGE.

10-20 AWARDS PER YEAR. WRITE FOR COMPLETE INFORMATION.

875

EDUCATIONAL FOUNDATION OF NATIONAL RESTAURANT ASSOC (UNDERGRADUATE SCHOLARSHIPS)

250 S WACKER DR; SUITE 1400
CHICAGO IL 60606
312/715-1010

AMOUNT: $500 - $10000
DEADLINE(S): MAR 1
FIELD(S): FOOD MANAGEMENT/SCIENCE

OPEN TO UNDERGRADUATE STUDENTS WITH GPA OF 3.2 OR HIGHER WHO ARE ENROLLED FULL TIME IN AN ACCREDITED FOODSERVICE/HOSPITALITY (OR RELATED AREA) PROGRAM RESULTING IN AN ASSOCIATES OR BACHELORS DEGREE.

APPROX 100 AWARDS PER YEAR. RENEWABLE WITH RE-APPLICATION. APPLICATIONS AVAILABLE DEC 1. WRITE FOR COMPLETE INFORMATION.

876

EDUCATIONAL FOUNDATION OF NATIONAL RESTAURANT ASSOC (UNDERGRADUATE SCHOLARSHIP PROGRAM)

250 S WACKER DR; SUITE 1400
CHICAGO IL 60606
312/715-1010

AMOUNT: $750 - $10000
DEADLINE(S): MAR 1
FIELD(S): FOODSERVICE; HOSPITALITY

OPEN TO FULL TIME UNDERGRADS IN A FOODSERVICE/HOSPITALITY DEGREE GRANTING PROGRAM BEGINNING WITH THE FALL TERM. MUST HAVE WORKED IN FOOD SERVICE INDUSTRY AND DEMONSTRATED CONSISTENT ACADEMIC ACHIEVEMENT.

MORE THAN 100 UNDERGRAD AWARDS PER YEAR.WRITE FOR COMPLETE INFORMATION.

877

GOLDEN GATE RESTAURANT ASSOCIATION (DAVID RUBENSTEIN MEMORIAL SCHOLARSHIP FOUNDATION AWARDS)

291 GEARY ST; SUITE 600
SAN FRANCISCO CA 94102
415/781-5348

AMOUNT: $1000 - $1500
DEADLINE(S): MAR 31
FIELD(S): HOTEL & RESTAURANT MANAGEMENT/FOOD SCIENCE

OPEN TO STUDENTS WHO HAVE COMPLETED THE FIRST SEMESTER OF COLLEGE AS A FOODSERVICE MAJOR AND HAVE A 2.75 OR BETTER GPA (4.0 SCALE) IN HOTEL & RESTAURANT COURSES.

SEVEN AWARDS PER YEAR. WRITE FOR COMPLETE INFORMATION.

878

HOTEL EMPLOYEES & RESTAURANT EMPLOYEES INTERNATIONAL UNION (EDWARD T. HANLEY SCHOLARSHIP)

1219 28TH STREET NW
WASHINGTON DC 20007
202/393-4373

AMOUNT: TUITION; FEES; ROOM & BOARD; VALUE OVER $6500 PER YEAR
DEADLINE(S): APR 1
FIELD(S): CULINARY ARTS

2 YR SCHOLARSHIP TO CULINARY INSTITUTE OF AMERICA IN NY. OPEN TO H.E.R.E. UNION MEMBERS (MINIMUM 1 YEAR) AND

CANDIDATES RECOMMENDED BY UNION MEMBERS. APPLICATIONS ARE BY THE VICE PRESIDENTIAL DISTRICT IN WHICH THE MEMBER LIVES.

RESIDENTS OF ODD NUMBERED DISTRICTS APPLY IN ODD NUMBERED YEARS; EVEN NUMBERED DISTRICTS IN EVEN YEARS. APPLICATIONS ARE PUBLISHED IN JAN, FEB & MAR EDITIONS OF "CATERING INDUSTRY EMPLOYEE." WRITE FOR COMPLETE INFORMATION.

879

ILLINOIS RESTAURANT ASSN (SCHOLARSHIP FUND)

350 WEST ONTARIO; 7TH FLOOR
CHICAGO IL 60610
312/787-4000

AMOUNT: VARIOUS

DEADLINE(S): VARIES

FIELD(S): FOOD MANAGEMENT; FOOD SCIENCE; CULINARY ARTS

OPEN TO ILLINOIS RESIDENTS FOR UNDERGRADUATE STUDY OF FOOD SERVICE MANAGEMENT; CULINARY ARTS; FOOD PROCESSING AND RELATED SUBJECTS AT ACCREDITED INSTITUTIONS IN THE USA.

WRITE FOR COMPLETE INFORMATION.

880

INSTITUTE OF FOOD TECHNOLOGISTS (FRESHMAN SCHOLARSHIPS)

221 N LA SALLE ST; #300
CHICAGO IL 60601
312/782-8424; FAX 312/782-8348

AMOUNT: $750 - $1000

DEADLINE(S): FEB 15

FIELD(S): FOOD SCIENCE; FOOD TECHNOLOGY

OPEN TO SCHOLASTICALLY OUTSTANDING HIGH SCHOOL GRADUATES OR HS SENIORS ENTERING COLLEGE FOR THE FIRST TIME IN AN APPROVED PROGRAM IN FOOD SCIENCE OR FOOD TECHNOLOGY.

15 SCHOLARSHIPS PER YEAR - ONE AT $1000; 14 AT $750. WRITE FOR COMPLETE INFORMATION.

881

INSTITUTE OF FOOD TECHNOLOGISTS (JUNIOR/SENIOR SCHOLARSHIPS)

221 N LA SALLE ST; #300
CHICAGO IL 60601
312/782-8424; FAX 312/782-8348

AMOUNT: $750 - $2000

DEADLINE(S): FEB 1

FIELD(S): FOOD SCIENCE; FOOD TECHNOLOGY

OPEN TO UNDERGRADUATE SOPHOMORES AND JUNIORS PURSUING AN APPROVED PROGRAM IN FOOD SCIENCE/TECHNOLOGY IN A USA OR CANADIAN INSTITUTION. APPLICANTS SHOULD BE SCHOLASTICALLY OUTSTANDING AND HAVE A WELL ROUNDED PERSONALITY.

FOR JUNIOR OR SENIOR YEAR OF STUDY. 55 JUNIOR/SENIOR AWARDS PER YEAR; RENEWABLE UPON REAPPLICATION. WRITE FOR COMPLETE INFORMATION.

882

INSTITUTE OF FOOD TECHNOLOGISTS (SOPHOMORE SCHOLARSHIPS)

221 N LA SALLE ST; #300
CHICAGO IL 60601
312/782-8424; FAX 312/782-8348

AMOUNT: $750 - $1000

DEADLINE(S): MAR 1

FIELD(S): FOOD SCIENCE; FOOD TECHNOLOGY

OPEN TO SCHOLASTICALLY OUTSTANDING COLLEGE FRESHMEN WHO HAVE A 2.5 OR BETTER GRADE POINT AVERAGE AND ARE EITHER PURSUING OR TRANSFERRING TO AN APPROVED PROGRAM IN FOOD SCIENCE/TECHNOLOGY.

17 AWARDS PER YEAR - 3 AT $1000; 14 AT $750. WRITE FOR COMPLETE INFORMATION.

883

MONTGOMERY COUNTY EXTENSION HOMEMAKER COUNCIL (MARY IRENE WATERS SCHOLARSHIP)

1311 LAYHILL ROAD
SILVER SPRING MD 20906
301-590-9638

AMOUNT: $1000

DEADLINE(S): MAR 31

FIELD(S): HOME ECONOMICS OR HUMAN ECOLOGY

OPEN TO GRADUATES OF MONTGOMERY COUNTY MD HIGH SCHOOLS OR PERMANENT MONTGOMERY COUNTY RESIDENTS WHO ARE COMPLETING OR HAVE COMPLETED THE SECOND YEAR AT A COLLEGE IN MARYLAND. MUST PLAN TO PURSUE A CAREER IN HOME ECONOMICS OR HUMAN ECOLOGY.

WRITE FOR COMPLETE INFORMATION.

884

NELLIE MARTIN CARMAN SCHOLARSHIP TRUST (SCHOLARSHIPS)
1121 244TH ST SW; #65
BOTHELL WA 98021
206/486-6575
AMOUNT: UP TO $1000
DEADLINE(S): MAR 15
FIELD(S): ALL FIELDS OF STUDY EXCEPT THOSE NOTED BELOW
OPEN TO SENIORS IN KING; PIERCE & SNOHOMISH COUNTY (WA) HIGH SCHOOLS WHO HAVE LIVED IN WASHINGTON AT LEAST 5 YRS. FOR UNDERGRADUATE STUDY IN WASHINGTON IN ALL FIELDS EXCEPT MUSIC; SCULPTURE; DRAWING; INTERIOR DESIGN & HOME ECONOMICS.
APPLICATIONS AVAILABLE ONLY THROUGH HIGH SCHOOLS. NOMINATION BY HS COUNSELOR IS REQUIRED. AWARDS ARE RENEWABLE. USA CITIZEN.

885

PHI UPSILON OMICRON NATIONAL OFFICE (JANICE CORY BULLOCK SCHOLARSHIP)
208 MOUNT HALL; 1050 CARMACK ROAD
COLUMBUS OH 43210
614/421-7860
AMOUNT: $500
DEADLINE(S): MAR 1
FIELD(S): HOME ECONOMICS
OPEN TO PHI U HOMEMAKERS WHO DESIRE TO CONTINUE AN EDUCATION FOR EITHER UNDERGRADUATE OR GRADUATE WORK IN HOME ECONOMICS WHICH WILL ENABLE THEM TO BE GAINFULLY EMPLOYED.
WRITE FOR COMPLETE INFORMATION.

886

PHI UPSILON OMICRON NATIONAL OFFICE (UNDERGRADUATE SCHOLARSHIPS)
208 MOUNT HALL; 1050 CARMACK ROAD
COLUMBUS OH 43210
614/421-7860
AMOUNT: $500
DEADLINE(S): MAR 1
FIELD(S): HOME ECONOMICS
OPEN TO PHI U MEMBERS WORKING TOWARD A BACCALAUREATE DEGREE. SELECTION BASED ON SCHOLASTIC RECORD; PARTICIPATION IN PHI U; STUDENT AHEA AND OTHER COLLEGIATE ACTIVITIES; STATEMENT OF PROFESSIONAL GOALS AND PERSONAL QUALIFICATIONS.
WRITE FOR COMPLETE INFORMATION.

887

SCHOOL FOOD SERVICE FOUNDATION (SCHOLARSHIPS AND LOANS)
1600 DUKE ST; 7TH FLOOR
ALEXANDRIA VA 22314
703/739-3900 OR 800/877-8822
AMOUNT: $150 - $1000
DEADLINE(S): APR 15
FIELD(S): FOOD SCIENCE & NUTRITION; FOOD SERVICE MANAGEMENT
OPEN TO ASFSA MEMBERS FOR GRADUATE OR UNDERGRADUATE STUDY IN THE ABOVE FIELDS. 3 SCHOLARSHIP PROGRAMS ARE OFFERED TO THOSE MEMBERS PLANNING A CAREER IN SCHOOL FOOD SERVICE. ONE OF THE SCHOLARSHIPS IS AVAILABLE TO CHILDREN OF ASFSA MEMBERS.
MUST DEMONSTRATE FINANCIAL NEED AND HAVE A GPA OF 2.7 OR BETTER. WRITE FOR COMPLETE INFORMATION.

888

STATLER FOUNDATION (SCHOLARSHIPS)
107 DELAWARE AVE; SUITE 508
BUFFALO NY 14202
716/852-1104
AMOUNT: $500 PER YEAR
DEADLINE(S): APR 15
FIELD(S): FOOD MANAGEMENT; CULINARY ARTS; HOTEL-MOTEL MANAGEMENT
OPEN TO UNDERGRADUATE OR GRADUATE STUDENTS WHO ARE ACCEPTED TO OR ENROLLED FULL TIME AT A USA INSTITUTION IN AN ACCREDITED PROGRAM OF STUDY IN ANY OF THE ABOVE AREAS.
APPROX 900 AWARDS PER YEAR. RENEWABLE. WRITE FOR COMPLETE INFORMATION.

889

TEXAS ELECTRIC COOPERATIVES INC (ANN LANE HOMEMAKER SCHOLARSHIP)
PO BOX 9589
AUSTIN TX 78766
512/454-0311
AMOUNT: $1000
DEADLINE(S): MAR 1
FIELD(S): HOME ECONOMICS
OPEN TO TEXAS RESIDENTS WHO ARE GRADUATING HIGH SCHOOL SENIORS AND ARE ACTIVE MEMBERS OF A LOCAL FUTURE HOMEMAKERS OF AMERICA CHAPTER. AWARD TENABLE AT ACCREDITED UNDERGRADUATE COLLEGE OR UNIVERSITY. USA CITIZEN.
WRITE FOR COMPLETE INFORMATION.

890

WOMEN GROCERS OF AMERICA (MARY MACEY SCHOLARSHIP PROGRAM)
1825 SAMUEL MORSE DR
RESTON VA 22090
703/437-5300
AMOUNT: $500
DEADLINE(S): JUN 1
FIELD(S): FOOD MANAGEMENT/SCIENCE
OPEN TO UNDERGRADUATE & GRADUATE STUDENTS PURSUING A COURSE OF STUDY LEADING TO A FOOD INDUSTRY RELATED CAREER. AWARDS ARE TENABLE AT RECOGNIZED COLLEGES & UNIVERSITIES.
WRITE FOR COMPLETE INFORMATION.

SCHOOL OF SOCIAL SCIENCE

891

ALPHA KAPPA ALPHA (LEADERSHIP FELLOWS GRANT)
5656 SO STONY ISLAND AVE
CHICAGO IL 60637
312/684-1282
AMOUNT: EXPENSES TO ATTEND 1 WEEK SEMINAR
DEADLINE(S): FEB 15
FIELD(S): SOCIAL SCIENCES
OPEN TO AKA SORORITY MEMBERS WHO HAVE MAINTAINED A 'B' AVERAGE OR BETTER; DEMONSTRATED LEADERSHIP & EXCELLED IN WRITING AN ASSIGNED ESSAY. APPLICANTS SHOULD BE IN THEIR JUNIOR OR SENIOR YEAR OF COLLEGE.
30 AWARDS PER YEAR. ESSAY THEME VARIES ANNUALLY. WRITE FOR COMPLETE INFORMATION.

892

CAPE CANAVERAL CHAPTER RETIRED OFFICERS ASSOC (SCHOLARSHIPS)
PO BOX 4186
PATRICK AFB FL 32925
WRITTEN INQUIRY
AMOUNT: APPROX $1500 PER YEAR
DEADLINE(S): MAY 31
FIELD(S): SCIENCE; MATHEMATICS; ENGINEERING; LIBERAL ARTS; CHEMISTRY
OPEN ONLY TO BREVARD COUNTY FLORIDA RESIDENTS WHO ARE UNDERGRADUATE JUNIORS OR SENIORS AT ANY 4-YEAR COLLEGE IN THE USA & THE SON OR DAUGHTER OF ACTIVE DUTY OR RETIRED MILITARY PERSONNEL. USA CITIZEN.
AWARDS RENEWABLE FOR ONE YEAR. WRITE TO THE SCHOLARSHIP PROGRAM COMMITTEE; ADDRESS ABOVE; FOR COMPLETE INFORMATION.

893

FLORIDA DEPT. OF EDUCATION (CHALLENGER ASTRONAUTS MEMORIAL SCHOLARSHIP PROGRAM)
OFFICE OF STUDENT FINANCIAL ASSISTANCE; KNOTT BLDG
TALLAHASSEE FL 32399
904/488-4095
AMOUNT: $4000 PER YEAR
DEADLINE(S): MAR 1
FIELD(S): LIBERAL ARTS; EDUCATION
FLORIDA RESIDENT FOR AT LEAST 1 YEAR FOR PURPOSES OTHER THAN EDUCATION. OPEN TO FLORIDA HIGH SCHOOL SENIORS WHO PLAN TO COMPLETE AN UNDERGRADUATE DEGREE IN LIBERAL ARTS OR PURSUE A TEACHING CAREER.
MUST BE NOMINATED BY DISTRICT SCHOOL BOARD BASED ON ACTIVITIES; RECOMMENDATIONS AND ESSAY ON 'THE CHALLENGE OF SPACE.' WRITE FOR COMPLETE INFORMATION.

894

INSTITUTE FOR HUMANE STUDIES (CLAUDE R. LAMBE FELLOWSHIPS)
GEORGE MASON UNIVERSITY; 4400 UNIVERSITY DR.
FAIRFAX VA 22030
703/323-1055
AMOUNT: $17500
DEADLINE(S): JAN 15
FIELD(S): SOCIAL SCIENCES; LAW; HUMANITIES
OPEN TO GRADUATE STUDENTS AND UNDERGRADS WHO WILL HAVE JUNIOR OR SENIOR STANDING AT ACCREDITED COLLEGES AND UNIVERSITIES THE NEXT ACADEMIC YEAR. AWARD IS TO SUPPORT STUDENTS WITH A DEMONSTRATED INTEREST IN THE CLASSICAL LIBERAL TRADITION.
RECIPIENT WILL BE INTENT ON PURSUING AN INTELLECTUAL/SCHOLARLY CAREER IN ONE OF THE ABOVE AREAS. WRITE FOR COMPLETE INFORMATION.

895

NELLIE MARTIN CARMAN SCHOLARSHIP TRUST (SCHOLARSHIPS)
1121 244TH ST SW; #65
BOTHELL WA 98021
206/486-6575
AMOUNT: UP TO $1000
DEADLINE(S): MAR 15
FIELD(S): ALL FIELDS OF STUDY EXCEPT THOSE NOTED BELOW
OPEN TO SENIORS IN KING; PIERCE & SNOHOMISH COUNTY (WA) HIGH SCHOOLS WHO HAVE LIVED IN WASHINGTON AT LEAST 5 YRS. FOR UNDERGRADUATE STUDY IN WASHINGTON IN ALL FIELDS EXCEPT MUSIC; SCULPTURE; DRAWING; INTERIOR DESIGN & HOME ECONOMICS.
APPLICATIONS AVAILABLE ONLY THROUGH HIGH SCHOOLS. NOMINATION BY HS COUNSELOR IS REQUIRED. AWARDS ARE RENEWABLE. USA CITIZEN.

COMMUNICATIONS

896

AMERICAN INSTITUTE OF POLISH CULTURE INC. (SCHOLARSHIPS)
1440 79TH STREET CAUSEWAY; SUITE 117
MIAMI FL 33141
305/864-2349
AMOUNT: $2500
DEADLINE(S): JAN 15
FIELD(S): JOURNALISM/PUBLIC RELATIONS
SCHOLARSHIPS TO ENCOURAGE YOUNG AMERICANS OF POLISH DESCENT TO PURSUE THE ABOVE PROFESSIONS. AWARD CAN BE USED AT ANY ACCREDITED AMERICAN COLLEGE. THE RULING CRITERIA FOR SELECTION ARE ACHIEVEMENT/TALENT & INVOLVEMENT IN PUBLIC LIFE.
AWARDS RENEWABLE. FOR FULL-TIME STUDY ONLY. CONTACT PROF. ZDZISLAW WESOLOWSKI AT ADDRESS ABOVE FOR COMPLETE INFORMATION.

897

AMERICAN SOCIETY OF NEWSPAPER EDITORS (MINORITY SCHOLARSHIPS)
PO BOX 17004; MINORITY AFFAIRS DIRECTOR
WASHINGTON DC 20041
703/648-1262
AMOUNT: $750
DEADLINE(S): NOV 15
FIELD(S): JOURNALISM
OPEN TO HIGH SCHOOL SENIORS OF BLACK; HISPANIC; ASIAN AMERICAN OR AMERICAN INDIAN ANCESTRY WHO HAVE HIGH SCHOOL GPA OF 2.5 OR BETTER AND ARE ENROLLED AS COLLEGE FRESHMEN FOR THE FALL TERM. AUTOBIOGRAPHY AND RECOMMENDATIONS REQUIRED.
60 AWARDS PER YEAR. WRITE FOR COMPLETE INFORMATION.

898

AMERICAN SOCIETY OF NEWSPAPER EDITORS (PROJECT FOCUS FOR MINORITY FRESHMEN)
PO BOX 17004; MINORITY AFFAIRS DIRECTOR
WASHINGTON DC 20041
703/648-1146
AMOUNT: WEEKLY STIPEND + $300 BONUS
DEADLINE(S): NOV 1 (POSTMARK)
FIELD(S): JOURNALISM (INTERNSHIPS)
PROGRAM OPEN TO MINORITY FRESHMEN AT ACCREDITED COLLEGES AND UNIVERSITIES IN THE USA. STUDENTS SELECTED TO PARTICIPATE RECEIVE PAID SUMMER INTERNSHIPS AT THEIR HOMETOWN OR NEARBY NEWSPAPER AND A $300 BONUS UPON COMPLETION OF THE PROGRAM.
USA CITIZEN OR LEGAL RESIDENT. STUDENTS APPLY DURING THE FALL SEMESTER OF THEIR FRESHMAN YEAR. WRITE FOR COMPLETE INFORMATION.

899

AMERICAN WOMEN IN RADIO & TELEVISION (HOUSTON INTERNSHIP PROGRAM)
APRILLE MEEK; AWRT-HOUSTON; PO BOX 980908
HOUSTON TX 77098
WRITTEN INQUIRY
AMOUNT: $500 PER YEAR
DEADLINE(S): MAR 1
FIELD(S): RADIO; TELEVISION; FILM & VIDEO; ADVERTISING; MARKETING
INTERNSHIPS OPEN TO STUDENTS WHO ARE JUNIORS; SENIORS OR GRADUATE STUDENTS AT GREATER HOUSTON AREA COLLEGES & UNIVERSITIES.
WRITE FOR COMPLETE INFORMATION.

900

ASIAN AMERICAN JOURNALISTS ASSOCIATION (SCHOLARSHIP AWARDS)
1765 SUTTER ST; ROOM 1000
SAN FRANCISCO CA 94115
415/346-2051
AMOUNT: UP TO $2000
DEADLINE(S): APR 15
FIELD(S): JOURNALISM; MASS COMMUNICATIONS
OPEN TO STUDENTS WITH A DEMONSTRATED ABILITY & SERIOUS CAREER INTEREST IN PRINT; PHOTO OR BROADCAST JOURNALISM. AWARDS BASED ON SCHOLASTIC ACHIEVEMENT; COMMITMENT TO JOURNALISM & TO THE ASIAN PACIFIC AMERICAN COMMUNITY; & FINANCIAL NEED.
FOR UNDERGRADUATE OR GRADUATE STUDY. WRITE FOR COMPLETE INFORMATION.

901

ASSOCIATED PRESS TELEVISION-RADIO ASSOCIATION OF CALIFORNIA/NEVADA (APTRA-CLETE ROBERTS MEMORIAL JOURNALISM SCHOLARSHIP AWARDS)
RACHEL AMBROSE; ASSOCIATED PRESS; 221 S FIGUEROA ST; #300
LOS ANGELES CA 90012
213/626-1200
AMOUNT: $1500
DEADLINE(S): DEC 18
FIELD(S): BROADCAST JOURNALISM
OPEN TO STUDENTS WITH A BROADCAST JOURNALISM CAREER OBJECTIVE WHO ARE STUDYING IN CALIFORNIA OR NEVADA. FOR UNDERGRADUATE OR GRADUATE STUDY.
WRITE FOR COMPLETE INFORMATION.

902

ASSOCIATION FOR EDUCATION IN JOURNALISM & MASS COMMUNICATION (CORRESPONDENTS FUND SCHOLARSHIPS)
UNIV OF SOUTH CAROLINA COLLEGE OF JOURNALISM
COLUMBIA SC 29208
803/777-2005
AMOUNT: UP TO $2000
DEADLINE(S): APR 30
FIELD(S): JOURNALISM; MASS COMMUNICATIONS; LIBERAL ARTS
OPEN TO CHILDREN OF PRINT OR BROADCAST JOURNALISTS WHO ARE FOREIGN CORRESPONDENTS FOR A USA NEWS MEDIUM. FOR UNDERGRADUATE; GRADUATE OR POST-GRADUATE STUDY AT ANY ACCREDITED COLLEGE OR UNIVERSITY IN THE USA.
PREFERENCE TO JOURNALISM OR COMMUNICATIONS MAJORS. 8-15 RENEWABLE AWARDS PER YEAR. WRITE FOR COMPLETE INFORMATION.

903

ASSOCIATION FOR EDUCATION IN JOURNALISM AND MASS COMMUNICATIONS (SUMMER JOURNALISM INTERNSHIP FOR MINORITIES)
NYU INST OF AFRO-AMERICAN AFFAIRS; 269 MERCER; SUITE 601
NEW YORK NY 10003
212/998-2130
AMOUNT: SALARY OF AT LEAST $200 PER WEEK
DEADLINE(S): NOV 3 TO REQUEST APPLICATION; DEC 15 TO SUBMIT APPLICATION.
FIELD(S): JOURNALISM; MASS COMMUNICATIONS; ADVERTISING; PUBLIC RELATIONS; PHOTO JOURNALISM; BROADCASTING
OPEN TO MEMBERS OF ETHNIC MINORITIES WHOSE CREDENTIALS REFLECT AN INTEREST IN AND COMMITMENT TO JOURNALISM. INTERNS WILL BE PLACED FOR 10 WEEKS IN AN ENTRY LEVEL POSITION WITH PARTICIPATING COMPANIES; PRIMARILY IN THE NY/NJ AREA.
WRITE FOR COMPLETE INFORMATION.

904

ATLANTA ASSOCIATION OF MEDIA WOMEN (SCHOLARSHIP)
A.S. REEVES; JOURNAL/CONSTITUTION; PO BOX 4689
ATLANTA GA 30302
404/526-5091
AMOUNT: $500 - $1000
DEADLINE(S): MAR 1
FIELD(S): JOURNALISM/COMMUNICATIONS
OPEN TO AFRICAN AMERICAN WOMEN RESIDING IN GEORGIA WHO ARE PURSUING AN UNDERGRADUATE DEGREE IN JOURNALISM OR COMMUNICATIONS IN A GEORGIA INSTITUTION. MUST HAVE THE DESIRE AND

INTENTION TO PURSUE A CAREER IN JOURNALISM OR COMMUNICATIONS.
FINANCIAL NEED IS CONSIDERED BUT NOT A DETERMINING FACTOR. WRITE FOR COMPLETE INFORMATION.

905

BALL STATE UNIVERSITY (DAVID LETTERMAN TELECOMMUNICATIONS SCHOLARSHIP PROGRAM)
DEPT OF TELECOMMUNICATIONS
MUNCIE IN 47306
317/285-1480
AMOUNT: 1ST FULL TUITION; 2ND 1/2 TUITION; 3RD 1/3 TUITION
DEADLINE(S): APR 1
FIELD(S): TELECOMMUNICATIONS
OPEN TO UNDERGRADUATE JUNIORS AT BALL STATE WHO HAVE DEMONSTRATED REASONABLE EXPECTATION OF BECOMING PROFESSIONALS IN THE TELECOMMUNICATIONS INDUSTRY. SCHOLARSHIPS ARE BASED ON 'CREATIVITY'; GRADES ARE NOT CONSIDERED.
ANY CREATIVE EFFORT CONNECTED WITH THE TELECOMMUNICATIONS FIELD WILL BE CONSIDERED. WRITE FOR COMPLETE INFORMATION.

906

BROADCAST EDUCATION ASSOCIATION (SCHOLARSHIPS IN BROADCASTING)
1771 N STREET NW
WASHINGTON DC 20036
202/429-5354
AMOUNT: $1250 - $3000
DEADLINE(S): JAN 15
FIELD(S): BROADCASTING
SCHOLARSHIPS ARE AWARDED FOR ONE SCHOLASTIC YEAR FOR DEGREE WORK AT THE JUNIOR; SENIOR OR GRADUATE LEVEL. APPLICANTS MUST SHOW EVIDENCE OF SUPERIOR ACADEMIC PERFORMANCE AND POTENTIAL. APPLICATIONS WILL NOT BE SENT OUT AFTER DEC 15.
SCHOLARSHIP WINNERS MUST STUDY AT A CAMPUS WHERE AT LEAST ONE DEPARTMENT IS A BEA INSTITUTIONAL MEMBER. WRITE FOR COMPLETE INFORMATION.

907

CALIFORNIA CHICANO NEWS MEDIA ASSN (JOEL GARCIA MEMORIAL SCHOLARSHIP COMPETITION)
C/O USC SCHOOL OF JOURNALISN (GFS 315)
LOS ANGELES CA 90089
213/743-7158
AMOUNT: UP TO $2000
DEADLINE(S): APR 15
FIELD(S): JOURNALISM; COMMUNICATIONS
OPEN TO ALL LATINO UNDERGRADUATE STUDENTS INTERESTED IN PURSUING CAREERS IN THE ABOVE AREAS. IT IS NOT NECESSARY TO BE A JOURNALISM OR COMMUNICATIONS MAJOR. AWARDS TENABLE AT ACCREDITED COLLEGES AND UNIVERSITIES IN CALIF. USA RESIDENT.
10 TO 30 AWARDS PER YEAR. WRITE FOR COMPLETE INFORMATION.

908

CENTRAL NEWSPAPERS INC (PULLIAM JOURNALISM FELLOWSHIPS)
C/O EDITOR; THE INDIANAPOLIS NEWS
INDIANAPOLIS IN 46206
317/633-9121
AMOUNT: $3810 STIPEND
DEADLINE(S): MAR 1
FIELD(S): JOURNALISM; PHOTOJOURNALISM
OPEN TO RECENT GRADUATES & TO UNDERGRADUATE SENIORS WHO WILL RECEIVE THEIR BACHELOR'S DEGREE BY JUNE. AWARD IS FOR A 10-WEEK WORK & STUDY INTERNSHIP AT ONE OF CNI'S NEWSPAPERS IN INDIANAPOLIS OR PHOENIX.
INCLUDES SESSIONS WITH A WRITING COACH & SEMINARS WITH LOCAL & NATIONAL JOURNALISTS. 20 AWARDS PER YEAR. CONTACT MR. RUSS PULLIAM; EDITOR; FOR COMPLETE INFORMATION.

909

CHARLES PRICE SCHOOL OF ADVERTISING AND JOURNALISM INC. (SCHOLARSHIP PROGRAM)
1700 WALNUT ST
PHILADELPHIA PA 19103
215/546-2747
AMOUNT: $500 - $1000
DEADLINE(S): VARIES
FIELD(S): ADVERTISING/JOURNALISM/PUBLIC RELATIONS

SCHOLARSHIPS FOR STUDY IN ABOVE FIELDS AT CHARLES PRICE SCHOOL OF ADVERTISING & JOURNALISM. UNDERGRADUATE JUNIORS AND SENIORS AND GRADUATE STUDENTS MAY APPLY. USA CITIZEN.

6 SCHOLARSHIPS PER YEAR. WRITE FOR COMPLETE INFORMATION.

910

COX NEWSPAPERS (MINORITY SCHOLARSHIP PROGRAM)

PO BOX 4689
ATLANTA GA 30302
404/526-5091

AMOUNT: TUITION + ALL EXPENSES FOR 4 YEARS

DEADLINE(S): APR 29

FIELD(S): NEWSPAPER (NEWS; ADVERTISING; BUSINESS OFFICE)

OPEN TO ATLANTA AREA HIGH SCHOOL SENIORS WHO ARE RACIAL MINORITIES AND ARE INTERESTED IN A CAREER IN THE NEWSPAPER INDUSTRY AND HAVE AT LEAST A 'B' GRADE POINT AVERAGE. MUST ATTEND GA STATE UNIV OR A COLLEGE IN THE ATLANTA UNIV CENTER.

AWARD INCLUDES PAID INTERNSHIP. WRITE FOR COMPLETE INFORMATION.

911

DAYTON FOUNDATION (LARRY FULLERTON PHOTOJOURNALISM SCHOLARSHIP)

2100 KETTERING TOWER
DAYTON OH 45423
513-222-0410

AMOUNT: $1000

DEADLINE(S): FEB 15

FIELD(S): PHOTOJOURNALISM

OPEN TO OHIO RESIDENTS WHO ARE FULL TIME UNDERGRAD STUDENTS AT AN OHIO COLLEGE; JUNIOR COLLEGE; OR SCHOOL WITH A STRUCTURED CURRICULUM & WHO PLAN TO PURSUE A PHOTOJOURNALISM CAREER. FINANCIAL NEED & PERSONAL CIRCUMSTANCES ARE CONSIDERED.

PORTFOLIO MUST BE SUBMITTED FOLLOWING GUIDELINES ESTABLISHED BY OHIO NEWS PHOTOGRAPHERS ASSOCIATION. WRITE FOR COMPLETE INFORMATION.

912

DOG WRITERS' EDUCATIONAL TRUST (SCHOLARSHIPS)

BERTA I. PICKETT; PO BOX 2220
PAYSON AZ 85547
602/474-8867

AMOUNT: $1000

DEADLINE(S): DEC 31

FIELD(S): VETERINARY MEDICINE; ANIMAL BEHAVIOR; JOURNALISM

OPEN TO APPLICANTS WHOSE PARENTS; GRANDPARENTS OR OTHER CLOSE RELATIVES (OR THE APPLICANT) ARE OR HAVE BEEN INVOLVED IN THE WORLD OF DOGS AS EXHIBITORS; BREEDERS; HANDLERS; JUDGES; CLUB OFFICERS OR OTHER ACTIVITIES.

SCHOLARSHIPS SUPPORT UNDERGRADUATE OR GRADUATE STUDY. 10 AWARDS PER YEAR. SEND SELF-ADDRESSED STAMPED ENVELOPE FOR COMPLETE INFORMATION AND APPLICATION.

913

DONALD W. REYNOLDS FOUNDATION, INC (THE) (SCHOLARSHIPS)

PO BOX 17017
FORT SMITH AR 72917
501/785-7808

AMOUNT: $2500 PER YEAR

DEADLINE(S): FEB 15

FIELD(S): JOURNALISM (PRINT)

OPEN TO COLLEGE STUDENTS ENTERING THEIR JUNIOR YEAR WHO ARE PREPARING FOR CAREERS IN COMMUNITY NEWSPAPER JOURNALISM. APPLICANTS MUST BE STUDENTS AT SPECIFIED COLLEGES IN AR; TX; UT; CA; OK; HI; MO; AND NV. MINIMUM OF 3.0 GPA REQUIRED.

RENEWABLE FOR SENIOR YEAR. CONTACT YOUR COLLEGE FINANCIAL AID OFFICE FOR INFORMATION. DO NOT WRITE OR CALL DONREY MEDIA GROUP.

914

DOW JONES NEWSPAPER FUND INC (EDITING INTERN PROGRAM FOR COLLEGE JUNIORS, SENIORS AND GRADUATE STUDENTS)

PO BOX 300
PRINCETON NJ 08543
609/452-2820

AMOUNT: $1000

DEADLINE(S): NOV 15

FIELD(S): JOURNALISM
OPEN TO COLLEGE JUNIORS, SENIORS & GRADUATE STUDENTS WITH A SINCERE DESIRE FOR A CAREER IN JOURNALISM. RECIPIENTS RECEIVE $1000 SCHOLARSHIP; FREE 2-WEEK PRE-INTERNSHIP RESIDENCY & SUMMER COPY EDITOR JOB ON DAILY PAPER AT REGULAR WAGES.
JOURNALISM MAJOR NOT REQUIRED. UP TO 45 AWARDS PER YEAR. APPLICATIONS AVAILABLE FROM SEP 1 TO NOV 1. WRITE FOR COMPLETE INFORMATION.

915

FREEDOM FORUM (SCHOLARSHIPS)
1101 WILSON BLVD
ARLINGTON VA 22209
703/528-0850
AMOUNT: $2500 - $4000
DEADLINE(S): JAN 31
FIELD(S): JOURNALISM
OPEN TO HIGH SCHOOL SENIORS AND UNDERGRADUATE OR GRADUATE COLLEGE STUDENTS WITH CAREER GOALS AND MAJORS IN PRINT OR BROADCAST JOURNALISM OR ADVERTISING. APPLICATIONS MUST BE REQUESTED BEFORE JAN 22.
WRITE FOR COMPLETE INFORMATION.

916

FUND FOR AMERICAN STUDIES (INSTITUTES ON POLITICAL JOURNALISM; BUSINESS & GOVERNMENT AFFAIRS & COMPARATIVE POLITICAL & ECONOMIC SYSTEMS)
1526 18TH ST NW
WASHINGTON DC 20036
202/986-0384
AMOUNT: UP TO $3500
DEADLINE(S): JAN 11 EARLY DECISION; MAR 15 GENERAL APPLICATION DEADLINE
FIELD(S): POLITICAL SCIENCE; ECONOMICS; JOURNALISM; BUSINESS ADMINISTRATION
SCHOLARSHIPS COVER COST TO ATTEND ANNUAL 6-WEEK SUMMER INSTITUTE AT GEORGETOWN UNIV. COURSES ARE WORTH 6 CREDITS & INCLUDE FOREIGN POLICY LECTURES; MEDIA DIALOGUE SERIES; SITE BRIEFINGS & CAREER DAYS. OPEN TO COLLEGE SOPHOMORES & JUNIORS.
APPROX 100 AWARDS PER YEAR. FOR FUND'S PROGRAMS ONLY. WRITE FOR COMPLETE INFORMATION.

917

FUND FOR INVESTIGATIVE JOURNALISM INC. (GRANTS FOR INVESTIGATIVE REPORTERS)
1755 MASSACHUSETTS AVE NW
WASHINGTON DC 20036
202/462-1844
AMOUNT: UP TO $1500
DEADLINE(S): NONE
FIELD(S): INVESTIGATIVE REPORTING BY WORKING JOURNALISTS
OPEN TO WORKING PRINT AND BROADCAST JOURNALISTS FOR SUPPORT OF INVESTIGATIONS INTO CONCEALED; OBSCURE AND COMPLEX MATTERS OF PUBLIC INTEREST. THE FUND SUPPORTS INVESTIGATIONS OF LOCAL AS WELL AS NATIONAL INTEREST.
WRITE FOR COMPLETE INFORMATION.

918

GLENN CARRINGTON FOUNDATION (ALASKA SCHOLARSHIP TO BENEFIT NATIVE ALASKANS)
927 LARKSPUR RD
OAKLAND CA 94610
510/763-9762
AMOUNT: UP TO $2000
DEADLINE(S): MAR 1
FIELD(S): BUSINESS; EDUCATION; ENVIRONMENT; POLITICAL SCIENCE; COMMUNICATIONS
OPEN TO ALASKA RESIDENTS COMMITTED TO HELPING NATIVE ALASKANS GOVERN; EDUCATE; DEVELOP BUSINESSES AND IMPROVE THEIR MANAGEMENT ABILITIES. MUST DEMONSTRATE PERSONAL AND FAMILY FINANCIAL NEED.
WRITE FOR COMPLETE INFORMATION.

919

INSTITUTE FOR HUMANE STUDIES (CLAUDE R. LAMBE FELLOWSHIPS)
GEORGE MASON UNIVERSITY; 4400 UNIVERSITY DRIVE
FAIRFAX VA 22030
703/323-1055
AMOUNT: $17500
DEADLINE(S): JAN 15
FIELD(S): SOCIAL SCIENCES; LAW; HUMANITIES
OPEN TO GRADUATE STUDENTS AND UNDERGRADS WHO WILL HAVE JUNIOR OR SENIOR STANDING AT ACCREDITED

COLLEGES AND UNIVERSITIES THE NEXT ACADEMIC YEAR. AWARD IS TO SUPPORT STUDENTS WITH A DEMONSTRATED INTEREST IN THE CLASSICAL LIBERAL TRADITION.
RECIPIENT WILL BE INTENT ON PURSUING AN INTELLECTUAL/SCHOLARLY CAREER IN ONE OF THE ABOVE AREAS. WRITE FOR COMPLETE INFORMATION.

920

INSTITUTE FOR HUMANE STUDIES (FELIX MORLEY MEMORIAL JOURNALISM COMPETITION)
GEORGE MASON UNIVERSITY; 4400 UNIVERSITY DRIVE
FAIRFAX VA 22030
703/323-1055
AMOUNT: $2500
DEADLINE(S): JUN 15
FIELD(S): JOURNALISM
OPEN TO STUDENT AND COLLEGE-AGE WRITERS. COMPETITION IS INTENDED TO ENCOURAGE WRITING THAT REFLECTS AN APPRECIATION OF THE CLASSICAL LIBERAL TRADITION.
WRITE FOR COMPLETE INFORMATION.

921

INTERNATIONAL DIV ASSN FOR EDUCATION IN JOURNALISM & MASS COMMUNICATION (MARY A. GARDNER SCHOLARSHIP)
PROFESSOR BULLION; 107 LORD HALL; UNIVERSITY OF MAINE
ORONO ME 04469
207/581-1283
AMOUNT: $500
DEADLINE(S): MAR 15
FIELD(S): JOURNALISM
OPEN TO UNDERGRADUATE STUDENTS HAVING AT LEAST ONE YEAR OF STUDY REMAINING WHO ARE ENROLLED FULL TIME IN AN ACCREDITED NEWS-EDITORIAL PROGRAM & HAVE AT LEAST A 3.0 GPA (4.0 SCALE).
WRITE FOR COMPLETE INFORMATION.

922

INTERNATIONAL RADIO & TELEVISION SOCIETY (IRTS SUMMER FELLOWSHIP PROGRAM)
MS. MARIA DE LEON; 420 LEXINGTON AVE.
NEW YORK NY 10170
212/867-6650
AMOUNT: HOUSING; STIPEND; TRAVEL
DEADLINE(S): NOV 23
FIELD(S): BROADCASTING; COMMUNICATIONS; SALES
ANNUAL 9-WEEK SUMMER FELLOWSHIP PROGRAM IN NEW YORK CITY OPEN TO OUTSTANDING FULL-TIME UNDERGRADUATE JUNIORS & SENIORS WITH A DEMONSTRATED INTEREST IN A CAREER IN COMMUNICATIONS.
WRITE FOR COMPLETE INFORMATION.

923

JOHN BAYLISS BROADCAST FOUNDATION (SCHOLARSHIP)
PO BOX 221070
CARMEL CA 93922
408/624-1536
AMOUNT: $2000
DEADLINE(S): APR 30
FIELD(S): RADIO BROADCASTING
OPEN TO UNDERGRADS IN THEIR JUNIOR OR SENIOR YEAR AND TO GRADUATE STUDENTS WHO ASPIRE TO A CAREER IN RADIO. APPLICANTS SHOULD HAVE A 3.0 OR BETTER GPA. FINANCIAL NEED IS A CONSIDERATION. USA CITIZEN OR LEGAL RESIDENT.
WRITE FOR COMPLETE INFORMATION.

924

JOHN M. WILL JOURNALISM SCHOLARSHIP FOUNDATION (SCHOLARSHIP)
PO BOX 290
MOBILE AL 36601
205/432-6751
AMOUNT: $2000
DEADLINE(S): 2ND FRIDAY IN APRIL
FIELD(S): JOURNALISM
OPEN TO FULL TIME STUDENTS MAJORING IN JOURNALISM WHO ARE RESIDENTS OF THE ALABAMA COUNTIES OF MOBILE; BALDWIN; ESCAMBIA; CLARKE; CONECUH; WASHINGTON OR MONROE; OR SANTA ROSA OR ESCAMBIA COUNTY FLORIDA; OR JACKSON OR GEORGE COUNTY; MISSISSIPPI
ALSO OPEN TO PERSONS CURRENTLY EMPLOYED IN JOURNALISM WHO WANT TO TAKE JOURNALISM RELATED TRAINING AS A FULL TIME STUDENT AT AN ACCREDITED COLLEGE. WRITE FOR COMPLETE INFORMATION.

925

JOURNALISM FOUNDATION OF METROPOLITAN ST LOUIS (SCHOLARSHIPS)
C/O PATRICK GAVEN; 900 N TUCKER BLVD
ST LOUIS MO 63101
314/340-8000
AMOUNT: $750-2500
DEADLINE(S): FEB 28
FIELD(S): JOURNALISM/COMMUNICATIONS
OPEN TO ST LOUIS METRO RESIDENTS ENTERING THEIR JUNIOR/SENIOR YEAR OF COLLEGE OR GRADUATE SCHOOL. MUST HAVE A DESIRE TO PURSUE A CAREER IN JOURNALISM & WRITING TALENT (SAMPLES).
17 OR MORE SCHOLARSHIPS PER YEAR. CONTACT PATRICIA RICE (CHAIRMAN) ADDRESS ABOVE FOR COMPLETE INFORMATION.

926

KCPQ TELEVISION (EWING C. KELLY SCHOLARSHIP PROGRAM)
4400 STEILACOOM BLVD SW; PO BOX 98828
TACOMA WA 98499
206/383-9501 OR 206/625-1313
AMOUNT: $500 - $3000
DEADLINE(S): APR 15
FIELD(S): BROADCASTING
OPEN TO GRADUATE OR UNDERGRADUATE STUDENTS WHO HAVE AT LEAST JUNIOR CLASS STANDING AND HAVE AT LEAST ONE YEAR TO GO BEFORE GRADUATION. MUST ATTEND ONE OF SEVERAL SPECIFIED WASHINGTON STATE UNIVERSITIES.
APPLICANTS SHOULD BE CAREER ORIENTED AND INTEND TO PURSUE A CAREER IN BROADCASTING. WRITE TO SCHOLARSHIP DIRECTOR ADEL HAUCK AT ABOVE ADDRESS FOR COMPLETE INFORMATION.

927

KNTV TELEVISION (MINORITY SCHOLARSHIP)
645 PARK AVE
SAN JOSE CA 95110
408/286-1111
AMOUNT: $750
DEADLINE(S): APR 1
FIELD(S): TELEVISION BROADCASTING
OPEN TO BLACK; HISPANIC; ASIAN/PACIFIC ISLANDER OR AMERICAN INDIAN STUDENTS WHO ARE RESIDENTS OF SANTA CLARA; SANTA CRUZ; MONTEREY OR SAN BENITO COUNTIES (CALIF.) AND ATTEND OR PLAN TO ATTEND AN ACCREDITED 4 YEAR INSTITUTION IN CALIFORNIA.
MUST ENROLL IN AT LEAST 12 SEMESTER UNITS EACH SEMESTER. CONSIDERATIONS INCLUDE INTEREST IN TV; FINANCIAL NEED; COMMUNITY INVOLVEMENT; ACADEMICS; CAREER ASPIRATIONS. WRITE FOR COMPLETE INFORMATION.

928

LOS ANGELES CHAPTER OF SOCIETY OF PROFESSIONAL JOURNALISTS - SIGMA DELTA CHI (BILL FARR SCHOLARSHIP)
T.W. MCGARRY; 4310 CORONET DRIVE
ENCINO CA 91316
818/345-5044
AMOUNT: $1000
DEADLINE(S): DEC 1
FIELD(S): JOURNALISM WRITING/EDITING/PHOTO
OPEN TO STUDENTS WHO WILL BE SENIORS OR GRAD STUDENTS IN THE FOLLOWING YEAR AND ARE EITHER LA RESIDENTS (WHO GO TO SCHOOL IN OR OUTSIDE THE LA AREA) OR ATTEND SCHOOL IN THE LA AREA (EVEN THOUGH THEY'RE NOT FROM LA).
LA AREA INCLUDES ORANGE COUNTY. WRITE FOR COMPLETE INFORMATION.

929

LOS ANGELES CHAPTER OF SOCIETY OF PROFESSIONAL JOURNALISTS (HELEN JOHNSON SCHOLARSHIP)
T.M. MCGARRY; 4310 CORONET DRIVE
ENCINO CA 91316
818/345-5044
AMOUNT: $1000
DEADLINE(S): DEC 1
FIELD(S): NEWS BROADCASTING - RADIO OR TELEVISION
OPEN TO UNDERGRADUATE OR GRADUATE STUDENT WHO HAS SHOWN ACCOMPLISHMENT AND POTENTIAL IN RADIO OR TV NEWS AND EITHER LIVES IN OR ATTENDS A 4-YEAR SCHOOL IN LOS ANGELES OR ORANGE COUNTY.
STUDENTS FROM LOS ANGELES/ORANGE COUNTY WHOSE FAMILIES CONTINUE TO LIVE IN THE AREA MAY ATTEND ANY 4-YEAR SCHOOL ANYWHERE. WRITE FOR COMPLETE INFORMATION.

930

LOS ANGELES CHAPTER OF SOCIETY OF PROFESSIONAL JOURNALISTS - SIGMA DELTA CHI (KEN INOUYE SCHOLARSHIP)

T.W. MCGARRY; 4310 CORONET DRIVE
ENCINO CA 91316
818/345-5044

AMOUNT: $1000
DEADLINE(S): DEC 1
FIELD(S): JOURNALISM - WRITING; EDITING; PHOTOGRAPHY

OPEN TO ETHNIC MINORITY STUDENTS WHO WILL BE A JUNIOR OR SENIOR OR GRAD STUDENT THE FOLLOWING YEAR. MUST RESIDE IN LOS ANGELES OR ORANGE COUNTY OR ATTEND A FOUR-YEAR SCHOOL IN THE AREA. DEMONSTRATE FINANCIAL NEED.

STUDENTS FROM LOS ANGELES OR ORANGE COUNTY WHOSE FAMILY CONTINUES TO LIVE IN THE AREA MAY ATTEND ANY 4-YEAR COLLEGE ANYWHERE. WRITE FOR COMPLETE INFORMATION.

931

LOS ANGELES CHAPTER OF SOCIETY OF PROFESSIONAL JOURNALISTS - SIGMA DELTA CHI (CARL GREENBURG PRIZE)

T.W. MCGARRY; 4310 CORONET DRIVE
ENCINO CA 91316
818/345-5044

AMOUNT: $1000
DEADLINE(S): DEC 1
FIELD(S): JOURNALISM

PRIZE AWARDED ANNUALLY FOR POLITICAL OR INVESTIGATIVE REPORTING TO STUDENT WHO IS EITHER AN LA AREA RESIDENT (WHO GOES TO SCHOOL IN OR OUTSIDE OF THE LA AREA) OR ATTENDS AN LA AREA SCHOOL (EVEN THOUGH NOT FROM LA)

LA AREA INCLUDES ORANGE COUNTY. WRITE FOR COMPLETE INFORMATION.

932

MIAMI INTERNATIONAL PRESS CLUB (SCHOLARSHIP PROGRAM)

C/O MIAMI HERALD; ONE HERALD PLAZA
MIAMI FL 33132
305/376-2784

AMOUNT: $500 - $2500
DEADLINE(S): APR 15
FIELD(S): JOURNALISM; BROADCASTING

DADE COUNTY (FLA) RESIDENT. SCHOLARSHIPS FOR UNDERGRADUATE STUDY AT ANY ACCREDITED COLLEGE OR UNIVERSITY IN THE ABOVE FIELDS. OPEN TO DESERVING DADE COUNTY HIGH SCHOOL SENIORS.

SCHOLARSHIPS ARE RENEWABLE. WRITE FOR COMPLETE INFORMATION OR CALL THE CLUB'S SECRETARY-TREASURER AT THE NUMBER ABOVE.

933

NATIONAL ASSN OF HISPANIC JOURNALISTS (MARK ZAMBRANO SCHOLARSHIP FUND)

NATIONAL PRESS BUILDING; SUITE 1193
WASHINGTON DC 20045
202/622-7145

AMOUNT: $1000
DEADLINE(S): DEC 31
FIELD(S): PRINT OR BROADCAST JOURNALISM; PHOTOJOURNALISM

OPEN TO UNDERGRAD JUNIORS & SENIORS AND GRAD STUDENTS WHO ARE COMMITTED TO PURSUING A CAREER IN PRINT OR BROADCAST JOURNALISM OR PHOTOJOURNALISM. IT IS NOT NECESSARY TO BE A JOURNALISM OR BROADCAST MAJOR NOR IS HISPANIC ANCESTRY REQUIRED.

AWARDS TENABLE AT ACCREDITED INSTITUTIONS IN THE USA & ITS TERRITORIES. WRITE FOR COMPLETE INFORMATION.

934

NATIONAL ASSN OF HISPANIC JOURNALISTS (NAHJ SCHOLARSHIP PROGRAM)

NATIONAL PRESS BUILDING; SUITE 1193
WASHINGTON DC 20045
202/622-7145

AMOUNT: VARIES
DEADLINE(S): MAR 11
FIELD(S): PRINT OR BROADCAST JOURNALISM; PHOTOJOURNALISM

OPEN TO HIGH SCHOOL SENIORS; UNDERGRADUATE & GRADUATE STUDENTS WHO ARE COMMITTED TO A CAREER IN PRINT OR BROADCAST JOURNALISM OR PHOTOJOURNALISM. IT IS NOT NECESSARY TO MAJOR IN THESE AREAS NOR IS IT REQUIRED TO BE OF HISPANIC ANCESTRY.

AWARDS TENABLE AT ACCREDITED 2-YEAR OR 4-YEAR SCHOOLS IN THE USA & ITS TERRITORIES. WRITE FOR COMPLETE INFORMATION.

935

NATIONAL ASSOCIATION OF BLACK JOURNALISTS (NABJ SCHOLARSHIP PROGRAM)
BOX 17212
WASHINGTON DC 20041
703/648-1270
AMOUNT: $2500
DEADLINE(S): MAR 31
FIELD(S): JOURNALISM
OPEN TO AFRICAN AMERICAN UNDERGRADUATE OR GRADUATE STUDENTS WHO ARE ACCEPTED TO OR ENROLLED IN AN ACCREDITED JOURNALISM PROGRAM MAJORING IN PRINT; PHOTO; RADIO; OR TELEVISION. GPA OF 2.5 OR BETTER (4.0 SCALE) IS REQUIRED.
12 AWARDS PER YEAR. WRITE FOR COMPLETE INFORMATION.

936

NATIONAL ASSOCIATION OF GOVERNMENT COMMUNICATORS (THOMAS PAINE AND THOMAS JEFFERSON SCHOLARSHIPS)
669 S WASHINGTON ST
ALEXANDRIA VA 22314
703/519-3902; FAX 703/519-7732
AMOUNT: $1000
DEADLINE(S): JUN 30
FIELD(S): GOVERNMENT COMMUNICATIONS
OPEN TO UNDERGRADUATE SOPHOMORES; JUNIORS AND SENIORS AND TO GRADUATE STUDENTS WHO PLAN CAREERS IN PUBLIC SECTOR COMMUNICATIONS. MONEY IS TO PAY FOR TUITION ONLY; NOT BOOKS. GPA OF 3.0 OR BETTER (4.0 SCALE) IS REQUIRED.
WRITE FOR COMPLETE INFORMATION.

937

NATIONAL BROADCASTING SOCIETY (ALPHA EPSILON RHO SCHOLARSHIPS)
UNIVERSITY OF SOUTH CAROLINA COLLEGE OF JOURNALISM
COLUMBIA SC 29208
803/777-3324
AMOUNT: $500 TO $1000
DEADLINE(S): MAR 1
FIELD(S): BROADCASTING
AWARDS FOR ACTIVE STUDENT MEMBERS OF ALPHA EPSILON RHO AS NOMINATED BY LOCAL CHAPTERS.
AWARDS RENEWABLE. CONTACT DR. JOHN LOPICIOLO EXECUTIVE SECRETARY ADDRESS ABOVE FOR COMPLETE INFORMATION.

938

NATIONAL FEDERATION OF PRESS WOMEN INC (HELEN M. MALLOCH SCHOLARSHIP)
PO BOX 99
BLUE SPRINGS MO 64013
816/229-1666
AMOUNT: $500 - $1000
DEADLINE(S): MAY 1
FIELD(S): JOURNALISM
WOMEN. UNDERGRADUATE JUNIOR/SENIOR OR GRADUATE STUDENT MAJORING IN JOURNALISM AT A COLLEGE OR UNIVERSITY OF THE STUDENT'S CHOICE.
WRITE FOR COMPLETE INFORMATION.

939

NATIONAL FEDERATION OF PRESS WOMEN INC (PROFESSIONAL EDUCATION SCHOLARSHIP)
PO BOX 99
BLUE SPRINGS MO 64013
816/229-1666
AMOUNT: $1000
DEADLINE(S): MAY 1
FIELD(S): JOURNALISM
FOR MEMBERS OF THE NATIONAL FEDERATION OF PRESS WOMEN WHO WANT TO CONTINUE OR RETURN TO COLLEGE AS A JOURNALISM MAJOR. FINANCIAL NEED IS A CONSIDERATION BUT IS NOT PARAMOUNT.
WRITE FOR COMPLETE INFORMATION.

940

NATIONAL ITALIAN AMERICAN FOUNDATION (COMMUNICATIONS SCHOLARSHIP)
DR. M. LOMBARDO; EDUCATION DIRECTOR; 666 11TH ST NW; SUITE 800
WASHINGTON DC 20001
202/638-2137
AMOUNT: $5000
DEADLINE(S): MAY 31
FIELD(S): COMMUNICATIONS; JOURNALISM
OPEN TO STUDENTS OF ITALIAN HERITAGE ENROLLED IN OR ENTERING COLLEGE AS JOURNALISM AND COMMUNICATION MAJORS. TWO SAMPLE WORKS ARE REQUIRED AND EVIDENCE OF FINANCIAL NEED MUST BE SUBMITTED.
WRITE FOR COMPLETE INFORMATION.

941

NATIONAL NEWSPAPER FOUNDATION (SERRILL SCHOLARSHIPS)
1627 'K' STREET NW; SUITE 400
WASHINGTON DC 20006
202/466-7200
AMOUNT: $250 - $1000
DEADLINE(S): JUN 15
FIELD(S): PRINT JOURNALISM
OPEN TO UNDERGRADUATE JUNIORS WHO ARE ENROLLED IN A USA COLLEGE OR UNIVERSITY. FOR THE STUDY OF PRINT JOURNALISM.
WRITE FOR COMPLETE INFORMATION.

942

NATIONAL RIGHT TO WORK COMMITTEE (WILLIAM B. RUGGLES JOURNALISM SCHOLARSHIP)
8001 BRADDOCK RD; SUITE 500
SPRINGFIELD VA 22160
703/321-9820
AMOUNT: $2000
DEADLINE(S): MAR 31
FIELD(S): JOURNALISM
SCHOLARSHIPS ARE OPEN TO UNDERGRADUATE AND GRADUATE STUDENTS MAJORING IN JOURNALISM AT ACCREDITED USA INSTITUTIONS OF HIGHER LEARNING WHO EXEMPLIFY THE DEDICATION TO PRINCIPLE & HIGH JOURNALISTIC STANDARDS OF THE LATE WILLIAM B. RUGGLES.
WRITE FOR COMPLETE INFORMATION.

943

NEW YORK FINANCIAL WRITERS' ASSOCIATION (SCHOLARSHIP PROGRAM)
PO BOX 21
SYOSSET NY 11791
516/921-7766
AMOUNT: $2000
DEADLINE(S): LATE DEC
FIELD(S): FINANCIAL JOURNALISM
OPEN TO UNDERGRADUATE & GRADUATE STUDENTS WHO ARE ENROLLED IN AN ACCREDITED COLLEGE OR UNIVERSITY IN METROPOLITAN NEW YORK CITY & ARE PURSUING A COURSE OF STUDY LEADING TO A FINANCIAL OR BUSINESS JOURNALISM CAREER.
WRITE FOR COMPLETE INFORMATION.

944

NEW YORK UNIVERSITY (GALLATIN DIVISION SPECIAL AWARDS & SCHOLARSHIPS)
715 BROADWAY; 6TH FLOOR
NEW YORK NY 10003
212/598-7077
AMOUNT: VARIES WITH AWARD
DEADLINE(S): NONE SPECIFIED
FIELD(S): PUBLISHING
VARIOUS SPECIAL AWARDS AND SCHOLARSHIPS ARE AVAILABLE TO UNDERGRADUATE AND GRADUATE STUDENTS ENROLLED IN THE GALLATIN DIVISION OF NEW YORK UNIVERSITY.
104 SPECIAL AWARDS AND SCHOLARSHIPS PER YEAR. CONTACT ADDRESS ABOVE FOR COMPLETE INFORMATION.

945

PEORIA JOURNAL STAR (SCHOLARSHIP PROGRAM)
1 NEWS PLAZA
PEORIA IL 61643
309/686-3027
AMOUNT: $1000 PER YEAR FOR 4 YEARS
DEADLINE(S): MAY 1
FIELD(S): NEWSPAPER JOURNALISM
OPEN TO HIGH SCHOOL SENIORS WHO RESIDE IN THE 'JOURNAL STAR' READERSHIP AREA FOR UNDERGRADUATE STUDY OF JOURNALISM.
SCHOLARSHIP RENEWABLE ANNUALLY FOR FOUR YEARS. WRITE FOR COMPLETE INFORMATION.

946

QUILL & SCROLL FOUNDATION (EDWARD J. NELL MEMORIAL SCHOLARSHIP)
UNIV OF IOWA SCHOOL OF JOURNALISM & MASS COMMUNICATION
IOWA CITY IA 52242
319/335-5795
AMOUNT: $500
DEADLINE(S): MAY 10
FIELD(S): JOURNALISM
OPEN TO HIGH SCHOOL SENIORS WHO ARE WINNERS IN THE NATIONAL WRITING/PHOTO OR YEARBOOK EXCELLENCE CONTEST SPONSORED BY QUILL & SCROLL AND WHO PLAN TO ENROLL IN AN ACCREDITED JOURNALISM PROGRAM. USA CITIZEN OR LEGAL RESIDENT.
CANDIDATES SHOULD ASK JOURNALISM TEACHER TO WRITE TO ADDRESS ABOVE FOR INFORMATION ON ADMINISTRATION OF THE CONTEST.

947

RADIO AND TELEVISION NEWS DIRECTORS FOUNDATION (BROADCAST JOURNALISM SCHOLARSHIP AWARDS)

1000 CONNECTICUT AVE NW; SUITE 615
WASHINGTON DC 20036
202/659-6510

AMOUNT: $1000 - $2000
DEADLINE(S): MAR 15
FIELD(S): RADIO & TELEVISION JOURNALISM

OPEN TO UNDERGRADUATE SOPHOMORES AND ABOVE AND MASTERS DEGREE CANDIDATES WHOSE CAREER OBJECTIVE IS RADIO AND TELEVISION NEWS. AWARDS ARE FOR 1 YEAR OF UNDERGRADUATE OR GRADUATE STUDY.

12 SCHOLARSHIPS AND 3 FELLOWSHIPS PER YEAR. NOT RENEWABLE. WRITE FOR COMPLETE INFORMATION.

948

RADIO FREE EUROPE/RADIO LIBERTY (MEDIA & OPINION RESEARCH ON EASTERN EUROPE & THE FORMER SOVIET UNION)

PERSONNEL DIVISION; 1201 CONNECTICUT AVE NW
WASHINGTON DC 20036
WRITTEN INQUIRY

AMOUNT: DAILY STIPEND OF 48 GERMAN MARKS PLUS ACCOMMODATIONS
DEADLINE(S): FEB 22
FIELD(S): COMMUNICATIONS; MARKET RESEARCH; STATISTICS; SOCIOLOGY; SOCIAL PSYCHOLOGY; EAST EUROPEAN STUDIES

INTERNSHIP OPEN TO GRADUATE STUDENT OR EXCEPTIONALLY QUALIFIED UNDERGRADUATE IN THE ABOVE AREAS WHO CAN DEMONSTRATE KNOWLEDGE OF QUANTITATIVE RESEARCH METHODS; COMPUTER APPLICATIONS AND PUBLIC OPINION SURVEY TECHNIQUES.

EAST EUROPEAN LANGUAGE SKILLS WOULD BE AN ADVANTAGE. WRITE FOR COMPLETE INFORMATION.

949

RALPH MCGILL SCHOLARSHIP FUND (SCHOLARSHIP PROGRAM)

C/O THE ATLANTA CONSTITUTION; PO BOX 4689
ATLANTA GA 30302
404/526-5091

AMOUNT: UP TO $2000
DEADLINE(S): MAY 1
FIELD(S): JOURNALISM

OPEN TO UNDERGRADUATE JUNIORS & SENIORS WHOSE ROOTS LIE IN THE 14 SOUTHERN STATES & INTEND TO PURSUE A CAREER IN DAILY OR WEEKLY NEWSPAPER WORK. MINIMUM 'B' AVERAGE. USA CITIZEN OR LEGAL RESIDENT.

APPROX 12-14 SCHOLARSHIPS PER YEAR. RENEWABLE. WRITE FOR COMPLETE INFORMATION.

950

SCRIPPS HOWARD FOUNDATION (SCRIPPS HOWARD FOUNDATION SCHOLARSHIPS)

312 WALNUT ST; 28TH FLOOR; PO BOX 5380
CINCINNATI OH 45201
513/977-3035

AMOUNT: $500 TO $3000
DEADLINE(S): DEC 20 FOR AN APPLICATION; FEB 25 FOR MAILING IN APPLICATION
FIELD(S): JOURNALISM; COMMUNICATIONS

PREFERENCE TO (BUT NOT LIMITED TO) FULL-TIME UNDERGRAD JUNIORS; SENIORS; GRAD STUDENTS OR PREVIOUS RECIPIENTS WHO ARE PREPARING TO WORK IN ANY PRINT OR BROADCAST MEDIA. USA CITIZEN OR LEGAL RESIDENT.

RENEWABLE WITH REAPPLICATION. SUBMIT LETTER WITH REQUEST FOR SCHOLARSHIP APPLICATION BEFORE DEC 20 STATING COLLEGE MAJOR AND CAREER GOAL.

951

SOCIETY FOR TECHNICAL COMMUNICATION (UNDERGRADUATE SCHOLARSHIPS)

901 N STUART ST; SUITE 304
ARLINGTON VA 22203
703/522-4114

AMOUNT: $1500
DEADLINE(S): FEB 15
FIELD(S): TECHNICAL COMMUNICATION

OPEN TO FULL-TIME UNDERGRADUATE STUDENTS WHO HAVE COMPLETED AT LEAST 1 YEAR OF STUDY & ARE ENROLLED IN AN ACCREDITED 2-YEAR OR 4-YEAR DEGREE PROGRAM FOR CAREER IN ANY AREA OF TECHNICAL COMMUNICATION.

AWARDS TENABLE AT RECOGNIZED COLLEGES & UNIVERSITIES IN USA & CANADA. 6 AWARDS PER YEAR. WRITE FOR COMPLETE INFORMATION.

952

SOCIETY OF BROADCAST ENGINEERS (HAROLD ENNES SCHOLARSHIP FUND)
PO BOX 20450
INDIANAPOLIS IN 46220
317/253-1640
AMOUNT: $1000
DEADLINE(S): JUL 1
FIELD(S): BROADCASTING
OPEN TO UNDERGRADUATE STUDENTS INTERESTED IN A CAREER IN BROADCASTING. TWO REFERENCES FROM SBE MEMBERS ARE NEEDED TO CONFIRM ELIGIBILITY. SUBMIT A STATEMENT OF PURPOSE AND A BRIEF BIOGRAPHY.
SEND SELF-ADDRESSED STAMPED ENVELOPE FOR APPLICATION AND COMPLETE INFORMATION.

953

SONOMA COUNTY PRESS CLUB (SCHOLARSHIP)
PO BOX 4692
SANTA ROSA CA 95402
WRITTEN INQUIRY
AMOUNT: $1000 FOR HIGH SCHOOL GRADUATE; $2000 FOR CONTINUING COLLEGE STUDENT
DEADLINE(S): APR 10
FIELD(S): JOURNALISM
OPEN TO SONOMA COUNTY (CA) HIGH SCHOOL SENIORS OR GRADUATES OR STUDENTS ATTENDING EITHER SANTA ROSA JUNIOR COLLEGE OR SONOMA STATE UNIVERSITY.
WRITE FOR COMPLETE INFORMATION.

954

UNITED METHODIST COMMUNICATIONS (LEONARD M. PERRYMAN COMMUNICATIONS SCHOLARSHIP FOR ETHNIC MINORITY STUDENTS)
475 RIVERSIDE DR; SUITE 1901
NEW YORK NY 10115
212/663-8900
AMOUNT: $2500
DEADLINE(S): MAR 30
FIELD(S): RELIGIOUS JOURNALISM
CHRISTIAN FAITH. SCHOLARSHIP OPEN TO ETHNIC MINORITY UNDERGRADUATE JUNIORS & SENIORS WHO ARE ENROLLED IN ACCREDITED SCHOOLS OF COMMUNICATION OR JOURNALISM (PRINT; ELECTRONIC OR AUDIOVISUAL). USA CITIZEN OR LEGAL RESIDENT.
CANDIDATES SHOULD PLAN TO PURSUE A CAREER IN RELIGIOUS COMMUNICATION. WRITE FOR COMPLETE INFORMATION.

955

UNIVERSITY OF MARYLAND (COLLEGE OF JOURNALISM SCHOLARSHIPS)
JOURNALISM BUILDING ROOM 1118
COLLEGE PARK MD 20742
301/405-2380
AMOUNT: $250 TO $1500
DEADLINE(S): FEB 15
FIELD(S): JOURNALISM
VARIETY OF JOURNALISM SCHOLARSHIPS; PRIZES AND AWARDS TENABLE AT THE UNIVERSITY OF MARYLAND. APPLICATIONS FORMS FOR ALL SCHOLARSHIPS ARE AVAILABLE AT THE ADDRESS ABOVE.
WRITE FOR COMPLETE INFORMATION.

956

VANDERBILT UNIVERSITY (THOROUGHBRED RACING ASSOCIATION FRED RUSSELL - GRANTLAND RICE SCHOLARSHIP)
2305 WEST END AVE
NASHVILLE TN 37203
615/322-2561
AMOUNT: $10000/YEAR (TOTAL AWARD $40000)
DEADLINE(S): JAN 1
FIELD(S): JOURNALISM
4 YEAR SCHOLARSHIP TO VANDERBILT UNIVERSITY OPEN TO HIGH SCHOOL SENIORS WHO WANT TO BECOME A SPORTS WRITER; HAVE DEMONSTRATED OUTSTANDING POTENTIAL IN THE FIELD & CAN MEET ENTRANCE REQUIREMENTS OF VANDERBILT'S COLLEGE OF ARTS & SCIENCE.
CONTACT SCHOLARSHIP COORDINATOR; ADDRESS ABOVE; FOR COMPLETE INFORMATION.

957

WILLIAM RANDOLPH HEARST FOUNDATION (JOURNALISM AWARDS PROGRAM)
90 NEW MONTGOMERY ST; #1212
SAN FRANCISCO CA 94105
415/543-6033
AMOUNT: $500 - $3000
DEADLINE(S): MONTHLY CONTESTS AT 92 ACCREDITED SCHOOLS OF JOURNALISM WITH A TOTAL OF $280300 AWARDED EACH YEAR.
FIELD(S): JOURNALISM; PHOTOJOURNALISM; BROADCAST NEWS

JOURNALISM AWARDS PROGRAM OFFERS MONTHLY COMPETITIONS OPEN TO UNDERGRADUATE COLLEGE JOURNALISM MAJORS WHO ARE CURRENTLY ENROLLED IN ONE OF THE 91 PARTICIPATING JOURNALISM SCHOOLS.

ENTRY FORMS AND DETAILS ON MONTHLY CONTESTS ARE ONLY AVAILABLE THROUGH THE JOURNALISM DEPARTMENT OF PARTICIPATING SCHOOLS.

958

WOMEN IN COMMUNICATIONS (SEATTLE PROFESSIONAL CHAPTER SCHOLARSHIPS FOR WASHINGTON STATE RESIDENTS)
610 LLOYD BLDG
SEATTLE WA 98101
206/682-9424
AMOUNT: $600 - $800
DEADLINE(S): MAR 1
FIELD(S): COMMUNICATIONS INCLUDING BUT NOT LIMITED TO PRINT & BROADCAST JOURNALISM; ADVERTISING & PUBLIC RELATIONS

OPEN TO WASHINGTON STATE RESIDENTS WHO ARE GRADUATE STUDENTS OR UNDERGRADUATES IN THEIR JUNIOR OR SENIOR YEAR AT A WASHINGTON STATE 4 YEAR COLLEGE OR UNIVERSITY AND ARE MAJORING IN COMMUNICATIONS.

AWARDS WILL BE BASED ON DEMONSTRATED EXCELLENCE IN COMMUNICATIONS; SCHOLASTIC ACHIEVEMENT & FINANCIAL NEED. WRITE FOR COMPLETE INFORMATION.

959

WOMEN IN COMMUNICATIONS - DETROIT CHAPTER (LUCY CORBETT; LENORE UPTON & MARY BUTLER SCHOLARSHIPS FOR MICHIGAN RESIDENTS)
PO BOX 688
HAMBURG MI 48139
313/791-1277
AMOUNT: $1000; $500
DEADLINE(S): APR 2
FIELD(S): COMMUNICATIONS

OPEN TO MICHIGAN RESIDENTS. SCHOLARSHIPS TO BE USED FOR TUITION BY UNDERGRADUATE JUNIOR OR SENIOR OR GRADUATE STUDENT WHO IS MAJORING IN COMMUNICATIONS OR JOURNALISM AT A COLLEGE OR UNIVERSITY IN THE STATE OF MICHIGAN.

WRITE FOR COMPLETE INFORMATION.

HISTORY

960

COMMITTEE ON INSTITUTIONAL COOPERATION (CIC PREDOCTORAL FELLOWSHIPS)
KIRKWOOD HALL RM 111; INDIANA UNIV
BLOOMINGTON IN 47405
812/855-0822
AMOUNT: $9500 + TUITION (5 YEARS)
DEADLINE(S): JAN 2
FIELD(S): HUMANITIES; SOCIAL SCIENCES; NATURAL SCIENCES; MATHEMATICS; ENGINEERING

PREDOCTORAL FELLOWSHIPS FOR USA CITIZENS OF AFRICAN AMERICAN; AMERICAN INDIAN; MEXICAN AMERICAN OR PUERTO RICAN HERITAGE. MUST HOLD OR EXPECT TO RECEIVE BACHELOR'S DEGREE BY LATE SUMMER FROM A REGIONALLY ACCREDITED COLLEGE OR UNIVERSITY.

AWARDS FOR SPECIFIED UNIVERSITIES IN IL; IN; IA; MI; MN; OH; WI; PA. WRITE FOR DETAILS.

961

DAUGHTERS OF THE AMERICAN REVOLUTION (AMERICAN HISTORY SCHOLARSHIPS)
1776 'D' ST NW
WASHINGTON DC 20006
202/879-3292
AMOUNT: $2000 PER YEAR FOR UP TO 4 YEARS
DEADLINE(S): FEB 1
FIELD(S): AMERICAN HISTORY

OPEN TO GRADUATING HIGH SCHOOL SENIORS PLANNING TO MAJOR IN AMERICAN HISTORY. MUST BE USA CITIZEN AND ATTEND AN ACCREDITED USA COLLEGE OR UNIVERSITY. AWARDS BASED ON ACADEMIC EXCELLENCE AND FINANCIAL NEED. DAR AFFILIATION NOT REQUIRED.

MUST BE SPONSORED BY A LOCAL DAR CHAPTER. WRITE FOR COMPLETE INFORMATION. SEND SELF-ADDRESSED STAMPED ENVELOPE.

962

DAUGHTERS OF THE AMERICAN REVOLUTION (ENID HALL GRISWOLD MEMORIAL SCHOLARSHIP PROGRAM)
OFFICE OF THE COMMITTEES; 1776 'D' ST NW
WASHINGTON DC 20006
202/879-3292

AMOUNT: $1000
DEADLINE(S): FEB 15
FIELD(S): HISTORY; POLITICAL SCIENCE; GOVERNMENT; ECONOMICS
OPEN TO UNDERGRADUATE JUNIORS & SENIORS ATTENDING AN ACCREDITED COLLEGE OR UNIVERSITY IN THE USA. AWARDS ARE JUDGED ON THE BASIS OF ACADEMIC EXCELLENCE AND FINANCIAL NEED. USA CITIZEN.
DAR AFFILIATION IS NOT REQUIRED BUT APPLICANTS MUST BE SPONSORED BY A LOCAL DAR CHAPTER. NOT RENEWABLE. WRITE FOR COMPLETE INFORMATION. SEND SELF-ADDRESSED STAMPED ENVELOPE.

963

HILLSDALE COLLEGE (FREEDOM AS VOCATION SCHOLARSHIP)
33 E COLLEGE ST
HILLSDALE MI 49242
517/437-7341
AMOUNT: VARIES
DEADLINE(S): NONE SPECIFIED
FIELD(S): BUSINESS; HISTORY; POLITICAL SCIENCE & ECONOMICS
OPEN TO HILLSDALE COLLEGE UNDERGRADUATES WHO MAINTAIN A 3.0 OR BETTER (4.0 SCALE) GPA AND COMMIT TO A SERIES OF COURSES IN THE ABOVE FIELDS. STUDENT MUST RANK IN TOP 20% OF CLASS AND TOP 10% OF TEST SCORES.
STUDENTS MUST POSSESS EXCELLENT COMMUNICATIONS AND PUBLIC SPEAKING SKILLS; LEADERSHIP SKILLS AND DEMONSTRATE OUTSTANDING CHARACTER AND CITIZENSHIP. WRITE FOR COMPLETE INFORMATION.

964

INSTITUTE FOR HUMANE STUDIES (CLAUDE R. LAMBE FELLOWSHIPS)
GEORGE MASON UNIVERSITY; 4400 UNIVERSITY DRIVE
FAIRFAX VA 22030
703/323-1055
AMOUNT: $17500
DEADLINE(S): JAN 15
FIELD(S): SOCIAL SCIENCES; LAW; HUMANITIES
OPEN TO GRADUATE STUDENTS AND UNDERGRADS WHO WILL HAVE JUNIOR OR SENIOR STANDING AT ACCREDITED COLLEGES AND UNIVERSITIES THE NEXT ACADEMIC YEAR. AWARD IS TO SUPPORT STUDENTS WITH A DEMONSTRATED INTEREST IN THE CLASSICAL LIBERAL TRADITION.
RECIPIENT WILL BE INTENT ON PURSUING AN INTELLECTUAL/SCHOLARLY CAREER IN ONE OF THE ABOVE AREAS. WRITE FOR COMPLETE INFORMATION.

965

NATIONAL FEDERATION OF THE BLIND (ORACLE CORPORATION SCHOLARSHIP)
814 4TH AVE; #200
GRINNELL IA 50112
515/236-3366
AMOUNT: $2500
DEADLINE(S): MAR 31
FIELD(S): HUMANITIES (ART; ENGLISH; FOREIGN LANGUAGES; HISTORY; PHILOSOPHY; RELIGION)
OPEN TO LEGALLY BLIND STUDENTS PURSUING OR PLANNING TO PURSUE A FULL TIME POST-SECONDARY COURSE OF STUDY IN THE TRADITIONAL HUMANITIES. AWARDS BASED ON ACADEMIC EXCELLENCE; COMMUNITY SERVICE; FINANCIAL NEED.
WRITE FOR COMPLETE INFORMATION.

966

NATIONAL FOUNDATION OF THE BLIND (HUMANITIES SCHOLARSHIP)
815 4TH AVE; #200
GRINNELL IA 50112
515/236-3366
AMOUNT: $2500
DEADLINE(S): MAR 31
FIELD(S): HUMANITIES (ART; ENGLISH; FOREIGN LANGUAGES; HISTORY; PHILOSOPHY; RELIGION)
OPEN TO LEGALLY BLIND STUDENTS PURSUING OR PLANNING TO PURSUE A POST-SECONDARY EDUCATION IN THE ABOVE AREAS. SCHOLARSHIPS ARE AWARDED ON BASIS OF ACADEMIC EXCELLENCE; COMMUNITY SERVICE AND FINANCIAL NEED.
WRITE FOR COMPLETE INFORMATION.

967

NATIONAL SPACE CLUB (DR. ROBERT H. GODDARD HISTORICAL ESSAY AWARD)
655 15TH ST NW; #300
WASHINGTON DC 20005
202/639-4210
AMOUNT: $1000

DEADLINE(S): DEC 1
FIELD(S): AEROSPACE HISTORY
ESSAY COMPETITION OPEN TO ANY USA CITIZEN ON A TOPIC DEALING WITH ANY SIGNIFICANT ASPECT OF THE HISTORICAL DEVELOPMENT OF ROCKETRY AND ASTRONAUTICS. ESSAYS SHOULD NOT EXCEED 5000 WORDS AND SHOULD BE FULLY DOCUMENTED.
WRITE FOR COMPLETE INFORMATION.

968

SOURISSEAU ACADEMY FOR STATE AND LOCAL HISTORY (RESEARCH GRANT)
C/O SAN JOSE STATE UNIVERSITY
SAN JOSE CA 95192
408/924-6510 OR 408/227-2657
AMOUNT: $500
DEADLINE(S): APR 1; NOV 1
FIELD(S): CALIFORNIA HISTORY
GRANTS ARE AVAILABLE TO SUPPORT UNDERGRADUATE AND GRADUATE RESEARCH ON CALIFORNIA HISTORY. PREFERENCE TO RESEARCH ON SANTA CLARA COUNTY HISTORY.
5-10 AWARDS PER YEAR ARE GRANTED FOR PROJECT EXPENSES. WRITE FOR COMPLETE INFORMATION.

969

U.S. INSTITUTE OF PEACE (NATIONAL PEACE ESSAY CONTEST)
PO BOX 27720; CENTRAL STATION
WASHINGTON DC 20038-7720
202/457-1700
AMOUNT: $100 TO $10000
DEADLINE(S): FEB 15
FIELD(S): AMERICAN HISTORY; AMERICAN FOREIGN POLICY
1500 WORD ESSAY CONTEST FOR COLLEGE SCHOLARSHIPS OPEN TO STUDENTS IN THE 9TH THROUGH 12TH GRADES. MUST BE USA CITIZENS. FIRST; SECOND AND THIRD PLACE WINNERS AT STATE AND NATIONAL LEVELS WILL RECEIVE COLLEGE SCHOLARSHIPS.
FIRST PLACE STATE WINNERS WILL RECEIVE ALL-EXPENSES-PAID TRIP TO WASHINGTON FOR THE WEEK-LONG AWARDS PROGRAM. 163 STATE WINNERS; 3 NATIONAL WINNERS. WRITE FOR COMPLETE INFORMATION.

970

U.S. MARINE CORPS HISTORICAL CENTER (COLLEGE INTERNSHIPS)
BUILDING 58; WASHINGTON NAVY YARD
WASHINGTON DC 20374
202/433-3839
AMOUNT: APPROX $500 FOR DAILY EXPENSES
DEADLINE(S): NONE SPECIFIED
FIELD(S): U.S. MILITARY HISTORY; HISTORIAN; LIBRARY SCIENCE; MUSEUM STUDIES
OPEN TO UNDERGRADUATE STUDENTS AT A COLLEGE OR UNIVERSITY WHICH WILL GRANT ACADEMIC CREDIT FOR WORK EXPERIENCE AS INTERNS AT THE ADDRESS ABOVE OR AT THE MARINE CORPS AIRGROUND MUSEUM IN QUANTICO VIRGINIA.
ALL INTERNSHIPS ARE REGARDED AS BEGINNING PROFESSIONAL-LEVEL HISTORIAN; CURATOR; LIBRARIAN OR ARCHIVIST POSITIONS. WRITE FOR COMPLETE INFORMATION.

971

WILLIAM RANDOLPH HEARST FOUNDATION (U.S. SENATE YOUTH PROGRAM)
90 NEW MONTGOMERY ST; SUITE 1212
SAN FRANCISCO CA 94105
415/543-4057; FAX 415/243-0760
AMOUNT: $2000 + ALL EXPENSES PAID WEEK IN WASHINGTON DC
DEADLINE(S): NONE SPECIFIED
FIELD(S): US GOVERNMENT; HISTORY; POLITICAL SCIENCE; ECONOMICS
OPEN TO ANY HIGH SCHOOL JUNIOR OR SENIOR WHO IS SERVING AS AN ELECTED STUDENT BODY OFFICER AT A USA HIGH SCHOOL. STUDENT RECEIVES A WEEK'S STAY IN WASHINGTON AS GUEST OF THE SENATE AND A $2000 SCHOLARSHIP.
STUDENT MUST BECOME A CANDIDATE FOR A DEGREE AT AN ACCREDITED USA COLLEGE OR UNIVERSITY WITHIN TWO YEARS OF HIGH SCHOOL GRADUATION. USA PERMANENT RESIDENT. CONTACT HIGH SCHOOL PRINCIPAL FOR COMPLETE INFORMATION.

LAW

972

AMERICAN SOCIETY OF CRIMINOLOGY (GENE CARTE STUDENT PAPER COMPETITION)
1314 KINNEAR ROAD; SUITE 212
COLUMBUS OH 43212
614/292-9207

AMOUNT: $300; $150; $100
DEADLINE(S): APR 15
FIELD(S): CRIMINOLOGY; CRIMINAL JUSTICE
ESSAY COMPETITION OPEN TO ANY STUDENT CURRENTLY ENROLLED FULL TIME IN AN ACADEMIC PROGRAM AT EITHER THE UNDERGRADUATE OR GRADUATE LEVEL. PAPERS MUST BE DIRECTLY RELATED TO CRIMINOLOGY AND MAY BE CONCEPTUAL AND/OR EMPIRICAL.
WRITE FOR COMPLETE INFORMATION.

973

ASSOCIATION OF FORMER AGENTS OF THE U.S. SECRET SERVICE - AFAUSS - (DIETRICH/CROSS/HANLY SCHOLARSHIPS)
PO BOX 11681
ALEXANDRIA VA 22312
WRITTEN INQUIRY
AMOUNT: $500 - $1500
DEADLINE(S): MAY 1
FIELD(S): LAW ENFORCEMENT; POLICE ADMINISTRATION
OPEN TO UNDERGRADUATE STUDENTS WHO HAVE COMPLETED AT LEAST ONE YEAR OF STUDY AND GRADUATE STUDENTS WORKING TOWARDS AN ADVANCED DEGREE IN THE ABOVE AREAS. USA CITIZEN.
WRITE FOR COMPLETE INFORMATION.

974

BOY SCOUTS OF AMERICA (J. EDGAR HOOVER FOUNDATION SCHOLARSHIPS)
1325 W.WALNUT HILL LN
IRVING TX 75015
214/580-2084
AMOUNT: $1000
DEADLINE(S): MAR 31
FIELD(S): LAW ENFORCEMENT
OPEN TO HIGH SCHOOL SENIORS WHO ARE REGISTERED EXPLORER SCOUTS; ACTIVE IN POST SPECIALIZING IN LAW ENFORCEMENT & HAVE DEMONSTRATED AN INTEREST IN PURSUING A CAREER IN LAW ENFORCEMENT. AWARDS FOR UNDERGRADUATE TUITION. USA CITIZEN.
SCHOLARSHIP FUNDS WILL REMAIN AVAILABLE TO WINNERS FOR A 24-MONTH PERIOD STARTING WITH SUMMER OR FALL SEMESTER OF THE YEAR SELECTED. WRITE FOR COMPLETE INFORMATION.

975

BOYS & GIRLS CLUBS OF SAN DIEGO (SPENCE REESE SCHOLARSHIP FUND)
3760 FOURTH AVE; SUITE 1
SAN DIEGO CA 92103
619/298-3520
AMOUNT: $2000 PER YEAR FOR 4 YEARS
DEADLINE(S): MAY 15
FIELD(S): MEDICINE; LAW; ENGINEERING; POLITICAL SCIENCE
OPEN TO MALE HIGH SCHOOL SENIORS PLANNING CAREER IN ABOVE FIELDS. PREFERENCE TO STUDENTS WITHIN A 250 MILE RADIUS OF SAN DIEGO. BOYS CLUB AFFILIATION IS NOT REQUIRED.
APPLICATIONS ARE AVAILABLE IN JANUARY. MUST ENCLOSE A SELF-ADDRESSED STAMPED ENVELOPE TO RECEIVE APPLICATION. A $10 PROCESSING FEE IS REQUIRED WITH COMPLETED APPLICATION. WRITE FOR COMPLETE INFORMATION.

976

EARL WARREN LEGAL TRAINING PROGRAM (SCHOLARSHIPS)
99 HUDSON ST; 16TH FLOOR
NEW YORK NY 10013
212/219-1900
AMOUNT: VARIES
DEADLINE(S): MAR 15
FIELD(S): LAW
SCHOLARSHIPS FOR ENTERING BLACK LAW STUDENTS. EMPHASIS ON APPLICANTS WHO WISH TO ENTER LAW SCHOOLS IN THE SOUTH. MUST SUBMIT PROOF OF ACCEPTANCE TO AN ACCREDITED LAW SCHOOL. US CITIZEN OR LEGAL RESIDENT.
US CITIZENS UNDER 35 YEARS OF AGE PREFERRED. WRITE FOR COMPLETE INFORMATION.

977

H. FLETCHER BROWN FUND (SCHOLARSHIPS)
C/O BANK OF DELAWARE; TRUST DEPT; PO BOX 791
WILMINGTON DE 19899
302/429-2827
AMOUNT: VARIES
DEADLINE(S): APR 15
FIELD(S): MEDICINE; DENTISTRY; LAW; ENGINEERING; CHEMISTRY

OPEN TO STUDENTS BORN IN DELAWARE; GRADUATED FROM A DELAWARE HIGH SCHOOL & STILL RESIDING IN DELAWARE. FOR FOUR YEARS OF STUDY (UNDERGRAD OR GRAD) LEADING TO A DEGREE THAT ENABLES APPLICANT TO PRACTICE IN CHOSEN FIELD.
SCHOLARSHIPS ARE BASED ON NEED; SCHOLASTIC ACHIEVEMENT; GOOD MORAL CHARACTER. RENEWABLE. WRITE FOR COMPLETE INFORMATION.

978

INSTITUTE FOR HUMANE STUDIES (CLAUDE R. LAMBE FELLOWSHIPS)
GEORGE MASON UNIVERSITY; 4400 UNIVERSITY DRIVE
FAIRFAX VA 22030
703/323-1055
AMOUNT: $17500
DEADLINE(S): JAN 15
FIELD(S): SOCIAL SCIENCES; LAW; HUMANITIES
OPEN TO GRADUATE STUDENTS AND UNDERGRADS WHO WILL HAVE JUNIOR OR SENIOR STANDING AT ACCREDITED COLLEGES AND UNIVERSITIES THE NEXT ACADEMIC YEAR. AWARD IS TO SUPPORT STUDENTS WITH A DEMONSTRATED INTEREST IN THE CLASSICAL LIBERAL TRADITION.
RECIPIENT WILL BE INTENT ON PURSUING AN INTELLECTUAL/SCHOLARLY CAREER IN ONE OF THE ABOVE AREAS. WRITE FOR COMPLETE INFORMATION.

979

INTERNATIONAL ASSN OF ARSON INVESTIGATORS (JOHN CHARLES WILSON SCHOLARSHIP FUND)
PO BOX 91119
LOUISVILLE KY 40291
502/239-7228
AMOUNT: $1000
DEADLINE(S): FEB 15
FIELD(S): POLICE SCIENCE; FIRE SCIENCE & AFFILIATED FIELDS
OPEN TO IAAI MEMBERS; THEIR IMMEDIATE FAMILY & NON-MEMBERS WHO ARE RECOMMENDED & SPONSORED BY MEMBERS IN GOOD STANDING. AWARDS ARE FOR UNDERGRADUATE STUDY IN ABOVE AREAS AT ACCREDITED 2-YEAR & 4-YEAR INSTITUTIONS.
WRITE FOR COMPLETE INFORMATION.

980

MARYLAND HIGHER EDUCATION COMMISSION (PROFESSIONAL SCHOOL SCHOLARSHIPS)
STATE SCHOLARSHIP ADMINISTRATION; 16 FRANCIS ST
ANNAPOLIS MD 21401
410/974-5370
AMOUNT: $200 - $1000
DEADLINE(S): MAR 1
FIELD(S): DENTISTRY; PHARMACY; MEDICINE; LAW; NURSING
OPEN TO MARYLAND RESIDENTS WHO HAVE BEEN ADMITTED AS FULL-TIME STUDENTS AT A PARTICIPATING GRADUATE INSTITUTION OF HIGHER LEARNING IN MARYLAND OR AN UNDERGRADUATE NURSING PROGRAM.
RENEWABLE UP TO 4 YEARS. WRITE FOR COMPLETE INFORMATION AND A LIST OF PARTICIPATING MARYLAND INSTITUTIONS.

981

NATIONAL BLACK POLICE ASSOCIATION (ALPHONSO DEAL SCHOLARSHIP AWARD)
3251 MT PLEASANT ST NW; 2ND FLOOR
WASHINGTON DC 20010
202/986-2070
AMOUNT: $500
DEADLINE(S): JUN 1
FIELD(S): LAW ENFORCEMENT - CRIMINAL JUSTICE
OPEN TO HIGH SCHOOL GRADUATES WHO HAVE BEEN ACCEPTED FOR ENROLLMENT IN A TWO OR FOUR YEAR COLLEGE. MUST HAVE A 2.5 OR BETTER GPA; BE A USA CITIZEN AND DEMONSTRATE FINANCIAL NEED.
WRITE FOR COMPLETE INFORMATION.

982

NATIONAL FEDERATION OF THE BLIND (HOWARD BROWN RICKARD SCHOLARSHIP)
814 4TH AVE; #200
GRINNELL IA 50112
515/236-3366
AMOUNT: $2500
DEADLINE(S): MAR 31
FIELD(S): NATURAL SCIENCES; ARCHITECTURE; ENGINEERING; MEDICINE; LAW
SCHOLARSHIPS FOR UNDERGRADUATE OR GRADUATE STUDY IN THE ABOVE AREAS. OPEN TO LEGALLY BLIND STUDENTS

ENROLLED FULL TIME AT ACCREDITED POST SECONDARY INSTITUTIONS.

AWARDS BASED ON ACADEMIC EXCELLENCE; SERVICE TO THE COMMUNITY AND FINANCIAL NEED. WRITE FOR COMPLETE INFORMATION.

983

STATE FARM COMPANIES FOUNDATION (EXCEPTIONAL STUDENT FELLOWSHIP AWARDS)
ONE STATE FARM PLAZA; SC-3
BLOOMINGTON IL 61710
309/766-2039
AMOUNT: $3000
DEADLINE(S): FEB 15
FIELD(S): BUSINESS RELATED FIELDS; COMPUTER SCIENCE; PRELAW; MATHEMATICS

OPEN TO EXCEPTIONAL CURRENT JUNIOR OR SENIOR UNDERGRADUATES IN THE ABOVE FIELDS. MUST BE NOMINATED BY DEAN OR DEPARTMENT HEAD. US CITIZEN. MUST BE COLLEGE JUNIOR OR SENIOR AT TIME OF APPLICATION.

50 FELLOWSHIPS PER ACADEMIC YEAR. APPLICATIONS AND NOMINATIONS AVAILABLE NOV 1. WRITE FOR COMPLETE INFORMATION.

POLITICAL SCIENCE

984

AMERICAN JEWISH COMMITTEE (HAROLD W. ROSENTHAL FELLOWSHIP)
2027 MASSACHUSETTS AVE NW
WASHINGTON DC 20036
202/265-2000
AMOUNT: $1650 STIPEND
DEADLINE(S): APR
FIELD(S): POLITICAL SCIENCE; GOVERNMENT SERVICE; FOREIGN AFFAIRS

OPEN TO COLLEGE SENIORS & GRAD STUDENTS. FELLOWSHIP PROVIDES OPPORTUNITY FOR A STUDENT TO SPEND A SUMMER WORKING IN THE OFFICE OF A MEMBER OF CONGRESS OR EXECUTIVE BRANCH ON FOREIGN AFFAIRS AND GOVERNMENT SERVICE ISSUES. US CITIZEN.

APPLICATIONS ARE AVAILABLE FROM THE ADDRESS ABOVE HOWEVER THEY MUST BE SUBMITTED WITH A RECOMMENDATION FROM YOUR DEAN. SELECTED FELLOWS WILL ALSO RECEIVE PREFERENTIAL TREATMENT FOR A EUROPEAN COMMUNITY 3-5 WEEK TRAVEL STUDY.

985

ASTRAEA NATIONAL LESBIAN ACTION FOUNDATION (MARGOT KARLE SCHOLARSHIP)
666 BROADWAY; ROOM 520
NEW YORK NY 10012
212/529-8021
AMOUNT: $500
DEADLINE(S): FEB 15; AUG 15
FIELD(S): POLITICAL SCIENCE; SOCIOLOGY

FOR WOMEN STUDENTS WHOSE CAREER PATH AND/OR EXTRACURRICULAR ACTIVITIES DEMONSTRATE POLITICAL AND/OR SOCIAL COMMITMENT ANALOGOUS TO THAT OF MARGOT KARLE (AN ATTORNEY WHO ACTIVELY FOUGHT FOR THE CIVIL RIGHTS OF GAYS & LESBIANS.)

FOR UNDERGRADUATE STUDY AT ONE OF THE SCHOOLS IN THE NEW YORK CITY UNIVERSITY SYSTEM. WRITE FOR COMPLETE INFORMATION.

986

BOYS & GIRLS CLUBS OF SAN DIEGO (SPENCE REESE SCHOLARSHIP FUND)
3760 FOURTH AVE; SUITE 1
SAN DIEGO CA 92103
619/298-3520
AMOUNT: $2000 PER YEAR FOR 4 YEARS
DEADLINE(S): MAY 15
FIELD(S): MEDICINE; LAW; ENGINEERING; POLITICAL SCIENCE

OPEN TO MALE HIGH SCHOOL SENIORS PLANNING CAREER IN ABOVE FIELDS. PREFERENCE TO STUDENTS WITHIN A 250 MILE RADIUS OF SAN DIEGO. BOYS CLUB AFFILIATION IS NOT REQUIRED.

APPLICATIONS ARE AVAILABLE IN JANUARY. MUST ENCLOSE A SELF-ADDRESSED STAMPED ENVELOPE TO RECEIVE APPLICATION. A $10 PROCESSING FEE IS REQUIRED WITH COMPLETED APPLICATION. WRITE FOR COMPLETE INFORMATION.

987

COMMITTEE ON INSTITUTIONAL COOPERATION (CIC PREDOCTORAL FELLOWSHIPS)
KIRKWOOD HALL RM 111; INDIANA UNIV
BLOOMINGTON IN 47405
812/855-0822
AMOUNT: $9500 + TUITION (5 YEARS)
DEADLINE(S): JAN 2
FIELD(S): HUMANITIES; SOCIAL SCIENCES; NATURAL SCIENCES; MATHEMATICS; ENGINEERING
PREDOCTORAL FELLOWSHIPS FOR USA CITIZENS OF AFRICAN AMERICAN; AMERICAN INDIAN; MEXICAN AMERICAN OR PUERTO RICAN HERITAGE. MUST HOLD OR EXPECT TO RECEIVE BACHELOR'S DEGREE BY LATE SUMMER FROM A REGIONALLY ACCREDITED COLLEGE OR UNIVERSITY.
AWARDS FOR SPECIFIED UNIVERSITIES IN IL; IN; IA; MI; MN; OH; WI; PA. WRITE FOR DETAILS.

988

DAUGHTERS OF THE AMERICAN REVOLUTION (ENID HALL GRISWOLD MEMORIAL SCHOLARSHIP PROGRAM)
OFFICE OF THE COMMITTEES; 1776 'D' ST NW
WASHINGTON DC 20006
202/879-3292
AMOUNT: $1000
DEADLINE(S): FEB 15
FIELD(S): HISTORY; POLITICAL SCIENCE; GOVERNMENT; ECONOMICS
OPEN TO UNDERGRADUATE JUNIORS & SENIORS ATTENDING AN ACCREDITED COLLEGE OR UNIVERSITY IN THE USA. AWARDS ARE JUDGED ON THE BASIS OF ACADEMIC EXCELLENCE AND FINANCIAL NEED. USA CITIZEN.
DAR AFFILIATION IS NOT REQUIRED BUT APPLICANTS MUST BE SPONSORED BY A LOCAL DAR CHAPTER. NOT RENEWABLE. WRITE FOR COMPLETE INFORMATION. SEND SELF-ADDRESSED STAMPED ENVELOPE.

989

FUND FOR AMERICAN STUDIES (INSTITUTES ON POLITICAL JOURNALISM; BUSINESS & GOVERNMENT AFFAIRS & COMPARATIVE POLITICAL & ECONOMIC SYSTEMS)
1526 18TH ST NW
WASHINGTON DC 20036
202/986-0384
AMOUNT: UP TO $3500
DEADLINE(S): JAN 11 EARLY DECISION; MAR 15 GENERAL APPLICATION DEADLINE
FIELD(S): POLITICAL SCIENCE; ECONOMICS; JOURNALISM; BUSINESS ADMINISTRATION
SCHOLARSHIPS COVER COST TO ATTEND ANNUAL 6-WEEK SUMMER INSTITUTE AT GEORGETOWN UNIV. COURSES ARE WORTH 6 CREDITS & INCLUDE FOREIGN POLICY LECTURES; MEDIA DIALOGUE SERIES; SITE BRIEFINGS & CAREER DAYS. OPEN TO COLLEGE SOPHOMORES & JUNIORS.
APPROX 100 AWARDS PER YEAR. FOR FUND'S PROGRAMS ONLY. WRITE FOR COMPLETE INFORMATION.

990

GLENN CARRINGTON FOUNDATION (ALASKA SCHOLARSHIP TO BENEFIT NATIVE ALASKANS)
927 LARKSPUR RD
OAKLAND CA 94610
510/763-9762
AMOUNT: UP TO $2000
DEADLINE(S): MAR 1
FIELD(S): BUSINESS; EDUCATION; ENVIRONMENT; POLITICAL SCIENCE; COMMUNICATIONS
OPEN TO ALASKA RESIDENTS COMMITTED TO HELPING NATIVE ALASKANS GOVERN; EDUCATE; DEVELOP BUSINESSES AND IMPROVE THEIR MANAGEMENT ABILITIES. MUST DEMONSTRATE PERSONAL AND FAMILY FINANCIAL NEED.
WRITE FOR COMPLETE INFORMATION.

991

HARRY S. TRUMAN SCHOLARSHIP FOUNDATION (SCHOLARSHIPS)
712 JACKSON PLACE NW
WASHINGTON DC 20006
202/395-4831
AMOUNT: UP TO $30000 OVER 4 YEARS
DEADLINE(S): DEC 2
FIELD(S): PUBLIC SERVICE; GOVERNMENT
OPEN TO FULL TIME STUDENTS; EITHER JUNIORS IN A 4-YEAR COLLEGE OR SOPHOMORES AT A 2-YEAR COLLEGE WHO ARE COMMITTED TO A CAREER IN GOVERNMENT OR PUBLIC SERVICE. MUST BE IN UPPER THIRD OF CLASS

AND HAVE OUTSTANDING LEADERSHIP POTENTIAL.

CANDIDATES MUST BE USA CITIZENS AND NOMINATED BY THEIR SCHOOLS. UP TO 92 SCHOLARSHIPS PER YEAR. WRITE FOR COMPLETE INFORMATION.

992

HILLSDALE COLLEGE (FREEDOM AS VOCATION SCHOLARSHIP)
33 E COLLEGE ST
HILLSDALE MI 49242
517/437-7341
AMOUNT: VARIES
DEADLINE(S): NONE SPECIFIED
FIELD(S): BUSINESS; HISTORY; POLITICAL SCIENCE & ECONOMICS

OPEN TO HILLSDALE COLLEGE UNDERGRADUATES WHO MAINTAIN A 3.0 OR BETTER (4.0 SCALE) GPA AND COMMIT TO A SERIES OF COURSES IN THE ABOVE FIELDS. STUDENT MUST RANK IN TOP 20% OF CLASS AND TOP 10% OF TEST SCORES.

STUDENTS MUST POSSESS EXCELLENT COMMUNICATIONS AND PUBLIC SPEAKING SKILLS; LEADERSHIP SKILLS AND DEMONSTRATE OUTSTANDING CHARACTER AND CITIZENSHIP. WRITE FOR COMPLETE INFORMATION.

993

ILLINOIS GOVERNOR'S SUMMER INTERNSHIP PROGRAM
2 1/2 STATE HOUSE
SPRINGFIELD IL 62706
217/782-4921
AMOUNT: $1000 PER MONTH
DEADLINE(S): FEB 15
FIELD(S): PUBLIC SERVICE

ILLINOIS RESIDENT. GOVERNOR'S SUMMER INTERNSHIP PROGRAM IS OPEN TO UNDERGRADUATE STUDENTS WHO HAVE COMPLETED AT LEAST 2 YEARS OF STUDY. INTERNS ARE PLACED WITH VARIOUS STATE AGENCIES IN CHICAGO & SPRINGFIELD. USA CITIZEN.

ACADEMIC CREDIT MAY BE ARRANGED. 140 INTERNSHIPS PER SUMMER. WRITE FOR COMPLETE INFORMATION.

994

INSTITUTE FOR HUMANE STUDIES (CLAUDE R. LAMBE FELLOWSHIPS)
GEORGE MASON UNIVERSITY; 4400 UNIVERSITY DRIVE
FAIRFAX VA 22030
703/323-1055
AMOUNT: $17500
DEADLINE(S): JAN 15
FIELD(S): SOCIAL SCIENCES; LAW; HUMANITIES

OPEN TO GRADUATE STUDENTS AND UNDERGRADS WHO WILL HAVE JUNIOR OR SENIOR STANDING AT ACCREDITED COLLEGES AND UNIVERSITIES THE NEXT ACADEMIC YEAR. AWARD IS TO SUPPORT STUDENTS WITH A DEMONSTRATED INTEREST IN THE CLASSICAL LIBERAL TRADITION.

RECIPIENT WILL BE INTENT ON PURSUING AN INTELLECTUAL/SCHOLARLY CAREER IN ONE OF THE ABOVE AREAS. WRITE FOR COMPLETE INFORMATION.

995

JUNIATA COLLEGE (BAKER PEACE AND CONFLICT STUDIES MERIT SCHOLARSHIP)
FINANCIAL AID OFFICE
HUNTINGDON PA 16652
814/643-4310
AMOUNT: $1000
DEADLINE(S): MAR 1
FIELD(S): INTERNATIONAL AFFAIRS

AWARDS ARE MADE BASED ON MERIT TO STUDENTS WHO ARE ACCEPTED AS INCOMING FRESHMEN AT JUNIATA COLLEGE & INTEND TO PURSUE THE PEACE AND CONFLICT STUDIES CURRICULUM.

STUDENT SHOULD RANK IN UPPER 20% OF GRADUATING H.S. CLASS & HAVE ABOVE AVERAGE SAT SCORES. SCHOLARSHIP IS RENEWABLE FOR UP TO 3 YEARS IF 3.0 GPA IS MAINTAINED.

996

LAVINIA ENGLE SCHOLARSHIP (UNDERGRADUATE WOMEN SCHOLARSHIPS)
C/O JUDITH HEIMANN; 6900 MARBURY RD
BETHESDA MD 20817
301/229-4647
AMOUNT: VARIES
DEADLINE(S): APR 15

FIELD(S): POLITICAL SCIENCE/GOVERNMENT/PUBLIC ADMINISTRATION

OPEN TO WOMEN RESIDING IN MONTGOMERY COUNTY MARYLAND. FOR UNDERGRADUATE STUDY AT A COLLEGE OR UNIVERSITY IN MARYLAND.

SEND SELF-ADDRESSED STAMPED ENVELOPE FOR APPLICATION AND COMPLETE INFORMATION.

997

NATIONAL ITALIAN AMERICAN FOUNDATION (CALIGUERI SCHOLARSHIP)

DR. M. LOMBARDO; EDUCATION DIRECTOR; 666 11TH ST NW; SUITE 800

WASHINGTON DC 20001

202/638-2137

AMOUNT: $1000

DEADLINE(S): MAY 31

FIELD(S): POLITICAL SCIENCE

OPEN TO UNDERGRADUATE AND GRADUATE STUDENTS OF ITALIAN HERITAGE MAJORING IN POLITICAL SCIENCE. APPLICANTS MUST PROVIDE EVIDENCE OF FINANCIAL NEED AND WRITE AN ESSAY (1 TYPED PAGE MAXIMUM) ON THEIR ITALIAN BACKGROUND.

WRITE FOR COMPLETE INFORMATION.

998

NEW YORK CITY DEPT. OF PERSONNEL (GOVERNMENT SCHOLARS INTERNSHIP PROGRAM)

2 WASHINGTON ST; 15TH FLOOR

NEW YORK NY 10004

212/487-5698

AMOUNT: $2500

DEADLINE(S): JAN 27

FIELD(S): PUBLIC ADMINISTRATION; URBAN PLANNING; GOVERNMENT; PUBLIC SERVICE; URBAN AFFAIRS

10-WEEK SUMMER INTERN PROGRAM OPEN TO UNDERGRADUATE SOPHOMORES; JUNIORS & SENIORS. PROGRAM PROVIDES STUDENTS WITH UNIQUE OPPORTUNITY TO LEARN ABOUT NY CITY GOVERNMENT. INTERNSHIPS AVAILABLE IN VIRTUALLY EVERY CITY AGENCY & MAYORAL OFFICE.

WRITE FOR COMPLETE INFORMATION.

999

NEW YORK CITY DEPT. OF PERSONNEL (URBAN FELLOWS PROGRAM)

2 WASHINGTON ST; 15TH FLOOR

NEW YORK NY 10004

212/487-5698

AMOUNT: $17000 STIPEND

DEADLINE(S): JAN 26

FIELD(S): PUBLIC ADMINISTRATION; URBAN PLANNING; GOVERNMENT; PUBLIC SERVICE; URBAN AFFAIRS

FELLOWSHIP PROGRAM PROVIDES ONE ACADEMIC YEAR (9 MONTHS) OF FULL-TIME WORK EXPERIENCE IN URBAN GOVERNMENT. OPEN TO GRADUATING COLLEGE SENIORS AND RECENT COLLEGE GRADUATES. USA CITIZEN.

WRITE FOR COMPLETE INFORMATION.

1000

U.S. DEPT. OF STATE (INTERNSHIPS)

PO BOX 9317

ARLINGTON VA 22219

703/875-7165; FAX 703/875-7243

AMOUNT: PAID INTERNSHIPS ARE AT GS-4 TO GS-6 LEVELS; SOME ARE UNPAID

DEADLINE(S): NOV 1 FOR SUMMER; MAR 1 FOR FALL; JUL 1 FOR SPRING

FIELD(S): INTERNATIONAL RELATIONS

OPEN TO CONTINUING COLLEGE OR UNIVERSITY JUNIORS; SENIORS OR GRAD STUDENTS WHO ARE USA CITIZENS AND HAVE COMPLETED SOME ACADEMIC STUDIES IN THE TYPE OF WORK THE STUDENT WISHES TO PERFORM FOR THE DEPARTMENT.

MUST BE ABLE TO PASS BACKGROUND INVESTIGATION. INTERNS SERVE ONE SEMESTER OR QUARTER DURING ACADEMIC YEAR OR 10 WEEKS DURING SUMMER. MOST ARE IN DC BUT SOME ARE ABROAD. WRITE FOR COMPLETE INFORMATION.

1001

U.S. INSTITUTE OF PEACE (NATIONAL PEACE ESSAY CONTEST)

PO BOX 27720; CENTRAL STATION

WASHINGTON DC 20038-7720

202/457-1700

AMOUNT: $100 TO $10000

DEADLINE(S): FEB 15

FIELD(S): AMERICAN HISTORY; AMERICAN FOREIGN POLICY

1500 WORD ESSAY CONTEST FOR COLLEGE SCHOLARSHIPS OPEN TO STUDENTS IN THE 9TH THROUGH 12TH GRADES. MUST BE USA CITIZENS. FIRST; SECOND AND THIRD PLACE WINNERS AT STATE AND NATIONAL LEVELS WILL RECEIVE COLLEGE SCHOLARSHIPS.

FIRST PLACE STATE WINNERS WILL RECEIVE ALL-EXPENSES-PAID TRIP TO WASHINGTON FOR THE WEEK-LONG AWARDS PROGRAM. 163 STATE WINNERS; 3 NATIONAL WINNERS. WRITE FOR COMPLETE INFORMATION.

1002

VASA ORDER OF AMERICA (THE L. EINAR AND EDITH NILSSON AWARD)

E.G. JOHNSON; VICE GRAND MASTER; 4406 SALMON POINT

STOCKTON CA 95219

209/478-7498

AMOUNT: $2000

DEADLINE(S): LL03-92

FIELD(S): POLITICAL SCIENCE

OPEN TO HIGH SCHOOL SENIORS OR COLLEGE UNDERGRADUATES FOR FULL TIME STUDY IN THE FIELD OF POLITICAL SCIENCE AT AN ACCREDITED COLLEGE OR UNIVERSITY. MUST DEMONSTRATE FINANCIAL NEED.

APPLICANTS MUST HAVE BEEN A VASA MEMBER IN ONE OF THE FOLLOWING DISTRICTS - CONNECTICUT NO. 1; MASSACHUSETTS NO. 2 OR RHODE ISLAND NO. 3. WRITE FOR COMPLETE INFORMATION.

1003

WASHINGTON CROSSING FOUNDATION (SCHOLARSHIP FUND)

EUGENE C. FISH ESQ.; PRESIDENT; PO BOX 1976

WASHINGTON CROSSING PA 18977

215/493-6577

AMOUNT: $5000

DEADLINE(S): JAN 15

FIELD(S): GOVERNMENT; PUBLIC SERVICE

OPEN TO USA HIGH SCHOOL SENIORS PLANNING CAREER IN GOVERNMENT SERVICE (LOCAL/STATE OR FEDERAL). $2000 FOR 1ST YEAR; $1000 PER YEAR FOR THE FOLLOWING 3 YEARS. TENABLE AT ANY ACCREDITED USA COLLEGE OR UNIVERSITY. USA CITIZEN.

ONE FACTOR WILL BE 200-WORD ESSAY ON WHY STUDENT IS CONSIDERING CAREER IN GOVERNMENT; INCLUDING ANY INSPIRATION TO BE DERIVED FROM THE LEADERSHIP OF GEORGE WASHINGTON CROSSING THE DELAWARE. WRITE FOR COMPLETE INFORMATION.

1004

WILLIAM RANDOLPH HEARST FOUNDATION (U.S. SENATE YOUTH PROGRAM)

90 NEW MONTGOMERY ST; SUITE 1212

SAN FRANCISCO CA 94105

415/543-4057; FAX 415/243-0760

AMOUNT: $2000 + ALL EXPENSES PAID WEEK IN WASHINGTON DC

DEADLINE(S): NONE SPECIFIED

FIELD(S): US GOVERNMENT; HISTORY; POLITICAL SCIENCE; ECONOMICS

OPEN TO ANY HIGH SCHOOL JUNIOR OR SENIOR WHO IS SERVING AS AN ELECTED STUDENT BODY OFFICER AT A USA HIGH SCHOOL. STUDENT RECEIVES A WEEK'S STAY IN WASHINGTON AS GUEST OF THE SENATE AND A $2000 SCHOLARSHIP.

STUDENT MUST BECOME A CANDIDATE FOR A DEGREE AT AN ACCREDITED USA COLLEGE OR UNIVERSITY WITHIN TWO YEARS OF HIGH SCHOOL GRADUATION. USA PERMANENT RESIDENT. CONTACT HIGH SCHOOL PRINCIPAL FOR COMPLETE INFORMATION.

PSYCHOLOGY

1005

AMERICAN FOUNDATION FOR THE BLIND (DELTA GAMMA FOUNDATION FLORENCE HARVEY MEMORIAL SCHOLARSHIP)

15 WEST 16TH ST

NEW YORK NY 10011

212/620-2000; TDD 212/620-2158

AMOUNT: $1000

DEADLINE(S): APR 1

FIELD(S): REHABILITATION AND/OR EDUCATION OF THE VISUALLY IMPAIRED AND BLIND

OPEN TO LEGALLY BLIND UNDERGRADUATE AND GRADUATE COLLEGE STUDENTS OF GOOD CHARACTER WHO HAVE EXHIBITED ACADEMIC EXCELLENCE AND ARE STUDYING IN THE FIELD OF EDUCATION AND/OR REHABILITATION OF THE VISUALLY IMPAIRED AND BLIND.

MUST BE USA CITIZEN. WRITE FOR COMPLETE INFORMATION.

1006

AMERICAN FOUNDATION FOR THE BLIND (RUDOLPH DILLMAN MEMORIAL SCHOLARSHIP)
15 WEST 16TH ST
NEW YORK NY 10011
212/620-2000; TDD 212/620-2158
AMOUNT: $2500
DEADLINE(S): APR 1
FIELD(S): REHABILITATION; EDUCATION OF BLIND & VISUALLY IMPAIRED
OPEN TO LEGALLY BLIND UNDERGRADUATE OR GRADUATE STUDENTS ACCEPTED TO OR ENROLLED IN AN ACCREDITED PROGRAM WITHIN THE BROAD AREAS OF REHABILITATION AND/OR EDUCATION OF THE BLIND AND VISUALLY IMPAIRED. USA CITIZEN.
THREE AWARDS PER YEAR. WRITE FOR COMPLETE INFORMATION.

1007

AMERICAN FOUNDATION FOR THE BLIND (TELESENSORY SCHOLARSHIP)
15 WEST 16TH ST
NEW YORK NY 10011
212/620-2000; TDD 212/620-2158
AMOUNT: $1000
DEADLINE(S): APR 1
FIELD(S): REHABILITATION; EDUCATION OF BLIND & VISUALLY IMPAIRED
OPEN TO LEGALLY BLIND UNDERGRADUATE & GRADUATE STUDENTS ACCEPTED TO OR ENROLLED IN AN ACCREDITED PROGRAM WITHIN THE BROAD AREAS OF REHABILITATION AND/OR EDUCATION OF THE BLIND AND VISUALLY IMPAIRED. USA CITIZEN.
WRITE FOR COMPLETE INFORMATION.

1008

COMMITTEE ON INSTITUTIONAL COOPERATION (CIC PREDOCTORAL FELLOWSHIPS)
KIRKWOOD HALL RM 111; INDIANA UNIV
BLOOMINGTON IN 47405
812/855-0822
AMOUNT: $9500 + TUITION (5 YEARS)
DEADLINE(S): JAN 2
FIELD(S): HUMANITIES; SOCIAL SCIENCES; NATURAL SCIENCES; MATHEMATICS; ENGINEERING
PREDOCTORAL FELLOWSHIPS FOR USA CITIZENS OF AFRICAN AMERICAN; AMERICAN INDIAN; MEXICAN AMERICAN OR PUERTO RICAN HERITAGE. MUST HOLD OR EXPECT TO RECEIVE BACHELOR'S DEGREE BY LATE SUMMER FROM A REGIONALLY ACCREDITED COLLEGE OR UNIVERSITY.
AWARDS FOR SPECIFIED UNIVERSITIES IN IL; IN; IA; MI; MN; OH; WI; PA. WRITE FOR DETAILS.

1009

EASTER SEAL SOCIETY OF IOWA (SCHOLARSHIPS & AWARDS)
PO BOX 4002
DES MOINES IA 50333
515/289-1933
AMOUNT: $400 - $600
DEADLINE(S): APR 15
FIELD(S): PHYSICAL REHABILITATION; MENTAL REHABILITATION; & RELATED AREAS
OPEN TO IOWA RESIDENTS WHO ARE FULL-TIME UNDERGRADUATE SOPHOMORES; JUNIORS; SENIORS OR GRADUATE STUDENTS AT ACCREDITED INSTITUTIONS; PLANNING A CAREER IN THE BROAD FIELD OF REHABILITATION; FINANCIALLY NEEDY & IN TOP 40% OF THEIR CLASS.
6 SCHOLARSHIPS PER YEAR. RENEWABLE. WRITE FOR COMPLETE INFORMATION.

1010

EPILEPSY FOUNDATION OF AMERICA (BEHAVIORAL SCIENCES STUDENT FELLOWSHIPS)
4351 GARDEN CITY DR; SUITE 406
LANDOVER MD 20785
301/459-3700
AMOUNT: $1500
DEADLINE(S): MAR 2
FIELD(S): EPILEPSY RELATED STUDY OR TRAINING PROJECTS.
OPEN TO UNDERGRAD AND GRAD STUDENTS IN NURSING; PSYCHOLOGY AND RELATED AREAS WHO PROPOSE A 3-MONTH EPILEPSY-RELATED PROJECT TO BE CARRIED OUT IN A USA INSTITUTION AT WHICH THERE ARE ONGOING EPILEPSY RESEARCH; SERVICE OR TRAINING PROGRAMS.
FELLOWSHIP MUST BE UNDERTAKEN DURING A FREE PERIOD IN THE STUDENT'S YEAR. WRITE FOR COMPLETE INFORMATION.

1011

INSTITUTE FOR HUMANE STUDIES (CLAUDE R. LAMBE FELLOWSHIPS)

GEORGE MASON UNIVERSITY; 4400 UNIVERSITY DRIVE
FAIRFAX VA 22030
703/323-1055

AMOUNT: $17500

DEADLINE(S): JAN 15

FIELD(S): SOCIAL SCIENCES; LAW; HUMANITIES

OPEN TO GRADUATE STUDENTS AND UNDERGRADS WHO WILL HAVE JUNIOR OR SENIOR STANDING AT ACCREDITED COLLEGES AND UNIVERSITIES THE NEXT ACADEMIC YEAR. AWARD IS TO SUPPORT STUDENTS WITH A DEMONSTRATED INTEREST IN THE CLASSICAL LIBERAL TRADITION.

RECIPIENT WILL BE INTENT ON PURSUING AN INTELLECTUAL/SCHOLARLY CAREER IN ONE OF THE ABOVE AREAS. WRITE FOR COMPLETE INFORMATION.

1012

NORTH CAROLINA OFFICE OF BUDGET AND MANAGEMENT (NC HEALTH; SCIENCES & MATH SCHOLARSHIP-LOAN PROGRAM)

116 WEST JONES ST; #2054
RALEIGH NC 27611
919/733-2164

AMOUNT: $2500 - $7500 PER YEAR

DEADLINE(S): JAN 8 - MAY 5

FIELD(S): HEALTH PROFESSIONS; SCIENCES; ENGINEERING

LOW-INTEREST SCHOLARSHIP LOANS OPEN TO NORTH CAROLINA RESIDENTS OF AT LEAST 1 YEAR WHO ARE PURSUING AN ASSOCIATES; UNDERGRADUATE OR GRADUATE DEGREE IN THE ABOVE AREAS AT AN ACCREDITED INSTITUTION IN THE USA.

LOANS MAY BE RETIRED AFTER GRADUATION BY WORKING (1 YEAR FOR EACH YEAR FUNDED) AT DESIGNATED INSTITUTIONS. WRITE FOR COMPLETE DETAILS.

1013

PARAPSYCHOLOGY FOUNDATION (EILEEN J. GARRETT RESEARCH SCHOLARSHIP)

228 EAST 71ST STREET
NEW YORK NY 10021
212/628-1550; FAX 212/628-1559

AMOUNT: $3000

DEADLINE(S): JUL 15

FIELD(S): PARAPSYCHOLOGY

OPEN TO ANY UNDERGRAD OR GRAD STUDENT WISHING TO PURSUE THE ACADEMIC STUDY OF THE SCIENCE OF PARAPSYCHOLOGY. FUNDING IS FOR STUDY; RESEARCH & EXPERIMENTATION ONLY. APPLICANTS MUST DEMONSTRATE PREVIOUS ACADEMIC INTEREST IN PARAPSYCHOLOGY.

APPROX 15 AWARDS PER YEAR. WRITE FOR COMPLETE INFORMATION.

1014

RADIO FREE EUROPE/RADIO LIBERTY (MEDIA & OPINION RESEARCH ON EASTERN EUROPE & THE FORMER SOVIET UNION)

PERSONNEL DIVISION; 1201 CONNECTICUT AVE NW
WASHINGTON DC 20036
WRITTEN INQUIRY

AMOUNT: DAILY STIPEND OF 48 GERMAN MARKS PLUS ACCOMMODATIONS

DEADLINE(S): FEB 22

FIELD(S): COMMUNICATIONS; MARKET RESEARCH; STATISTICS; SOCIOLOGY; SOCIAL PSYCHOLOGY; EAST EUROPEAN STUDIES

INTERNSHIP OPEN TO GRADUATE STUDENT OR EXCEPTIONALLY QUALIFIED UNDERGRADUATE IN THE ABOVE AREAS WHO CAN DEMONSTRATE KNOWLEDGE OF QUANTITATIVE RESEARCH METHODS; COMPUTER APPLICATIONS AND PUBLIC OPINION SURVEY TECHNIQUES.

EAST EUROPEAN LANGUAGE SKILLS WOULD BE AN ADVANTAGE. WRITE FOR COMPLETE INFORMATION.

1015

SOCIETY FOR THE SCIENTIFIC STUDY OF SEX (STUDENT RESEARCH GRANT)

PO BOX 208
MT VERNON IA 52314
319/895-8407

AMOUNT: $500

DEADLINE(S): FEB 1 & SEP 1

FIELD(S): HUMAN SEXUALITY

OPEN TO ANY STUDENT ENROLLED IN A DEGREE GRANTING PROGRAM AT AN ACCREDITED INSTITUTION. CAN BE MASTERS THESIS OR DOCTORAL DISSERTATION BUT THIS IS NOT A REQUIREMENT.

WRITE TO KATHRYN KELLEY PHD AT ABOVE ADDRESS FOR APPLICATION AND COMPLETE INFORMATION.

SOCIOLOGY

1016

AMERICAN SOCIOLOGICAL ASSOCIATION (MINORITY OPPORTUNITY SUMMER TRAINING PROGRAM)
1722 N STREET NW
WASHINGTON DC 20036
202/833-3410
AMOUNT: $1000 STIPEND + TRAVEL AND ROOM AND BOARD
DEADLINE(S): DEC 31
FIELD(S): SOCIOLOGY
INTENSIVE SUMMER INSTITUTE AT EITHER THE UNIVERSITY OF MICHIGAN OR UNIVERSITY OF CALIFORNIA BERKELEY OFFERING UNDERGRADUATES AN INTRODUCTION TO GRADUATE STUDY IN SOCIOLOGY. CREDIT IS GIVEN FOR COURSEWORK.
WRITE FOR COMPLETE INFORMATION.

1017

ASTRAEA NATIONAL LESBIAN ACTION FOUNDATION (MARGOT KARLE SCHOLARSHIP)
666 BROADWAY; ROOM 520
NEW YORK NY 10012
212/529-8021
AMOUNT: $500
DEADLINE(S): FEB 15; AUG 15
FIELD(S): POLITICAL SCIENCE; SOCIOLOGY
FOR WOMEN STUDENTS WHOSE CAREER PATH AND/OR EXTRACURRICULAR ACTIVITIES DEMONSTRATE POLITICAL AND/OR SOCIAL COMMITMENT ANALOGOUS TO THAT OF MARGOT KARLE (AN ATTORNEY WHO ACTIVELY FOUGHT FOR THE CIVIL RIGHTS OF GAYS & LESBIANS.)
FOR UNDERGRADUATE STUDY AT ONE OF THE SCHOOLS IN THE NEW YORK CITY UNIVERSITY SYSTEM. WRITE FOR COMPLETE INFORMATION.

1018

B'NAI B'RITH YOUTH ORGANIZATION (SCHOLARSHIP PROGRAM)
1640 RHODE ISLAND AVENUE NW
WASHINGTON DC 20036
202/857-6633
AMOUNT: $2500 PER YEAR
DEADLINE(S): EACH SPRING
FIELD(S): SOCIAL WORK
JEWISH FAITH. FIRST OR SECOND-YEAR GRADUATE STUDENTS ATTENDING ACCREDITED GRADUATE SCHOOLS OF SOCIAL WORK OR COLLEGE SENIORS PLANNING TO ATTEND A GRADUATE SCHOOL OF SOCIAL WORK.
SHOW EVIDENCE OF GOOD SCHOLARSHIP; INTEREST IN WORKING FOR JEWISH AGENCIES & HAVE KNOWLEDGE OF JEWISH COMMUNAL STRUCTURE & INSTITUTIONS. RENEWABLE. WRITE FOR COMPLETE INFORMATION.

1019

EASTER SEAL SOCIETY OF IOWA (SCHOLARSHIPS & AWARDS)
PO BOX 4002
DES MOINES IA 50333
515/289-1933
AMOUNT: $400 - $600
DEADLINE(S): APR 15
FIELD(S): PHYSICAL REHABILITATION; MENTAL REHABILITATION; & RELATED AREAS
OPEN TO IOWA RESIDENTS WHO ARE FULL-TIME UNDERGRADUATE SOPHOMORES; JUNIORS; SENIORS OR GRADUATE STUDENTS AT ACCREDITED INSTITUTIONS; PLANNING A CAREER IN THE BROAD FIELD OF REHABILITATION; FINANCIALLY NEEDY & IN TOP 40% OF THEIR CLASS.
6 SCHOLARSHIPS PER YEAR. RENEWABLE. WRITE FOR COMPLETE INFORMATION.

1020

INSTITUTE FOR HUMANE STUDIES (CLAUDE R. LAMBE FELLOWSHIPS)
GEORGE MASON UNIVERSITY; 4400 UNIVERSITY DRIVE
FAIRFAX VA 22030
703/323-1055
AMOUNT: $17500
DEADLINE(S): JAN 15
FIELD(S): SOCIAL SCIENCES; LAW; HUMANITIES
OPEN TO GRADUATE STUDENTS AND UNDERGRADS WHO WILL HAVE JUNIOR OR SENIOR STANDING AT ACCREDITED COLLEGES AND UNIVERSITIES THE NEXT

ACADEMIC YEAR. AWARD IS TO SUPPORT STUDENTS WITH A DEMONSTRATED INTEREST IN THE CLASSICAL LIBERAL TRADITION.

RECIPIENT WILL BE INTENT ON PURSUING AN INTELLECTUAL/SCHOLARLY CAREER IN ONE OF THE ABOVE AREAS. WRITE FOR COMPLETE INFORMATION.

1021

INTERNATIONAL ASSOCIATION OF FIRE CHIEFS FOUNDATION (SCHOLARSHIP PROGRAM)

1329 18TH STREET NW
WASHINGTON DC 20036
202/833-3420

AMOUNT: $250

DEADLINE(S): AUG 15

FIELD(S): BUSINESS & URBAN ADMINISTRATION; ENGINEERING; FIRE SCIENCE

OPEN TO MEMBERS OF A FIRE SERVICE OF A STATE; COUNTY; PROVINCIAL; MUNICIPAL; COMMUNITY; INDUSTRIAL OR FEDERAL FIRE DEPARTMENT.

18 SCHOLARSHIPS PER YEAR. RENEWABLE. WRITE FOR COMPLETE DETAILS.

1022

JEWISH VOCATIONAL SERVICE (MARCUS & THERESA LEVIE EDUCATIONAL FUND SCHOLARSHIPS)

1 SOUTH FRANKLIN STREET
CHICAGO IL 60606
312/346-6700 EXT 2214

AMOUNT: $5000

DEADLINE(S): MAR 1

FIELD(S): SOCIAL WORK; MEDICINE; DENTISTRY; NURSING & OTHER RELATED PROFESSIONS & VOCATIONS

OPEN TO COOK COUNTY RESIDENTS OF THE JEWISH FAITH WHO PLAN CAREERS IN THE HELPING PROFESSIONS. MUST SHOW FINANCIAL NEED. FOR UNDERGRADUATE; GRADUATE OR VOCATIONAL STUDY. APPLICATIONS AVAILABLE BEGINNING DEC 1 FROM SCHOLARSHIP SECRETARY.

85-100 AWARDS PER YEAR. RENEWAL POSSIBLE WITH REAPPLICATION. WRITE FOR COMPLETE INFORMATION.

1023

NEW YORK CITY DEPT. OF PERSONNEL (GOVERNMENT SCHOLARS INTERNSHIP PROGRAM)

2 WASHINGTON ST; 15TH FLOOR
NEW YORK NY 10004
212/487-5698

AMOUNT: $2500

DEADLINE(S): JAN 27

FIELD(S): PUBLIC ADMINISTRATION; URBAN PLANNING; GOVERNMENT; PUBLIC SERVICE; URBAN AFFAIRS

10-WEEK SUMMER INTERN PROGRAM OPEN TO UNDERGRADUATE SOPHOMORES; JUNIORS & SENIORS. PROGRAM PROVIDES STUDENTS WITH UNIQUE OPPORTUNITY TO LEARN ABOUT NY CITY GOVERNMENT. INTERNSHIPS AVAILABLE IN VIRTUALLY EVERY CITY AGENCY & MAYORAL OFFICE.

WRITE FOR COMPLETE INFORMATION.

1024

NEW YORK CITY DEPT. OF PERSONNEL (URBAN FELLOWS PROGRAM)

2 WASHINGTON ST; 15TH FLOOR
NEW YORK NY 10004
212/487-5698

AMOUNT: $17000 STIPEND

DEADLINE(S): JAN 26

FIELD(S): PUBLIC ADMINISTRATION; URBAN PLANNING; GOVERNMENT; PUBLIC SERVICE; URBAN AFFAIRS

FELLOWSHIP PROGRAM PROVIDES ONE ACADEMIC YEAR (9 MONTHS) OF FULL-TIME WORK EXPERIENCE IN URBAN GOVERNMENT. OPEN TO GRADUATING COLLEGE SENIORS AND RECENT COLLEGE GRADUATES. USA CITIZEN.

WRITE FOR COMPLETE INFORMATION.

1025

RADIO FREE EUROPE/RADIO LIBERTY (MEDIA & OPINION RESEARCH ON EASTERN EUROPE & THE FORMER SOVIET UNION)

PERSONNEL DIVISION; 1201 CONNECTICUT AVE NW
WASHINGTON DC 20036
WRITTEN INQUIRY

AMOUNT: DAILY STIPEND OF 48 GERMAN MARKS PLUS ACCOMMODATIONS

DEADLINE(S): FEB 22

FIELD(S): COMMUNICATIONS; MARKET RESEARCH; STATISTICS; SOCIOLOGY; SOCIAL PSYCHOLOGY; EAST EUROPEAN STUDIES

INTERNSHIP OPEN TO GRADUATE STUDENT OR EXCEPTIONALLY QUALIFIED UNDERGRADUATE IN THE ABOVE AREAS WHO CAN DEMONSTRATE KNOWLEDGE OF QUANTITATIVE RESEARCH METHODS; COMPUTER APPLICATIONS AND PUBLIC OPINION SURVEY TECHNIQUES.

EAST EUROPEAN LANGUAGE SKILLS WOULD BE AN ADVANTAGE. WRITE FOR COMPLETE INFORMATION.

SCHOOL OF VOCATIONAL ED

1026

AID ASSOCIATION FOR LUTHERANS (VOCATIONAL/TECHNICAL SCHOLARSHIP PROGRAM)
4321 N BALLARD RD
APPLETON WI 54915
414/734-5721
AMOUNT: $500 FULL TIME; $250 PART TIME
DEADLINE(S): NOV 30
FIELD(S): VOCATIONAL/TECHNICAL

OPEN TO AAL MEMBERS WHO ARE ENROLLED OR PLAN TO ENROLL IN AN ACCREDITED VOC/TECH INSTITUTE OR 2 YEAR COLLEGE FULL TIME OR HALF TIME IN PURSUIT OF AN ASSOCIATE DEGREE OR VOCATIONAL DIPLOMA.

APPLICANTS MUST HAVE IN FORCE AN AAL CERTIFICATE OF MEMBERSHIP AND INSURANCE OR ANNUITY IN THEIR OWN NAME AT TIME OF APPLICATION. ASSOCIATE MEMBERS NOT ELIGIBLE. WRITE FOR COMPLETE INFORMATION.

1027

AMERICAN BOARD OF FUNERAL SERVICE EDUCATION (SCHOLARSHIPS)
14 CRESTWOOD RD
CUMBERLAND ME 04021
207/829-5715
AMOUNT: $250; $500
DEADLINE(S): MAR 15; SEP 15
FIELD(S): FUNERAL SERVICE

OPEN TO STUDENTS WHO HAVE COMPLETED AT LEAST ONE TERM OF STUDY IN AN ACCREDITED PROGRAM IN FUNERAL SERVICE. APPLICANTS MUST SUBMIT IRS FORM 1040 TO DEMONSTRATE NEED AND BE A USA CITIZEN.

APPROX 70 SCHOLARSHIPS PER YEAR. ADDRESS INQUIRIES TO THE SCHOLARSHIP CHAIRMAN ADDRESS ABOVE.

1028

AMERICAN INSTITUTE OF BAKING (SCHOLARSHIPS)
1213 BAKERS WAY
MANHATTAN KS 66502
913/537-4750
AMOUNT: PARTIAL OR FULL TUITION
DEADLINE(S): NOV 1; MAY 1
FIELD(S): BAKING INDUSTRY (INCLUDING ELECTRICAL & ELECTRONIC MAINTENANCE)

AWARD IS FOR TUITION FOR A 16 OR 10 WEEK COURSE IN BAKING SCIENCE AND TECHNOLOGY OR MAINTENANCE ENGINEERING AT THE INSTITUTE. EXPERIENCE IN BAKING OR MECHANICS OR AN APPROVED ALTERNATIVE IS REQUIRED. USA CITIZEN.

AWARDS ARE INTENDED FOR PEOPLE WHO PLAN TO SEEK NEW POSITIONS IN THE BAKING AND MAINTENANCE ENGINEERING FIELDS.

1029

AVIATION DISTRIBUTORS AND MANUFACTURERS ASSOCIATION INTERNATIONAL (ADMA INTERNATIONAL SCHOLARSHIP FUND)
1900 ARCH STREET
PHILADELPHIA PA 19103
215/564-3484
AMOUNT: $1000
DEADLINE(S): APR 10
FIELD(S): AVIATION MANAGEMENT; PROFESSIONAL PILOT

OPEN TO STUDENTS SEEKING A CAREER IN AVIATION MANAGEMENT OR AS PROFESSIONAL PILOTS. EMPHASIS MAY BE IN GENERAL AVIATION; AIRWAY SCIENCE MANAGEMENT; AVIATION MAINTENANCE; FLIGHT ENGINEER OR AIRWAY A/C SYSTEMS MANAGEMENT.

APPLICANTS MUST BE STUDYING IN THE AVIATION FIELD IN A FOUR-YEAR SCHOOL HAVING AN AVIATION PROGRAM AND MUST HAVE COMPLETED AT LEAST TWO YEARS OF THEIR PROGRAM. WRITE FOR COMPLETE INFORMATION.

1030

AVIATION MAINTENANCE EDUCATION FUND (AMEF SCHOLARSHIP PROGRAM)
PO BOX 2826
REDMOND WA 98073
206/828-3917
AMOUNT: $250 - $1000
DEADLINE(S): NONE
FIELD(S): AVIATION MAINTENANCE TECHNOLOGY
AMEF SCHOLARSHIP PROGRAM OPEN TO ANY WORTHY APPLICANT WHO IS ENROLLED IN A FEDERAL AVIATION ADMINISTRATION (FAA) CERTIFIED AVIATION MAINTENANCE TECHNOLOGY PROGRAM.
WRITE FOR COMPLETE INFORMATION.

1031

BUSINESS AND PROFESSIONAL WOMEN'S FOUNDATION (CAREER ADVANCEMENT SCHOLARSHIPS)
2012 MASSACHUSETTS AVE NW
WASHINGTON DC 20036
202/293-1200
AMOUNT: $500 - $1000
DEADLINE(S): APR 15 POSTMARK (APPS AVAILABLE ONLY OCT 1 - APR 1)
FIELD(S): COMPUTER SCIENCE; EDUCATION; PARALEGAL; ENGINEERING; SCIENCE (EXCEPT HEALTH CARE)
OPEN TO WOMEN (30 OR OLDER) WITHIN 12-24 MONTHS OF COMPLETING UNDERGRAD OR GRAD STUDY IN USA (INCLUDING PUERTO RICO & THE VIRGIN ISLANDS). SHOULD LEAD TO ENTRY OR REENTRY INTO THE WORK FORCE OR IMPROVE CAREER ADVANCEMENT CHANCES.
MUST SHOW FINANCIAL NEED. SEND SELF-ADDRESSED STAMPED ($.52) #10 ENVELOPE FOR APPLICATION & COMPLETE INFORMATION. NOT FOR STUDY AT DOCTORAL LEVEL.

1032

CALIFORNIA STUDENT AID COMMISSION (CAL GRANT 'C' PROGRAM)
PO BOX 510624
SACRAMENTO CA 94245
916/445-0880
AMOUNT: UP TO $2001 (TUITION); UP TO $449 (TRAINING RELATED COSTS)
DEADLINE(S): MAR 2
FIELD(S): VOCATIONAL-TECHNICAL
CALIFORNIA RESIDENT. OPEN TO VOCATIONAL-TECHNICAL STUDENTS ENROLLED IN ELIGIBLE 4-MONTH TO 2-YEAR PROGRAMS IN CALIF. GRANTS SUPPORT TUITION & TRAINING RELATED COSTS. USA CITIZEN; LEGAL RESIDENT OR ELIGIBLE NON-CITIZEN.
APPROX 1500 GRANTS PER YEAR. RENEWABLE. CONTACT YOUR COUNSELOR; FINANCIAL AID OFFICE OR ADDRESS ABOVE FOR COMPLETE INFORMATION.

1033

CDS INTERNATIONAL INC. (CONGRESS-BUNDESTAG YOUTH EXCHANGE PROGRAM)
330 SEVENTH AVE
NEW YORK NY 10001
212/760-1400; FAX 212/268-1288
AMOUNT: TRAVEL; TUITION; INSURANCE; HOST FAMILY PAYMENT
DEADLINE(S): DEC 31
FIELD(S): BUSINESS; VOC/TECH FIELDS
YEAR LONG WORK/STUDY PROGRAMS IN GERMANY FOR USA CITIZENS AGE 18-24 AND IN THE USA FOR GERMAN CITIZENS AGE 18-21. PROGRAM FOR AMERICANS INCLUDES 2 MONTHS LANGUAGE STUDY; 4 MONTHS STUDY IN A TECH OR PROFESSIONAL SCHOOL & 6 MONTH INTERNSHIP.
PROFESSIONAL TARGET AND APPLICABLE WORK EXPERIENCE REQUIRED. PARTICIPANTS MUST PROVIDE THEIR OWN SPENDING MONEY OF $300-$350 A MONTH. WRITE FOR COMPLETE INFORMATION.

1034

CIVIL AIR PATROL (VOCATIONAL-TECHNICAL GRANTS)
CAP NATIONAL HEADQUARTERS/TT
MAXWELL AIR FORCE BASE AL 36112
205/293-5332
AMOUNT: $750
DEADLINE(S): APR 1
FIELD(S): VOCATIONAL-TECHNICAL AEROSPACE STUDIES
OPEN TO CAP MEMBERS WHO ARE QUALIFIED AND INTERESTED IN FURTHERING THEIR EDUCATION IN SPECIAL AEROSPACE COURSES AT ACCREDITED VOCATIONAL-TECHNICAL INSTITUTIONS.
WRITE FOR COMPLETE INFORMATION.

1035

EAA AVIATION FOUNDATION (SCHOLARSHIP PROGRAM)
WHITMAN REGIONAL AIRPORT; PO BOX 3065
OSHKOSH WI 54903
414/426-4888
AMOUNT: $200 TO $1500
DEADLINE(S): APR 1
FIELD(S): AVIATION
TEN DIFFERENT SCHOLARSHIP PROGRAMS OPEN TO WELL ROUNDED INDIVIDUALS INVOLVED IN SCHOOL AND COMMUNITY ACTIVITIES AS WELL AS AVIATION. APPLICANTS' ACADEMIC RECORDS SHOULD VERIFY THEIR ABILITY TO COMPLETE THEIR EDUCATIONAL PROGRAM.
FINANCIAL NEED IS A CONSIDERATION. WRITE FOR COMPLETE INFORMATION.

1036

EASTERN NEW ENGLAND NINETY-NINES INC. (MARJOURIE VAN VLIET AVIATION MEMORIAL SCHOLARSHIP)
207 SANDY POND RD
LINCOLN MA 01773
617/259-0222
AMOUNT: $2000
DEADLINE(S): JAN 31
FIELD(S): AERONAUTICS; AVIATION MAINTENANCE; FLIGHT TRAINING
OPEN TO HIGH SCHOOL SENIORS OR BEYOND WHO LIVE IN ONE OF THE NEW ENGLAND STATES; PLAN A CAREER IN AVIATION AND HAVE APPLIED TO AN AVIATION RELATED EDUCATION OR TRAINING PROGRAM. SHOW FINANCIAL NEED.
CAN USE FOR TUITION AND/OR FLIGHT TRAINING. WRITE FOR COMPLETE INFORMATION.

1037

EMPIRE COLLEGE (DEAN'S SCHOLARSHIP)
3033 CLEVELAND
SANTA ROSA CA 95403
707/546-4000
AMOUNT: $250 - $1500
DEADLINE(S): APR 15
FIELD(S): COURT REPORTING; ACCOUNTING; SECRETARIAL; LEGAL; MEDICAL (CLINICAL & ADMINISTRATIVE); TRAVEL & TOURISM; GENERAL BUSINESS.
OPEN TO HIGH SCHOOL SENIORS WHO MEET ADMISSION REQUIREMENTS AND WANT TO ATTEND EMPIRE COLLEGE IN SANTA ROSA CALIF. USA CITIZENSHIP REQUIRED.
TEN SCHOLARSHIPS PER YEAR. CONTACT MS. MARLENE MARELLO - HIGH SCHOOL DIRECTOR - FOR COMPLETE INFORMATION.

1038

GEMOLOGICAL INSTITUTE OF AMERICA (HOME STUDY AND RESIDENT SCHOLARSHIPS)
FINANCIAL AID OFFC; 1660 STEWART ST.
SANTA MONICA CA 90404
310/829-2991
AMOUNT: $500 - $700
DEADLINE(S): APR 1
FIELD(S): GEMOLOGY
A VARIETY OF SCHOLARSHIPS OFFERED TO USA CITIZENS OR PERMANENT RESIDENTS WHO ARE AT LEAST 17 YEARS OF AGE AND ARE EMPLOYED IN THE JEWELRY INDUSTRY OR WHO PLAN TO ENTER THE FIELD.
THE MARY ABELSON RESIDENT SCHOLARSHIP OFFERS ONE FULL OR PARTIAL TUITION AWARD FOR GRADUATE JEWELER PROGRAMS EVERY OTHER YEAR. HOME STUDY SCHOLARSHIPS ARE FOR UNDERGRADS. WRITE FOR COMPLETE INFORMATION.

1039

HILGENFELD FOUNDATION FOR MORTUARY EDUCATION (SCHOLARSHIP GRANTS)
PO BOX 4311
FULLERTON CA 92634
WRITTEN INQUIRY
AMOUNT: VARIES
DEADLINE(S): NONE
FIELD(S): FUNERAL SERVICE AND EDUCATION
GRANTS AVAILABLE TO QUALIFIED INDIVIDUALS AND ORGANIZATIONS WITH INTEREST IN FUNERAL SERVICE. PREFERENCE GIVEN TO SOUTHERN CALIFORNIA RESIDENTS.
GRANT FUNDS AVAILABLE FOR INDIVIDUALS ENTERING THE FUNERAL SERVICE PROFESSION AND FOR INDIVIDUALS PURSUING ADVANCED DEGREES TO ADVANCE IN THE TEACHING PROFESSION.

1040

INTERNATIONAL ASSN OF ARSON INVESTIGATORS (JOHN CHARLES WILSON SCHOLARSHIP FUND)
PO BOX 91119
LOUISVILLE KY 40291
502/239-7228

AMOUNT: $1000
DEADLINE(S): FEB 15
FIELD(S): POLICE SCIENCE; FIRE SCIENCE & AFFILIATED FIELDS
OPEN TO IAAI MEMBERS; THEIR IMMEDIATE FAMILY & NON-MEMBERS WHO ARE RECOMMENDED & SPONSORED BY MEMBERS IN GOOD STANDING. AWARDS ARE FOR UNDERGRADUATE STUDY IN ABOVE AREAS AT ACCREDITED 2-YEAR & 4-YEAR INSTITUTIONS.
WRITE FOR COMPLETE INFORMATION.

1041

INTERNATIONAL ASSOCIATION OF FIRE CHIEFS FOUNDATION (SCHOLARSHIP PROGRAM)
1329 18TH STREET NW
WASHINGTON DC 20036
202/833-3420
AMOUNT: $250
DEADLINE(S): AUG 15
FIELD(S): BUSINESS & URBAN ADMINISTRATION; ENGINEERING; FIRE SCIENCE
OPEN TO MEMBERS OF A FIRE SERVICE OF A STATE; COUNTY; PROVINCIAL; MUNICIPAL; COMMUNITY; INDUSTRIAL OR FEDERAL FIRE DEPARTMENT.
18 SCHOLARSHIPS PER YEAR. RENEWABLE. WRITE FOR COMPLETE DETAILS.

1042

INTERNATIONAL WOMEN HELICOPTER PILOTS (WHIRLY-GIRLS SCHOLARSHIPS)
DIANE C. DOWD; 100 GREEN POND RD
SHERMAN CT 06784
203/354-6511
AMOUNT: $4000
DEADLINE(S): OCT 30
FIELD(S): HELICOPTER FLIGHT TRAINING
WOMEN. TWO AWARDS FOR HELICOPTER FLIGHT TRAINING. ONE AWARDED TO LICENSED HELICOPTER PILOT TO OBTAIN ADVANCED HELICOPTER RATING(S). ONE AWARDED TO LICENSED FIXED WING; BALLOON; OR GLIDER PILOT TO OBTAIN HELICOPTER TRANSITION.
ONLY SERIOUS WOMEN WHO WANT TO MAKE HELICOPTER FLYING THEIR CAREER NEED APPLY. FINANCIAL NEED IS A CONSIDERATION. WRITE FOR COMPLETE INFORMATION.

1043

MARYLAND HIGHER EDUCATION COMMISSION (REIMBURSEMENT OF FIREFIGHTER & RESCUE SQUAD MEMBERS)
STATE SCHOLARSHIP ADMINISTRATION; 16 FRANCIS ST
ANNAPOLIS MD 21401
410/974-5370
AMOUNT: TUITION REIMBURSEMENT UP TO $2300
DEADLINE(S): JUL 1
FIELD(S): FIRE SERVICE OR EMERGENCY MEDICAL TECHNOLOGY
OPEN TO MARYLAND RESIDENTS AFFILIATED WITH AN ORGANIZED FIRE DEPARTMENT OR RESCUE SQUAD IN MARYLAND. FOR FULL OR PART TIME STUDY AT A MARYLAND INSTITUTION. REIMBURSEMENT MADE ONE YEAR AFTER SUCCESSFUL COMPLETION OF COURSE(S).
FOR UNDERGRADUATE OR GRADUATE STUDY IN MARYLAND. RENEWABLE. WRITE FOR COMPLETE INFORMATION.

1044

MARYLAND HIGHER EDUCATION COMMISSION (TOLBERT GRANTS)
STATE SCHOLARSHIP ADMINISTRATION; 16 FRANCIS ST
ANNAPOLIS MD 21401
410/974-5370
AMOUNT: $200 - $1500
DEADLINE(S): ROLLING DEADLINE
FIELD(S): VOCATIONAL-TECHNICAL (PRIVATE CAREER SCHOOLS)
MARYLAND RESIDENT. GRANTS TO SUPPORT TRAINING AT MARYLAND PRIVATE CAREER (VOCATIONAL - TECHNICAL) SCHOOLS. FOR FULL TIME STUDY. MUST DEMONSTRATE FINANCIAL NEED.
RENEWABLE FOR ONE YEAR. APPLICANTS MUST BE NOMINATED BY THEIR SCHOOLS. WRITE FOR COMPLETE INFORMATION.

1045

MIDWAY COLLEGE (INSTITUTIONAL AID PROGRAM-SCHOLARSHIPS AND GRANTS)
FINANCIAL AID OFFICE
MIDWAY KY 40347
606/846-4421
AMOUNT: VARIES
DEADLINE(S): MAR 15
FIELD(S): NURSING; PARALEGAL; BILINGUAL BUSINESS; FRENCH STUDIES; SPANISH STUDIES; EQUINE STUDIES

SCHOLARSHIPS & GRANTS OPEN TO WOMEN WHO ARE ACCEPTED FOR ENROLLMENT AT MIDWAY COLLEGE. AWARDS SUPPORT UNDERGRADUATE STUDY IN THE ABOVE AREAS.

APPROX 200 AWARDS PER YEAR. CONTACT ADDRESS ABOVE FOR COMPLETE DETAILS.

1046

MINNESOTA FEDERATION OF TEACHERS (CHARLIE CARPENTER VOCATIONAL SCHOLARSHIP)

168 AURORA AVE
ST PAUL MN 55103
612/227-8583

AMOUNT: $1000

DEADLINE(S): FIRST FRIDAY IN MARCH

FIELD(S): VOCATIONAL/TECHNICAL

OPEN TO SENIORS IN MINNESOTA HIGH SCHOOLS OR THOSE WHO HAVE GRADUATED FROM A MN HIGH SCHOOL. APPLICANTS MUST BE RECOMMENDED BY 2 HIGH SCHOOL TEACHERS ON THE BASIS OF FINANCIAL NEED; ACADEMIC ACHIEVEMENT; LEADERSHIP ABILITY; CHARACTER.

TENABLE AT ANY ACCREDITED VOCATIONAL SCHOOL. WRITE FOR COMPLETE INFORMATION.

1047

MOONEY AIRCRAFT PILOTS ASSOCIATION SAFETY FOUNDATION (AL AND ART MOONEY SCHOLARSHIP PROGRAM)

MARK BUNZEL; AVTEX CORP; 2105 S BASCOM AVE; #290
CAMPBELL CA 95008
408/245-2374

AMOUNT: $1000

DEADLINE(S): JUL 1

FIELD(S): AVIATION (FLIGHT SAFETY)

OPEN TO STUDENTS HAVING A CAREER OBJECTIVE WHICH WOULD PROMOTE FLIGHT SAFETY WHO HAVE COMPLETED HALF OF THEIR COURSE OF STUDY. MUST BE A MEMBER OF MAPA OR BE SPONSORED BY A MEMBER. ESSAY ON HOW CAREER WILL PROMOTE FLIGHT SAFETY IS REQUIRED

CANDIDATES SHOULD HAVE 3.0 OR BETTER GPA. CONTACT DENNIS MCGUIRE AT ABOVE ADDRESS FOR APPLICATION FORM AND COMPLETE INFORMATION.

1048

NATIONAL BUSINESS AIRCRAFT ASSOCIATION (SCHOLARSHIPS)

1200 18TH ST NW
WASHINGTON DC 20036
202/783-9000; FAX 202/331-8364

AMOUNT: $500

DEADLINE(S): OCT 31

FIELD(S): AVIATION

OPEN TO COLLEGE SOPHOMORES; JUNIORS OR SENIORS WHO WILL BE CONTINUING IN SCHOOL THE FOLLOWING ACADEMIC YEAR IN AN AVIATION RELATED BACCALAUREATE OR GRADUATE PROGRAM. MUST BE USA CITIZEN AND HAVE 3.0 OR BETTER GPA.

10 AWARDS PER YEAR. WRITE FOR COMPLETE INFORMATION.

1049

NEW HAMPSHIRE ELECTRICAL CONTRACTORS ASSOC. (PHIL MORAN SCHOLARSHIP FUND)

PO BOX 1032
CONCORD NH 03302
603/224-3532

AMOUNT: $1000

DEADLINE(S): MAY 1

FIELD(S): ELECTRICITY (INDUSTRIAL; COMMERCIAL; RESIDENTIAL)

OPEN TO STUDENTS WHO RESIDE IN NEW HAMPSHIRE AND WERE OR WILL BE IN THE TOP 50% OF THEIR HIGH SCHOOL GRADUATING CLASS. STUDIES MUST RELATE TO RESIDENTIAL; COMMERCIAL OR INDUSTRIAL ELECTRICITY ('NOT' ELECTRONICS OR ELECTRICAL ENGINEERING).

WRITE FOR COMPLETE INFORMATION.

1050

ORGAN HISTORICAL SOCIETY (E. POWER BIGGS FELLOWSHIP)

PO BOX 26811
RICHMOND VA 23261
804/353-9226

AMOUNT: SEE BELOW

DEADLINE(S): DEC 31

FIELD(S): HISTORIC PIPE ORGANS

FELLOWSHIP TO ENCOURAGE STUDENTS AND OTHERS TO BECOME INVOLVED IN THE APPRECIATION OF HISTORIC PIPE ORGANS BY SPONSORING ATTENDANCE AT THE OHS ANNUAL CONVENTION.

3-4 AWARDS PER YEAR. CONTACT JULIE E. STEPHENS; BIGGS COMMITTEE CHAIR; ADDRESS ABOVE FOR COMPLETE INFORMATION.

1051

PROFESSIONAL AVIATION MAINTENANCE ASSOCIATION (CAREERQUEST SCHOLARSHIPS)
500 NORTHWEST PLAZA; SUITE 1016
ST ANN MO 63074
314/739-2580
AMOUNT: $1000 PER YEAR
DEADLINE(S): APPLY BETWEEN JAN 1 & FEB 15 OR SEP 1 & FEB 15
FIELD(S): AVIATION MAINTENANCE
OPEN TO STUDENTS PURSUING AIRFRAME AND POWERPLANT (A&P) TECHNICIAN CERTIFICATION THROUGH AN FAA PART 147 AVIATION MAINTENANCE TECHNICIAN SCHOOL. MUST HAVE COMPLETED 25% OF REQUIRED CURRICULUM; HAVE A 3.0 OR BETTER GPA.
6 AWARDS PER YEAR; 3 IN SPRING; 3 IN FALL. APPLICATION MUST BE SUBMITTED THROUGH STUDENT'S SCHOOL. MUST DEMONSTRATE FINANCIAL NEED. WRITE FOR COMPLETE INFORMATION.

1052

PROFESSIONAL AVIATION MAINTENANCE ASSOCIATION (PAMA SCHOLARSHIP FUND)
500 NORTHWEST PLAZA; #1016
ST ANN MO 63074
314/739-2580
AMOUNT: VARIES
DEADLINE(S): APPLY BETWEEN JUL 1 & NOV 30
FIELD(S): AVIATION MAINTENANCE
OPEN TO STUDENTS ENROLLED IN AN INSTITUTION TO OBTAIN AN AIRFRAME AND POWERPLANT (A&P) LICENSE WHO HAVE COMPLETED 25% OF THE REQUIRED CURRICULUM. MUST HAVE 3.0 OR BETTER GPA; DEMONSTRATE FINANCIAL NEED AND BE RECOMMENDED BY INSTRUCTOR.
APPLICATIONS TO BE SUBMITTED THROUGH STUDENT'S SCHOOL. WRITE FOR COMPLETE INFORMATION.

1053

U.S. DEPT. OF INTERIOR; BUREAU OF INDIAN AFFAIRS (INDIAN EMPLOYMENT ASSISTANCE GRANTS)
18TH AND C ST NW; C490/MS 390 SIB
WASHINGTON DC 20240
202/208-2570
AMOUNT: $4800 TO $5500
DEADLINE(S): NONE
FIELD(S): VOCATIONAL-TECHNICAL
OPEN TO MEMBERS OF TRIBES OR BANDS WHO RESIDE ON OR NEAR A RESERVATION UNDER THE JURISDICTION OF BIA. GRANTS FOR ADULT VOCATIONAL TRAINING AND JOB PLACEMENT SERVICES FOR INDIVIDUAL INDIANS WHO ARE UNEMPLOYED OR UNDER EMPLOYED.
3500 GRANTS PER YEAR. APPLICATIONS ARE AVAILABLE THROUGH TRIBAL CONTRACT OFFICE OR HOME AGENCY. FUNDS FOR VOCATIONAL TRAINING AND JOB PLACEMENT ONLY - NOT FOR A FORMAL DEGREE.

1054

U.S. DEPT. OF VETERANS AFFAIRS (VOCATIONAL REHABILITATION)
810 VERMONT AVE NW (28)
WASHINGTON DC 20420
VA REGIONAL OFFICE IN EACH STATE
AMOUNT: TUITION; BOOKS; FEES; EQUIPMENT
DEADLINE(S): WITHIN 12 YEARS FROM DATE OF NOTIFICATION OF ENTITLEMENT TO VA
FIELD(S): VOCATIONAL-TECHNICAL
OPEN TO USA MILITARY VETERANS WHO WERE DISABLED DURING ACTIVE DUTY; WERE HONORABLY DISCHARGED AND ARE IN NEED OF REHABILITATION SERVICES TO OVERCOME AN EMPLOYMENT HANDICAP. AT LEAST A 20% DISABILITY RATING USUALLY IS REQUIRED.
PROGRAM WILL PROVIDE COLLEGE; TRADE; TECHNICAL; ON-JOB OR ON-FARM TRAINING. ALSO MAY BE AT HOME OR IN A SPECIAL REHAB FACILITY IF VET'S DISABILITY REQUIRES. CONTACT NEAREST VA OFFICE FOR COMPLETE INFORMATION.

1055

VERTICAL FLIGHT FOUNDATION (UNDERGRADUATE/GRADUATE SCHOLARSHIPS)
217 N WASHINGTON ST
ALEXANDRIA VA 22314
703/684-6777
AMOUNT: UP TO $2000
DEADLINE(S): FEB 1
FIELD(S): MECHANICAL ENGINEERING; ELECTRICAL ENGINEERING; AEROSPACE ENGINEERING

ANNUAL SCHOLARSHIPS OPEN TO UNDERGRADUATE & GRADUATE STUDENTS IN THE ABOVE AREAS WHO ARE INTERESTED IN PURSUING CAREERS IN SOME ASPECT OF HELICOPTER OR VERTICAL FLIGHT. FOR FULL TIME STUDY AT ACCREDITED SCHOOL OF ENGINEERING.

WRITE FOR COMPLETE INFORMATION.

1056

VIOLIN SOCIETY OF AMERICA (KAPLAN-GOODKIND MEMORIAL SCHOLARSHIPS)

85-07 ABINGDON RD
KEW GARDENS NY 11415
718/849-1373

AMOUNT: $500 (AVERAGE)
DEADLINE(S): NONE
FIELD(S): VIOLIN MAKING; RESTORATION & REPAIR

SCHOLARSHIPS TO STUDY THE 'ART OF VIOLIN MAKING' AT AN ACCREDITED SCHOOL IN THE USA. NOT LIMITED BY RESIDENCE; COLOR; RACE; RELIGION OR SEX. TALENT AND NEED ARE THE MAIN CRITERIA FOR SELECTION OF RECIPIENTS. USA CITIZEN.

SCHOLARSHIPS RENEWABLE. CONTACT ADDRESS ABOVE FOR COMPLETE INFORMATION.

GENERAL

1057

AAAA SCHOLARSHIP FOUNDATION INC. (SCHOLARSHIPS AND LOANS)

49 RICHMONDVILLE AVE
WESTPORT CT 06880
203/226-8184; FAX 203/222-9863

AMOUNT: $1000 - $12000
DEADLINE(S): MAY 1
FIELD(S): ALL FIELDS OF STUDY

OPEN TO MEMBERS OF ARMY AVIATION ASSN OF AMERICA (AAAA); THEIR SPOUSES; UNMARRIED SIBLINGS AND UNMARRIED CHILDREN. SCHOLARSHIPS AND LOANS AVAILABLE FOR FALL ENTRY AS A FULL TIME STUDENT IN AN ACCREDITED COLLEGE OR UNIVERSITY.

MINIMUM OF 30 SCHOLARSHIPS AND FIVE INTEREST FREE LOANS WILL BE AWARDED. WRITE FOR COMPLETE INFORMATION.

1058

ABBIE M. GRIFFIN EDUCATIONAL FUND (SCHOLARSHIPS)

C/O WINER & BENNETT; 111 CONCORD ST
NASHUA NH 03060
603/882-5157

AMOUNT: $300 - $2000
DEADLINE(S): MAY 1
FIELD(S): ALL AREAS OF STUDY

OPEN ONLY TO RESIDENTS OF MERRIMACK NH. AWARDS TO ENTERING FRESHMEN ONLY FOR FULL-TIME UNDERGRADUATE STUDY AT AN ACCREDITED COLLEGE OR UNIVERSITY.

10-15 AWARDS PER YEAR. WRITE FOR COMPLETE INFORMATION.

1059

ABE AND ANNIE SEIBEL FOUNDATION (INTEREST FREE EDUCATIONAL LOAN FUND)

C/O US NATIONAL BANK; PO BOX 179
GALVESTON TX 77553
409/763-1151

AMOUNT: UP TO $3000 A YEAR
DEADLINE(S): FEB 28
FIELD(S): ALL FIELDS OF STUDY

OPEN TO TEXAS RESIDENTS WHO WILL BE OR ARE ENROLLED (FOR AT LEAST 12 CREDIT HOURS PER SEMESTER) AS AN UNDERGRADUATE STUDENT AT A TEXAS COLLEGE OR UNIVERSITY. MUST MAINTAIN 3.0 OR BETTER GPA. FOR STUDY LEADING TO FIRST 4-YEAR DEGREE.

WRITE FOR COMPLETE INFORMATION.

1060

ACME ELECTRIC (JAMES A. COMSTOCK MEMORIAL SCHOLARSHIP)

NORSTAR TRUST CO; 10 FOUNTAIN PLAZA
BUFFALO NY 14202
716/847-7232

AMOUNT: 25% OF ANNUAL TUITION
DEADLINE(S): JAN 31
FIELD(S): ALL FIELDS OF STUDY

OPEN TO CHILDREN OF ACME ELECTRIC EMPLOYEES WHO RESIDE IN THE AREA SURROUNDING ACME ELECTRIC PLANTS. AWARDS ARE BASED ON GRADES; NEED; COMMUNITY SERVICE.

WRITE FOR COMPLETE INFORMATION.

1061

AFS INTERCULTURAL PROGRAMS (INTERNATIONAL EXCHANGE STUDENT PROGRAM)
313 EAST 43RD STREET
NEW YORK NY 10017
212/949-4242 OR 800/AFS-INFO
AMOUNT: VARIES
DEADLINE(S): FALL AND SPRING
FIELD(S): ALL AREAS OF STUDY
INTERNAT'L EXCHANGE OF HIGH SCHOOL STUDENTS. STUDENTS LIVE WITH HOST FAMILIES AND ATTEND LOCAL SECONDARY SCHOOLS. STUDENTS GO TO AND FROM 50 COUNTRIES. SCHOLARSHIP ASSISTANCE FOR SUMMER; SCHOOL YEAR & SEMESTER.
ALL PARTICIPANTS RECEIVE SOME SCHOLARSHIP ASSISTANCE. 10000 PARTICIPANTS WORLDWIDE. WRITE FOR COMPLETE INFORMATION.

1062

AHEPA EDUCATIONAL FOUNDATION (SCHOLARSHIPS)
1909 'Q' ST NW; SUITE 500
WASHINGTON DC 20009
202/232-6300
AMOUNT: $1000 - $4000
DEADLINE(S): MAY 1
FIELD(S): ALL FIELDS OF STUDY
VARIOUS SCHOLARSHIPS FOR UNDERGRADUATE AND GRADUATE STUDY; SOME FOR SPECIFIC SCHOOLS IN GREECE. AHEPA IS THE PARENT ORGANIZATION OF DAUGHTERS OF PENELOPE; MAIDS OF ATHENA & SONS OF PERICLES. SUMMER INTERNSHIPS IN DC ALSO ARE AVAILABLE.
MEMBERSHIP IN AHEPA ORGANIZATIONS IS NOT MANDATORY BUT MEMBERS WILL BE GIVEN PREFERENCE. WRITE FOR COMPLETE INFORMATION.

1063

AID ASSOCIATION FOR LUTHERANS (ALL-COLLEGE SCHOLARSHIP PROGRAM)
4321 N BALLARD RD
APPLETON WI 54919
414/734-5721
AMOUNT: $500 - $2000
DEADLINE(S): NOV 30
FIELD(S): ALL FIELDS OF STUDY
OPEN TO HIGH SCHOOL SENIORS WHO HOLD AN AAL CERTIFICATE OF MEMBERSHIP IN THEIR OWN NAME BEFORE APPLICATION DEADLINE. FOR UNDERGRADUATE STUDY AT AN ACCREDITED COLLEGE OR UNIVERSITY IN USA.
775 AWARDS PER YEAR; 275 OF WHICH ARE RENEWABLE. WRITE FOR COMPLETE INFORMATION.

1064

AID ASSOCIATION FOR LUTHERANS (LUTHERAN CAMPUS SCHOLARSHIP PROGRAM)
4321 N BALLARD RD
APPLETON WI 54919
414/734-5721
AMOUNT: $200 - $1000
DEADLINE(S): VARIES WITH SCHOOL
FIELD(S): ALL FIELDS OF STUDY
OPEN TO AAL MEMBERS ENROLLED OR PLANNING TO ENROLL IN AN UNDERGRADUATE DEGREE PROGRAM AT ONE OF THE 49 LUTHERAN POST SECONDARY INSTITUTIONS IN THE USA. STUDENTS CAN ATTEND FULL OR HALF TIME.
APPROXIMATELY 1000 AWARDS PER YEAR. WRITE FOR COMPLETE INFORMATION.

1065

AIR FORCE AID SOCIETY (GRANTS PROGRAM)
1745 JEFFERSON DAVIS HWY; #202
ARLINGTON VA 22202
703/692-9313
AMOUNT: $1000
DEADLINE(S): MAR 31
FIELD(S): ALL FIELDS OF STUDY
GRANTS ARE OPEN TO UNDERGRADUATE STUDENTS WHO ARE DEPENDENT CHILDREN OF ACTIVE DUTY; RETIRED OR DECEASED MEMBERS OF THE US AIR FORCE. FOR FULL-TIME STUDY AT AN ACCREDITED INSTITUTION. USA CITIZEN OR LEGAL RESIDENT.
MUST MAINTAIN AT LEAST A 2.0 GPA (4.0 SCALE). WRITE FOR COMPLETE INFORMATION.

1066

AIR FORCE AID SOCIETY (LOANS)
1745 JEFFERSON DAVIS HWY; #202
ARLINGTON VA 22202
703/692-9313

AMOUNT: $100 - $7500
DEADLINE(S): NONE
FIELD(S): ALL FIELDS OF STUDY
OPEN TO ACTIVE OR RETIRED AIR FORCE/AIR NATIONAL GUARD OR AIR FORCE RESERVE MEMBERS AND THEIR SPOUSES; WIDOWS OR CHILDREN.
LOANS RENEWABLE. ALL LEVELS OF STUDY. US CITIZEN OR LEGAL RESIDENT. WRITE FOR COMPLETE INFORMATION.

1067

AIR FORCE SERGEANTS' ASSOCIATION (SCHOLARSHIP AWARDS PROGRAM)
PO BOX 50
TEMPLE HILLS MD 20757
301/899-3500
AMOUNT: $1000 - $2500
DEADLINE(S): APR 15
FIELD(S): ALL FIELDS OF STUDY
OPEN TO SINGLE DEPENDENT CHILDREN (UNDER 23) OF AFSA MEMBERS OR ITS AUXILIARY. FOR UNDERGRADUATE STUDY AT ACCREDITED INSTITUTIONS ONLY. AWARDS ARE BASED ON ACADEMIC EXCELLENCE.
FOR APPLICATION AND COMPLETE INFORMATION SEND SELF-ADDRESSED STAMPED (75 CENTS) BUSINESS SIZE ENVELOPE TO AFSA/AMF SCHOLARSHIPS ADMINISTRATOR; 5211 AUTH RD; SUITLAND MD 20757.

1068

AIRLINE PILOTS ASSOCIATION (SCHOLARSHIP PROGRAM)
1625 MASSACHUSETTS AVE NW
WASHINGTON DC 20036
202/797-4050
AMOUNT: $3000 PER YEAR FOR UP TO 4 YEARS
DEADLINE(S): APR 1
FIELD(S): ALL FIELDS OF STUDY
OPEN TO UNDERGRADUATE SONS OR DAUGHTERS OF MEDICALLY RETIRED OR DECEASED PILOT MEMBERS OF THE AIRLINE PILOTS ASSOCIATION. ACADEMIC CAPABILITY AND FINANCIAL NEED CONSIDERED. RENEWABLE FOR UP TO 3 YEARS.
WRITE FOR COMPLETE INFORMATION ONLY IF ABOVE QUALIFICATIONS ARE MET.

1069

AIRMEN MEMORIAL FOUNDATION (AMF SCHOLARSHIP AWARDS PROGRAM)
5211 AUTH ROAD
SUITLAND MD 20746
800/638-0594
AMOUNT: $500 - $3000
DEADLINE(S): APR 15 (APPS AVAILABLE NOV 1-MAR 31)
FIELD(S): ALL FIELDS OF STUDY
OPEN TO UNMARRIED DEPENDENT CHILDREN (UNDER 25) OF AIR FORCE ENLISTED PERSONNEL (ACTIVE OR RETIRED) OF ALL COMPONENTS; INCLUDING AIR NATIONAL GUARD & RESERVES. FOR UNDERGRADUATE STUDY AT ANY ACCREDITED ACADEMIC OR TRADE/TECHNICAL SCHOOL.
SEND SELF-ADDRESSED STAMPED (75 CENTS) BUSINESS SIZE ENVELOPE TO AFSA/AMF SCHOLARSHIP PROGRAM; PO BOX 50; TEMPLE HILLS MD 20746 FOR APPLICATION AND COMPLETE INFORMATION. APPLICATIONS AVAILABLE NOV 1- MAR 31.

1070

ALABAMA COMMISSION ON HIGHER EDUCATION (SCHOLARSHIPS; GRANTS; LOANS; WORK STUDY PROGRAMS)
SUITE 221/ONE COURT SQUARE
MONTGOMERY AL 36197
WRITTEN INQUIRY
AMOUNT: VARIES
DEADLINE(S): NONE SPECIFIED
FIELD(S): ALL FIELDS OF STUDY
THE COMMISSION ADMINISTERS A NUMBER OF FINANCIAL AID PROGRAMS TENABLE AT POST SECONDARY INSTITUTIONS IN ALABAMA. SOME AWARDS ARE NEED BASED.
WRITE FOR THE 'FINANCIAL AID SOURCES IN ALABAMA' BROCHURE OR CONTACT HIGH SCHOOL GUIDANCE COUNSELOR OR COLLEGE FINANCIAL AID OFFICER.

1071

ALABAMA DEPARTMENT OF VETERANS AFFAIRS (G.I. DEPENDENT CHILDREN SCHOLARSHIP PROGRAM)
PO BOX 1509
MONTGOMERY AL 36102
205/242-5077
AMOUNT: VARIES
DEADLINE(S): NONE

FIELD(S): ALL FIELDS OF STUDY

ALABAMA RESIDENT. OPEN TO DEPENDENT CHILDREN (UNDER 26 YEARS OLD) OF VETERANS WHO WERE ALABAMA RESIDENTS FOR AT LEAST 5 YEARS PRIOR TO ACTIVE DUTY & DIED AS RESULT OF MILITARY SERVICE; WAS/IS MIA OR POW OR BECAME 20% - 100% DISABLED.

AWARDS TENABLE AT STATE SUPPORTED INSTITUTIONS IN ALABAMA. TOTALLY DISABLED VETS NOT ORIGINAL ALABAMA RESIDENTS MAY QUALIFY AFTER 5 YEARS OF ALA. RESIDENCY. WRITE FOR COMPLETE INFORMATION.

1072

ALABAMA DEPARTMENT OF VETERANS AFFAIRS (G.I. UNREMARRIED WIFE/WIDOW SCHOLARSHIP PROGRAM)

PO BOX 1509
MONTGOMERY AL 36102
205/242-5077

AMOUNT: VARIES
DEADLINE(S): NONE
FIELD(S): ALL FIELDS OF STUDY

OPEN TO UNREMARRIED WIFE OR WIDOW OF VETERAN WHO WAS AN ALABAMA RESIDENT FOR AT LEAST 5 YEARS PRIOR TO ACTIVE DUTY & DIED AS RESULT OF MILITARY SERVICE; WAS/IS MIA OR POW OR BECAME 20% - 100% DISABLED.

VETS NOT ORIGINAL ALA. RESIDENTS BUT WITH 100% SERVICE CONNECTED DISABILITY MAY QUALIFY AFTER 5 YEARS ALA. RESIDENCY. AWARDS TENABLE AT STATE SUPPORTED ALA. INSTITUTIONS. WRITE FOR COMPLETE INFORMATION.

1073

ALASKA COMMISSION ON POST-SECONDARY EDUCATION (STUDENT LOAN PROGRAM; FAMILY LOAN PROGRAM)

PO BOX 110505
JUNEAU AK 99811
907/465-2962

AMOUNT: $5500 - $6500
DEADLINE(S): MAY 15
FIELD(S): ALL AREAS OF STUDY

OPEN TO ALASKA RESIDENTS OF AT LEAST 2 YEARS. THESE LOW-INTEREST LOANS (8% STUDENT; 5% FAMILY) SUPPORT FULL-TIME STUDY AT ANY ACCREDITED VOCATIONAL; UNDERGRADUATE OR GRADUATE INSTITUTION.

UP TO $5500 AVAILABLE FOR VOCATIONAL OR UNDERGRADUATE STUDY AND UP TO $6500 FOR GRADUATE STUDY. RENEWABLE. WRITE FOR COMPLETE INFORMATION.

1074

ALASKA COMMISSION ON POST-SECONDARY EDUCATION (STATE EDUCATIONAL INCENTIVE GRANT PROGRAM)

BOX 110505
JUNEAU AK 99811
907/465-2962 EXT 106

AMOUNT: $100 - $1500
DEADLINE(S): MAY 31
FIELD(S): ALL FIELDS OF STUDY

OPEN TO ALASKA RESIDENTS OF AT LEAST 2 YEARS WHO ARE ACCEPTED TO OR ENROLLED IN THEIR FIRST UNDERGRADUATE DEGREE OR COMPARABLE CERTIFICATE PROGRAM AT AN ACCREDITED INSTITUTION (IN-STATE OR OUT-OF-STATE). DEMONSTRATE NEED.

315 GRANTS PER YEAR. WRITE FOR COMPLETE INFORMATION.

1075

ALBERT BAKER FUND (STUDENT LOANS)

5 THIRD ST; #717
SAN FRANCISCO CA 94103
415/543-7028

AMOUNT: $1200 - $2000
DEADLINE(S): JUL 1
FIELD(S): ALL AREAS OF STUDY

OPEN TO STUDENTS WHO ARE MEMBERS OF THE MOTHER CHURCH - THE FIRST CHURCH OF CHRIST SCIENTIST IN BOSTON - AND ARE ACTIVE AS CHRISTIAN SCIENTISTS. STUDENT MUST HAVE OTHER PRIMARY LENDER AND BE ENROLLED IN AN ACCREDITED COLLEGE OR UNIVERSITY.

FOREIGN STUDENTS MUST HAVE COSIGNER WHO IS A USA CITIZEN. AVERAGE OF 160 AWARDS PER YEAR. WRITE FOR COMPLETE INFORMATION.

1076

ALCOA FOUNDATION (ALCOA FOUNDATION SCHOLARSHIPS)

1501 ALCOA BLDG; MELLON SQUARE
PITTSBURGH PA 15219
WRITTEN INQUIRY

AMOUNT: $2000 PER YEAR
DEADLINE(S): SEP 15

FIELD(S): ALL AREAS OF STUDY
OPEN TO HIGH SCHOOL SENIORS WHO ARE DEPENDENT CHILDREN OF ALCOA-USA EMPLOYEES. SCHOLARSHIPS ARE AWARDED FOR 4 YEARS OF FULL-TIME UNDERGRADUATE STUDY. USA CITIZEN.
45-55 AWARDS PER YEAR. WRITE FOR COMPLETE INFORMATION.

1077

ALEXANDER GRAHAM BELL ASSOCIATION FOR THE DEAF (ELSIE BELL GROSVENOR SCHOLARSHIP AWARDS)
3417 VOLTA PLACE NW
WASHINGTON DC 20007
202/337-5220
AMOUNT: $500 - $1000
DEADLINE(S): APR 15
FIELD(S): ALL AREAS OF STUDY
OPEN TO ORAL DEAF STUDENTS WHO WERE BORN WITH PROFOUND HEARING IMPAIRMENT OR WHO SUFFERED SUCH IMPAIRMENT BEFORE ACQUIRING LANGUAGE. MUST BE ACCEPTED INTO A FULL-TIME ACADEMIC PROGRAM FOR HEARING STUDENTS.
MUST RESIDE IN OR ATTEND COLLEGE IN WASHINGTON DC METROPOLITAN AREA. WRITE FOR COMPLETE INFORMATION.

1078

ALEXANDER GRAHAM BELL ASSOCIATION FOR THE DEAF (LUCILE A. ABT & MAUDE WINKLER SCHOLARSHIPS)
3417 VOLTA PLACE NW
WASHINGTON DC 20007
202/337-5220
AMOUNT: $500 - $1000
DEADLINE(S): APR 15
FIELD(S): ALL AREAS OF STUDY
OPEN TO ORAL DEAF STUDENTS BORN WITH A PROFOUND HEARING IMPAIRMENT OR WHO SUFFERED SUCH A LOSS BEFORE ACQUIRING LANGUAGE. MUST BE ACCEPTED INTO A FULL-TIME ACADEMIC PROGRAM FOR HEARING STUDENTS. PREFERENCE TO NORTH AMERICA CITIZENS.
5 AWARDS PER YEAR. WRITE FOR COMPLETE INFORMATION.

1079

ALEXANDER GRAHAM BELL ASSOCIATION FOR THE DEAF (HERBERT P. FEIBELMAN JR. INTERNATIONAL PARENTS' ORGANIZATION SCHOLARSHIP AWARD)
3417 VOLTA PLACE NW
WASHINGTON DC 20007
202/337-5220 (VOICE OR TDD)
AMOUNT: $1000
DEADLINE(S): APR 15
FIELD(S): ALL AREAS OF STUDY
OPEN TO ORAL DEAF STUDENTS WHO WERE BORN WITH PROFOUND HEARING IMPAIRMENT OR WHO SUFFERED SUCH A LOSS BEFORE ACQUIRING LANGUAGE. MUST BE ACCEPTED INTO A FULL-TIME ACADEMIC PROGRAM FOR HEARING STUDENTS. NORTH AMERICA CITIZEN.
WRITE FOR COMPLETE INFORMATION.

1080

ALEXANDER GRAHAM BELL ASSOCIATION FOR THE DEAF (ORAL HEARING IMPAIRED SECTION SCHOLARSHIP AWARD)
3417 VOLTA PLACE NW
WASHINGTON DC 20007
202/337-5220
AMOUNT: $1000
DEADLINE(S): APR 15
FIELD(S): ALL AREAS OF STUDY
OPEN TO ORAL DEAF STUDENTS WHO WERE BORN WITH A PROFOUND HEARING IMPAIRMENT OR WHO SUFFERED SUCH A LOSS BEFORE ACQUIRING LANGUAGE. MUST BE ACCEPTED INTO A FULL-TIME ACADEMIC PROGRAM FOR HEARING STUDENTS. NORTH AMERICA CITIZEN.
WRITE FOR COMPLETE INFORMATION.

1081

ALEXANDER GRAHAM BELL ASSOCIATION FOR THE DEAF (AUXILIARY OF THE NAT'L RURAL LETTER CARRIERS ASSOC & ALLIE RANEY HUNT SCHOLARSHIPS)
3417 VOLTA PLACE NW
WASHINGTON DC 20007
202/337-5220
AMOUNT: $500
DEADLINE(S): APR 15
FIELD(S): ALL AREAS OF STUDY
OPEN TO STUDENTS WHO ARE ORAL DEAF OR WERE BORN WITH A PROFOUND HEARING

IMPAIRMENT OR SUFFERED LOSS BEFORE ACQUIRING LANGUAGE. MUST BE ACCEPTED INTO A FULL-TIME ACADEMIC PROGRAM FOR HEARING STUDENTS. NORTH AMERICA CITIZEN.
WRITE FOR COMPLETE INFORMATION.

1082

ALEXANDER GRAHAM BELL ASSOCIATION FOR THE DEAF (VOLTA SCHOLARSHIP AWARDS)
3417 VOLTA PLACE NW
WASHINGTON DC 20007
202/337-5220
AMOUNT: $500
DEADLINE(S): APR 15
FIELD(S): ALL AREAS OF STUDY
OPEN TO ORAL DEAF STUDENTS BORN WITH PROFOUND HEARING IMPAIRMENT OR WHO SUFFERED SUCH A LOSS BEFORE ACQUIRING LANGUAGE. MUST BE ACCEPTED INTO A FULL-TIME ACADEMIC PROGRAM FOR HEARING STUDENTS. PREFERENCE TO NORTH AMERICAN CITIZENS.
WRITE FOR COMPLETE INFORMATION.

1083

ALGONQUIN COUNCIL; BOY SCOUTS OF AMERICA (COLLEGE LOAN PROGRAM)
PO BOX 149; 34 DELOSS ST
FRAMINGHAM MA 01781
617/872-6551
AMOUNT: $1000
DEADLINE(S): NONE
FIELD(S): ALL AREAS
OPEN TO EXPLORER SCOUT WITH A MINIMUM OF 3 YEARS AS A REGISTERED MEMBER OF THE ALGONQUIN COUNCIL. MUST DEMONSTRATE GOOD SCHOLARSHIP ABILITY AND FINANCIAL NEED.
WRITE FOR COMPLETE INFORMATION.

1084

ALMANOR SCHOLARSHIP FUND (SCHOLARSHIPS)
PO BOX 796
CHESTER CA 96020
916/258-2111
AMOUNT: $1200
DEADLINE(S): SEP 1
FIELD(S): ALL AREAS OF STUDY
OPEN TO GRADUATES OF CHESTER (CALIF.) HIGH SCHOOL WHO ARE RESIDENTS OF CHESTER AND HAVE AT LEAST A 3.0 GPA. AWARDS ARE FOR FULL TIME STUDY AT ANY ACCREDITED COLLEGE OR UNIVERSITY. USA CITIZEN OR LEGAL RESIDENT.
WRITE FOR COMPLETE INFORMATION.

1085

ALPHA KAPPA ALPHA (DOMESTIC TRAVEL TOUR GRANT)
5656 SO STONY ISLAND AVE
CHICAGO IL 60637
312/684-1282
AMOUNT: $1000 VALUE
DEADLINE(S): JAN 31 (ODD-NUMBERED YEARS)
FIELD(S): ALL FIELDS OF STUDY
OPEN TO ALL FEMALE HIGH SCHOOL JUNIORS & SENIORS IN USA WITH AT LEAST A 'B' AVG. THE GRANT PROVIDES AN OPPORTUNITY FOR YOUNG WOMEN TO GAIN PRIMARY KNOWLEDGE ON VARIED PLACES THROUGH STRUCTURED TRAVEL TOURS. AKA MEMBERSHIP 'NOT' REQUIRED.
30 AWARDS EVERY 2 YEARS (ODD-NUMBERED YEARS). WRITE FOR COMPLETE INFORMATION.

1086

AMALGAMATED CLOTHING AND TEXTILE WORKERS UNION (ACTWU SCHOLARSHIP)
15 UNION SQUARE WEST
NEW YORK NY 10003
212/242-0700
AMOUNT: $1000
DEADLINE(S): MAR 15
FIELD(S): ALL FIELDS OF STUDY
THREE WINNERS ARE SELECTED EACH YEAR FOR SCHOLARSHIPS TO ANY TWO OR FOUR YEAR DEGREE GRANTING COLLEGE. AWARDS ARE MADE ONLY TO INCOMING FRESHMEN WHO ARE THE SON OR DAUGHTER OF A UNION MEMBER IN GOOD STANDING FOR TWO YEARS OR MORE.
SCHOLARSHIP IS RENEWABLE FOR ONE ADDITIONAL YEAR. WRITE FOR COMPLETE INFORMATION.

1087

AMAX FOUNDATION INC (SCHOLARSHIP PROGRAM)
200 PARK AVE
NEW YORK NY 10166
212/856-4250

AMOUNT: UP TO $4000
DEADLINE(S): NOV 1
FIELD(S): ALL AREAS OF STUDY
SCHOLARSHIP PROGRAM FOR DEPENDENT CHILDREN OF AMAX INC EMPLOYEES. OPEN TO HIGH SCHOOL SENIORS; UNDERGRADUATE FRESHMEN & SOPHOMORES.
CONTACT ADDRESS ABOVE FOR COMPLETE INFORMATION.

1088
AMERICAN ASSOCIATION OF UNIVERSITY WOMEN - HONOLULU BRANCH (PACIFIC FELLOWSHIP)
1802 KEEAUMOKU STREET
HONOLULU HI 96822
808/537-4702
AMOUNT: VARIES WITH NEED - COVERS HOUSING; MEDICAL INSURANCE; SOME EDUCATIONAL & RESEARCH EXPENSES
DEADLINE(S): APR 15 - NOV 30
FIELD(S): CAREER SUPPORT AT ANY LEVEL
OPEN TO WOMEN FROM THE SOUTH PACIFIC OR ASIA FOR STUDY AND RESEARCH AT ANY INSTITUTION IN HAWAII IN AN AREA RELATED TO IMPROVEMENT OF THEIR PROFESSIONAL KNOWLEDGE.
MUST DEMONSTRATE FINANCIAL NEED. WRITE FOR COMPLETE INFORMATION.

1089
AMERICAN ASSOCIATION OF UNIVERSITY WOMEN - HONOLULU BRANCH (RUTH E. BLACK SCHOLARSHIP)
1802 KEEAUMOKU STREET
HONOLULU HI 96822
808/537-4702
AMOUNT: VARIES
DEADLINE(S): MAR 1
FIELD(S): ALL FIELDS OF STUDY
OPEN TO WOMEN WHO ARE LEGAL RESIDENTS OF HAWAII. FOR UNDERGRADUATE STUDY AT AN ACCREDITED COLLEGE OR UNIVERSITY IN HAWAII. MUST DEMONSTRATE FINANCIAL NEED.
WRITE FOR COMPLETE INFORMATION.

1090
AMERICAN COUNCIL OF THE BLIND (FLOYD QUALLS MEMORIAL SCHOLARSHIPS)
1155 15TH ST NW; STE 720
WASHINGTON DC 20005
202/467-5081
AMOUNT: $1000 - $2000
DEADLINE(S): MAR 15
FIELD(S): ALL FIELDS OF STUDY
SCHOLARSHIPS OPEN TO LEGALLY BLIND APPLICANTS WHO HAVE BEEN ACCEPTED TO OR ARE ENROLLED IN AN ACCREDITED INSTITUTION FOR VOCATIONAL; TECHNICAL; UNDERGRADUATE; GRADUATE OR PROFESSIONAL STUDIES. USA CITIZEN OR LEGAL RESIDENT.
WRITE FOR COMPLETE INFORMATION.

1091
AMERICAN EXPRESS FOUNDATION (SCHOLARSHIP PROGRAM)
PROGRAMS COORDINATOR; WORLD FINANCIAL CENTER; AMERICAN EXPRESS TOWER
NEW YORK NY 10285
212/640-5661
AMOUNT: $500 - $3000
DEADLINE(S): NONE
FIELD(S): ALL FIELDS OF STUDY
OPEN TO HIGH SCHOOL SENIORS WHO ARE CHILDREN OF AMERICAN EXPRESS EMPLOYEES. FOR UNDERGRADUATE STUDY AT ANY ACCREDITED COLLEGE OR UNIVERSITY.
WRITE FOR COMPLETE INFORMATION.

1092
AMERICAN FEDERATION OF STATE; COUNTY & MUNICIPAL EMPLOYEES (AFSCME FAMILY SCHOLARSHIP PROGRAM)
1625 'L' STREET NW; EDUCATION DEPT
WASHINGTON DC 20036
202/452-4800
AMOUNT: $2000 PER YEAR FOR 4 YEARS
DEADLINE(S): DEC 31
FIELD(S): ALL AREAS OF STUDY
OPEN TO HIGH SCHOOL SENIORS WHO ARE DEPENDENT CHILDREN OF ACTIVE AFSCME MEMBERS. AWARDS FOR FULL-TIME UNDERGRADUATE STUDY AT ANY ACCREDITED 4-YEAR COLLEGE OR UNIVERSITY. USA CITIZEN OR LEGAL RESIDENT.
RENEWABLE. WRITE FOR COMPLETE INFORMATION.

1093
AMERICAN FOUNDATION FOR THE BLIND (HELEN KELLER SCHOLARSHIP FUND)
15 WEST 16TH ST
NEW YORK NY 10011
212/620-2000; TDD 212/620-2158

AMOUNT: $1000 - $3000
DEADLINE(S): APR 1
FIELD(S): ALL AREAS OF STUDY
OPEN TO COLLEGE OR UNIVERSITY STUDENTS WHO ARE LEGALLY BLIND AND DEAF FOR HELP WITH THEIR READING; TUTORING OR EQUIPMENT ACQUISITION EXPENSES. STUDENT MUST BE USA CITIZEN AND SUBMIT PROOF OF BOTH LEGAL BLINDNESS AND DEAFNESS.
THIS SCHOLARSHIP IS NOT AVAILABLE FOR 1992 WRITE FOR COMPLETE INFORMATION.

1094

AMERICAN LEGION - DEPARTMENT OF NEW JERSEY (STUTZ MEMORIAL SCHOLARSHIP)
WAR MEMORIAL BUILDING
TRENTON NJ 08608
WRITTEN INQUIRY
AMOUNT: $1000 PER YEAR (4 YEARS)
DEADLINE(S): MAR 1
FIELD(S): ALL FIELDS OF STUDY
OPEN TO CHILDREN OF MEMBERS OR DECEASED MEMBERS OF THE AMERICAN LEGION DEPARTMENT OF NEW JERSEY. APPLICANTS MUST BE A MEMBER OF THE GRADUATING CLASS OF A SENIOR HIGH SCHOOL AND USE THE AWARD THE YEAR IT IS RECEIVED.
FINANCIAL NEED IS A CONSIDERATION. WRITE FOR COMPLETE INFORMATION.

1095

AMERICAN LEGION AUXILIARY - DEPT OF MN (SCHOLARSHIPS)
DEPT OF MINNESOTA STATE VETERANS SERVICE BUILDING
ST PAUL MN 55155
612/224-7634
AMOUNT: $500
DEADLINE(S): MAR 5
FIELD(S): ALL AREAS OF STUDY
OPEN TO MINNESOTA RESIDENTS WHO ARE THE CHILDREN OR GRANDCHILDREN OF MILITARY VETERANS WHO SERVED DURING TIME OF AN ARMED CONFLICT. MUST BE HIGH SCHOOL SENIOR OR GRADUATE WITH AT LEAST A 'C' GRADE AVERAGE AND DEMONSTRATE FINANCIAL NEED.
WRITE FOR COMPLETE INFORMATION.

1096

AMERICAN LEGION AUXILIARY NATIONAL HEADQUARTERS (AMERICAN LEGION AUXILIARY NATIONAL PRESIDENT'S SCHOLARSHIPS)
777 N MERIDIAN ST
INDIANAPOLIS IN 46204
317/635-6291
AMOUNT: $1500 - $2000
DEADLINE(S): MAR 15
FIELD(S): ALL AREAS OF STUDY
OPEN TO CHILDREN OF VETERANS OF WWI; WWII; KOREAN WAR OR VIETNAM WAR WHO ARE HIGH SCHOOL SENIORS OR HIGH SCHOOL GRADUATES WHO HAVE NOT ATTENDED AN INSTITUTE OF HIGHER LEARNING AT THE TIME OF AWARD.
10 AWARDS PER YEAR. FOR DETAILS WRITE TO THE AMERICAN LEGION AUXILIARY IN YOUR LOCAL AREA ONLY. DO NOT WRITE TO THE ADDRESS ABOVE. THE PROGRAM IS ADMINISTERED BY 5 REGIONAL DIVISIONS (2 AWARDS PER DIVISION.)

1097

AMERICAN LOGISTICS ASSOCIATION-NEW YORK CHAPTER (CDR. WILLIAM S. STUHR SCHOLARSHIP FUND)
1200 FIFTH AVE
NEW YORK NY 10029
212/876-8180; FAX 212/722-0139
AMOUNT: $1000 PER YEAR FOR 4 YEARS
DEADLINE(S): VARIES
FIELD(S): ALL AREAS OF STUDY
OPEN TO HIGH SCHOOL SENIORS WHO ARE DEPENDENTS OF ACTIVE DUTY OR RETIRED MEMBERS OF THE US MILITARY AND LIVE WITHIN A 100 MILE RADIUS OF NEW YORK CITY. FOR STUDY AT AN ACCREDITED COLLEGE OR UNIVERSITY.
ONE SCHOLARSHIP FOR EACH OF THE FIVE SERVICES IS AVAILABLE FOR DEPENDENTS OF THAT SERVICE. APPLICANTS SHOULD BE IN TOP 10% OF CLASS AND DEMONSTRATE FINANCIAL NEED. WRITE FOR COMPLETE INFORMATION.

1098

AMERICAN MENSA EDUCATION & RESEARCH FOUNDATION (SCHOLARSHIPS)
2626 E 14TH ST
BROOKLYN NY 11235
WRITTEN INQUIRY

AMOUNT: $200 TO $1000
DEADLINE(S): JAN 31
FIELD(S): ALL FIELDS OF STUDY
OPEN TO STUDENTS ENROLLED FOR THE ACADEMIC YEAR FOLLOWING THE AWARD IN A DEGREE PROGRAM IN AN ACCREDITED AMERICAN INSTITUTION OF POST SECONDARY EDUCATION. APPLICANTS MUST SUBMIT AN ESSAY DESCRIBING CAREER; VOCATIONAL AND ACADEMIC GOALS.
ESSAY SHOULD BE FEWER THAN 550 WORDS AND MUST BE SPECIFIC RATHER THAN GENERAL. IT MUST BE ON AN OFFICIAL APPLICATION. SEND SELF-ADDRESSED STAMPED ENVELOPE FOR APPLICATION AND COMPLETE INFORMATION.

1099

AMERICAN NATIONAL CAN COMPANY (SCHOLARSHIP PROGRAM)
8770 W BRYNMAWR AVE; #10-N
CHICAGO IL 60631
312/399-3000
AMOUNT: $500 TO $3000
DEADLINE(S): MAR 15
FIELD(S): ALL FIELDS OF STUDY
MUST BE HIGH SCHOOL SENIOR TO APPLY AND THE SON OR DAUGHTER OF AN EMPLOYEE OF THE AMERICAN CAN COMPANY WITH MINIMUM 3 YEARS SERVICE.
10 SCHOLARSHIPS ARE AVAILABLE PER YEAR. RENEWABLE TO 4 YEARS. WRITE FOR COMPLETE INFORMATION.

1100

AMERICAN POSTAL WORKERS UNION/AFL-CIO (E.C. HALLBECK MEMORIAL SCHOLARSHIP PROGRAM)
1300 'L' STREET NW
WASHINGTON DC 20005
202/842-4268
AMOUNT: $1000 PER YEAR FOR 4 YEARS
DEADLINE(S): MAR 1
FIELD(S): ALL FIELDS OF STUDY
OPEN TO HIGH SCHOOL SENIORS WHO ARE DEPENDENT CHILDREN OF AMERICAN POSTAL WORKERS UNION MEMBERS (ACTIVE OR DECEASED). AWARDS TENABLE AT ACCREDITED COLLEGES & UNIVERSITIES.
WRITE FOR COMPLETE INFORMATION.

1101

AMERICAN RADIO RELAY LEAGUE FOUNDATION (EDWARD D. JAIKINS MEMORIAL SCHOLARSHIP FUND)
225 MAIN ST
NEWINGTON CT 06111
203/666-1541
AMOUNT: $500
DEADLINE(S): FEB 15
FIELD(S): ALL AREAS OF STUDY
OPEN TO STUDENTS WHO ARE RESIDENTS OF THE FCC EIGHTH CALL DISTRICT (MICHIGAN; OHIO; W VIRGINIA); ATTEND AN ACCREDITED INSTITUTION WITHIN THAT CALL DISTRICT; HAVE 3.0 GPA OR BETTER & ARE AT LEAST GENERAL CLASS LICENSED RADIO AMATEURS.
WRITE FOR COMPLETE INFORMATION.

1102

AMERICAN RADIO RELAY LEAGUE FOUNDATION (NEW ENGLAND FEMARA SCHOLARSHIP)
225 MAIN ST
NEWINGTON CT 06111
203/666-1541
AMOUNT: $600
DEADLINE(S): FEB 15
FIELD(S): ALL FIELDS OF STUDY
OPEN TO RESIDENTS OF THE SIX NEW ENGLAND STATES WHO ARE RADIO AMATEURS HOLDING AT LEAST A TECHNICIAN'S LICENSE.
WRITE FOR COMPLETE INFORMATION.

1103

AMERICAN RADIO RELAY LEAGUE FOUNDATION (YOU'VE GOT A FRIEND IN PENNSYLVANIA SCHOLARSHIP FUND)
225 MAIN ST
NEWINGTON CT 06111
203/666-1541
AMOUNT: $1000
DEADLINE(S): FEB 15
FIELD(S): ALL FIELDS OF STUDY
PREFERENCE TO PENNSYLVANIA RESIDENTS WHO ARE ARRL MEMBERS; AT LEAST GENERAL CLASS LICENSED RADIO AMATEURS & HAVE AN 'A' GRADE POINT AVERAGE IN GRADED COURSES (SPORTS & PHYSICAL EDUCATION GRADES EXCLUDED).
WRITE FOR COMPLETE INFORMATION.

1104

AMERICAN SAMOA GOVERNMENT (FINANCIAL AID PROGRAM)

DEPT OF EDUCATION; OFFICE OF STUDENT FINANCIAL PROGRAM
PAGO PAGO AMERICAN SAMOA 96799
684/633-4255

AMOUNT: $5000
DEADLINE(S): APR 30
FIELD(S): ALL FIELDS OF STUDY

SCHOLARSHIPS OPEN TO RESIDENTS OF AMERICAN SAMOA. AWARDS SUPPORT UNDERGRADUATE & GRADUATE STUDY AT ALL ACCREDITED COLLEGES & UNIVERSITIES. APPLICANTS FROM OFF ISLANDS MAY BE ELIGIBLE IF THEIR PARENTS ARE CITIZENS OF AMERICAN SAMOA.

APPROX 50 AWARDS PER YEAR. RENEWABLE. WRITE FOR COMPLETE INFORMATION.

1105

AMERICAN STERILIZER CO. (FOUNDERS MEMORIAL SCHOLARSHIP FUND)

2424 WEST 23RD ST
ERIE PA 16506
814/870-8448

AMOUNT: $3000
DEADLINE(S): MAR 29
FIELD(S): ALL AREAS OF STUDY

OPEN TO DEPENDENTS OF EMPLOYEES OF AMERICAN STERILIZER. FOR UNDERGRADUATE OR GRADUATE STUDY IN COLLEGES OR UNIVERSITIES OR TRADE SCHOOLS. MUST DEMONSTRATE FINANCIAL NEED.

WRITE FOR COMPLETE INFORMATION

1106

AMVETS NATIONAL SCHOLARSHIP PROGRAM (SCHOLARSHIPS)

4647 FORBES BOULEVARD
LANHAM MD 20706
301/459-9600; FAX 301/459-7924

AMOUNT: $1000 PER YEAR
DEADLINE(S): JUN 1
FIELD(S): ALL FIELDS OF STUDY

OPEN TO HIGH SCHOOL SENIORS WHO ARE THE CHILDREN OR GRANDCHILDREN OF AN AMERICAN MILITARY VETERAN. APPLICANTS MUST DEMONSTRATE FINANCIAL NEED AND ACADEMIC ACHIEVEMENT AND BE USA CITIZENS.

VETERANS WHO HAVE EXHAUSTED ALL GOVERNMENT FINANCIAL AID ALSO MAY APPPLY UNDER 'SPECIAL CONSIDERATION' CATEGORY. AWARD RENEWABLE FOR UP TO 4 YEARS. WRITE FOR COMPLETE INFORMATION.

1107

ANITA H. RICHARD TRUST (DAVID CARLYLE III SCHOLARSHIP)

353 CHICAGO AVE
SAVANNA IL 61074
815/273-2839

AMOUNT: $2000 PER SEMESTER FOR 4 YEARS
DEADLINE(S): APR 15 EVERY FOUR YEARS
FIELD(S): ALL AREAS OF STUDY

OPEN TO GRADUATING SENIORS OF CARROL COUNTY ILLINOIS HIGH SCHOOLS. AWARDS ARE TENABLE AT ACCREDITED UNDERGRADUATE COLLEGES & UNIVERSITIES. MAINTAIN AT LEAST A 2.0 GPA ON 4.0 SCALE. USA CITIZEN. MUST DEMONSTRATE FINANCIAL NEED.

A JUNIOR COLLEGE IS ACCEPTABLE IF STUDENT INTENDS TO ENROLL AT A COLLEGE OR UNIVERSITY FOR THE THIRD AND FOURTH YEAR. WRITE FOR COMPLETE INFORMATION.

1108

APPALOOSA YOUTH FOUNDATION (YOUTH EDUCATIONAL SCHOLARSHIPS)

PO BOX 8403
MOSCOW ID 83843
208/882-5578

AMOUNT: $1000
DEADLINE(S): JUN 10
FIELD(S): ALL FIELDS OF STUDY

OPEN TO MEMBERS OF THE APPALOOSA YOUTH ASSN OR THE APPALOOSA HORSE CLUB; CHILDREN OF APPALOOSA HORSE CLUB MEMBERS AND TO INDIVIDUALS SPONSORED BY A REGIONAL CLUB OR RACING ASSOCIATION.

11 SCHOLARSHIPS PER YEAR. RENEWABLE. CONTACT THE YOUTH COORDINATOR AT ADDRESS ABOVE FOR COMPLETE INFORMATION.

1109

ARCTIC EDUCATION FOUNDATION (SHAREHOLDER SCHOLARSHIPS)

BOX 129
BARROW AK 99723
907/852-8633

AMOUNT: VARIES ACCORDING TO NEED
DEADLINE(S): NONE SPECIFIED
FIELD(S): ALL AREAS OF STUDY
OPEN TO ARCTIC SLOPE REGIONAL CORPORATION SHAREHOLDERS AND THEIR CHILDREN. FOR FULL TIME UNDERGRADUATE OR GRADUATE STUDY AT ANY ACCREDITED INSTITUTION OF HIGHER EDUCATION. MUST MAINTAIN 2.0 OR BETTER GPA AND DEMONSTRATE FINANCIAL NEED.
AVAILABLE FOR STUDIES LEADING TO TWO OR FOUR YEAR DEGREES. WRITE FOR COMPLETE INFORMATION.

1110

ARKANSAS DEPARTMENT OF HIGHER EDUCATION (STUDENT ASSISTANCE GRANT PROGRAM)
114 EAST CAPITOL
LITTLE ROCK AR 72201
501/342-9300
AMOUNT: $100 - $800
DEADLINE(S): AWARDED FIRST COME FIRST SERVED UNTIL FUNDS ARE EXHAUSTED
FIELD(S): ALL FIELDS OF STUDY
US CITIZEN OR LEGAL RESIDENT. RESIDENT OF ARKANSAS ATTENDING AN UNDERGRADUATE INSTITUTION IN ARKANSAS. DEMONSTRATE FINANCIAL NEED AND SATISFACTORY ACADEMIC PROGRESS.
10000 GRANTS PER YEAR. WRITE FOR COMPLETE INFORMATION.

1111

ARKANSAS STUDENT LOAN GUARANTEE FOUNDATION (LOAN PROGRAM)
219 SOUTH VICTORY
LITTLE ROCK AR 72201
501/371-2634
AMOUNT: $2625 1ST & 2ND YR UNDERGRADS; $4000 3RD & 4TH YR; $7500 GRADUATE (PER YEAR)
DEADLINE(S): APR 15
FIELD(S): ALL FIELDS OF STUDY LEADING TO A DEGREE OR CERTIFICATE
LOANS OPEN TO ARKANSAS RESIDENT OR NON-RESIDENT ENROLLED AT ELIGIBLE ARKANSAS POST-SECONDARY EDUCATIONAL INSTITUTION. DEMONSTRATE FINANCIAL NEED. USA CITIZEN OR LEGAL RESIDENT.
WRITE FOR COMPLETE INFORMATION.

1112

ARLINE P. PADELFORD SCHOLARSHIP TRUST (SCHOLARSHIPS)
C/O STATE STREET BANK & TRUST CO; PO BOX 351
BOSTON MA 02101
617/786-3000
AMOUNT: $600
DEADLINE(S): NONE SPECIFIED
FIELD(S): ALL AREAS OF STUDY
SCHOLARSHIPS FOR WORTHY AND DESERVING STUDENTS AT TAUNTON (MA.) HIGH SCHOOL TO PURSUE COLLEGE OR TECHNICAL EDUCATION.
12 SCHOLARSHIPS PER YEAR. CONTACT TAUNTON HIGH GUIDANCE COUNSELOR FOR COMPLETE INFORMATION.

1113

ARMCO FOUNDATION (SCHOLARSHIP PROGRAM FOR SONS & DAUGHTERS OF ARMCO EMPLOYEES)
300 INTERPACE PARKWAY
PARSIPPANY NJ 07054
201-316-5274
AMOUNT: $2000 PER YEAR FOR UP TO 4 YEARS
DEADLINE(S): NOV 30
FIELD(S): ALL AREAS OF STUDY
MUST BE SON OR DAUGHTER OF ELIGIBLE ARMCO EMPLOYEE; HIGH SCHOOL SENIOR WHO WILL GRADUATE IN CURRENT ACADEMIC YEAR AND ENTER AN ACCREDITED USA COLLEGE OR UNIVERSITY IN THE NEXT ACADEMIC YEAR.
AWARDS RENEWABLE FOR UP TO 3 YEARS. WRITE FOR COMPLETE INFORMATION.

1114

ARMENIAN ASSEMBLY OF AMERICA (SCHOLARSHIP INFORMATION)
122 ‘C’ STREET NW; SUITE 350
WASHINGTON DC 20001
201/393-3434
AMOUNT: VARIES
DEADLINE(S): VARIOUS
FIELD(S): ALL AREAS OF STUDY
THE ARMENIAN ASSEMBLY PREPARES AN ANNUAL BOOKLET TITLED ‘DIRECTORY OF FINANCIAL AID FOR STUDENTS OF ARMENIAN DESCENT.’ IT DESCRIBES NUMEROUS SCHOLARSHIP; LOAN & GRANT PROGRAMS

THAT ARE AVAILABLE FROM SOURCES IN THE ARMENIAN COMMUNITY.
THE DIRECTORY IS FREE & IS AVAILABLE FROM THE ADDRESS ABOVE.

1115

ARMENIAN RELIEF SOCIETY OF NORTH AMERICA INC. (GRANTS)
80 BIGELOW AVE
WATERTOWN MA 02172
617/923-3801
AMOUNT: $400-$1000
DEADLINE(S): APR 1
FIELD(S): ALL FIELDS OF STUDY
OPEN TO UNDERGRADUATES OF ARMENIAN ANCESTRY WHO ARE ATTENDING AN ACCREDITED 2 OR 4 YEAR COLLEGE OR UNIVERSITY IN THE USA AND HAVE COMPLETED AT LEAST ONE SEMESTER. AWARDS BASED ON NEED; MERIT; INVOLVEMENT IN ARMENIAN COMMUNITY.
WRITE TO SCHOLARSHIP COMMITTEE; ADDRESS ABOVE; FOR COMPLETE INFORMATION.

1116

ARMENIAN STUDENTS' ASSOCIATION OF AMERICA INC. (SCHOLARSHIPS; FELLOWSHIPS)
C. WILLIAMSON; SCHOLARSHIP ADM; 395 CONCORD AVE
BELMONT MA 02178
617/484-9548
AMOUNT: $500 - $1500
DEADLINE(S): APR 1 (REQUEST APPLICATION BY FEB 15)
FIELD(S): ALL FIELDS OF STUDY
FOR FULL TIME GRADUATE OR UNDERGRADUATE STUDY IN USA BY STUDENT OF ARMENIAN DESCENT. UNDERGRADS MUST HAVE COMPLETED AT LEAST 1 YEAR OF POST-SECONDARY SCHOOLING; DEMONSTRATE FINANCIAL NEED AND HAVE GOOD ACADEMIC RECORD.
50 SCHOLARSHIPS AND 10 FELLOWSHIPS PER YEAR. RENEWABLE. WRITE FOR COMPLETE INFORMATION.

1117

ARTHUR C. & FLORENCE S. BOEHMER FUND (SCHOLARSHIPS)
C/O RINN & ELLIOT; PO BOX 1827
LODI CA 95240
209/369-2781
AMOUNT: YEARLY INCOME
DEADLINE(S): JUN 1
FIELD(S): MEDICAL
OPEN TO STUDENTS WHO ARE GRADUATES OF A HIGH SCHOOL WITHIN THE LODI (SAN JOAQUIN COUNTY, CA) UNIFIED SCHOOL DISTRICT. FOR UNDERGRADUATE; GRADUATE OR POST-GRADUATE STUDY IN THE FIELD OF MEDICINE AT AN ACCREDITED INSTITUTION IN CALIFORNIA.
GRADE POINT AVERAGE OF 2.9 OR BETTER REQUIRED. SCHOLARSHIPS ARE RENEWABLE. WRITE FOR COMPLETE INFORMATION.

1118

ARTHUR C. & LUCIA S. PALMER FOUNDATION INC. (GRANTS)
471 PENNSYLVANIA AVE
WAVERLY NY 14892
607/565-4603
AMOUNT: $3000
DEADLINE(S): APR 1
FIELD(S): ALL FIELDS OF STUDY
GRANTS OPEN TO STUDENTS WHO ARE RESIDENTS OF TIOGA COUNTY, NY OR BRADFORD COUNTY, PA. FINANCIAL NEED IS DISCUSSED DURING A REQUIRED INTERVIEW. AWARDS BASED ON MOTIVATION & FINANCIAL NEED.
WRITE FOR COMPLETE INFORMATION.

1119

ASSOCIATION FOR EDUCATION & REHABILITATION OF THE BLIND & VISUALLY IMPAIRED (FERRELL SCHOLARSHIP FUND)
206 N WASHINGTON ST; SUITE 320
ALEXANDRIA VA 22314
703/548-1884
AMOUNT: VARIES
DEADLINE(S): APR 15 OF EVEN NUMBERED YEARS
FIELD(S): CAREER FIELD IN SERVICES TO THE BLIND
OPEN TO LEGALLY BLIND STUDENTS ENROLLED IN A COLLEGE OR UNIVERSITY PROGRAM RELATED TO BLIND SERVICES SUCH AS ORIENTATION AND MOBILITY; SPECIAL EDUCATION; REHABILITATION TEACHING; VISION REHABILITATION.
FOR UNDERGRADUATE; GRADUATE OR POST-GRADUATE STUDY. WRITE FOR COMPLETE INFORMATION.

1120

ASSOCIATION ON AMERICAN INDIAN AFFAIRS INC. (ADOLPH VAN PELT SCHOLARSHIPS)
245 5TH AVE; SUITE 1801
NEW YORK NY 10016
212/689-8270; FAX 212/685-4692
AMOUNT: $500 - $800
DEADLINE(S): JUN 1
FIELD(S): ALL FIELDS OF STUDY
OPEN TO UNDERGRADUATE AND GRADUATE STUDENTS OF NATIVE AMERICAN HERITAGE WHO CAN DEMONSTRATE FINANCIAL NEED AND MERIT. APPLICANTS MUST PROVE THEIR NATIVE AMERICAN HERITAGE (AT LEAST 25%).
15-25 AWARDS PER YEAR RENEWABLE FOR UP TO FOUR YEARS. WRITE FOR COMPLETE INFORMATION.

1121

ASSOCIATION ON AMERICAN INDIAN AFFAIRS INC. (EMERGENCY AID & HEALTH PROFESSION SCHOLARSHIPS)
245 FIFTH AVENUE; SUITE 1801
NEW YORK NY 10016
212/689-8270
AMOUNT: UP TO $300
DEADLINE(S): NONE
FIELD(S): ALL FIELDS OF STUDY
AMERICAN INDIAN OR ALASKAN NATIVE. PROOF OF TRIBAL AFFILIATION REQUIRED. EMERGENCY AID IS OFFERED ON FIRST COME FIRST SERVED BASIS WHEN FUNDS ARE AVAILABLE. STUDENTS SHOULD INQUIRE ONLY AFTER BEGINNING CLASSES.
WRITE FOR COMPLETE INFORMATION. ENCLOSE SELF-ADDRESSED STAMPED ENVELOPE.

1122

ASSOCIATION OF THE SONS OF POLAND (SCHOLARSHIP PROGRAM)
333 HACKENSACK ST
CARLSTADT NJ 07072
201/935-2807
AMOUNT: $1000 SCHOLARSHIP; $100 ACHIEVEMENT AWARD
DEADLINE(S): MAY 14
FIELD(S): ALL FIELDS OF STUDY
OPEN TO HIGH SCHOOL STUDENTS WHO HAVE BEEN MEMBERS OF THE ASSOCIATION OF THE SONS OF POLAND FOR AT LEAST 2 YEARS AND ARE INSURED BY THE ASSOCIATION. MUST BE ENTERING AN ACCREDITED COLLEGE IN SEPTEMBER OF THE YEAR OF HIGH SCHOOL GRADUATION.
USA CITIZEN. WRITE FOR COMPLETE INFORMATION.

1123

AUTOMOTIVE HALL OF FAME INC. (SCHOLARSHIP PROGRAM)
PO BOX 1727
MIDLAND MI 48641
517/631-5760
AMOUNT: $250 - $2000
DEADLINE(S): JUN 30
FIELD(S): ALL FIELDS OF STUDY
OPEN TO FULL TIME UNDERGRADUATE COLLEGE STUDENTS WHO HAVE A SINCERE INTEREST IN PURSUING AN AUTOMOTIVE CAREER UPON GRADUATION FROM COLLEGE. MUST BE AT LEAST A SOPHOMORE WHEN SCHOLARSHIP IS GRANTED BUT FRESHMEN MAY SEND IN APPLICATION.
16-24 AWARDS PER YEAR. RENEWABLE WITH REAPPLICATION. WRITE FOR COMPLETE INFORMATION.

1124

AUXILIARY TO SONS OF UNION VETERANS OF THE CIVIL WAR (SCHOLARSHIP)
616 W SUMMIT ST
ALLIANCE OH 44601
216/823-6919
AMOUNT: $350
DEADLINE(S): JAN 1
FIELD(S): HISTORY
OPEN TO DESCENDENTS OF VETERANS OF THE CIVIL WAR WHO ARE HIGH SCHOOL SENIORS OR 1ST YEAR COLLEGE STUDENTS. FOR THE STUDY OF HISTORY.
WRITE FOR COMPLETE INFORMATION.

1125

AYN RAND INSTITUTE (ANTHEM CONTEST)
PO BOX 6099; DEPT DB
INGLEWOOD CA 90312
310/306-9232; FAX 310/306-4925
AMOUNT: $1000 (FIRST PLACE); $200 (10 SECONDS); $100 (20 THIRDS)
DEADLINE(S): MAR 30
FIELD(S): ALL FIELDS OF STUDY
OPEN TO HIGH SCHOOL 9TH AND 10TH GRADERS. CASH AWARDS FOR ESSAYS ON AYN RAND'S NOVELETTE 'ANTHEM.' AWARDS ARE TO

ENCOURAGE ANALYTICAL THINKING AND WRITING EXCELLENCE AND INTRODUCE YOUNG PEOPLE TO THE NOVELETTE'S PHILOSOPHICAL MEANING.
WRITE FOR COMPLETE INFORMATION.

1126

AYN RAND INSTITUTE (FOUNTAINHEAD ESSAY CONTEST)
PO BOX 6004; DEPT DB
INGLEWOOD CA 90312
310/306-9232; FAX 310/306-4925
AMOUNT: $5000-FIRST PRIZE; $1000-SECOND PRIZE (5); $500-THIRD PRIZE (10)
DEADLINE(S): APR 15
FIELD(S): ALL FIELDS OF STUDY
ESSAY COMPETITION OPEN TO HIGH SCHOOL JUNIORS & SENIORS. CONTEST IS TO ENCOURAGE ANALYTICAL THINKING AND WRITING EXCELLENCE & TO INTRODUCE STUDENTS TO THE PHILOSOPHIC AND PSYCHOLOGICAL MEANING OF AYN RAND'S NOVEL 'THE FOUNTAINHEAD.'
16 AWARDS PER YEAR. WRITE FOR COMPLETE INFORMATION.

1127

BAKERY; CONFECTIONERY AND TOBACCO WORKERS INTERNATIONAL UNION (SCHOLARSHIP PROGRAM)
10401 CONNECTICUT AVE
KENSINGTON MD 20895
301/933-8600
AMOUNT: $1000 PER YEAR FOR A MAX OF 4 YEARS
DEADLINE(S): DEC 31
FIELD(S): ALL FIELDS OF STUDY
UNDERGRADUATE SCHOLARSHIPS ARE AWARDED EACH YEAR TO WINNERS OF A COMPETITION THAT IS OPEN TO MEMBERS AND CHILDREN OF MEMBERS OF BC&TWIU. APPLICANTS MUST BE HIGH SCHOOL STUDENTS ENTERING COLLEGE FOR THE FIRST TIME.
8 SCHOLARSHIPS PER YEAR. WRITE FOR COMPLETE INFORMATION.

1128

BALSO FOUNDATION (SCHOLARSHIPS)
493 WEST MAIN STREET
CHESHIRE CT 06410
203/272-5381
AMOUNT: VARIES
DEADLINE(S): APR 15
FIELD(S): ALL FIELDS OF STUDY
OPEN TO RESIDENTS OF CHESHIRE CT. SCHOLARSHIPS ARE FOR FULL-TIME UNDERGRADUATE STUDY & ARE AWARDED BASED ON ACADEMIC & FINANCIAL NEED. USA CITIZEN.
10 TO 15 AWARDS PER YEAR. RENEWABLE. WRITE FOR COMPLETE INFORMATION.

1129

BANK ONE OHIO TRUST CO. (FLORENCE B. STOUCH & CLYDE W. STOUCH FOUNDATION SCHOLARSHIP FUND)
PO BOX 1428; TRUST DEPT; 401 MARKET ST
STEUBENVILLE OH 43952
614/282-3665
AMOUNT: $750 - $1000
DEADLINE(S): NONE
FIELD(S): ALL FIELDS OF STUDY
OPEN TO RESIDENTS OF JEFFERSON COUNTY, OHIO WHO WILL ATTEND OHIO STATE UNIVERSITY AND YORK COUNTY, PENNSYLVANIA WHO WILL ATTEND THE UNIVERSITY OF PENNSYLVANIA. MUST NOT BE ANARCHIST OR FAVOR VIOLENT OVERTHROW OF U.S. GOVERNMENT.
MUST DEMONSTRATE FINANCIAL NEED. SCHOLARSHIPS AVAILABLE THROUGH STUDENT'S HIGH SCHOOL. RENEWABLE UP TO 8 YEARS. WRITE FOR COMPLETE INFORMATION.

1130

BAXTER FOUNDATION (SCHOLARSHIP PROGRAM FOR CHILDREN OF BAXTER INTERNATIONAL EMPLOYEES)
ONE BAXTER PARKWAY
DEERFIELD IL 60015
708/948-4604
AMOUNT: $1000
DEADLINE(S): MAR 1
FIELD(S): ALL AREAS OF STUDY
OPEN TO CHILDREN OF BAXTER INT'L EMPLOYEES WITH AT LEAST 3 YEARS SERVICE. APPLICANTS TO BE UNDER 23 & ENROLLED OR PLANNING TO ENROLL IN A FULL TIME UNDERGRADUATE PROGRAM AT ACCREDITED COLLEGE; UNIVERSITY OR VOCATIONAL / TECHNICAL SCHOOL.
RENEWABLE. 100 AWARDS ANNUALLY. WRITE FOR COMPLETE INFORMATION.

1131

BEATRICE AND FRANCIS THOMPSON SCHOLARSHIP FUND (SCHOLARSHIP)
MS. DIANE DUFFY; CO-TRUSTEE/SECRETARY; 417 SUMMIT AVENUE
ORADELL NJ 07649
WRITTEN INQUIRY ONLY
AMOUNT: $2000 TO $4000
DEADLINE(S): NOV 1 FOR SPRING SEMESTER; MAR 1 FOR FALL
FIELD(S): ALL AREAS OF STUDY
OPEN TO UNDERGRADUATE OR VOC/TECH STUDENTS WHOSE PARENTS ARE BOTH DEAD. APPLICANTS SHOULD HAVE A 2.5 OR BETTER GPA. FINANCIAL NEED IS A CONSIDERATION. RENEWABLE.
USA CITIZEN OR LEGAL RESIDENT. WRITE FOR COMPLETE INFORMATION.

1132

BELLARMINE COLLEGE (PHILIP MORRIS CAREER SCHOLARSHIP PROGRAM)
2001 NEWBURG ROAD
LOUISVILLE KY 40205
502/452-8131
AMOUNT: UP TO $1500
DEADLINE(S): MAY 15; JUL 15; DEC 15
FIELD(S): ALL AREAS OF STUDY
SCHOLARSHIPS OPEN TO STUDENTS (AGE 23 OR OLDER) WHO ARE ADMITTED TO BUT NOT CURRENTLY ATTENDING AN ACCREDITED LOUISVILLE AREA COLLEGE OR UNIVERSITY IN AN UNDERGRADUATE DEGREE PROGRAM.
180 SCHOLARSHIPS PER YEAR. RENEWABLE FOR 2 ADDITIONAL YEARS BASED UPON ACADEMIC ACHIEVEMENT. WRITE FOR COMPLETE INFORMATION.

1133

BEMENT EDUCATIONAL GRANTS COMMITTEE (DIOCESE OF WESTERN MASSACHUSETTS UNDERGRADUATE GRANTS)
37 CHESTNUT ST
SPRINGFIELD MA 01103
413/737-4786
AMOUNT: UP TO $750
DEADLINE(S): FEB 15
FIELD(S): ALL FIELDS OF STUDY
UNDERGRADUATE GRANTS FOR UNMARRIED STUDENTS WHO ARE ACTIVE EPISCOPALIANS IN THE DIOCESE OF WESTERN MASSACHUSETTS. HIGH GPA. FINANCIAL NEED. INTERVIEW REQUIRED AS ARRANGED.
60-70 AWARDS PER YEAR. RENEWABLE WITH REAPPLICATION. WRITE FOR COMPLETE INFORMATION.

1134

BERYL BUCK INSTITUTE FOR EDUCATION (SCHOLARSHIPS)
CAROL HORAN; 18 COMMERCIAL BLVD
NOVATO CA 94949
415/883-0122
AMOUNT: $500 - $2000
DEADLINE(S): MAR 31
FIELD(S): ALL FIELDS OF STUDY
OPEN TO MARIN COUNTY CALIF RESIDENTS WHO HAVE LIVED IN THE COUNTY SINCE SEP 1 OF THE YEAR PRIOR TO SUBMITTING AN APPLICATION. SCHOLARSHIPS TENABLE AT ACCREDITED COLLEGES & UNIVERSITIES AND VOCATIONAL OR TRADE PROGRAMS.
CONTACT HIGH SCHOOL OR COLLEGE COUNSELOR OR ADDRESS ABOVE FOR COMPLETE INFORMATION.

1135

BETA THETA PI GENERAL FRATERNITY (SCHOLARSHIPS & FELLOWSHIPS)
ADMINISTRATIVE OFFICE; 208 EAST HIGH ST
OXFORD OH 45056
513/523-7591
AMOUNT: $750 - $1500
DEADLINE(S): APR
FIELD(S): ALL FIELDS OF STUDY
OPEN TO UNDERGRADUATE AND GRADUATE STUDENTS WHO ARE BETA THETA PI MEMBERS IN GOOD STANDING AND HAVE A COMPETITIVE GRADE POINT AVERAGE.
30 SCHOLARSHIPS AND 8 FELLOWSHIPS PER YEAR; NON-RENEWABLE. WRITE FOR COMPLETE INFORMATION.

1136

BLINDED VETERANS ASSOCIATION (KATHERN F. GRUBER SCHOLARSHIP PROGRAM)
477 H STREET NW
WASHINGTON DC 20001-2694
202/371-8880
AMOUNT: $2000
DEADLINE(S): APR 15
FIELD(S): ALL AREAS OF STUDY

OPEN TO CHILDREN & SPOUSES OF BLINDED VETERANS. THE VET MUST BE LEGALLY BLIND; EITHER SERVICE OR NON-SERVICE CONNECTED. MUST BE ACCEPTED OR ALREADY ENROLLED FULL-TIME IN AN ACCREDITED UNDERGRAD OR GRAD PROGRAM AND USA CITIZEN.

12 AWARDS PER YEAR. WRITE FOR COMPLETE INFORMATION.

1137

BOCES GENESEO MIGRANT CENTER (G. & J. MATTERA NATIONAL SCHOLARSHIP FUND)
HOLCOMB BLDG; ROOM 210
GENESEO NY 14454
716/245-5681
AMOUNT: UP TO $250
DEADLINE(S): NONE
FIELD(S): ALL FIELDS OF STUDY
OPEN TO MIGRANT FARMWORKERS IN THE USA AND THEIR DEPENDENT CHILDREN. AWARDS USUALLY SUPPORT UNDERGRADUATE STUDY BUT SOME SUPPORT HIGH SCHOOL GRADUATION AND GRADUATE STUDY.

60 AWARDS PER YEAR. RENEWABLE. WRITE FOR COMPLETE INFORMATION.

1138

BOETTCHER FOUNDATION (SCHOLARSHIPS)
600 17TH ST; SUITE 2210 SOUTH
DENVER CO 80202
303/534-1938
AMOUNT: TUITION + $2300 STIPEND
DEADLINE(S): FEB 1
FIELD(S): ALL FIELDS OF STUDY
OPEN TO COLORADO RESIDENTS WHO ARE IN THE TOP 7% OF THEIR HIGH SCHOOL CLASS & HAVE BEEN ACCEPTED AS AN INCOMING FRESHMAN AT A COLLEGE OR UNIVERSITY IN THE STATE OF COLORADO. USA CITIZEN.

40 AWARDS PER YEAR. WRITE FOR COMPLETE INFORMATION OR CONSULT YOUR COLORADO HIGH SCHOOL COUNSELOR.

1139

BOYE SCHOLARSHIP FUND (SCHOLARSHIPS)
WELLS FARGO PRIVATE BANKING GROUP; PO BOX 2511
SACRAMENTO CA 95812
916/440-4433
AMOUNT: NOT SPECIFIED
DEADLINE(S): NONE GIVEN
FIELD(S): ALL AREAS OF STUDY
OPEN TO RESIDENTS OF SACRAMENTO COUNTY (CA) WHO GRADUATED FROM A HIGH SCHOOL IN THE SACRAMENTO CITY SCHOOL DISTRICT.
WRITE FOR COMPLETE INFORMATION.

1140

BRANCH-WILBUR FUND INC. (GRANTS)
1600 EAST AVENUE
ROCHESTER NY 14610
WRITTEN INQUIRY
AMOUNT: $500 - $5000
DEADLINE(S): DEC
FIELD(S): ALL AREAS OF STUDY
OPEN TO FOREIGN STUDENTS RESIDING OR STUDYING IN THE ROCHESTER NEW YORK AREA. GRANTS AWARDED BASED ON NEED AND USUALLY LAST UNTIL A DEGREE (AA, AS, BA OR BS) IS OBTAINED.

EIGHT AWARDS PER YEAR. WRITE FOR COMPLETE INFORMATION.

1141

BRIDGESTONE/FIRESTONE INC. (SCHOLARSHIP PROGRAM FOR SONS AND DAUGHTERS OF EMPLOYEES)
1200 FIRESTONE PARKWAY
AKRON OH 44317
216/379-6802
AMOUNT: $2000
DEADLINE(S): FEB 1
FIELD(S): ALL FIELDS OF STUDY
OPEN TO SONS OR DAUGHTERS OF BRIDGESTONE/FIRESTONE EMPLOYEES WHO HAVE AT LEAST ONE YEAR OF SERVICE; RETIRED OR FULL TIME WORKERS. MUST BE USA CITIZEN.

NOT RENEWABLE. WRITE FOR COMPLETE INFORMATION.

1142

BRITISH AMERICAN EDUCATIONAL FOUNDATION (SCHOLARS' PROGRAM)
135 EAST 65TH ST
NEW YORK NY 10021
212/772-3890
AMOUNT: UP TO $17000
DEADLINE(S): MAY 1
FIELD(S): ALL FIELDS OF STUDY
OPEN TO AMERICAN HIGH SCHOOL SENIORS WHO ARE 18 OR YOUNGER AND WANT TO SPEND A YEAR AT AN INDEPENDENT

BOARDING SCHOOL IN THE UNITED KINGDOM PRIOR TO ENTERING COLLEGE. FINANCIAL AID FORM IS USED TO EVALUATE FINANCIAL NEED.
WRITE FOR COMPLETE INFORMATION.

1143

BRUNSWICK FOUNDATION (SCHOLARSHIPS)
ONE BRUNSWICK PLAZA
SKOKIE IL 60077
708/470-4646
AMOUNT: $1000 PER SEMESTER
DEADLINE(S): MAY 1
FIELD(S): ALL AREAS OF STUDY
OPEN ONLY TO SONS AND DAUGHTERS OF FULL-TIME BRUNSWICK EMPLOYEES—HIGH SCHOOL SENIOR SCHOLARSHIP & COLLEGE UNDERGRADUATE SCHOLARSHIP. FOR UNDERGRADUATE STUDY ONLY.
45 AWARDS PER YEAR. FOR FULL-TIME STUDY ONLY. PARENTS SHOULD CONTACT THEIR BRUNSWICK PERSONNEL OFFICE FOR COMPLETE INFORMATION.

1144

BUCKNELL UNIVERSITY (GERTRUDE J. DEPPEN & VORIS AUTEN TEETOTALING NON-ATHLETE SCHOLARSHIP FUND)
FINANCIAL AID OFFICE
LEWISBURG PA 17837
717/524-1331
AMOUNT: VARIES
DEADLINE(S): NONE
FIELD(S): ALL AREAS OF STUDY
OPEN TO STUDENTS WHO HAVE LIVED IN MOUNT CARMEL, PA FOR LAST 10 YEARS; GRADUATED FROM MT CARMEL HIGH SCHOOL & DO NOT USE ALCOHOL; TOBACCO; NARCOTICS OR ENGAGE IN STRENUOUS ATHLETIC CONTESTS.
AWARD TENABLE AT BUCKNELL UNIVERSITY.

1145

BUFFALO FOUNDATION (SCHOLARSHIPS)
237 MAIN ST
BUFFALO NY 14203
716/852-2857
AMOUNT: VARIES
DEADLINE(S): MAY 10
FIELD(S): ALL FIELDS OF STUDY
SCHOLARSHIPS OPEN TO RESIDENTS OF ERIE COUNTY, NY. AWARDS ARE LIMITED TO ONE MEMBER PER FAMILY PER YEAR & ARE TENABLE AT RECOGNIZED UNDERGRADUATE COLLEGES & UNIVERSITIES.
APPROX 400 AWARDS PER YEAR. WRITE FOR COMPLETE INFORMATION.

1146

BUSINESS AND PROFESSIONAL WOMEN'S FOUNDATION (AVON PRODUCTS FOUNDATION SCHOLARSHIP)
2012 MASSACHUSETTS AVE NW
WASHINGTON DC 20036
202/293-1200
AMOUNT: $1000
DEADLINE(S): APR 15 POSTMARK (APPS AVAILABLE OCT 1-APR 1 ONLY)
FIELD(S): ALL FIELDS OF STUDY
OPEN TO WOMEN OVER 25 OR OLDER ACCEPTED INTO AN ACCREDITED PROGRAM AT A USA, PUERTO RICO OR VIRGIN ISLAND INSTITUTION WHO ARE WITHIN 12-24 MONTHS OF GRADUATION. MUST BE IN BUSINESS RELATED FIELD; SHOW FINANCIAL NEED & BE A USA CITIZEN.
FOR UNDERGRAD OR GRAD STUDY EXCEPT AT DOCTORATE LEVEL. SEND STAMPED ($.52) SELF-ADDRESSED #10 ENVELOPE FOR APPLICATION AND COMPLETE INFORMATION. FOR FULL OR PART TIME STUDY. WRITE FOR COMPLETE INFORMATION.

1147

BUTLER MANUFACTURING COMPANY FOUNDATION (SCHOLARSHIP PROGRAM)
BMA TOWER; PO BOX 419917; PENN VALLEY PARK
KANSAS CITY MO 64141
816/968-3208
AMOUNT: $2000 PER YEAR
DEADLINE(S): NONE
FIELD(S): ALL AREAS OF STUDY
OPEN TO CHILDREN OF BUTLER EMPLOYEES WHO HAVE BEEN EMPLOYED FOR ONE YEAR OR MORE & CURRENTLY EMPLOYED FULL-TIME. SCHOLARSHIPS TO BE USED FOR UNDERGRADUATE STUDY ONLY. USA CITIZEN.
8 SCHOLARSHIPS PER YEAR. RENEWABLE FOR 4 YEARS. WRITE FOR COMPLETE INFORMATION.

1148

C. BASCOM SLEMP FOUNDATION (SCHOLARSHIPS)
STAR BANK NA; PO BOX 5208
CINCINNATI OH 45201
513/632-4579

AMOUNT: $2000
DEADLINE(S): OCT 1
FIELD(S): ALL FIELDS OF STUDY
OPEN ONLY TO RESIDENTS OF LEE OR WISE COUNTIES IN VIRGINIA. FOR UNDERGRADUATE STUDY.
30 AWARDS PER YEAR. WRITE FOR COMPLETE INFORMATION.

1149
C.G. FULLER FOUNDATION (SCHOLARSHIPS)
C/0 NCNB NATIONAL BANK OF SC; BOX 2307
COLUMBIA SC 29202
803/758-2317
AMOUNT: $2000
DEADLINE(S): FEB 15
FIELD(S): ALL AREAS OF STUDY
OPEN TO SOUTH CAROLINA RESIDENTS ATTENDING ACCREDITED UNDERGRADUATE COLLEGES & UNIVERSITIES IN SOUTH CAROLINA. AT LEAST 3.0 GPA ON 4.0 SCALE. USA CITIZEN.
APPROX 10 AWARDS PER YEAR. WRITE FOR COMPLETE INFORMATION.

1150
CALIFORNIA DEPARTMENT OF VETERANS AFFAIRS (CALIFORNIA VETERANS DEPENDENTS EDUCATIONAL ACT)
PO BOX 942895
SACRAMENTO CA 94295
916/653-2573
AMOUNT: CAL STATE UNIVERSITY TUITION & FEE WAIVER
DEADLINE(S): VARIES
FIELD(S): ALL FIELDS OF STUDY
OPEN TO SPOUSES & DEPENDENT CHILDREN OF VETERANS WHO (AS A RESULT OF MILITARY SERVICE) WERE DISABLED; KILLED IN ACTION; POW OR MIA OR WHOSE DEATH WAS SERVICE RELATED. AWARDS ARE FOR UNDERGRAD STUDY AT CALIFORNIA PUBLIC COLLEGES.
APPLICANT'S ANNUAL INCOME CANNOT EXCEED $5000 PER YEAR (INCLUDING SUPPORT FROM PARENTS.) 2000 AWARDS PER YEAR. WRITE FOR COMPLETE INFORMATION.

1151
CALIFORNIA DEPT. OF VOCATIONAL REHABILITATION (TUITION ASSISTANCE PROGRAM)
CONTACT YOUR LOCAL
DEPT. OF REHABILITATION OFFICE
DO NOT TELEPHONE
AMOUNT: TUITION ASSISTANCE
DEADLINE(S): NONE
FIELD(S): ALL AREAS OF STUDY LEADING TO GAINFUL EMPLOYMENT
TUITION ASSISTANCE PROGRAM FOR CALIF RESIDENTS WHO HAVE BEEN STRUCK WITH A DISEASE OR DISABILITY AND NOW NEED RETRAINING OR EDUCATION FOR A NEW CAREER. ONLY PROGRAMS LEADING TO A RECOGNIZABLE AND EMPLOYABLE SKILL WILL BE FUNDED.
CONTACT YOUR NEAREST CALIF DEPT OF REHABILITATION OFFICE. ONLY PROGRAMS RESULTING IN MARKETABLE SKILLS THAT LEAD TO EMPLOYMENT WILL BE CONSIDERED.

1152
CALIFORNIA GOVERNOR'S COMMITTEE FOR EMPLOYMENT OF DISABLED PERSONS (HAL CONNOLLY SCHOLAR-ATHLETE AWARD)
C/O EDD/MIC 41; PO BOX 826880
SACRAMENTO CA 94280
916/323-2545
AMOUNT: $1000 1ST; $500 2ND; $250 3RD
DEADLINE(S): MAR 1
FIELD(S): ALL FIELDS OF STUDY
MUST HAVE COMPETED DURING HIGH SCHOOL IN VARSITY LEVEL OR EQUIVALENT ATHLETICS AND HAVE A DISABILITY. ACADEMIC AND ATHLETIC HISTORIES MUST DEMONSTRATE THE QUALITIES OF LEADERSHIP AND ACCOMPLISHMENT. AGE 19 OR UNDER.
PRIMARY CONSIDERATION WILL BE GIVEN TO APPLICANTS WHOSE NOMINATION MATERIALS DOCUMENT SCHOLASTIC APTITUDE AND EXEMPLARY PERSONAL ACHIEVEMENT.

1153
CALIFORNIA MASONIC FOUNDATION (GENERAL FUND & AMARANTH FUND SCHOLARSHIP PROGRAMS)
1111 CALIFORNIA ST
SAN FRANCISCO CA 94108
415/776-7000
AMOUNT: $750 - $1000
DEADLINE(S): MAY 15
FIELD(S): ALL AREAS OF STUDY
UNDERGRADUATE SCHOLARSHIPS OPEN TO ANY CALIFORNIA RESIDENT WHO IS ACCEPTED TO

OR ENROLLED IN AN ACCREDITED COLLEGE OR TECHNICAL SCHOOL IN THE USA. NO RELIGIOUS OR MEMBERSHIP REQUIREMENTS. USA CITIZEN.

AMARANTH FUND LIMITED TO FEMALE CALIFORNIA RESIDENTS UNDER AGE 21. AWARDS RENEWABLE. APPLICATIONS ACCEPTED BETWEEN FEB 2 AND MAY 15. APPLICANTS MAY ATTEND SCHOOLS OUTSIDE OF CALIFORNIA. WRITE FOR COMPLETE INFORMATION.

1154 ___

CALIFORNIA STUDENT AID COMMISSION (CAL GRANT 'A' PROGRAM)

PO BOX 510624
SACRAMENTO CA 94245
916/445-0880

AMOUNT: $768 - $1746 (STATE SCHOOLS); $594 - $4452 (INDEPENDENT SCHOOLS)

DEADLINE(S): MAR 2

FIELD(S): ALL FIELDS OF STUDY

CALIFORNIA RESIDENT. OPEN TO LOW & MIDDLE-INCOME UNDERGRADUATE STUDENTS ATTENDING ELIGIBLE SCHOOLS IN CALIF. GRANTS SUPPORT TUITION & FEE COSTS. SELECTION BASED ON NEED & GRADES. USA CITIZEN; LEGAL RESIDENT OR ELIGIBLE NON-CITIZEN.

APPROX 17400 GRANTS PER YEAR. RENEWABLE. CONTACT YOUR COUNSELOR; FINANCIAL AID OFFICE OR ADDRESS ABOVE FOR COMPLETE INFORMATION.

1155 ___

CALIFORNIA STUDENT AID COMMISSION (CAL GRANT 'B' PROGRAM)

PO BOX 510624
SACRAMENTO CA 94245
916/445-0880

AMOUNT: $594 - $1196 (LIVING ALLOWANCE); $786 (AVG. STATE SCHOOL TUITION); $4452 (AVG. INDEPENDENT SCHOOL TUITION)

DEADLINE(S): MAR 2

FIELD(S): ALL FIELDS OF STUDY

CALIF RESIDENT. OPEN TO VERY LOW INCOME UNDERGRADUATE STUDENTS WITH HIGH POTENTIAL ATTENDING ELIGIBLE 2 & 4 YEAR COLLEGES IN CALIF. GRANTS SUPPORT LIVING ALLOWANCE & TUITION/FEE COSTS. USA CITIZEN; LEGAL RESIDENT OR ELIGIBLE NON-CITIZEN.

APPROX 12250 GRANTS PER YEAR. RENEWABLE. CONTACT YOUR COUNSELOR; FINANCIAL AID OFFICE OR ADDRESS ABOVE FOR COMPLETE INFORMATION.

1156 ___

CALIFORNIA STUDENT AID COMMISSION (LAW ENFORCEMENT PERSONNEL DEPENDENTS GRANT PROGRAM)

PO BOX 510624
SACRAMENTO CA 94245
916/322-2294

AMOUNT: UP TO $1500 PER YEAR

DEADLINE(S): NONE

FIELD(S): ALL FIELDS OF STUDY

OPEN TO THE NATURAL OR ADOPTED CHILD OF A CALIF LAW ENFORCEMENT OFFICER KILLED OR TOTALLY DISABLED IN THE PERFORMANCE OF HIS/HER DUTY. FOR UNDERGRAD OR GRAD STUDY AT ELIGIBLE CALIFORNIA SCHOOLS. MUST BE CALIFORNIA RESIDENT AND USA CITIZEN.

AWARDS LIMITED TO A MAXIMUM OF $6000 OVER SIX YEARS. MAY BE USED FOR TUITION; FEES; BOOKS; SUPPLIES; LIVING EXPENSES. WRITE FOR COMPLETE INFORMATION.

1157 ___

CALIFORNIA STATE PTA (STUDENT LOAN PROGRAM)

930 GEORGIA ST; PO BOX 15015
LOS ANGELES CA 90015
213/620-1100

AMOUNT: $700 PER YEAR LOWER DIVISION; $900 UPPER DIVISION; $1100 GRADUATE

DEADLINE(S): MAY 15; NOV 15

FIELD(S): ALL FIELDS OF STUDY

LOANS AT 6% INTEREST OPEN TO FULL TIME STUDENTS WHO ARE CALIFORNIA RESIDENTS AND USA CITIZENS ATTENDING OR ACCEPTED BY AN ACCREDITED CALIFORNIA COLLEGE; UNIVERSITY; COMMUNITY COLLEGE OR TRADE OR TECHNICAL SCHOOL.

APPLICANTS MUST DEMONSTRATE FINANCIAL NEED AND RESPONSIBILITY. A CO-MAKER IS REQUIRED. PAYMENT OF INTEREST ONLY IS REQUIRED TWICE EACH YEAR WHILE ENROLLED FULL TIME. WRITE FOR COMPLETE INFORMATION.

1158

CALIFORNIA TEACHERS ASSN. (CTA SCHOLARSHIPS)
PO BOX 921; 1705 MURCHISON DRIVE
BURLINGAME CA 94011
415/697-1400
AMOUNT: $2000
DEADLINE(S): FEB 15
FIELD(S): ALL AREAS OF STUDY
OPEN TO ACTIVE CTA MEMBERS OR THEIR DEPENDENT CHILDREN FOR UNDERGRADUATE OR GRADUATE STUDY. APPLICATIONS AVAILABLE IN OCTOBER OF EACH YEAR FROM CTA HUMAN RIGHTS DEPARTMENT AT ADDRESS ABOVE.
TWENTY SCHOLARSHIPS PER YEAR. WRITE FOR COMPLETE INFORMATION.

1159

CALIFORNIA YOUNG WOMAN OF THE YEAR INC. (SCHOLARSHIPS)
PO BOX 1863
SANTA ROSA CA 95402
707/576-7505
AMOUNT: $10000
DEADLINE(S): MAR 1
FIELD(S): ALL FIELDS OF STUDY
COMPETITION OPEN TO GIRLS IN THEIR JUNIOR YEAR OF HIGH SCHOOL WHO ARE USA CITIZENS AND CALIFORNIA RESIDENTS. WINNER RECEIVES $10000 COLLEGE SCHOLARSHIP; RUNNERS UP SHARE UP TO $30000 IN AWARDS. FOR UNDERGRADUATE OR GRADUATE STUDY.
AWARD CAN BE USED FOR BOOKS; FEES & TUITION AT ANY COLLEGE IN THE WORLD. WRITE TO C. (TING) GUGGIANA; ADDRESS ABOVE; FOR COMPLETE INFORMATION.

1160

CAMP FOUNDATION (SCHOLARSHIP GRANTS)
PO BOX 813
FRANKLIN VA 23851
804-562-3439
AMOUNT: NOT SPECIFIED
DEADLINE(S): NONE GIVEN
FIELD(S): ALL FIELDS OF STUDY
OPEN TO GRADUATING HIGH SCHOOL SENIORS IN THE CITY OF FRANKLIN AND THE COUNTIES OF ISLE OF WIGHT AND SOUTHAMPTON, VA OR TO RESIDENTS OF THESE AREAS WHO GRADUATED FROM HIGH SCHOOL ELSEWHERE. FOR UNDERGRADUATE STUDY.
THESE AWARDS ARE MADE LOCALLY NOT ON A NATIONWIDE BASIS. ONLY THOSE WHO MEET RESIDENCY REQUIREMENTS SHOULD WRITE FOR COMPLETE INFORMATION.

1161

CAPITAL CITIES/ABC INC. (MERIT SCHOLARSHIP PROGRAM)
HUMAN RESOURCES; 77 W 66TH ST
NEW YORK NY 10023
212/456-7777
AMOUNT: $500 - $2000 PER YEAR
DEADLINE(S): OCT
FIELD(S): ALL AREAS OF STUDY
OPEN TO DEPENDENT CHILDREN OF CAPITAL CITIES/ABC EMPLOYEES FOR 1 YEAR OR MORE. STUDENTS MUST TAKE THE PRELIMINARY SCHOLARSHIP APTITUDE TEST/NATIONAL MERIT SCHOLARSHIP QUALIFYING TEST (PSAT/NMSQT) IN OCT OF THEIR HIGH SCHOOL JUNIOR YEAR.
AWARDS RENEWABLE FOR UP TO 4 YEARS. SELECTION OF RECIPIENTS IS DETERMINED BY THE NATIONAL MERIT SCHOLARSHIP CORP; 1 AMERICAN PLAZA; EVANSTON IL 60201. CONTACT THEM OR YOUR H.S. COUNSELOR FOR FURTHER INFORMATION.

1162

CENTRAL SCHOLARSHIP BUREAU (INTEREST-FREE LOANS)
4001 CLARKS LANE
BALTIMORE MD 21215
410/358-8668
AMOUNT: $500 - $8000 (MAX THRU GRAD SCHOOL)
DEADLINE(S): JUN 1; DEC 1
FIELD(S): ALL FIELDS OF STUDY
INTEREST-FREE LOANS FOR RESIDENTS OF METROPOLITAN BALTIMORE AREA WHO HAVE EXHAUSTED ALL OTHER AVAILABLE AVENUES OF FUNDING. AID IS OFFERED FOR STUDY AT ANY ACCREDITED UNDERGRAD OR GRADUATE INSTITUTION.
AWARDS ARE MADE ON A NON-COMPETITIVE BASIS TO ANYONE WITH A SOUND EDUCATIONAL PLAN. 100 LOANS PER YEAR. MUST APPLY FIRST THROUGH GOVERNMENT AND SCHOOL. WRITE FOR COMPLETE INFORMATION.

1163

CHARLES B. KEESEE EDUCATIONAL FUND INC. (SCHOLARSHIPS)
PO BOX 431
MARTINSVILLE VA 24114
703/632-2229
AMOUNT: VARIES
DEADLINE(S): MAR 1
FIELD(S): ALL FIELDS OF STUDY
OPEN TO ELIGIBLE RESIDENTS OF VIRGINIA & NORTH CAROLINA WHO ATTEND SCHOOL OR COLLEGE IN VIRGINIA THAT IS AFFILIATED WITH VIRGINIA BAPTIST GENERAL ASSOCIATION OR A SEMINARY OF SOUTHERN BAPTIST CONVENTION. USA CITIZEN.
750 AWARDS PER YEAR. WRITE FOR COMPLETE INFORMATION.

1164

CHARLES H. HOOD FUND (H.P. HOOD INC. SCHOLARSHIPS)
500 RUTHERFORD AVE.
BOSTON MA 02129
617/242-0600
AMOUNT: $4000 PER YEAR
DEADLINE(S): JAN 15
FIELD(S): ALL FIELDS OF STUDY
OPEN ONLY TO SONS AND DAUGHTERS OF EMPLOYEES OF H.P. HOOD INC. ONE PROGRAM IS FOR HIGH SCHOOL SENIORS AND ONE IS FOR COLLEGE UPPER CLASSMEN.
THREE TO FOUR AWARDS PER PROGRAM PER YEAR. WRITE FOR COMPLETE INFORMATION.

1165

CHATHAM COLLEGE (DIVISIONAL & HONORS SCHOLARSHIP PROGRAM)
WOODLAND ROAD; OFFICE OF ADMISSIONS
PITTSBURGH PA 15232
412/365-1290
AMOUNT: UP TO $10000 PER YEAR
DEADLINE(S): FEB 1
FIELD(S): ALL FIELDS OF STUDY
WOMEN ONLY. AWARDS OPEN TO ENTERING FRESHMEN ACCEPTED AT CHATHAM COLLEGE. SELECTION BASED ON HIGH SCHOOL RECORD; SAT-ACT SCORES; TEACHER/COUNSELOR RECOMMENDATIONS; INTERVIEW; EXTRACURRICULAR ACTIVITIES & ESSAY.
APPROXIMATELY 50 AWARDS PER YEAR RENEWABLE FOR UP TO 4 YEARS. WRITE FOR COMPLETE INFORMATION.

1166

CHAUTAUQUA REGION COMMUNITY FOUNDATION INC. (SCHOLARSHIP GRANTS)
104 HOTEL JAMESTOWN BLDG
JAMESTOWN NY 14701
716/661-3390
AMOUNT: VARIES
DEADLINE(S): APR 8
FIELD(S): ALL FIELDS OF STUDY
SCHOLARSHIPS ARE OPEN TO STUDENTS WHO LIVE IN THE VICINITY OF JAMESTOWN, NY WITH PREFERENCE TO STUDENTS IN 12 SCHOOL DISTRICTS IN SOUTHERN CHAUTAUQUA COUNTY. FOR FULL TIME STUDY.
WRITE FOR COMPLETE INFORMATION.

1167

CHEROKEE NATION (HIGHER EDUCATION NEED BASED GRANT PROGRAM)
PO BOX 948
TAHLEQUAH OK 74465
918/456-0671
AMOUNT: VARIES
DEADLINE(S): APR 1
FIELD(S): ALL AREAS OF STUDY
GRANTS AVAILABLE TO MEMBERS OF THE CHEROKEE NATION OF OKLAHOMA. AWARDS ARE TENABLE AT ACCREDITED UNDERGRADUATE 2-YEAR & 4-YEAR COLLEGES & UNIVERSITIES IN THE USA. USA CITIZEN. STUDENTS MUST BE ELIGIBLE FOR PELL GRANTS.
500 AWARDS PER YEAR. WRITE FOR COMPLETE INFORMATION.

1168

CHINESE CHRISTIAN HERALD CRUSADES (CHINESE COLLEGIATE MERIT SCHOLARSHIP FOR NEW YORK SCHOOLS)
DR. K.C. TAM; 136 HENRY ST
NEW YORK NY 10002
212/227-8181
AMOUNT: $500 TO $1500
DEADLINE(S): NONE SPECIFIED
FIELD(S): ALL FIELDS OF STUDY
OPEN TO CHINESE STUDENTS WHO ARE NOT USA CITIZENS AND WHO ARE ATTENDING A

SCHOOL WITHIN A 50 MILE RADIUS OF NEW YORK CITY.
TWO UNDERGRADUATE AND TWO GRADUATE AWARDS EACH YEAR. WRITE FOR COMPLETE INFORMATION.

1169

CHINESE PROFESSIONAL CLUB OF HOUSTON (SCHOLARSHIP PROGRAM)
11302 FALLBROOK DR; SUITE 304
HOUSTON TX 77065
713/955-0115
AMOUNT: $600 - $1500
DEADLINE(S): NOV 15
FIELD(S): ALL AREAS OF STUDY
OPEN TO HIGH SCHOOL SENIORS OF CHINESE DESCENT WHO RESIDE IN THE GREATER HOUSTON METROPOLITAN AREA. FOR STUDY AT AN ACCREDITED COLLEGE OR UNIVERSITY IN THE USA.
10 SCHOLARSHIPS PER YEAR; NOT RENEWABLE. WRITE FOR COMPLETE INFORMATION.

1170

CHRISTIAN RECORD SERVICES INC. (SCHOLARSHIPS)
4444 SOUTH 52ND STREET
LINCOLN NE 68516
402/488-0981
AMOUNT: $500 - $1000
DEADLINE(S): APR 1
FIELD(S): ALL FIELDS OF STUDY
UNDERGRADUATE SCHOLARSHIPS AVAILABLE TO LEGALLY BLIND STUDENTS WHO ARE ATTENDING SCHOOL IN THE USA. MUST DEMONSTRATE FINANCIAL NEED AND BE A USA CITIZEN.
10-15 AWARDS PER YEAR. WRITE FOR COMPLETE INFORMATION.

1171

CHRYSLER CORPORATION FUND (SCHOLARSHIP PROGRAM)
CITIZENS SCHOLARSHIP FOUNDATION OF AMERICA; PO BOX 297
ST PETER MN 56082
507/931-1682
AMOUNT: $500 - $3000 PER YEAR
DEADLINE(S): MAR 15
FIELD(S): ALL AREAS OF STUDY
OPEN TO CHILDREN OF REGULAR FULL TIME EMPLOYEES OF CHRYSLER CORP AND ITS USA BASED SUBSIDIARIES. FOR STUDY AT A 4-YEAR COLLEGE OR UNIVERSITY; VOC/TECH SCHOOL; NURSING SCHOOL OR SECRETARIAL/BUSINESS SCHOOL. MUST DEMONSTRATE FINANCIAL NEED.
FOR STUDENTS 21 OR UNDER WHO ARE NOT IN THEIR FINAL YEAR OF STUDIES. RENEWABLE FOR UP TO 4 YEARS. WRITE FOR COMPLETE INFORMATION.

1172

CHRYSLER CORPORATION FUND (THE LEE IACOCCA SCHOLARS PROGRAM)
CITIZENS' SCHOLARSHIP FOUNDATION OF AMERICA; PO BOX 297
ST PETER MN 56082
507/931-1682
AMOUNT: $2000 - $5000
DEADLINE(S): MAR 15 OF SENIOR YEAR IN HIGH SCHOOL
FIELD(S): ALL AREAS OF STUDY
OPEN TO CHILDREN OF REGULAR; FULL TIME CHRYSLER CORP EMPLOYEES AND ITS USA BASED SUBSIDIARIES. APPLICATION CAN BE MADE ONLY DURING SENIOR YEAR OF HIGH SCHOOL. FOR UNDERGRADUATE STUDY AT AN ACCREDITED FOUR YEAR COLLEGE OR UNIVERSITY.
AWARD IS TO RECOGNIZE AND REWARD EXCEPTIONAL HIGH SCHOOL ACHIEVEMENT. MUST DEMONSTRATE FINANCIAL NEED. WRITE FOR COMPLETE INFORMATION.

1173

CITIBANK EMPLOYEES FOUNDATION (CITICORP SCHOLARSHIP PROGRAM)
C/O EDUCATIONAL TESTING SERVICE; PO BOX 6730
PRINCETON NJ 08541
609-921-9000
AMOUNT: $2500 - $3000 (4 YR COLLEGE); $750 - $1500 (VOC TECH SCHOOL)
DEADLINE(S): NOV 30
FIELD(S): ALL AREAS OF STUDY
OPEN ONLY TO HIGH SCHOOL SENIORS WHO ARE DEPENDENTS OF CITICORP EMPLOYEES. WINNERS ARE CHOSEN BASED ON THEIR SAT SCORES & RANK IN CLASS. THE SIZE OF THE AWARD WILL VARY ACCORDING TO FINANCIAL NEED.
MUST SUBMIT FAF FORM TO SHOW FINANCIAL NEED. WRITE FOR COMPLETE INFORMATION.

1174

CLARA ABBOTT FOUNDATION (AWARD PROGRAM)
EXECUTIVE DIRECTOR
ABBOT PARK IL 60064
708/937-3377
AMOUNT: UP TO $1800
DEADLINE(S): JAN - MAR
FIELD(S): ALL FIELDS OF STUDY
AWARDS ARE AVAILABLE TO SONS AND DAUGHTERS (AGED 17-29) OF ABBOTT LABORATORIES EMPLOYEES FOR UNDERGRADUATE STUDY.
WRITE FOR COMPLETE INFORMATION.

1175

CLARK FOUNDATION (SCHOLARSHIP PROGRAM)
PO BOX 427
COOPERSTOWN NY 13326
607/547-9927
AMOUNT: $500 - $5000
DEADLINE(S): NONE
FIELD(S): ALL AREAS OF STUDY
OPEN TO GRADUATES OF HIGH SCHOOLS IN THE FOLLOWING DISTRICTS - CHERRY VALLEY; COOPERSTOWN; EDMESTON; LAURENS; MILFORD; RICHFIELD SPRINGS; SCENEVUS; SPRINGFIELD; VAN HORNSVILLE; WEST WINFIELD; WORCESTER. 700 SCHOLARSHIPS PER YEAR. RENEWABLE
MUST HAVE HIGH SCHOOL DIPLOMA; RANK IN THE UPPER ONE-THIRD OF GRADUATING CLASS AND HAVE A 3.0 OR BETTER GPA.

1176

CLYDE L. AND MARY C. SCHAULL (EDUCATIONAL TRUST FUND)
1519 FISHER ROAD
MECHANICSBURG PA 17055
717/691-4097
AMOUNT: $200 - $1400 ANNUALLY
DEADLINE(S): APR 25
FIELD(S): ALL AREAS OF STUDY
OPEN ONLY TO GRADUATES OF MECHANICSBURG (PA) HIGH SCHOOL. FOR UNDERGRADUATE STUDY. MUST DEMONSTRATE FINANCIAL NEED.
WRITE FOR COMPLETE INFORMATION.

1177

COCA-COLA SCHOLARS FOUNDATION (SCHOLARSHIPS)
ONE BUCKHEAD PLAZA #1000; 3060 PEACHTREE RD NW
ATLANTA GA 30305
404/237-1300
AMOUNT: $5000; $1000 PER YEAR
DEADLINE(S): OCT 31 OF H.S. SENIOR YEAR
FIELD(S): ALL FIELDS OF STUDY
OPEN TO HIGH SCHOOL SENIORS IN PARTICIPATING USA COCA-COLA BOTTLERS TERRITORIES (CURRENTLY 90%+ ARE PARTICIPATING) WHO ARE PLANNING TO PURSUE A POST-SECONDARY DEGREE AT AN ACCREDITED COLLEGE OR UNIVERSITY IN THE USA.
MAJOR SELECTION CRITERIA ARE LEADERSHIP; CHARACTER AND ACHIEVEMENT. 50 4-YEAR $20000 SCHOLARSHIPS & 100 4-YEAR $4000 SCHOLARSHIPS. CONTACT SCHOOL GUIDANCE COUNSELER OR WRITE TO ADDRESS ABOVE FOR COMPLETE INFORMATION.

1178

COLLEGE FOUNDATION INC. (FEDERAL PLUS LOANS UNDER NC INSURED STUDENT LOAN PROGRAM)
2100 YONKERS RD; PO BOX 12100
RALEIGH NC 27605
919/821-4771
AMOUNT: DIFFERENCE BETWEEN COST OF ATTENDING AND OTHER FINANCIAL AID RECEIVED
DEADLINE(S): VARIES
FIELD(S): ALL FIELDS OF STUDY
FOR PARENT OF STUDENT WHO IS DEPENDENT (BY FEDERAL DEFINITION) AND ENROLLED IN ELIGIBLE USA COLLEGE. IF THE STUDENT IS AT A COLLEGE NOT IN NC BORROWER MUST BE LEGAL NC RESIDENT. MUST MEET NATION-WIDE FEDERAL PLUS LOANS REQUIREMENTS.
APPROXIMATELY 2600 LOANS PER YEAR. MUST REAPPLY EACH YEAR. WRITE FOR COMPLETE INFORMATION.

1179

COLLEGE FOUNDATION INC. (FEDERAL SUPPLEMENTAL LOANS FOR STUDENTS UNDER THE NC INSURED STUDENT LOAN PROGRAM)
2100 YONKERS RD; PO BOX 12100
RALEIGH NC 27605
919/821-4771

AMOUNT: $4000 - $5000 PER YEAR UNDERGRADS; UP TO $10000 PER YEAR GRADS
DEADLINE(S): VARIES
FIELD(S): ALL AREAS OF STUDY
FOR LEGAL RESIDENTS OF NC ENROLLED IN ELIGIBLE COLLEGES IN OR OUT OF STATE OR FOR OUT-OF-STATE STUDENTS ATTENDING ELIGIBLE COLLEGES IN NC MUST MEET ELIGIBILITY REQUIREMENTS OF THE NATIONWIDE FEDERAL SUPPLEMENTAL LOANS FOR STUDENTS.
APPROXIMATELY 3500 LOANS PER YEAR. MUST REAPPLY ANNUALLY. WRITE FOR COMPLETE INFORMATION.

1180

COLLEGE FOUNDATION INC. (NORTH CAROLINA INSURED STUDENT LOAN PROGRAM - STAFFORD LOANS)
PO BOX 12100; 2100 YONKERS ROAD
RALEIGH NC 27605
919/821-4771
AMOUNT: MAX OF $2625; $4000 OR $7500 PER YEAR DEPENDING ON LEVEL OF STUDY
DEADLINE(S): VARIES
FIELD(S): ALL FIELDS OF STUDY
OPEN TO LEGAL RESIDENTS OF NC ENROLLED IN AN ELIGIBLE IN-STATE OR OUT-OF-STATE COLLEGE OR AN OUT-OF-STATE STUDENT ATTENDING AN ELIGIBLE NC COLLEGE. MUST MEET NATIONWIDE ELIGIBILITY REQUIREMENTS OF STAFFORD LOANS.
APPROXIMATELY 36000 LOANS PER YEAR. FINANCIAL NEED MUST BE ESTABLISHED AND NEW LOAN APPLICATION REQUIRED YEARLY. WRITE FOR COMPLETE INFORMATION.

1181

COLLEGE FOUNDATION INC. (NORTH CAROLINA STUDENT INCENTIVE GRANT)
PO BOX 12100; 2100 YONKERS ROAD
RALEIGH NC 27605
919/821-4771
AMOUNT: $1500 MAX
DEADLINE(S): MAR 15
FIELD(S): ALL FIELDS OF STUDY
UNDERGRADUATE GRANTS TO STUDENTS WHO ARE US CITIZENS; RESIDENTS OF NORTH CAROLINA AND ATTENDING OR PLANNING TO ATTEND COLLEGE IN NORTH CAROLINA. MUST DEMONSTRATE SUBSTANTIAL FINANCIAL NEED.
APPROXIMATELY 3000 GRANTS PER YEAR; RENEWABLE TO A MAXIMUM OF 5 YEARS OF UNDERGRADUATE STUDY. WRITE FOR COMPLETE INFORMATION.

1182

COLORADO MASONS BENEVOLENT FUND ASSOCIATION (SCHOLARSHIP PROGRAM)
1130 PANORAMA DRIVE
COLORADO SPRINGS CO 80904
719/471-9587
AMOUNT: UP TO $20000 OVER FOUR YEARS
DEADLINE(S): MAR 15
FIELD(S): ALL FIELDS OF STUDY
OPEN TO SENIORS IN COLORADO PUBLIC HIGH SCHOOLS WHO PLAN TO ATTEND A COLORADO COLLEGE OR UNIVERSITY. MUST BE COLORADO RESIDENT BUT MASONIC AFFILIATION IS NOT REQUIRED. NEED IS CONSIDERED BUT IS NOT PARAMOUNT.
APPLICATIONS ARE MAILED EARLY IN NOVEMBER TO ALL COLORADO PUBLIC SCHOOLS & MASONIC LODGES. CONTACT COLORADO SCHOOLS AND LOCAL MASONIC LODGES. DO NOT WRITE TO ADDRESS ABOVE.

1183

COMINCO LTD. (HIGHER EDUCATION AWARDS)
200 BURRARD ST
VANCOUVER BC V6C 3L7 CANADA
604/682-0611
AMOUNT: $700 - $1000
DEADLINE(S): AUG 15
FIELD(S): ALL AREAS OF STUDY
OPEN TO ELIGIBLE SONS; DAUGHTERS & WARDS OF COMINCO LTD EMPLOYEES & PENSIONERS. AWARDS ARE OFFERED TO ENCOURAGE STUDENTS OF GOOD SCHOLASTIC ACCOMPLISHMENT TO PURSUE THEIR EDUCATION AT AN ACCREDITED COLLEGE FOR AT LEAST 2 YEARS.
APPROX 40 AWARDS PER YEAR. WRITE FOR COMPLETE INFORMATION.

1184

COMMUNICATIONS WORKERS OF AMERICA (RAY HACKNEY SCHOLARSHIP FUND)
30 E PADONIA RD; PADONIA CENTER #205
TIMONIUM MD 21093
202/728-2300

AMOUNT: $1000 PER YEAR FOR 4 YEARS
DEADLINE(S): MAR 31
FIELD(S): ALL AREAS OF STUDY
OPEN ONLY TO CWA MEMBERS OR THE SONS OR DAUGHTERS OF CWA MEMBERS. APPLICANTS MUST BE HIGH SCHOOL GRADUATES OR GRADUATE IN THE YEAR THEY APPLY.
8 AWARDS PER YEAR. WRITE FOR COMPLETE INFORMATION.

1185

COMMUNITY FOUNDATION OF GREATER LORAIN COUNTY (LORAIN YOUTH CENTER SCHOLARSHIP FUND)
1865 N RIDGE RD. E; SUITE A
LORAIN OH 44055
216/277-0142
AMOUNT: $1000
DEADLINE(S): MAY 1
FIELD(S): ALL FIELDS OF STUDY
OPEN TO STUDENTS IN THE 4 LORAIN HIGH SCHOOLS WHO LIVE IN THE CITY OF LORAIN AND APPLY FOR THE SCHOLARSHIP IN THE YEAR OF HIGH SCHOOL GRADUATION. MUST SHOW FINANCIAL NEED & ACADEMIC ABILITY AND BE ACTIVE IN EXTRACURRICULAR ACTIVITIES.
APPLICATION ACCEPTANCE BEGINS AROUND JAN 30. WRITE FOR COMPLETE INFORMATION.

1186

COMMUNITY FOUNDATION OF GREATER LORAIN COUNTY (WALTER AND VIRGINIA NORD SCHOLARSHIP FUND)
1865 N RIDGE RD. E; SUITE A
LORAIN OH 44055
216/277-0142 OR 216/323-4445
AMOUNT: $1000
DEADLINE(S): FEB 1
FIELD(S): ALL FIELDS OF STUDY
OPEN TO RESIDENTS OF LORAIN COUNTY WHO APPLY FOR SCHOLARSHIP IN THE YEAR OF GRADUATION FROM A LORAIN COUNTY HIGH SCHOOL. MUST BE IN UPPER THIRD OF GRADUATING CLASS AND DEMONSTRATE FINANCIAL NEED.
APPLICATION ACCEPTANCE BEGINS AROUND JAN 30. WRITE FOR COMPLETE INFORMATION.

1187

CONE MILLS CORPORATION (SCHOLARSHIP PROGRAM)
1201 MAPLE ST
GREENSBORO NC 27405
919/379-6697
AMOUNT: $500 - $2500 PER YEAR
DEADLINE(S): NOV 30
FIELD(S): ALL FIELDS OF STUDY
OPEN TO CHILDREN OF CONE MILLS EMPLOYEES. PARENTS MUST HAVE WORKED FOR CONE MILLS FOR 1 YEAR BY DEC 1 OF THE YEAR SCHOLARSHIP IS APPLIED FOR AND BE EMPLOYED AT THE TIME AWARDS ARE MADE. FOR UNDERGRADUATE STUDY. AWARDS ARE BASED ON FINANCIAL NEED.
MUST APPLY DURING SENIOR YR OF HIGH SCHOOL. UP TO 10 4-YR SCHOLARSHIPS AND 15 VOC-TECH AWARDS PER YEAR. CONTACT CATHY COLTRANE; ADDRESS ABOVE; FOR COMPLETE INFORMATION.

1188

CONNECTICUT DEPT. OF HIGHER EDUCATION (STATE SCHOLASTIC GRANT PROGRAM)
61 WOODLAND ST
HARTFORD CT 06015
203/566-2618
AMOUNT: $300 - $2000
DEADLINE(S): FEB 15
FIELD(S): ALL FIELDS OF STUDY
OPEN TO CONN HIGH SCHOOL SENIORS & GRADUATES WHO RANKED IN TOP 20% OF THEIR HIGH SCHOOL CLASS OR SCORED ABOVE 1100 ON SAT EXAM. FOR UNDERGRADUATE STUDY AT A NEW ENGLAND COLLEGE OR UNIVERSITY. USA CITIZEN OR LEGAL RESIDENT.
3000 AWARDS PER YEAR. WRITE FOR COMPLETE INFORMATION.

1189

CONNECTICUT DEPT. OF HIGHER EDUCATION. (STUDENT FINANCIAL ASSISTANCE PROGRAMS)
61 WOODLAND ST
HARTFORD CT 06105
203/566-2618
AMOUNT: VARIES WITH PROGRAM
DEADLINE(S): VARIES
FIELD(S): ALL FIELDS OF STUDY

VARIOUS STATE AND FEDERAL PROGRAMS PROVIDING FINANCIAL AID TO CONNECTICUT STUDENTS. PROGRAMS INCLUDE TUITION WAIVERS FOR VETERANS AND SENIOR CITIZENS; WORK STUDY PROGRAMS; LOANS AND SCHOLARSHIPS AND GRANTS.

MOST PROGRAMS EMPHASIZE FINANCIAL NEED. WRITE FOR BROCHURE LISTING PROGRAMS AND APPLICATION INFORMATION.

1190

CONRAD & MARCEL SCHLUMBERGER (SCHOLARSHIPS)

PO BOX 2175
HOUSTON TX 77252
WRITTEN INQUIRY
AMOUNT: VARIES
DEADLINE(S): MAR 31
FIELD(S): ALL FIELDS OF STUDY

SON OR DAUGHTER OF A SCHLUMBERGER EMPLOYEE. SENIOR IN HIGH SCHOOL ENTERING COLLEGE FOR THE FIRST TIME AS A FRESHMAN OR UNDER ADVANCED PLACEMENT.

WRITE TO THE SCHOLARSHIP COMMITTEE FOR COMPLETE INFORMATION.

1191

CONRAIL-CONSOLIDATED RAIL CORPORATION (FRANK THOMSON SCHOLARSHIPS FOR MALES)

ROOM 1010; SIX PENN CENTER
PHILADELPHIA PA 19103
215/977-1764
AMOUNT: $2000
DEADLINE(S): APR 1
FIELD(S): ENGINEERING

OPEN ONLY TO HIGH SCHOOL SENIORS WHO ARE SONS OF CONRAIL OR PREDECESSOR RAILROAD COMPANY EMPLOYEES. MUST TAKE SAT AND CERTAIN ACHIEVEMENT TESTS.

APPROXIMATELY 12 SCHOLARSHIPS AWARDED ON BASIS OF BOTH FINANCIAL NEED AND COMPETITIVE EXAMS. RENEWABLE UP TO 4 YEARS. WRITE FOR COMPLETE INFORMATION.

1192

CONRAIL-CONSOLIDATED RAIL CORPORATION (WOMEN'S AID SCHOLARSHIPS FOR MEN AND WOMEN)

ROOM 1010 SIX PENN CENTER
PHILADELPHIA PA 19103
215/977-1764
AMOUNT: $200-1500
DEADLINE(S): APR 1
FIELD(S): ALL AREAS OF STUDY

OPEN TO HIGH SCHOOL SENIORS WHO ARE CHILDREN OF CONRAIL; PENN CENTRAL OR PREDECESSOR R.R. CO EMPLOYEES. MUST DEMONSTRATE NEED AND TAKE SAT; TSWE AND TWO ACHIEVEMENT TESTS. FOR UNDERGRADUATE STUDY.

12 TO 15 SCHOLARSHIPS BASED ON FINANCIAL NEED AND COMPETITIVE EXAMS. RENEWABLE UP TO 4 YEARS. WRITE FOR COMPLETE INFORMATION.

1193

COREY WRIGHT MEMORIAL SCHOLARSHIP

CLAIR WRIGHT; 123 SANTA TERESA WAY
SALINAS CA 93906
WRITTEN INQUIRY
AMOUNT: VARIES WITH FUNDS AVAILABLE
DEADLINE(S): MAY 15
FIELD(S): ALL FIELDS OF STUDY

OPEN TO HIGH SCHOOL SENIORS RESIDING IN MONTEREY COUNTY, CA WHO ARE ACHIEVING SUCCESS DESPITE A MAJOR OBSTACLE. MUST HAVE A 'C' OR BETTER AVERAGE ON LAST REPORT CARD. FOR UNDERGRAD STUDY AT A RECOGNIZED 2 OR 4 YEAR COLLEGE OR TRADE SCHOOL.

'MAJOR OBSTACLES' COULD INCLUDE DRUG OR ALCOHOL PROBLEMS; EMOTIONAL OR PHYSICAL ABUSE; LEARNING PROBLEMS; DEATH IN THE FAMILY. SEND SASE FOR COMPLETE INFORMATION.

1194

COSTAS G. LEMONOPOULOS SCHOLARSHIP TRUST (SCHOLARSHIPS)

NATIONAL ASSN. OF LETTER CARRIERS; 100 INDIANA AVE NW
WASHINGTON DC 20001
WRITTEN INQUIRY
AMOUNT: NOT SPECIFIED
DEADLINE(S): JUN 1
FIELD(S): ALL FIELDS OF STUDY

OPEN TO CHILDREN OF ACTIVE; RETIRED OR DECEASED NALC MEMBERS TO ATTEND FLORIDA STATE SUPPORTED COLLEGES; UNIVERSITIES OR ST. PETERSBURG (FLA) JUNIOR COLLEGE.

WRITE FOR COMPLETE INFORMATION.

1195

COUNCIL OF CITIZENS WITH LOW VISION INTERNATIONAL (CCLVI TELESENSORY SCHOLARSHIP)
5707 BROCKTON DR; #302
INDIANAPOLIS IN 46220
800/733-2258 OR 317/254-1185; FAX 317/251-6588
AMOUNT: $1000
DEADLINE(S): MAR 15
FIELD(S): ALL AREAS OF STUDY
OPEN TO AN UNDERGRADUATE OR GRADUATE STUDENT WHO IS VISION IMPAIRED BUT NOT LEGALLY BLIND.
WRITE FOR COMPLETE INFORMATION.

1196

CSX CORPORATION (SCHOLARSHIP PROGRAM)
RASP SCHOLARSHIP SERVICE; PO BOX 5151
RICHMOND VA 23220
800/533-4723 OR 804/282-0337
AMOUNT: $2500
DEADLINE(S): MAY 1
FIELD(S): ALL AREAS OF STUDY
UNDERGRADUATE SCHOLARSHIPS OPEN TO DEPENDENTS OF ACTIVE CSX EMPLOYEES FOR AT LEAST ONE YEAR WHO PLAN TO ATTEND FULL TIME AN ACCREDITED COLLEGE OR UNIVERSITY IN AN ASSOCIATE OR BACHELOR'S DEGREE PROGRAM. MUST HAVE GPA OF 3.5 OR BETTER.
100 SCHOLARSHIPS PER YEAR; RENEWABLE WITH REAPPLICATION. FINANCIAL NEED IS A CONSIDERATION. WRITE FOR COMPLETE INFORMATION.

1197

CUBAN AMERICAN TEACHER ASSOCIATION (SCHOLARSHIPS)
DR. ALBERT C. DEL CALVO; 12037 PEORIA ST
SUN VALLEY CA 91352
213/668-2666
AMOUNT: $300 - $1000
DEADLINE(S): APR 1
FIELD(S): ALL FIELDS OF STUDY
OPEN TO HIGH SCHOOL STUDENTS OF CUBAN DESCENT WHO ARE PLANNING TO CONTINUE THEIR EDUCATION AT THE COLLEGE LEVEL. APPLICANTS SHOULD HAVE AT LEAST A 'B' AVERAGE; DEMONSTRATE AN INTEREST IN THEIR CULTURAL HERITAGE & SPEAK ACCEPTABLE SPANISH.
PARTICIPATION IN SCHOOL AND COMMUNITY AFFAIRS ALSO IS CONSIDERED. WRITE FOR COMPLETE INFORMATION.

1198

D.D. HACHAR CHARITABLE TRUST FUND (UNDERGRADUATE SCHOLARSHIPS)
LAREDO NATIONAL BANK - TRUSTEE; PO BOX 59
LAREDO TX 78042
512/723-1151 EXT 670
AMOUNT: VARIES
DEADLINE(S): LAST FRI OF APR; LAST FRI OF OCT
FIELD(S): ALL AREAS OF STUDY
OPEN TO RESIDENTS OF LAREDO (WEBB COUNTY) TEXAS. SCHOLARSHIPS AVAILABLE FOR UNDERGRADUATE STUDY; COLLEGE FRESHMEN AND SOPHOMORES MUST MAINTAIN MINIMUM 2.0 GPA; JUNIORS AND SENIORS AT LEAST 2.5 GPA. ENROLLED FULL TIME STUDENT.
ANNUAL FAMILY INCOME CANNOT EXCEED $44000. USA CITIZEN. WRITE FOR COMPLETE INFORMATION.

1199

DALLAS TIMES HERALD (GOLDEN HERALD SCHOLARSHIPS)
1101 PACIFIC AVE
DALLAS TX 75202
214/720-6501
AMOUNT: $1000
DEADLINE(S): MAR
FIELD(S): ALL AREAS OF STUDY
SCHOLARSHIPS OPEN TO DALLAS AREA HIGH SCHOOL SENIORS WHO HAVE USED THEIR ACADEMIC TALENTS FOR THE BETTERMENT OF THEIR SCHOOLS AND COMMUNITIES. MUST BE NOMINATED BY HIGH SCHOOL.
11 FIRST PLACE AWARDS; 22 HONORABLE MENTION SCHOLARSHIPS AND ENGRAVED MEMENTOS. CONTACT ADDRESS ABOVE FOR COMPLETE INFORMATION.

1200

DANISH SISTERHOOD IN AMERICA (SCHOLARSHIP PROGRAM)
2916 NORTH 121ST ST
MILWAUKEE WI 53222
WRITTEN INQUIRY ONLY
AMOUNT: VARIES
DEADLINE(S): VARIES

FIELD(S): ALL AREAS OF STUDY

OPEN TO MEMBERS OF THE DANISH SISTERHOOD OF AMERICA. VARIOUS AWARD PROGRAMS FOR VOCATIONAL; UNDERGRADUATE AND GRADUATE STUDY.

WRITE TO THE ATTN OF LORRAINE MATTSEN ZEMBINSKI (NATIONAL TRUSTEE) FOR COMPLETE INFORMATION.

1201

DAUGHTERS OF PENELOPE (ANNUAL SCHOLARSHIPS)

1909 Q ST NW; SUITE 500
WASHINGTON DC 20009
202/234-9741

AMOUNT: $500 - $1000

DEADLINE(S): JUN 20

FIELD(S): ALL FIELDS OF STUDY

UNDERGRADUATE STUDY. OPEN TO FEMALES OF GREEK DESCENT WHO ARE MEMBERS OF DAUGHTERS OF PENELOPE OR MAID OF ATHENA; OR THE DAUGHTER OF A MEMBER OF DAUGHTERS OF PENELOPE OR ORDER OF AHEPA. ACADEMIC PERFORMANCE & NEED ARE MAIN CONSIDERATIONS.

RENEWABLE. WRITE FOR COMPLETE INFORMATION.

1202

DAUGHTERS OF THE AMERICAN REVOLUTION (AMERICAN INDIANS SCHOLARSHIP)

MISS SUSANNE W. O'MALLEY; NATIONAL CHAIRMAN; 1101 ELDON DRIVE
MITCHELLVILLE MD 20715
202/628-1776 OR 202/879-3292

AMOUNT: $500

DEADLINE(S): AUG 1; DEC 1

FIELD(S): ALL FIELDS OF STUDY

OPEN TO AMERICAN INDIANS (BOTH YOUTH AND ADULTS) STRIVING TO GET AN EDUCATION. FUNDS HELP STUDENTS OF ANY TRIBE IN ANY STATE BASED ON NEED; ACADEMIC ACHIEVEMENT AND AMBITION.

SEND SELF-ADDRESSED STAMPED ENVELOPE TO ADDRESS ABOVE FOR COMPLETE INFORMATION.

1203

DAUGHTERS OF THE AMERICAN REVOLUTION (LILLIAN AND ARTHUR DUNN SCHOLARSHIPS)

1776 'D' ST NW
WASHINGTON DC 20006
202/879-3292

AMOUNT: $1000 PER YEAR FOR 4 YEARS

DEADLINE(S): FEB 15

FIELD(S): ALL FIELDS OF STUDY

OPEN TO GRADUATING HIGH SCHOOL SENIORS WHO ARE SPONSORED BY THEIR MOTHER'S DAR CHAPTER. AWARD IS FOR UNDERGRADUATE STUDY AND CAN BE RENEWED WITH ANNUAL TRANSCRIPT REVIEW AND APPROVAL. USA CITIZEN.

WRITE FOR COMPLETE INFORMATION. SEND SELF-ADDRESSED STAMPED ENVELOPE.

1204

DAUGHTERS OF THE CINCINNATI (SCHOLARSHIP PROGRAM)

122 EAST FIFTY-EIGHTH STREET
NEW YORK NY 10022
212/319-6915

AMOUNT: UP TO $1500 PER YEAR FOR 4 YEARS

DEADLINE(S): MAR 15

FIELD(S): ALL FIELDS OF STUDY

OPEN TO HIGH SCHOOL SENIORS WHO ARE DAUGHTERS OF COMMISSIONED OFFICERS (ACTIVE; RETIRED OR DECEASED) IN REGULAR USA ARMY; NAVY; AIR FORCE; MARINE CORPS OR COAST GUARD. FOR UNDERGRADUATE STUDY AT ANY ACCREDITED FOUR YEAR INSTITUTION.

AWARDS BASED ON NEED & MERIT. INCLUDE PARENT'S RANK AND BRANCH OF SERVICE WHEN WRITING FOR APPLICATION OR FURTHER INFORMATION.

1205

DAUGHTERS OF UNION VETERANS OF THE CIVIL WAR (GRAND ARMY OF THE REPUBLIC LIVING MEMORIAL SCHOLARSHIP)

503 SOUTH WALNUT
SPRINGFIELD IL 62704
WRITTEN INQUIRY

AMOUNT: $200

DEADLINE(S): APR 30

FIELD(S): ALL FIELDS OF STUDY

OPEN TO LINEAL DESCENDANTS OF A UNION VETERAN OF THE CIVIL WAR. MUST BE A JUNIOR OR SENIOR IN COLLEGE; IN GOOD SCHOLASTIC STANDING; OF GOOD MORAL CHARACTER AND HAVE A FIRM BELIEF IN THE USA FORM OF GOVERNMENT.

4-5 AWARDS PER YEAR. SEND STAMPED SELF-ADDRESSED ENVELOPE FOR COMPLETE INFORMATION.

1206

DAVID WASSERMAN SCHOLARSHIP FUND INC (AWARD PROGRAM)
ADIRONDACK CENTER; ROUTE 30 N
AMSTERDAM NY 12010
518/843-2800
AMOUNT: $300 PER YEAR
DEADLINE(S): APR 15
FIELD(S): ALL AREAS OF STUDY
OPEN TO BONA FIDE RESIDENTS OF MONTGOMERY COUNTY NY WHO ARE PURSUING AN UNDERGRADUATE DEGREE AND ARE USA CITIZENS.
20-25 AWARDS PER YEAR. RENEWABLE. MAKE REQUESTS FOR INFORMATION AND APPLICATIONS IN WRITING.

1207

DAVIS-ROBERTS SCHOLARSHIP FUND INC. (SCHOLARSHIPS TO DE MOLAYS & JOBS DAUGHTERS)
PO BOX 1974
CHEYENNE WY 82003
307/632-2948
AMOUNT: VARIES
DEADLINE(S): JUN 15
FIELD(S): ALL AREAS OF STUDY
OPEN TO WYOMING RESIDENTS WHO ARE OR HAVE BEEN A DE MOLAY OR JOBS DAUGHTER IN THE STATE OF WYOMING. SCHOLARSHIPS FOR FULL-TIME UNDERGRADUATE STUDY. FINANCIAL NEED IS A CONSIDERATION.
12 TO 14 AWARDS ANNUALLY. RENEWABLE. WRITE FOR COMPLETE INFORMATION.

1208

DELAWARE HIGHER EDUCATION COMMISSION (SCHOLARSHIP FUND)
820 N FRENCH ST; 4TH FLOOR
WILMINGTON DE 19801
302/577-3240
AMOUNT: $200 - $1000
DEADLINE(S): APR 15
FIELD(S): ALL FIELDS OF STUDY
OPEN TO THOSE WHO HAVE LIVED IN DELAWARE FOR AT LEAST ONE YEAR. AWARDS ARE FOR FULL TIME UNDERGRADUATE STUDY AT ACCREDITED COLLEGES AND UNIVERSITIES. FINANCIAL NEED IS THE PRIMARY CONSIDERATION.
1300 SCHOLARSHIPS PER YEAR. RENEWABLE. WRITE FOR COMPLETE INFORMATION.

1209

DELTA GAMMA FOUNDATION (SCHOLARSHIPS; FELLOWSHIPS; LOANS)
3250 RIVERSIDE DR
COLUMBUS OH 43221
614/481-8169
AMOUNT: $1000 - $2500
DEADLINE(S): MAR 1; APR 1
FIELD(S): ALL AREAS OF STUDY
SCHOLARSHIPS; FELLOWSHIPS & LOANS OPEN TO DELTA GAMMA MEMBERS & THEIR DEPENDENTS. AWARDS MAY BE USED FOR UNDERGRADUATE OR GRADUATE STUDY.
APPROX 60 AWARDS PER YEAR. CONTACT THE GRANTS & LOANS CHAIRMAN ADDRESS ABOVE FOR COMPLETE INFORMATION.

1210

DEMOLAY FOUNDATION INC. (SCHOLARSHIPS)
10200 N EXECUTIVE HILLS BLVD
KANSAS CITY MO 64153
816/891-8333
AMOUNT: $800
DEADLINE(S): APR 1
FIELD(S): ALL AREAS OF STUDY
FOR UNDERGRADUATE FRESHMEN OR SOPHOMORES WITH A 2.0 GPA OR BETTER. ALTHOUGH DEMOLAY MEMBERSHIP IS NOT REQUIRED MEMBERS ARE GIVEN PRIORITY. CONSIDERATIONS ARE LEADERSHIP; ACADEMIC ACHIEVEMENT AND GOALS.
10 GRANTS PER YEAR. WRITE FOR COMPLETE INFORMATION.

1211

DEPARTMENT OF VETERANS AFFAIRS (SURVIVORS AND DEPENDENTS EDUCATIONAL ASSISTANCE PROGRAM)
DEPARTMENT OF VETERANS BENEFITS
WASHINGTON DC 20420
VA REGIONAL OFFICE IN EACH STATE
AMOUNT: $404 PER MONTH FOR FULL TIME STUDY
DEADLINE(S): VARIES
FIELD(S): ALL AREAS OF STUDY
EDUCATIONAL SUPPORT FOR CHILDREN (AGED 18-26) AND SPOUSES/WIDOWS OF VETERANS WHO ARE DISABLED/DECEASED DUE TO MILITARY SERVICE OR ARE CLASSIFIED CURRENTLY AS PRISONER OF WAR OR MISSING IN ACTION. TRAINING IN APPROVED INSTITUTION.

SPOUSES ARE ELIGIBLE UP TO 10 YEARS AFTER DETERMINATION OF ELIGIBILITY. CONTACT THE NEAREST VA OFFICE FOR COMPLETE INFORMATION.

1212

DEPT OF VETERANS AFFAIRS (SURVIVORS' AND DEPENDENTS' EDUCATIONAL SCHOLARSHIP ASSISTANCE PROGRAM)

VETERANS BENEFITS ADMINISTRATION
WASHINGTON DC 20420
VA REGIONAL OFFICE IN EACH STATE

AMOUNT: $404 PER MONTH FOR FULL TIME STUDY

DEADLINE(S): VARIES

FIELD(S): ALL FIELDS OF STUDY

EDUCATIONAL SUPPORT FOR ELIGIBLE CHILDREN (AGED 18-26) AND SPOUSES/WIDOWS OF VETERANS WHO ARE DISABLED/DECEASED DUE TO MILITARY SERVICE OR ARE CURRENT POW OR MIA. FOR TRAINING AT AN APPROVED INSTITUTION.

SPOUSES ARE ELIGIBLE UP TO 10 YEARS AFTER DETERMINATION OF ELIGIBILITY. CONTACT YOUR NEAREST VA REGIONAL OFFICE FOR COMPLETE INFORMATION.

1213

DESCENDANTS OF THE SIGNERS OF THE DECLARATION OF INDEPENDENCE (SCHOLARSHIP GRANT)

12 RED FOX COURT
GREENVILLE SC 29615
803/297-9770

AMOUNT: $1200 - $2000

DEADLINE(S): MAR 15

FIELD(S): ALL AREAS OF STUDY

UNDERGRAD & GRAD AWARDS FOR STUDENTS WHO ARE DSDI MEMBERS AND CAN PROVE THEY ARE A DIRECT DESCENDANT OF A SIGNER OF THE DECLARATION OF INDEPENDENCE. MUST BE FULL TIME STUDENT ENROLLED IN A RECOGNIZED USA 4-YEAR COLLEGE OR UNIVERSITY.

APPLICANTS SHOULD NAME THEIR ANCESTOR-SIGNER WHEN REQUESTING APPLICATION OR THEY WILL NOT RECEIVE A RESPONSE. 6 TO 9 AWARDS PER YEAR RENEWABLE WITH REAPPLICATION. WRITE FOR COMPLETE INFORMATION.

1214

DISABLED AMERICAN VETERANS (SCHOLARSHIPS)

PO BOX 14301
CINCINNATI OH 45250
606/441-7300

AMOUNT: $200 - $3000

DEADLINE(S): NOV 15

FIELD(S): ALL FIELDS OF STUDY

OPEN TO DEPENDENTS OF US MILITARY VETERANS WITH RECOGNIZED SERVICE CONNECTED DISABILITIES. FOR HIGH SCHOOL SENIORS AND GED RECIPIENTS UNDER 26 WHO HAVEN'T ATTENDED COLLEGE PREVIOUSLY. MUST DEMONSTRATE FINANCIAL NEED AND BE USA CITIZEN.

WRITE FOR COMPLETE INFORMATION.

1215

DISABLED AMERICAN VETERANS AUXILIARY (DAVA STUDENT LOANS)

3725 ALEXANDRIA PIKE
COLD SPRING KY 41076
606/441-7300

AMOUNT: UP TO MAXIMUM OF $1000 FOR 4 YEARS

DEADLINE(S): APR 25

FIELD(S): ALL FIELDS OF STUDY

CITIZEN OF U.S. WHO HAS BEEN ACCEPTED BY AN INSTITUTION OF HIGHER EDUCATION. CHILDREN WHOSE LIVING MOTHER IS A LIFE MEMBER OF DAV AUXILIARY OR IF MOTHER DECEASED; FATHER MUST BE A LIFE MEMBER FOR AT LEAST 1 YEAR.

40-42 LOANS PER YEAR. RENEWABLE. WRITE FOR COMPLETE INFORMATION.

1216

DISTRICT OF COLUMBIA (STATE STUDENT INCENTIVE GRANT PROGRAM)

2100 M.L. KING JR. AVE SE; SUITE 401
WASHINGTON DC 20020
202/727-3688

AMOUNT: $400 - $1500

DEADLINE(S): LAST FRIDAY IN JUNE

FIELD(S): ALL FIELDS OF STUDY EXCEPT LAW & MEDICINE

OPEN TO CITIZENS OR LEGAL RESIDENTS OF USA WHO HAVE LIVED IN DC FOR AT LEAST 15 CONSECUTIVE MONTHS; HAVE AT LEAST A 2.0 GPA; CAN DEMONSTRATE FINANCIAL NEED; AND ARE ENROLLED IN AN ELIGIBLE USA INSTITUTION.

RENEWABLE SCHOLARSHIPS FOR UNDERGRADUATE STUDY. MUST HAVE HIGH SCHOOL DIPLOMA OR EQUIVALENT. WRITE FOR COMPLETE INFORMATION.

1217

DOLPHIN SCHOLARSHIP FOUNDATION (SCHOLARSHIPS)

405 DILLINGHAM BLVD; NORFOLK NAVAL STATION
NORFOLK VA 23511
804/451-3660

AMOUNT: $1750
DEADLINE(S): APR 15
FIELD(S): ALL FIELDS OF STUDY

CHILDREN OF MEMBERS OR FORMER MEMBERS OF THE SUBMARINE FORCE WHO QUALIFIED IN SUBMARINES AND SERVED IN THE SUBMARINE FORCE FOR AT LEAST 5 YEARS AFTER QUALIFICATION OR FOR AT LEAST 6 YEARS IN DIRECT SUPPORT OF THE SUBMARINE FORCE.

FOR STUDENTS SEEKING BA OR BS DEGREE. FINANCIAL NEED IS A CONSIDERATION. SEND SELF-ADDRESSED STAMPED ENVELOPE (BUSINESS SIZE) FOR COMPLETE INFORMATION.

1218

DOUGLASS COLLEGE (NEW JERSEY STATE FEDERATION OF WOMEN'S CLUBS CITIZENSHIP INSTITUTE SCHOLARSHIPS)

FINANCIAL AID OFFICE
NEW BRUNSWICK NJ 08903
908/932-7057

AMOUNT: VARIES
DEADLINE(S): NONE SPECIFIED
FIELD(S): ALL FIELDS OF STUDY

OPEN TO WOMEN WHO ARE NEW JERSEY RESIDENTS AND WHO ATTENDED GIRLS CITIZENSHIP INSTITUTE WHILE A HIGH SCHOOL JUNIOR.

MUST ATTEND DOUGLASS COLLEGE. NOT RENEWABLE. WRITE FOR COMPLETE INFORMATION.

1219

DOUGLASS COLLEGE (NEW JERSEY STATE FEDERATION OF WOMEN'S CLUBS CONTINUING EDUCATION SCHOLARSHIPS)

FINANCIAL AID OFFICE
NEW BRUNSWICK NJ 08903
908/932-7057

AMOUNT: VARIES
DEADLINE(S): NONE SPECIFIED
FIELD(S): ALL FIELDS OF STUDY

OPEN TO WOMEN WHO RESIDE IN NEW JERSEY AND ARE RETURNING TO COLLEGE ON A PART TIME BASIS. MUST ATTEND DOUGLASS COLLEGE.

WRITE FOR COMPLETE INFORMATION.

1220

DOYLE SCHOLARSHIP PROGRAM (SCHOLARSHIPS)

1501 MENDOCINO AVE
SANTA ROSA CA 95401
707/527-4740

AMOUNT: VARIES
DEADLINE(S): MAR 1
FIELD(S): ALL FIELDS OF STUDY

APPLICANTS MUST BE ENROLLED AT SANTA ROSA JUNIOR COLLEGE. APPLICATIONS FOR THE DOYLE SCHOLARSHIP PROGRAM ARE MADE THROUGH THE SRJC SCHOLARSHIP OFFICE. AWARDS ARE BASED ON SCHOLASTIC ACHIEVEMENT AND FINANCIAL NEED.

NUMBER OF AWARDS PER YEAR VARIES. CONTACT SRJC SCHOLARSHIP OFFICE FOR COMPLETE INFORMATION.

1221

EASTER SEAL SOCIETY OF IOWA INC. (JAMES L. & LAVON MADDEN MALLORY ANNUAL DISABILITY SCHOLARSHIP PROGRAM)

PO BOX 4002
DES MOINES IA 50333
515/289-1933

AMOUNT: $1000
DEADLINE(S): APR 15
FIELD(S): ALL FIELDS OF STUDY

OPEN TO IOWA RESIDENTS WHO HAVE A PERMANENT DISABILITY AND ARE GRADUATING HIGH SCHOOL SENIORS. AWARD SUPPORTS UNDERGRADUATE STUDY AT A RECOGNIZED COLLEGE OR UNIVERSITY.

WRITE FOR COMPLETE INFORMATION.

1222

EBELL OF LOS ANGELES SCHOLARSHIP PROGRAM (FLINT SCHOLARSHIPS & EBELL SCHOLARSHIPS)

743 SOUTH LUCERNE BLVD
LOS ANGELES CA 90005
213/931-1277

AMOUNT: $2000 ($200/MONTH FOR 10 MONTHS)
DEADLINE(S): JUN 1
FIELD(S): ALL AREAS OF STUDY
OPEN TO UNMARRIED LOS ANGELES COUNTY RESIDENTS WHO ARE UNDERGRADUATE SOPHOMORES; JUNIORS OR SENIORS ENROLLED IN A LOS ANGELES COUNTY COLLEGE OR UNIVERSITY. MAINTAIN A 3.25 AVERAGE FOR RENEWAL. USA CITIZEN.
50-60 AWARDS PER YEAR. WRITE FOR COMPLETE INFORMATION.

1223

EDUCATIONAL COMMUNICATIONS SCHOLARSHIP FOUNDATION (ANNUAL SCHOLARSHIP AWARD PROGRAM)
721 N MC KINLEY RD
LAKE FOREST IL 60045
708/295-6650
AMOUNT: $1000
DEADLINE(S): JUN 1 (REQUEST APPLICATIONS BY MAR 15)
FIELD(S): ALL FIELDS OF STUDY
OPEN TO CURRENT HIGH SCHOOL STUDENTS WHO ARE USA CITIZENS AND HAVE TAKEN THE SAT OR ACT EXAMINATION. AWARDS BASED ON GPA; ACHIEVEMENT TEST SCORES; LEADERSHIP; WORK EXPERIENCE; ESSAY; FINANCIAL NEED.
100 SCHOLARSHIPS PER YEAR. WRITE FOR COMPLETE INFORMATION. INCLUDE NAME; HOME ADDRESS; CURRENT YEAR IN HIGH SCHOOL AND APPROXIMATE GRADE POINT AVERAGE.

1224

EDWARD ARTHUR MELLINGER EDUCATIONAL FOUNDATION INC. (SCHOLARSHIPS AND LOANS)
PO BOX 278; 1025 EAST BROADWAY
MONMOUTH IL 61462
309/734-2419
AMOUNT: $750 MAXIMUM
DEADLINE(S): MAY 1
FIELD(S): ALL AREAS OF STUDY
SCHOLARSHIPS ARE AVAILABLE TO STUDENTS WHO RESIDE IN WESTERN ILLINOIS AND EASTERN IOWA WHO ARE ENROLLED IN UNDERGRADUATE PROGRAMS. LOANS ARE AVAILABLE FOR GRADUATE STUDY.
250 AWARDS PER YEAR. RENEWABLE. WRITE FOR COMPLETE INFORMATION.

1225

EDWARD RUTLEDGE CHARITY (COLLEGE SCHOLARSHIPS)
BOX 758
CHIPPEWA FALLS WI 54729
715/723-6618
AMOUNT: $1700
DEADLINE(S): JUL 1
FIELD(S): ALL FIELDS OF STUDY
SCHOLARSHIPS OPEN TO RESIDENTS OF CHIPPEWA COUNTY WISCONSIN. AWARDS ARE FOR FULL TIME UNDERGRADUATE STUDY AT RECOGNIZED COLLEGES & UNIVERSITIES. GRADES AND FINANCIAL NEED ARE CONSIDERATIONS. USA CITIZEN.
35 AWARDS PER YEAR. RENEWABLE. CONTACT ADDRESS ABOVE FOR COMPLETE INFORMATION.

1226

EDWARDS SCHOLARSHIP FUND (UNDERGRADUATE AND GRADUATE SCHOLARSHIPS)
10 POST OFFICE SQUARE SO; SUITE 1230
BOSTON MA 02109
617/426-4434
AMOUNT: $250 TO $2500
DEADLINE(S): MAR 1
FIELD(S): ALL FIELDS OF STUDY
OPEN ONLY TO BOSTON RESIDENTS UNDER AGE 25 WHO CAN DEMONSTRATE FINANCIAL NEED; SCHOLASTIC ABILITY AND GOOD CHARACTER. FOR UNDERGRADUATE OR GRADUATE STUDY BUT UNDERGRADS RECEIVE PREFERENCE. FAMILY HOME MUST BE WITHIN BOSTON CITY LIMIT.
APPLICANTS MUST HAVE LIVED IN BOSTON FROM AT LEAST THE BEGINNING OF THEIR JUNIOR YEAR IN HIGH SCHOOL. WRITE FOR COMPLETE INFORMATION.

1227

EISENHOWER MEMORIAL SCHOLARSHIP FOUNDATION (UNDERGRADUATE SCHOLARSHIPS)
303 NORTH CURRY PIKE
BLOOMINGTON IN 47404
812/332-2257
AMOUNT: $2500-$10000
DEADLINE(S): VARIES
FIELD(S): ALL AREAS OF STUDY

OPEN TO INDIANA HIGH SCHOOL SENIORS IN GOOD STANDING WHO HAVE NEVER ATTENDED COLLEGE; HAVE FAITH IN A DIVINE BEING; AND A FIRM BELIEF IN THE FREE ENTERPRISE SYSTEM AND THE AMERICAN WAY OF LIFE. FINANCIAL NEED IS NOT A CONSIDERATION.

THE AWARDS ARE LIMITED TO CERTAIN INDIANA COLLEGES. WRITE FOR COMPLETE INFORMATION.

1228

ELKS NATIONAL FOUNDATION (UNDERGRADUATE SCHOLARSHIPS)
2750 LAKE VIEW AVE
CHICAGO IL 60614
312/929-2100
AMOUNT: $1000 - $5000
DEADLINE(S): JAN 15 (CAN VARY WITH LOCAL LODGE)
FIELD(S): ALL FIELDS OF STUDY

SCHOLARSHIPS ARE OFFERED TO GRADUATING HIGH SCHOOL SENIORS WHO ARE USA CITIZENS AND RESIDE WITHIN THE JURISDICTION OF A LOCAL LODGE OF THE BPO ELKS OF THE USA. MEMBERSHIP IS NOT REQUIRED.

CRITERIA FOR SELECTION ARE FINANCIAL NEED; LEADERSHIP AND SCHOLARSHIP. OBTAIN APPLICATION FORMS FROM LOCAL ELKS LODGES AFTER NOV 1; NOT FROM ADDRESS ABOVE.

1229

EMANUEL STERNBERGER EDUCATIONAL FUND (LOAN PROGRAM)
PO BOX 1735
GREENSBORO NC 27401
919/275-6316
AMOUNT: $1000 FIRST YEAR; $2000 SUBSEQUENT YEARS; MAXIMUM $5000
DEADLINE(S): APR 30
FIELD(S): ALL FIELDS OF STUDY

OPEN TO RESIDENTS OF NORTH CAROLINA WHO ARE ENTERING THEIR JUNIOR OR SENIOR YEAR OF COLLEGE OR ARE A GRADUATE STUDENT. CONSIDERATIONS INCLUDE GRADES; ECONOMIC SITUATION; REFERENCES; CREDIT RATING.

PERSONAL INTERVIEW IS REQUIRED. CAN BE USED AT ANY COLLEGE OR UNIVERSITY. WRITE FOR COMPLETE INFORMATION.

1230

ENGLISH-SPEAKING UNION (LUCY DALBIAC LUARD SCHOLARSHIP)
16 EAST 69TH ST
NEW YORK NY 10021
212/879-6800
AMOUNT: FULL TUITION & EXPENSES
DEADLINE(S): DEC 1
FIELD(S): ALL FIELDS OF STUDY

OPEN TO STUDENTS ATTENDING A UNITED NEGRO COLLEGE OR HOWARD OR HAMPTON UNIVERSITIES. FULL SCHOLARSHIP TO SPEND UNDERGRADUATE JUNIOR YEAR AT A UNIVERSITY IN ENGLAND. USA CITIZEN.

APPLICATION MUST BE MADE THROUGH STUDENT'S COLLEGE OR UNIVERSITY. INFORMATION AND APPLICATIONS ARE SENT EACH FALL TO THE ACADEMIC DEAN/VP FOR ACADEMIC AFFAIRS AT PARTICIPATING SCHOOLS.

1231

ETHEL N. BOWEN FOUNDATION (SCHOLARSHIPS)
PO BOX 1559
BLUEFIELD WV 24701
304/325-8181
AMOUNT: VARIES
DEADLINE(S): APR 30
FIELD(S): ALL AREAS OF STUDY

UNDERGRADUATE AND OCCASIONAL GRADUATE SCHOLARSHIPS OPEN TO RESIDENTS OF SOUTHWEST VIRGINIA.

20-25 AWARDS PER YEAR. WRITE FOR COMPLETE INFORMATION.

1232

FALCON FOUNDATION (SCHOLARSHIPS)
5450 TECH CENTER DR; STE 405
COLORADO SPRINGS CO 80919
719/594-4440
AMOUNT: $3000
DEADLINE(S): MAR 31
FIELD(S): ALL AREAS OF STUDY

SCHOLARSHIPS TO ATTEND PRIVATE PREPARATORY SCHOOLS FOR STUDENTS WHO PLAN TO SEEK ADMISSION TO THE US AIR FORCE ACADEMY. OPEN TO SINGLE STUDENTS AGE 17-21; IN EXCELLENT HEALTH & HIGHLY MOTIVATED TO ATTEND ACADEMY. USA CITIZEN.

100 AWARDS PER YEAR. WRITE FOR COMPLETE INFORMATION.

1233

FAY T. BARNES SCHOLARSHIP TRUST (SCHOLARSHIP PROGRAM)
TEXAS COMMERCE BANK; PO BOX 550
AUSTIN TX 78789
512/479-2629
AMOUNT: $2500 PER YEAR FOR 4 YEARS
DEADLINE(S): JAN 15
FIELD(S): ALL AREAS OF STUDY
OPEN TO HIGH SCHOOL STUDENTS IN THE TEXAS COUNTIES OF TRAVIS AND WILLIAMSON. AWARDS ARE MADE BASED ON SCHOLARSHIP; CITIZENSHIP AND NEED. FOR STUDY AT TEXAS COLLEGES OR UNIVERSITIES ONLY.
APPLY THROUGH HIGH SCHOOL COUNSELOR ONLY. DO NOT MAKE DIRECT APPLICATION TO THE TRUST.

1234

FEDERAL EMPLOYEE EDUCATION & ASSISTANCE FUND (FEEA SCHOLARSHIP PROGRAM)
8441 W BOWLES AVE; SUITE 200
LITTLETON CO 80123
303/933-7580; 800/323-4140; FAX 303/933-7587
AMOUNT: $250 - $1000
DEADLINE(S): JUN 1 (APPLICATIONS AVAILABLE MAR THRU MAY)
FIELD(S): ALL FIELDS OF STUDY
OPEN TO CIVILIAN FEDERAL AND POSTAL EMPLOYEES (WITH AT LEAST 3 YEARS SERVICE) AND THEIR DEPENDENT FAMILY MEMBERS. MUST BE ENROLLED OR PLAN TO ENROLL IN A COURSE THAT WILL LEAD TO A 2-YEAR; 4-YEAR OR GRADUATE DEGREE. GPA OF 3.0 OR BETTER.
AWARDS ARE MERIT BASED. WINNERS MAY REAPPLY AND RECOMPETE EACH YEAR. SEND SELF-ADDRESSED STAMPED ENVELOPE (BUSINESS SIZE) FOR COMPLETE INFORMATION.

1235

FEDERAL EMPLOYEE EDUCATION & ASSISTANCE FUND (FEEA TERI LOAN PROGRAM)
8441 W BOWLES AVE; SUITE 200
LITTLETON CO 80123
303/933-7850; 800/323-4140; FAX 303/933-7587
AMOUNT: $2000 - $20000 PER YEAR
DEADLINE(S): NONE
FIELD(S): ALL FIELDS OF STUDY
LOANS OPEN TO ANY FEDERAL EMPLOYEE (INCLUDING POSTAL AND MILITARY) & THEIR DEPENDENTS OR SURVIVORS. FOR UNDERGRADUATE; GRADUATE OR POST-GRADUATE STUDY AT ANY ACCREDITED 2-YEAR OR 4-YEAR INSTITUTION. USA CITIZEN OR LEGAL RESIDENT.
SEND SELF-ADDRESSED STAMPED ENVELOPE FOR COMPLETE INFORMATION.

1236

FIELD CO-OPERATIVE ASSOCIATION (MISSISSIPPI RESIDENT LOANS)
PO BOX 5054
JACKSON MS 39216
601/939-9295
AMOUNT: $2000
DEADLINE(S): 2 MONTHS PRIOR TO REGISTRATION
FIELD(S): ALL FIELDS OF STUDY
OPEN ONLY TO MISSISSIPPI RESIDENTS WHO ARE UNDERGRADUATE JUNIORS & GRADUATE STUDENTS WITH SATISFACTORY ACADEMIC STANDING. DEMONSTRATE EVIDENCE OF NEED & PROMISE OF FINANCIAL RESPONSIBILITY. USA CITIZEN OR LEGAL RESIDENT.
THESE ARE LOANS NOT SCHOLARSHIPS. LOANS ARE RENEWABLE. WRITE FOR COMPLETE INFORMATION.

1237

FIFTH MARINE DIVISION ASSN (SCHOLARSHIPS)
C/O W.A. ARMOND; 260 S NORWINDEN DR
SPRINGFIELD PA 19064
215/543-4660
AMOUNT: $500 PER SEMESTER MAXIMUM
DEADLINE(S): JUN 1
FIELD(S): ALL FIELDS OF STUDY
OPEN TO CHILDREN OF ASSOCIATION MEMBERS FOR UNDERGRADUATE STUDY. SHOW EVIDENCE OF FINANCIAL NEED AND AN ABILITY LEVEL APPROPRIATE TO PROPOSED PROGRAM OF STUDY. LIMITED TO RESIDENTS OF THE USA WHO ARE HIGH SCHOOL GRADUATES OR EQUIVALENT.
RENEWABLE FOR NOT MORE THAN EIGHT SEMESTERS OF UNDERGRADUATE STUDY. WRITE FOR COMPLETE INFORMATION.

1238

FIRST CAVALRY DIVISION ASSOCIATION (SCHOLARSHIPS)
302 N MAIN
COPPERAS COVE TX 76522
WRITTEN INQUIRY
AMOUNT: $600 PER YEAR UP TO 4 YEARS MAX
DEADLINE(S): NONE SPECIFIED
FIELD(S): ALL FIELDS OF STUDY
AWARDS TO CHILDREN OF SOLDIERS WHO DIED OR WERE DECLARED 100% DISABLED FROM INJURIES WHILE SERVING WITH THE 1ST CALVARY DIVISION DURING & SINCE THE VIETNAM WAR OR DURING DESERT STORM.
IF DEATH OCCURRED AFTER 3/1/80 DECEASED PARENT MUST HAVE BEEN AN ASSOCIATION MEMBER AND SERVING WITH THE DIVISION AT THE TIME OF DEATH. WRITE FOR COMPLETE INFORMATION.

1239

FIRST COMMERCIAL BANK (NAT'L ADVISORY BOARD SCHOLARSHIP PROGRAM)
PO BOX 1471
LITTLE ROCK AR 72203
501/371-6758
AMOUNT: 50% OF FEES + ROOM & BOARD
DEADLINE(S): FEB 1
FIELD(S): ALL AREAS OF STUDY
SCHOLARSHIPS OPEN TO ARKANSAS RESIDENTS WHO ARE HIGH SCHOOL SENIORS AND PLAN TO ATTEND AN ACCREDITED ARKANSAS COLLEGE OR UNIVERSITY THAT OFFERS A BACHELOR'S DEGREE.
RENEWABLE FOR UP TO 4 YEARS. WRITE FOR COMPLETE INFORMATION.

1240

FIRST FLORIDA BANK NA (ETHEL TWEED SCHOLARSHIP TRUST)
PO BOX 11311; TRUST DEPT
ST PETERSBURG FL 33733
813/892-3896
AMOUNT: $125/MO FOR 9 MOS OVER 4 YEAR PERIOD
DEADLINE(S): APR 1
FIELD(S): ALL AREAS OF STUDY
SCHOLARSHIPS OPEN TO ST PETERSBURG FLORDIA HIGH SCHOOL SENIORS. AWARDS SUPPORT UNDERGRADUATE STUDY AT ACCREDITED COLLEGES & UNIVERSITIES. USA CITIZEN OR LEGAL RESIDENT.
APPLICATIONS AVAILABLE FROM ST PETERSBURG, FL HIGH SCHOOL GUIDANCE COUNSELORS.

1241

FIRST MARINE DIVISION ASSOCIATION; INC. (SCHOLARSHIP PROGRAM)
PO BOX 220840
CHANTILLY VA 22022
703/550-7516
AMOUNT: VARIES
DEADLINE(S): NOT SPECIFIED
FIELD(S): ALL AREAS OF STUDY
FOR DEPENDENT OF PERSON WHO SERVED IN THE FIRST MARINE DIVISION OR IN A UNIT ATTACHED TO OR IN SUPPORT OF THE DIVISION AND IS DECEASED FROM ANY CAUSE OR 100% DISABLED.
FOR UNDERGRADUATE STUDY. WRITE FOR COMPLETE INFORMATION.

1242

FLEET RESERVE ASSOCIATION (SCHOLARSHIPS AND AWARDS)
FRA SCHOLARSHIP ADMINISTRATOR; 125 N WEST ST
ALEXANDRIA VA 22314
202/785-2768
AMOUNT: APPROX $500
DEADLINE(S): APR 15
FIELD(S): ALL AREAS OF STUDY
OPEN TO CHILDREN/SPOUSES OF FLEET RESERVE ASSN MEMBERS. DEPENDENTS OF RETIRED OR DECEASED MEMBERS ALSO MAY APPLY. FOR UNDERGRADUATE STUDY. AWARDS BASED ON FINANCIAL NEED; SCHOLASTIC STANDING; CHARACTER; LEADERSHIP QUALITIES.
'DEPENDENT CHILD' IS DEFINED AS UNMARRIED; UNDER 21; OR UNDER 23 IF CURRENTLY ENROLLED IN COLLEGE. WRITE FOR COMPLETE INFORMATION.

1243

FLORENCE EVANS BUSHEE FOUNDATION (SCHOLARSHIPS)
ONE BEACON STREET
BOSTON MA 02108
617/573-0462
AMOUNT: VARIES
DEADLINE(S): MAY 1
FIELD(S): ALL FIELDS OF STUDY
OPEN ONLY TO UNDERGRADUATE COLLEGE STUDENTS WHO RESIDE IN THE

MASSACHUSETTS TOWNS OF BYFIELD; GEORGETOWN; NEWBURY; NEWBURYPORT; ROWLEY; SALISBURY OR WEST NEWBURY.
APPROX 120 GRANTS PER YEAR. WRITE FOR COMPLETE INFORMATION.

1244

FLORIDA DEPT. OF EDUCATION ('CHAPPIE' JAMES MOST PROMISING TEACHER SCHOLARSHIP LOAN PROGRAM)
OFFICE OF STUDENT FINANCIAL ASSISTANCE; FLORIDA EDUCATION CENTER ; ROOM 1344
TALLAHASSEE FL 32399
904/488-4095
AMOUNT: $4000
DEADLINE(S): MAR 1
FIELD(S): TEACHING
SCHOLARSHIP LOANS FOR OUTSTANDING FLORIDA HIGH SCHOOL SENIORS WHO PLAN TO PURSUE A TEACHING CAREER IN FLORIDA. UP TO $4000 PER ACADEMIC YEAR. MUST ENROLL FULL TIME AT AN ELIGIBLE FLORIDA INSTITUTION.
LOAN IS REPAID BY TEACHING IN FLORIDA AFTER GRADUATION OR IN CASH. WRITE FOR COMPLETE INFORMATION.

1245

FLORIDA DEPT. OF EDUCATION (COLLEGE CAREER WORK EXPERIENCE PROGRAM)
OFFICE OF STUDENT FINANCIAL ASSISTANCE; FLORIDA EDUCATION CENTER; ROOM 1344
TALLAHASSEE FL 32399
904/487-0049
AMOUNT: VARIES
DEADLINE(S): SET BY EACH PARTICIPATING INSTITUTION
FIELD(S): ALL FIELDS OF STUDY
FLORIDA RESIDENT FOR AT LEAST 1 YEAR. UNDERGRADUATE STUDENTS WITH FINANCIAL NEED ENROLLED AT LEAST 1/2 TIME AT AN ELIGIBLE FLORIDA INSTITUTION.
PROVIDES STUDENTS WITH OFF-CAMPUS EMPLOYMENT IN JOBS RELATED TO THEIR DECLARED MAJOR AREA OF STUDY OR CAREER INTEREST. WRITE FOR COMPLETE INFORMATION.

1246

FLORIDA DEPT. OF EDUCATION (CONFEDERATE MEMORIAL SCHOLARSHIPS)
OFFICE OF STUDENT FINANCIAL ASSISTANCE; KNOTT BLDG
TALLAHASSEE FL 32399
904/488-6181
AMOUNT: $150 PER YEAR
DEADLINE(S): APR 1 POSTMARK
FIELD(S): ALL FIELDS OF STUDY
FLORIDA RESIDENT AND A LINEAL DESCENDANT OF A CONFEDERATE SOLDIER/OR SAILOR AND CERTIFIED AS SUCH BY A CHAPTER OF THE UNITED DAUGHTERS OF THE CONFEDERACY. ENROLLED AS FULL TIME UNDERGRADUATE STUDENT AT A PUBLIC FLORIDA INSTITUTION.
AWARDED ON A ONE-YEAR BASIS BUT MAY BE RENEWED ANNUALLY PROVIDED ALL ELIGIBILITY REQUIREMENTS ARE MET. CONTACT ADDRESS ABOVE FOR COMPLETE INFORMATION.

1247

FLORIDA DEPT. OF EDUCATION (FLORIDA STUDENT ASSISTANCE GRANTS)
OFFICE OF STUDENT FINANCIAL ASSISTANCE; 1344 FLORIDA EDUCATION CENTER
TALLAHASSEE FL 32399
904/487-0049
AMOUNT: $200 - $1500
DEADLINE(S): APR 15
FIELD(S): ALL FIELDS OF STUDY
US CITIZEN OR LEGAL RESIDENT. FLORIDA RESIDENT FOR AT LEAST 1 YEAR. FULL TIME UNDERGRADUATE AT ELIGIBLE FLORIDA INSTITUTION. DEMONSTRATE FINANCIAL NEED.
RENEWABLE. WRITE FOR COMPLETE INFORMATION.

1248

FLORIDA DEPT. OF EDUCATION (FLORIDA STUDENTS REGENTS SCHOLARSHIP)
OFFICE OF STUDENT FINANCIAL ASSISTANCE; 1344 FLORIDA EDUCATION CENTER
TALLAHASSEE FL 32399
904/488-4234
AMOUNT: $5000
DEADLINE(S): NONE
FIELD(S): ALL FIELDS OF STUDY
SCHOLARSHIP AWARDED TO STUDENTS WHO SERVE/OR HAVE SERVED AS STUDENT MEMBERS OF THE FLORIDA BOARD OF REGENTS.
WRITE FOR COMPLETE INFORMATION.

1249

FLORIDA DEPT. OF EDUCATION (FLORIDA TUITION VOUCHER GRANTS)
OFFICE OF STUDENT FINANCIAL ASSISTANCE; 1344 FLORIDA EDUCATION CENTER
TALLAHASSEE FL 32399
904/487-0049
AMOUNT: UP TO $1000
DEADLINE(S): SET BY PARTICIPATING INSTITUTION
FIELD(S): ALL FIELDS OF STUDY EXCEPT THEOLOGY
US CITIZEN OR LEGAL RESIDENT. FLORIDA RESIDENT FOR AT LEAST 1 YEAR. FULL TIME UNDERGRADUATE AT ELIGIBLE FLORIDA INSTITUTIONS MAY APPLY. NEED IS NOT CONSIDERED.
WRITE FOR COMPLETE INFORMATION.

1250

FLORIDA DEPT. OF EDUCATION (FLORIDA UNDERGRADUATE SCHOLARS' FUND)
OFFICE OF STUDENT FINANCIAL ASSISTANCE; 1344 FLORIDA EDUCATION CENTER
TALLAHASSEE FL 32399
904/487-0049
AMOUNT: $1000-1500
DEADLINE(S): FEB 15 - APR 1
FIELD(S): ALL FIELDS OF STUDY
OPEN TO USA CITIZENS OR LEGAL RESIDENTS WHO HAVE BEEN FLORIDA RESIDENTS FOR AT LEAST 1 YEAR. MERIT PROGRAM CREATED TO ENCOURAGE FLORIDA'S TOP HIGH SCHOOL SENIORS TO ATTEND A FLORIDA COLLEGE OR UNIVERSITY.
WRITE FOR COMPLETE INFORMATION.

1251

FLORIDA DEPT. OF EDUCATION (GUARANTEED STUDENT LOAN PROGRAM & PARENTS' PLUS LOANS)
OFFICE OF STUDENT FINANCIAL ASSISTANCE; FLORIDA EDUCATION CENTER; SUITE 1344
TALLAHASSEE FL 32399
904/488-4095
AMOUNT: $2625 PER ACADEMIC YEAR; MAX $12500 UNDERGRAD & $25000 UNDERGRADUATE/GRADUATE COMBINED
DEADLINE(S): NONE SPECIFIED
FIELD(S): ALL FIELDS OF STUDY
US CITIZEN OR LEGAL RESIDENT. RESIDENT OF FLORIDA FOR AT LEAST 12 MONTHS. ENROLLED OR HAVE BEEN ACCEPTED AT LEAST 1/2 TIME IN ELIGIBLE FLORIDA INSTITUTION.
PARENTS WHO ARE RESIDENTS OF FLORIDA AND BORROWING FOR AN ELIGIBLE STUDENT ATTENDING A FLORIDA SCHOOL MAY BORROW UP TO $4000 PER ACADEMIC YEAR.

1252

FLORIDA DEPT. OF EDUCATION (JOSE MARTI SCHOLARSHIP CHALLENGE GRANT FUND)
OFFICE OF STUDENT FINANCIAL ASSISTANCE; KNOTT BLDG
TALLAHASSEE FL 32399
904/487-0049
AMOUNT: $2000 PER YEAR
DEADLINE(S): APR 1
FIELD(S): ALL FIELDS OF STUDY
US CITIZEN OR LEGAL RESIDENT. HISPANIC-AMERICAN & FLORIDA RESIDENT FOR AT LEAST 1 YEAR. ENROLLED AS FULL-TIME UNDERGRADUATE OR GRADUATE STUDENT AT ELIGIBLE FLORIDA INSTITUTION.
NEED BASED AWARD IS $2000 PER YEAR FOR A MAX OF 8 SEMESTERS (12 QUARTERS) FOR UNDERGRADS OR A MAX OF 4 SEMESTERS (6 QUARTERS) FOR GRADUATE STUDY. WRITE FOR COMPLETE INFORMATION.

1253

FLORIDA DEPT. OF EDUCATION (PUBLIC SCHOOL WORK EXPERIENCE PROGRAM)
OFFICE OF STUDENT FINANCIAL ASSISTANCE; 1344 FLORIDA EDUCATION CENTER
TALLAHASSEE FL 32399
904/487-0049
AMOUNT: VARIES
DEADLINE(S): SET BY EACH PARTICIPATING INSTITUTION
FIELD(S): ALL FIELDS OF STUDY
FLORIDA RESIDENT FOR AT LEAST 2 YEARS. UNDERGRADUATE STUDENTS WITH FINANCIAL NEED WHO HAVE COMPLETED FRESHMAN YEAR & ENROLLED AT LEAST 1/2 TIME AT AN ELIGIBLE FLORIDA INSTITUTION.
PROVIDES STUDENTS WITH EMPLOYMENT AS TEACHER AIDES OR SCIENCE LABORATORY ASSISTANTS IN A PUBLIC SCHOOL IN FLORIDA. WRITE FOR COMPLETE INFORMATION.

1254

FLORIDA DEPT. OF EDUCATION (SCHOLARSHIPS FOR CHILDREN OF DECEASED OR DISABLED VETERANS)
OFFICE OF STUDENT FINANCIAL ASSISTANCE; 1344 FLORIDA EDUCATION CENTER
TALLAHASSEE FL 32399
904/487-0049
AMOUNT: THE AMOUNT OF TUITION & FEES PER ACADEMIC YEAR
DEADLINE(S): APR 1 POSTMARK
FIELD(S): ALL FIELDS OF STUDY
US CITIZEN. 5-YEAR FLORIDA RESIDENT. ENROLLED FULL TIME IN FLORIDA PUBLIC INSTITUTION. CHILDREN OF DECEASED OR 100% DISABLED WAR VETERANS/POW'S/OR MIA'S.
SCHOLARSHIPS ARE RENEWABLE. WRITE FOR COMPLETE INFORMATION.

1255

FLORIDA DEPT. OF EDUCATION (SEMINOLE/MICCOSUKEE INDIAN SCHOLARSHIPS)
OFFICE OF STUDENT FINANCIAL ASSISTANCE; KNOTT BLDG
TALLAHASSEE FL 32399
904/487-0049
AMOUNT: VARIES
DEADLINE(S): NONE
FIELD(S): ALL FIELDS OF STUDY
USA CITIZEN AND FLORIDA RESIDENT WHO IS A MEMBER OF SEMINOLE OR MICCOSUKEE INDIAN TRIBE AND IS ENROLLED AS FULL OR PART TIME UNDERGRADUATE OR GRADUATE STUDENT AT AN ELIGIBLE FLORIDA INSTITUTION. MUST DEMONSTRATE FINANCIAL NEED.
SCHOLARSHIPS ARE RENEWABLE. WRITE FOR COMPLETE INFORMATION.

1256

FLUOR CORPORATION (EMPLOYEE DEPENDENTS' SCHOLARSHIP PROGRAM)
3333 MICHELSON DR; CORP RELATIONS DEPT
IRVINE CA 92730
714/975-6799
AMOUNT: $500 - $1500
DEADLINE(S): APR 1
FIELD(S): ALL AREAS OF STUDY
OPEN TO STUDENTS ENROLLED FULL TIME IN AN ACCREDITED COLLEGE; UNIVERSITY OR VOC-TECH SCHOOL WHO IS A DEPENDENT OF A FULL TIME FLUOR CORP EMPLOYEE WITH AT LEAST ONE YEAR OF CONTINUOUS SERVICE.
WRITE FOR COMPLETE INFORMATION.

1257

FOUNDATION FOR AMATEUR RADIO (SCHOLARSHIPS)
6903 RHODE ISLAND AVE
COLLEGE PARK MD 20740
WRITTEN INQUIRY
AMOUNT: VARIES EACH YEAR
DEADLINE(S): JUN 1
FIELD(S): ALL AREAS OF STUDY
PROGRAM OPEN TO 'ACTIVE LICENSED' RADIO AMATEURS ONLY. SINCE THIS SPECIALIZED PROGRAM CHANGES SO MUCH EACH YEAR THE FOUNDATION ANNUALLY PLACES ANNOUNCEMENTS WITH COMPLETE ELIGIBILITY REQUIREMENTS IN THE AMATEUR RADIO MAGAZINES.
TO DETERMINE YOUR ELIGIBILITY LOOK FOR ANNOUNCEMENTS IN MAGAZINES SUCH AS QST; CQ; 73; WORLDRADIO; ETC. WRITE FOR COMPLETE INFORMATION.

1258

FOUNDATION FOR EXCEPTIONAL CHILDREN (SCHOLARSHIP AWARDS)
1920 ASSOCIATION DRIVE
RESTON VA 22091
703/620-1054
AMOUNT: $500 & $1000
DEADLINE(S): FEB 1
FIELD(S): ALL FIELDS OF STUDY
UNDERGRADUATE AWARDS IN 4 CATEGORIES. 1. STUDENTS WITH DISABILITIES. 2. ETHNIC MINORITY STUDENTS WITH DISABILITIES. 3. GIFTED/TALENTED STUDENTS WITH DISABILITIES. 4. ETHNIC MINORITY GIFTED/TALENTED WITH DISABILITIES.
APPLY ONLY IN ONE CATEGORY. MUST BE ENTERING FRESHMAN. WRITE FOR COMPLETE INFORMATION.

1259

FRANCIS NATHANIEL AND KATHERYN PADGET FOUNDATION (UNDERGRADUATE SCHOLARSHIPS)
PO BOX 1178
GREENWOOD SC 29646
803/942-1402

AMOUNT: $400 - $600 PER YEAR
DEADLINE(S): MAY 10 FOR RENEWALS; JUN 10 FOR NEW STUDENTS
FIELD(S): ALL AREAS OF STUDY
OPEN TO RESIDENTS OF LAUREN COUNTY SC WHO ARE OF THE PROTESTANT FAITH AND ARE SEEKING A BA OR BS DEGREE. PREFERENCE TO STUDENTS WITH A 3.0 OR BETTER GPA ALTHOUGH EXCEPTIONS ARE MADE. MOST GRANTS GO TO STUDENTS BETWEEN THE AGES OF 18 AND 30
WRITE FOR COMPLETE INFORMATION.

1260

FRANCIS OUIMET CADDIE SCHOLARSHIP FUND (SCHOLARSHIPS)
190 PARK RD
WESTON MA 02193
617/891-6400
AMOUNT: $500 - $5000
DEADLINE(S): DEC 1
FIELD(S): ALL FIELDS OF STUDY
OPEN TO MASSACHUSETTS RESIDENTS WHO ARE COLLEGE STUDENTS AND HAVE CADDIED OR SERVICED GOLF IN SOME CAPACITY FOR THREE OR MORE YEARS AT A MASSACHUSETTS GOLF CLUB. MUST DEMONSTRATE FINANCIAL NEED.
200-250 AWARDS PER YEAR. RENEWABLE. WRITE FOR COMPLETE INFORMATION.

1261

FRED A. BRYAN COLLEGIATE STUDENTS FUND (TRUST FUND SCHOLARSHIPS)
NORWEST BANK INDIANA NA; 112 W JEFFERSON BLVD
SOUTH BEND IN 46601
219/237-3314
AMOUNT: $1400 - $1600
DEADLINE(S): MAR 31
FIELD(S): ALL FIELDS OF STUDY
OPEN TO MALE GRADUATES OF HIGH SCHOOLS IN SOUTH BEND AND ST JOSEPH COUNTY IND. PREFERENCE TO THOSE WHO ARE OR HAVE BEEN BOY SCOUTS. AWARD IS FOR UNDERGRADUATE STUDY AT A RECOGNIZED COLLEGE OR UNIVERSITY. MUST DEMONSTRATE FINANCIAL NEED.
RENEWABLE FOR UP TO 4 YEARS. WRITE FOR COMPLETE INFORMATION.

1262

FRED B. & RUTH B. ZIGLER FOUNDATION (SCHOLARSHIPS)
PO BOX 986; 324 BROADWAY
JENNINGS LA 70546
318/824-2413
AMOUNT: $1250 PER SEMESTER
DEADLINE(S): MAR 10
FIELD(S): ALL AREAS OF STUDY
SCHOLARSHIPS OPEN TO GRADUATING SENIORS AT JEFFERSON DAVIS PARISH (LA) HIGH SCHOOLS. AWARDS ARE TENABLE AT RECOGNIZED COLLEGES & UNIVERSITIES.
10-18 SCHOLARSHIPS PER YEAR. RENEWABLE FOR UP TO 4 YEARS. WRITE FOR COMPLETE INFORMATION.

1263

FREEDOM FROM RELIGION FOUNDATION (STUDENT ESSAY CONTEST)
PO BOX 750
MADISON WI 53701
608/256-5800
AMOUNT: $1000; $500; $200
DEADLINE(S): AUG. 1 (POSTMARK)
FIELD(S): ALL FIELDS OF STUDY
ESSAY CONTEST ON TOPICS RELATED TO CHURCH-STATE ENTANGLEMENT IN PUBLIC SCHOOLS; GROWING UP A 'FREETHINKER' IN A RELIGIOUS ORIENTED SOCIETY; OR TUITION CREDITS FOR EDUCATION.
OPEN TO ANY COLLEGE STUDENT OR HIGH SCHOOL SENIOR WHO WILL BE ATTENDING COLLEGE IN THE SUMMER OR FALL. WRITE FOR COMPLETE INFORMATION.

1264

FREEMAN E. FAIRFIELD - MEEKER CHARITABLE TRUST (FAIRFIELD SCHOLARSHIP PROGRAM)
FIRST INTERSTATE BANK OF DENVER; PO BOX 5825
DENVER CO 80217
303/293-2211
AMOUNT: $650 PER YEAR
DEADLINE(S): NONE
FIELD(S): ALL AREAS OF STUDY
OPEN TO GRADUATES OF MEEKER HIGH SCHOOL (RIO BLANCO COUNTY) COLO FOR UNDERGRADUATE STUDY.
69 AWARDS PER YEAR; RENEWABLE. WRITE FOR COMPLETE INFORMATION.

1265

FRIENDS OF THE NATIONAL ZOO (TRAINEESHIPS)
NATIONAL ZOOLOGICAL PARK
WASHINGTON DC 20008
202/673-4955
AMOUNT: $2400 STIPEND
DEADLINE(S): FEB 22 (POSTMARK)
FIELD(S): MOST FIELDS OF STUDY
SUMMER OR FALL TRAINEESHIP PROGRAMS IN WASHINGTON DC ARE OFFERED BY THE NATIONAL ZOO TO STUDENTS IN A VARIETY OF DISCIPLINES INCLUDING VETERINARY MEDICINE; HORTICULTURE; FACILITIES DESIGN; PUBLIC AFFAIRS; PHOTOGRAPHY.
FOR ADVANCED UNDERGRADUATE STUDENTS OR RECENT GRADUATES. MINORITIES AND WOMEN ARE ENCOURAGED TO APPLY. WRITE FOR COMPLETE INFORMATION.

1266

FROZEN FOOD ASSOCIATION OF NEW ENGLAND (SCHOLARSHIP PROGRAM)
77 GREAT ROAD
ACTON MA 01720
508/263-1171
AMOUNT: $1000
DEADLINE(S): APR 1
FIELD(S): ALL AREAS OF STUDY
SCHOLARSHIPS OPEN TO PERMANENT RESIDENTS OF THE 6 NEW ENGLAND STATES. APPLICANT OR AN IMMEDIATE FAMILY MEMBER MUST BE EMPLOYED BY AN FFANE MEMBER. AWARDS SUPPORT UNDERGRADUATE STUDY AT ACCREDITED 2 OR 4 YEAR INSTITUTIONS.
12 AWARDS PER YEAR. CONTACT ADDRESS ABOVE FOR COMPLETE INFORMATION.

1267

FULLER E. CALLAWAY FOUNDATION (HATTON LOVEJOY SCHOLARSHIP)
209 BROOME STREET
LA GRANGE GA 30240
404/884-7348
AMOUNT: $3300 PER SCHOOL YEAR
DEADLINE(S): FEB 15
FIELD(S): ALL FIELDS OF STUDY
OPEN TO HIGH SCHOOL GRADUATES WHO HAVE LIVED IN TROUP COUNTY, GA FOR AT LEAST TWO YEARS AND RANK IN THE UPPER 25 PERCENT OF THEIR CLASS.
10 SCHOLARSHIPS PER YEAR. WRITE FOR COMPLETE INFORMATION.

1268

GABRIEL J. BROWN TRUST (LOW-INTEREST LOAN FUND)
112 AVENUE 'E' WEST
BISMARCK ND 58501
701/223-5916
AMOUNT: VARIES
DEADLINE(S): JUN 15
FIELD(S): ALL FIELDS OF STUDY
SPECIAL LOW-INTEREST LOANS (6%) OPEN TO RESIDENTS OF NORTH DAKOTA WHO HAVE COMPLETED AT LEAST 2 YEARS OF UNDERGRADUATE STUDY AT A RECOGNIZED COLLEGE OR UNIVERSITY & HAVE A GPA OF 2.5 OR BETTER. USA CITIZEN.
APPROX 75 LOANS PER YEAR. RENEWABLE. CONTACT ADDRESS ABOVE FOR COMPLETE INFORMATION.

1269

GEORGE ABRAHAMIAN FOUNDATION (SCHOLARSHIPS FOR LOCAL ARMENIANS)
945 ADMIRAL STREET
PROVIDENCE RI 02904
401/831-2887
AMOUNT: VARIES
DEADLINE(S): SEP 1
FIELD(S): ALL AREAS OF STUDY
OPEN TO UNDERGRADUATE AND GRADUATE STUDENTS WHO ARE USA CITIZENS OF ARMENIAN ANCESTRY WHO LIVE IN PROVIDENCE RI; ARE OF GOOD CHARACTER; HAVE THE ABILITY TO LEARN AND CAN DEMONSTRATE FINANCIAL NEED.
RENEWABLE. WRITE FOR COMPLETE INFORMATION.

1270

GEORGE E. ANDREWS TRUST
BLACKHAWK STATE BANK; PO BOX 719
BELOIT WI 53512
608/364-8917
AMOUNT: $2000
DEADLINE(S): FEB 1
FIELD(S): ALL FIELDS OF STUDY
OPEN TO SENIORS AT BELOIT MEMORIAL OR BELOIT CATHOLIC HIGH SCHOOL. SCHOLARSHIP AWARDED ALTERNATELY BETWEEN THESE TWO SCHOOLS. AWARDS BASED ON SCHOLASTIC STANDINGS; FINANCIAL NEED; MORAL CHARACTER; INDUSTRIOUSNESS; OTHER FACTORS.
WRITE FOR COMPLETE INFORMATION.

1271

GEORGE GROTEFEND SCHOLARSHIP FUND (GROTEFEND SCHOLARSHIP)
1644 MAGNOLIA AVE
REDDING CA 96001
916/225-0227
AMOUNT: $150 - $400
DEADLINE(S): APR 20 (APPLICATION SUBMISSION)
FIELD(S): ALL FIELDS OF STUDY
SCHOLARSHIPS OPEN TO APPLICANTS WHO COMPLETED ALL 4 YEARS OF HIGH SCHOOL IN SHASTA COUNTY, CALIFORNIA. AWARDS SUPPORT ALL LEVELS OF STUDY AT RECOGNIZED COLLEGES & UNIVERSITIES. USA CITIZEN OR LEGAL RESIDENT.
300 AWARDS PER YEAR. WRITE FOR COMPLETE INFORMATION.

1272

GEORGE M. PULLMAN EDUCATIONAL FOUNDATION (SCHOLARSHIP AND COUNSELING PROGRAM)
5020 S LAKE SHORE DR; SUITE 307
CHICAGO IL 60615
312/363-6191
AMOUNT: VARIES
DEADLINE(S): DEC 1 - HIGH SCHOOL SENIORS; MAY 1 - UNDERGRADUATES
FIELD(S): ALL FIELDS OF STUDY
UNDERGRADUATE SCHOLARSHIPS OPEN TO COOK COUNTY, ILL RESIDENTS WHO ARE HIGH SCHOOL SENIORS OR ADVANCED UNDERGRADUATES.
CONTACT YOUR HIGH SCHOOL GUIDANCE COUNSELOR OR WRITE FOR COMPLETE INFORMATION.

1273

GEORGE T. WELCH (SCHOLARSHIPS)
C/O TRUST DEPT; PO BOX 1796
WALLA WALLA WA 99362
509/525-2000
AMOUNT: VARIES
DEADLINE(S): APR 1
FIELD(S): ALL AREAS OF STUDY
OPEN ONLY TO USA CITIZENS WHO RESIDE IN WALLA WALLA COUNTY, WASHINGTON. MUST BE SINGLE AND ABLE TO DEMONSTRATE FINANCIAL NEED.
APPROXIMATELY 60 AWARDS PER YEAR. CONTACT DENNIS GISI AT ADDRESS ABOVE FOR COMPLETE INFORMATION.

1274

GEORGIA BOARD OF REGENTS (SCHOLARSHIPS)
244 WASHINGTON STREET SW
ATLANTA GA 30334
404/656-2200
AMOUNT: $500 FOR JUNIOR COLLEGE/$750 FOR 4-YEAR COLLEGE AND $1000 FOR GRADUATE SCHOOL STUDENTS.
DEADLINE(S): NONE SPECIFIED
FIELD(S): ALL AREAS OF STUDY
LEGAL GEORGIA RESIDENT WHO IS ENROLLED OR ACCEPTED IN AN INSTITUTION OF THE UNIVERSITY SYSTEM OF GEORGIA. GPA (BASED ON HIGH SCHOOL AND SAT SCORES) IN UPPER 25% OF CLASS. DEMONSTRATED FINANCIAL NEED.
WRITE FOR COMPLETE INFORMATION.

1275

GHIDOTTI FOUNDATION (SCHOLARSHIPS)
WELLS FARGO PRIVATE BANKING GROUP; PO BOX 2511
SACRAMENTO CA 95812
916/440-4433
AMOUNT: NOT SPECIFIED
DEADLINE(S): NONE GIVEN
FIELD(S): ALL AREAS OF STUDY
OPEN TO GRADUATES OF PUBLIC OR PRIVATE HIGH SCHOOLS LOCATED WITHIN THE BOUNDARIES OF NEVADA COUNTY, CA.
WRITE FOR COMPLETE INFORMATION.

1276

GLASS; MOLDERS; POTTERY; PLASTICS & ALLIED WORKERS INT'L UNION (SCHOLARSHIP PROGRAM)
PO BOX 607
MEDIA PA 19063
215/565-5051
AMOUNT: $2500 PER YEAR FOR 4 YEARS
DEADLINE(S): NOV 1
FIELD(S): ALL FIELDS OF STUDY
OPEN TO DEPENDENT CHILDREN OF UNION MEMBERS. APPLICANTS MUST RANK IN THE TOP 1/4 OF HIGH SCHOOL SENIOR CLASS. CHILDREN OF INTERNATIONAL UNION OFFICERS ARE NOT ELIGIBLE. AWARDS

TENABLE AT ACCREDITED UNDERGRADUATE COLLEGES & UNIVERSITIES.
WRITE FOR COMPLETE INFORMATION.

1277 ———————————————

GRACO FOUNDATION (GRACO INC. & DAVID A. KOCH SCHOLARSHIP PROGRAMS)
PO BOX 1441
MINNEAPOLIS MN 55440
612/623-6684
AMOUNT: $750 - $2000
DEADLINE(S): MAR 15
FIELD(S): ALL FIELDS OF STUDY
OPEN ONLY TO DEPENDENT CHILDREN OF REGULAR FULL-TIME EMPLOYEES OF GRACO INC. APPLICANTS MUST BE UNDER AGE 26.
WRITE FOR COMPLETE INFORMATION. E.M. JAROS IS CONTACT PERSON.

1278 ———————————————

GRAHAM-FANCHER SCHOLARSHIP TRUST
149 JOSEPHINE ST; SUITE A
SANTA CRUZ CA 95060
408/423-3640
AMOUNT: VARIES
DEADLINE(S): MAY 1
FIELD(S): ALL AREAS OF STUDY
RESIDENTS OF NORTHERN SANTA CRUZ COUNTY. MUST BE GRADUATING SENIORS FROM HIGH SCHOOLS LOCATED IN NORTHERN SANTA CRUZ COUNTY. SCHOLARSHIP; SCHOOL ACTIVITIES; COMMUNITY ACTIVITIES AND FINANCIAL NEED ARE CONSIDERATIONS.
20 AWARDS PER ACADEMIC YEAR. WRITE FOR COMPLETE INFORMATION.

1279 ———————————————

GRAND LODGE OF ILLINOIS (ILLINOIS ODD FELLOW-REBEKAH SCHOLARSHIP AWARD)
PO BOX 248; 305 NORTH KICKAPOO ST
LINCOLN IL 62656
217/735-2561
AMOUNT: UP TO $1000
DEADLINE(S): DEC 1 TO REQUEST APPLICATION; MAR 1 FOR RETURN OF APPLICATION
FIELD(S): ALL AREAS OF STUDY
ILLINOIS RESIDENT. SCHOLARSHIPS FOR UNDERGRADUATE STUDY. APPLICANTS MUST USE THE OFFICIAL ODD FELLOW-REBEKAH SCHOLARSHIP FORM; SUBMIT OFFICIAL TRANSCRIPT OF LATEST GRADES & DEMONSTRATE NEED. USA CITIZEN.
CONTACT ADDRESS ABOVE FOR COMPLETE INFORMATION AND APPLICATION FORMS.

1280 ———————————————

GRAND RAPIDS FOUNDATION (THE) - (UNDERGRADUATE EDUCATIONAL GRANTS)
161 OTTAWA NW; SUITE 209-C
GRAND RAPIDS MI 49503
616/454-1751
AMOUNT: $250 - $2500
DEADLINE(S): JAN 1 - APR 15
FIELD(S): ALL FIELDS OF STUDY
KENT COUNTY RESIDENTS. GRANTS AVAILABLE TO STUDENTS ATTENDING COLLEGE IN THE LOCAL AREA OR WESTERN MICHIGAN. FUNDING AVAILABLE FOR ADVANCED STUDY IN MUSIC AT SCHOOLS OUTSIDE MICHIGAN. US CITIZEN. DEMONSTRATE NEED.
WRITE FOR COMPLETE INFORMATION.

1281 ———————————————

GRAPHIC COMMUNICATIONS INTERNATIONAL UNION (GCIU-AJ DE ANDRADE SCHOLARSHIP AWARDS PROGRAM)
1900 L STREET NW
WASHINGTON DC 20036
202/462-1400
AMOUNT: $2000 (PAYABLE $500 PER YEAR)
DEADLINE(S): FEB 15
FIELD(S): ALL AREAS
OPEN TO CITIZENS OF USA OR CANADA WHO ARE GRADUATING HIGH SCHOOL SENIORS AND ARE DEPENDENTS OF GRAPHIC COMMUNICATIONS INTERNATIONAL UNION MEMBERS.
10 AWARDS PER YEAR. WRITE FOR COMPLETE INFORMATION.

1282 ———————————————

GREATER WORCESTER COMMUNITY FOUNDATION (SCHOLARSHIP PROGRAM)
44 FRONT ST; SUITE 530
WORCESTER MA 01608
508/775-0980
CANCELLED
AMOUN
DEAD
FIELD AREAS OF STUDY
THE FOUNDATION ADMINISTERS 16 SCHOLARSHIP FUNDS; SOME OF WHICH ARE RESTRICTED TO RESIDENTS OF A SPECIFIC

GEOGRAPHIC AREA OR TO THOSE PURSUING A PARTICULAR FIELD OF STUDY [illegible]IPIENTS ARE SELECTED ON A CO[illegible]SIS.
CONSIDERATIONS [illegible] AND NON-A[illegible]ND D[illegible]NANCIAL NEED.
A[illegible]ONS AVAILABLE IN GUIDANCE OFFICES OF ALL WORCESTER COUNTY SCHOOLS OR WRITE TO ADDRESS ABOVE.

CANCELLED

1283

GTE (SCHOLARSHIP PROGRAMS)
C/O EDUCATIONAL TESTING SERVICE; PO BOX 6730
PRINCETON NJ 08541
609/921-9000
AMOUNT: VARIES
DEADLINE(S): NOV 15
FIELD(S): ALL AREAS OF STUDY
OPEN TO HIGH SCHOOL SENIORS WHO ARE DEPENDENT CHILDREN OF FULL-TIME ACTIVE EMPLOYEES OF GTE DOMESTIC SUBSIDIARIES. STUDENTS MUST PLAN TO BEGIN FULL TIME STUDY AT AN ACCREDITED UNDERGRADUATE COLLEGE OR UNIVERSITY IN THE FOLLOWING ACADEMIC YEAR.
ALL GTE SCHOLARSHIP AWARD RECIPIENTS ARE SELECTED ON A COMPETITIVE BASIS BY INDEPENDENT ORGANIZATIONS EXPERIENCED IN THE SELECTION OF AWARD WINNERS.

1284

GTE CORPORATION
ONE STAMFORD FORUM
STAMFORD CT 06904
203/965-2948
AMOUNT: $500 - $3000
DEADLINE(S): NONE SPECIFIED
FIELD(S): ALL AREAS OF STUDY
OPEN TO HIGH SCHOOL SENIORS WHO ARE ENROLLING IN AN ACCREDITED UNDERGRADUATE PROGRAM AND ARE CHILDREN OF FULL TIME ACTIVE GTE EMPLOYEES AND GTE'S DOMESTIC SUBSIDIARIES.
WRITE FOR COMPLETE INFORMATION.

1285

GUIDEPOSTS MAGAZINE (YOUTH WRITING CONTEST SCHOLARSHIP)
16 E 34TH ST
NEW YORK NY 10016
212/251-8100
AMOUNT: $1000 - $6000
DEADLINE(S): DEC 2
FIELD(S): ALL FIELDS OF STUDY
OPEN TO ANY HIGH SCHOOL JUNIOR OR SENIOR (USA OR FOREIGN CITIZEN) WHO WRITES AN ORIGINAL 1200-WORD PERSONAL EXPERIENCE STORY (IN ENGLISH) IN WHICH THE WRITER'S FAITH IN GOD PLAYED A ROLE. STORIES SHOULD BE TRUE & WRITTEN IN THE 1ST PERSON.
THE TOP 30 STORIES WILL RECEIVE THESE PRIZES—1ST/$6000 2ND/$5000 3RD/$4000 4TH/$3000 5TH/$2000 6TH-10TH/$1000 AND 1ST-30TH PORTABLE ELECTRONIC TYPEWRITERS. STORIES SHOULD BE SUBMITTED BETWEEN SEP 1 & THE MONDAY AFTER THANKSGIVING.

1286

H&R BLOCK FOUNDATION (SCHOLARSHIP FOUNDATION)
4410 MAIN STREET
KANSAS CITY MO 64111
816/753-6900
AMOUNT: $2000
DEADLINE(S): APR 10
FIELD(S): ALL AREAS OF STUDY
FOR CHILDREN OF ELIGIBLE EMPLOYEES OF H&R BLOCK INC/OR ONE OF ITS OWNED SUBSIDIARIES. BASED ON ACADEMIC CAPABILITY AND FINANCIAL NEED. MUST BE ENROLLED FULL TIME.
35 AWARDS PER YEAR. CONTACT ADDRESS ABOVE FOR COMPLETE INFORMATION.

1287

H.P. HOOD INC. (SCHOLARSHIPS)
CHARLES H. HOOD FUND; 500 RUTHERFORD AVE
BOSTON MA 02129
617/242-0600
AMOUNT: $3500 PER YEAR
DEADLINE(S): JAN 15
FIELD(S): ALL AREAS OF STUDY
OPEN TO SONS AND DAUGHTERS OF EMPLOYEES OF H.P. HOOD INC. AND AGRI-MARK INC. ONE PROGRAM IS FOR HIGH SCHOOL SENIORS AND ONE IS FOR COLLEGE UPPER CLASSMEN.
THREE TO FOUR AWARDS PER PROGRAM PER YEAR. WRITE FOR COMPLETE INFORMATION.

1288

H.T. EWALD FOUNDATION (SCHOLARSHIP AWARDS)
15175 E JEFFERSON AVE
GROSSE POINTE MI 48230
313/821-2000
AMOUNT: $400 TO $2500
DEADLINE(S): MAY 1
FIELD(S): ALL FIELDS OF STUDY
OPEN TO RESIDENTS OF THE METROPOLITAN DETROIT (MI) AREA WHO WILL BE ENTERING COLLEGE AS A FRESHMAN. AWARDS ARE AVAILABLE FOR UP TO 4-YEARS OF UNDERGRADUATE WORK BASED ON FINANCIAL NEED; ACADEMIC ACHIEVEMENT; EXTRACURRICULAR ACTIVITIES.
10 TO 15 AWARDS PER YEAR. WRITE FOR COMPLETE INFORMATION.

1289

HARNESS HORSEMEN INTERNATIONAL FOUNDATION (J.L. HAUCK MEMORIAL SCHOLARSHIP FUND)
525 HIGHWAY 33; SUITE 3
ENGLISHTOWN NJ 07726
908/446-3346
AMOUNT: $4000
DEADLINE(S): JUN 1
FIELD(S): ALL FIELDS OF STUDY
OPEN TO SONS & DAUGHTERS OF HARNESS HORSEMEN INTERNATIONAL ASSN MEMBERS. SCHOLARSHIP SUPPORTS UNDERGRADUATE STUDY AT ANY RECOGNIZED COLLEGE OR UNIVERSITY.
RENEWABLE. WRITE FOR COMPLETE INFORMATION.

1290

HARNESS TRACKS OF AMERICA (HARRY M. STEVENS-LADBROKE RACING & PENNSYLVANIA-ROSECROFT RACEWAY SCHOLARSHIPS)
35 AIRPORT RD; #420
MORRISTOWN NJ 07960
201/285-9090
AMOUNT: $2500 - $3000
DEADLINE(S): MAY 30
FIELD(S): ALL FIELDS OF STUDY
OPEN TO YOUNG PERSONS ACTIVELY ENGAGED IN THE SPORT OF HARNESS RACING & CHILDREN OF PERSONS WHO ARE LICENSED AS A GROOM; TRAINER; DRIVER; ETC. AWARDS SUPPORT UNDERGRADUATE OR GRADUATE STUDY.
5 TO 6 SCHOLARSHIPS PER YEAR. RENEWABLE. WRITE FOR COMPLETE INFORMATION.

1291

HARRY E. & FLORENCE W. SNAYBERGER MEMORIAL FOUNDATION (GRANT AWARD)
C/O PENNSYLVANIA NATIONAL BANK & TRUST COMPANY; TRUST DEPT; CENTER & NORWEGIAN
POTTSVILLE PA 17901
717/622-4200
AMOUNT: VARIES
DEADLINE(S): LAST WORKING DAY IN FEBRUARY
FIELD(S): ALL AREAS OF STUDY
APPLICANTS MUST BE RESIDENTS OF SCHUYLKILL COUNTY, PA AND APPLY FOR PHEAA AND PELL GRANTS. FAILURE TO QUALIFY FOR THESE GRANTS DOES NOT HARM CHANCES OF RECEIVING THE SNAYBERGER GRANT HOWEVER.
CONTACT MRS. CAROLYN B. BERNATONIS TRUST SECRETARY ADDRESS ABOVE.

1292

HARVARD UNIVERSITY - NIEMAN FOUNDATION (FELLOWSHIPS FOR JOURNALISTS)
WALTER LIPPMAN HOUSE; ONE FRANCIS AVE
CAMBRIDGE MA 02138
617/495-2237; FAX 617/495-8976
AMOUNT: STIPEND; FEES; CHILD CARE ALLOWANCE
DEADLINE(S): JAN 31 AMERICAN JOURNALISTS; MAR 1 FOREIGN JOURNALISTS
FIELD(S): ALL FIELDS OF STUDY
OPEN TO FULL TIME NEWS OR EDITORIAL EMPLOYEES OR PHOTOGRAPHERS WITH THE GENERAL INTEREST MEDIA (PRINT OR ELECTRONIC). THERE ARE NO EDUCATIONAL PREREQUISITES BUT A MINIMUM OF 3 YEARS EXPERIENCE AS A PROFESSIONAL JOURNALIST IS REQUIRED.
FELLOWS RECEIVE NEITHER COURSE CREDIT NOR DEGREES. AMERICAN JOURNALISTS MUST BE USA CITIZENS; FOREIGN JOURNALISTS MUST BE FLUENT IN SPOKEN AND WRITTEN ENGLISH. WRITE FOR COMPLETE INFORMATION.

1293

HARVARD/RADCLIFFE OFFICE OF ADMISSIONS AND FINANCIAL AID (SCHOLARSHIPS; GRANTS; LOANS & WORK STUDY PROGRAMS)

3RD FLOOR - BYERLY HALL; 8 GARDEN ST.
CAMBRIDGE MA 02138
617/495-1581

AMOUNT: VARIES
DEADLINE(S): NONE
FIELD(S): ALL FIELDS OF STUDY

ALL FINANCIAL AID IS NEED BASED EXCEPT FOR STUDENTS DESCENDED FROM ORIGINAL DONORS NAMED DOWNER; PENNOYER; MACHSONDALE & ELLIS WHO MAY BE ELIGIBLE FOR ASSISTANCE. NEED BASED FUNDS AVAILABLE TO ALL WHO ARE ADMITTED AND CAN SHOW NEED.

APPLICANTS MUST BE ACCEPTED FOR ADMISSION TO HARVARD BEFORE THEY WILL BE CONSIDERED FOR FUNDING. MANY FACTORS OTHER THAN FAMILY INCOME ARE CONSIDERED. WRITE FOR COMPLETE INFORMATION.

1294

HATTIE M. STRONG FOUNDATION (NO-INTEREST LOANS)

1735 EYE ST NW; RM 705
WASHINGTON DC 20006
202/331-1619

AMOUNT: UP TO $2500
DEADLINE(S): APPLY JAN 1 - MAR 31
FIELD(S): ALL FIELDS OF STUDY

OPEN TO USA UNDERGRADUATE & GRADUATE STUDENTS IN THEIR LAST YEAR OF STUDY IN THE USA OR ABROAD. LOANS ARE MADE SOLELY ON THE BASIS OF INDIVIDUAL MERIT. THERE IS NO INTEREST & NO COLLATERAL REQUIREMENT. USA CITIZEN.

APPROX 240 AWARDS PER YEAR. FINANCIAL NEED IS A CONSIDERATION. WRITE GIVING PERSONAL HISTORY; SCHOOL ATTENDED; SUBJECT STUDIED; DATE EXPECTED TO COMPLETE STUDIES & AMOUNT OF FUNDS NEEDED. SEND SELF-ADDRESSED STAMPED ENVELOPE.

1295

HAUSS-HELMS FOUNDATION INC. (GRANT PROGRAM-SCHOLARSHIPS)

PO BOX 25
WAPAKONETA OH 45895
419/738-4911

AMOUNT: UP TO $4500
DEADLINE(S): APR 15
FIELD(S): ALL FIELDS OF STUDY

UNDERGRADUATE SCHOLARSHIPS. OPEN TO RESIDENTS OF EITHER AUGLAIZE OR ALLEN COUNTY, OHIO WHO ARE RECOMMENDED BY THEIR HIGH SCHOOL PRINCIPAL; RESPONSIBLE FACULTY MEMBER OR THEIR GUIDANCE COUNSELOR. USA CITIZEN.

195 SCHOLARSHIPS PER YEAR. RENEWABLE WITH REAPPLICATION. WRITE FOR COMPLETE INFORMATION.

1296

HAWAII COMMUNITY FOUNDATION (SCHOLARSHIPS)

222 MERCHANT ST; 2ND FLOOR
HONOLULU HI 96813
808/537-6333

AMOUNT: VARIES
DEADLINE(S): MAR 1
FIELD(S): ALL AREAS OF STUDY

VARIETY OF SCHOLARSHIPS OPEN TO HAWAII RESIDENTS WHO CAN DEMONSTRATE FINANCIAL NEED AND ARE ATTENDING AN ACCREDITED TWO OR FOUR YEAR COLLEGE OR UNIVERSITY. EACH AWARD HAS SPECIFIC ELIGIBILITY REQUIREMENTS.

WRITE FOR A BROCHURE LISTING THE VARIOUS SCHOLARSHIPS AND THEIR REQUIREMENTS.

1297

HAWAII EDUCATIONAL LOAN PROGRAM (PLUS/SLS)

1314 S KING ST; #961
HONOLULU HI 96814
808/536-3731

AMOUNT: $4000
DEADLINE(S): NONE
FIELD(S): ALL AREAS OF STUDY

THIS IS A PARENTAL LOAN FOR EITHER PARENTS OF (DEPENDENT) UNDERGRADUATES; INDEPENDENT UNDERGRADUATES OR GRADUATE STUDENTS. THE LOAN MUST BE REPAID. VARIABLE INTEREST RATE CHANGES ANNUALLY.

WRITE FOR COMPLETE INFORMATION.

1298

HERBERT LEHMAN EDUCATION FUND (SCHOLARSHIPS)

99 HUDSON STREET; #1600
NEW YORK NY 10013
WRITTEN INQUIRY

AMOUNT: $1200
DEADLINE(S): APR 15
FIELD(S): ALL FIELDS OF STUDY
OPEN TO NEEDY AFRICAN AMERICAN HIGH SCHOOL STUDENTS PLANNING TO BEGIN UNDERGRADUATE STUDY AT RECENTLY DESEGREGATED AND PUBLICLY SUPPORTED DEEP SOUTH INSTITUTIONS HAVING A BELOW AVERAGE ENROLLMENT OF AFRICAN AMERICANS.
USA CITIZENS. 50-100 AWARDS PER YEAR. RENEWABLE. ALL REQUESTS FOR APPLICATION FORMS MUST BE IN WRITING AND REQUESTED BY THE APPLICANT.

1299

HERMAN O. WEST FOUNDATION (SCHOLARSHIP PROGRAM)
PO BOX 808; HUMAN RESOURCES DEPT.
PHOENIXVILLE PA 19460
215/935-4626
AMOUNT: UP TO $2000 PER YEAR
DEADLINE(S): FEB 28
FIELD(S): ALL AREAS OF STUDY
OPEN TO CHILDREN OF WEST COMPANY EMPLOYEES FOR UNDERGRADUATE STUDY AT AN ACCREDITED FOUR YEAR COLLEGE OR UNIVERSITY. FOR HIGH SCHOOL GRADUATES WHO WILL ENTER COLLEGE THE FALL FOLLOWING GRADUATION.
PARENT SHOULD OBTAIN APPLICATION FROM HUMAN RESOURCES DEPARTMENT. FOR CHILDREN OF WEST COMPANY EMPLOYEES ONLY.

1300

HERSCHEL C. PRICE EDUCATIONAL FOUNDATION (GRANTS PROGRAM)
PO BOX 412
HUNTINGTON WV 25708
304/529-3852
AMOUNT: $250 TO $1500 PER SEMESTER
DEADLINE(S): OCT 1; APR 1
FIELD(S): ALL FIELDS OF STUDY
SCHOLARSHIPS ARE GIVEN PRIMARILY TO STUDENTS WHO ARE RESIDENTS OF WEST VIRGINIA IN ATTENDANCE AT WV INSTITUTIONS AT THE UNDERGRADUATE LEVEL. SOME GRADUATE AWARDS ARE AVAILABLE. USA CITIZEN.
WRITE FOR COMPLETE INFORMATION.

1301

HORACE SMITH FUND (WALTER S. BARR SCHOLARSHIP FELLOWSHIP & LOAN FUND)
PO BOX 3034; 1441 MAIN ST
SPRINGFIELD MA 01101
413/739-4222
AMOUNT: VARIES
DEADLINE(S): DEC 31 (SCHOLARSHIPS); FEB 1 (FELLOWSHIPS); JUL 1 (LOANS)
FIELD(S): ALL AREAS OF STUDY
OPEN TO GRADUATES OF HAMPDEN COUNTY MASS SECONDARY SCHOOLS FOR UNDERGRADUATE OR GRADUATE STUDY. FINANCIAL NEED IS OF PRIMARY IMPORTANCE. SCHOLARSHIP/FELLOWSHIP APPLICATIONS AVAILABLE AFTER SEP 1; LOAN APPLICATIONS AFTER APR 1.
SCHOLARSHIPS ARE FOR SENIORS FROM AGAWAM; CHICOPEE; E LONGMEADOW; LONGMEADOW; LUDLOW; SPRINGFIELD; W SPRINGFIELD & WILBRAHAM HIGH SCHOOLS. RENEWABLE. WRITE FOR COMPLETE INFORMATION.

1302

HOWARD AND MAMIE NICHOLS SCHOLARSHIP TRUST (SCHOLARSHIPS)
WELLS FARGO BANK TRUST DEPT.; 2222 W SHAW AVE; SUITE 11
FRESNO CA 93711
209/442-6232 OR 805/395-0920
AMOUNT: VARIES
DEADLINE(S): FEB 28
FIELD(S): ALL FIELDS OF STUDY
OPEN TO GRADUATES OF KERN COUNTY CALIF HIGH SCHOOLS FOR FULL-TIME UNDERGRADUATE OR GRADUATE STUDY AT A POST-SECONDARY INSTITUTION. MUST DEMONSTRATE FINANCIAL NEED AND HAVE A 2.0 OR BETTER GPA.
APPROXIMATELY 100 AWARDS PER YEAR. RENEWABLE WITH REAPPLICATION. WRITE FOR COMPLETE INFORMATION.

1303

HOYT FOUNDATION (MAY EMMA HOYT FUND SCHOLARSHIPS)
PO BOX 1488
NEW CASTLE PA 16103
WRITTEN INQUIRY
AMOUNT: VARIES
DEADLINE(S): NONE GIVEN

FIELD(S): ALL FIELDS OF STUDY
OPEN TO RESIDENTS OF LAWRENCE COUNTY, PA FOR UNDERGRADUATE STUDY. THERE ARE NO RESTRICTIONS ON THE CHOICE OF A COLLEGE.
WRITE FOR COMPLETE INFORMATION.

1304

HUALAPAI TRIBAL COUNCIL (SCHOLARSHIP PROGRAM)
PO BOX 179
PEACH SPRINGS AZ 86434
602/769-2216
AMOUNT: $700
DEADLINE(S): 2 WEEKS BEFORE EACH SEMESTER
FIELD(S): ALL AREAS OF STUDY
SCHOLARSHIPS ARE OFFERED TO STUDENTS WHO ARE ENROLLED FULL TIME AND MAINTAIN PASSING GRADES. APPLICANTS MUST BE A MEMBER OF THE HUALAPAI TRIBE.
CONTACT LINDA E. HAVATONE ADDRESS ABOVE.

1305

HUNT MANUFACTURING CO. FOUNDATION (COLLEGE AID FOR DEPENDENTS)
230 SOUTH BROAD STREET; SUITE 1300
PHILADELPHIA PA 19102
215/732-7700
AMOUNT: $1000 - $2000
DEADLINE(S): APR 15
FIELD(S): ALL AREAS OF STUDY
SCHOLARSHIPS OPEN ONLY TO DEPENDENTS OF HUNT MANUFACTURING EMPLOYEES. FOR UNDERGRADUATE STUDY AT RECOGNIZED COLLEGES AND UNIVERSITIES.
4-6 AWARDS PER YEAR. WRITE FOR COMPLETE INFORMATION.

1306

IDAHO STATE BOARD OF EDUCATION (SCHOLARSHIP PROGRAMS)
LBJ BUILDING - ROOM 307; 650 WEST STATE ST
BOISE ID 83720
208/334-2270
AMOUNT: $1500 - $5000
DEADLINE(S): VARIOUS
FIELD(S): ALL AREAS OF STUDY
VARIOUS SCHOLARSHIP PROGRAMS OPEN TO IDAHO RESIDENTS WHO ARE GRADUATES OF IDAHO HIGH SCHOOLS. SUBMIT SCORES ON ACT (ACADEMIC & VOCATIONAL). FOR UNDERGRADUATE STUDY AT RECOGNIZED COLLEGES & UNIVERSITIES.
WRITE FOR COMPLETE INFORMATION.

1307

ILLINOIS DEPARTMENT OF THE AMERICAN LEGION (SCHOLARSHIPS)
PO BOX 2910
BLOOMINGTON IL 61702
309/663-0361
AMOUNT: $500
DEADLINE(S): MAR 15
FIELD(S): ALL FIELDS OF STUDY
SCHOLARSHIPS ARE OPEN TO DEPENDENT CHILDREN OF ILLINOIS AMERICAN LEGION MEMBERS. AWARDS ARE TENABLE AT RECOGNIZED UNDERGRADUATE COLLEGES & UNIVERSITIES. USA CITIZEN.
20 SCHOLARSHIPS PER YEAR. WRITE FOR COMPLETE INFORMATION.

1308

ILLINOIS DEPARTMENT OF THE AMERICAN LEGION (SCOUTING SCHOLARSHIP)
PO BOX 2910
BLOOMINGTON IL 61701
309/663-0361
AMOUNT: $500 & $100
DEADLINE(S): APR 30
FIELD(S): ALL AREAS OF STUDY
OPEN TO SCOUTS OR EXPLORER SCOUTS WHO ARE RESIDENTS OF ILLINOIS. ESSAY OF 500 WORDS ON THE LEGION'S AMERICANISM AND SCOUTING PROGRAM IS REQUIRED.
ONE $500 AND FOUR $100 SCHOLARSHIPS PER YEAR. WRITE FOR COMPLETE INFORMATION.

1309

ILLINOIS STUDENT ASSISTANCE COMMISSION (STATE & FEDERAL SCHOLARSHIPS; FELLOWSHIPS; GRANTS; LOANS)
106 WILMONT ROAD
DEERFIELD IL 60015
708/948-8550
AMOUNT: VARIES WITH PROGRAM
DEADLINE(S): VARIES
FIELD(S): ALL AREAS OF STUDY
COMMISSION ADMINISTERS A NUMBER OF STATE AND FEDERAL SCHOLARSHIP; FELLOWSHIP; GRANT AND LOAN PROGRAMS FOR ILLINOIS RESIDENTS.
WRITE FOR COMPLETE INFORMATION.

1310

INDEPENDENCE FEDERAL SAVINGS BANK (GUARANTEED STUDENT LOAN PROGRAM)
1835 K STREET NW; SUITE 300
WASHINGTON DC 20006
202/626-0473 OR 800/733-0473
AMOUNT: $2625 - $4000 UNDERGRADS; UP TO $7500 GRADUATES
DEADLINE(S): NONE
FIELD(S): ALL FIELDS OF STUDY
LOANS OPEN TO US CITIZENS WHO ARE ACCEPTED FOR ENROLLMENT OR ENROLLED IN A SCHOOL APPROVED BY THE US DEPT OF EDUCATION; HAVE A SATISFACTORY ACADEMIC RECORD AND CAN DEMONSTRATE FINANCIAL NEED.
WRITE FOR COMPLETE INFORMATION.

1311

INDIANA STATE STUDENT ASSISTANCE COMMISSION (HIGHER EDUCATION & FREEDOM OF CHOICE GRANTS)
150 W MARKET ST; SUITE 500
INDIANAPOLIS IN 46204
317/232-2350
AMOUNT: $200 - $4000
DEADLINE(S): MAR 1
FIELD(S): ALL FIELDS OF STUDY
OPEN TO INDIANA RESIDENTS WHO ARE ACCEPTED TO OR ENROLLED IN ELIGIBLE INDIANA INSTITUTIONS AS FULL TIME UNDERGRADUATE STUDENTS. USA CITIZEN OR LEGAL RESIDENT.
APPROX 49000 GRANTS & AWARDS PER YEAR. FINANCIAL NEED IS A CONSIDERATION BASED ON CHOICE OF COLLEGE. WRITE FOR COMPLETE INFORMATION.

1312

INLAND STEEL - RYERSON FOUNDATION (ALL-INLAND SCHOLARSHIP PROGRAM)
30 WEST MONROE
CHICAGO IL 60603
312/899-3420
AMOUNT: $500 TO $2250
DEADLINE(S): NONE
FIELD(S): ALL AREAS OF STUDY
OPEN TO HIGH SCHOOL SENIORS WHO ARE CHILDREN OF INLAND STEEL EMPLOYEES. AWARDS MADE ON BASIS OF CLASS STANDING (GPA) AND FINANCIAL NEED AS DETERMINED BY FINANCIAL AID FORM. RENEWABLE.
40 TO 50 AWARDS PER YEAR. WRITE FOR COMPLETE INFORMATION.

1313

INTERCOLLEGIATE TENNIS COACHES ASSOCIATION (SCHOLARSHIP)
PO BOX 71
PRINCETON NJ 08544
609/258-6332
AMOUNT: $1000
DEADLINE(S): MAY 1
FIELD(S): ALL FIELDS OF STUDY
SCHOLARSHIPS FOR GRADUATE STUDY OPEN TO SENIOR UNDERGRADUATES WHO HAVE OUTSTANDING ACADEMIC RECORDS; HOLD VARSITY TENNIS LETTERS; AND HAVE BEEN RECOGNIZED FOR THEIR EXTRACURRICULAR ACHIEVEMENTS.
EIGHT AWARDS PER YEAR. WRITE FOR COMPLETE INFORMATION.

1314

INTERNATIONAL ALLIANCE OF THEATRICAL STAGE EMPLOYEES AND MOVING PICTURE MACHINE OPERATORS (RICHARD F. WALSH FOUNDATION)
1515 BROADWAY; SUITE 601
NEW YORK NY 10036
212/730-1770
AMOUNT: $750
DEADLINE(S): DEC 31
FIELD(S): ALL FIELDS OF STUDY
SCHOLARSHIP IS OFFERED TO HIGH SCHOOL SENIORS WHO ARE CHILDREN OF MEMBERS IN GOOD STANDING. AWARDS ARE BASED ON TRANSCRIPTS; SAT SCORES; LETTER(S) OF RECOMMENDATION FROM CLERGY OR TEACHER.
AWARD RENEWABLE FOR 4 YEARS. WRITE FOR COMPLETE INFORMATION.

1315

INTERNATIONAL ASSN. OF BRIDGE STRUCTURAL AND ORNAMENTAL IRON WORKERS (JOHN H. LYONS SCHOLARSHIP PROGRAM)
1750 NEW YORK AVE NW; SUITE 400
WASHINGTON DC 20006
202/383-4800
AMOUNT: $1500 PER YEAR MAXIMUM

DEADLINE(S): JAN 15
FIELD(S): ALL AREAS OF STUDY
OPEN TO CHILDREN OF MEMBERS OR DECEASED MEMBERS IN GOOD STANDING AT THE TIME OF DEATH. APPLICANTS MUST RANK IN THE UPPER HALF OF HIGH SCHOOL GRADUATING CLASS. FOR UNDERGRADUATE STUDY IN USA OR CANADA.
SCHOLARSHIPS WILL BE AWARDED FOR ONE YEAR AND MAY BE RENEWED FOR THREE ACADEMIC YEARS. WRITE FOR COMPLETE INFORMATION.

1316

INTERNATIONAL ASSOCIATION OF MACHINISTS AND AEROSPACE WORKERS (IAM SCHOLARSHIP COMPETITION)
9000 MACHINISTIS PLACE; ROOM 301
UPPER MARLBORO MD 20772
301/967-4708
AMOUNT: $1000 - $2000
DEADLINE(S): DEC 1
FIELD(S): ALL FIELDS OF STUDY
MEMBER OR DEPENDENT CHILD OF A MEMBER WITH 2 YEARS CONTINUOUS MEMBERSHIP. FOR BEGINNING UNDERGRADUATE STUDY ONLY. ENCLOSE SELF-ADDRESSED STAMPED BUSINESS SIZE ENVELOPE WITH EACH APPLICATION REQUEST.
WRITE FOR COMPLETE INFORMATION.

1317

INTERNATIONAL BROTHERHOOD OF TEAMSTERS (SCHOLARSHIP FUND)
25 LOUISIANA AVENUE NW
WASHINGTON DC 20001
202/624-8735
AMOUNT: $1000 - $1500 PER YEAR
DEADLINE(S): NOV 30 (TO LOCAL UNION)
FIELD(S): ALL FIELDS OF STUDY
OPEN TO HIGH SCHOOL SENIORS WHO ARE DEPENDENT CHILDREN OF TEAMSTER MEMBERS. FOR STUDENTS IN TOP 15% OF THEIR CLASS WITH EXCELLENT APTITUDE SCORES. USA OR CANADIAN CITIZEN. MUST DEMONSTRATE FINANCIAL NEED.
25 SCHOLARSHIPS PER YEAR. TOP 10 ARE FOR $1500 & RENEWABLE UP TO 4 YEARS. REMAINING 15 ARE FOR $1000 AND FOR 1 YEAR ONLY. WRITE FOR COMPLETE INFORMATION.

1318

INTERNATIONAL CHRISTIAN YOUTH EXCHANGE (ICYE SCHOLARSHIP PROGRAMS)
134 W 26TH ST; SUITE 401
NEW YORK NY 10001
212/206-7307; FAX 212/633-9085
AMOUNT: UP TO $1500
DEADLINE(S): MAY 15
FIELD(S): INTERNATIONAL EXCHANGE
OPEN TO PEOPLE AGE 16-30 WHO WANT TO GO ABROAD WITH ICYE FOR ONE YEAR OR PARTICIPATE IN SUMMER ICYE WORKCAMPS OUTSIDE THE USA.
WRITE FOR COMPLETE INFORMATION.

1319

INTERNATIONAL LADIES GARMENT WORKERS UNION (NATIONAL SCHOLARSHIP FUND)
1710 BROADWAY
NEW YORK NY 10019
212/265-7000
AMOUNT: $2500 TOTAL OVER 4 YEARS
DEADLINE(S): DEC 31
FIELD(S): ALL FIELDS OF STUDY
OPEN TO SONS OR DAUGHTERS OF UNION MEMBERS IN GOOD STANDING FOR AT LEAST 3 YEARS. MUST SUBMIT SAT OR ACT SCORES. APPLICATIONS ACCEPTED ONLY FROM HIGH SCHOOL SENIORS.
10 SCHOLARSHIPS PER YEAR. WRITE FOR COMPLETE INFORMATION.

1320

INTERNATIONAL LADIES GARMENT WORKERS UNION (ILGWU SCHOLARSHIPS)
ONE NORTH HOWARD STREET
BALTIMORE MD 21201
301/685-0884
AMOUNT: $2500
DEADLINE(S): APR 1
FIELD(S): ALL FIELDS OF STUDY
OPEN TO CHILDREN OF CURRENT MEMBERS OF UPPER SOUTH DEPT. ILGWU WITH 3 YEARS GOOD STANDING IN UNION. AWARDS ARE TENABLE AT ACCREDITED UNDERGRADUATE COLLEGES & UNIVERSITIES.
WRITE FOR COMPLETE INFORMATION.

1321

INTERNATIONAL LADIES GARMENT WORKERS UNION (PHILADELPHIA - SOUTH JERSEY DISTRICT COUNCIL SCHOLARSHIP AWARDS)

EDUCATION DIRECTOR; 35 S 4TH ST
PHILADELPHIA PA 19106
215/351-0750

AMOUNT: $600
DEADLINE(S): APR 15
FIELD(S): ALL AREAS OF STUDY

OPEN TO HIGH SCHOOL STUDENTS WHO ARE CHILDREN OF PHILADELPHIA-SOUTH JERSEY DISTRICT COUNCIL ILGWU MEMBERS (FOR AT LEAST 2 YEARS) OR TO CHILDREN OF MEMBERS WHO HAVE DIED (WITHIN LAST 2 YEARS).

STUDENTS CURRENTLY ENROLLED IN COLLEGE ARE NOT ELIGIBLE TO APPLY. WRITE FOR COMPLETE INFORMATION.

1322

INTERNATIONAL ONEXIOCA (FOUNDERS MEMORIAL AWARD)

911 BARTLETT PLACE
WINDSOR CA 95492
WRITTEN INQUIRY ONLY

AMOUNT: $250
DEADLINE(S): JAN 7
FIELD(S): ALL FIELDS OF STUDY

ANNUAL AWARD IN MEMORY OF HERNESTO K ONEXIOCA/FOUNDER. ANYONE WITH THE NAME OF ONEXIOCA (WHO IS NOT A BLOOD/OR MARRIAGE RELATIVE) & BORN ON JAN 1 IS ELIGIBLE TO APPLY.

ALL INQUIRIES MUST INCLUDE PROOF OF NAME AND BIRTH DATE. THOSE WITHOUT SUCH PROOF WILL NOT BE ACKNOWLEDGED.

1323

INTERNATIONAL SOCIETY FOR CLINICAL LABORATORY TECHNOLOGY (SCHOLARSHIP)

818 OLIVE ST; #918
ST LOUIS MO 63101
314/241-1445

AMOUNT: VARIES
DEADLINE(S): JUL 31
FIELD(S): ALL FIELDS OF STUDY

OPEN TO ISCLT MEMBERS AND THEIR DEPENDENT CHILDREN. REQUIRES GRADUATION FROM AN ACCREDITED HIGH SCHOOL OR EQUIVALENT.

WRITE FOR COMPLETE INFORMATION.

1324

INTERNATIONAL UNION OF BRICKLAYERS AND ALLIED CRAFTSMEN (HARRY C. BATES MERIT SCHOLARSHIP PROGRAM)

815 FIFTEENTH STREET NW
WASHINGTON DC 20005
202/783-3788

AMOUNT: $500 - $2000 PER YEAR UP TO 4 YEARS
DEADLINE(S): OCT PSAT TESTS
FIELD(S): ALL AREAS OF STUDY

OPEN TO NATURAL OR LEGALLY ADOPTED CHILDREN OF CURRENT; RETIRED OR DECEASED BAC MEMBERS. COMPETITION IS ADMINISTERED BY NATIONAL MERIT SCHOLARSHIP CORP. WHICH CONDUCTS PSAT/NMSQT DURING OCTOBER OF STUDENT'S JUNIOR YEAR OF HIGH SCHOOL.

APPLICANTS MUST BE NATIONAL MERIT SEMIFINALISTS. AWARD TENABLE AT ANY ACCREDITED UNIVERSITY OR COMMUNITY COLLEGE THE STUDENT ATTENDS FULL TIME. WRITE FOR COMPLETE INFORMATION.

1325

INTERNATIONAL UNION OF ELECTRONIC; ELECTRICAL; SALARIED; MACHINE & FURNITURE WORKERS (JB CAREY; DJ FITZMAURICE & WH BYWATER SCHOLARSHIPS)

1126 16TH ST NW; DEPT SOCIAL ACTION
WASHINGTON DC 20036
202/296-1200

AMOUNT: $1000 JBC; $2000 DJF; $3000 WHB
DEADLINE(S): APR 15
FIELD(S): ALL AREAS OF STUDY

PROGRAMS OPEN TO DEPENDENTS OF UNION MEMBERS. JB CAREY SCHOLARSHIPS SUPPORT UNDERGRADUATE STUDY FOR 1 YEAR IN ALL AREAS OF STUDY. DJ FITZMAURICE SCHOLARSHIPS SUPPORT UNDERGRADUATE STUDY FOR 1 YEAR IN ENGINEERING ONLY.

WH BYWATER SCHOLARSHIP AVAILABLE ONLY TO CHILDREN OF ELECTED LOCAL UNION OFFICIALS. 10 AWARDS PER YEAR. CONTACT UNION REPRESENTATIVE FOR COMPLETE INFORMATION.

1326

IOWA AMERICAN LEGION (BASEBALL TOURNAMENT SCHOLARSHIP)
720 LYON ST
DES MOINES IA 50309
515/282-5068
AMOUNT: $1000
DEADLINE(S): NONE SPECIFIED
FIELD(S): ALL AREAS OF STUDY
OPEN TO PARTICIPANTS IN THE LEGION SPONSORED SENIOR BASEBALL TOURNAMENT WHO PORTRAY OUTSTANDING SPORTSMANSHIP; TEAM PLAY AND ATHLETIC ABILITY. FOR STUDY IN IOWA COLLEGES AND UNIVERSITIES.
WRITE FOR COMPLETE INFORMATION.

1327

IOWA AMERICAN LEGION (BOY SCOUT OF THE YEAR CONTEST SCHOLARSHIP)
720 LYON ST
DES MOINES IA 50309
515/282-5068
AMOUNT: $1000
DEADLINE(S): NONE SPECIFIED
FIELD(S): ALL AREAS OF STUDY
OPEN TO IOWA BOY SCOUTS WHO HAVE RECEIVED THE EAGLE SCOUT AWARD. SCHOLARSHIP IS GIVEN BASED ON SCOUT'S OUTSTANDING SERVICE TO HIS RELIGIOUS INSTITUTION; SCHOOL AND COMMUNITY. FOR UNDERGRADUATE STUDY AT AN IOWA COLLEGE OR UNIVERSITY.
WRITE FOR COMPLETE INFORMATION.

1328

IOWA AMERICAN LEGION (ORATORICAL CONTEST SCHOLARSHIP)
720 LYON ST
DES MOINES IA 50309
515/282-5068
AMOUNT: $2000 (1ST PRIZE); $600 (2ND); $400 (3RD)
DEADLINE(S): NONE SPECIFIED
FIELD(S): ALL AREAS OF STUDY
ORATORICAL CONTEST OPEN TO IOWA HIGH SCHOOL STUDENTS IN THE 9TH THROUGH 12TH GRADES. PRIZES ARE IN THE FORM OF SCHOLARSHIPS TO ATTEND A COLLEGE OR UNIVERSITY IN IOWA.
WRITE FOR COMPLETE INFORMATION.

1329

IOWA AMERICAN LEGION (OUTSTANDING CITIZEN OF BOYS STATE SCHOLARSHIP)
720 LYON ST
DES MOINES IA 50309
515/282-5068
AMOUNT: $1500
DEADLINE(S): NONE SPECIFIED
FIELD(S): ALL AREAS OF STUDY
OPEN TO MALES WHO ATTEND BOYS STATE. FOR UNDERGRADUATE STUDY AT A COLLEGE OR UNIVERSITY IN IOWA.
WRITE FOR COMPLETE INFORMATION.

1330

IOWA COLLEGE STUDENT AID COMMISSION (IOWA TUITION GRANT PROGRAM)
201 JEWETT BUILDING; 9TH AND GRAND AVE
DES MOINES IA 50309
515/281-3501
AMOUNT: $2650
DEADLINE(S): APR 20
FIELD(S): ALL FIELDS OF STUDY
OPEN TO IOWA RESIDENTS ENROLLED OR PLANNING TO ENROLL AS AN UNDERGRADUATE AT PRIVATELY SUPPORTED ELIGIBLE COLLEGES OR UNIVERSITIES; BUSINESS SCHOOLS OR HOSPITAL NURSING PROGRAMS IN IOWA. MUST DEMONSTRATE NEED.
USA CITIZEN OR LEGAL RESIDENT. 10140 GRANTS PER YEAR. RENEWABLE. WRITE FOR COMPLETE INFORMATION.

1331

IOWA COLLEGE STUDENT AID COMMISSION (IOWA STAFFORD LOAN PROGRAM; IOWA PLUS/SLS LOANS)
201 JEWETT BLDG; 9TH & GRAND AVE
DES MOINES IA 50309
515/281-3501
AMOUNT: $2625 - $4000 UNDERGRAD; $7500 GRAD
DEADLINE(S): NONE
FIELD(S): ALL FIELDS OF STUDY
LOANS OPEN TO IOWA RESIDENT ENROLLED IN OR ATTENDING AN APPROVED INSTITUTION. MUST BE USA CITIZEN OR LEGAL RESIDENT AND DEMONSTRATE NEED.
WRITE FOR COMPLETE INFORMATION.

1332

IOWA COLLEGE STUDENT AID COMMISSION (STATE OF IOWA SCHOLARSHIPS)
201 JEWETT BUILDING; 9TH & GRAND AVE
DES MOINES IA 50309
515/281-3501
AMOUNT: $500 - $2000 (4 YEAR MAXIMUM)
DEADLINE(S): DEC 1
FIELD(S): ALL FIELDS OF STUDY
OPEN TO IOWA HIGH SCHOOL SENIORS WHO ARE IN THE TOP 15% OF THEIR CLASS AND PLAN TO ATTEND AN ELIGIBLE IOWA COLLEGE OR UNIVERSITY. CONSIDERATIONS INCLUDE ACT TEST SCORE; FINANCIAL NEED AND UNITS IN SPECIFIED SUBJECTS.
2000 SCHOLARSHIPS PER YEAR. RENEWABLE. CONTACT YOUR COUNSELOR OR ADDRESS ABOVE FOR COMPLETE INFORMATION.

1333

IOWA DEPT OF PUBLIC DEFENSE-VETERANS AFFAIRS DIV (WAR ORPHANS EDUCATIONAL SCHOLARSHIP AID)
7700 NW BEAVER DR; CAMP DODGE
JOHNSTON IA 50131
515/278-9331
AMOUNT: $400 - $2000
DEADLINE(S): NONE SPECIFIED
FIELD(S): ALL AREAS OF STUDY
RESIDENT OF IOWA FOR AT LEAST 2 YEARS PRIOR TO APPLICATION. CHILD OF PARENT WHO DIED IN OR AS A RESULT OF MILITARY SERVICE. HIGH SCHOOL GRADUATE OR EQUIVALENT. ATTEND A POST-SECONDARY INSTITUTION IN IOWA.
RENEWABLE. WRITE FOR COMPLETE INFORMATION.

1334

IOWA FEDERATION OF LABOR AFL-CIO (ANNUAL SCHOLARSHIP PROGRAM)
2000 WALKER ST
DES MOINES IA 50317
515/262-9571
AMOUNT: $1500
DEADLINE(S): MAR 16
FIELD(S): ALL AREAS OF STUDY
COMPETITION BASED ON ESSAY OPEN ONLY TO IOWA HIGH SCHOOL SENIORS.
WRITE FOR COMPLETE INFORMATION.

1335

ITALIAN CATHOLIC FEDERATION INC. (COLLEGE SCHOLARSHIPS TO HIGH SCHOOL SENIORS)
PO BOX 640449; 1801 VAN NESS AVE; #330
SAN FRANCISCO CA 94164
415/673-8240
AMOUNT: $350
DEADLINE(S): MAR 15
FIELD(S): ALL AREAS OF STUDY
SCHOLARSHIPS ARE FOR GRADUATING SENIORS OF ITALIAN ANCESTRY AND CATHOLIC FAITH. WINNERS MAY ATTEND ANY ACCREDITED INSTITUTION. FOR STUDENTS WHO ARE RESIDENTS OF STATES WHERE THE FEDERATION IS LOCATED (CALIF; NEVADA & ILLINOIS).
MINIMUM GPA OF 3.0 ON 4.0 SCALE. 190 SCHOLARSHIPS PER YEAR. FOR FURTHER INFORMATION SEND STAMPED; SELF-ADDRESSED ENVELOPE TO ADDRESS ABOVE.

1336

J. WOOD PLATT CADDIE SCHOLARSHIP TRUST (SCHOLARSHIPS)
DRAWER 808
SOUTHEASTERN PA 19399
215/687-2340
AMOUNT: UP TO $6000
DEADLINE(S): APR 30
FIELD(S): ALL FIELDS OF STUDY
OPEN TO HIGH SCHOOL SENIORS & UNDERGRADUATE STUDENTS WHO HAVE SERVED AS A CADDIE AT A GOLF ASSN OF PHILADELPHIA MEMBER CLUB; HAVE FINANCIAL NEED & HAVE CAPABILITY TO SUCCESSFULLY COMPLETE THEIR UNDERGRADUATE DEGREE.
RENEWABLE. WRITE FOR COMPLETE INFORMATION.

1337

J.H. BAKER SCHOLARSHIP FUND (SCHOLARSHIPS)
C/O TOM DECHANT CPA; PO BOX 280
LA CROSSE KS 67548
913/222-2537
AMOUNT: $1600 PER YEAR
DEADLINE(S): JUL 31
FIELD(S): ALL FIELDS OF STUDY

OPEN TO GRADUATES OF HIGH SCHOOLS IN THE KANSAS COUNTIES OF RUSH; BARTON; ELLIS; NESS AND PAWNEE. MUST BE UNDER 25 YEARS OF AGE. SELECTION IS BASED ON ACADEMIC PERFORMANCE; CHARACTER; ABILITY AND NEED.

CONTACT ADDRESS ABOVE FOR COMPLETE INFORMATION.

1338

JACK IN THE BOX RESTAURANTS (ESSAY AND PHOTO SCHOLARSHIP COMPETITION)

C/O ANDERSON COMMUNICATIONS CO; 3 CORPORATE PLAZA; SUITE 200

NEWPORT BEACH CA 92660

714/644-4414

AMOUNT: $1000

DEADLINE(S): VARIES YEARLY

FIELD(S): ALL FIELDS OF STUDY

OPEN TO HIGH SCHOOL SENIORS IN ARIZONA; CALIFORNIA; HAWAII OR WASHINGTON. ESSAY AND PHOTO CONTEST TO ENCOURAGE STUDENTS TO PURSUE A COLLEGE EDUCATION AND REWARD CREATIVITY WITHOUT EMPHASIZING SCHOLASTIC ACHIEVEMENT.

16 AWARDS PER YEAR; THEME CHANGES ANNUALLY. WRITE FOR COMPLETE INFORMATION.

1339

JACKSONVILLE UNIVERSITY (SCHOLARSHIPS & GRANTS PROGRAMS)

DIRECTOR OF STUDENT FINANCIAL ASSISTANCE

JACKSONVILLE FL 32211

904/744-3950

AMOUNT: VARIES

DEADLINE(S): JAN 1 TO MAR 15

FIELD(S): ALL AREAS OF STUDY

JACKSONVILLE UNIVERSITY OFFERS NUMEROUS SCHOLARSHIPS; GRANTS-IN-AID; SERVICE AWARDS AND CAMPUS EMPLOYMENT. FINANCIAL NEED IS NOT NECESSARILY A CONSIDERATION. EARLY APPLICATIONS ARE ADVISED.

200 AWARDS PER YEAR FOR STUDY ONLY AT JACKSONVILLE UNIVERSITY. WRITE FOR COMPLETE INFORMATION.

1340

JAMES G.K. MCCLURE EDUCATIONAL AND DEVELOPMENT FUND (WESTERN NORTH CAROLINA SCHOLARSHIPS)

11 SUGAR HOLLOW RD

FAIRVIEW NC 28730

704/628-1044

AMOUNT: $300 TO $1500

DEADLINE(S): MAY 15

FIELD(S): ALL FIELDS OF STUDY

OPEN TO STUDENTS RESIDING IN WESTERN NORTH CAROLINA WHO ARE ENTERING THE FRESHMAN CLASS OF A NORTH CAROLINA COLLEGE OR UNIVERSITY. FINANCIAL NEED IS A CONSIDERATION.

WRITE FOR COMPLETE INFORMATION.

1341

JAMES M. HOFFMAN SCHOLARSHIP (UNDERGRADUATE SCHOLARSHIP)

SOUTHTRUST BANK OF CALHOUN COUNTY, PO BOX 1000

ANNISTON AL 36202

205/238-1000 EXT 338

AMOUNT: VARIES

DEADLINE(S): MAR 1

FIELD(S): ALL FIELDS OF STUDY

OPEN TO HIGH SCHOOL SENIORS ATTENDING SCHOOLS WITHIN CALHOUN COUNTY ALABAMA. FOR UNDERGRADUATE STUDY AT ACCREDITED COLLEGES AND UNIVERSITIES. MUST SUBMIT COPIES OF PARENTS' W-2 FORMS.

WRITE TO ATTENTION OF PHILLIP D. STUART FOR COMPLETE INFORMATION.

1342

JAMES W. COLGAN FUND (UNDERGRADUATE LOANS)

C/O FLEET BANK OF MASS; PO BOX 9003

SPRINGFIELD MA 01101

413/787-8700; 413/787-8570

AMOUNT: $1500 - $2000

DEADLINE(S): JUN 30

FIELD(S): ALL FIELDS OF STUDY

EDUCATIONAL LOANS AVAILABLE TO MASSACHUSETTS RESIDENTS UNDER AGE 30 WHO ARE ENROLLED AS AN UNDERGRADUATE COLLEGE STUDENT IN OR OUTSIDE OF MASSACHUSETTS. FINANCIAL NEED AND GRADES ARE TAKEN INTO CONSIDERATION.

LOANS ARE RENEWABLE. WRITE FOR COMPLETE INFORMATION.

1343

JAMES Z. NAURISON SCHOLARSHIP FUND (SCHOLARSHIPS)
PO BOX 9006
SPRINGFIELD MA 01101
413/787-8570
AMOUNT: $400 - $2000
DEADLINE(S): APR 15
FIELD(S): ALL FIELDS OF STUDY
OPEN TO UNDERGRADUATE AND GRADUATE STUDENTS WHO ARE RESIDENTS OF THE MASSACHUSETTS COUNTIES OF BERKSHIRE; FRANKLIN; HAMPDEN OR HAMPSHIRE OR OF THE CITY OF SUFFIELD OR ENFIELD CONNECTICUT. AWARDS BASED ON FINANCIAL NEED & ACADEMIC RECORD.
APPROXIMATELY 300 AWARDS PER YEAR. SELF-ADDRESSED STAMPED ENVELOPE MUST ACCOMPANY REQUESTS FOR APPLICATION.

1344

JAPANESE AMERICAN CITIZENS LEAGUE (ABE & ESTER HAGIWARA STUDENT AID AWARD)
1765 SUTTER ST
SAN FRANCISCO CA 94115
415/921-5225
AMOUNT: VARIES
DEADLINE(S): APR 1
FIELD(S): ALL FIELDS OF STUDY
OPEN TO JACL MEMBERS OR THEIR CHILDREN OR ANY AMERICAN OF JAPANESE ANCESTRY. SCHOLARSHIP MAY BE USED FOR ANY LEVEL OF STUDY. USA CITIZEN OR LEGAL RESIDENT. MUST SUBMIT FAF FORM AS PROOF OF FINANCIAL NEED.
SEND STAMPED SELF-ADDRESSED ENVELOPE FOR COMPLETE INFORMATION.

1345

JAPANESE AMERICAN CITIZENS LEAGUE (FRESHMAN SCHOLARSHIPS)
1765 SUTTER ST
SAN FRANCISCO CA 94115
415/921-5225
AMOUNT: VARIES
DEADLINE(S): MAR 1
FIELD(S): ALL FIELDS OF STUDY
OPEN TO JACL MEMBERS OR THEIR CHILDREN OR ANY AMERICAN OF JAPANESE ANCESTRY. FOR HIGH SCHOOL SENIORS WHO ARE PLANNING TO ATTEND A TRADE SCHOOL; BUSINESS SCHOOL; COLLEGE OR UNIVERSITY. USA CITIZEN OR LEGAL RESIDENT.
14 SCHOLARSHIPS PER YEAR. SEND STAMPED SELF-ADDRESSED ENVELOPE FOR COMPLETE INFORMATION.

1346

JAPANESE AMERICAN CITIZENS LEAGUE (UNDERGRADUATE SCHOLARSHIPS)
1765 SUTTER ST
SAN FRANCISCO CA 94115
415/921-5225
AMOUNT: VARIES
DEADLINE(S): APR 1
FIELD(S): ALL FIELDS OF STUDY
OPEN TO JACL MEMBERS OR THEIR CHILDREN OR ANY AMERICAN OF JAPANESE ANCESTRY. FOR UNDERGRADUATE STUDENTS CURRENTLY ENROLLED IN OR PLANNING TO RE-ENTER A TRADE SCHOOL; BUSINESS SCHOOL; COLLEGE OR UNIVERSITY. USA CITIZEN OR LEGAL RESIDENT.
5 SCHOLARSHIPS PER YEAR. SEND STAMPED SELF-ADDRESSED ENVELOPE FOR COMPLETE INFORMATION.

1347

JEANNETTE RANKIN FOUNDATION (WOMEN'S EDUCATION FUND)
PO BOX 6653
ATHENS GA 30604
WRITTEN INQUIRY
AMOUNT: $1000
DEADLINE(S): JAN 15 TO REQUEST APPLICATION; MAR 1 FOR RETURN OF APPLICATION
FIELD(S): ALL FIELDS OF STUDY (UNDERGRADUATE & TECHNICAL)
OPEN TO FEMALE USA CITIZENS WHO ARE 35 OR OLDER TO PURSUE A CERTIFIED COURSE OF TRAINING OR UNDERGRADUATE EDUCATION. CRITICAL FINANCIAL NEED AND ACHIEVABLE GOALS ARE THE MAJOR CRITERIA FOR SELECTION. FOR UNDERGRADUATE STUDY ONLY.
AWARD MONEY CAN BE USED FOR ANY PURPOSE THAT WILL FURTHER THE AWARDEE'S EDUCATION INCLUDING CHILD CARE; TRANSPORTATION; BOOKS; TUITION. WRITE FOR COMPLETE INFORMATION.

1348

JENNIE G. AND PEARL ABELL EDUCATION TRUST (GRANTS PROGRAM)

PO BOX 487; 717 MAIN ST
ASHLAND KS 67831
316/635-2228

AMOUNT: VARIES
DEADLINE(S): JUN 15
FIELD(S): ALL AREAS OF STUDY EXCEPT VOC/TECH

GRANTS FOR UNDERGRADUATE STUDY ARE OPEN TO STUDENTS WHO ARE GRADUATES OF CLARK COUNTY (KANSAS) HIGH SCHOOLS OR RESIDE IN CLARK COUNTY, KANSAS AND CAN DEMONSTRATE FINANCIAL NEED.

WRITE FOR COMPLETE INFORMATION.

1349

JESSIE BAKER SCHOLARSHIP TRUST (SCHOLARSHIPS FOR BROOME COUNTY, NY STUDENTS)

MARINE MIDLAND BANK TRUST DEPT.; PO BOX 4203
BUFFALO NY 14240
WRITTEN INQUIRY

AMOUNT: $50 TO $1000
DEADLINE(S): NONE GIVEN
FIELD(S): ALL FIELDS OF STUDY

OPEN TO HIGH SCHOOL STUDENTS WHO RESIDE IN BROOME COUNTY, NY. MUST APPLY WHEN THEY ARE SENIORS IN THEIR LOCAL HIGH SCHOOL AND REAPPLY EACH YEAR WHILE ATTENDING COLLEGE. FAILURE TO REAPPLY WILL RESULT IN INELIGIBILITY FOR FUTURE SCHOLARSHIPS

FINANCIAL NEED IS A CONSIDERATION. WRITE FOR COMPLETE INFORMATION OR CONTACT SCHOOL COUNSELOR.

1350

JEWISH FAMILY AND CHILDREN'S SERVICES (ANNA AND CHARLES STOCKWITZ CHILDREN AND YOUTH FUND)

1600 SCOTT STREET
SAN FRANCISCO CA 94115
415/561-1226

AMOUNT: $5000 PER YEAR (STUDENT LOANS)
DEADLINE(S): NONE
FIELD(S): ALL FIELDS OF STUDY

LOANS AND GRANTS OPEN TO UNDERGRADUATE STUDENTS OF THE JEWISH FAITH AGE 25 OR YOUNGER WHO RESIDE IN SAN FRANCISCO; SAN MATEO; SANTA CLARA; MARIN OR SONOMA COUNTY. LOAN REPAYMENT IS FLEXIBLE; INTEREST USUALLY AT 80% OF CURRENT PRIME RATE.

GRANT APPLICANTS MUST DEMONSTRATE FINANCIAL NEED; LOAN APPLICANTS MUST SHOW ABILITY TO REPAY. CONTACT LOCAL JFCS OFFICE FOR COMPLETE INFORMATION.

1351

JEWISH FAMILY AND CHILDREN'S SERVICES (COLLEGE LOAN FUND)

1600 SCOTT ST
SAN FRANCISCO CA 94115
415/561-1226

AMOUNT: $5000 MAXIMUM (STUDENT LOAN)
DEADLINE(S): NONE
FIELD(S): ALL FIELDS OF STUDY

OPEN TO WORTHY COLLEGE STUDENTS OF THE JEWISH FAITH WITH LIMITED RESOURCES BUT WITH A DEMONSTRATED ABILITY TO REPAY. MUST RESIDE IN SAN FRANCISCO; SAN MATEO; SANTA CLARA; MARIN OR SONOMA COUNTY.

GUARANTORS OR CO-MAKERS ARE REQUIRED BUT NOT COLLATERAL. REPAYMENT TERMS FLEXIBLE; INTEREST USUALLY SET AT 80% OF CURRENT PRIME RATE. CONTACT LOCAL JFCS OFFICE FOR FORMS AND COMPLETE INFORMATION.

1352

JEWISH FAMILY AND CHILDREN'S SERVICES (FOGEL LOAN FUND)

1600 SCOTT STREET
SAN FRANCISCO CA 94115
415/561-1226

AMOUNT: VARIES
DEADLINE(S): NONE
FIELD(S): ALL FIELDS OF STUDY

LOANS TO HELP INDIVIDUALS OF ALL AGES FOR COLLEGE OR VOCATIONAL STUDIES AND FOR PERSONAL; BUSINESS OR PROFESSIONAL PURPOSES. APPLICANT MUST BE OF THE JEWISH FAITH AND HAVE SOUND PLAN FOR REPAYMENT.

SHOULD BE RESIDENT OF SAN FRANCISCO; SAN MATEO; SANTA CLARA; MARIN OR SONOMA COUNTY. GUARANTOR OR CO-MAKERS REQUIRED BUT NO COLLATERAL IS NEEDED. CONTACT JFCS OFFICE FOR COMPLETE INFORMATION.

1353

JEWISH FAMILY AND CHILDREN'S SERVICES (JACOB RASSEN MEMORIAL SCHOLARSHIP FUND)
1600 SCOTT STREET
SAN FRANCISCO CA 94115
415/561-1226
AMOUNT: UP TO $2000
DEADLINE(S): NONE
FIELD(S): STUDY TRIP TO ISRAEL
OPEN TO JEWISH STUDENT UNDER AGE 22 WITH DEMONSTRATED ACADEMIC ACHIEVEMENT AND FINANCIAL NEED WITH A DESIRE TO ENHANCE JEWISH IDENTITY AND INCREASE KNOWLEDGE OF AND CONNECTION TO ISRAEL.
MUST RESIDE IN SAN FRANCISCO; SAN MATEO; SANTA CLARA; MARIN OR SONOMA COUNTY. CONTACT LOCAL JFCS OFFICE FOR FORMS AND COMPLETE INFORMATION.

1354

JEWISH FAMILY AND CHILDREN'S SERVICES (STANLEY OLSON YOUTH SCHOLARSHIP FUND)
1600 SCOTT STREET
SAN FRANCISCO CA 94115
415/561-1226
AMOUNT: UP TO $2500
DEADLINE(S): NONE
FIELD(S): ALL AREAS OF STUDY (PREFERENCE TO ENGLISH MAJORS)
OPEN TO UNDERGRADUATE OR GRADUATE STUDENTS OF JEWISH FAITH WHO ARE 25 OR YOUNGER; HAVE DEMONSTRATED ACADEMIC ACHIEVEMENT AND FINANCIAL NEED AND HAVE BEEN ACCEPTED FOR ENROLLMENT IN A COLLEGE OR UNIVERSITY.
MUST RESIDE IN SAN FRANCISCO; SAN MATEO; SANTA CLARA; MARIN OR SONOMA COUNTY. CONTACT LOCAL JFCS OFFICE FOR APPLICATIONS AND COMPLETE INFORMATION.

1355

JEWISH FAMILY AND CHILDREN'S SERVICES (VIVIENNE CAMP COLLEGE SCHOLARSHIP FUND)
1600 SCOTT STREET
SAN FRANCISCO CA 94115
415/561-1226
AMOUNT: $5000 PER YEAR
DEADLINE(S): MAY 1
FIELD(S): ALL AREAS OF STUDY
OPEN TO STUDENTS OF JEWISH FAITH FOR UNDERGRADUATE OR VOCATIONAL STUDY. APPLICANTS SHOULD HAVE DEMONSTRATED ACADEMIC ACHIEVEMENT; FINANCIAL NEED; BROAD BASED EXTRA-CURRICULAR ACTIVITIES AND COMMUNITY INVOLVEMENT.
MUST HAVE BEEN ACCEPTED TO A CALIFORNIA COLLEGE OR VOCATIONAL SCHOOL AND RESIDE IN SAN FRANCISCO; SAN MATEO; SANTA CLARA; MARIN OR SONOMA COUNTY. CONTACT LOCAL JFCS OFFICE FOR FORMS AND COMPLETE INFORMATION.

1356

JEWISH FOUNDATION FOR EDUCATION OF WOMEN (GRANTS & LOANS)
330 WEST 58TH STREET
NEW YORK NY 10019
212/265-2565
AMOUNT: VARIES
DEADLINE(S): JAN 31
FIELD(S): ALL AREAS OF STUDY
OPEN TO WOMEN WHO LIVE WITHIN A 50-MILE RADIUS OF NEW YORK CITY. FOR UNDERGRADUATE AND LIMITED GRADUATE STUDY. MUST BE USA CITIZEN AND DEMONSTRATE FINANCIAL NEED. NO RELIGIOUS AFFILIATION REQUIRED.
APPROXIMATELY 150 GRANTS AND/OR LOANS PER YEAR. WRITE FOR COMPLETE INFORMATION.

1357

JEWISH SOCIAL SERVICE AGENCY OF METROPOLITAN WASHINGTON (LOAN FUND)
6123 MONTROSE ROAD
ROCKVILLE MD 20852
301/881-3700
AMOUNT: UP TO $2000
DEADLINE(S): JUN 1
FIELD(S): ALL FIELDS OF STUDY
OPEN TO JEWISH APPLICANTS 18 OR OLDER WHO ARE WITHIN TWO YEARS OF COMPLETING AN UNDERGRADUATE OR GRADUATE DEGREE OR A VOCATIONAL TRAINING PROGRAM AND ARE RESIDENTS OF THE WASHINGTON METROPOLITAN AREA. NO INTEREST LOAN; ONE TIME AWARD.
USA CITIZEN OR PERMANENT RESIDENT WHO WILL SEEK CITIZENSHIP. WRITE FOR COMPLETE INFORMATION.

1358

JEWISH SOCIAL SERVICE AGENCY OF METROPOLITAN WASHINGTON (UNDERGRADUATE SCHOLARSHIP FUND)
6123 MONTROSE ROAD
ROCKVILLE MD 20852
301/881-3700
AMOUNT: UP TO $3500/YEAR
DEADLINE(S): JUN 1
FIELD(S): ALL FIELDS OF STUDY
OPEN TO JEWISH UNDERGRADUATES NO OLDER THAN 30 WHO ARE ENROLLED IN AN ACCREDITED UNDERGRADUATE FOUR-YEAR DEGREE PROGRAM AND ARE FROM THE WASHINGTON METROPOLITAN AREA. SPECIAL CONSIDERATION IS GIVEN TO REFUGEES.
RENEWABLE. AWARDS BASED ON FINANCIAL NEED. WRITE FOR COMPLETE INFORMATION.

1359

JEWISH SOCIAL SERVICE AGENCY OF METROPOLITAN WASHINGTON (IRENE STAMBLER VOCATIONAL OPPORTUNITIES GRANT PROGRAM)
6123 MONTROSE ROAD
ROCKVILLE MD 20852
301/881-3700
AMOUNT: UP TO $2500
DEADLINE(S): NONE
FIELD(S): ALL FIELDS OF STUDY
OPEN TO JEWISH WOMEN WHO ARE RESIDENTS OF THE WASHINGTON METROPOLITAN AREA AND NEED TO IMPROVE THEIR EARNING POWER BECAUSE OF DIVORCE; SEPARATION OR DEATH OF THEIR SPOUSES.
GRANTS MAY BE USED TO COMPLETE AN EDUCATIONAL OR VOCATIONAL PROGRAM OR START OR EXPAND A SMALL BUSINESS. WRITE FOR COMPLETE INFORMATION.

1360

JOHN W. AND ROSE E. WATSON SCHOLARSHIP FOUNDATION (UNDERGRADUATE SCHOLARSHIPS)
5800 WEISS STREET
SAGINAW MI 48603
517/799-7910
AMOUNT: VARIES BY YEAR
DEADLINE(S): MAR 15
FIELD(S): ALL FIELDS OF STUDY
OPEN TO RESIDENTS OF SAGINAW COUNTY, MI WHO GRADUATED FROM A SAGINAW COUNTY CATHOLIC HIGH SCHOOL.
WRITE FOR COMPLETE INFORMATION.

1361

JOHNSON AND WALES UNIVERSITY (GAEBE EAGLE SCOUT SCHOLARSHIPS)
8 ABBOT PLACE
PROVIDENCE RI 02903
401/456-1000
AMOUNT: $300
DEADLINE(S): APR 30
FIELD(S): ALL FIELDS OF STUDY
OPEN TO UNDERGRADUATE FRESHMEN WHO HAVE BEEN ACCEPTED AT JOHNSON AND WALES UNIVERSITY. MUST BE EAGLE SCOUT WHO HAS RECEIVED THE RELIGIOUS AWARD OF HIS FAITH.
ALL ELIGIBLE FRESHMAN RECEIVE AWARD OF $300. WRITE FOR COMPLETE INFORMATION.

1362

JOHNSON CONTROLS FOUNDATION (SCHOLARSHIP PROGRAM)
5757 N GREEN BAY AVE; BOX 591
MILWAUKEE WI 53201
414/228-2179 OR 414/228-2135
AMOUNT: $1750 PER YEAR ($7000 OVER 4 YRS)
DEADLINE(S): NONE SPECIFIED
FIELD(S): ALL AREAS OF STUDY
ELIGIBILITY FOR SCHOLARSHIPS LIMITED TO CHILDREN OF EMPLOYEES OF JOHNSON CONTROLS INC. MUST BE IN UPPER 30% OF HIGH SCHOOL GRADUATING CLASS AND MUST MAINTAIN STANDARDS IN COLLEGE FOR RENEWAL. SCHOLARSHIPS FOR FULL TIME STUDY ONLY.
CONTACT JON DEHLINGER; CORP HUMAN RES CONSULTANT; JOHNSON CONTROLS INC.; FOR COMPLETE INFORMATION.

1363

JORDAAN FOUNDATION INC. (SCHOLARSHIP)
PO BOX 360
LARNED KS 67550
316/285-3157
AMOUNT: $2000 ANNUALLY
DEADLINE(S): APR 15
FIELD(S): ALL FIELDS OF STUDY
OPEN ONLY TO SENIORS GRADUATING FROM PAWNEE COUNTY (KANSAS) HIGH SCHOOL

WHO PLAN TO ATTEND A KANSAS COLLEGE OR UNIVERSITY. MUST DEMONSTRATE FINANCIAL NEED.

APPLICATIONS AVAILABLE THROUGH PAWNEE COUNTY HIGH SCHOOL.

1364

JOSTENS FOUNDATION (LEADER SCHOLARSHIP PROGRAM)
5501 NORMAN CENTER DRIVE
MINNEAPOLIS MN 55437
507/931-1682
AMOUNT: $1000
DEADLINE(S): DEC 10
FIELD(S): ALL FIELDS OF STUDY

OPEN TO GRADUATING HS SENIORS IN THE USA; ITS TERRITORIES AND AMERICAN SCHOOLS OVERSEAS. FOR STUDENTS WHO HAVE SHOWN LEADERSHIP QUALITIES & WILL ENROLL IN AN ACCREDITED UNDERGRADUATE PROGRAM. FOR FIRST YEAR OF FULL TIME STUDY.

300 AWARDS ANNUALLY. NOT FOR DEPENDENTS OF JOSTENS EMPLOYEES. DEADLINE DATE SUBJECT TO CHANGE; CONTACT SCHOOL'S GUIDANCE DEPT AT BEGINNING OF SCHOOL YEAR. WRITE FOR COMPLETE INFORMATION.

1365

JUNIATA COLLEGE (FREDERICK & MARY F. BECKLEY SCHOLARSHIP FUND FOR NEEDY 'LEFT-HANDED' FRESHMEN)
FINANCIAL AID OFFICE
HUNTINGDON PA 16652
814/643-4310
AMOUNT: $700 - $1000
DEADLINE(S): NONE
FIELD(S): ALL FIELDS OF STUDY

AWARDS ARE OPEN TO NEEDY 'LEFT-HANDED' STUDENTS WHO HAVE JUNIOR OR SENIOR STANDING AT JUNIATA COLLEGE.

WRITE FOR COMPLETE INFORMATION.

1366

JUNIOR LEAGUE OF NORTHERN VIRGINIA (SCHOLARSHIPS)
7921 JONES BRANCH DR; #320
MCLEAN VA 22102
703/893-0258
AMOUNT: $500 TO $2000
DEADLINE(S): DEC 15
FIELD(S): ALL FIELDS OF STUDY

OPEN TO WOMEN WHO ARE 28 YEARS OLD OR OLDER & ACCEPTED TO OR ENROLLED IN AN ACCREDITED COLLEGE OR UNIVERSITY AS AN UNDERGRADUATE OR GRADUATE STUDENT. MUST BE USA CITIZEN; NORTHERN VIRGINIA RESIDENT; AND DEMONSTRATE FINANCIAL NEED.

8-10 AWARDS PER YEAR. WRITE FOR COMPLETE INFORMATION.

1367

KAMEHAMEHA SCHOOLS (FINANCIAL AID PROGRAMS)
DEPT. OF FINANCIAL AID; KAPALAMA HEIGHTS
HONOLULU HI 96817
808/842-8216
AMOUNT: $100 - $1000
DEADLINE(S): APR 15
FIELD(S): ALL AREAS OF STUDY

OPEN TO HAWAII RESIDENT OF HAWAIIAN DESCENT WHO IS A GRADUATE OF A HAWAIIAN HIGH SCHOOL. FOR FULL TIME UNDERGRADUATE OR GRADUATE STUDY IN USA. MUST DEMONSTRATE FINANCIAL NEED.

WRITE FOR COMPLETE INFORMATION.

1368

KANSAS AMERICAN LEGION (SCHOLARSHIPS)
1314 SW TOPEKA BLVD
TOPEKA KS 66612
WRITTEN INQUIRY
AMOUNT: $150 - $1000
DEADLINE(S): FEB 15; JUL 15
FIELD(S): ALL FIELDS OF STUDY

VARIETY OF SCHOLARSHIPS AND AWARDS FOR KANSAS RESIDENTS TO ATTEND KANSAS COLLEGES; UNIVERSITIES OR TRADE SCHOOLS. SOME ARE LIMITED TO LEGION MEMBERS AND/OR DESIGNATED FIELDS OF STUDY.

WRITE FOR COMPLETE INFORMATION.

1369

KANSAS BOARD OF REGENTS (GRANTS)
700 SW HARRISON; SUITE 1410
TOPEKA KS 66603
913/296-3517
AMOUNT: UP TO $1700
DEADLINE(S): MAR 15
FIELD(S): ALL FIELDS OF STUDY

GRANTS OPEN ONLY TO KANSAS RESIDENTS WHO ARE FULL TIME UNDERGRADUATE

STUDENTS AT ELIGIBLE KANSAS INDEPENDENT COLLEGES & UNIVERSITIES. USA CITIZEN. FINANCIAL NEED IS A CONSIDERATION.
3600 GRANTS PER YEAR. RENEWABLE. WRITE FOR COMPLETE INFORMATION.

1370

KANSAS BOARD OF REGENTS (STATE SCHOLARS AWARDS)
SUITE 609; CAPITOL TOWER; 400 SW EIGHTH
TOPEKA KS 66603
913/296-3517
AMOUNT: UP TO $1000
DEADLINE(S): MAR 15
FIELD(S): ALL FIELDS OF STUDY
OPEN ONLY TO KANSAS RESIDENTS WHO WERE DESIGNATED STATE SCHOLARS AS SENIORS IN KANSAS HIGH SCHOOLS AND ARE ENROLLED AT AN ELIGIBLE POST-SECONDARY SCHOOL IN KANSAS. FINANCIAL NEED IS A CONSIDERATION.
1200 SCHOLARSHIPS PER YEAR. RENEWABLE. WRITE FOR COMPLETE INFORMATION.

1371

KANSAS COMMISSION ON VETERANS' AFFAIRS (SCHOLARSHIPS)
700 SW JACKSON ST; #701
TOPEKA KS 66603
913/296-3976
AMOUNT: FREE TUITION AND FEES IN STATE SUPPORTED INSTITUTIONS
DEADLINE(S): PRIOR TO ENROLLMENT
FIELD(S): ALL AREAS OF STUDY
OPEN TO DEPENDENT CHILD OF PERSON WHO ENTERED USA MILITARY SERVICE AS A RESIDENT OF KANSAS & WAS PRISONER OF WAR; MISSING OR KILLED IN ACTION OR DIED AS A RESULT OF SERVICE CONNECTED DISABILITIES INCURRED DURING SERVICE IN VIETNAM.
RENEWABLE TO MAXIMUM OF 12 SEMESTERS. WRITE FOR COMPLETE INFORMATION.

1372

KEENA SCHOLARSHIP FUND (SCHOLARSHIPS)
WELLS FARGO PRIVATE BANKING GROUP; PO BOX 2511
SACRAMENTO CA 95812
916/440-4433
AMOUNT: NOT SPECIFIED
DEADLINE(S): NONE GIVEN
FIELD(S): ALL AREAS OF STUDY
OPEN TO RESIDENTS OF PLACER COUNTY (CA) WHO GRADUATED FROM PLACER COUNTY UNION HIGH SCHOOL.
WRITE FOR COMPLETE INFORMATION.

1373

KENTUCKY CENTER FOR VETERANS AFFAIRS (BENEFITS FOR VETERANS & THEIR DEPENDENTS)
545 S 3RD ST; ROOM 123
LOUISVILLE KY 40202
501/595-4447
AMOUNT: VARIES
DEADLINE(S): NONE
FIELD(S): ALL FIELDS OF STUDY
KENTUCKY RESIDENTS. OPEN TO VETERANS & DEPENDENT CHILDREN; NAT'L GUARDSMEN; SPOUSES & NON-REMARRIED WIDOWS OF PERMANENTLY & TOTALLY DISABLED WAR VETERANS WHO SERVED DURING PERIODS OF FEDERALLY RECOGNIZED HOSTILITIES OR WAS POW OR MIA.
WRITE FOR COMPLETE INFORMATION.

1374

KENTUCKY HIGHER EDUCATION ASSISTANCE AUTHORITY (GRANTS PROGRAM)
1050 US-127 SOUTH
FRANKFORT KY 40601
502/564-7990
AMOUNT: $300 TO $1400
DEADLINE(S): APR 1 PRIORITY DATE
FIELD(S): ALL FIELDS OF STUDY
US CITIZEN OR LEGAL RESIDENT. KENTUCKY RESIDENT. ENROLLEDOR PLAN TO ENROLL AS UNDERGRADUATE FULL TIME IN NONRELIGIOUS DEGREE PROGRAM AT AN ELIGIBLE KENTUCKY INSTITUTION.
RENEWABLE WITH REAPPLICATION. WRITE FOR COMPLETE INFORMATION.

1375

KENTUCKY HIGHER EDUCATION ASSISTANCE AUTHORITY (STUDENT LOAN PROGRAM)
1050 US-127 SOUTH; SUITE 102
FRANKFORT KY 40601
502/564-7990
AMOUNT: $2625 FRESHMAN/SOPHOMORE; $4000 JUNIOR/SENIOR; $7500 GRADUATE
DEADLINE(S): VARIES

FIELD(S): ALL FIELDS OF STUDY
US CITIZEN OR LEGAL RESIDENT. KENTUCKY RESIDENT ENROLLED/OR ACCEPTED FOR ENROLLMENT ON AT LEAST A HALF-TIME BASIS AT AN ELIGIBLE POST-SECONDARY EDUCATIONAL INSTITUTION.
WRITE FOR COMPLETE INFORMATION.

1376

KNIGHTS OF COLUMBUS (EDUCATIONAL TRUST FUND)
PO DRAWER 1670
NEW HAVEN CT 06507
203/772-2130 EXT. 332
AMOUNT: VARIES
DEADLINE(S): NONE SPECIFIED
FIELD(S): ALL AREAS OF STUDY
OPEN TO CHILDREN OF K.C. MEMBERS WHO DIED IN MILITARY SERVICE OR BECAME TOTALLY AND PERMANENTLY DISABLED FROM CAUSES DIRECTLY CONNECTED WITH PERIOD OF CONFLICT OR FROM DUTIES AS A POLICEMAN OR FIREMAN.
MUST ATTEND CATHOLIC COLLEGE. UNSPECIFIED NUMBER OF AWARDS PER YEAR. WRITE FOR COMPLETE INFORMATION.

1377

KNIGHTS OF COLUMBUS (PRO DEO PRO PATRIA SCHOLARSHIPS)
PO DRAWER 1670
NEW HAVEN CT 06507
203/772-2130 EXT. 332
AMOUNT: $1000
DEADLINE(S): FEB 1
FIELD(S): ALL AREAS OF STUDY
OPEN TO STUDENTS ENROLLING IN A CATHOLIC COLLEGE WHO CAN SUBMIT EVIDENCE OF SATISFACTORY ACADEMIC PERFORMANCE. MUST BE A MEMBER OR DEPENDENT OF A KNIGHTS OF COLUMBUS MEMBER OR A DECEASED MEMBER IN GOOD STANDING.
20 SCHOLARSHIPS PER YEAR. TEN AT ANY CATHOLIC COLLEGE AND TEN AT THE CATHOLIC UNIVERSITY OF AMERICA. RENEWABLE UP TO 4 YEARS.

1378

KNIGHTS OF COLUMBUS (SQUIRES SCHOLARSHIP PROGRAM)
PO DRAWER 1670
NEW HAVEN CT 06507
203/772-2130
AMOUNT: $1000
DEADLINE(S): MAR 1
FIELD(S): ALL AREAS OF STUDY
OPEN TO STUDENTS ENTERING THEIR FRESHMAN YEAR AT A CATHOLIC COLLEGE WHO ARE MEMBERS IN GOOD STANDING OF THE COLUMBIAN SQUIRES AND HAVE DEMONSTRATED ACADEMIC EXCELLENCE.
RENEWABLE UP TO FOUR YEARS. WRITE FOR COMPLETE INFORMATION.

1379

KNIGHTS TEMPLAR EDUCATIONAL FOUNDATION (SPECIAL LOW-INTEREST LOANS)
507 N ELSTON; SUITE 101
CHICAGO IL 60630
312/777-3300
AMOUNT: $6000 PER STUDENT MAXIMUM
DEADLINE(S): VARIES
FIELD(S): ALL FIELDS OF STUDY
SPECIAL LOW-INTEREST LOANS (5% FIXED RATE). NO PAYMENTS WHILE IN SCHOOL. REPAYMENTS START AFTER GRADUATION OR WHEN YOU LEAVE SCHOOL. OPEN TO VOC-TECH STUDENTS OR JUNIOR/SENIOR UNDERGRADUATE STUDENTS OR GRADUATE STUDENTS.
USA CITIZEN OR LEGAL RESIDENT. REQUEST INFORMATION FROM CHARLES R. NEUMANN; GRAND RECORDER-SECRETARY.

1380

LADIES OF NORTHANTS (SCHOLARSHIP)
PO BOX 6609
CODDINGTOWN CA 95406
WRITTEN INQUIRY
AMOUNT: $250
DEADLINE(S): FEB 8
FIELD(S): NUCLEAR ENGINEERING
THE LADIES OF NORTHANTS OFFERS A SCHOLARSHIP TO A WOMAN OVER 40 WHO MIGRATED TO THE UNITED STATES FROM NORTHAMPTONSHIRE ENGLAND AND IS COMMITTED TO A CAREER IN NUCLEAR ENGINEERING. FOR UNDERGRADUATE OR GRADUATE STUDY.
PREFERENCE TO NATIVES OF THE VILLAGE OF PODINGTON WHO HAVE A 3.75 OR BETTER GRADE POINT AVERAGE (4.0 SCALE) AND CAN DEMONSTRATE FINANCIAL NEED. WRITE FOR COMPLETE INFORMATION.

1381

LEAGUE OF UNITED LATIN AMERICAN CITIZENS (LULAC-SANTA FE PACIFIC HISPANIC AMERICAN SCHOLARSHIP PROGRAM)

777 N CAPITOL ST NE; SUITE 305
WASHINGTON DC 20002
708/995-6000
AMOUNT: VARIES
DEADLINE(S): NONE SPECIFIED
FIELD(S): ALL FIELDS OF STUDY

OPEN TO HIGH SCHOOL GRADUATES OF HISPANIC ORIGIN WHO ARE ENROLLED IN AN UNDERGRADUATE COLLEGE OR UNIVERSITY. FIRST CONSIDERATION GIVEN TO STUDENTS RESIDING IN STATES IN WHICH SANTA FE PACIFIC CORP & ITS SUBSIDIARIES OPERATE.

USA CITIZEN OR LEGAL RESIDENT. SEE HIGH SCHOOL COUNSELOR OR WRITE FOR COMPLETE INFORMATION.

1382

LEMBERG SCHOLARSHIP LOAN FUND (SCHOLARSHIP-LOANS)

60 EAST 42ND ST; SUITE 1814
NEW YORK NY 10165
WRITTEN INQUIRY
AMOUNT: VARIES WITH NEED
DEADLINE(S): APR 1
FIELD(S): ALL AREAS OF STUDY

SPECIAL NO-INTEREST SCHOLARSHIP-LOANS OPEN TO JEWISH MEN & WOMEN PURSUING ANY UNDERGRADUATE; GRADUATE OR PROFESSIONAL DEGREE. RECIPIENTS ASSUME AN OBLIGATION TO REPAY THEIR LOANS WITHIN 10 YEARS AFTER THE COMPLETION OF THEIR STUDIES.

WRITE FOR COMPLETE INFORMATION.

1383

LEOLA W. & CHARLES H. HUGG TRUST (JAMES N. & LILLIAN C. WHEELESS MEMORIAL SCHOLARSHIPS)

FIRST CITY TEXAS - HOUSTON NA; PO BOX 809
HOUSTON TX 77001
WRITTEN INQUIRY ONLY
AMOUNT: NOT STATED
DEADLINE(S): NONE GIVEN
FIELD(S): ALL AREAS OF STUDY

SCHOLARSHIPS OPEN TO WORTHY UNDERGRADUATE STUDENTS WHO RESIDED IN AND ATTENDED THEIR LAST TWO YEARS OF HIGH SCHOOL IN WILLIAMSON COUNTY, TEXAS.

WRITE FOR COMPLETE INFORMATION.

1384

LEONARD H. BULKELEY SCHOLARSHIP FUND (SCHOLARSHIP GRANTS)

C/O R.N. WOODWORTH; TREASURER; 17 CROCKER ST
NEW LONDON CT 06320
203/442-6291
AMOUNT: $1000 (APPROX)
DEADLINE(S): APR 1
FIELD(S): ALL FIELDS OF STUDY

OPEN ONLY TO RESIDENTS OF NEW LONDON; CT FOR UNDERGRADUATE STUDY IN AN ACCREDITED COLLEGE OR UNIVERSITY. MUST DEMONSTRATE FINANCIAL NEED.

WRITE FOR COMPLETE INFORMATION.

1385

LEOPOLD SCHEPP FOUNDATION (UNDERGRADUATE AWARDS)

551 FIFTH AVE; SUITE 2525
NEW YORK NY 10176
212/986-3078
AMOUNT: VARIES
DEADLINE(S): JUN 1 - DEC 31
FIELD(S): ALL FIELDS OF STUDY

UNDERGRADUATES SHOULD WRITE DETAILING THEIR EDUCATION TO DATE; YEAR IN SCHOOL; LENGTH OF COURSE OF STUDY; VOCATIONAL GOAL; FINANCIAL NEED; AGE; CITIZENSHIP; COLLEGE CHOICE AND AVAILABILITY FOR INTERVIEW IN NEW YORK CITY.

APPROXIMATELY 75 NEW AWARDS PER YEAR WITH ANOTHER 75 RENEWALS. APPLICANTS SHOULD ALREADY BE IN COLLEGE AND NOT OLDER THAN 30. HIGH SCHOOL SENIORS MAY NOT APPLY. PRINT OR TYPE NAME AND ADDRESS.

1386

LEVI STRAUSS & CO. (EMPLOYEE DEPENDENT SCHOLARSHIP)

LYNNE SONENBERG; COMMUNITY AFFAIRS; 1155 BATTERY ST
SAN FRANCISCO CA 94120
415/544-3662
AMOUNT: $1000 - $2000
DEADLINE(S): FEB 15
FIELD(S): ALL FIELDS OF STUDY

FOR DEPENDENTS OF LEVI STRAUSS & CO EMPLOYEES. FOR FULL TIME

UNDERGRADUATE OR VOCATIONAL STUDY. USA CITIZEN.
APPROXIMATELY 65 SCHOLARSHIPS PER YEAR. RENEWABLE. WRITE FOR COMPLETE INFORMATION.

1387

LLOYD D. SWEET SCHOLARSHIP FOUNDATION (SCHOLARSHIPS)
BOX 217 (C/O MRS. BETTY SPRINKLE)
CHINOOK MT 59523
406/357-3374
AMOUNT: VARIES
DEADLINE(S): MAR 2
FIELD(S): ALL AREAS OF STUDY
SCHOLARSHIPS OPEN TO MONTANA RESIDENTS WHO ARE GRADUATES OF CHINOOK HIGH SCHOOL. AWARDS ARE FOR FULL TIME UNDERGRADUATE OR GRADUATE STUDY AT ACCREDITED COLLEGES & UNIVERSITIES IN THE USA.
APPROX 100 AWARDS PER YEAR. WRITE FOR COMPLETE INFORMATION.

1388

LOUISIANA DEPARTMENT OF VETERANS AFFAIRS (AWARDS PROGRAM)
PO BOX 94095; CAPITOL STATION
BATON ROUGE LA 70804
504/922-0500; FAX 504/922-0511
AMOUNT: VARIES
DEADLINE(S): VARIES
FIELD(S): ALL FIELDS OF STUDY
LOUISIANA RESIDENT. OPEN TO CHILDREN (AGED 16-25) & WIDOWS/SPOUSES OF DECEASED/DISABLED (100%) WAR VETERANS WHO WERE LOUISIANA RESIDENT FOR AT LEAST 1 YEAR PRIOR TO SERVICE. FOR UNDERGRADUATE STUDY AT STATE SUPPORTED SCHOOLS IN LOUISIANA.
APPROXIMATELY 200 AWARDS PER YEAR. RENEWABLE UP TO 4 YEARS. WRITE FOR COMPLETE INFORMATION.

1389

LOUISIANA REHABILITATION SERVICES (VOCATIONAL AID FOR THE HANDICAPPED)
1755 FLORIDA ST
BATON ROUGE LA 70804
504/342-2285
AMOUNT: SEE BELOW
DEADLINE(S): NONE
FIELD(S): ALL AREAS OF STUDY
SEVERELY DISABLED PERSONS IN LOUISIANA FOUND ELIGIBLE FOR VOCATIONAL REHABILITATION SERVICES CAN RECEIVE FULL TUITION IF THEY ALSO MEET THE AGENCY'S CRITERIA FOR COLLEGE TRAINING.
PROGRAM IS INTENDED TO INCREASE THE EMPLOYABILITY OF THE DISABLED. THEREFORE ONLY PROGRAMS RESULTING IN INCREASED EMPLOYABILITY WILL BE APPROVED. WRITE FOR COMPLETE INFORMATION.

1390

LOUISIANA STUDENT FINANCIAL ASSISTANCE COMMISSION (SCHOLARSHIP; GRANT; LOAN PROGRAMS)
PO BOX 91202
BATON ROUGE LA 70821
504/922-1011; FAX 504/922-1089
AMOUNT: VARIED
DEADLINE(S): APR 1
FIELD(S): ALL AREAS OF STUDY
VARIOUS PROGRAMS FOR UNDERGRADUATE AND GRADUATE STUDY ADMINISTERED BY THE OSFA. OPEN TO LOUISIANA RESIDENTS. SOME PROGRAMS BASED ON FINANCIAL NEED; OTHERS ON ACADEMIC STANDING AND/OR SPECIFIC PROGRAMS OF STUDY.
CHECK WITH HIGH SCHOOL COUNSELOR OR WRITE FOR COMPLETE INFORMATION.

1391

LUTHERAN BROTHERHOOD (SCHOLARSHIPS)
625 FOURTH AVE SOUTH
MINNEAPOLIS MN 55415
800/328-7168
AMOUNT: \$800 - \$1500
DEADLINE(S): FEB 12
FIELD(S): ALL FIELDS OF STUDY
UNDERGRADUATE SCHOLARSHIPS OPEN TO LUTHERAN BROTHERHOOD MEMBERS. RECIPIENTS ARE CHOSEN BY AN INDEPENDENT PANEL OF JUDGES ON BASIS OF SCHOLASTIC ACHIEVEMENT (MINIMUM H.S. GPA OF 3.5) SCHOOL & COMMUNITY INVOLVEMENT & FUTURE PLANS.
\$500 AWARD FOR PUBLIC SCHOOL; \$1000 AWARD FOR PRIVATE NON LUTHERAN SCHOOL; \$2000 AWARD FOR LUTHERAN SCHOOL. RENEWABLE. WRITE FOR COMPLETE INFORMATION.

1392

LUTHERAN BROTHERHOOD (STAFFORD STUDENT LOANS)
625 FOURTH AVE SOUTH
MINNEAPOLIS MN 55415
800/328-7168
AMOUNT: $2650 - $7500
DEADLINE(S): NONE
FIELD(S): ALL FIELDS OF STUDY
LOANS OPEN TO LUTHERAN STUDENTS ON A FIRST-COME FIRST-SERVED BASIS WHO HAVE BEEN ACCEPTED FOR ADMISSION BY AN ELIGIBLE HIGHER EDUCATION INSTITUTION AND ARE MAKING SATISFACTORY PROGRESS. MUST MEET FEDERAL REQUIREMENTS.
CONTACT ADDRESS ABOVE FOR COMPLETE INFORMATION.

1393

MAINE BUREAU OF VETERAN SERVICES (GRANTS FOR DEPENDENTS)
STATE HOUSE; STATION 117
AUGUSTA ME 04333
207/626-4464
AMOUNT: FREE TUITION AT STATE SUPPORTED MAINE SCHOOLS
DEADLINE(S): NONE
FIELD(S): ALL AREAS OF STUDY
MAINE RESIDENTS. UNDERGRADUATE GRANTS FOR CHILDREN AGED 17-21 AND SPOUSES OR WIDOWS OF MILITARY VETERANS WHO ARE TOTALLY DISABLED DUE TO SERVICE OR WHO DIED IN SERVICE. US CITIZEN OR LEGAL RESIDENT.
VETERAN MUST HAVE LIVED IN MAIN AT TIME OF ENTERING SERVICE OR FOR 5 YEARS PRIOR TO APPLICATION. STUDENTS IN PRIVATE SCHOOLS CAN RECEIVE UP TO $300 PER YEAR. RENEWABLE FOR 8 SEMESTERS. WRITE FOR COMPLETE INFORMATION.

1394

MAINE EDUCATION ASSISTANCE DIVISION (HIGHER EDUCATION INTEREST-FREE LOANS)
STATE HOUSE STATION; #119
AUGUSTA ME 04333
207/289-2183 (IN STATE 800/228-3734)
AMOUNT: $1500 PER YEAR
DEADLINE(S): APR 1
FIELD(S): ALL FIELDS OF STUDY; PREFERENCE TO EDUCATION MAJORS
MAINE RESIDENTS. HIGH SCHOOL SENIORS; COLLEGE STUDENTS & TEACHERS ARE ELIGIBLE TO APPLY FOR INTEREST FREE LOANS. LOANS ARE COMPETITIVE & BASED ON ACADEMIC MERIT; RELEVANCE OF FIELD OF STUDY ETC.
400 NEW AWARDS PER YEAR. RENEWABLE. WRITE FOR COMPLETE INFORMATION.

1395

MAINE EDUCATION ASSISTANCE DIVISION - FINANCE AUTHORITY OF MAINE (SCHOLARSHIPS)
STATE HOUSE STATION; #119
AUGUSTA ME 04333
207/289-2183
AMOUNT: $500 (PUBLIC INSITITUTIONS); $1000 (PRIVATE)
DEADLINE(S): MAY 1
FIELD(S): ALL FIELDS OF STUDY
OPEN TO MAINE RESIDENTS ATTENDING COLLEGE IN THE NEW ENGLAND AREA. AWARDS ARE FOR FULL TIME UNDERGRADUATE STUDY.
8000 AWARDS PER YEAR. APPLICATION IS THE MAINE FINANCIAL AID FORM AVAILABLE IN COLLEGE FINANCIAL AID OFFICE.

1396

MAKARIOS SCHOLARSHIP FUND INC. (SCHOLARSHIPS)
13 EAST 40TH STREET
NEW YORK NY 10016
212/696-4590
AMOUNT: $1000
DEADLINE(S): MAY 1
FIELD(S): ALL AREAS OF STUDY
OPEN TO STUDENTS OF CYPRIOT OR GREEK ORIGIN. AWARDS SUPPORT FULL TIME UNDERGRADUATE OR GRADUATE STUDY AT AN ACCREDITED COLLEGE OR UNIVERSITY IN THE USA. MUST DEMONSTRATE FINANCIAL NEED.
6 AWARDS PER YEAR. WRITE FOR COMPLETE INFORMATION.

1397

MARGARET W. AND IRVIN W. LESHER FOUNDATION (SCHOLARSHIPS)
PO BOX 374
OIL CITY PA 16301
814/677-5085

AMOUNT: UP TO $2000
DEADLINE(S): APR 15
FIELD(S): ALL AREAS OF STUDY
OPEN TO GRADUATES OF THE JOINT UNION, HIGH SCHOOL DISTRICT IN CLARION COUNTY PENNSYLVANIA FOR UNDERGRADUATE STUDY. US CITIZEN OR LEGAL RESIDENT.
71 SCHOLARSHIPS PER YEAR. WRITE TO SCHOLARSHIP ADMINISTRATOR STEPHEN P. KOSAK AT ADDRESS ABOVE FOR COMPLETE INFORMATION.

1398

MARIN EDUCATIONAL FOUNDATION (UNDERGRADUATE SCHOLARSHIP PROGRAM)
1010 'B' STREET; SUITE 300
SAN RAFAEL CA 94901
415/459-4240
AMOUNT: $500 - $2800
DEADLINE(S): MAR 1
FIELD(S): ALL FIELDS OF STUDY
OPEN TO MARIN COUNTY RESIDENTS FOR UNDERGRADUATE STUDY IN TWO OR FOUR YEAR COLLEGES; VOCATIONAL-TECHNICAL AND FIFTH YEAR TEACHING CREDENTIAL PROGRAMS. MUST BE ENROLLED AT LEAST HALF TIME AND DEMONSTRATE FINANCIAL NEED.
WRITE FOR COMPLETE INFORMATION.

1399

MARION BRILL SCHOLARSHIP FOUNDATION INC. (UNDERGRADUATE SCHOLARSHIPS)
97 WEST ST; PO BOX 420
ILION NY 13357
315/895-7771
AMOUNT: $100 - $500
DEADLINE(S): JAN 15
FIELD(S): ALL AREAS OF STUDY
UNDERGRADUATE SCHOLARSHIPS OPEN TO RESIDENTS OF ILION (HERKIMER COUNTY) NY WHO GRADUATED FROM ILION CENTRAL SCHOOL DISTRICT. MUST DEMONSTRATE FINANCIAL NEED TO SATISFACTION OF SCREENING COMMITTEE. FAF FORM REQUIRED.
WRITE FOR COMPLETE INFORMATION.

1400

MARION BURK KNOTT SCHOLARSHIP FUND (SCHOLARSHIPS)
C/O ST MARY'S SEMINARY & UNIVERSITY; 5400 ROLAND AVE
BALTIMORE MD 21210
301/323-4300
AMOUNT: FULL TUITION
DEADLINE(S): NONE SPECIFIED
FIELD(S): ALL FIELDS OF STUDY
OPEN TO CATHOLIC STUDENTS TO ATTEND PARISH ELEMENTARY OR CATHOLIC SECONDARY SCHOOL IN BALTIMORE CITY OR THE COUNTIES OF BALTIMORE; CARROLL; FREDERICK; HARFORD OR HOWARD; OR ONE OF THE THREE CATHOLIC COLLEGES IN MARYLAND.
PRIMARILY AN ACADEMIC SCHOLARSHIP; WITH STUDENT INVOLVEMENT IN CHURCH; SCHOOL AND COMMUNITY TAKEN INTO ACCOUNT. WRITE FOR COMPLETE INFORMATION.

1401

MARJORIE S. CARTER BOY SCOUT SCHOLARSHIP TRUST (SCHOLARSHIPS)
PO BOX 527
WEST CHATHAM MA 02669
508/945-1225
AMOUNT: $1500 PER YEAR
DEADLINE(S): APR 15
FIELD(S): ALL AREAS OF STUDY
OPEN TO HIGH SCHOOL SENIORS WHO RESIDE IN ONE OF THE SIX NEW ENGLAND STATES AND ARE MEMBERS OF THE NEW ENGLAND COUNCIL OF BOY SCOUTS OF AMERICA. MUST BE ENTERING COLLEGE FOR THE FIRST TIME IN THE FALL.
FINANCIAL NEED IS A CONSIDERATION. THE TRUST HAS ITS OWN FINANCIAL AID FORM. WRITE FOR COMPLETE INFORMATION.

1402

MARQUETTE UNIVERSITY (SOUTH AFRICAN SCHOLARSHIP PROGRAM)
ALUMNI MEMORIAL UNION 425
MILWAUKEE WI 53233
414/288-7289
AMOUNT: TUITION; LAB FEES; SPECIAL COURSE FEES
DEADLINE(S): MAR 15
FIELD(S): ALL AREAS OF UNDERGRADUATE STUDY

ONE AWARD TO NON-WHITE SOUTH AFRICAN CITIZEN WHO CAN MEET THE ADMISSION REQUIREMENTS FOR ACADEMIC; PERSONAL AND ENGLISH LANGUAGE ABILITIES. MUST HAVE FINANCIAL SPONSOR FOR LIVING EXPENSES.

THE MAXIMUM DURATION OF ANY SCHOLARSHIP IS NORMALLY FOUR CALENDAR YEARS WITH THE DURATION REDUCED PROPORTIONATELY FOR STUDENTS WHO RECEIVE TRANSFER CREDIT.

1403

MARTIN LUTHER KING JR. SCHOLARSHIP FOUNDATION (SCHOLARSHIPS)

PO BOX 751
PORTLAND OR 97207
503-229-3000

AMOUNT: FULL TUITION

DEADLINE(S): JUL 31 - FALL; DEC 2 - WINTER; MAR 3 - SPRING

FIELD(S): ALL AREAS OF STUDY

OPEN TO STUDENTS AT ALL LEVELS OF STUDY WHO RESIDE IN OREGON AND PLAN TO ATTEND OR ALREADY ATTEND AN OREGON SCHOOL. A GPA OF 3.0 OR BETTER AND PROOF OF ADMISSION TO A POST-SECONDARY INSTITUTION REQUIRED.

WRITE FOR COMPLETE INFORMATION.

1404

MARY M. AARON MEMORIAL TRUST

1190 CIVIC CENTER BLVD
YUBA CITY CA 95997
WRITTEN INQUIRY

AMOUNT: APPROX $375 - $750

DEADLINE(S): MAR 15

FIELD(S): ALL AREAS OF STUDY

OPEN TO ANY NEEDY STUDENT FROM SUTTER COUNTY, CA ATTENDING AN ACCREDITED 2-YEAR (APPROX $375) OR 4-YEAR (APPROX $750) CALIFORNIA COLLEGE OR UNIVERSITY. GRANTS BASED ON FINANCIAL NEED. GRADES & ACTIVITIES ARE NOT CONSIDERED.

WRITE FOR COMPLETE INFORMATION.

1405

MARYLAND HIGHER EDUCATION COMMISSION (DISTINGUISHED SCHOLAR AWARDS)

STATE SCHOLARSHIP ADMINISTRATION; 16 FRANCIS ST
ANNAPOLIS MD 21401
410/974-5370

AMOUNT: $3000

DEADLINE(S): APPLY IN SPRING OF JUNIOR YEAR IN HIGH SCHOOL

FIELD(S): ALL FIELDS OF STUDY

OPEN TO MARYLAND HIGH SCHOOL STUDENTS WHO ARE NATIONAL MERIT OR ACHIEVEMENT FINALISTS. ADDITIONAL AWARDS GIVEN TO ACADEMICALLY GIFTED OR TALENTED STUDENTS. FOR UNDERGRADUATE STUDY IN MARYLAND.

RENEWABLE UP TO 4 YEARS. DISTINGUISHED SCHOLAR WINNERS WHO WISH TO BE TEACHERS ARE ALSO ELIGIBLE FOR $3000 TEACHER EDUCATION SCHOLARSHIPS. CONTACT HIGH SCHOOL COUNSELOR OR ADDRESS ABOVE FOR DETAILS.

1406

MARYLAND HIGHER EDUCATION COMMISSION (EDWARD T. CONROY MEMORIAL SCHOLARSHIPS)

STATE SCHOLARSHIP ADMINISTRATION; 16 FRANCIS ST
ANNAPOLIS MD 21401
410/974-5370

AMOUNT: UP TO $2400 FOR TUITION & MANDATORY FEES

DEADLINE(S): JUL 15

FIELD(S): ALL FIELDS OF STUDY

OPEN TO DEPENDENT CHILDREN OF 100% DISABLED OR KILLED IN THE LINE OF MILITARY DUTY WHO WERE MARYLAND RESIDENTS AT THE TIME OF DISABILITY OR DEATH AND TO DEPENDENT CHILDREN OF MIA'S OR POW'S OF THE VIETNAM CONFLICT. USA CITIZEN.

FOR UNDERGRADUATE OR GRADUATE STUDY; FULL OR PART TIME. WRITE FOR COMPLETE INFORMATION.

1407

MARYLAND HIGHER EDUCATION COMMISSION (GENERAL STATE SCHOLARSHIPS PROGRAM)

STATE SCHOLARSHIP ADMINISTRATION; 16 FRANCIS ST
ANNAPOLIS MD 21401
410/974-5370

AMOUNT: $200 - $2500

DEADLINE(S): MAR 1

FIELD(S): ALL AREAS OF STUDY

OPEN TO MARYLAND RESIDENTS FOR FULL TIME UNDERGRADUATE STUDY IN MARYLAND . MUST DEMONSTRATE FINANCIAL NEED. NURSING STUDENTS MAY ATTEND PART TIME. SAT OR ACT REQUIRED.

RENEWABLE WITH REAPPLICATION FOR UP TO 3 YEARS. WRITE FOR COMPLETE INFORMATION.

1408

MARYLAND HIGHER EDUCATION COMMISSION (HOUSE OF DELEGATE SCHOLARSHIPS)

STATE SCHOLARSHIP ADMINISTRATION; 16 FRANCIS ST
ANNAPOLIS MD 21401
410/974-5370

AMOUNT: VARIABLE - MINIMUM $200
DEADLINE(S): ESTABLISHED BY INDIVIDUAL DELEGATES
FIELD(S): ALL FIELDS OF STUDY

MARYLAND RESIDENT. FOR STUDENTS LIVING IN DISTRICT OF MEMBER OF HOUSE OF DELEGATES. UNDERGRADUATE OR GRADUATE STUDY IN MARYLAND OR OUT-OF-STATE WITH UNIQUE MAJOR. US CITIZEN OR LEGAL RESIDENT.

DURATION UP TO 4 YEARS; 2-4 SCHOLARSHIPS PER DISTRICT. ALSO FOR FULL OR PART TIME STUDY AT CERTAIN PRIVATE CAREER SCHOOLS AND DIPLOMA SCHOOLS OF NURSING. WRITE TO YOUR DELEGATE FOR COMPLETE INFORMATION.

1409

MARYLAND HIGHER EDUCATION COMMISSION (SENATORIAL SCHOLARSHIP PROGRAM)

STATE SCHOLARSHIP ADMINISTRATION; 16 FRANCIS ST
ANNAPOLIS MD 21401
410/974-5370

AMOUNT: $400 - $2000
DEADLINE(S): MAR 1
FIELD(S): ALL FIELDS OF STUDY

OPEN TO MARYLAND RESIDENTS FOR UNDERGRAD STUDY AT MD DEGREE GRANTING INSTITUTIONS; CERTAIN PRIVATE CAREER SCHOOLS & NURSING DIPLOMA SCHOOLS IN MARYLAND. FOR FULL OR PART TIME STUDY. SAT OR ACT REQUIRED.

STUDENTS WITH UNIQUE MAJORS OR WITH IMPAIRED HEARING MAY ATTEND OUT OF STATE. DURATION IS 1-4 YEARS WITH AUTOMATIC RENEWAL UNTIL DEGREE IS GRANTED. WRITE FOR COMPLETE INFORMATION.

1410

MASSACHUSETTS COMPANY (THE M. GENEVA GRAY SCHOLARSHIP FUND)

TRUST DEPT; 125 HIGH ST
BOSTON MA 02110
617/556-2335

AMOUNT: UP TO $1000
DEADLINE(S): JUN 15
FIELD(S): ALL FIELDS OF STUDY

OPEN TO UNDERGRADUATE STUDENTS WHO ARE UNABLE TO QUALIFY FOR SCHOLARSHIPS DUE TO PARENTAL OR INDIVIDUAL INCOME LIMITATIONS OR ARE UNABLE TO COMPLETE THEIR EDUCATION BECAUSE OF LACK OF FINANCES.

CANDIDATES FROM MIDDLE INCOME FAMILIES ($25000 - $50000) WITH SEVERAL CHILDREN TO BE EDUCATED ARE FAVORED. THERE ARE NO ACADEMIC REQUIREMENTS OTHER THAN ENROLLMENT IN GOOD STANDING. WRITE FOR COMPLETE INFORMATION.

1411

MASSACHUSETTS HIGHER EDUCATION COORDINATING COUNCIL (WAR ORPHANS SCHOLARSHIP PROGRAM)

330 STUART STREET; 3RD FLOOR
BOSTON MA 02116
617/727-9420

AMOUNT: UP TO $750 PER YEAR
DEADLINE(S): MAR 1
FIELD(S): ALL AREAS OF STUDY

OPEN TO PERMANENT MASSACHUSETTS RESIDENTS (AGED 17-23) WHO ARE DEPENDENT CHILDREN OF VETERANS WHO DIED DURING MILITARY SERVICE (WHILE RESIDENT OF MASS). AWARDS TENABLE AT RECOGNIZED UNDERGRADUATE INSTITUTIONS.

WRITE FOR COMPLETE INFORMATION.

1412

MASSACHUSETTS HIGHER EDUCATION COORDINATING COUNCIL (GENERAL SCHOLARSHIP PROGRAM)

330 STUART STREET; 3RD FLOOR
BOSTON MA 02116
617/727-9420

AMOUNT: $200 - $1600
DEADLINE(S): MAY 1
FIELD(S): ALL FIELDS OF STUDY
OPEN TO PERMANENT RESIDENTS OF MASSACHUSETTS. AWARDS ARE FOR UNDERGRADUATE STUDY AT ACCREDITED COLLEGES AND UNIVERSITIES IN MASSACHUSETTS.
40000-50000 AWARDS PER YEAR. WRITE FOR COMPLETE INFORMATION.

1413

MASSACHUSETTS HIGHER EDUCATION COORDINATING COUNCIL (FIRE - POLICE - CORRECTION SCHOLARSHIP PROGRAM)
330 STUART ST; 3RD FLOOR
BOSTON MA 02116
617/727-9420
AMOUNT: TUITION COSTS
DEADLINE(S): NONE SPECIFIED
FIELD(S): ALL FIELDS OF STUDY
OPEN TO PERMANENT RESIDENTS OF MASSACHUSETTS WHOSE PARENT DIED IN THE LINE OF DUTY AS A FIRE; POLICE OR CORRECTION OFFICER. AWARDS ARE FOR FULL TIME UNDERGRADUATE STUDY AT A MASSACHUSETTS COLLEGE OR UNIVERSITY.
WRITE FOR COMPLETE INFORMATION.

1414

MASSACHUSETTS SCHOLARSHIP OFFICE (NATIONAL GUARD EDUCATIONAL ASSISTANCE SCHOLARSHIP PROGRAM)
330 STUART STREET; 3RD FLOOR
BOSTON MA 02116
617/727-9420
AMOUNT: TUITION WAIVER
DEADLINE(S): NONE
FIELD(S): ALL AREAS OF STUDY
PROGRAM OPEN TO UNDERGRADUATE STUDENTS WHO ARE ENROLLED AT A MASSACHUSETTS PUBLIC COLLEGE OR UNIVERSITY & ARE ACTIVE MEMBERS OF THE MASSACHUSETTS NATIONAL GUARD OR THE MASSACHUSETTS AIR NATIONAL GUARD.
CONTACT THE VETERANS OFFICE AT YOUR COLLEGE OR ADDRESS ABOVE FOR COMPLETE INFORMATION.

1415

MASSACHUSETTS SCHOLARSHIP OFFICE (VETERANS TUITION EXEMPTION PROGRAM)
330 STUART STREET; 3RD FLOOR
BOSTON MA 02116
617/727-9420
AMOUNT: TUITION EXEMPTION
DEADLINE(S): NONE
FIELD(S): ALL AREAS OF STUDY
OPEN TO MILITARY VETERANS WHO ARE PERMANENT RESIDENTS OF MASSACHUSETTS. AWARDS ARE TENABLE AT MASSACHUSETTS POST-SECONDARY INSTITUTIONS.
CONTACT VETERANS AGENT AT COLLEGE OR ADDRESS ABOVE FOR COMPLETE INFORMATION.

1416

MCCURDY MEMORIAL SCHOLARSHIP FOUNDATION (EMILY SCOFIELD SCHOLARSHIP FUND)
134 WEST VAN BUREN STREET
BATTLE CREEK MI 49017
616/962-9591
AMOUNT: $100 - $1000
DEADLINE(S): MAR 31
FIELD(S): ALL AREAS OF STUDY
SCHOLARSHIPS FOR RESIDENTS OF CALHOUN COUNTY, MICHIGAN. MUST BE UNDERGRADUATE.
4-5 SCHOLARSHIPS PER YEAR. RENEWABLE WITH REAPPLICATION AND SATISFACTORY GRADES. WRITE FOR COMPLETE INFORMATION.

1417

MCCURDY MEMORIAL SCHOLARSHIP FOUNDATION (MCCURDY SCHOLARSHIP)
134 WEST VAN BUREN STREET
BATTLE CREEK MI 49017
616/962-9591
AMOUNT: $1000
DEADLINE(S): MAR 31
FIELD(S): ALL FIELDS OF STUDY
MUST BE RESIDENT OF CALHOUN COUNTY, MICHIGAN. MUST BE UNDERGRADUATE IN COLLEGE LEVEL OF STUDY.
7 SCHOLARSHIPS PER YEAR. RENEWABLE WITH REAPPLICATION AND SATISFACTORY GRADES. WRITE FOR COMPLETE INFORMATION.

1418

MCDONNELL DOUGLAS SCHOLARSHIP FOUNDATION (SCHOLARSHIP PROGRAM FOR EMPLOYEE DEPENDENTS)

3855 LAKEWOOD BLVD; MC 802-11
LONG BEACH CA 90846
310/593-2612

AMOUNT: $1500 - $4000

DEADLINE(S): 1ST FRIDAY IN MAR

FIELD(S): ALL FIELDS OF STUDY

OPEN TO HIGH SCHOOL SENIORS WHO HAVE A PARENT EMPLOYED BY MCDONNELL DOUGLAS CORP-WEST. POINTS GIVEN FOR SCHOLASTIC STANDING; STUDENT GOVERNMENT PARTICIPATION (LEADERSHIP); ATHLETICS; EXTRACURRICULAR & COMMUNITY ACTIVITIES; SAT/ACT SCORES.

40-45 SCHOLARSHIPS PER YEAR. RENEWABLE. WRITE FOR COMPLETE INFORMATION.

1419

MERCHANTS NATIONAL BANK (CLAUDE & INA BREY MEMORIAL ENDOWMENT FUND)

C/O TRUST DEPT; PO BOX 178
TOPEKA KS 66601
913/291-1118

AMOUNT: $500

DEADLINE(S): APR 15

FIELD(S): ALL FIELDS OF STUDY

SCHOLARSHIPS OPEN TO FOURTH DEGREE KANSAS GRANGE MEMBERS. AWARDS TENABLE AT RECOGNIZED UNDERGRADUATE COLLEGES & UNIVERSITIES. USA CITIZEN.

8 AWARDS PER YEAR. RENEWABLE. FOR COMPLETE INFORMATION WRITE TO MARLENE BUSH; PO BOX 186; MELVERN KS 66510.

1420

MERIT GASOLINE FOUNDATION (SCHOLARSHIP PROGRAM)

551 WEST LANCASTER AVE
HAVERFORD PA 19041
215/527-7900

AMOUNT: $1000 - $3000

DEADLINE(S): MAY 15

FIELD(S): ALL FIELDS OF STUDY

OPEN TO CHILDREN AND STEP CHILDREN OF QUALIFIED MERIT OIL CO. EMPLOYEES OR RETIRED; TOTALLY DISABLED OR DECEASED EMPLOYEES. FOR UNDERGRADUATE STUDY. AMOUNT OF AWARD DEPENDS ON FINANCIAL NEED OF RECIPIENT.

UP TO FOUR NEW SCHOLARSHIPS ARE AVAILABLE EACH YEAR. SCHOLARSHIPS ARE RENEWABLE. WRITE FOR COMPLETE INFORMATION.

1421

MEXICAN AMERICAN BUSINESS AND PROFESSIONAL SCHOLARSHIP ASSOCIATION (SCHOLARSHIP PROGRAM)

PO BOX 22292
LOS ANGELES CA 90022
WRITTEN INQUIRY ONLY

AMOUNT: $100 - $1000

DEADLINE(S): MAY 1 (POSTMARK)

FIELD(S): ALL FIELDS OF STUDY

OPEN TO LOS ANGELES COUNTY RESIDENTS WHO ARE OF MEXICAN-AMERICAN DESCENT AND ARE ENROLLED FULL TIME IN AN UNDERGRADUATE PROGRAM. AWARDS ARE BASED ON FINANCIAL NEED AND PAST ACADEMIC PERFORMANCE.

WRITE FOR COMPLETE INFORMATION.

1422

MEXICAN AMERICAN WOMEN'S NATIONAL ASSOCIATION (RAQUEL MARQUEZ FRANKEL SCHOLARSHIP FUND)

1101 17TH ST NW; SUITE 803
WASHINGTON DC 20036
WRITTEN INQUIRY

AMOUNT: $200 - $1000

DEADLINE(S): DEC 31

FIELD(S): ALL FIELDS OF STUDY

OPEN TO WOMEN OF HISPANIC BACKGROUND WHO ARE ENROLLED IN UNDERGRADUATE OR GRADUATE PROGRAMS AT ACCREDITED COLLEGES; UNIVERSITIES OR VOCATIONAL PROGRAMS. MUST DEMONSTRATE FINANCIAL NEED. THERE IS A $10 APPLICATION FEE.

WRITE FOR COMPLETE INFORMATION.

1423

MICHIGAN COMMISSION ON INDIAN AFFAIRS; MICHIGAN DEPT. OF CIVIL RIGHTS (TUITION WAIVER PROGRAM)

PO BOX 30026
LANSING MI 48909
517/373-0654

AMOUNT: TUITION (ONLY) WAIVER

DEADLINE(S): 8 WEEKS PRIOR TO CLASS REGISTRATION
FIELD(S): ALL AREAS
OPEN TO ANY MICHIGAN RESIDENT WHO IS AT LEAST 1/4 NORTH AMERICAN INDIAN (CERTIFIED BY THEIR TRIBAL NATION) & WILLING TO ATTEND ANY PUBLIC MICHIGAN COMMUNITY COLLEGE; COLLEGE OR UNIVERSITY.
AWARD IS FOR ALL LEVELS OF STUDY AND IS RENEWABLE. MUST BE MICHIGAN RESIDENTS FOR AT LEAST 12 MONTHS BEFORE CLASS REGISTRATION. WRITE FOR COMPLETE INFORMATION.

1424

MICHIGAN DEPARTMENT OF EDUCATION (MICHIGAN COMPETITIVE SCHOLARSHIPS)
STUDENT FINANCIAL ASSISTANCE SERVICES; PO BOX 30008
LANSING MI 48909
517/373-3394
AMOUNT: $100 - $1200
DEADLINE(S): FEB 15 FOR FRESHMEN
FIELD(S): ALL FIELDS OF STUDY/MICHIGAN RESIDENTS
OPEN TO USA CITIZENS WHO HAVE LIVED IN MICHIGAN AT LEAST A YEAR AND ARE ENROLLED AT LEAST HALF TIME IN AN ELIGIBLE MICHIGAN COLLEGE. MUST DEMONSTRATE FINANCIAL NEED AND SUBMIT ACT SCORES.
SCHOLARSHIPS RENEWABLE. FACT SHEETS ARE AVAILABLE FROM HIGH SCHOOL COUNSELORS. WRITE FOR COMPLETE INFORMATION.

1425

MICHIGAN DEPARTMENT OF EDUCATION (MICHIGAN TUITION GRANTS)
STUDENT FINANCIAL ASSISTANCE SERVICES; PO BOX 30008
LANSING MI 48909
517/373-3394
AMOUNT: $100 - $2100
DEADLINE(S): VARIES
FIELD(S): ALL FIELDS OF STUDY
OPEN TO MICHIGAN RESIDENTS WHO ENROLLED AT LEAST HALF TIME AT INDEPENDENT NON-PROFIT MICHIGAN INSTITUTIONS (LIST AVAILABLE FROM ABOVE ADDRESS). BOTH UNDERGRADUATE AND GRADUATE STUDENTS WHO CAN DEMONSTRATE FINANCIAL NEED ARE ELIGIBLE.
GRANTS RENEWABLE. WRITE FOR COMPLETE INFORMATION.

1426

MICHIGAN GUARANTY AGENCY (STAFFORD; SLS; PLUS LOANS)
PO BOX 30047
LANSING MI 48909
517/373-0760
AMOUNT: UP TO $7500
DEADLINE(S): NONE SPECIFIED
FIELD(S): ALL AREAS OF STUDY
GUARANTEED STUDENT LOANS AVAILABLE TO STUDENTS OR PARENTS OF STUDENTS WHO ARE ENROLLED IN AN ELIGIBLE INSTITUTION.
WRITE FOR COMPLETE INFORMATION.

1427

MICHIGAN VETERANS TRUST FUND (TUITION GRANTS PROGRAM)
BOX 30026; 611 WEST OTTAWA
LANSING MI 48909
517/335-1629
AMOUNT: TUITION
DEADLINE(S): NONE
FIELD(S): ALL AREAS OF STUDY
OPEN TO MICHIGAN RESIDENTS OF AT LEAST 12 MONTHS PRECEDING ENROLLMENT WHO ARE AGE 16-22; CHILD OF MICHIGAN VETERAN WHO WAS KILLED IN ACTION OR LATER DIED DUE TO SERVICE CONNECTED CAUSE OR IS TOTALLY DISABLED DUE TO SERVICE CONNECTED CAUSE.
GRANTS ARE FOR UNDERGRADUATE STUDY AT MICHIGAN TAX-SUPPORTED SCHOOLS. WRITE FOR COMPLETE INFORMATION.

1428

MIDAS INTERNATIONAL CORPORATION (SCHOLARSHIP TRUST)
225 N MICHIGAN AVE
CHICAGO IL 60601
312/565-7500
AMOUNT: VARIES
DEADLINE(S): MAR 1
FIELD(S): ALL AREAS OF STUDY
MIDAS SCHOLARSHIP TRUST IS OPEN TO DEPENDENTS OF CURRENT MIDAS EMPLOYEES WHO HAVE ONE OR MORE YEARS OF SERVICE WITH THE COMPANY.
CONTACT ADDRESS ABOVE FOR COMPLETE INFORMATION.

1429

MILITARY ORDER OF THE PURPLE HEART (SONS; DAUGHTERS & GRANDCHILDREN SCHOLARSHIP PROGRAM)

NATIONAL HEADQUARTERS; 5413-B BACKLICK ROAD
SPRINGFIELD VA 22151
703/642-5360

AMOUNT: $1000 PER YEAR
DEADLINE(S): JUL 15
FIELD(S): ALL AREAS OF STUDY

OPEN TO CHILDREN & GRANDCHILDREN OF MILITARY ORDER OF PURPLE HEART MEMBERS. APPLICANTS MUST DEMONSTRATE ACADEMIC ACHIEVEMENT & ENROLL IN A FULL TIME PROGRAM OF STUDY AT ANY LEVEL. USA CITIZEN OR LEGAL RESIDENT.

FINANCIAL NEED IS A CONSIDERATION. SCHOLARSHIPS RENEWABLE UP TO 4 YEARS PROVIDED 2.5 GPA IS MAINTAINED. WRITE FOR COMPLETE INFORMATION.

1430

MILTON AND HATTIE KUTZ FOUNDATION (UNDERGRADUATE SCHOLARSHIPS FOR DELAWARE RESIDENTS)

101 GARDEN OF EDEN ROAD
WILMINGTON DE 19803
302/478-6200

AMOUNT: $1000 PER YEAR (APPROX)
DEADLINE(S): APR 15
FIELD(S): ALL FIELDS OF STUDY

OPEN TO DELAWARE RESIDENTS FOR UNDERGRADUATE STUDY. AWARDS BASED ON FINANCIAL NEED; SAT SCORES; INDIVIDUAL'S POTENTIAL AND RECOMMENDATIONS; OUTSIDE ACTIVITIES/WORK.

RENEWABLE UP TO 4 YEARS; 10-15 AWARDS PER YEAR INCLUDING RENEWALS. WRITE FOR COMPLETE INFORMATION.

1431

MINNESOTA CHIPPEWA TRIBE (SCHOLARSHIP FUND)

PO BOX 217
CASS LAKE MN 56633
218/335-8584

AMOUNT: UP TO $3000
DEADLINE(S): JUN 1
FIELD(S): ALL FIELDS OF STUDY

OPEN TO ENROLLED MEMBERS OF THE MINNESOTA CHIPPEWA TRIBE AND THOSE ELIGIBLE FOR ENROLLMENT. AWARDS ARE TENABLE AT RECOGNIZED UNDERGRADUATE AND GRADUATE INSTITUTIONS. USA CITIZEN.

APPROX 850 AWARDS PER YEAR. WRITE FOR COMPLETE INFORMATION.

1432

MINNESOTA FEDERATION OF TEACHERS (FLORA ROGGE COLLEGE SCHOLARSHIP)

168 AURORA AVE
ST PAUL MN 55103
612/227-8583 OR 1/800/652-9710

AMOUNT: $1000
DEADLINE(S): MAR 4
FIELD(S): ALL AREAS OF STUDY

OPEN TO MINNESOTA HIGH SCHOOL SENIORS OR GRADUATES OF MINNESOTA HIGH SCHOOLS. FOR STUDY AT ANY ACCREDITED COLLEGE OR UNIVERSITY. RECOMMENDATIONS FROM TWO SENIOR HIGH SCHOOL INSTRUCTORS ARE REQUIRED.

AWARD BASED ON FINANCIAL NEED; ACADEMIC ACHIEVEMENT; LEADERSHIP ABILITY AND CHARACTER. WRITE FOR COMPLETE INFORMATION.

1433

MINNESOTA HIGHER EDUCATION COORDINATING BOARD (GRANTS)

CAPITOL SQUARE BLDG; SUITE 400; 550 CEDAR ST
ST PAUL MN 55101
612/296-3974

AMOUNT: $100 - $5848
DEADLINE(S): MAY 31
FIELD(S): ALL FIELDS OF STUDY

OPEN TO MINNESOTA RESIDENTS TO ATTEND ELIGIBLE MN COLLEGES & UNIVERSITIES. CANDIDATES MAY NOT HOLD 4 YEAR DEGREE OR HAVE ATTENDED COLLEGE FOR 4 YEARS; MAY NOT BE IN DEFAULT ON A STUDENT LOAN OR DELINQUENT IN CHILD SUPPORT PAYMENTS.

65000 AWARDS PER YEAR. WRITE FOR COMPLETE INFORMATION.

1434

MINNESOTA STATE DEPARTMENT OF VETERANS AFFAIRS (DECEASED VETERANS' DEPENDENTS SCHOLARSHIPS)
VETERANS SERVICE BLDG; BENEFITS DIV
ST PAUL MN 55155
612/296-2562
AMOUNT: TUITION + $350
DEADLINE(S): NONE
FIELD(S): ALL AREAS OF STUDY
OPEN TO MINN RESIDENT FOR AT LEAST 2 YEARS WHO IS SON/DAUGHTER OF VETERAN WHO WAS KILLED OR DIED AS A RESULT OF SERVICE-CAUSED CONDITION. PARENT MUST HAVE BEEN RESIDENT OF MINN AT TIME OF ENTRY INTO SERVICE. USA CITIZEN OR LEGAL RESIDENT.
AWARDS TENABLE AT MINN UNDERGRADUATE COLLEGES & UNIVERSITIES. SCHOLARSHIPS ARE RENEWABLE UP TO A BACHELORS DEGREE. WRITE FOR COMPLETE INFORMATION.

1435

MINNESOTA STATE DEPARTMENT OF VETERANS AFFAIRS (VETERANS GRANTS)
VETERANS SERVICE BLDG; BENEFITS DIV
ST PAUL MN 55155
612/296-2562
AMOUNT: $350
DEADLINE(S): NONE
FIELD(S): ALL AREAS OF STUDY
OPEN TO VETERANS WHO WERE RESIDENTS OF MINNESOTA AT THE TIME OF THEIR ENTRY INTO THE ARMED FORCES OF THE USA & WERE HONORABLY DISCHARGED AFTER HAVING SERVED ON ACTIVE DUTY FOR AT LEAST 181 CONSECUTIVE DAYS. USA CITIZEN OR LEGAL RESIDENT.
GRANTS MAY BE USED FOR TUITION AT ANY POST SECONDARY INSTITUTION WITHIN MINNESOTA. NOT RENEWABLE. WRITE FOR COMPLETE INFORMATION.

1436

MINNESOTA TEAMSTERS JOINT COUNCIL NO. 32 (SCHOLARSHIP AWARDS)
EDUCATION COMMITTEE; 3001 UNIVERSITY AVE SE
MINNEAPOLIS MN 55414
612/331-6767
AMOUNT: $1000
DEADLINE(S): APR 30
FIELD(S): ALL FIELDS OF STUDY
OPEN TO GRADUATING SENIORS OF MN HIGH SCHOOLS WHO ARE DEPENDENT CHILDREN OF MEMBERS OR DECEASED MEMBERS OF MN TEAMSTERS JOINT COUNCIL NO. 32. FOR STUDY AT ANY COLLEGE OR UNIVERSITY OR VOC-TECH INSTITUTE IN MINNESOTA. MUST HAVE GPA OF 3.0 OR
APPLICATIONS AVAILABLE FROM HIGH SCHOOL COUNSELORS. WRITE FOR COMPLETE INFORMATION.

1437

MINNIE PEARL SCHOLARSHIP PROGRAM
2000 CHURCH STREET; BOX 111
NASHVILLE TN 37236
800/545-HEAR (VOICE/TDD)
AMOUNT: $2000 (OR AMOUNT OF TUITION WHICHEVER IS LESS)
DEADLINE(S): MAR 16
FIELD(S): ALL AREAS OF STUDY
OPEN TO MAINSTREAM HIGH SCHOOL SENIORS WITH A SIGNIFICANT BI-LATERAL HEARING LOSS; A 3.0 OR BETTER GPA; WHO ARE ENROLLED IN OR HAVE BEEN ACCEPTED BY AN ACCREDITED COLLEGE; UNIVERSITY OR TECH SCHOOL. FOR FULL TIME STUDY.
NUMBER OF AWARDS VARIES EACH YEAR. RENEWABLE THROUGHOUT COLLEGE CAREER. WRITE FOR COMPLETE INFORMATION.

1438

MIRAMAR OFFICERS WIVES CLUB (SCHOLARSHIPS)
PO BOX 45241 N.A.S. MIRAMAR
SAN DIEGO CA 92145
WRITTEN INQUIRY
AMOUNT: $700 AVE
DEADLINE(S): APR 15
FIELD(S): ALL AREAS OF STUDY
OPEN TO SPOUSES AND CHILDREN OF OFFICER OR ENLISTED NAVY; MARINE CORPS OR COAST GUARD MEMBERS ON ACTIVE DUTY; RETIRED WITH PAY OR DECEASED. RECIPIENTS MUST RESIDE IN THE SAN DIEGO AREA.
WRITE FOR COMPLETE INFORMATION.

1439

MISSISSIPPI BOARD OF TRUSTEES OF STATE INSTITUTIONS OF HIGHER LEARNING (LAW ENFORCEMENT OFFICERS AND FIREMEN SCHOLARSHIP PROGRAM)
3825 RIDGEWOOD RD
JACKSON MS 39211
601/982-6570
AMOUNT: TUITION; ROOM; REQUIRED FEES
DEADLINE(S): NONE SPECIFIED
FIELD(S): ALL AREAS OF STUDY
OPEN TO CHILDREN OR STEP-CHILDREN OR SPOUSE OF MISSISSIPPI LAW ENFORCEMENT OFFICERS OR FULL TIME FIREMEN WHO WERE FATALLY INJURED OR WERE TOTALLY DISABLED WHILE ON DUTY. CHILDREN MUST BE UNDER AGE 23.
TUITION FREE SCHOLARSHIPS FOR 8 SEMESTERS AT ANY STATE SUPPORTED COLLEGE OR UNIVERSITY IN MISSISSIPPI. WRITE FOR COMPLETE INFORMATION.

1440

MISSISSIPPI BOARD OF TRUSTEES OF STATE INSTITUTIONS OF HIGHER LEARNING (SOUTHEAST ASIA POW/MIA SCHOLARSHIP PROGRAM)
3825 RIDGEWOOD RD
JACKSON MS 39211
601/982-6570
AMOUNT: TUITION; ROOM; REQUIRED FEES
DEADLINE(S): NONE SPECIFIED
FIELD(S): ALL AREAS OF STUDY
OPEN TO DEPENDENT CHILDREN OF MILITARY VETERANS FORMERLY OR CURRENTLY LISTED AS MISSING IN ACTION IN SOUTHEAST ASIA OR AS A PRISONER OF WAR AS A RESULT OF MILITARY ACTION AGAINST THE US NAVAL VESSEL PUEBLO.
TUITION FREE SCHOLARSHIPS FOR 8 SEMESTERS AT ANY STATE SUPPORTED MISSISSIPPI COLLEGE OR UNIVERSITY. WRITE FOR COMPLETE INFORMATION.

1441

MISSISSIPPI BOARD OF TRUSTEES OF STATE INSTITUTIONS OF HIGHER LEARNING (STATE STUDENT INCENTIVE GRANT)
3825 RIDGEWOOD RD
JACKSON MS 39211
601/982-6570
AMOUNT: $200 - $1500
DEADLINE(S): NONE
FIELD(S): ALL FIELDS OF STUDY
OPEN TO FULL TIME UNDERGRADUATE STUDENTS WHO ARE MISSISSIPPI RESIDENTS AND CAN DEMONSTRATE FINANCIAL NEED TO THE SATISFACTION OF THE MISSISSIPPI INSTITUTION IN WHICH THEY ARE ENROLLED.
APPLICATIONS MUST BE OBTAINED FROM THE INSTITUTION THE STUDENT ATTENDS.

1442

MISSOURI COORDINATING BOARD FOR HIGHER EDUCATION (MISSOURI STUDENT GRANT PROGRAM)
PO BOX 1438; 101 ADAMS ST
JEFFERSON CITY MO 65102
314/751-3940
AMOUNT: $100 TO $1500
DEADLINE(S): JAN 1 - APR 30
FIELD(S): ALL FIELDS OF STUDY
UNDERGRADUATE GRANTS OPEN TO MISSOURI RESIDENTS WHO ARE USA CITIZENS. MISSOURI FFS OR MISSOURI FAF REQUIRED.
8300 GRANTS PER YEAR. WRITE FOR COMPLETE INFORMATION.

1443

MISSOURI COORDINATING BOARD FOR HIGHER EDUCATION (MISSOURI GUARANTEED STUDENT LOAN PROGRAM)
PO BOX 1438; 101 ADAMS ST
JEFFERSON CITY MO 65102
314/751-3940
AMOUNT: UP TO $23000 (TOTAL) FOR UNDERGRADUATE STUDY; $8500 PER YEAR FOR GRADUATE STUDENTS TO A MAXIMUM OF $65000 (BOTH UNDERGRAD & GRAD)
DEADLINE(S): BY END OF ACADEMIC PERIOD
FIELD(S): ALL FIELDS OF STUDY
OPEN TO MISSOURI RESIDENTS OR STUDENTS ATTENDING SCHOOL IN MISSOURI. US CITIZEN OR LEGAL RESIDENT.
WRITE FOR COMPLETE INFORMATION.

1444

MISSOURI COORDINATING BOARD FOR HIGHER EDUCATION (HIGHER EDUCATION ACADEMIC SCHOLARSHIP PROGRAM)
PO BOX 1438; 101 ADAMS ST
JEFFERSON CITY MO 65102
314/751-3940
AMOUNT: $2000

DEADLINE(S): JUN 1
FIELD(S): ALL FIELDS OF STUDY
UNDERGRADUATE SCHOLARSHIPS FOR MISSOURI RESIDENTS WHO ARE US CITIZENS. MUST BE HIGH SCHOOL GRADUATE ACCEPTED OR ENROLLED FULL TIME AS AN UNDERGRADUATE & HAVE A COMPOSITE ACT OR SAT SCORE IN TOP 3% FOR MISSOURI SCHOOLS.
RENEWABLE YEARLY AS AN UNDERGRADUATE. WRITE FOR COMPLETE INFORMATION.

1445 ---

MOBIL CORPORATION (DESERT STORM VETERANS SCHOLARSHIPS)
3225 GALLOWS ROAD
FAIRFAX VA 22037
WRITTEN INQUIRY ONLY
AMOUNT: $1000 TO $5000
DEADLINE(S): VARIES WITH INSTITUTION
FIELD(S): ALL FIELDS OF STUDY
OPEN TO VETERANS OF OPERATION DESERT STORM/DESERT SHIELD; THEIR SPOUSES AND CHILDREN. THE SPOUSES AND CHILDREN OF THOSE WHO DIED IN THE OPERATIONS RECEIVE HIGHEST PRIORITY. FOR FULL TIME UNDERGRADUATE STUDY LEADING TO A BACHELOR'S DEGREE.
SCHOLARSHIPS ARE RENEWABLE AND AVAILABLE AT 20 USA COLLEGES AND UNIVERSITIES. FINANCIAL NEED IS A CONSIDERATION. WRITE FOR LIST OF PARTICIPATING SCHOOLS AND COMPLETE INFORMATION.

1446 ---

MODERN WOODMEN OF AMERICA (FRATERNAL COLLEGE SCHOLARSHIP PROGRAM)
1701 FIRST AVENUE
ROCK ISLAND IL 61201
WRITTEN INQUIRY ONLY
AMOUNT: $500 - $2000
DEADLINE(S): JAN 1
FIELD(S): ALL FIELDS OF STUDY
OPEN TO HIGH SCHOOL SENIORS WHO HAVE BEEN BENEFICIAL MEMBERS OF MODERN WOODMEN FOR AT LEAST TWO YEARS AND ARE IN THE UPPER HALF OF THEIR GRADUATING CLASS. FOR USE AT ANY ACCREDITED FOUR-YEAR COLLEGE IN THE USA.
36 AWARDS PER YEAR RENEWABLE FOR FOUR YEARS. WRITE FOR COMPLETE INFORMATION.

1447 ---

MODERN WOODMEN OF AMERICA (FRATERNAL VOCATIONAL-TECHNICAL SCHOLARSHIP PROGRAM)
1701 FIRST AVENUE
ROCK ISLAND IL 61201
WRITTEN INQUIRY
AMOUNT: $600 - $1000
DEADLINE(S): JAN 1
FIELD(S): ALL FIELDS OF STUDY
OPEN TO HIGH SCHOOL SENIORS OR GRADUATES WITHIN THE LAST THREE YEARS WHO HAVE NOT PURSUED VOC-TECH TRAINING. MUST HAVE BEEN A BENEFICIAL MEMBER OF MODERN WOODMEN FOR AT LEAST TWO YEARS.
FOR STUDY IN AN ACCREDITED VOC-TECH SCHOOL OR COMMUNITY COLLEGE IN THE USA. 12 AWARDS PER YEAR RENEWABLE FOR TWO YEARS. WRITE FOR COMPLETE INFORMATION.

1448 ---

MONTANA UNIVERSITY SYSTEM (INDIAN FEES WAIVER PROGRAM)
2500 BROADWAY
HELENA MT 59620
WRITTEN INQUIRY
AMOUNT: WAIVER OF REGISTRATION & INCIDENTAL FEES
DEADLINE(S): NONE
FIELD(S): ALL FIELDS OF STUDY
ONE-FOURTH OR MORE INDIAN BLOOD & MONTANA RESIDENT FOR AT LEAST A YEAR BEFORE ENROLLING IN THE MONTANA UNIVERSITY SYSTEM. MUST DEMONSTRATE FINANCIAL NEED. EACH UNIT OF THE MONTANA UNIVERSITY SYSTEM MAKES ITS OWN RULES GOVERNING SELECTION.
500 WAIVERS PER YEAR. WRITE FOR COMPLETE INFORMATION.

1449 ---

MONTANA UNIVERSITY SYSTEM (MONTANA GUARANTEED STUDENT LOAN PROGRAM)
35 SOUTH LAST CHANCE GULCH
HELENA MT 59620
406/444-6594
AMOUNT: $2625 - $4000 PER YEAR UNDERGRADS; $7500 PER YEAR GRADS
DEADLINE(S): NONE
FIELD(S): ALL FIELDS OF STUDY

THE MGSLP IS NOT A LENDER; IT DOES NOT MAKE LOANS TO STUDENTS. RATHER IT GUARANTEES THEIR LOANS WHICH ARE MADE BY REGULAR LENDING INSTITUTIONS SUCH AS BANKS; SAVINGS AND LOAN ASSNS; MUST DEMONSTRATE FINANCIAL NEED.

MUST BE A RESIDENT OF MONTANA ATTENDING AN ELIGIBLE MONTANA SCHOOL. WRITE FOR COMPLETE INFORMATION.

1450

MONTANA UNIVERSITY SYSTEM (MONTANA STATE STUDENT INCENTIVE GRANTS)
35 SO LAST CHANCE GULCH
HELENA MT 59620
406/444-6594
AMOUNT: UP TO $600
DEADLINE(S): NONE
FIELD(S): ALL FIELDS OF STUDY

OPEN TO MONTANA RESIDENTS WHO ARE FULL TIME UNDERGRADUATE STUDENTS ATTENDING ACCREDITED SCHOOLS IN MONTANA. MUST DEMONSTRATE NEED.

1150 AWARDS PER YEAR. CONTACT FINANCIAL AID OFFICE OF THE SCHOOL YOU PLAN TO ATTEND OR ADDRESS ABOVE FOR COMPLETE INFORMATION.

1451

MOTHER JOSEPH ROGAN MARYMOUNT FOUNDATION (GRANT PROGRAM & LOAN PROGRAM)
C/O JOSEPH E. LYNCH; 2217 CLAYVILLE CT
CHESTERFIELD MO 63017
314/391-6248
AMOUNT: $400 TO $750
DEADLINE(S): MAY 1
FIELD(S): ALL AREAS OF STUDY

GRANTS AND LOANS FOR STUDENTS WHO ARE USA CITIZENS; LIVE IN THE METROPOLITAN ST LOUIS AREA AND ARE ENTERING OR ENROLLED IN A HIGH SCHOOL; VOCATIONAL/TECHNICAL SCHOOL; COLLEGE OR UNIVERSITY.

WRITE FOR COMPLETE INFORMATION.

1452

MUSKEGON COUNTY COMMUNITY FOUNDATION (SCHOLARSHIP PROGRAM)
425 WEST WESTERN AVE; SUITE 304
MUSKEGON MI 49440
616/722-4538
AMOUNT: $500+
DEADLINE(S): APR 16
FIELD(S): ALL FIELDS OF STUDY

OPEN TO MUSKEGON COUNTY MICHIGAN RESIDENTS ONLY. SCHOLARSHIPS FOR 2-YEAR OR 4-YEAR UNDERGRADUATE STUDY OR GRADUATE SCHOOL. USA CITIZEN OR LEGAL RESIDENT. FINANCIAL NEED AND ACADEMIC STANDING ARE CONSIDERATIONS.

284 AWARDS PER YEAR (130 ARE RENEWALS). WRITE FOR COMPLETE INFORMATION.

1453

NAACP NATIONAL HEADQUARTERS (AGNES JONES JACKSON SCHOLARSHIP)
4805 MT HOPE DR
BALTIMORE MD 21215
301/358-8900
AMOUNT: $1500 - $2500
DEADLINE(S): APR 30
FIELD(S): ALL AREAS OF STUDY

UNDERGRADUATE ($1500) & GRADUATE ($2500) SCHOLARSHIPS OPEN TO APPLICANTS WHO HAVE BEEN NAACP MEMBERS FOR AT LEAST 1 YEAR & WILL BE UNDER AGE OF 25 ON APR 30. MINIMUM GPA OF 2.5-HIGH SCHOOL; 2.0-UNDERGRADUATE & 3.0-GRADUATE STUDENT.

SEND LEGAL SIZE SELF-ADDRESSED STAMPED ENVELOPE TO ADDRESS ABOVE FOR APPLICATION AND COMPLETE INFORMATION.

1454

NAACP NATIONAL HEADQUARTERS (ROY WILKINS SCHOLARSHIP)
4805 MOUNT HOPE DR
BALTIMORE MD 21215
301/358-8900
AMOUNT: $1000
DEADLINE(S): APR 30
FIELD(S): ALL FIELDS OF STUDY

OPEN TO GRADUATING HIGH SCHOOL SENIORS WHO ARE MEMBERS OF THE NAACP. APPLICANTS MUST HAVE AT LEAST A 2.5 (C+) GRADE POINT AVERAGE.

WRITE FOR COMPLETE INFORMATION.

1455

NATIONAL 4-H COUNCIL (NATIONAL 4-H AWARD PROGRAMS)
7100 CONNECTICUT AVE
CHEVY CHASE MD 20815
301/961-2800

AMOUNT: $750 - $1500
DEADLINE(S): NONE SPECIFIED
FIELD(S): ALL FIELDS OF STUDY
PRESENT OR FORMER 4-H MEMBERS ARE ELIGIBLE FOR MULTITUDE OF SCHOLARSHIP & AWARD PROGRAMS FOR POST-SECONDARY EDUCATION. CONTACT YOUR LOCAL 4-H AGENT OR STATE LEADER FOR INFORMATION & APPLICATIONS.
THE 4-H DIGEST (A SUMMARY OF SCHOLARSHIP PROGRAMS) & NATIONAL 4-H COLLEGE SCHOLARSHIP PROGRAMS CHECKLIST SHOULD BE AVAILABLE FROM YOUR LOCAL OR STATE AGENT. IF NOT SEND SELF-ADDRESSED STAMPED ENVELOPE TO ADDRESS ABOVE FOR DETAILS.

1456

NATIONAL AMPUTATION FOUNDATION (SCHOLARSHIPS)
12-45 150TH ST
WHITESTONE NY 11357
718/767-0596
AMOUNT: $250
DEADLINE(S): NONE
FIELD(S): ALL FIELDS OF STUDY
OPEN TO ANY HIGH SCHOOL SENIOR WHO IS AN AMPUTEE. AWARDS SUPPORT UNDERGRADUATE STUDY AT ANY RECOGNIZED COLLEGE OR UNIVERSITY.
5 AWARDS PER YEAR. WRITE FOR COMPLETE INFORMATION.

1457

NATIONAL ART MATERIALS TRADE ASSN. (NAMTA SCHOLARSHIPS)
178 LAKEVIEW AVE
CLIFTON NJ 07011
201/546-6400
AMOUNT: VARIES
DEADLINE(S): MAR 15
FIELD(S): ALL AREAS OF STUDY
OPEN TO NAMTA EMPLOYEES; MEMBERS AND THEIR RELATIVES OR TO INDIVIDUALS IN AN ORGANIZATION RELATED TO ART OR THE ART MATERIALS INDUSTRY. FOR UNDERGRADUATE OR GRADUATE STUDY.
SELECTION BASED ON FINANCIAL NEED; GRADES; ACTIVITIES; INTERESTS AND CAREER CHOICE. WRITE FOR COMPLETE INFORMATION.

1458

NATIONAL ASSOCIATION OF LETTER CARRIERS (WILLIAM C. DOHERTY SCHOLARSHIP PROGRAM)
100 INDIANA AVE NW
WASHINGTON DC 20001
202/393-4695
AMOUNT: $800
DEADLINE(S): MAR 31
FIELD(S): ALL FIELDS OF STUDY
OPEN TO HIGH SCHOOL SENIORS WHO ARE SONS; DAUGHTERS OR LEGALLY ADOPTED STEPCHILDREN OF AN ACTIVE; RETIRED OR DECEASED MEMBER OF THE NATIONAL ASSOCIATION OF LETTER CARRIERS.
15 SCHOLARSHIPS PER YEAR. RENEWABLE FOR 4 CONSECUTIVE YEARS. SEE THE JUL-NOV 'POSTAL RECORD' FOR COMPLETE INFORMATION.

1459

NATIONAL ASSOCIATION OF SECONDARY SCHOOL PRINCIPALS (NATIONAL HONOR SOCIETY SCHOLARSHIPS)
1904 ASSOCIATION DR
RESTON VA 22091
INQUIRE OF H.S. PRINCIPAL OR COUNSELOR
AMOUNT: $1000
DEADLINE(S): FEB 1
FIELD(S): ALL FIELDS OF STUDY
OPEN TO NATIONAL HONOR SOCIETY MEMBERS. EACH CHAPTER NOMINATES TWO SENIORS TO COMPETE FOR SCHOLARSHIPS AT THE NATIONAL LEVEL.
250 SCHOLARSHIPS PER YEAR. CONTACT YOUR NHS CHAPTER; HIGH SCHOOL PRINCIPAL OR GUIDANCE COUNSELOR FOR COMPLETE INFORMATION.

1460

NATIONAL COLLEGIATE ATHLETIC ASSOCIATION (GRANTS TO UNDERGRADUATES WHO HAVE EXHAUSTED INSTITUTIONAL FINANCIAL AID OPPORTUNITY)
URSULA R. WALSH; PO BOX 1906
MISSION KS 66201
913/339-1906
AMOUNT: TUITION; BOARD & ROOM; BOOKS; FEES
DEADLINE(S): MAY 15 POSTMARK
FIELD(S): ALL AREAS OF STUDY

OPEN TO NCAA STUDENT-ATHLETES WHO HAVE RECEIVED BUT EXHAUSTED INSTITUTIONAL ELIGIBILITY FOR ATHLETICS-RELATED FINANCIAL AID AND ARE WITHIN 30 SEMESTER HOURS (45 QUARTER HOURS) OF GRADUATION. FINANCIAL INFORMATION WILL BE REQUIRED.

APPLICATION AND DOCUMENTATION MUST BE SUBMITTED BY STUDENT'S DIRECTOR OF ATHLETICS. MUST HAVE GPA OF 2.0 OR BETTER. WRITE FOR COMPLETE INFORMATION.

1461

NATIONAL COLLEGIATE ATHLETIC ASSOCIATION (WALTER BYERS POSTGRADUATE SCHOLARSHIP)
PO BOX 1906
MISSION KS 66201
WRITTEN INQUIRY ONLY
AMOUNT: $7500 + EXPENSE ALLOWANCE
DEADLINE(S): FEB 5
FIELD(S): ALL AREAS OF STUDY

OPEN TO NCAA STUDENT-ATHLETES WHO ARE GRADUATING SENIORS WITH A GPA OF 3.5 OR BETTER AND HAVE BEEN ACCEPTED INTO A GRADUATE DEGREE PROGRAM AT AN ACCREDITED NON-PROFIT EDUCATIONAL INSTITUTION. FOR FULL TIME STUDY.

AWARD GOES TO ONE MALE; ONE FEMALE STUDENT ATHLETE AND IS RENEWABLE FOR A SECOND YEAR. MUST BE NOMINATED BY FACULTY ATHLETICS REPRESENTATIVE.

1462

NATIONAL COUNCIL OF JEWISH WOMEN-GREATER BOSTON SECTION (AMELIA GREENBAUM SCHOLARSHIP PROGRAM)
75 HARVARD AVENUE
ALLSTON MA 02134
617/783-9660
AMOUNT: APPROX $400
DEADLINE(S): APR 30
FIELD(S): ALL AREAS OF STUDY

OPEN TO JEWISH WOMEN WHO ARE RESIDENTS OF BOSTON OR VICINITY WHO ATTEND A MASSACHUSETTS COLLEGE OR UNIVERSITY AS AN UNDERGRADUATE. MUST DEMONSTRATE FINANCIAL NEED.

10 AWARDS PER YEAR. WRITE FOR COMPLETE INFORMATION.

1463

NATIONAL FEDERATION OF THE BLIND (BLIND EDUCATOR OF TOMORROW AWARD)
814 4TH AVE
GRINNELL IA 50112
515/236-3366
AMOUNT: $4000
DEADLINE(S): MAR 31
FIELD(S): ALL FIELDS OF STUDY

OPEN TO LEGALLY BLIND WOMAN BETWEEN THE AGES OF 17 AND 25 WHO IS PURSUING OR PLANNING TO PURSUE A FULL TIME POST-SECONDARY COURSE OF STUDY. AWARD IS BASED ON ACADEMIC EXCELLENCE; SERVICE TO THE COMMUNITY AND FINANCIAL NEED.

WRITE FOR COMPLETE INFORMATION.

1464

NATIONAL FEDERATION OF THE BLIND (EZRA DAVIS-AMERICAN BROTHERHOOD FOR THE BLIND SCHOLARSHIP)
814 4TH AVE; #200
GRINNELL IA 50112
515/236-3366
AMOUNT: $6000
DEADLINE(S): MAR 31
FIELD(S): ALL FIELDS OF STUDY

OPEN TO LEGALLY BLIND STUDENTS PURSUING OR PLANNING TO PURSUE A FULL TIME POST-SECONDARY COURSE OF STUDY. AWARDS ARE BASED ON ACADEMIC EXCELLENCE; COMMUNITY SERVICE AND FINANCIAL NEED.

WRITE FOR COMPLETE INFORMATION.

1465

NATIONAL FEDERATION OF THE BLIND (FRANK WALTON HORN MEMORIAL SCHOLARSHIP)
814 4TH AVE; #200
GRINNELL IA 50112
515/236-3366
AMOUNT: $2500
DEADLINE(S): MAR 31
FIELD(S): ALL FIELDS OF STUDY

SCHOLARSHIP FOR LEGALLY BLIND STUDENTS STUDYING (OR PLANNING TO STUDY) AT ANY POST-SECONDARY LEVEL. FOR ALL FIELDS OF STUDY BUT PREFERENCE WILL BE GIVEN TO ARCHITECTURE AND ENGINEERING MAJORS.

AWARDS BASED ON ACADEMIC EXELLENCE; SERVICE TO THE COMMUNITY; FINANCIAL NEED. WRITE FOR COMPLETE INFORMATION.

1466

NATIONAL FEDERATION OF THE BLIND (HERMIONE GRANT CALHOUN SCHOLARSHIPS)
814 4TH AVE; #200
GRINNELL IA 50112
515/236-3366
AMOUNT: $2000
DEADLINE(S): MAR 31
FIELD(S): ALL FIELDS OF STUDY
SCHOLARSHIPS OPEN TO LEGALLY BLIND FEMALE UNDERGRADUATE AND GRADUATE STUDENTS. AWARDS BASED ON ACADEMIC EXCELLENCE; SERVICE TO THE COMMUNITY; FINANCIAL NEED.
WRITE FOR COMPLETE INFORMATION.

1467

NATIONAL FEDERATION OF THE BLIND (KITCHER-KILLIAN MEMORIAL SCHOLARSHIP)
814 4TH AVE
GRINNELL IA 50112
515/236-3366
AMOUNT: $2000
DEADLINE(S): MAR 31
FIELD(S): ALL FIELDS OF STUDY
OPEN TO LEGALLY BLIND STUDENT WHO IS PURSUING OR PLANNING TO PURSUE A FULL TIME POST-SECONDARY COURSE OF STUDY. AWARD IS BASED ON ACADEMIC EXCELLENCE; SERVICE TO THE COMMUNITY AND FINANCIAL NEED.
WRITE FOR COMPLETE INFORMATION.

1468

NATIONAL FEDERATION OF THE BLIND (MELVA T. OWEN MEMORIAL SCHOLARSHIP)
814 4TH AVE; #200
GRINNELL IA 50112
515/236-3366
AMOUNT: $2500
DEADLINE(S): MAR 31
FIELD(S): ALL FIELDS OF STUDY
OPEN TO LEGALLY BLIND STUDENTS FOR ALL POST-SECONDARY AREAS OF STUDY DIRECTED TOWARDS ATTAINING FINANCIAL INDEPENDENCE. EXCLUDES RELIGION AND THOSE SEEKING ONLY TO FURTHER THEIR GENERAL AND CULTURAL EDUCATION.
AWARDS BASED ON ACADEMIC EXCELLENCE; SERVICE TO THE COMMUNITY AND FINANCIAL NEED. WRITE FOR COMPLETE INFORMATION.

1469

NATIONAL FEDERATION OF THE BLIND (SCHOLARSHIPS)
814 4TH AVE; #200
GRINNELL IA 50112
515/236-3366
AMOUNT: $2000 - $4000
DEADLINE(S): MAR 31
FIELD(S): ALL FIELDS OF STUDY
16 SCHOLARSHIPS (2 FOR $4000 EA; 5 FOR $2500 EA; 9 FOR $2000 EA) WILL BE GIVEN. APPLICANTS MUST BE LEGALLY BLIND AND STUDYING (OR PLANNING TO STUDY) FULL TIME AT THE POST-SECONDARY LEVEL.
AWARDS ARE ON THE BASIS OF ACADEMIC EXCELLENCE; COMMUNITY SERVICE AND FINANCIAL NEED. WRITE FOR COMPLETE INFORMATION.

1470

NATIONAL FEDERATION OF THE BLIND OF CONNECTICUT (SCHOLARSHIPS & AWARDS)
135 BURNSIDE AVE; SUITE A-2
EAST HARTFORD CT 06108
203/289-1971
AMOUNT: $1250 - $3000
DEADLINE(S): SEP 15
FIELD(S): ALL AREAS OF STUDY
FOR LEGALLY BLIND APPLICANTS WHO ARE CONNECTICUT RESIDENTS OR NON-RESIDENTS STUDYING IN CONNECTICUT. PROGRAMS FOR UNDERGRADUATE STUDY; VOCATIONAL-TECHNICAL TRAINING; PERSONAL ADVANCEMENT. US CITIZEN OR LEGAL RESIDENT.
WRITE OR PHONE FOR COMPLETE INFORMATION.

1471

NATIONAL HISPANIC SCHOLARSHIP FUND (SCHOLARSHIPS)
PO BOX 728
NOVATO CA 94948
WRITTEN INQUIRY
AMOUNT: VARIES

DEADLINE(S): APR 1 - JUN 15
FIELD(S): ALL FIELDS OF STUDY
OPEN TO US CITIZENS OR PERMANENT RESIDENTS OF HISPANIC PARENTAGE ENROLLED FULL TIME AS UNDERGRADUATE OR GRADUATE STUDENT IN USA COLLEGE OR UNIVERSITY. APPLICANTS MUST HAVE COMPLETED AT LEAST 15 UNITS/CREDITS PRIOR TO FALL REGISTRATION.
COMMUNITY COLLEGE UNITS MUST BE TRANSFERABLE TO A 4-YEAR INSTITUTION. FINANCIAL NEED IS A CONSIDERATION. SEND BUSINESS SIZE SELF-ADDRESSED STAMPED ENVELOPE FOR COMPLETE INFORMATION.

1472

NATIONAL ITALIAN AMERICAN FOUNDATION (AGNES E. VAGHI CORNARO AND NIAF-CORNARO SCHOLARSHIPS)
DR. M. LOMBARDO; EDUCATION DIRECTOR; 666 11TH ST NW; SUITE 800
WASHINGTON DC 20001
202/638-2137
AMOUNT: $1000
DEADLINE(S): MAY 31
FIELD(S): ALL FIELDS OF STUDY
OPEN TO ITALIAN-AMERICAN UNDERGRADUATE WOMEN WHO SUBMIT EVIDENCE OF FINANCIAL NEED AND AN ESSAY (1 TYPED PAGE MAXIMUM) DESCRIBING THEIR ITALIAN BACKGROUND.
WRITE FOR COMPLETE INFORMATION.

1473

NATIONAL ITALIAN AMERICAN FOUNDATION (CHRISTOPHER COLUMBUS SCHOLARSHIP)
DR. M. LOMBARDO; EDUCATION DIRECTOR; 666 11TH ST NW; SUITE 800
WASHINGTON DC 20001
202/638-2137
AMOUNT: $1000
DEADLINE(S): MAY 31
FIELD(S): ALL FIELDS OF STUDY
OPEN TO UNDERGRADUATES OF ITALIAN HERITAGE WHO PREPARE A 3 PAGE DOUBLE SPACED TYPED ESSAY ON THE TOPIC "COLUMBUS; THE ENTREPRENEUR IN MODERN-DAY SOCIETY." EVIDENCE OF FINANCIAL NEED IS REQUIRED WITH APPLICATION.
ESSAY SHOULD RELATE RESEARCH ON COLUMBUS' LIFE TO INDICATE HOW HE WOULD EXPRESS HIS SENSE OF ADVENTURE TODAY. WRITE FOR COMPLETE INFORMATION.

1474

NATIONAL ITALIAN AMERICAN FOUNDATION (GENERAL UNDERGRADUATE AND FIERI SCHOLARSHIPS)
DR. M. LOMBARDO; EDUCATION DIRECTOR; 666 11TH ST. NW; SUITE 800
WASHINGTON DC 20001
202/638-2137
AMOUNT: $1000
DEADLINE(S): MAY 31
FIELD(S): ALL FIELDS OF STUDY
OPEN TO UNDERGRADUATES OF ITALIAN HERITAGE CURRENTLY ENROLLED OR ENTERING COLLEGE. APPLICATION REQUIRES AN ESSAY DESCRIBING ITALIAN BACKGROUND AND EVIDENCE OF FINANCIAL NEED.
WRITE FOR COMPLETE INFORMATION.

1475

NATIONAL ITALIAN AMERICAN FOUNDATION (GUIDO ZERILLI-MARIMO FELLOWSHIPS)
DR. M. LOMBARDO; EDUCATION DIRECTOR; 666 11TH ST NW; SUITE 800
WASHINGTON DC 20001
202/638-2137
AMOUNT: $5000
DEADLINE(S): MAY 13
FIELD(S): ALL FIELDS OF STUDY
OPEN TO UNDERGRADUATE OR GRADUATE STUDENTS AT NEW YORK UNIVERSITY WHO ARE OF ITALIAN HERITAGE AND WISH TO STUDY IN ITALY. STUDENTS MUST SHOW EVIDENCE OF ACCEPTANCE TO AN ITALIAN UNIVERSITY OR AN AMERICAN UNIVERSITY WITH A SCHOOL IN ITALY.
EVIDENCE OF FINANCIAL NEED TO BE SUBMITTED WITH APPLICATION. WRITE FOR COMPLETE INFORMATION.

1476

NATIONAL ITALIAN AMERICAN FOUNDATION (JOHN FRISELLA SCHOLARSHIP)
DR. M. LOMBARDO; EDUCATION DIRECTOR; 666 11TH ST. NW; SUITE 800
WASHINGTON DC 20001
202/638-2137
AMOUNT: $1000
DEADLINE(S): MAY 31
FIELD(S): ALL FIELDS OF STUDY
OPEN TO UNDERGRADUATES FROM THE ST LOUIS (MO) AREA WHO ARE OF ITALIAN

HERITAGE. EVIDENCE OF FINANCIAL NEED AND AN ESSAY (1 TYPED PAGE MAXIMUM) DESCRIBING ITALIAN BACKGROUND ARE REQUIRED WITH APPLICATION.
WRITE FOR COMPLETE INFORMATION.

1477

NATIONAL ITALIAN AMERICAN FOUNDATION (ROBERT J. DIPIETRO SCHOLARSHIP)
DR. M. LOMBARDO; EDUCATION DIRECTOR; 666 11TH ST NW; SUITE 800
WASHINGTON DC 20001
202/638-2137
AMOUNT: $1000
DEADLINE(S): MAY 31
FIELD(S): ALL FIELDS OF STUDY
OPEN TO UNDERGRADUATE AND GRADUATE STUDENTS OF ITALIAN HERITAGE WHO ARE NO OLDER THAN 25. APPLICANTS SHOULD INCLUDE AN ESSAY OF 400 TO 600 WORDS ON HOW THEY INTEND TO PRESERVE THEIR ETHNICITY THROUGHOUT LIFE.
WRITE FOR COMPLETE INFORMATION.

1478

NATIONAL ITALIAN AMERICAN FOUNDATION (SILVIO CONTE INTERNSHIP)
DR. M. LOMBARDO; EDUCATION DIRECTOR; 666 11TH ST NW; SUITE 800
WASHINGTON DC 20001
202/638-2137
AMOUNT: $1000
DEADLINE(S): MAY 31
FIELD(S): ALL FIELDS OF STUDY
OPEN TO UNDERGRADUATE AND GRADUATE STUDENTS OF ITALIAN DESCENT INTERESTED IN INTERNING FOR ONE SEMESTER ON CAPITOL HILL IN WASHINGTON. STUDENT IS EXPECTED TO WRITE A PAPER ABOUT THE INTERNSHIP AND HOW IT WILL BENEFIT HIS/HER CAREER.
WRITE FOR COMPLETE INFORMATION.

1479

NATIONAL MERIT SCHOLARSHIP CORPORATION
1560 SHERMAN AVE; SUITE 200
EVANSTON IL 60201
708/866-5100
AMOUNT: NON-RENEWABLE $2000; RENEWABLE $250-$2000 (OR MORE)
DEADLINE(S): SEE PSAT/NMSQT STUDENT BULLETIN
FIELD(S): ALL AREAS OF STUDY
OPEN TO STUDENTS WHO ENTER THE COMPETITION FOR SCHOLARSHIPS BY TAKING THE PSAT/NMSQT IN OCTOBER OF THEIR JUNIOR YEAR IN HIGH SCHOOL. USA CITIZENSHIP REQUIRED.
7000 SCHOLARSHIPS PER YEAR; SOME RENEWABLE; SOME ARE NOT. CONTACT SCHOOL COUNSELOR FOR COMPLETE INFORMATION.

1480

NATIONAL OFFICE PRODUCTS ASSOCIATION
301 NORTH FAIRFAX ST
ALEXANDRIA VA 22314
703/549-9040
AMOUNT: $2000
DEADLINE(S): MAR 15
FIELD(S): ALL FIELDS OF STUDY
OPEN TO APPLICANTS WHO ARE EMPLOYED BY (OR RELATED TO AN EMPLOYEE OF) A MEMBER COMPANY OF THE NATIONAL OFFICE PRODUCTS ASSOCIATION. MEMBERSHIP STATUS WILL BE VERIFIED.
80 SCHOLARSHIPS PER YEAR. WRITE FOR COMPLETE INFORMATION.

1481

NATIONAL SCIENCE TEACHERS ASSN SCHOLARSHIP COMPETITION (DURACELL/NSTA SCHOLARSHIP COMPETITION)
1742 CONNECTICUT AVE NW
WASHINGTON DC 20009
202/328-5800
AMOUNT: $100 - $10000
DEADLINE(S): JAN 15
FIELD(S): ALL FIELDS OF STUDY
DESIGN COMPETITION OPEN TO ALL USA HIGH SCHOOL STUDENTS WHO CREATE & BUILD AN ORIGINAL WORKING DEVICE POWERED BY 1 OR MORE DURACELL BATTERIES. 41 AWARDS. TENABLE AT ANY ACCREDITED USA COLLEGE OR UNIVERSITY. USA CITIZEN OR LEGAL RESIDENT.
OFFICIAL ENTRY FORMS ARE AVAILABLE FROM SCIENCE TEACHERS OR BY WRITING TO NSTA AT THE ADDRESS ABOVE. WRITE FOR COMPLETE INFORMATION.

1482

NATIONAL SLOVAK SOCIETY (PETER V. ROVNIANEK SCHOLARSHIP FUND)
2325 E CARSON ST
PITTSBURGH PA 15203
412/488-1890
AMOUNT: VARIES
DEADLINE(S): JUL 1
FIELD(S): ALL FIELDS OF STUDY
OPEN TO DESERVING & NEEDY HIGH SCHOOL SENIORS ENROLLING IN A 2 OR 4 YEAR COLLEGE; UNIVERSITY OR TRADE SCHOOL. APPLICANTS MUST HAVE BEEN A BENEFICIAL MEMBER OF THE SOCIETY FOR AT LEAST 2 YEARS BEFORE APPLYING.
WRITE FOR COMPLETE INFORMATION.

1483

NATIONAL SOCIETY OF THE SONS OF THE AMERICAN REVOLUTION (EAGLE SCOUT SCHOLARSHIP)
1000 S FOURTH ST
LOUISVILLE KY 40203
502/589-1776
AMOUNT: $5000 1ST; $1000 2ND
DEADLINE(S): DEC 31
FIELD(S): ALL FIELDS OF STUDY
OPEN TO THE CURRENT CLASS OF EAGLE SCOUTS WHO PASSED THEIR BOARD OF REVIEW BETWEEN JUL 1 AND THE FOLLOWING JUN 30 OF EACH YEAR. COLLEGE PLANS DO NOT HAVE TO BE COMPLETE IN ORDER TO RECEIVE THE CASH SCHOLARSHIPS.
WRITE FOR COMPLETE INFORMATION.

1484

NATIONAL TWENTY AND FOUR (MEMORIAL SCHOLARSHIPS)
C/O ETHEL M. MATUSCHKA; 6000 LUCERNE CT; #2
MEQUON WI 53092
WRITTEN INQUIRY
AMOUNT: MAXIMUM OF $500
DEADLINE(S): MAY 1
FIELD(S): ALL AREAS OF STUDY
OPEN TO MEMBERS & DEPENDENTS OF MEMBERS BETWEEN THE AGES OF 16 AND 25. SELECTION IS BASED ON FINANCIAL NEED; SCHOLASTIC STANDING & SCHOOL ACTIVITIES.
WRITE FOR COMPLETE INFORMATION ONLY IF ABOVE QUALIFICATIONS ARE MET.

1485

NATIONAL WELSH-AMERICAN FOUNDATION (EXCHANGE SCHOLARSHIP PROGRAM)
MRS. OLWEN JOYCE ANDERSON; BOX 173 RD #3
SELINSGROVE PA 17870
717/345-5745
AMOUNT: $5000
DEADLINE(S): MAR 1
FIELD(S): ALL FIELDS OF STUDY
OPEN TO USA CITIZENS OF WELSH DESCENT WHO ASPIRE TO UNDERGRADUATE OR GRADUATE DEGREES AT RECOGNIZED USA INSTITUTIONS. APPLICANTS SHOULD BE NO MORE THAN 36. FOR STUDY OF WELSH-ORIENTED SUBJECTS AT A COLLEGE IN WALES.
WELSH FAMILY TIES ARE IMPORTANT. WRITE FOR COMPLETE INFORMATION.

1486

NATIVE SONS OF THE GOLDEN WEST (ANNUAL HIGH SCHOOL PUBLIC SPEAKING CONTEST)
414 MASON ST; SUITE 300
SAN FRANCISCO CA 94102
415/392-1223
AMOUNT: $600 - $1600
DEADLINE(S): JAN 1
FIELD(S): ALL FIELDS OF STUDY
PUBLIC SPEAKING COMPETITION OPEN TO CALIFORNIA HIGH SCHOOL STUDENTS UNDER AGE 20. SPEECHES SHOULD BE 7-9 MINUTES IN LENGTH & MAY BE MADE ON ANY SUBJECT RELATED TO CALIFORNIA'S PAST OR PRESENT.
DISTRICT ELIMINATIONS TAKE PLACE IN MARCH & APRIL. FINALS ARE IN MAY. WRITE FOR COMPLETE INFORMATION.

1487

NAVY SUPPLY CORPS FOUNDATION (SCHOLARSHIPS)
U.S. NAVY SUPPLY CORPS SCHOOL
ATHENS GA 30606
404/354-4111
AMOUNT: $2000
DEADLINE(S): FEB 15
FIELD(S): ALL FIELDS OF STUDY
OPEN TO CHILDREN OF NAVY SUPPLY CORPS OFFICERS (INCLUDING WARRANT) & SUPPLY CORPS ASSOCIATED ENLISTED RATINGS ON ACTIVE DUTY; IN RESERVE STATUS; RETIRED WITH PAY OR DECEASED. FOR

UNDERGRADUATE STUDY AT ACCREDITED 2-YR/4-YR COLLEGES.

APPROX 50 AWARDS PER YEAR. WRITE FOR COMPLETE INFORMATION.

1488

NAVY WIVES CLUBS OF AMERICA (SCHOLARSHIPS)

MRS. DIANA BOWER; DIRECTOR; NCWA SCHOLARSHIP FDN.; 16015 TERRY ST
BELTON MO 64012
816/331-2427

AMOUNT: NOT SPECIFIED
DEADLINE(S): APR 15
FIELD(S): ALL FIELDS OF STUDY

OPEN TO CHILDREN OF ENLISTED MEMBERS OF THE USA NAVY; MARINE CORPS OR COAST GUARD WHO ARE ON ACTIVE DUTY; RETIRED WITH PAY; OR DECEASED. FOR UNDERGRADUATE STUDY. MUST DEMONSTRATE FINANCIAL NEED.

APPLICANTS MUST BE PREVIOUSLY APPROVED FOR ADMISSION TO AN ACCREDITED SCHOOL. 26 AWARDS PER YEAR. SEND SELF-ADDRESSED STAMPED LONG ENVELOPE FOR COMPLETE INFORMATION.

1489

NAVY/MARINE CORPS RELIEF SOCIETY (NRS EDUCATION GRANTS)

801 NORTH RANDOLPH ST; RM 1228
ARLINGTON VA 22203
202/696-4904

AMOUNT: $1000
DEADLINE(S): NONE SPECIFIED
FIELD(S): ALL AREAS OF STUDY

UNDERGRADUATE GRANTS OPEN TO UNMARRIED DEPENDENT CHILDREN (UNDER AGE 23) OF US NAVY & US MARINE CORPS PERSONNEL WHO DIED WHILE ON ACTIVE DUTY OR DURING RETIREMENT AFTER 20+ YEARS OF SERVICE. USA CITIZEN OR LEGAL RESIDENT.

RENEWABLE. WRITE FOR COMPLETE DETAILS.

1490

NAVY/MARINE CORPS ROTC (COLLEGE SCHOLARSHIPS)

4015 WILSON BLVD
ARLINGTON VA 22203
WRITTEN INQUIRY

AMOUNT: TUITION; BOOKS; FEES; $100 PER MONTH
DEADLINE(S): DEC 1
FIELD(S): ALL FIELDS OF STUDY (US MARINE CORPS OFFICER)

OPEN TO USA CITIZENS BETWEEN THE AGES OF 17 AND 21 WHO ARE PHYSICALLY QUALIFIED AND WILL HAVE HIGH SCHOOL DIPLOMA BY END OF AUGUST. MUST HAVE NO QUALMS ABOUT BEARING ARMS AND DEFENDING THE USA CONSTITUTION.

FOR FOUR YEARS OF UNDERGRADUATE STUDY LEADING TO COMMISSION AS A RESERVE OFFICER IN THE US NAVY OR MARINE CORPS. SEE USN/USMC RECRUITER OR WRITE FOR COMPLETE INFORMATION.

1491

NCR SCHOLARSHIP FOUNDATION PROGRAM

C/O EDUCATIONAL TESTING SERVICE; PO BOX 6730
PRINCETON NJ 08541
609/921-9000

AMOUNT: $500 - $5000
DEADLINE(S): L.FEB
FIELD(S): ALL AREAS OF STUDY

FOR DEPENDENTS OF NCR CORP EMPLOYEES ONLY. PURPOSE IS TO HONOR & RECOGNIZE ACADEMIC ACHIEVEMENT AMONG OUTSTANDING STUDENTS FROM AROUND THE WORLD. SELECTION OF WINNERS IS BASED SOLELY ON MERIT WITHOUT REGARD TO FINANCIAL NEED.

CONTACT ADDRESS ABOVE FOR APPLICATION AND COMPLETE INFORMATION.

1492

NEGRO EDUCATIONAL EMERGENCY DRIVE (NEED SCHOLARSHIP PROGRAM)

643 LIBERTY AVE; 17TH FL
PITTSBURGH PA 15222
412/566-2760

AMOUNT: $100 - $1000
DEADLINE(S): APR 30
FIELD(S): ALL AREAS OF STUDY

PENNSYLVANIA RESIDENT. OPEN TO BLACK RESIDENTS WITH A HIGH SCHOOL DIPLOMA OR GED WHO RESIDE IN ALLEGHENY; ARMSTRONG; BEAVER; BUTLER; WASHINGTON OR WESTMORELAND COUNTIES. USA CITIZEN.

400 SCHOLARSHIPS PER YEAR. RENEWABLE. WRITE FOR COMPLETE INFORMATION.

1493

NEVADA DEPT OF EDUCATION (STUDENT INCENTIVE GRANT PROGRAM)
CAPITOL COMPLEX; 400 W KING ST
CARSON CITY NV 89701
702/687-5915
AMOUNT: UP TO $2500
DEADLINE(S): NONE SPECIFIED
FIELD(S): ALL FIELDS OF STUDY
STUDENT INCENTIVE GRANTS AVAILABLE TO NEVADA RESIDENTS ENROLLED IN ELIGIBLE NEVADA INSTITUTIONS.
APPLICATION MUST BE MADE THROUGH THE FINANCIAL AID OFFICE OF ELIGIBLE PARTICIPATING INSTITUTIONS.

1494

NEW BEDFORD PORT SOCIETY - LADIES BRANCH (LIMITED SCHOLARSHIP GRANT)
15 JOHNNY CAKE HILL
NEW BEDFORD MA 02740
WRITTEN INQUIRY ONLY
AMOUNT: $300 - $400
DEADLINE(S): MAY 1
FIELD(S): ALL AREAS OF STUDY
OPEN TO RESIDENTS OF GREATER NEW BEDFORD MA WHO ARE DESCENDED FROM SEAFARERS SUCH AS WHALING MASTERS AND OTHER FISHERMEN. FOR UNDERGRADUATE STUDY.
RENEWABLE. WRITE FOR COMPLETE INFORMATION.

1495

NEW BRITIAN LABOR COUNCIL AFL-CIO (BEYER-ROPIAK SCHOLARSHIP)
1 GROVE ST. #315B
NEW BRITIAN CT 06051
WRITTEN INQUIRY
AMOUNT: $500
DEADLINE(S): JUN 1
FIELD(S): ALL AREAS OF STUDY
SON/DAUGHTER/OR WARD OF AFL-CIO MEMBER WHOSE LOCAL IS AFFILIATED WITH NEW BRITIAN CENTRAL LABOR COUNCIL. FULL TIME UNDERGRADUATE STUDY ONLY.
WRITE FOR COMPLETE INFORMATION.

1496

NEW ENGLAND BOARD OF HIGHER EDUCATION (NEW ENGLAND REGIONAL STUDENT PROGRAM)
45 TEMPLE PL
BOSTON MA 02111
617/357-9620
AMOUNT: TUITION REDUCTION (AVG VALUE $2900)
DEADLINE(S): VARIES
FIELD(S): ALL FIELDS OF STUDY
UNDER THIS PROGRAM NEW ENGLAND RESIDENTS MAY ATTEND PUBLIC COLLEGES & UNIVERSITIES IN OTHER NEW ENGLAND STATES AT A REDUCED TUITION RATE FOR CERTAIN DEGREE PROGRAMS WHICH ARE NOT AVAILABLE IN THEIR OWN STATE'S PUBLIC INSTITUTIONS.
5883 AWARDS LAST YEAR. WRITE FOR COMPLETE INFORMATION.

1497

NEW ENGLAND EDUCATION LOAN MARKETING CORPORATION (NELLIE MAE - EXCEL & SHARE LOANS)
50 BRAINTREE HILL PARK; SUITE 300
BRAINTREE MA 02184-1763
617/849-1325
AMOUNT: $2000 - $20000
DEADLINE(S): NONE SPECIFIED
FIELD(S): ALL FIELDS OF STUDY
VARIETY OF LOANS AVAILABLE FOR UNDERGRADUATE AND GRADUATE STUDY AT ACCREDITED DEGREE GRANTING COLLEGES OR UNIVERSITIES. VARIED REPAYMENT AND INTEREST RATE OPTIONS. CUMULATIVE MAXIMUM LOAN OF $80000 PER STUDENT.
WRITE FOR COMPLETE INFORMATION.

1498

NEW HAMPSHIRE AMERICAN LEGION (SCHOLARSHIPS)
DEPARTMENT ADJUTANT; STATE HOUSE ANNEX
CONCORD NH 03301
WRITTEN INQUIRY ONLY
AMOUNT: $1000
DEADLINE(S): MAY 1
FIELD(S): ALL FIELDS OF STUDY
VARIOUS SCHOLARSHIPS AND AWARDS OPEN TO NEW HAMPSHIRE RESIDENTS FOR COLLEGE OR VOCATIONAL/TECHNICAL SCHOOL STUDIES. SOME ARE LIMITED TO CHILDREN OF LEGION MEMBERS.
WRITE FOR COMPLETE INFORMATION.

1499

NEW HAMPSHIRE CHARITABLE FUND (STUDENT AID SCHOLARSHIP FUNDS)
PO BOX 1335; 1 SOUTH ST
CONCORD NH 03301
603/225-6641
AMOUNT: $100 - $3000
DEADLINE(S): APR 24
FIELD(S): ALL AREAS OF STUDY
MORE THAN 90 SEPARATE SCHOLARSHIP AND LOAN PROGRAMS FOR NEW HAMPSHIRE RESIDENTS ARE ADMINISTERED BY THE NHCF. STUDENT MUST BE ENROLLED IN AN ACCREDITED 2-YEAR OR 4-YEAR COLLEGE OR UNIVERSITY. MUST BE LEGAL RESIDENT OF NEW HAMPSHIRE.
WRITE FOR COMPLETE INFORMATION.

1500

NEW HAMPSHIRE HIGHER EDUCATION ASSISTANCE FOUNDATION (FEDERAL FAMILY EDUCATION LOAN PROGRAM)
PO BOX 877; 143 N MAIN ST
CONCORD NH 03301
603/225-6612 OR 800/525-2577
AMOUNT: VARIES WITH PROGRAM
DEADLINE(S): NONE
FIELD(S): ALL FIELDS OF STUDY
OPEN TO NEW HAMPSHIRE RESIDENTS PURSUING A COLLEGE EDUCATION IN OR OUT OF STATE AND TO NON-RESIDENTS WHO ATTEND A NEW HAMPSHIRE COLLEGE OR UNIVERSITY. THE FOUNDATION ADMINISTERS A VARIETY OF STUDENT AND PARENT LOAN PROGRAMS.
USA CITIZEN. WRITE FOR COMPLETE INFORMATION.

1501

NEW JERSEY DEPT. OF HIGHER EDUCATION (DISTINGUISHED SCHOLARS PROGRAM)
OFFICE OF STUDENT ASSISTANCE; CN 540
TRENTON NJ 08625
609/588-3230; 800/792-8670 IN NJ
AMOUNT: $1000 PER YEAR FOR 4 YEARS
DEADLINE(S): FALL
FIELD(S): ALL AREAS OF STUDY
NEW JERSEY RESIDENT. PROGRAM OPEN TO ACADEMICALLY OUTSTANDING NJ HIGH SCHOOL STUDENTS WHO INTEND TO GO TO A NJ COLLEGE OR UNIVERSITY. US CITIZEN OR LEGAL RESIDENT.
STUDENTS MAY NOT APPLY DIRECTLY TO THE PROGRAM. APPLICATIONS MUST BE MADE THROUGH THE HIGH SCHOOL. CONTACT GUIDANCE COUNSELOR OR ADDRESS ABOVE FOR COMPLETE INFORMATION.

1502

NEW JERSEY DEPT. OF HIGHER EDUCATION (EDUCATIONAL OPPORTUNITY FUND GRANTS)
OFFICE OF STUDENT ASSISTANCE; CN 540
TRENTON NJ 08625
609/588-3230; 800/792-8670 IN NJ
AMOUNT: $200-$1950 UNDERGRAD; $200-$4000 GRADUATE STUDENT
DEADLINE(S): OCT 1; MAR 1
FIELD(S): ALL AREAS OF STUDY
NEW JERSEY RESIDENT FOR AT LEAST 12 MONTHS PRIOR TO APPLICATION. GRANTS FOR ECONOMICALLY AND EDUCATIONALLY DISADVANTAGED STUDENTS. FOR UNDERGRADUATE OR GRADUATE STUDY IN NEW JERSEY. MUST DEMONSTRATE NEED. US CITIZEN OR LEGAL RESIDENT.
GRANTS RENEWABLE. WRITE FOR COMPLETE INFORMATION.

1503

NEW JERSEY DEPT. OF HIGHER EDUCATION (GARDEN STATE SCHOLARSHIPS)
OFFICE OF STUDENT ASSISTANCE; CN 540
TRENTON NJ 08625
609/588-3230; 800/792-8670 IN NJ
AMOUNT: $500 PER YEAR FOR 4 YEARS
DEADLINE(S): OCT 1; MAR 1
FIELD(S): ALL AREAS OF STUDY
RESIDENT OF NEW JERSEY FOR AT LEAST 12 MONTHS PRIOR TO RECEIVING AWARD. FOR UNDERGRADUATE STUDY IN NJ. DEMONSTRATE SCHOLASTIC ACHIEVEMENT & NEED. US CITIZEN OR LEGAL RESIDENT.
RENEWABLE. WRITE FOR COMPLETE INFORMATION.

1504

NEW JERSEY DEPT. OF HIGHER EDUCATION (HIGHER EDUCATION LOAN PROGRAM)
OFFICE OF STUDENT ASSISTANCE; CN 540
TRENTON NJ 08625
609/588-3200; 800/792-8670 IN NJ
AMOUNT: $2625 UNDERGRAD; $7500 GRADUATE STUDENT

DEADLINE(S): 2 MONTHS PRIOR TO DATE OF NEED
FIELD(S): ALL AREAS OF STUDY
US CITIZENS OR LEGAL RESIDENTS. RESIDENTS OF NEW JERSEY FOR 6 MONTHS PRIOR TO FILING APPLICATION OR OUT-OF-STATE STUDENT ATTENDING SCHOOL IN NJ. APPLIES TO ALL LEVELS OF STUDY.
WRITE FOR COMPLETE INFORMATION.

1505
NEW JERSEY DEPT. OF HIGHER EDUCATION (PUBLIC TUITION BENEFIT PROGRAM)
OFFICE OF STUDENT ASSISTANCE; CN 540
TRENTON NJ 08625
609/588-3230; 800/792-8670 IN NJ
AMOUNT: PARTIAL - FULL TUITION
DEADLINE(S): OCT 1; MAR 1
FIELD(S): ALL AREAS OF STUDY
NEW JERSEY RESIDENT. OPEN TO DEPENDENTS OF EMERGENCY SERVICE PERSONNEL & LAW OFFICERS KILLED IN THE LINE OF DUTY IN NJ. FOR UNDERGRADUATE STUDY IN NJ. US CITIZEN OR LEGAL RESIDENT.
GRANTS RENEWABLE. WRITE FOR COMPLETE INFORMATION.

1506
NEW JERSEY DEPT. OF HIGHER EDUCATION (POW/MIA DEPENDENT'S GRANTS)
OFFICE OF STUDENT ASSISTANCE; CN 540
TRENTON NJ 08625
609/588-3200; 800/792-8670 IN NJ
AMOUNT: FULL TUITION
DEADLINE(S): OCT 1; MAR 1
FIELD(S): ALL AREAS OF STUDY
NEW JERSEY RESIDENTS. OPEN TO DEPENDENT CHILDREN OF USA MILITARY SERVICE PERSONNEL WHO WERE OFFICIALLY DECLARED POW OR MIA AFTER JAN 1 1960. GRANTS WILL PAY UNDERGRADUATE TUITION AT ANY ACCREDITED PUBLIC OR INDEPENDENT COLLEGE/UNIV IN NJ.
WRITE FOR COMPLETE INFORMATION.

1507
NEW JERSEY DEPT. OF HIGHER EDUCATION (TUITION AID GRANTS)
OFFICE OF STUDENT ASSISTANCE; CN 540
TRENTON NJ 08625
609/588-3230; 800/792-8670 IN NJ
AMOUNT: $400 - $4580
DEADLINE(S): OCT 1; MAR 1
FIELD(S): ALL AREAS OF STUDY
NEW JERSEY RESIDENT FOR AT LEAST 12 MONTHS. FOR STUDENTS WHO ARE OR INTEND TO BE ENROLLED AS FULL-TIME UNDERGRADUATE IN ANY COLLEGE OR UNIVERSITY IN NEW JERSEY. US CITIZEN OR LEGAL RESIDENT.
GRANTS RENEWABLE. WRITE FOR COMPLETE INFORMATION.

1508
NEW JERSEY DEPT. OF HIGHER EDUCATION (VETERANS TUITION CREDIT PROGRAM)
OFFICE OF STUDENT ASSISTANCE; CN 540
TRENTON NJ 08625
609/588-3200; 800/792-8670 IN NJ
AMOUNT: $400 FULL TIME; $200 HALF TIME
DEADLINE(S): OCT 1; MAR 1
FIELD(S): ALL AREAS OF STUDY
OPEN TO USA VETERANS WHO SERVED BETWEEN DEC 31 1960 - AUG 1 1974 & WERE RESIDENTS OF NJ AT TIME OF INDUCTION OR DISCHARGE. APPLIES TO ALL LEVELS OF STUDY.
WRITE FOR COMPLETE INFORMATION.

1509
NEW JERSEY STATE GOLF ASSOC (SCHOLARSHIPS)
RAINTREE; 14 WOODMERE CT
FREEHOLD NJ 07728
201/780-3562 AFTER 6 PM
AMOUNT: $800 - $2500
DEADLINE(S): MAY 1
FIELD(S): ALL FIELDS OF STUDY
OPEN TO STUDENTS WHO HAVE SERVED AS A CADDIE AT A NEW JERSEY GOLF CLUB WHICH IS A MEMBER OF THE NJ STATE GOLF ASSOCIATION. FOR FULL TIME UNDERGRADUATE STUDY AT AN ACCREDITED COLLEGE OR UNIVERSITY.
AWARDS ARE BASED ON SCHOLASTIC ACHIEVEMENT; FINANCIAL NEED; SAT SCORES; CHARACTER & LENGTH OF SERVICE AS A CADDIE. 30+ NEW AWARDS PER YEAR. RENEWABLE FOR 3 ADDITIONAL YEARS. WRITE FOR COMPLETE INFORMATION.

1510
NEW MEXICO EDUCATIONAL ASSISTANCE FOUNDATION (STUDENT INCENTIVE GRANT)
PO BOX 27020
ALBUQUERQUE NM 87125
505/345-3371

AMOUNT: UP TO $2000
DEADLINE(S): NONE
FIELD(S): ALL AREAS/NEW MEXICO RESIDENTS
OPEN TO NEW MEXICO RESIDENTS WHO ARE ENROLLED AT LEAST HALF TIME IN A PUBLIC OR PRIVATE UNDERGRADUATE INSTITUTION IN NEW MEXICO. NMEAF IS FISCAL ADMINISTRATIVE AGENT; INDIVIDUAL SCHOOLS MAKE AWARDS BASED ON FINANCIAL NEED.
APPROXIMATELY 2700 GRANTS PER YEAR. CONTACT COLLEGE FINANCIAL AID OFFICER FOR COMPLETE INFORMATION.

1511

NEW MEXICO VETERANS' SERVICE COMMISSION (SCHOLARSHIP PROGRAM)
PO BOX 2324
SANTA FE NM 87503
505/827-6300
AMOUNT: FULL TUITION + $300
DEADLINE(S): NONE
FIELD(S): ALL AREAS OF STUDY
OPEN TO NEW MEXICO RESIDENTS (AGED 17-25) WHO ARE SON OR DAUGHTER OF PERSON WHO WAS KILLED IN ACTION OR DIED AS A RESULT OF MILITARY SERVICE IN THE U.S. ARMED FORCES DURING A PERIOD OF ARMED CONFLICT.
VETERAN MUST HAVE BEEN NM RESIDENT AT TIME OF ENTRY INTO SERVICE AND MUST HAVE SERVED DURING A PERIOD OF ARMED CONFLICT. APPROX 13 FULL TUITION SCHOLARSHIPS FOR UNDERGRADS PER YEAR. WRITE FOR COMPLETE INFORMATION.

1512

NEW YORK COUNCIL NAVY LEAGUE SCHOLARSHIP FUND (SCHOLARSHIPS)
1 WORLD TRADE CENTER; SUITE 2611
NEW YORK NY 10048
212/912-1798
AMOUNT: $2500
DEADLINE(S): JUN 15
FIELD(S): ALL AREAS OF STUDY
UNDERGRADUATE SCHOLARSHIPS FOR DEPENDENTS OF REGULAR NAVY; MARINE CORPS AND COAST GUARD PERSONNEL WHO ARE SERVING ON ACTIVE DUTY; RETIRED WITH PAY; DISABLED OR WHO DIED IN LINE OF DUTY OR AFTER RETIREMENT.
LIMITED TO RESIDENTS OF NEW YORK; NEW JERSEY AND CONNECTICUT. WRITE FOR COMPLETE INFORMATION.

1513

NEW YORK STATE EDUCATION DEPARTMENT (AWARDS; SCHOLARSHIPS & FELLOWSHIPS)
STATE & FEDERAL SCHOLARSHIP & FELLOWSHIP UNIT; CULTURAL EDUCATION CENTER
ALBANY NY 12230
WRITTEN INQUIRY
AMOUNT: VARIES
DEADLINE(S): VARIES
FIELD(S): ALL FIELDS OF STUDY
VARIOUS STATE AND FEDERAL PROGRAMS ADMINISTERED BY THE NY STATE EDUCATION DEPARTMENT OPEN TO RESIDENTS OF NEW YORK STATE. ONE YEAR'S NY RESIDENCY IMMEDIATELY PRECEDING EFFECTIVE DATE OF AWARD IS REQUIRED.
WRITE FOR COMPLETE INFORMATION.

1514

NEW YORK STATE HIGHER EDUCATION SERVICES CORPORATION (STATE & FEDERAL SCHOLARSHIPS; FELLOWSHIPS; GRANTS; LOANS)
STUDENT INFORMATION; 99 WASHINGTON AVE
ALBANY NY 12255
518/473-7087
AMOUNT: VARIES WITH PROGRAM
DEADLINE(S): VARIES
FIELD(S): ALL FIELDS OF STUDY
THE CORPORATION ADMINISTERS A VARIETY OF FEDERAL AND STATE SCHOLARSHIPS; FELLOWSHIPS; GRANTS AND LOANS. OPEN TO NEW YORK STATE RESIDENTS. SOME PROGRAMS CARRY A SERVICE OBLIGATION FOR EACH YEAR SUPPORT IS RECEIVED.
WRITE FOR COMPLETE INFORMATION.

1515

NEW YORK TELEPHONE (SCHOLARSHIP PROGRAM FOR BLACK AND HISPANIC STUDENTS)
COTE; PO BOX 2810
CHERRY HILL NJ 08034
609/573-9400
AMOUNT: $1000
DEADLINE(S): APR 30
FIELD(S): ALL FIELDS OF STUDY

OPEN TO BLACK OR HISPANIC STUDENTS WHO RESIDE IN NEW YORK AND ARE ENROLLED FULL TIME AS SECOND SEMESTER FRESHMEN IN A TWO-YEAR UNDERGRADUATE PROGRAM LEADING TO AN ASSOCIATE DEGREE. MUST BE ENROLLED IN AN ACCREDITED NEW YORK STATE SCHOOL.

FINANCIAL NEED IS A CONSIDERATION. NOT RENEWABLE. WRITE FOR COMPLETE INFORMATION.

1516

NEWTON PUBLIC SCHOOLS (CHAFFIN EDUCATIONAL FUND SCHOLARSHIP & LOAN PROGRAMS)
100 WALNUT STREET
NEWTONVILLE MA 02160
617/552-7681
AMOUNT: $500 PER SEMESTER; $4000 MAXIMUM
DEADLINE(S): NONE
FIELD(S): ALL FIELDS OF STUDY

OPEN TO GRADUATES OF NEWTON PUBLIC HIGH SCHOOLS. PREFERENCE TO STUDENTS ENROLLING IN 4-YEAR ACCREDITED UNDERGRADUATE PROGRAM.

APPROX 27 AWARDS PER YEAR. RENEWABLE TO MAXIMUM OF $4000. WRITE FOR COMPLETE INFORMATION.

1517

NON COMMISSIONED OFFICERS ASSOCIATION (SCHOLARSHIPS)
PO BOX 33610
SAN ANTONIO TX 78265
512/653-6161
AMOUNT: $750 - $1000
DEADLINE(S): MAR 31
FIELD(S): ALL FIELDS OF STUDY

UNDERGRADUATE & VOCATIONAL SCHOLARSHIPS OPEN TO CHILDREN AND SPOUSES OF MEMBERS. CHILDREN OF MEMBERS MUST BE UNDER AGE 25 TO RECEIVE INITIAL GRANTS.

25 AWARDS PER YEAR. FULL TIME STUDENTS WHO MAINTAIN AT LEAST A 3.0 GPA MAY REAPPLY EACH YEAR FOR SCHOLARSHIP RENEWAL. WRITE FOR COMPLETE INFORMATION.

1518

NORTH AMERICAN PHILIPS CORPORATION (SCHOLARSHIP PROGRAM)
100 EAST 42ND STREET
NEW YORK NY 10017
212/850-5000
AMOUNT: $2500; $500 - $1500
DEADLINE(S): MAR 1 (APPLY IN JAN)
FIELD(S): ALL AREAS STUDY

OPEN TO DEPENDENT CHILDREN OF NORTH AMERICAN PHILIPS EMPLOYEES. APPLICANTS MUST BE HIGH SCHOOL SENIORS WHO EXPECT TO GRADUATE DURING THE CURRENT YEAR. CONSIDERATIONS INCLUDE ACADEMIC RECORD; SAT OR ACT SCORES & BIOGRAPHICAL QUESTIONNAIRE.

52 AWARDS PER YEAR. FINANCIAL NEED IS CONSIDERATION EXCEPT FOR TWO $2500 AWARDS WHICH ARE MERIT BASED ONLY. PARTICIPATION IN EXTRACURRICULAR ACTIVITIES AND SPORTS ARE CONSIDERED. WRITE FOR COMPLETE INFORMATION.

1519

NORTH CAROLINA DIVISION OF SERVICES FOR THE BLIND (REHABILITATION ASSISTANCE FOR VISUALLY HANDICAPPED)
309 ASHE AVE
RALEIGH NC 27606
919/733-9700
AMOUNT: TUITION; FEES; BOOKS AND SUPPLIES
DEADLINE(S): NONE
FIELD(S): ALL AREAS OF STUDY

NORTH CAROLINA RESIDENT. LEGALLY BLIND OR HAVE A PROGRESSIVE EYE CONDITION WHICH MAY RESULT IN BLINDNESS THEREBY CREATING AN EMPLOYMENT HANDICAP FOR THE INDIVIDUAL. UNDERGRAD OR GRAD STUDENT AT NC SCHOOL.

WRITE FOR COMPLETE INFORMATION.

1520

NORTH CAROLINA DIVISION OF VETERANS AFFAIRS (DEPENDENTS SCHOLARSHIP PROGRAM)
325 N SALISBURY ST; SUITE 1065
RALEIGH NC 27603
919/733-3851
AMOUNT: $1200 - $3000 (PRIVATE COLLEGE); TUITION & FEES & ROOM AND BOARD (PUBLIC COLLEGE)
DEADLINE(S): MAY 31

FIELD(S): ALL FIELDS OF STUDY

UNDERGRADUATE SCHOLARSHIPS OPEN TO CHILDREN OF VETERANS WHO DIED AS A RESULT OF WARTIME SERVICE OR WERE DISABLED; POW; MIA OR RECEIVED PENSION FROM THE VA. VETERAN ENTERED SERVICE AS NC RESIDENT OR APPLICANT NC RESIDENT SINCE BIRTH.

AWARDS TENABLE AT PRIVATE & PUBLIC COLLEGES IN NORTH CAROLINA. 350-400 AWARDS PER YEAR. RENEWABLE UP TO 4 YEARS. WRITE FOR COMPLETE INFORMATION.

1521

NORTH CAROLINA STATE EDUCATION ASSISTANCE AUTHORITY (STUDENT FINANCIAL AID FOR NORTH CAROLINIANS)

PO BOX 2688
CHAPEL HILL NC 27515
919/549-8614

AMOUNT: VARIES

DEADLINE(S): VARIOUS

FIELD(S): ALL FIELDS OF STUDY

THE STATE OF NC; PRIVATE NC ORGANIZATIONS & THE FEDERAL GOVERNMENT FUND NUMEROUS SCHOLARSHIP; GRANT; WORK-STUDY & LOAN PROGRAMS FOR NORTH CAROLINA RESIDENTS AT ALL LEVELS OF STUDY.

THE NC STATE EDUCATION ASSISTANCE AUTHORITY ANNUALLY PUBLISHES A FINANCIAL AID BOOKLET DESCRIBING IN DETAIL VARIOUS PROGRAMS FOR NORTH CAROLINA RESIDENTS. A COPY IS AVAILABLE FREE TO NC RESIDENT UNDERGRADUATES FROM THE ADDRESS ABOVE.

1522

NORTH CAROLINA STATE UNIVERSITY (JOHN GATLING SCHOLARSHIP PROGRAM)

2118 PULLEN HALL; BOX 7342
RALEIGH NC 27695
919/515-3671

AMOUNT: $6000 PER YEAR

DEADLINE(S): APPLY FOR ADMISSION TO NC STATE BY FEB 1

FIELD(S): ALL FIELDS OF STUDY

IF YOU WERE BORN WITH SURNAME OF 'GATLIN' OR 'GATLING' THIS PROGRAM WILL PROVIDE $6000 TOWARD THE COST OF ATTENDING NC STATE UNIV AS AN UNDERGRADUATE PROVIDED YOU MEET NC STATE UNIV ENTRANCE AND TRANSFER REQUIREMENTS. USA CITIZEN.

AWARD IS RENEWABLE EACH YEAR IF YOU STUDY FULL TIME (24 OR MORE CREDITS PER YEAR) & MAINTAIN AT LEAST 2.0 GPA. CONTACT THE NCSU MERIT AWARDS PROGRAM COORDINATOR AT ADDRESS ABOVE FOR COMPLETE INFORMATION.

1523

NORTH DAKOTA INDIAN SCHOLARSHIP PROGRAM (SCHOLARSHIPS)

STATE CAPITOL BUILDING; 10TH FLOOR
BISMARCK ND 58505
701/224-2166

AMOUNT: UP TO $2000

DEADLINE(S): JUN 30

FIELD(S): ALL FIELDS OF STUDY

OPEN TO NORTH DAKOTA RESIDENTS WHO HAVE AT LEAST 1/4 DEGREE INDIAN BLOOD OR ARE AN ENROLLED MEMBER OF A NORTH DAKOTA TRIBE. AWARDS ARE TENABLE AT RECOGNIZED UNDERGRADUATE COLLEGES & UNIVERSITIES IN NORTH DAKOTA. USA CITIZEN.

100-150 SCHOLARSHIPS PER YEAR. RENEWABLE. WRITE FOR COMPLETE INFORMATION.

1524

NORTH DAKOTA STUDENT FINANCIAL ASSISTANCE AGENCY (GRANTS)

STATE CAPITOL; 10TH FLOOR; 600 EAST BLVD
BISMARCK ND 58505
701/224-4114

AMOUNT: UP TO $600

DEADLINE(S): APR 15

FIELD(S): ALL FIELDS OF STUDY

OPEN TO RESIDENTS OF NORTH DAKOTA FOR UNDERGRADUATE STUDY AT COLLEGES & UNIVERSITIES IN THE STATE OF NORTH DAKOTA. USA CITIZEN OR LEGAL RESIDENT.

2400 AWARDS PER YEAR. RENEWABLE. WRITE FOR COMPLETE INFORMATION.

1525

OHEF SHOLOM TEMPLE (SARAH COHEN SCHOLARSHIP FUND)

RALEIGH AVENUE AT STOCKLEY GARDENS
NORFOLK VA 23507
804/625-4295

AMOUNT: VARIES

DEADLINE(S): BEFORE END OF SPRING SEMESTER

FIELD(S): ALL AREAS OF STUDY

OPEN TO RESIDENTS OF NORFOLK VA WHO HAVE HIGH ACADEMIC STANDING AND A MARKED POTENTIAL FOR SERVICE TO THE COMMUNITY. HALF OF THOSE RECEIVING AWARD MUST BE OF THE JEWISH FAITH AND ONE-HALF MUST BE NON-JEWISH.

FOR UNDERGRADUATE STUDY AT A RECOGNIZED COLLEGE OR UNIVERSITY WHICH GRANTS A DEGREE. MUST SHOW FINANCIAL NEED. WRITE FOR COMPLETE INFORMATION.

1526

OHIO BOARD OF REGENTS (OHIO ACADEMIC SCHOLARSHIP PROGRAM)

30 EAST BROAD STREET; 36TH FLOOR
COLUMBUS OH 43266-0417
614/466-1190

AMOUNT: $1000

DEADLINE(S): FEB 23

FIELD(S): ALL FIELDS OF STUDY

OPEN TO SENIORS AT ELIGIBLE OHIO HIGH SCHOOLS WHO ARE OHIO RESIDENTS AND ENROLLED OR INTEND TO BE ENROLLED AS FULL TIME UNDERGRADUATE STUDENTS IN ELIGIBLE OHIO INSTITUTIONS OF HIGHER EDUCATION. USA CITIZEN.

1000 AWARDS PER YEAR. SCHOLARSHIPS ARE AUTOMATICALLY RENEWABLE FOR UP TO FOUR YEARS OF UNDERGRADUATE STUDY PROVIDED SATISFACTORY PROGRESS IS MADE. WRITE FOR COMPLETE INFORMATION.

1527

OHIO BOARD OF REGENTS (OHIO INSTRUCTIONAL GRANTS)

30 EAST BROAD STREET; ROOM 3600
COLUMBUS OH 43266-0417
614/466-7420

AMOUNT: $216 - $1326 PUBLIC INST; $540 - $3306 PRIVATE INST; $372 - $2268 PROPRIETARY INST

DEADLINE(S): LAST FRIDAY IN SEPTEMBER

FIELD(S): ALL AREAS OF STUDY

OPEN TO OHIO RESIDENTS WHO ARE USA CITIZENS ENROLLED AS FULL TIME STUDENTS IN AN ELIGIBLE OHIO INSTITUTION OF HIGHER EDUCATION. MUST BE IN GOOD FINANCIAL STANDING AND DEMONSTRATE FINANCIAL NEED.

90000 RENEWABLE GRANTS PER YEAR. WRITE FOR COMPLETE INFORMATION.

1528

OHIO BOARD OF REGENTS (OHIO STUDENT CHOICE GRANT)

30 EAST BROAD STREET; ROOM 3600
COLUMBUS OH 43266-0417
614/466-1190

AMOUNT: VARIES

DEADLINE(S): DETERMINED BY INSTITUTION

FIELD(S): ALL FIELDS OF STUDY EXCEPT THEOLOGY OR RELIGION

OPEN TO OHIO RESIDENTS WHO ARE USA CITIZENS AND ARE ENROLLED AS FULL TIME UNDERGRADUATE STUDENTS AT AN ELIGIBLE PRIVATE NON-PROFIT OHIO COLLEGE OR UNIVERSITY. NOT FOR STUDIES LEADING TO DEGREES IN RELIGION OR THEOLOGY.

23000 AWARDS PER YEAR RENEWABLE FOR A MAXIMUM OF 5 YEARS. WRITE FOR COMPLETE INFORMATION.

1529

OHIO BOARD OF REGENTS (STUDENT GRANT PROGRAM)

30 E BROAD ST; 36TH FLOOR
COLUMBUS OH 43266
614/466-7420

AMOUNT: VARIES

DEADLINE(S): VARIES

FIELD(S): ALL APPROVED DEGREE PROGRAMS (NOT LEADING TO THEOLOGY)

OPEN TO OHIO RESIDENTS ATTENDING ELIGIBLE OHIO PRIVATE INSTITUTIONS. MUST BE A FULL TIME STUDENT IN A BACHELOR'S DEGREE PROGRAM & HAVE NOT ATTENDED COLLEGE ON A FULL TIME BASIS PRIOR TO JUL 1 1984.

UNSPECIFIED NUMBER OF GRANTS PER YEAR. RENEWABLE. WRITE FOR COMPLETE INFORMATION.

1530

OHIO NATIONAL GUARD TUITION GRANT PROGRAM

ADJ GEN DEPT; ATTN AGOH-TG; 2825 W GRANVILLE RD
COLUMBUS OH 43235
614/889-7032

AMOUNT: FOR STATE SCHOOLS 60% OF TUITION; FOR PVT SCHOOLS 60% OF AVG STATE SCHOOL FEES

DEADLINE(S): JUL 1; NOV 1; FEB 1; APR 1

FIELD(S): ALL FIELDS OF STUDY

OPEN TO RESIDENTS OF OHIO WITH AN ENLISTED OBLIGATION OF SIX YEARS IN THE OHIO NATIONAL GUARD. PROVIDES 12 QUARTERS OR 8 SEMESTER HOURS.

WRITE TO THE TUITION GRANT OFFICE AT ABOVE ADDRESS FOR COMPLETE INFORMATION.

1531

OHIO UNIVERSITY (CHARLES KILBURGER SCHOLARSHIP)

ASST DIR STUDENT SERVICES; 1570 GRANVILLE PIKE

LANCASTER OH 43130

614/654-6711

AMOUNT: TUITION

DEADLINE(S): FEB 1

FIELD(S): ALL FIELDS OF STUDY

SCHOLARSHIP OPEN TO SENIORS GRADUATING FROM A FAIRFIELD COUNTY (OHIO) HIGH SCHOOL WHO WILL ENROLL AT OHIO UNIVERSITY LANCASTER FOR AT LEAST TWO YEARS. FOR UNDERGRADUATE STUDY ONLY. USA CITIZEN.

APPLICATIONS AVAILABLE ONLY FROM HIGH SCHOOL COUNSELORS. MUST DEMONSTRATE FINANCIAL NEED.

1532

OHIO WAR ORPHANS SCHOLARSHIP BOARD (SCHOLARSHIPS)

3600 STATE OFFICE TOWER; 30 BROAD ST

COLUMBUS OH 43266

614/466-1190

AMOUNT: FULL TUITION AT PUBLIC SCHOOLS; EQUIVALENT AMOUNT AT PRIVATE SCHOOLS

DEADLINE(S): JUL 1

FIELD(S): ALL AREAS OF STUDY

OHIO RESIDENT & DEPENDENT OF VETERAN WHO SERVED FOR AT LEAST 90 DAYS DURING WAR & AS A RESULT IS NOW 60% OR MORE DISABLED OR 100% DISABLED FOR ANY REASON OR IS DECEASED.

350 AWARDS PER YEAR. WRITE FOR COMPLETE INFORMATION.

1533

OMEGA PSI PHI FRATERNITY (FOUNDERS MEMORIAL SCHOLARSHIPS)

2714 GEORGIA AVE NW

WASHINGTON DC 20001

202/667-7158

AMOUNT: $500

DEADLINE(S): MAY 15

FIELD(S): ALL AREAS OF STUDY

OPEN ONLY TO MEMBERS OF OMEGA PSI PHI FRATERNITY WHO WILL BE COLLEGE SOPHOMORES OR JUNIORS AND WHO HAVE A 3.0 OR BETTER GRADE POINT AVERAGE.

WRITE TO THE OMEGA PSI PHI FRATERNITY DISTRICT SCHOLARSHIP CHAIRMAN FOR COMPLETE INFORMATION.

1534

OPERATING ENGINEERS LOCAL UNION NO. 3 (IUOE SCHOLARSHIP PROGRAM)

1620 SOUTH LOOP RD

ALAMEDA CA 94501

510/478-4700

AMOUNT: UP TO $1000

DEADLINE(S): MAR 1

FIELD(S): ALL AREAS OF STUDY

OPEN TO DEPENDENT CHILDREN OF MEMBERS OF IUOE LOCAL NO. 3 WHO ARE HIGH SCHOOL SENIORS WITH AT LEAST A 3.0 GPA. AWARDS TENABLE AT RECOGNIZED UNDERGRADUATE COLLEGES & UNIVERSITIES. USA CITIZEN.

WRITE FOR COMPLETE INFORMATION.

1535

OPTIMIST INTERNATIONAL (ORATORICAL CONTEST/SCHOLARSHIP)

4494 LINDELL BLVD

ST LOUIS MO 63108

314/371-6000

AMOUNT: $1500

DEADLINE(S): JAN 15

FIELD(S): ALL AREAS OF STUDY

ORATORICAL CONTEST FOR STUDENTS 16 YEARS OR YOUNGER AS OF JAN 1. ENTRY MUST BE THROUGH AN OPTIMIST CLUB.

CONTACT LOCAL OPTIMIST CLUB FOR COMPLETE INFORMATION.

1536

ORDER OF THE EASTERN STAR (GRAND CHAPTER OF CALIFORNIA SCHOLARSHIPS)

870 MARKET STREET; SUITE 722

SAN FRANCISCO CA 94102

WRITTEN INQUIRY

AMOUNT: $250 - $500 (2 YEAR COLLEGE); $500 - $1000 (4 YEAR COLLEGE)

DEADLINE(S): APR 1

FIELD(S): ALL FIELDS OF STUDY

OPEN TO CALIFORNIA RESIDENTS WHO ARE ACCEPTED TO OR ENROLLED AT A CALIFORNIA COLLEGE OR UNIVERSITY OR TRADE SCHOOL AND HAVE AT LEAST A 3.5 GPA (4.0 SCALE). MUST DEMONSTRATE FINANCIAL NEED AND BE USA CITIZEN.

WRITE TO MRS. DIANE SILVA; GRAND SECRETARY; ADDRESS ABOVE; FOR COMPLETE INFORMATION.

1537

OREGON DEPARTMENT OF VETERANS' AFFAIRS (EDUCATIONAL SCHOLARSHIP AID FOR OREGON VETERANS)

700 SUMMER ST NE; SUITE 150
SALEM OR 97310
800/692-9666

AMOUNT: $35 - $50 PER MONTH

DEADLINE(S): NONE

FIELD(S): ALL FIELDS OF STUDY

RESIDENT OF OREGON FOR TWO YEARS PRIOR TO MILITARY SERVICE AND AT TIME OF ENROLLMENT. MUST BE A USA CITIZEN WITH A QUALIFYING MILITARY SERVICE RECORD. FOR STUDY IN AN ACCREDITED OREGON SCHOOL.

APPLICANTS MUST HAVE ARMED FORCES EXPEDITIONARY MEDAL OR THE VIETNAM SERVICE MEDAL OR BE A VETERAN OF THE KOREAN CONFLICT (ACTIVE DUTY). 30 AWARDS PER YEAR. WRITE FOR COMPLETE INFORMATION.

1538

OREGON STATE SCHOLARSHIP COMMISSION (OREGON CASH AWARDS;OREGON NEED GRANTS)

1445 WILLAMETTE STREET
EUGENE OR 97401
503/346-1240

AMOUNT: UP TO $864 (CASH AWARD); UP TO $1920 (NEED GRANTS)

DEADLINE(S): APR 1

FIELD(S): ALL AREAS OF STUDY

OPEN TO OREGON RESIDENTS ENROLLED FULL TIME IN ANY 2 OR 4 YEAR NON-PROFIT COLLEGE OR UNIVERSITY IN OREGON. MUST BE USA CITIZEN OR LEGAL RESIDENT AND DEMONSTRATE FINANCIAL NEED.

IT IS NOT NECESSARY TO TAKE SAT/ACT FOR NEED GRANTS. 22000 AWARDS AND GRANTS PER YEAR. RENEWABLE. WRITE FOR COMPLETE INFORMATION.

1539

OREGON STATE SCHOLARSHIP COMMISSION (OREGON GUARANTEED STUDENT LOANS)

1445 WILLAMETTE ST
EUGENE OR 97401
503/346-3200

AMOUNT: $2625 - $4000 UNDERGRAD; $7500 GRADUATE (ANNUAL MAXIMUM)

DEADLINE(S): NONE SPECIFIED

FIELD(S): ALL FIELDS OF STUDY

OPEN TO USA CITIZENS OR PERMANENT RESIDENTS WHO ARE ATTENDING AN ELIGIBLE OREGON INSTITUTION AND TO OREGON RESIDENTS ATTENDING ANY ELIGIBLE INSTITUTION OUTSIDE OF OREGON AT LEAST HALF TIME.

WRITE FOR COMPLETE INFORMATION.

1540

OREGON STATE SCHOLARSHIP COMMISSION (PRIVATE SCHOLARSHIP PROGRAMS ADMINISTERED BY THE COMMISSION)

1445 WILLAMETTE ST
EUGENE OR 97401
503/346-1240 OR 800/452-8807

AMOUNT: $250 - $3000

DEADLINE(S): VARIES

FIELD(S): ALL FIELDS OF STUDY

70 DIFFERENT PRIVATE SCHOLARSHIP PROGRAMS ARE ADMINISTERED BY THE COMMISSION AND ARE OPEN TO OREGON RESIDENTS. SOME ARE TIED TO A SPECIFIC FIELD AND/OR LEVEL OF STUDY BUT IN GENERAL THEY ARE AVAILABLE TO ALL LEVELS AND FIELDS OF STUDY.

WRITE FOR COMPLETE INFORMATION.

1541

ORPHAN FOUNDATION OF AMERICA (SCHOLARSHIP PROGRAM)

PO BOX 14261
WASHINGTON DC 20044
WRITTEN INQUIRIES ONLY

AMOUNT: $250 - $1000

DEADLINE(S): JUN 15

FIELD(S): ALL AREAS OF STUDY

PROGRAM OPEN TO 'ORPHANS' (AS DEFINED BY THE ORPHAN FOUNDATION OF AMERICA) WHO HAVE 'NOT BEEN ADOPTED.' AWARDS TENABLE AT ANY RECOGNIZED UNDERGRADUATE OR VOCATIONAL SCHOOL

IN THE USA. USA CITIZEN OR LEGAL RESIDENT.

50+ SCHOLARSHIPS PER YEAR. RENEWABLE WITH REAPPLICATION. WRITE FOR COMPLETE INFORMATION.

1542

ORVILLE REDENBACHER'S SECOND START SCHOLARSHIP PROGRAM

PO BOX 4137

BLAIR NE 68009

WRITTEN INQUIRY ONLY

AMOUNT: $1000

DEADLINE(S): MAY 1

FIELD(S): ALL AREAS OF STUDY

OPEN TO ADULTS OVER AGE 30 WHO ARE RETURNING TO COLLEGE OR ENTERING COLLEGE TO PURSUE A DEGREE FOR THE FIRST TIME. APPLICATIONS ACCEPTED FROM MAR 1 TO MAY 1.

CONTACT SCHOOL'S FINANCIAL AID OFFICE OR WRITE TO THE ADDRESS ABOVE FOR COMPLETE INFORMATION.

1543

OSHKOSH FOUNDATION (SCHOLARSHIPS)

PO BOX 1726

OSHKOSH WI 54902

414/426-3993

AMOUNT: VARIES

DEADLINE(S): APR 1

FIELD(S): ALL FIELDS OF STUDY

OPEN TO STUDENTS OF OSHKOSH (WISC) HIGH SCHOOLS. APPLICATION SHOULD BE MADE DURING SENIOR YEAR THROUGH HIGH SCHOOL COUNSELOR. MUST BE USA CITIZEN. FINANCIAL NEED IS A CONSIDERATION. MUST BE A RESIDENT OF OSHKOSH AND/OR WINNEBAGO COUNTY WI.

CONTACT HIGH SCHOOL COUNSELOR FOR COMPLETE INFORMATION.

1544

PACIFIC COCA COLA/THRIFTWAY STORES/SEATTLE SEAHAWKS

1150 124TH AVE; PO BOX C-93346

BELLEVUE WA 98009

206/455-2000 EXT 770

AMOUNT: $1500

DEADLINE(S): APR 19

FIELD(S): ALL FIELDS OF STUDY

OPEN TO STUDENTS ATTENDING HIGH SCHOOL IN WESTERN WASHINGTON - YAKIMA AND WENATCHEE AREAS ONLY. STUDENTS MAY APPLY IF THEY PLAN TO ENROLL FULL TIME IN ONE OF 9 PARTICIPATING WASHINGTON INSTITUTIONS AND HAVE GPA OF 3.5 OR BETTER.

SELECTION CRITERIA INCLUDE GRADES (60%); LEADERSHIP POTENTIAL; SCHOOL AND COMMUNITY INVOLVEMENT; EMPLOYMENT; FAMILY RESPONSIBILITY. 18 AWARDS PER YEAR. WRITE FOR COMPLETE INFORMATION.

1545

PARENTS WITHOUT PARTNERS (INTERNATIONAL SCHOLARSHIP)

8807 COLESVILLE RD

SILVER SPRING MD 20910

301/588-9355

AMOUNT: VARIES

DEADLINE(S): MAR 15

FIELD(S): ALL FIELDS OF STUDY

OPEN TO THE CHILDREN OF PARENTS WITHOUT PARTNERS MEMBERS. FOR UNDERGRADUATE STUDY AT ANY ACCREDITED COLLEGE OR UNIVERSITY. MUST DEMONSTRATE FINANCIAL NEED.

WRITE FOR COMPLETE INFORMATION.

1546

PARKE-DAVIS (EPILEPSY SCHOLARSHIP PROGRAM)

INTRAMED; 1800 AVE OF THE AMERICAS

NEW YORK NY 10036

800/972-7503

AMOUNT: $3000

DEADLINE(S): MAR 1

FIELD(S): ALL FIELDS OF STUDY

OPEN TO OUTSTANDING HIGH SCHOOL SENIORS OR COLLEGE FRESHMEN; SOPHOMORES OR JUNIORS WHO ARE UNDER A PHYSICIAN'S CARE FOR EPILEPSY. APPLICANTS MUST HAVE COMPLETED A COLLEGE APPLICATION OR ENROLLMENT AND BE UNDER TREATMENT FOR EPILEPSY.

CONSIDERATIONS INCLUDE ACADEMIC ACHIEVEMENT AND EXTRACURRICULAR ACTIVITIES. OBTAIN APPLICATIONS FROM YOUR PHYSICIAN.

1547

PAUL AND MARY HAAS FOUNDATION (SCHOLARSHIP GRANTS)
PO BOX 2928
CORPUS CHRISTI TX 78403
512/887-6955
AMOUNT: $750 PER SEMESTER
DEADLINE(S): AT LEAST 3 MONTHS PRIOR TO EACH SEMESTER
FIELD(S): ALL FIELDS OF STUDY
PROGRAM OPEN TO CORPUS CHRISTI, TX RESIDENTS. AWARDS SUPPORT THE FULL TIME PURSUIT OF THEIR FIRST UNDERGRADUATE DEGREE OR VOCATIONAL CERTIFICATE AT A RECOGNIZED INSTITUTION.
APPROX 100 AWARDS PER YEAR. MUST PROVE FINANCIAL NEED. WRITE FOR COMPLETE INFORMATION.

1548

PENNSYLVANIA DEPARTMENT OF MILITARY AFFAIRS-BUREAU OF VETERANS AFFAIRS (SCHOLARSHIPS)
FORT INDIANTOWN GAP
ANNVILLE PA 17003
717/865-8904 OR 717/865-8910
AMOUNT: $500 - $4000
DEADLINE(S): NONE
FIELD(S): ALL AREAS OF STUDY
OPEN TO CHILD OF A MILITARY VETERAN WHO DIED OR WAS TOTALLY DISABLED AS A RESULT OF WAR; ARMED CONFLICT OR TERRORIST ATTACK. MUST HAVE LIVED IN PENNSYLVANIA FOR 5 YEARS PRIOR TO APPLICATION; BE AGE 16-23 AND DEMONSTRATE FINANCIAL NEED.
70 AWARDS PER YEAR. RENEWABLE. FOR STUDY AT PENNSYLVANIA SCHOOLS. MUST BE USA CITIZEN. WRITE FOR COMPLETE INFORMATION.

1549

PENNSYLVANIA HIGHER EDUCATION ASSISTANCE AGENCY (ROBERT C. BYRD SCHOLARSHIP PROGRAM)
PO BOX 8114
HARRISBURG PA 17105
717/975-3320
AMOUNT: $1500 PER YEAR
DEADLINE(S): APR 15
FIELD(S): ALL FIELDS OF STUDY
OPEN TO PENN HIGH SCHOOL SENIORS IN THE TOP 5 PERCENT OF THEIR GRADUATING CLASS WITH A 3.5 OR BETTER GPA & AN SAT SCORE OF 1100 OR HIGHER. MUST BE USA CITIZEN & HAVE BEEN ACCEPTED FOR ENROLLMENT IN AN INSTITUTION OF HIGHER EDUCATION.
RENEWABLE TO A MAXIMUM OF FOUR YEARS. WRITE FOR COMPLETE INFORMATION.

1550

PENNSYLVANIA STEEL FOUNDRY FOUNDATION (SCHOLARSHIPS)
THIRD AND ARCH STREETS
HAMBURG PA 19526
215/562-7533
AMOUNT: VARIES
DEADLINE(S): MAY 1
FIELD(S): ALL FIELDS OF STUDY
SCHOLARSHIPS FOR QUALIFIED EMPLOYEES AND QUALIFIED CHILDREN OF EMPLOYEES IN NEED OF FINANCIAL ASSISTANCE AT AN ACCREDITED FOUR-YEAR COLLEGE OR UNIVERSITY. FOR FULL TIME UNDERGRADUATE STUDY.
ONLY EMPLOYEES OF PENNSYLVANIA STEEL FOUNDRY & MACHINE COMPANY QUALIFY. WRITE FOR COMPLETE INFORMATION.

1551

PERRY & STELLA TRACY SCHOLARSHIP FUND (SCHOLARSHIPS)
WELLS FARGO PRIVATE BANKING GROUP; PO BOX 2511
SACRAMENTO CA 95812
916/440-4449
AMOUNT: $350 - $750
DEADLINE(S): NONE
FIELD(S): ALL AREAS OF STUDY
OPEN TO APPLICANTS WHO ARE GRADUATES OF EL DORADO COUNTY HIGH SCHOOLS OR HAVE RESIDED IN EL DORADO COUNTY CA FOR AT LEAST 2 YEARS. AWARDS ARE TENABLE AT RECOGNIZED UNDERGRADUATE COLLEGES & UNIVERSITIES.
APPROX 125 AWARDS PER YEAR. RENEWABLE. CONTACT HIGH SCHOOL COUNSELOR FOR COMPLETE INFORMATION. DO NOT CONTACT WELLS FARGO.

1552

PETER G. FLINN SCHOLARSHIP AWARD (SCHOLARSHIPS)

BANK ONE TRUST GROUP; PO BOX 68
MARION IN 46952
317/668-3525
AMOUNT: VARIES
DEADLINE(S): APR
FIELD(S): ALL FIELDS OF STUDY

OPEN TO STUDENTS WHO HAVE BEEN RESIDENTS OF GRANT COUNTY (INDIANA) FOR AT LEAST ONE YEAR PRIOR TO GRADUATION FROM A GRANT COUNTY HIGH SCHOOL. AWARDS ARE TENABLE AT RECOGNIZED UNDERGRADUATE COLLEGES & UNIVERSITIES.

RENEWABLE UP TO 4 YEARS. SEND SELF-ADDRESSED STAMPED ENVELOPE FOR COMPLETE INFORMATION.

1553

PHI KAPPA THETA NATIONAL FOUNDATION (SCHOLARSHIP PROGRAM)

C/O GREGORY STEIN; 111-55 77TH AVE
FOREST HILLS NY 11375
718/793-2193
AMOUNT: VARIES
DEADLINE(S): APR 30
FIELD(S): ALL AREAS OF STUDY

UNDERGRADUATE SCHOLARSHIPS ARE LIMITED TO MEMBERS OF PHI KAPPA THETA FRATERNITY. APPLICATIONS ARE SENT TO ALL CHAPTERS AND EXTRAS ARE AVAILABLE AT NATIONAL OFFICE. NOT AVAILABLE TO HIGH SCHOOL OR GRADUATE STUDENTS.

EIGHT SCHOLARSHIPS ANNUALLY. FINANCIAL NEED IS A CONSIDERATION BUT IS RELATIVE TO THE OTHER APPLICANTS. WRITE FOR COMPLETE INFORMATION.

1554

PHILADELPHIA COLLEGE OF TEXTILES AND SCIENCE (SCHOLARSHIP PROGRAM)

SCHOOLHOUSE LANE & HENRY AVENUE
PHILADELPHIA PA 19144
215/951-2800
AMOUNT: $2000 - $10000
DEADLINE(S): MAY 1
FIELD(S): ALL AREAS OF STUDY

OPEN TO HIGH SCHOOL SENIORS IN THE TOP 1/5 OF THEIR CLASS. FOR STUDY AT PHILADELPHIA COLLEGE OF TEXTILES & SCIENCE. MUST SUBMIT SAT OR ACT SCORE AND BE USA CITIZEN. SCHOLARSHIP RENEWABLE IF GPA OF 3.0 OR BETTER IS MAINTAINED.

WRITE FOR COMPLETE INFORMATION.

1555

PHILIP MORRIS SCHOLARSHIP PROGRAM (VOC-TECH; IN-COLLEGE; & GRADUATE/PROFESSIONAL SCHOLARSHIPS)

PO BOX 6730
PRINCETON NJ 08541
WRITTEN INQUIRY ONLY
AMOUNT: UP TO $5000 PER YEAR
DEADLINE(S): NOV 15
FIELD(S): ALL FIELDS OF STUDY

OPEN TO CHILDREN OF FULL TIME EMPLOYEES OF PHILIP MORRIS COMPANY OR ITS SUBSIDIARIES FOR FULL TIME STUDY AT ACCREDITED COLLEGES; UNIVERSITIES OR VOC-TECH SCHOOLS. FINANCIAL NEED DETERMINES AMOUNT OF AWARD.

WRITE FOR COMPLETE INFORMATION.

1556

PICKETT AND HATCHER EDUCATIONAL FUND INC. (LOANS)

PO BOX 8169
COLUMBUS GA 31908
404/327-6586
AMOUNT: $3000 PER YEAR
DEADLINE(S): MAY 15
FIELD(S): ALL FIELDS OF STUDY EXCEPT LAW; MEDICINE & MINISTRY

OPEN TO USA CITIZENS WHO ARE LEGAL RESIDENTS OF AND ATTEND COLLEGES LOCATED IN THE SOUTHEASTERN PORTION OF THE UNITED STATES. LOANS NOT MADE FOR GRADUATE STUDIES OR FOR STUDIES IN VOCATIONAL/TECHNICAL SCHOOLS.

WRITE FOR APPLICATIONS AND COMPLETE INFORMATION IN OCTOBER OR NOVEMBER OF THE YEAR PRECEDING THE ACADEMIC YEAR IN WHICH LOAN WILL BE NEEDED.

1557

PITNEY BOWES (JAMES L. TURRENTINE SCHOLARSHIPS)

1 ELMCROFT RD
STAMFORD CT 06926
203/351-6203
AMOUNT: $2500
DEADLINE(S): DEC 31
FIELD(S): ALL AREAS OF STUDY

SCHOLARSHIPS OPEN TO CHILDREN OF PITNEY BOWES EMPLOYEES. APPLICANTS SHOULD BE IN THEIR SENIOR YEAR OF HIGH SCHOOL AND PLAN TO ENTER COLLEGE THE FALL IMMEDIATELY FOLLOWING GRADUATION.

30 AWARDS PER YEAR. MUST RANK IN UPPER THIRD OF CLASS.

1558 ———

PORTUGUESE CONTINENTAL UNION (SCHOLARSHIPS)

899 BOYLSTON STREET

BOSTON MA 02115

617/536-2916

AMOUNT: VARIES

DEADLINE(S): FEB 15 TO MAR 31

FIELD(S): ALL AREAS OF STUDY

OPEN TO PORTUGUESE CONTINENTAL UNION MEMBERS WHO ARE ENROLLED IN AN UNDERGRADUATE OR GRADUATE PROGRAM AT AN ACCREDITED COLLEGE OR UNIVERSITY. ONE YEAR MEMBERSHIP REQUIRED.

FINANCIAL NEED IS A CONSIDERATION. WRITE FOR COMPLETE INFORMATION.

1559 ———

POTLATCH FOUNDATION FOR HIGHER EDUCATION (UNDERGRADUATE SCHOLARSHIPS)

PO BOX 8162

WALNUT CREEK CA 94596

510/947-4725

AMOUNT: $1200

DEADLINE(S): FEB 15

FIELD(S): ALL AREAS OF STUDY

SCHOLARSHIP APPLICANT'S PERMANENT RESIDENCE OR HIGH SCHOOL MUST BE LOCATED WITHIN 30 MILES OF A POTLATCH CORP. FACILITY. THE MAJORITY OF SCHOLARSHIPS ARE AWARDED TO STUDENTS RESIDING NEAR COMPANY FACILITIES IN IDAHO; MINN AND ARKANSAS.

MUST NOT HAVE GRADUATED FROM COLLEGE. CONTACT JOYCE LABOURG; ADDRESS ABOVE; FOR COMPLETE INFORMATION.

1560 ———

PRESBYTERIAN CHURCH-USA (NATIVE AMERICAN EDUCATION GRANTS)

FINANCIAL AID FOR STUDIES; CHURCH VOCATION UNIT; 100 WITHERSPOON ST

LOUISVILLE KY 40202

502/569-5760

AMOUNT: $200 - $1500

DEADLINE(S): JUN 1

FIELD(S): ALL FIELDS OF STUDY

OPEN TO NATIVE AMERICAN INDIANS; ALEUTS & ESKIMOS WHO HAVE COMPLETED AT LEAST ONE SEMESTER OF WORK AT AN ACCREDITED INSTITUTION OF HIGHER EDUCATION. PREFERENCE TO PRESBYTERIAN STUDENTS AT THE UNDERGRADUATE LEVEL. MUST BE USA CITIZEN.

RENEWAL IS BASED ON CONTINUED FINANCIAL NEED AND SATISFACTORY ACADEMIC PROGRESS. WRITE FOR COMPLETE INFORMATION.

1561 ———

PRESBYTERIAN CHURCH-USA (NATIONAL PRESBYTERIAN COLLEGE SCHOLARSHIPS)

NCPS CHURCH VOCATIONS UNIT; 100 WITHERSPOON ST

LOUISVILLE KY 40202

502/569-5745

AMOUNT: $500 - $1400

DEADLINE(S): DEC 1

FIELD(S): ALL FIELDS OF STUDY

SCHOLARSHIPS FOR INCOMING FRESHMEN AT ONE OF THE PARTICIPATING COLLEGES RELATED TO THE CHURCH. APPLICANTS MUST BE SUPERIOR HIGH SCHOOL SENIORS & CONFIRMED MEMBERS OF THE PRESBYTERIAN CHURCH-USA. USA CITIZEN OR LEGAL RESIDENT.

APPLICATION AND BROCHURE AVAILABLE AFTER SEP 1. FINANCIAL NEED IS A CONSIDERATION. WRITE FOR COMPLETE INFORMATION.

1562 ———

PRESBYTERIAN CHURCH-USA (SAMUEL ROBINSON SCHOLARSHIPS)

100 WITHERSPOON ST

LOUISVILLE KY 40202

502/569-5745

AMOUNT: $1000

DEADLINE(S): APR 1

FIELD(S): ALL FIELDS OF STUDY

OPEN TO UNDERGRADUATE STUDENTS ENROLLED IN ONE OF THE 69 COLLEGES RELATED TO THE PRESBYTERIAN CHURCH. APPLICANTS MUST SUCCESSFULLY RECITE THE ANSWERS TO THE WESTMINSTER SHORTER CATECHISM AND WRITE A 2000 WORD ESSAY.

20-30 AWARDS PER YEAR. WRITE FOR COMPLETE INFORMATION.

1563

PRESBYTERIAN CHURCH-USA (STUDENT LOAN FUND)
CHURCH VOCATIONS UNIT; 100 WITHERSPOON ST
LOUISVILLE KY 40202
502/569-5735
AMOUNT: UP TO $1000 PER YEAR
DEADLINE(S): NONE SPECIFIED
FIELD(S): ALL FIELDS OF STUDY
LOANS OPEN TO COMMUNICANT MEMBERS OF THE PRESBYTERIAN CHURCH (USA) WHO ARE USA CITIZENS OR PERMANENT RESIDENTS. FOR FULL TIME UNDERGRADUATE OR GRADUATE STUDY. NO INTEREST WHILE IN SCHOOL; REPAYABLE AT 8% APR THEREAFTER.
GPA OF 2.0 OR BETTER REQUIRED. THOSE PREPARING FOR PROFESSIONAL CHURCH OCCUPATIONS CAN BORROW UP TO $2000 PER ACADEMIC YEAR. WRITE FOR COMPLETE INFORMATION.

1564

PRESBYTERIAN CHURCH-USA (STUDENT OPPORTUNITY MINORITY SCHOLARSHIPS)
CHURCH VOCATIONS UNIT; 100 WITHERSPOON ST
LOUISVILLE KY 40202
502/569-5760
AMOUNT: $100 - $1400
DEADLINE(S): APR 1
FIELD(S): ALL FIELDS OF STUDY
OPEN TO MINORITY (BLACK; HISPANIC; ASIAN; NATIVE AMERICAN) HIGH SCHOOL SENIORS WHO ARE MEMBERS OF THE PRESBYTERIAN CHURCH & ENTERING COLLEGE AS FULL TIME FRESHMEN. USA CITIZEN OR LEGAL RESIDENT.
110-130 AWARDS PER YEAR. RENEWAL OF AWARDS IS DEPENDENT ON CONTINUED FINANCIAL NEED AND SATISFACTORY ACADEMIC PROGRESS. WRITE FOR COMPLETE INFORMATION.

1565

PRESIDENT'S COMMITTEE ON EMPLOYMENT OF PEOPLE WITH DISABILITIES (NATIONAL POSTER SCHOLARSHIP PROGRAM)
1331 F ST NW
WASHINGTON DC 20004
202/376-6200; FAX 202/376-6219; TDD 202/376-6205
AMOUNT: $500
DEADLINE(S): MAR 1
FIELD(S): ALL FIELDS OF STUDY
OPEN TO STUDENTS GRADES 9 - 12 AND UNDERGRADUATES AT SCHOOLS IN THE USA; PUERTO RICO; THE VIRGIN ISLANDS OR THE DISTRICT OF COLUMBIA. POSTER CONTEST ON THE SUBJECT OF EMPLOYMENT OPPORTUNITIES FOR PEOPLE WITH DISABILITIES.
WRITE FOR COMPLETE INFORMATION.

1566

PRESIDENT'S COMMITTEE ON EMPLOYMENT OF PEOPLE WITH DISABILITIES (NATIONAL JOURNALISM SCHOLARSHIP PROGRAM)
1331 F ST NW
WASHINGTON DC 20004
202/376-6200; FAX 202/376-6219; TDD 202/376-6205
AMOUNT: $1000 TO $3000
DEADLINE(S): MAR 1
FIELD(S): ALL FIELDS OF STUDY
OPEN TO 16 TO 19 YEAR OLDS WHO HAVE NOT ENTERED A POST-SECONDARY SCHOOL AS OF MAR 1 AND WHO LIVES IN THE USA; THE VIRGIN ISLANDS; PUERTO RICO OR DISTRICT OF COLUMBIA. WRITING CONTEST RELATED TO SKILLS AND ABILITIES OF THE DISABLED.
WRITE FOR COMPLETE INFORMATION.

1567

PRINCE GEORGE'S CHAMBER OF COMMERCE FOUNDATION (SCHOLARSHIP)
4640 FORBES BLVD; SUITE 200
LANHAM MD 20706
301/731-5000
AMOUNT: FULL TUITION AT MARYLAND SCHOOLS; PARTIAL TUITION OUT OF STATE SCHOOLS
DEADLINE(S): MAY 1
FIELD(S): ALL FIELDS OF STUDY
OPEN TO RESIDENTS OF PRINCE GEORGES COUNTY, MD FOR UNDERGRADUATE STUDY. USA CITIZEN. FINANCIAL NEED IS A CONSIDERATION.
WRITE FOR COMPLETE INFORMATION.

1568

PROFESSIONAL BOWLERS ASSOCIATION (BILLY WELU MEMORIAL SCHOLARSHIP)
1720 MERRIMAN RD; PO BOX 5118
AKRON OH 44334
216/836-5568
AMOUNT: $500
DEADLINE(S): MAY 31

FIELD(S): ALL FIELDS OF STUDY

THE SCHOLARSHIP IS DESIGNED TO ASSIST UNDERGRADUATE STUDENTS WHO ARE PRESENTLY ENROLLED IN COLLEGE & ARE CURRENTLY REPRESENTING THEIR SCHOOLS IN BOWLING AS A TEAM MEMBER; COACH OR TRAINER.

THE AIM OF THE PBA IS TO SUPPORT AND PROMOTE THE SPORT OF BOWLING. WRITE FOR COMPLETE INFORMATION.

1569

PROFESSIONAL HORSEMEN'S ASSOCIATION OF AMERICA INC. (FINANCIAL ASSISTANCE)

PO BOX 572; LONG HILL RD
NEW VERNON NJ 07976
201/538-3797

AMOUNT: $500
DEADLINE(S): MAY 1
FIELD(S): ALL AREAS OF STUDY

MEMBERS OR DEPENDENTS OF MEMBERS OF THE PROFESSIONAL HORSEMEN'S ASSOCIATION RECEIVE FIRST CONSIDERATION FOR FINANCIAL ASSISTANCE. AWARDS CAN BE USED FOR COLLEGE OR TRADE SCHOOL.

WRITE TO MR. ALEX FORMAN; SCHOLARSHIP COMMITTEE CHAIRMAN; ADDRESS ABOVE FOR COMPLETE INFORMATION.

1570

PUBLIC EMPLOYEES ROUNDTABLE (PUBLIC SERVICE SCHOLARSHIPS)

PO BOX 14270
WASHINGTON DC 20044
202/927-5000; FAX 202/927-5001

AMOUNT: $500 - $1000
DEADLINE(S): MAY 15
FIELD(S): ALL FIELDS OF STUDY

OPEN TO GRADUATE STUDENTS & UNDERGRADUATE SOPHOMORES; JUNIORS; SENIORS WHO ARE PLANNING A CAREER IN GOVERNMENT. MINIMUM OF 3.5 CUMULATIVE GPA. PREFERENCE TO APPLICANTS WITH SOME PUBLIC SERVICE WORK EXPERIENCE (PAID OR UNPAID).

10 TO 15 AWARDS PER YEAR. APPLICATIONS AVAILABLE AS OF FEB 1. SEND SELF-ADDRESSED STAMPED ENVELOPE FOR APPLICATION.

1571

QUAKER CHEMICAL FOUNDATION (SCHOLARSHIPS)

ELM & LEE STREETS
CONSHOHOCKEN PA 19428
215/828-4119

AMOUNT: UP TO $4000
DEADLINE(S): DEC
FIELD(S): ALL AREAS OF STUDY

MUST BE DEPENDENT OF EMPLOYEE. $4000 PER YEAR IS AVAILABLE FOR FOUR YEARS OF BACCALAUREATE STUDY. $2000 FOR FOUR YEARS OF NON-BACCALAUREATE STUDY. $1500 PER YEAR IS AVAILABLE FOR FOUR YEARS FOR CHILDREN FROM SELECTED HIGH SCHOOLS.

NUMBER OF AWARDS PER YEAR VARIES. CONTACT KATHLEEN MAGUE ADMINISTRATIVE ASSISTANT ADDRESS ABOVE FOR COMPLETE INFORMATION. FOR UNDERGRADUATE STUDY ONLY.

1572

RACINE EDUCATION COUNCIL (EDUCATIONAL ASSISTANCE GRANTS PROGRAM)

310 FIFTH ST; #101
RACINE WI 53403
414/631-5600

AMOUNT: VARIES
DEADLINE(S): JUN 30; OCT 31
FIELD(S): ALL FIELDS OF STUDY

MUST BE RESIDENT OF RACINE WI. GRANTS ARE MAINLY FOR MINORITY YOUTHS WHO ARE HIGH SCHOOL GRADUATES. MUST BE U.S. CITIZEN.

100 AWARDS PER YEAR. CONTACT MARY DAY; EXECUTIVE DIRECTOR; ADDRESS ABOVE; FOR COMPLETE INFORMATION.

1573

RECORDING FOR THE BLIND (MARY P. OENSLAGER SCHOLASTIC ACHIEVEMENT AWARDS)

20 ROSZEL RD
PRINCETON NJ 08540
609/452-0606

AMOUNT: $500 - $3000
DEADLINE(S): FEB 1
FIELD(S): ALL AREAS OF STUDY

ANNUAL AWARDS OPEN TO OUTSTANDING LEGALLY BLIND UNDERGRADUATE SENIORS WHO GRADUATE FROM AN ACCREDITED

4-YEAR COLLEGE OR UNIVERSITY IN THE USA; HAVE 3.0 OR HIGHER GPA (4.0 SCALE) & ARE A REGISTERED RFB BORROWER.
WRITE FOR COMPLETE INFORMATION.

1574

RHODE ISLAND HIGHER EDUCATION ASSISTANCE AUTHORITY (LOAN PROGRAM; PLUS LOANS)
560 JEFFERSON BLVD
WARWICK RI 02886
401/277-2050
AMOUNT: UP TO $4000 UNDERGRADUATE; UP TO $7500 GRADUATE
DEADLINE(S): NONE SPECIFIED
FIELD(S): ALL FIELDS OF STUDY
OPEN TO RHODE ISLAND RESIDENTS OR NON-RESIDENTS ATTENDING AN ELIGIBLE RHODE ISLAND SCHOOL. MUST BE USA CITIZENS OR LEGAL RESIDENTS AND BE ENROLLED AT LEAST HALF TIME. RHODE ISLAND RESIDENTS MAY ATTEND SCHOOLS OUTSIDE THE STATE.
MUST DEMONSTRATE FINANCIAL NEED. WRITE FOR CURRENT INTEREST RATES AND COMPLETE INFORMATION.

1575

RHODE ISLAND HIGHER EDUCATION ASSISTANCE AUTHORITY (UNDERGRADUATE GRANT & SCHOLARSHIP PROGRAM)
560 JEFFERSON BLVD
WARWICK RI 02886
401/277-2050
AMOUNT: $250 - $700
DEADLINE(S): MAR 1
FIELD(S): ALL FIELDS OF STUDY
OPEN TO RHODE ISLAND RESIDENTS WHO ARE ENROLLED OR PLANNING TO ENROLL AT LEAST 1/2 TIME AT AN ELIGIBLE POST-SECONDARY INSTITUTION. USA CITIZEN OR LEGAL RESIDENT.
MUST DEMONSTRATE FINANCIAL NEED. WRITE FOR COMPLETE INFORMATION.

1576

RIPON COLLEGE (DISTINGUISHED HONOR SCHOLARSHIP; PICKARD SCHOLARSHIP)
PO BOX 248; 300 SEWARD ST; ADMISSIONS OFFICE
RIPON WI 54971
414/748-8102
AMOUNT: $2500 (DHS); $6500 & $13000 (PICKARD)
DEADLINE(S): MAR 1
FIELD(S): ALL AREAS OF STUDY
ENTERING FRESHMEN. PICKARD SCHOLARSHIPS AND DISTINGUISHED HONOR SCHOLARSHIPS WILL BE AWARDED ON BASIS OF TOTAL HIGH SCHOOL RECORD; RECOMMENDATIONS; AND INTERVIEW.
80 AWARDS PER YEAR. THERE ARE 9 $6500 PICKARD SCHOLARSHIPS AND ONE FOR $13000. MUST APPLY AND BE ACCEPTED FOR ADMISSION AT RIPON COLLEGE. WRITE FOR COMPLETE INFORMATION.

1577

RIPON COLLEGE (ROTC HONOR SCHOLARSHIP)
PO BOX 248; 300 SEWARD ST; ADMISSIONS OFFICE
RIPON WI 54971
414/748-8102
AMOUNT: $1500
DEADLINE(S): MAR 1
FIELD(S): ALL AREAS OF STUDY
ENTERING FRESHMEN. DISTINGUISHED HONOR SCHOLARSHIPS WILL BE AWARDED ON BASIS OF TOTAL HIGH SCHOOL RECORD; RECOMMENDATIONS & INTERVIEW.
15 AWARDS PER YEAR. MUST APPLY AND BE ACCEPTED FOR ADMISSION AT RIPON COLLEGE. WRITE FOR COMPLETE INFORMATION.

1578

ROCKWELL INTERNATIONAL (ROCKWELL NATIONAL MERIT SCHOLARSHIP PROGRAM)
2201 SEAL BEACH BLVD
SEAL BEACH CA 90740
310/797-5783
AMOUNT: $500 - $2000 PER YEAR
DEADLINE(S): NONE
FIELD(S): ALL FIELDS OF STUDY
OPEN TO CHILDREN OF ELIGIBLE ACTIVE OR FORMER EMPLOYEES OF ROCKWELL INTERNATIONAL. USA CITIZENSHIP REQUIRED.
CONTACT ROCKWELL COLLEGE RELATIONS DEPARTMENT OR WRITE TO ADDRESS ABOVE FOR COMPLETE INFORMATION.

1579

ROTARY FOUNDATION OF ROTARY INTERNATIONAL (ACADEMIC YEAR AMBASSADORIAL SCHOLARSHIPS)
1 ROTARY CENTER; 1560 SHERMAN AV
EVANSTON IL 60201
708/866-3000
AMOUNT: FULL TUITION & LIVING EXPENSES UP TO US$20000
DEADLINE(S): CHECK WITH LOCAL ROTARY CLUB
FIELD(S): ALL FIELDS OF STUDY
OPEN TO HIGH SCHOOL GRADS WHO ARE PURSUING UNIVERSITY STUDIES AND WILL HAVE 2 YEARS OF COURSEWORK WHEN SCHOLARSHIP BEGINS AND TO THOSE PURSUING VOCATIONAL STUDIES WHO HAVE BEEN EMPLOYED IN A RECOGNIZED VOCATION FOR AT LEAST 2 YEARS.
FOR STUDY IN ANOTHER COUNTRY WHERE ROTARY CLUBS ARE LOCATED. APPLICATIONS MUST BE SUBMITTED THROUGH LOCAL ROTARY CLUBS. DEADLINES CAN BE AS EARLY AS MAR & AS LATE AS JUL 15.

1580

ROTARY FOUNDATION OF ROTARY INTERNATIONAL (MULTI YEAR AMBASSADORIAL SCHOLARSHIP)
ONE ROTARY CENTER; 1560 SHERMAN AVE
EVANSTON IL 60201
313/866-3000
AMOUNT: UP TO $10000 PER YEAR
DEADLINE(S): CHECK WITH LOCAL ROTARY CLUB
FIELD(S): ALL FIELDS OF STUDY
SCHOLARSHIP IS FOR 2 OR 3 YEARS OF STUDY ABROAD AT A STUDY INSTITUTION ASSIGNED BY ROTARY FOUNDATION. SCHOLAR MUST BE ENROLLED IN A SPECIFIC UNIVERSITY DEGREE PROGRAM AND HAVE COMPLETED AT LEAST 2 YEARS OF UNIVERSITY COURSEWORK.
APPLICANTS MUST SPEAK LANGUAGE OF HOST COUNTRY. DEADLINE MAY BE AS EARLY AS MAR OR AS LATE AS JULY 15. CONTACT LOCAL ROTARY CLUB FOR COMPLETE INFORMATION.

1581

ROUCH FOUNDATION (A.P. ROUCH AND LOUISE ROUCH SCHOLARSHIP GRANT)
C/O TRUST DEPT. TWIN FALLS BANK & TRUST COMPANY
TWIN FALLS ID 83303
208/733-1722 EXT. 221
AMOUNT: VARIES
DEADLINE(S): MAY 1
FIELD(S): ALL AREAS OF STUDY
OPEN TO ORPHANED; POOR OR UNDERPRIVILEGED BOYS AND GIRLS WHO LIVE IN TWIN FALLS IDAHO AND THE IMMEDIATE VICINITY. AWARDS CAN BE USED AT IDAHO SCHOOLS. MUST DEMONSTRATE FINANCIAL NEED.
NUMBER OF AWARDS PER YEAR VARIES. RENEWABLE. CONTACT ASSISTANT TRUST OFFICER JANICE STOVER AT ABOVE ADDRESS FOR COMPLETE INFORMATION.

1582

ROYAL A. & MILDRED D. EDDY STUDENT LOAN TRUST FUND; LOUISE I. LATSHAW STUDENT LOAN TRUST FUND (STUDENT LOANS)
2999 MC COOL RD
PORTAGE IN 46368
WRITTEN INQUIRY
AMOUNT: $2000 MAX
DEADLINE(S): FIRST APPLIED BASIS
FIELD(S): ALL FIELDS OF STUDY
LOAN FUND AVAILABLE TO UNDERGRADUATE JUNIORS AND SENIORS WHO ARE USA CITIZENS. LOAN PRINCIPAL AND INTEREST IS TO BE REPAID IN FULL AND TWO CREDITWORTHY CO-SIGNERS ARE REQUIRED. INTEREST RATE IS 10%. FOR STUDY IN USA ONLY.
REPAYMENT IN MONTHLY INSTALLMENTS IS TO START NOT LATER THAN FIVE MONTHS AFTER GRADUATION. WRITE FOR COMPLETE INFORMATION.

1583

ROYAL NEIGHBORS OF AMERICA (FRATERNAL SCHOLARSHIPS)
230 16TH STREET
ROCK ISLAND IL 61201
309/788-4561
AMOUNT: $500 - $2000
DEADLINE(S): 3RD FRIDAY IN SEP
FIELD(S): ALL AREAS OF STUDY

OPEN TO RNA MEMBERS OF AT LEAST 2 YEARS WHO ARE IN THE UPPER QUARTER OF THEIR CLASS OR ARE RECOMMENDED BY THEIR HIGH SCHOOL PRINCIPAL. AWARDS TENABLE AT RECOGNIZED UNDERGRADUATE COLLEGES & UNIVERSITIES.

22 SCHOLARSHIPS FOR FRESHMEN YEAR ONLY & 10 SCHOLARSHIPS THAT ARE RENEWABLE FOR 3 YEARS. WRITE FOR COMPLETE INFORMATION.

1584

S.R. PRITCHETT SCHOLARSHIP FUND (SCHOLARSHIPS)

WELLS FARGO PRIVATE BANKING GROUP; PO BOX 2511

SACRAMENTO CA 95812

916/440-4433

AMOUNT: NOT SPECIFIED

DEADLINE(S): NONE GIVEN

FIELD(S): ALL AREAS OF STUDY

UNDERGRADUATE SCHOLARSHIPS OPEN TO GRADUATES OF LOS MOLINAS HIGH SCHOOL IN THE VINA AREA SCHOOL DISTRICT IN TEHAMA COUNTY; CA.

WRITE FOR COMPLETE INFORMATION.

1585

SACHS FOUNDATION (SCHOLARSHIP PROGRAM)

90 S CASCADE AVE; SUITE 1410

COLORADO SPRINGS CO 80903

719/633-2353

AMOUNT: $3000

DEADLINE(S): MAR 1

FIELD(S): ALL AREAS OF STUDY

OPEN TO BLACK RESIDENTS OF COLORADO WHO ARE HIGH SCHOOL GRADUATES; USA CITIZENS; HAVE A 3.4 OR BETTER GPA AND CAN DEMONSTRATE FINANCIAL NEED. AWARDS ARE FOR UNDERGRADUATE OR GRADUATE STUDY AT ANY ACCREDITED COLLEGE OR UNIVERSITY.

50 SCHOLARSHIPS PER YEAR. RENEWABLE IF STUDENT MAINTAINS A 2.5 OR BETTER GPA. GRANTS ARE FOR UP TO 4 YEARS IN DURATION. WRITE FOR COMPLETE INFORMATION.

1586

SACRAMENTO SCOTTISH RITE OF FREEMASONRY (CHARLES M. GOETHE MEMORIAL SCHOLARSHIP)

PO BOX 19497

SACRAMENTO CA 95819

916/452-5881

AMOUNT: VARIES

DEADLINE(S): JUN 10

FIELD(S): ALL FIELDS OF STUDY

FOR ANY FIELD OF STUDY BUT PREFERENCE TO STUDENTS MAJORING IN EUGENICS OR BIOLOGICAL SCIENCES. GRANTS ARE LIMITED TO STUDENTS WHO ARE MEMBERS OR SENIOR MEMBERS OF THE ORDER OF DEMOLAY.

ALSO OPEN TO CHILDREN OF MEMBERS OR DECEASED MEMBERS OF A CALIFORNIA MASONIC LODGE. WRITE FOR COMPLETE INFORMATION.

1587

SAINT ANDREW'S SOCIETY OF THE STATE OF NEW YORK (GRADUATE SCHOLARSHIP PROGRAM)

71 W 23RD ST 10TH FL

NEW YORK NY 10010

212/807-1730

AMOUNT: UP TO $12000

DEADLINE(S): NOV 30

FIELD(S): ALL FIELDS OF STUDY

OPEN TO UNDERGRADUATE SENIORS AT ACCREDITED USA INSTITUTIONS WHO ARE OF SCOTTISH ANCESTRY. SCHOLARSHIPS ARE FOR A YEAR OF GRADUATE STUDY AT A SCOTTISH UNIVERSITY.

PREFERENCE TO APPLICANTS WHO HAVE NOT STUDIED IN GREAT BRITAIN. FINANCIAL NEED IS A CONSIDERATION. WRITE FOR COMPLETE INFORMATION.

1588

SAN DIEGO COUNTY CITIZENS SCHOLARSHIP FOUNDATION (RUTH JENKINS SCHOLARSHIP FUND)

1665 FROUDE STREET

SAN DIEGO CA 92107

619/223-6000

AMOUNT: VARIES

DEADLINE(S): NONE GIVEN

FIELD(S): ALL AREAS OF STUDY

OPEN TO HIGH SCHOOL SENIORS WHO LIVE IN SAN DIEGO COUNTY; CA AND ARE HIGH

SCHOOL SENIORS OF AFRICAN-AMERICAN DESCENT. MUST HAVE BEEN ACCEPTED FOR ENROLLMENT IN A FOUR YEAR COLLEGE OR UNIVERSITY OR A JUNIOR COLLEGE.

APPLICATIONS ARE AVAILABLE FROM HIGH SCHOOL GUIDANCE COUNSELORS OR FROM THE ADDRESS ABOVE.

1589

SAN FRANCISCO STATE UNIVERSITY (OVER-60 PROGRAM)

ADMISSIONS OFFICE; 1600 HOLLOWAY AVE
SAN FRANCISCO CA 94132
415/338-2037

AMOUNT: ADMISSIONS AND REGISTRATION FEES WAIVER

DEADLINE(S): NONE

FIELD(S): ALL FIELDS

OPEN TO CALIFORNIA RESIDENTS OVER 60 YEARS OF AGE WHO HAVE LIVED IN THE STATE FOR AT LEAST ONE YEAR BY SEPTEMBER 20TH. MUST MEET THE UNIVERSITY'S REGULAR ADMISSIONS STANDARDS. TOTAL COST IS $3 PER SEMESTER.

WRITE ADMISSIONS OFFICE FOR COMPLETE INFORMATION.

1590

SAN JOSE GI FORUM SCHOLARSHIP FOUNDATION INC. (SCHOLARSHIP PROGRAM)

100 SKYPORT DR; MC218
SAN JOSE CA 95115
408/947-6885

AMOUNT: $500-$6000

DEADLINE(S): MAR 15

FIELD(S): ALL AREAS OF STUDY

SCHOLARSHIPS FOR HISPANIC STUDENTS WHO GRADUATE FROM SANTA CLARA COUNTY HIGH SCHOOLS.

APPROXIMATELY 65 SCHOLARSHIPS PER YEAR. WRITE FOR COMPLETE INFORMATION.

1591

SAN JOSE STATE UNIVERSITY (SCHOLARSHIPS)

FINANCIAL AID OFFICE SJSU; ONE WASHINGTON SQUARE
SAN JOSE CA 95192
408/924-6063

AMOUNT: $50 - $1000

DEADLINE(S): JAN 1 - MAR 1

FIELD(S): ALL FIELDS OF STUDY

SCHOLARSHIPS ARE AWARDED COMPETITIVELY TO STUDENTS ENROLLED AT SAN JOSE STATE ON THE BASIS OF GRADE POINT AVERAGE. MOST REQUIRE A DEMONSTRATION OF FINANCIAL NEED.

STUDENTS INTERESTED IN GRADUATE FELLOWSHIPS AND ASSISTANTSHIPS SHOULD APPLY DIRECTLY TO THEIR DEPARTMENT DEAN'S OFFICE. 450 SCHOLARSHIPS PER YEAR. WRITE FOR COMPLETE INFORMATION.

1592

SAN RAFAEL INDOOR SPORTS CLUB INC. (SCHOLARSHIPS FOR DISABLED STUDENTS)

C/O COLLEGE OF MARIN; FINANCIAL AID OFFICE
KENTFIELD CA 94904
415/924-3549

AMOUNT: $300 PER YEAR

DEADLINE(S): MAY 1

FIELD(S): ALL AREAS OF STUDY

OPEN TO STUDENTS ENROLLED IN OR PLANNING TO ENROLL IN THE DISABLED STUDENTS PROGRAM AT THE COLLEGE OF MARIN. MUST HAVE A COURSE LOAD OF SIX UNITS OR MORE AND MAINTAIN A 3.0 OR BETTER GPA.

WRITE FOR COMPLETE INFORMATION.

1593

SANTA BARBARA FOUNDATION (STUDENT LOAN PROGRAM)

15 E CARRILLO ST
SANTA BARBARA CA 93101
805/963-1873

AMOUNT: VARIES

DEADLINE(S): JAN 31

FIELD(S): ALL AREAS OF STUDY

OPEN TO SANTA BARBARA COUNTY HIGH SCHOOL GRADUATES OR STUDENTS WITH STRONG SANTA BARBARA TIES. APPLICATION MAY BE MADE FOR 3 YEARS OF UNDERGRADUATE STUDY BY USA CITIZENS OR PERMANENT RESIDENTS. FINANCIAL NEED IS A CONSIDERATION.

APPLICANTS SHOULD HAVE ATTENDED SANTA BARBARA COUNTY SCHOOLS SINCE THE 7TH GRADE. UP TO 550 AWARDS PER YEAR. APPLICATIONS AVAILABLE OCT 1 TO JAN 15. WRITE FOR COMPLETE INFORMATION.

1594

SANTA FE PACIFIC FOUNDATION (NATIONAL MERIT SCHOLARSHIPS)
1700 E GOLF RD
SCHAUMBURG IL 60173
WRITTEN INQUIRY
AMOUNT: $2000 - $3500
DEADLINE(S): NONE SPECIFIED
FIELD(S): ALL FIELDS OF STUDY
OPEN TO CHILDREN OF EMPLOYEES OF SANTA FE PACIFIC AND AFFILIATE COMPANIES. AWARDS ARE FOR STUDENTS WHO WILL COMPLETE HIGH SCHOOL AND ENTER AN ACCREDITED USA COLLEGE DURING THE SAME YEAR.
RENEWABLE FOR UP TO 4 YEARS. WRITE FOR COMPLETE INFORMATION.

1595

SARA LEE CORPORATION (STUDENT LOAN PROGRAM)
3 FIRST NATIONAL PLAZA
CHICAGO IL 60602
312/726-2600
AMOUNT: $1000 - $2500
DEADLINE(S): NONE
FIELD(S): ALL FIELDS OF STUDY
PROGRAM OPEN TO FULL TIME EMPLOYEES OF SARA LEE CORPORATION & THEIR DEPENDENT CHILDREN. SUPPORTS STUDY AT ACCREDITED COLLEGES & UNIVERSITIES.
WRITE FOR COMPLETE INFORMATION.

1596

SCHOLARSHIP FOUNDATION OF ST LOUIS (INTEREST-FREE UNDERGRADUATE LOAN PROGRAM)
8215 CLAYTON ROAD
ST LOUIS MO 63117
314/725-7990
AMOUNT: $2000
DEADLINE(S): APR 15
FIELD(S): ALL AREAS OF STUDY
RESIDENTS OF THE ST LOUIS AREA WHO ARE HIGH SCHOOL GRADUATES AND WHO CAN DEMONSTRATE FINANCIAL NEED. LOANS ARE INTEREST-FREE. SIX YEARS TO REPAY FOLLOWING GRADUATION.
LOANS ARE RENEWABLE UP TO A MAXIMUM OF $12000 PER PERSON PROVIDED STUDENT IS IN GOOD ACADEMIC STANDING AND CONTINUES TO SHOW NEED. WRITE FOR COMPLETE INFORMATION.

1597

SCHOOL CRIME PREVENTION PROJECT (BROWN/SCOTT SCHOLARSHIP)
1550 THE ALAMEDA; NO. 209
SAN JOSE CA 95126
408/923-5836
AMOUNT: $500
DEADLINE(S): MAY 15
FIELD(S): ALL FIELDS OF STUDY
ESSAY CONTEST OPEN TO STUDENTS WHO WRITE AN ESSAY ABOUT SCHOOL CRIME AND HOW TO PREVENT IT. CONTEST IS OPEN TO ALL AGES WITH NO RESTRICTIONS AS TO GRADES. ESSAY CAN BE OF ANY LENGTH.
ESSAYS BECOME THE PROPERTY OF THE SCHOOL CRIME PREVENTION PROJECT COMMITTEE. WRITE FOR COMPLETE INFORMATION.

1598

SCREEN ACTORS GUILD FOUNDATION (JOHN L. DALES SCHOLARSHIP FUND)
7065 HOLLYWOOD BLVD
HOLLYWOOD CA 90028
213/856-6670
AMOUNT: VARIES
DEADLINE(S): MAR 1
FIELD(S): ALL AREAS OF STUDY
SCHOLARSHIPS OPEN TO SAG MEMBERS WITH AT LEAST 5 YEARS MEMBERSHIP OR DEPENDENT CHILDREN OF MEMBERS WITH AT LEAST 8 YEARS MEMBERSHIP. AWARDS ARE FOR ANY LEVEL OF UNDERGRADUATE; GRADUATE OR POST-GRADUATE STUDY.
FINANCIAL NEED IS A CONSIDERATION. RENEWABLE YEARLY WITH REAPPLICATION. WRITE FOR COMPLETE INFORMATION.

1599

SEABEE MEMORIAL SCHOLARSHIP ASSOCIATION INC. (SCHOLARSHIPS)
C/O NAVAL FACILITIES ENGINEERING COMMAND CODE-00E; 200 STOVAL ST
ALEXANDRIA VA 22332
202/325-8557
AMOUNT: $1150
DEADLINE(S): APR 15
FIELD(S): ALL AREAS OF STUDY
SCHOLARSHIPS ARE AVAILABLE FOR CHILDREN OF REGULAR; RESERVE; RETIRED OR DECEASED OFFICERS OR ENLISTED MEMBERS WHO HAVE SERVED OR WHO ARE NOW

SERVING WITH THE NAVAL CIVIL ENGINEER CORPS (SEABEES).

16 AWARDS PER YEAR. RENEWABLE UP TO 4 YEARS. WRITE FOR COMPLETE INFORMATION.

1600

SEAFARERS' WELFARE PLAN (CHARLIE LOGAN SCHOLARSHIP PROGRAM FOR SEAMEN)

5201 AUTH WAY
CAMP SPRINGS MD 20746
301/899-0675

AMOUNT: $6000 - $15000
DEADLINE(S): APR 15
FIELD(S): ALL AREAS OF STUDY

OPEN TO SEAMAN WHO HAS NOT LESS THAN 2 YEARS OF ACTUAL EMPLOYMENT ON VESSELS OF COMPANIES SIGNATORY TO THE SEAFARERS' WELFARE PLAN. MUST HAVE HAD 125 DAYS EMPLOYMENT IN PREVIOUS CALENDAR YEAR.

RENEWABLE UP TO 2 YEARS. WRITE FOR COMPLETE INFORMATION.

1601

SEAFARERS' WELFARE PLAN (CHARLIE LOGAN SCHOLARSHIP PROGRAM FOR DEPENDENTS)

5201 AUTH WAY
CAMP SPRINGS MD 20746
301/899-0675

AMOUNT: $10000
DEADLINE(S): APR 15
FIELD(S): ALL AREAS OF STUDY

OPEN TO DEPENDENT CHILDREN OF SEAMEN WHO HAVE BEEN EMPLOYED FOR AT LEAST 3 YEARS BY A CONTRIBUTOR TO SEAFARER'S WELFARE PLAN. STUDENT MUST BE HS (OR EQUIV) GRAD IN UPPER 1/3 OF CLASS; UNMARRIED & UNDER 19 YEARS OF AGE.

WRITE FOR COMPLETE INFORMATION.

1602

SECOND MARINE DIVISION ASSOCIATION (SCHOLARSHIP FUND)

PO BOX 8180
CAMP LEJEUNE NC 28542
WRITTEN INQUIRY

AMOUNT: $700
DEADLINE(S): JUN 1
FIELD(S): ALL AREAS

OPEN TO UNMARRIED DEPENDENTS OF INDIVIDUALS WHO ARE NOW SERVING OR HAVE SERVED IN THE USMC 2ND MARINE DIVISION. AWARDS FOR UNDERGRADUATE STUDY ONLY. REQUESTS FOR APPLICATION SHOULD BE IN THE STUDENT'S OWN HANDWRITING.

INCLUDE SELF-ADDRESSED STAMPED ENVELOPE WITH APPLICATION REQUEST.

1603

SELBY FOUNDATION (SCHOLARSHIP PROGRAM)

1800 SECOND ST; SUITE 905
SARASOTA FL 34236
813/957-0442

AMOUNT: $500 - $2000
DEADLINE(S): APR 30
FIELD(S): ALL FIELDS OF STUDY

FOR UNDERGRADUATE STUDY BY RESIDENTS OF SARASOTA OR MANATEE COUNTY FLORIDA WHO ARE ATTENDING AN ACCREDITED COLLEGE AND HAVE A GPA OF 3.0 OR BETTER. MUST BE USA CITIZEN AND DEMONSTRATE FINANCIAL NEED.

650 RENEWABLE SCHOLARSHIPS AND GRANTS PER YEAR. WRITE FOR COMPLETE INFORMATION.

1604

SEMINOLE TRIBE OF FLORIDA (HIGHER EDUCATION AWARDS)

6073 STIRLING ROAD
HOLLYWOOD FL 33024
305/321-1047

AMOUNT: VARIES
DEADLINE(S): APR 15; JUL 15; NOV 15
FIELD(S): ALL AREAS OF STUDY

OPEN TO ENROLLED MEMBERS OF THE SEMINOLE TRIBE OF FLORIDA OR TO THOSE ELIGIBLE TO BECOME A MEMBER. FOR UNDERGRADUATE OR GRADUATE STUDY AT AN ACCREDITED COLLEGE OR UNIVERSITY.

AWARDS RENEWABLE. WRITE FOR COMPLETE INFORMATION.

1605

SENECA NATION HIGHER EDUCATION (EDUCATION GRANTS)

BOX 231
SALAMANCA NY 14779
716/945-1790

AMOUNT: UP TO $5000
DEADLINE(S): JUL 15; DEC 31; MAY 20
FIELD(S): ALL AREAS OF STUDY
ENROLLED MEMBERS OF THE SENECA NATION OF INDIANS WHO ARE IN NEED OF FUNDING FOR POST-SECONDARY EDUCATION AND ARE ACCEPTED IN AN ACCREDITED PROGRAM OF STUDY. FUNDS MAY BE USED TOWARD ASSOCIATES; BACHELORS; MASTERS OR DOCTORS DEGREE.
AWARD IS BASED ON FINANCIAL NEED. WRITE FOR COMPLETE INFORMATION.

1606

SERVICE EMPLOYEES INTERNATIONAL UNION (SCHOLARSHIP PROGRAM)
1313 'L' ST NW
WASHINGTON DC 20005
800/448-7348
AMOUNT: $750
DEADLINE(S): VARIES
FIELD(S): ALL AREAS OF STUDY
SCHOLARSHIPS OPEN TO SERVICE EMPLOYEES INTERNATIONAL UNION MEMBERS (IN GOOD STANDING) & THEIR DEPENDENT CHILDREN. AWARDS TENABLE AT RECOGNIZED UNDERGRADUATE COLLEGES & UNIVERSITIES.
11 SCHOLARSHIPS ARE AWARDED ANNUALLY. RENEWABLE UP TO FOUR YEARS. WRITE FOR COMPLETE INFORMATION.

1607

SHOE SUPPLIERS ASSOCIATION OF AMERICA (UNDERGRADUATE SCHOLARSHIPS)
MARY E. GERRY; EXECUTIVE VICE PRES; 9 HILLSIDE AVE
WOBURN MA 01801
617/935-3445
AMOUNT: $1000
DEADLINE(S): NONE
FIELD(S): ALL AREAS OF STUDY
OPEN TO DEPENDENT CHILDREN OF ANY SHOE INDUSTRY EMPLOYEE. AWARDS ARE FOR UNDERGRADUATE STUDY AT ACCREDITED COLLEGES & UNIVERSITIES.
WRITE FOR COMPLETE INFORMATION.

1608

SICO FOUNDATION (SCHOLARSHIPS)
SCHOLARSHIPS COORDINATOR
MOUNT JOY PA 17552
717/653-1411
AMOUNT: $1000 PER YEAR
DEADLINE(S): FEB 15
FIELD(S): ALL AREAS OF STUDY
HIGH SCHOOL SENIOR WHOSE RESIDENCE IS THE STATE OF DELAWARE OR THE PENNSYLVANIA COUNTIES OF ADAMS; BERKS; CHESTER; CUMBERLAND; DAUPHIN; DELAWARE; LANCASTER; LEBANON OR YORK.
ALSO AVAILABLE TO RESIDENTS OF NEW JERSEY COUNTIES OF ATLANTIC; CAPE MAY; CUMBERLAND; GLOUCESTER AND SALEM AND TO RESIDENTS OF CECIL COUNTY MARYLAND. WRITE FOR COMPLETE INFORMATION.

1609

SOCIETY OF DAUGHTERS OF HOLLAND DAMES (SCHOLARSHIPS)
'THORLAND' - VALLEY ROAD
LOCUST VALLEY NY 11560
515/671-8833
AMOUNT: $500
DEADLINE(S): MAY 1
FIELD(S): ALL AREAS OF STUDY
OPEN TO APPLICANTS OF DUTCH DESCENT WHO WILL BE AN UNDERGRADUATE JUNIOR OR SENIOR AT AN ACCREDITED USA COLLEGE OR UNIVERSITY. DEMONSTRATE HIGH SCHOLASTIC STANDING AND GOOD MORAL CHARACTER. USA CITIZEN. FINANCIAL NEED IS A CONSIDERATION.
RENEWABLE FOR SENIOR YEAR UPON REAPPLICATION AND REEVALUATION. WRITE FOR COMPLETE INFORMATION AND INCLUDE PROOF OF DUTCH ANCESTRY.

1610

SOCIETY OF DAUGHTERS OF THE U.S. ARMY (SCHOLARSHIPS)
4242 EAST-WEST HWY; APT 910
CHEVY CHASE MD 20815
703/538-5540
AMOUNT: $750
DEADLINE(S): MAR 31
FIELD(S): ALL AREAS OF STUDY
OPEN TO DAUGHTERS; STEP & GRAND DAUGHTERS OF COMMISSIONED OFFICERS OF THE US ARMY WHO ARE ON ACTIVE DUTY; ARE RETIRED OR WHO DIED WHILE ON ACTIVE DUTY OR AFTER ELIGIBLE RETIREMENT. MUST DEMONSTRATE FINANCIAL NEED AND MERIT.

APPROXIMATELY 8 SCHOLARSHIPS PER YEAR; RENEWABLE. INCLUDE QUALIFYING PARENT'S NAME; RANK; SOCIAL SECURITY NUMBER AND DATES OF SERVICE. SEND STAMPED SELF-ADDRESSED ENVELOPE BETWEEN NOV 1 AND MAR 1.

1611

SOCIETY OF THE FIRST DIVISION FOUNDATION (SCHOLARSHIPS)
5 MONTGOMERY AVE
PHILADELPHIA PA 19118
WRITTEN INQUIRY
AMOUNT: $500 PER YEAR (4 YEARS MAXIMUM)
DEADLINE(S): JUN 1
FIELD(S): ALL FIELDS OF STUDY
OPEN TO HIGH SCHOOL SENIORS WHO ARE THE CHILDREN OR GRANDCHILDREN OF SOLDIERS WHO SERVED IN THE US ARMY 1ST INFANTRY DIVISION. AWARD BASED ON SCHOLASTIC ACHIEVEMENTS; CAREER OBJECTIVES; ESSAY. FOR UNDERGRAD STUDY AT 2 OR 4 YEAR COLLEGE.
WRITE FOR COMPLETE INFORMATION.

1612

SONS OF ITALY FOUNDATION (NATIONAL LEADERSHIP GRANTS)
219 'E' STREET NE
WASHINGTON DC 20002
202/547-2900
AMOUNT: $2000
DEADLINE(S): MAR 15
FIELD(S): ALL FIELDS OF STUDY
NATIONAL LEADERSHIP GRANT COMPETITION IS OPEN TO ANY FULL TIME STUDENT OF ITALIAN HERITAGE STUDYING AT AN ACCREDITED COLLEGE OR UNIVERSITY. FOR UNDERGRADUATE OR GRADUATE STUDY.
WRITE FOR COMPLETE INFORMATION. ALSO CONTACT LOCAL AND STATE LODGES WHICH ALSO OFFER SCHOLARSHIPS TO MEMBERS AND THEIR CHILDREN.

1613

SONS OF NORWAY FOUNDATION (ASTRID G. GATES SCHOLARSHIP FUND)
1455 WEST LAKE ST
MINNEAPOLIS MN 55408
WRITTEN INQUIRY
AMOUNT: $250 - $750
DEADLINE(S): MAR 1
FIELD(S): ALL FIELDS OF STUDY
APPLICANTS MUST BE BETWEEN THE AGES OF 17 & 22 AND BE CURRENT MEMBERS OF SONS OF NORWAY OR CHILDREN OR GRANDCHILDREN OF CURRENT SONS OF NORWAY MEMBERS. MUST DEMONSTRATE FINANCIAL NEED.
WRITE FOR COMPLETE INFORMATION.

1614

SOROPTIMIST FOUNDATIONS (SOROPTIMIST INTERNATIONAL OF THE AMERICAS - TRAINING AWARDS PROGRAM)
1616 WALNUT STREET
PHILADELPHIA PA 19103
215/732-0512
AMOUNT: $3000 (54 AWARDS) PLUS 1 ADDITIONAL CASH AWARD OF $10000
DEADLINE(S): DEC 15
FIELD(S): ALL FIELDS OF STUDY
OPEN TO MATURE WOMEN HEADS OF HOUSEHOLD FURTHERING THEIR SKILLS & TRAINING TO UPGRADE EMPLOYMENT STATUS. PREFERENCE TO WOMEN ENTERING VOCATIONAL OR TECHNICAL TRAINING OR COMPLETING AN UNDERGRAD DEGREE. NOT AVAILABLE FOR GRADUATE WORK.
54 REGIONAL AWARDS IN USA & 17 OTHER COUNTRIES & TERRITORIES EACH YEAR. CONTACT LOCAL CLUB FOR COMPLETE INFORMATION.

1615

SOUTH BAY BOARD OF REALTORS (SCHOLARSHIP PROGRAM)
PO BOX 549
REDONDO BEACH CA 90277
310/379-2439
AMOUNT: $1000
DEADLINE(S): MAY 3
FIELD(S): ALL AREAS OF STUDY
OPEN TO RESIDENTS OF REDONDO BEACH; HERMOSA BEACH OR MANHATTAN BEACH (CALIF). STUDENTS SHOULD WRITE DESCRIBING THEIR ACTIVITIES OUTSIDE OF ACADEMIC PURSUITS AND THE PROGRAM THEY WISH TO PURSUE IN COLLEGE. FOR UNDERGRADUATE STUDY.
WRITE FOR COMPLETE INFORMATION.

1616

SOUTH CAROLINA DEPARTMENT OF VETERANS AFFAIRS (TUITION SCHOLARSHIPS FOR CHILDREN OF VETERANS)

1205 PENDLETON STREET
COLUMBIA SC 29201
803/734-0200

AMOUNT: TUITION WAIVER

DEADLINE(S): NONE

FIELD(S): ALL FIELDS OF STUDY

SOUTH CAROLINA RESIDENT. FOR CHILDREN OF VETERANS WHO WERE LEGAL RESIDENTS OF SOUTH CAROLINA AT TIME OF ENTRY INTO MILITARY SERVICE & WHO DURING SERVICE - WERE KILLED IN ACTION; DIED OF DISEASE; POW; MIA OR TOTALLY DISABLED. USA CITIZEN.

FOR UNDERGRADUATE STUDY AT SOUTH CAROLINA STATE SUPPORTED SCHOOLS. WRITE FOR COMPLETE INFORMATION.

1617

SOUTH CAROLINA STUDENT LOAN CORPORATION

PO BOX 21487
COLUMBIA SC 29221
803/798-0916

AMOUNT: $2625 PER YEAR FROSH/SOPH; $4000 PER YEAR JR/SR; $7500 PER YEAR GRAD

DEADLINE(S): 30 DAYS BEFORE END OF LOAN PERIOD

FIELD(S): ALL AREAS OF STUDY

OPEN TO USA CITIZENS OR ELIGIBLE NON-CITIZENS. MUST BE ENROLLED OR ACCEPTED FOR ENROLLMENT AT AN ELIGIBLE POST-SECONDARY SCHOOL. AMOUNT OF LOAN DETERMINED BY COST OF SCHOOL AND FINANCIAL NEED.

INTEREST BEGINS AT 8% AND INCREASES TO 10% AT FIFTH YEAR OF REPAYMENT. LOAN MUST BE RENEWED ANNUALLY. WRITE FOR COMPLETE INFORMATION.

1618

SOUTH CAROLINA TUITION GRANTS COMMITTEE (HIGHER EDUCATION TUITION GRANTS PROGRAM)

PO BOX 12159; 1ST FLOOR KEENAN BLDG
COLUMBIA SC 29211
803/734-1200

AMOUNT: UP TO $3990

DEADLINE(S): NONE SPECIFIED

FIELD(S): ALL FIELDS OF STUDY

OPEN TO RESIDENTS OF SOUTH CAROLINA WHO ARE ACCEPTED TO OR ENROLLED IN ELIGIBLE PRIVATE POST-SECONDARY INSTITUTIONS IN SOUTH CAROLINA. DEMONSTRATE FINANCIAL NEED AND ACADEMIC MERIT. USA CITIZEN OR LEGAL RESIDENT.

APPROX 8000 GRANTS PER YEAR. RENEWABLE. CONTACT FINANCIAL AID OFFICE OR ADDRESS ABOVE FOR COMPLETE INFORMATION.

1619

SOUTH DAKOTA DEPT. OF EDUCATION AND CULTURAL AFFAIRS (STATE STUDENT INCENTIVE GRANT)

700 GOVERNORS DR
PIERRE SD 57501
605/773-3134

AMOUNT: $100 - $600

DEADLINE(S): APR 1

FIELD(S): ALL FIELDS OF STUDY

PROGRAM OPEN TO RESIDENTS OF SOUTH DAKOTA WHO ARE ENROLLED AT AN APPROVED UNDERGRADUATE COLLEGE; UNIVERSITY; PROPRIETARY OR VOCATIONAL SCHOOL WITHIN THE STATE ON AT LEAST A HALF-TIME BASIS. USA CITIZEN OR LEGAL RESIDENT.

900 AWARDS PER YEAR. AWARDS ARE RENEWABLE UNTIL ATTAINMENT OF THE BACHELOR'S DEGREE. WRITE FOR COMPLETE INFORMATION.

1620

SOUTH DAKOTA DEPT. OF EDUCATION AND CULTURAL AFFAIRS (TUITION EQUALIZATION GRANT 'TEG' PROGRAM)

700 GOVERNORS DR
PIERRE SD 57501
605/773-3134

AMOUNT: $100 - $250

DEADLINE(S): APR 1

FIELD(S): ALL FIELDS OF STUDY

OPEN TO RESIDENTS OF SOUTH DAKOTA ATTENDING AN APPROVED UNDERGRADUATE PRIVATE COLLEGE OR UNIVERSITY WITHIN THE STATE ON A FULL TIME BASIS. USA CITIZEN OR LEGAL RESIDENT.

600 AWARDS PER YEAR. WRITE FOR COMPLETE INFORMATION.

1621

SOUTH DAKOTA DEPT. OF EDUCATION AND CULTURAL AFFAIRS (SUPERIOR SCHOLAR PROGRAM)

700 GOVERNORS DR
PIERRE SD 57501
605/773-3134

AMOUNT: UP TO $1500
DEADLINE(S): JUN 1
FIELD(S): ALL FIELDS OF STUDY

THIS PROGRAM AIDS SOUTH DAKOTA RESIDENTS WHO BECOME SD NATIONAL MERIT SCHOLARSHIP SEMIFINALISTS. STUDENTS MUST ATTEND A PARTICIPATING SOUTH DAKOTA COLLEGE.

60 AWARDS PER YEAR. AWARDS ARE RENEWABLE IF THE STUDENT ENROLLS IN A MINIMUM OF 15 SEMESTER HOURS AND MAINTAINS A 3.0 GRADE POINT AVERAGE. WRITE FOR COMPLETE INFORMATION.

1622

SOUTH DAKOTA DIVISION OF VETERANS AFFAIRS (AID TO VETERANS)

500 E CAPITOL AVE
PIERRE SD 57501
605/773-3269; FAX 605/773-5380

AMOUNT: FREE TUITION IN STATE SUPPORTED SCHOOLS
DEADLINE(S): NONE SPECIFIED
FIELD(S): ALL FIELDS OF STUDY

OPEN TO SD RESIDENTS WHO SERVED IN THE USA MILITARY BETWEEN JUNE 15, 1950 AND MAY 7, 1975 AND HAVE EXHAUSTED THEIR GI BILL AND OTHER FEDERAL EDUCATIONAL BENEFITS. ENTITLED TO 1 MONTH OF EDUCATION PER MONTH OF MILITARY SERVICE UP TO 4 YEARS.

MILITARY DISCHARGE MUST HAVE BEEN OTHER THAN DISHONORABLE AND BENEFIT MUST BE USED WITHIN 20 YEARS OF CESSATION OF HOSTILITIES OR 6 YEARS FROM DISCHARGE; WHICHEVER IS LATER. WRITE FOR COMPLETE INFORMATION.

1623

SOUTH DAKOTA DIVISION OF VETERANS AFFAIRS (AID TO DEPENDENTS OF DECEASED VETERANS)

500 E CAPITOL AVE
PIERRE SD 57501
605/773-3269; FAX 605/773-5380

AMOUNT: FREE TUITION
DEADLINE(S): NONE SPECIFIED
FIELD(S): ALLB FIELDS OF STUDY

PROGRAM AIDS SOUTH DAKOTA RESIDENTS WHO ARE UNDER 25 YEARS OF AGE AND ARE CHILDREN OF VETERANS WHO DIED FROM ANY CAUSE WHILE A MEMBER OF THE USA ARMED FORCES AND LIVED IN SD FOR AT LEAST 6 MONTHS PRIOR TO ENTRY INTO ACTIVE SERVICE.

STUDENTS MUST BE ENROLLED IN AN UNDERGRADUATE PROGRAM AT A STATE-SUPPORTED COLLEGE OR UNIVERSITY WITHIN SOUTH DAKOTA. WRITE FOR COMPLETE INFORMATION.

1624

SOUTH DAKOTA EDUCATION ASSISTANCE CORPORATION (GUARANTEED STUDENT LOAN PROGRAM - STAFFORD; PLUS AND SLS LOANS)

115 FIRST AVE SW
ABERDEEN SD 57401
605/225-6423

AMOUNT: VARIES
DEADLINE(S): NONE
FIELD(S): ALL AREAS OF STUDY

SOUTH DAKOTA RESIDENT ENROLLED IN AN ELIGIBLE SCHOOL ON AT LEAST A HALF-TIME BASIS. US CITIZEN OR LEGAL RESIDENT.

LOANS ARE RENEWABLE. WRITE FOR COMPLETE INFORMATION.

1625

STANFORD UNIVERSITY (EAGLE SCOUT SCHOLARSHIP AWARD)

FINANCIAL AID OFFICE
STANFORD CA 94305
415/497-3059

AMOUNT: VARIES
DEADLINE(S): FEB 1
FIELD(S): ALL AREAS OF STUDY

OPEN TO EAGLE SCOUTS WHO LIVE IN ARIZONA; CALIFORNIA; HAWAII; NEVADA; UTAH; OR ROCK SPRINGS, WYOMING WHO ARE SEEKING A BACHELOR'S DEGREE AT STANFORD UNIVERSITY. MUST HAVE GOOD ACADEMIC STANDING AND RECOMMENDATION OF SCOUT EXECUTIVE.

WRITE FOR COMPLETE DETAILS.

1626

STATE COLLEGE AND UNIVERSITY SYSTEMS OF WEST VIRGINIA - CENTRAL OFFICE (WV HIGHER EDUCATION GRANT PROGRAM)
PO BOX 4007
CHARLESTON WV 25364
304/347-1211
AMOUNT: $350 TO $1964
DEADLINE(S): JAN 1; MAR 1
FIELD(S): ALL AREAS OF STUDY
OPEN TO HIGH SCHOOL GRADS WHO HAVE LIVED IN WV FOR 1 YEAR PRIOR TO APPLICATION & ARE ENROLLED FULL TIME AS AN UNDERGRAD IN AN APPROVED WV OR PA EDUCATIONAL INSTITUTION. MUST BE USA CITIZEN & DEMONSTRATE FINANCIAL NEED.
USA CITIZENSHIP REQUIRED. APPROX 5000 GRANTS PER YEAR. RENEWABLE UP TO 8 SEMESTERS. WRITE FOR COMPLETE INFORMATION.

1627

STATE FARM COMPANIES FOUNDATION (SCHOLARSHIP AWARD PROGRAM)
ONE STATE FARM PLAZA
BLOOMINGTON IL 61710
309/766-2039
AMOUNT: $2000 TO $6000 PER YEAR FOR 4 YEARS
DEADLINE(S): DEC 31
FIELD(S): ALL FIELDS OF STUDY
OPEN TO CHILDREN OF FULL TIME STATE FARM AGENTS OR FULL TIME STATE FARM EMPLOYEES OF THE STATE FARM COMPANIES. STUDENTS QUALIFY FROM SCORES MADE IN NATIONAL MERIT SCHOLARSHIP COMPETITION.
20 SCHOLARSHIPS PER YEAR. RENEWABLE UP TO FOUR YEARS.

1628

STEVEN KNEZEVICH TRUST (GRANTS)
100 E WISCONSIN AVE; SUITE 1020
MILWAUKEE WI 53202
414/271-6364
AMOUNT: $100 TO $800
DEADLINE(S): NOV 1
FIELD(S): ALL AREAS OF STUDY
UNDERGRADUATE & GRADUATE GRANTS FOR STUDENTS OF SERBIAN DESCENT. MUST ESTABLISH EVIDENCE OF ANCESTRAL HERITAGE. IT IS COMMON PRACTICE FOR STUDENTS TO BE INTERVIEWED IN MILWAUKEE PRIOR TO GRANTING THE AWARD.
ADDRESS INQUIRIES TO STANLEY HACK. INCLUDE SELF-ADDRESSED STAMPED ENVELOPE.

1629

STUDENT AID FOUNDATION (LOANS)
1393 SHEFFIELD PARKWAY
MARIETTA GA 30062
404/973-0256
AMOUNT: UNDERGRADUATES $2500 PER YEAR; GRADUATE STUDENTS $3000 PER YEAR
DEADLINE(S): APR 15
FIELD(S): ALL AREAS OF STUDY
LOANS AVAILABLE ONLY TO WOMEN WHO ARE RESIDENTS OF GEORGIA OR ARE ATTENDING SCHOOLS IN GEORGIA. GRADES; FINANCIAL NEED; PERSONAL INTEGRITY AND SENSE OF RESPONSIBILITY ARE CONSIDERATIONS.
35 LOANS PER YEAR. RENEWABLE WITH REAPPLICATION.

1630

STUDENTS' FINANCIAL SERVICES (COLLEGEAIRE LOAN PROGRAM)
PO BOX 88370
ATLANTA GA 30356
404/952-2500
AMOUNT: VARIES
DEADLINE(S): NONE
FIELD(S): ALL FIELDS OF STUDY
COLLEGE FINANCING LOAN PROGRAM OFFERING LINE OF CREDIT RANGING FROM DOUBLE A SAVINGS DEPOSIT FOR A 1 OR 2 YEAR COLLEGE PROGRAM TO 2 1/2 TIMES THE DEPOSIT FOR A 4 YEAR PROGRAM. SAVINGS IS RETURNED WITH INTEREST WHEN CREDIT LINE IS REPAID.
COLLEGAIRE LOAN PROGRAM IS OFFERED BY CITIZENS BANK. WRITE FOR COMPLETE INFORMATION.

1631

SUDBURY FOUNDATION STUDENT AID PROGRAM (LOANS/SCHOLARSHIPS)
278 OLD SUDBURY ROAD
SUDBURY MA 01776
508/443-0849
AMOUNT: $500 - $4000 PER YEAR
DEADLINE(S): JUN 1

FIELD(S): ALL AREAS OF STUDY
OPEN TO LINCOLN-SUDBURY HIGH SCHOOL (MASS) GRADUATING SENIORS OR DEPENDENTS OF SUDBURY RESIDENTS FOR POST-SECONDARY STUDIES INCLUDING VOCATIONAL TRAINING. LOW INTEREST LOANS AND LOAN/SCHOLARSHIP COMBINATIONS ARE AVAILABLE.
MUST DEMONSTRATE FINANCIAL NEED. ACADEMIC AND NON-ACADEMIC FACTORS ARE CONSIDERED IN EVALUATING LOAN REQUESTS.

1632

SUNKIST GROWERS INC. (A.W. BODINE - SUNKIST MEMORIAL SCHOLARSHIP)
PO BOX 7888
VAN NUYS CA 91409
818/379-7510
AMOUNT: $1000
DEADLINE(S): MAR 1
FIELD(S): ALL FIELDS OF STUDY
OPEN TO CALIFORNIA AND ARIZONA UNDERGRADUATES WHO COME FROM AN AGRICULTURAL BACKGROUND AND ARE IN NEED OF FINANCIAL ASSISTANCE. CONFIDENTIAL APPLICATION INCLUDES PERSONAL AND FINANCIAL INFORMATION.
WRITE FOR COMPLETE INFORMATION.

1633

SWEDISH INSTITUTE (SCHOLARSHIPS FOR STUDY OR RESEARCH IN SWEDEN)
PO BOX 7434
S-103 91 STOCKHOLM SWEDEN
WRITTEN INQUIRY
AMOUNT: SEK 6700 PER MONTH
DEADLINE(S): APPLICATIONS AVAILABLE ONLY BETWEEN SEP 1 AND DEC 1
FIELD(S): ALL FIELDS OF STUDY
OPEN TO STUDENTS & RESEARCHERS WHO ARE NOT SWEDISH CITIZENS. FOR STUDY OR RESEARCH IN SWEDEN WHEN IT CANNOT BE DONE EQUALLY AS WELL IN ANOTHER COUNTRY. DURATION IS NORMALLY 1 ACADEMIC YEAR. KNOWLEDGE OF SWEDISH OR ENGLISH REQUIRED.
AWARDS TENABLE AT ANY SWEDISH UNIVERSITY; EDUCATIONAL INSTITUTION OR FOR INDEPENDENT RESEARCH. WRITE FOR COMPLETE INFORMATION.

1634

SWISS BENEVOLENT SOCIETY OF CHICAGO (SCHOLARSHIP FUND)
6440 N BOSWORTH AVE
CHICAGO IL 60626
WRITTEN INQUIRY
AMOUNT: $750 - $2500
DEADLINE(S): INQUIRY FEB 1; APPLICATION MAR 1
FIELD(S): ALL AREAS OF STUDY
UNDERGRADUATE SCHOLARSHIPS OPEN TO SWISS NATIONALS OR THOSE OF PROVEN SWISS DESCENT WHO ARE PERMANENT RESIDENTS OF ILLINOIS OR SOUTHERN WISCONSIN & ACCEPTED TO OR ENROLLED IN ACCREDITED COLLEGES OR UNIVERSITIES. MINIMUM 3.5 GPA.
SWISS STUDENTS STUDYING IN THE USA ON A STUDENT OR VISITORS VISA ARE NOT ELIGIBLE. WRITE FOR COMPLETE INFORMATION.

1635

SWISS BENEVOLENT SOCIETY OF SAN FRANCISCO (SWISS UNDERGRADUATE SCHOLARSHIP FUND)
465 MONTGOMERY; SUITE 1500
SAN FRANCISCO CA 94104
415/788-2272
AMOUNT: VARIES
DEADLINE(S): MAY 15
FIELD(S): ALL AREAS OF STUDY
UNDERGRAD SCHOLARSHIPS AT USA COLLEGES OPEN TO SWISS NATIONALS OR THOSE OF SWISS DESCENT WITH AT LEAST 1 GRANDPARENT OF SWISS NATIONALITY WHO HAVE LIVED WITHIN A 150 MILE RADIUS OF THE S.F. CITY HALL FOR 3 YEARS PRIOR TO APPLICATION DATE.
50-60 AWARDS PER YEAR. LIMITED TO SCHOOLS IN CALIFORNIA. WRITE FOR COMPLETE INFORMATION.

1636

TAILHOOK FOUNDATION (SCHOLARSHIP AWARDS)
PO BOX 40
BONITA CA 91908
619/689-9223
AMOUNT: $1500
DEADLINE(S): JUL 15
FIELD(S): ALL FIELDS OF STUDY

OPEN TO CURRENT OR FORMER MEMBERS OF THE US NAVY; MARINE CORPS OR COAST GUARD WHO SERVED AS AN AVIATOR; FLIGHT OFFICER OR AIR CREWMAN OR ABOARD A US NAVY AIRCRAFT CARRIER IN ANY CAPACITY.

AWARDS ARE BASED ON EDUCATIONAL ACHIEVEMENT; MERIT; CITIZENSHIP AND FINANCIAL NEED. WRITE FOR COMPLETE INFORMATION.

1637

TEEN MAGAZINE (MISS TEENAGE AMERICA PROGRAM)
8490 SUNSET BLVD
LOS ANGELES CA 90069
310/854-2222
AMOUNT: $15000 + COMPLETE WARDROBE; OTHER PRIZES
DEADLINE(S): JUN 15
FIELD(S): ALL FIELDS OF STUDY

OPEN TO YOUNG WOMEN BETWEEN THE AGES OF 13 AND 18. CANDIDATES ARE JUDGED ON SCHOLASTIC ACHIEVEMENT; INDIVIDUAL ACCOMPLISHMENT; COMMUNITY SERVICE; POISE; APPEARANCE AND PERSONALITY. COMPETITION IS HELD IN LOS ANGELES CA.

APPLICATIONS AVAILABLE IN MAGAZINE STARTING IN MARCH AND FROM KMART STORES. WRITE FOR COMPLETE INFORMATION.

1638

TEXAS A & M UNIVERSITY (ACADEMIC EXCELLENCE AWARDS)
STUDENT FINANCIAL AID OFFICE
COLLEGE STATION TX 77843
409/845-5852
AMOUNT: $500 - $1500
DEADLINE(S): MAR 1
FIELD(S): ALL FIELDS OF STUDY

OPEN TO FULL TIME UNDERGRADUATE & GRADUATE STUDENTS AT TEXAS A & M UNIVERSITY. AWARDS ARE INTENDED TO RECOGNIZE & ASSIST STUDENTS WHO ARE MAKING EXCELLENT SCHOLASTIC PROGRESS.

APPROX 500 AWARDS PER YEAR. AWARDS GRANTED FOR ONE YEAR. APPLICATIONS ARE AVAILABLE AT THE STUDENT FINANCIAL AID OFFICE DURING JANUARY & FEBRUARY.

1639

TEXAS A & M UNIVERSITY (OPPORTUNITY AWARDS; ACADEMIC ACHIEVEMENT SCHOLARSHIPS)
STUDENT FINANCIAL AID OFFICE
COLLEGE STATION TX 77843
409/845-3236
AMOUNT: $500 - $2000
DEADLINE(S): JAN 15
FIELD(S): ALL FIELDS OF STUDY

THESE PROGRAMS ARE DESIGNED TO PROVIDE SCHOLARSHIPS TO TEXAS A&M UNIV FOR COLLEGE FRESHMEN & OUTSTANDING HIGH SCHOOL GRADUATES. SELECTION IS BASED ON LEADERSHIP ABILITY; SAT SCORES & HIGH SCHOOL RECORD. USA CITIZEN OR PERMANENT RESIDENT.

APPROX 500 AWARDS PER YEAR. AWARDS ARE GRANTED FOR 1-4 YEARS. CONTACT FINANCIAL AID OFFICE FOR COMPLETE INFORMATION.

1640

TEXAS A & M UNIVERSITY (PRESIDENTS ACHIEVEMENT AWARDS FOR MINORITY STUDENTS)
OFFICE OF HONORS PROGRAMS & ACADEMIC SCHOLARSHIPS
COLLEGE STATION TX 77843
409/845-1957
AMOUNT: $2500 PER YEAR FOR 4 YEARS
DEADLINE(S): JAN 15
FIELD(S): ALL FIELDS OF STUDY

THIS COMPETITIVE ACADEMIC SCHOLARSHIP PROGRAM PROVIDES 4-YEAR SCHOLARSHIPS FOR AFRICAN-AMERICAN AND HISPANIC HIGH SCHOOL SENIORS WHO WILL BE ATTENDING TEXAS A&M UNIVERSITY. USA CITIZEN OR PERMANENT RESIDENT.

APPROX 300 AWARDS PER YEAR. WRITE FOR COMPLETE INFORMATION.

1641

TEXAS A & M UNIVERSITY (PRESIDENT'S ENDOWED SCHOLARSHIPS; LECHNER FELLOWSHIPS; MC FADDEN SCHOLARSHIPS)
OFFICE OF HONORS PROGRAMS & ACADEMIC SCHOLARSHIPS
COLLEGE STATION TX 77843
409/845-1957
AMOUNT: $2000 - $3000 PER YEAR OVER 4 YEARS
DEADLINE(S): JAN 15
FIELD(S): ALL FIELDS OF STUDY

OPEN TO HIGH SCHOOL SENIORS WHO WILL BE ATTENDING TEXAS A&M; SCORED 1250 OR HIGHER ON THEIR SAT (OR EQUIVALENT OF 30 ON ACT) AND RANK IN THE TOP 15% OF HIGH SCHOOL GRADUATING CLASS OR ARE NATIONAL MERIT SCHOLARSHIP SEMI FINALISTS.

USA CITIZEN OR LEGAL RESIDENT. APPROX 350 AWARDS PER YEAR. WRITE FOR COMPLETE INFORMATION.

1642

TEXAS COMMERCE BANK (FRANKLIN LINDSEY STUDENT LOAN FUND)

PO BOX 550
AUSTIN TX 78789
512/476-6611

AMOUNT: UP TO $3000 PER ACADEMIC YEAR
DEADLINE(S): MAY 1
FIELD(S): ALL FIELDS OF STUDY

LOANS AVAILABLE TO STUDENTS WHO HAVE COMPLETED AT LEAST 1 YEAR AT A TEXAS COLLEGE OR UNIVERSITY & HAVE MAINTAINED NO LESS THAN A 'C' AVERAGE FOR ALL COURSEWORK.

WRITE FOR COMPLETE INFORMATION.

1643

TEXAS HIGHER EDUCATION COORDINATING BOARD (SCHOLARSHIPS; GRANTS & LOANS)

PO BOX 12788; CAPITOL STATION
AUSTIN TX 78711
512/483-6340

AMOUNT: VARIES
DEADLINE(S): VARIES WITH PROGRAM
FIELD(S): ALL FIELDS OF STUDY

OPEN TO TEXAS RESIDENTS ATTENDING TEXAS INSTITUTIONS. NUMEROUS STATE-ADMINISTERED STUDENT FINANCIAL AID PROGRAMS INCLUDING SCHOLARSHIPS; GRANTS & LOANS.

CONTACT YOUR SCHOOL'S FINANCIAL AID OFFICE OR WRITE TO THE ADDRESS ABOVE FOR THE BOOKLET 'FINANCIAL AID FOR TEXAS STUDENTS' WHICH DESCRIBES ALL PROGRAMS IN DETAIL.

1644

THETA DELTA CHI EDUCATIONAL FOUNDATION (SCHOLARSHIP)

135 BAY STATE ROAD
BOSTON MA 02215
WRITTEN INQUIRY

AMOUNT: $1000
DEADLINE(S): APR 30
FIELD(S): ALL FIELDS OF STUDY

SCHOLARSHIPS OPEN TO ACTIVE MEMBERS OF THETA DELTA CHI. CONSIDERATIONS INCLUDE PAST SERVICE TO THE FRATERNITY; SCHOLASTIC ACHIEVEMENTS AND PROMISE AND FINANCIAL NEED. PREFERENCE TO UNDERGRADS BUT GRADUATE STUDENTS WILL BE CONSIDERED.

WRITE FOR COMPLETE INFORMATION.

1645

THIRD MARINE DIVISION ASSOCIATION (SCHOLARSHIPS)

PO BOX 634
INVERNESS FL 32651
WRITTEN INQUIRY

AMOUNT: $400 - $2400
DEADLINE(S): APR 15
FIELD(S): ALL FIELDS OF STUDY

UNDERGRAD SCHOLARSHIPS FOR DEPENDENT CHILDREN OF USMC & USN PERSONNEL WHO DIED AS A RESULT OF SERVICE IN VIETNAM OR THE SOUTHEAST ASIA OPPERATIONS 'DESERT SHIELD' AND 'DESERT STORM' AS A RESULT OF SERVICE WITH THE 3D MARINE DIV.

ALSO OPEN TO CHILDREN OF ASSOCIATION MEMBERS (LIVING OR DEAD) WHO HELD MEMBERSHIP 2 YEARS OR MORE. MUST DEMONSTRATE FINANCIAL NEED. AWARDS RENEWABLE. WRITE FOR COMPLETE INFORMATION.

1646

THIRTY-SEVENTH DIVISION VETERANS ASSOCIATION (SCHOLARSHIPS)

65 SOUTH FRONT STREET; ROOM 707
COLUMBUS OH 43215
614/228-3788

AMOUNT: $500
DEADLINE(S): APR 1
FIELD(S): ALL AREAS OF STUDY

OPEN TO DEPENDENT CHILDREN OF 37TH DIVISION VETERANS WHO SERVED IN WORLD WAR II OR THE KOREAN CONFLICT. FINANCIAL NEED IS A CONSIDERATION PARTICULARLY IF THE FATHER IS DECEASED.

2 SCHOLARSHIPS PER YEAR. PAID-UP MEMBERS GIVEN PREFERENCE.

1647

THOMAS J. WATSON FOUNDATION (FELLOWSHIP PROGRAM)
217 ANGELL ST
PROVIDENCE RI 02906
401/274-1952
AMOUNT: $15000 SINGLE; $21000 WITH ACCOMPANYING FINANCIAL AND LEGAL DEPENDENT
DEADLINE(S): NOV 1
FIELD(S): ALL FIELDS OF STUDY
OPEN TO GRADUATING SENIORS AT THE 52 USA COLLEGES ON THE FOUNDATION'S ROSTER. FELLOWSHIP PROVIDES FOR ONE YEAR OF INDEPENDENT STUDY AND TRAVEL ABROAD IMMEDIATELY FOLLOWING GRADUATION.
CANDIDATES MUST BE NOMINATED BY THEIR COLLEGE. UP TO 65 AWARDS PER YEAR. WRITE FOR LIST OF PARTICIPATING INSTITUTIONS AND COMPLETE INFORMATION.

1648

TIMKEN COMPANY EDUCATIONAL FUND, INC. (SCHOLARSHIP PROGRAM)
1835 DUEBER AVENUE SW
CANTON OH 44706
216/471-3987
AMOUNT: TUITION + BOOKS; FEES & 80% ROOM & BOARD
DEADLINE(S): NOV 1
FIELD(S): ALL AREAS OF STUDY
UNDERGRADUATE SCHOLARSHIPS OPEN TO HIGH SCHOOL STUDENTS IN TOP 1/3 OF THEIR CLASS WHO ARE DEPENDENT CHILDREN OF EMPLOYEES OF TIMKEN COMPANY; LATROBE STEEL COMPANY OR CANADIAN TIMKEN LTD. USA OR CANADIAN CITIZEN.
WRITE FOR COMPLETE INFORMATION.

1649

TOWSON STATE UNIVERSITY
SCHOLARSHIP OFFICE
TOWSON MD 21204
301/321-3702
AMOUNT: VARIES
DEADLINE(S): VARIOUS
FIELD(S): ALL FIELDS OF STUDY
NUMEROUS SCHOLARSHIP AND AWARD PROGRAMS AVAILABLE TO ENTERING FRESHMEN AND TO GRADUATE AND TRANSFER STUDENTS.
WRITE FOR SCHOLARSHIPS AND AWARDS BOOKLET WHICH DESCRIBES EACH PROGRAM IN DETAIL.

1650

TRANSPORT WORKERS UNION OF AMERICA (MICHAEL J. QUILL SCHOLARSHIP FUND)
80 WEST END AVE
NEW YORK NY 10023
212/873-6000
AMOUNT: $1200
DEADLINE(S): MAY 1
FIELD(S): ALL FIELDS OF STUDY
OPEN TO HIGH SCHOOL SENIORS (UNDER 21) WHO ARE DEPENDENTS OF TWU MEMBERS IN GOOD STANDING OR OF A DECEASED MEMBER WHO WAS IN GOOD STANDING AT TIME OF DEATH. DEPENDENT BROTHERS OR SISTERS OF MEMBERS IN GOOD STANDING ALSO MAY APPLY.
15 SCHOLARSHIPS PER YEAR. RENEWABLE UP TO 4 YEARS. WRITE FOR COMPLETE INFORMATION.

1651

TULANE UNIVERSITY (SCHOLARSHIPS & FELLOWSHIPS)
ADMISSIONS OFFICE
NEW ORLEANS LA 70118
504/865-5731
AMOUNT: VARIES
DEADLINE(S): VARIOUS
FIELD(S): ALL AREAS OF STUDY
NUMEROUS SCHOLARSHIP & FELLOWSHIP PROGRAMS FOR UNDERGRADUATE & GRADUATE STUDY AT TULANE UNIVERSITY. THERE ALSO IS AN HONORS PROGRAM FOR OUTSTANDING STUDENTS ACCEPTED FOR ENROLLMENT AT TULANE.
WRITE FOR COMPLETE INFORMATION.

1652

TUPPERWARE HOME PARTIES (SCHOLARSHIPS)
PO BOX 2353
ORLANDO FL 32802
407/826-5050
AMOUNT: VARIES
DEADLINE(S): JAN 15
FIELD(S): ALL AREAS OF STUDY
UNDERGRADUATE SCHOLARSHIPS OPEN TO INDEPENDENT TUPPERWARE DEALERS;

MANAGERS & THEIR DEPENDENT CHILDREN AND TO CHILDREN OF FRANCHISED DISTRIBUTORS. AWARDS TENABLE AT ANY RECOGNIZED COLLEGE OR UNIVERSITY. USA CITIZEN OR LEGAL RESIDENT.

WRITE FOR COMPLETE INFORMATION.

1653

TWO/TEN INTERNATIONAL FOOTWEAR FOUNDATION (SCHOLARSHIP PROGRAM)

56 MAIN STREET
WATERTOWN MA 02172
617/923-4500 OR 800/346-3210

AMOUNT: $200 - $2000
DEADLINE(S): DEC 16
FIELD(S): ALL FIELDS OF STUDY

OPEN TO CHILDREN OF FOOTWEAR; LEATHER & ALLIED INDUSTRIES WORKERS (FOR AT LEAST 1 YEAR) OR TO STUDENTS WHO WILL WORK AT LEAST 500 HOURS IN THESE INDUSTRIES IN THE YEAR BEFORE A SCHOLARSHIP WILL BE USED.

FOR UNDERGRAD STUDY AT 2 OR 4 YEAR COLLEGE OR AT VOC-TECH OR NURSING SCHOOL. 200+ SCHOLARSHIPS PER YEAR. USA RESIDENT. WRITE FOR COMPLETE INFORMATION.

1654

TY COBB EDUCATIONAL FOUNDATION (UNDERGRADUATE SCHOLARSHIP PROGRAM)

PO BOX 725
FOREST PARK GA 30051
WRITTEN INQUIRY

AMOUNT: $2000
DEADLINE(S): JUN 15
FIELD(S): ALL AREAS OF STUDY

OPEN TO RESIDENTS OF GEORGIA WHO HAVE COMPLETED AT LEAST ONE ACADEMIC YEAR WITH 'B' AVERAGE IN AN ACCREDITED COLLEGE. DEMONSTRATE FINANCIAL NEED.

RENEWABLE WITH REAPPLICATION AND COMPLETION OF 45 QUARTER OR 30 SEMESTER CREDIT HOURS. WRITE FOR COMPLETE INFORMATION.

1655

U.S. AIR FORCE ACADEMY (ACADEMY APPOINTMENT)

2304 CADET DR; SUITE 300
USAF ACADEMY CO 80840
719/472-2520

AMOUNT: FULL TUITION; ALL COSTS; SALARY
DEADLINE(S): JAN 31
FIELD(S): ALL FIELDS OF STUDY

APPOINTMENT IS FOR A 4-YEAR UNDERGRADUATE DEGREE FOLLOWED BY A COMMISSION AS A SECOND LIEUTENANT IN THE USAF. RECIPIENTS ARE OBLIGATED TO SIX YEARS OF ACTIVE DUTY. MUST BE USA CITIZEN BETWEEN 17 AND 22. SAT/ACT SCORES REQUIRED.

NOMINATION IS REQUIRED FOR APPOINTMENT. WRITE FOR INFORMATION ON OBTAINING NOMINATION AND FOR DETAILED ADMISSION REQUIREMENTS.

1656

U.S. ARMY EMERGENCY RELIEF (UNDERGRADUATE SCHOLARSHIP AND LOAN PROGRAMS)

200 STOVALL ST
ALEXANDRIA VA 22332
703/960-3982

AMOUNT: UP TO $1000 PER YEAR
DEADLINE(S): MAR 1
FIELD(S): ALL AREAS OF STUDY

OPEN TO UNMARRIED DEPENDENT CHILDREN OF ACTIVE; RETIRED OR DECEASED MEMBERS OF THE US ARMY. APPLICANTS MAY NOT HAVE REACHED THEIR 22ND BIRTHDAY BEFORE JUN 1 OF THE SCHOOL YEAR THAT BEGINS THE FOLLOWING SEPTEMBER. FOR UNDERGRADUATE STUDY.

SSL AND PLUS LOANS ALSO ARE AVAILABLE. MUST SUBMIT FINANCIAL AID FORM AND OFFICIAL HIGH SCHOOL TRANSCRIPT. WRITE FOR COMPLETE INFORMATION.

1657

U.S. ARMY ROTC (SCHOLARSHIPS)

SCHOLARSHIP OFFICE; 4807 ROCKSIDE RD; SUITE 310
INDEPENDENCE OH 44131
216/642-8844

AMOUNT: $1000 PER YEAR + UP TO $8000 FOR TUITION AND $800 IN ALLOWANCES
DEADLINE(S): JUL 15; DEC 1; APR 1
FIELD(S): ALL AREAS OF STUDY

OPEN TO OHIO RESIDENTS WHO ARE USA CITIZENS BETWEEN THE AGES OF 17 AND 25. FOR UNDERGRADUATE STUDY AT COLLEGES HAVING ARMY ROTC PROGRAMS. MUST HAVE 2.5 GPA AND MEET PHYSICAL STANDARDS.

4000 SCHOLARSHIPS PER YEAR OF WHICH 500 ARE LIMITED TO CANDIDATES FOR BS IN NURSING. WRITE FOR COMPLETE INFORMATION.

1658

U.S. COAST GUARD MUTUAL ASSISTANCE (ADMIRAL ROLAND STUDENT LOAN PROGRAM)
COAST GUARD HEADQUARTERS (GZMA)
WASHINGTON DC 20593
202/267-1683
AMOUNT: UP TO $2700 PER YEAR (UNDERGRADUATES); $7500 (GRADUATES)
DEADLINE(S): NONE SPECIFIED
FIELD(S): ALL AREAS OF STUDY
FOR MEMBERS & DEPENDENTS OF COAST GUARD MUTUAL ASSISTANCE MEMBERS WHO ARE ENROLLED AT LEAST ONE-HALF TIME IN AN APPROVED POST-SECONDARY SCHOOL.
LOANS RENEWABLE FOR UP TO FOUR YEARS. MUST REAPPLY ANNUALLY. WRITE FOR COMPLETE INFORMATION.

1659

U.S. DEPT. OF EDUCATION (ROBERT C. BYRD HONORS SCHOLARSHIP PROGRAM)
400 MARYLAND AVE SW; (RM 3118A; ROB-NCR)
WASHINGTON DC 20202
202/708-7861
AMOUNT: $1500/YEAR
DEADLINE(S): VARIES BY STATE
FIELD(S): ALL FIELDS OF STUDY
OPEN TO OUTSTANDING HIGH SCHOOL GRADUATES WHO HAVE BEEN ACCEPTED FOR ENROLLMENT AT AN INSTITUTION OF HIGHER EDUCATION AND ARE USA CITIZENS OR PERMANENT RESIDENTS. FOR UP TO FOUR YEARS OF STUDY.
STATE EDUCATIONAL AGENCIES RECEIVE FUNDING FROM THE US DEPARTMENT OF EDUCATION. APPLY THROUGH STATE EDUCATIONAL AGENCY OR CONTACT SCHOOL COUNSELOR FOR COMPLETE INFORMATION.

1660

U.S. DEPT. OF EDUCATION (TRIO PROGRAM)
400 MARYLAND AVE SW; ROOM 3060; ROB-3
WASHINGTON DC 20202
202/732-3270
AMOUNT: NOT SPECIFIED
DEADLINE(S): VARIES
FIELD(S): ALL FIELDS OF STUDY
SPECIAL PROGRAMS SEEK TO IDENTIFY STUDENTS FROM DISADVANTAGED BACKGROUNDS AND PREPARE THEM FOR SUCCESSFUL ENTRY; RETENTION AND COMPLETION OF A POST-SECONDARY EDUCATION.
TRIO SERVICES ARE DESIGNED TO IMPROVE ACADEMIC PERFORMANCE; INCREASE MOTIVATION AND FACILITATE TRANSITION FROM ONE LEVEL OF EDUCATION TO THE NEXT. WRITE FOR COMPLETE INFORMATION.

1661

U.S. DEPT. OF INTERIOR; BUREAU OF INDIAN AFFAIRS (HIGHER EDUCATION GRANT PROGRAM)
MS 3530; MIB 5422
WASHINGTON DC 20240
202/208-4871
AMOUNT: VARIES DEPENDING ON NEED
DEADLINE(S): VARIES
FIELD(S): ALL AREAS OF STUDY
OPEN TO ENROLLED MEMBERS OF INDIAN TRIBES OR ALASKA NATIVE DESCENDANTS ELIGIBLE TO RECEIVE SERVICES FROM THE SECRETARY OF THE INTERIOR. FOR STUDY LEADING TO ASSOCIATES; BACHELORS OR GRADUATE DEGREE.
MUST DEMONSTRATE FINANCIAL NEED. CONTACT HOME AGENCY; TRIBE OR BIA AREA OFFICE - OR FINANCIAL AID OFFICE AT CHOSEN COLLEGE.

1662

U.S. MARINE CORPS SCHOLARSHIP FOUNDATION INC. (SCHOLARSHIPS)
PO BOX 3008
PRINCETON NJ 08543
609/921-3534
AMOUNT: $500 - $2500
DEADLINE(S): FEB 1 (APPLICATIONS AVAILABLE SEPT 1)
FIELD(S): ALL AREAS OF STUDY
OPEN TO CHILDREN OF US MARINE CORPS MEMBERS OR THE DEPENDENT CHILDREN OF FORMER MARINES FOR UNDERGRADUATE OR VOCATIONAL STUDY. APPLICANT'S GROSS FAMILY INCOME SHOULD NOT EXCEED $35000.

RENEWABLE WITH WRITTEN REAPPLICATION EACH YEAR. WRITE FOR COMPLETE INFORMATION.

1663

U.S. SUBMARINE VETERANS OF WWII (SCHOLARSHIP PROGRAM)

DOLPHIN SCHOLARSHIP FDN; 405 DILLINGHAM BLVD; NORFOLK NAVAL STATION

NORFOLK VA 23511

804/440-5819

AMOUNT: VARIES

DEADLINE(S): APR 15

FIELD(S): ALL FIELDS OF STUDY

FOR CHILDREN OF PAID-UP REGULAR MEMBERS OF US SUBMARINE VETERANS OF WWII. APPLICANT MUST BE AN UNMARRIED HIGH SCHOOL SENIOR OR HAVE GRADUATED FROM HIGH SCHOOL NO MORE THAN 4 YEARS PRIOR TO APPLYING AND UNDER AGE 24.

LIST THOSE SUBMARINES IN WHICH YOUR SPONSOR SERVED DURING WWII AND INCLUDE SPONSOR'S MEMBERSHIP CARD NUMBER WHEN REQUESTING APPLICATION.

1664

UNION PACIFIC RAILROAD (EMPLOYEE DEPENDENT SCHOLARSHIP PROGRAM)

1416 DODGE ST; ROOM 320

OMAHA NE 68179

402/271-3489

AMOUNT: $750

DEADLINE(S): FEB 1

FIELD(S): ALL AREAS OF STUDY

OPEN TO HIGH SCHOOL SENIORS IN TOP 1/4 OF THEIR CLASS WHO ARE DEPENDENT CHILDREN OF CURRENT OR RETIRED FULL TIME UP RAILROAD EMPLOYEES. AWARDS TENABLE AT ANY RECOGNIZED UNDERGRADUATE COLLEGE OR UNIVERSITY.

50 AWARDS PER YEAR. RENEWABLE. WRITE FOR COMPLETE INFORMATION.

1665

UNITED DAUGHTERS OF THE CONFEDERACY (SCHOLARSHIPS)

BUSINESS OFFICE; MEMORIAL BLDG; 328 NORTH BLVD

RICHMOND VA 23220

804/355-1636

AMOUNT: $400 - $1500

DEADLINE(S): FEB 15

FIELD(S): ALL AREAS OF STUDY

OPEN TO DESCENDANTS OF WORTHY CONFEDERATE VETERANS. APPLICANTS WHO ARE COLLATERAL DESCENDANTS MUST BE ACTIVE MEMBERS OF THE UNITED DAUGHTERS OF THE CONFEDERACY OR OF THE CHILDREN OF THE CONFEDERACY & MUST BE SPONSORED BY A UDC CHAPTER.

MOST AWARDS FOR UNDERGRADUATE STUDY. FOR COMPLETE INFORMATION SEND STAMPED SELF-ADDRESSED #10 ENVELOPE TO ADDRESS ABOVE OR CONTACT THE EDUCATION DIRECTOR IN THE DIVISION WHERE YOU RESIDE.

1666

UNITED FEDERATION OF TEACHERS (COLLEGE SCHOLARSHIP FUND)

260 PARK AVE SOUTH

NEW YORK NY 10010

212/529-2110

AMOUNT: $4000 ($1000 PER YEAR)

DEADLINE(S): DEC 6

FIELD(S): ALL FIELDS OF STUDY

OPEN TO NEW YORK CITY RESIDENTS WHO ATTEND NEW YORK CITY PUBLIC HIGH SCHOOLS. SCHOLARSHIPS SUPPORT UNDERGRADUATE STUDY AT RECOGNIZED COLLEGES & UNIVERSITIES. FINANCIAL NEED AND ACADEMIC STANDING ARE CONSIDERATIONS.

APPROX 250 AWARDS PER YEAR. RENEWABLE. WRITE FOR COMPLETE INFORMATION.

1667

UNITED FOOD & COMMERCIAL WORKERS INTERNATIONAL UNION (UFCW SCHOLARSHIP PROGRAM)

1775 'K' STREET NW

WASHINGTON DC 20006

201/223-3111

AMOUNT: $1000 PER YEAR FOR 4 YEARS

DEADLINE(S): DEC 31

FIELD(S): ALL FIELDS OF STUDY

OPEN TO UFCW MEMBERS OR HIGH SCHOOL SENIORS WHO ARE CHILDREN OF MEMBERS. APPLICANTS MUST MEET CERTAIN ELIGIBILITY REQUIREMENTS. AWARDS FOR FULL TIME STUDY ONLY.

14 AWARDS PER YEAR. CONTACT WILLIAM WYNN; PRESIDENT; ADDRESS ABOVE FOR COMPLETE INFORMATION.

1668

UNITED FOOD & COMMERCIAL WORKERS UNION - LOCAL 555 (SCHOLARSHIP PROGRAM)
PO BOX 23555
TIGARD OR 97223
503/684-2822
AMOUNT: $900 - $1200
DEADLINE(S): MAR 15
FIELD(S): ALL FIELDS OF STUDY
PROGRAM OPEN ONLY TO LOCAL 555 MEMBERS (IN GOOD STANDING FOR AT LEAST 1 YEAR); THEIR CHILDREN & SPOUSES. SCHOLARSHIPS MAY BE USED AT ANY ACCREDITED UNIVERSITY; COLLEGE; TECHNICAL-VOCATIONAL SCHOOL; JUNIOR COLLEGE OR COMMUNITY COLLEGE.
WRITE FOR COMPLETE INFORMATION ONLY IF YOU ARE A UFCW LOCAL 555 MEMBER OR RELATIVE OF A MEMBER.

1669

UNITED NEGRO COLLEGE FUND (SCHOLARSHIPS)
EDUCATIONAL SERVICES DEPARTMENT; 500 E 62ND ST
NEW YORK NY 10021
212/326-1100
AMOUNT: $500 TO $7500 PER YEAR
DEADLINE(S): VARIES
FIELD(S): ALL AREAS OF STUDY
SCHOLARSHIPS AVAILABLE TO STUDENTS WHO ENROLL IN ONE OF THE 41 UNITED NEGRO COLLEGE FUND MEMBER INSTITUTIONS. FINANCIAL NEED MUST BE ESTABLISHED THROUGH THE FINANCIAL AID OFFICE AT A UNCF COLLEGE.
FOR INFORMATION AND A LIST OF THE UNCF CAMPUSES WRITE TO THE ADDRESS ABOVE.

1670

UNITED PAPERWORKERS INTERNATIONAL UNION (SCHOLARSHIP PROGRAM)
PO BOX 1475
NASHVILLE TN 37202
615/834-8590
AMOUNT: $1000
DEADLINE(S): MAR 15
FIELD(S): ALL FIELDS OF STUDY
SCHOLARSHIPS OPEN TO HIGH SCHOOL SENIORS WHO ARE SONS OR DAUGHTERS OF PAID-UP UNION MEMBERS OF AT LEAST ONE YEAR. AWARDS TENABLE AT ACCREDITED UNDERGRADUATE COLLEGES & UNIVERSITIES. USA OR CANADIAN CITIZEN.
22 AWARDS PER YEAR. RECIPIENTS ARE ASKED TO TAKE AT LEAST 1 LABOR COURSE DURING THEIR COLLEGE CAREER. FINANCIAL NEED IS A CONSIDERATION. WRITE FOR COMPLETE INFORMATION.

1671

UNITED STATES JAYCEES (WAR MEMORIAL FUND SCHOLARSHIP PROGRAM)
PO BOX 7
TULSA OK 74102
WRITTEN INQUIRY
AMOUNT: $1000
DEADLINE(S): MAR 1
FIELD(S): ALL FIELDS OF STUDY
OPEN TO USA CITIZENS. SPECIAL CONSIDERATION TO HIGH SCHOOL SENIORS PREPARING TO ENTER COLLEGE AS FIRST QUARTER FRESHMEN. MUST BE ENROLLED IN OR ACCEPTED FOR ADMISSION TO A COLLEGE OR UNIVERSITY AND DEMONSTRATE FINANCIAL NEED.
APPLICATIONS AVAILABLE ONLY BETWEEN JULY 1 AND FEB 1. SEND SELF-ADDRESSED STAMPED BUSINESS SIZE ENVELOPE AND $5 APPLICATION FEE TO JWMF DEPT 94922; TULSA OK 74194-0001.

1672

UNITED STEELWORKERS OF AMERICA-DISTRICT 7 (HUGH CARCELLA SCHOLARSHIP PROGRAM)
1017 W 9TH AVE; #A & B
KING OF PRUSSIA PA 19406
215/265-7577
AMOUNT: $750 - $3000
DEADLINE(S): MAR 15
FIELD(S): ALL AREAS OF STUDY
MUST BE MEMBER IN GOOD STANDING; OR SON OR DAUGHTER OR LEGAL WARD OF MEMBER OF UNITED STEELWORKERS OF AMERICA DISTRICT 7 LOCAL UNION; PARTICIPATING IN THE SCHOLARSHIP PROGRAM. MUST BE ENTERING FRESHMAN PURSUING A BS DEGREE.
8 SCHOLARSHIPS PER YEAR. RENEWABLE. WRITE FOR COMPLETE INFORMATION.

1673

UNITED STUDENT AID FUNDS INC. (GUARANTEED STUDENT LOAN PROGRAM; PLUS LOANS)
1912 CAPITOL AVE; #320
CHEYENNE WY 82001
307/635-3259
AMOUNT: $2645 - $4000 UNDERGRADUATES; $7500 GRADUATES
DEADLINE(S): NONE
FIELD(S): ALL FIELDS OF STUDY
LOW-INTEREST LOANS ARE AVAILABLE TO WYOMING RESIDENTS WHO ARE CITIZENS OR PERMANENT RESIDENTS OF THE USA & ENROLLED AT LEAST 1/2 TIME IN SCHOOL. MUST DEMONSTRATE FINANCIAL NEED.
WRITE FOR COMPLETE INFORMATION.

1674

UNITED TRANSPORTATION UNION (SCHOLARSHIP PROGRAM)
14600 DETROIT AVENUE
CLEVELAND OH 44107
216/228-9400
AMOUNT: $500
DEADLINE(S): MAR 31
FIELD(S): ALL AREAS OF STUDY
OPEN TO USA OR CANADIAN CITIZENS WHO ARE HIGH SCHOOL GRADUATES UNDER AGE 25 AND ARE EITHER UTU MEMBERS OR THE CHILDREN OR GRANDCHILDREN OF UTU MEMBERS. MUST MAINTAIN SATISFACTORY ACADEMIC RECORD.
50 SCHOLARSHIPS PER YEAR. RENEWABLE UP TO 4 YEARS. AWARDED ON LOTTERY SYSTEM. WRITE FOR COMPLETE INFORMATION.

1675

UNIVERSITY OF NEBRASKA AT LINCOLN (REGENTS; DAVID; DAVIS; NATIONAL MERIT & DEPARTMENTAL SCHOLARSHIPS)
16 ADMINISTRATION BLDG
LINCOLN NE 68588
401/472-2030
AMOUNT: VARIES
DEADLINE(S): DEC 15 PRECEDING FALL SEMESTER
FIELD(S): ALL AREAS OF STUDY
OPEN TO NEBRASKA HIGH SCHOOL GRADUATES WHO HAVE TAKEN THE ACT OR SAT AND SENT SCORES TO UNL. VARIETY OF SCHOLARSHIPS AVAILABLE; SOME FOR MINORITIES; SOME BASED ON FINANCIAL NEED; VARIOUS OTHER REQUIREMENTS.
BY SUBMITTING APPLICATION FOR FRESHMAN SCHOLARSHIPS, STUDENT IS COMPETING FOR APPROXIMATELY 1500 OTHER INDIVIDUAL SCHOLARSHIP PROGRAMS AT UNL. WRITE FOR COMPLETE INFORMATION.

1676

UNIVERSITY OF NEW MEXICO (SCHOLARSHIPS)
MESA HALL NORTH
ALBUQUERQUE NM 87131
505/277-6090
AMOUNT: VARYING AMOUNTS TO $2000
DEADLINE(S): FEB 1
FIELD(S): ALL FIELDS OF STUDY
THE UNIVERSITY OF NEW MEXICO AWARDS TO ELIGIBLE FIRST-TIME FRESHMEN MORE THAN 1000 SCHOLARSHIPS FROM SIX MAJOR SCHOLARSHIP PROGRAMS. CONSIDERATIONS INCLUDE EXTRACURRICULAR ACTIVITIES AND PERSONAL STATEMENT. USA CITIZEN.
CONTACT DEPARTMENT OF STUDENT FINANCIAL AID AND SCHOLARSHIPS; ADDRESS ABOVE; FOR COMPLETE INFORMATION.

1677

UNIVERSITY OF OXFORD-SOMERVILLE COLLEGE (JANET WATSON BURSARY)
COLLEGE SECRETARY; SOMERVILLE COLLEGE
OXFORD OX2 6HD ENGLAND
865-270600
AMOUNT: 2400 POUNDS STERLING
DEADLINE(S): APR 1
FIELD(S): ALL FIELDS OF STUDY
BURSARY IS OFFERED FOR A USA WOMAN GRADUATE WISHING TO READ FOR A FURTHER DEGREE AT OXFORD AS A MEMBER OF THE COLLEGE. SOMERVILLE ADMITS ONLY WOMEN. USA CITIZEN.
RENEWABLE FOR A SECOND YEAR. WRITE FOR COMPLETE INFORMATION.

1678

UNIVERSITY OF WINDSOR (UNDERGRADUATE SCHOLARSHIPS)
STUDENT AWARDS OFFICE
WINDSOR ONTARIO N9B 3P4 CANADA
519/253-4232
AMOUNT: APPROX $600
DEADLINE(S): MAY 31; DEC 31
FIELD(S): ALL FIELDS OF STUDY

FOR USA CITIZENS WHO HAVE SUPERIOR GRADES AND WISH TO STUDY AT WINDSOR UNIVERSITY. IN-COURSE AWARDS ARE AVAILABLE TO THOSE WHO ARE ALREADY ENROLLED. STUDENT MUST COMPLETE ALL ADMISSIONS REQUIREMENTS.

RENEWABLE FOR THREE YEARS IF QUALIFYING AVERAGE IS MAINTAINED. WRITE FOR COMPLETE INFORMATION AND A CATALOG OF AVAILABLE UNDERGRADUATE SCHOLARSHIPS.

1679

URANN FOUNDATION (SCHOLARSHIP PROGRAM)

ROBERT C. LEBOEUF; ADMINISTRATOR; PO BOX 1788

BROCKTON MA 02403

617/588-7744

AMOUNT: VARIES

DEADLINE(S): APR 15

FIELD(S): ALL AREAS OF STUDY

SCHOLARSHIP PROGRAM OPEN TO CHILDREN OF CRANBERRY GROWERS & THEIR EMPLOYEES (IN THE STATE OF MASSACHUSETTS ONLY). AWARDS ARE TENABLE AT ELIGIBLE 2-YEAR & 4-YEAR UNDERGRADUATE COLLEGES & UNIVERSITIES.

WRITE FOR COMPLETE INFORMATION.

1680

UTAH BOARD OF REGENTS (STUDENT INCENTIVE GRANTS; EDUCATIONALLY DISADVANTAGED FUND)

355 W NORTH TEMPLE #3 TRIAD SUITE 550

SALT LAKE CITY UT 84180

SCHOOL FINANCIAL AID OFFICE

AMOUNT: $2500; $100-$1500

DEADLINE(S): NONE SPECIFIED

FIELD(S): ALL AREAS OF STUDY

UTAH RESIDENT ATTENDING ELIGIBLE UTAH SCHOOL. PURPOSE OF THESE AWARDS IS TO MAKE INCENTIVE GRANTS AVAILABLE TO STUDENTS WITH SUBSTANTIAL FINANCIAL NEED TO ENABLE THEM TO ATTEND OR CONTINUE THEIR STUDIES. US CITIZEN OR LEGAL RESIDENT.

2000 AWARDS PER YEAR. AWARDS ARE MADE THROUGH FINANCIAL AID OFFICE AT EACH ELIGIBLE INSTITUTION. WRITE FOR COMPLETE INFORMATION.

1681

UTILITY WORKERS UNION OF AMERICA (SCHOLARSHIP PROGRAM)

815 16TH STREET NW

WASHINGTON DC 20006

WRITTEN INQUIRY

AMOUNT: $2000

DEADLINE(S): JAN 1 OF JUNIOR YEAR IN HIGH SCHOOL

FIELD(S): ALL FIELDS OF STUDY

SCHOLARSHIPS ARE FOR SONS AND DAUGHTERS OF UTILITY WORKERS UNION MEMBERS IN GOOD STANDING. WINNERS ARE SELECTED FROM THE GROUP OF HIGH SCHOOL JUNIORS WHO TAKE THE NATIONAL MERIT SCHOLARSHIP EXAMS.

2 FOUR-YEAR SCHOLARSHIPS AWARDED ANNUALLY.

1682

VASA ORDER OF AMERICA (COLLEGE OR VOCATIONAL AWARDS)

E.G. JOHNSON; VICE GRAND MASTER; 4406 SALMON POINT

STOCKTON CA 95219

209/478-7498

AMOUNT: $750

DEADLINE(S): JAN 15

FIELD(S): ALL FIELDS OF STUDY

OPEN TO STUDENTS PLANNING TO CONTINUE ACADEMIC EDUCATION IN A COLLEGE OR VOCATIONAL SCHOOL ON A FULL TIME EQUIVALENT BASIS. ONE YEAR MEMBERSHIP IN THE VASA ORDER OF AMERICA IS REQUIRED. MUST DEMONSTRATE FINANCIAL NEED.

NINE AWARDS PER YEAR. WRITE FOR COMPLETE INFORMATION.

1683

VASA ORDER OF AMERICA (OSCAR AND MILDRED LARSON AWARD)

E.G. JOHNSON; VICE GRAND MASTER; 4406 SALMON POINT

STOCKTON CA 95219

209/478-7498

AMOUNT: $2500 PER YEAR/4 YEARS

DEADLINE(S): JAN 15

FIELD(S): OPEN TO RESIDENTS OF THE USA; CANADA OR SWEDEN WHO WERE BORN IN SWEDEN OR ARE OF SWEDISH ANCESTRY. APPLICANTS MUST BE ENROLLED OR

ACCEPTED AS A FULL TIME UNDERGRAD OR GRAD STUDENT IN AN ACCREDITED 4-YEAR COLLEGE OR UNIVERSITY IN THE USA.
FINANCIAL NEED IS A CONSIDERATION. RENEWABLE. WRITE FOR COMPLETE INFORMATION.

1684

VASA ORDER OF AMERICA (THE FERNSTROM AWARD)
E.G. JOHNSON; VICE GRAND MASTER; 4406 SALMON POINT
STOCKTON CA 95219
209/478-7498
AMOUNT: $750
DEADLINE(S): JAN 15
FIELD(S): ALL FIELDS OF STUDY
OPEN TO HIGH SCHOOL SENIORS OR COLLEGE UNDERGRADUATES PLANNING TO CONTINUE THEIR EDUCATION ON A FULL TIME BASIS. ONE YEAR OF MEMBERSHIP IN THE VASA ORDER OF AMERICA IS REQUIRED. MUST DEMONSTRATE FINANCIAL NEED.
WRITE FOR COMPLETE INFORMATION.

1685

VASA ORDER OF AMERICA (THE GLADYS A. AND RUSSELL M. BIRTWISTLE AWARD)
E.G. JOHNSON; VICE GRAND MASTER; 4406 SALMON POINT
STOCKTON CA 95219
209/478-7498
AMOUNT: $2000
DEADLINE(S): JAN 15
FIELD(S): ALL FIELDS OF STUDY
OPEN TO HIGH SCHOOL SENIORS OR COLLEGE UNDERGRADUATES WHO PLAN TO CONTINUE THEIR EDUCATION FULL TIME AT AN ACCREDITED INSTITUTION OF HIGHER LEARNING. MUST DEMONSTRATE FINANCIAL NEED.
APPLICANTS MUST HAVE BEEN A VASA MEMBER IN ONE OF THE FOLLOWING DISTRICTS FOR AT LEAST ONE YEAR - CONNECTICUT NO.1; MASSACHUSETTS NO. 2; RHODE ISLAND NO. 3. WRITE FOR COMPLETE INFORMATION.

1686

VASA ORDER OF AMERICA (THE IRMA AND KNUTE CARLSON AWARD)
E.G. JOHNSON; VICE GRAND MASTER; 4406 SALMON POINT
STOCKTON CA 95219
209/478-7498
AMOUNT: $750
DEADLINE(S): JAN 15
FIELD(S): ALL FIELDS OF STUDY
OPEN TO UPPER CLASS COLLEGE STUDENTS (JUNIORS OR SENIORS) OR GRADUATE STUDENTS WHO HAVE BEEN A MEMBER OF THE VASA ORDER OF AMERICA FOR AT LEAST ONE YEAR. MUST DEMONSTRATE FINANCIAL NEED.
WRITE FOR COMPLETE INFORMATION.

1687

VERMONT STATE LABOR COUNCIL AFL-CIO (JAMES CROSS SCHOLARSHIP)
PO BOX 858; 149 STATE ST
MONTPELIER VT 05602
802/223-5229
AMOUNT: $1500
DEADLINE(S): MAR 15
FIELD(S): ALL AREAS OF STUDY
VERMONT RESIDENT. OPEN TO GRADUATING HIGH SCHOOL SENIORS WHO ARE DEPENDENT CHILDREN OF MEMBERS OF A UNION AFFILIATED WITH THE VERMONT AFL-CIO. AWARDS TENABLE AT RECOGNIZED UNDERGRADUATE COLLEGES & UNIVERSITIES.
CONTACT ADDRESS ABOVE FOR COMPLETE DETAILS.

1688

VERMONT STUDENT ASSISTANCE CORPORATION (INCENTIVE GRANTS)
CHAMPLAIN MILL; PO BOX 2000
WINOOSKI VT 05404
802/655-9602
AMOUNT: $300 - $4950 (AVERAGE $1210)
DEADLINE(S): MAR 1
FIELD(S): ALL FIELDS OF STUDY
OPEN TO VERMONT RESIDENTS ENROLLED AS FULL TIME UNDERGRADUATE STUDENTS IN APPROVED DEGREE PROGRAMS. MUST DEMONSTRATE FINANCIAL NEED AND BE USA CITIZEN OR LEGAL RESIDENT.
WRITE FOR COMPLETE INFORMATION.

1689

VIKKI CARR SCHOLARSHIP FOUNDATION (SCHOLARSHIPS)
PO BOX 5126
BEVERLY HILLS CA 90210
WRITTEN INQUIRY
AMOUNT: UP TO $3000
DEADLINE(S): APR 1

FIELD(S): ALL AREAS OF STUDY

OPEN TO MEXICAN-AMERICAN CALIFORNIA RESIDENTS BETWEEN THE AGES OF 17 AND 22. AWARDS ARE FOR UNDERGRADUATE STUDY AT ACCREDITED COLLEGES & UNIVERSITIES. USA CITIZEN.

5-10 AWARDS PER YEAR. APPLICATIONS AVAILABLE JAN 1. SEND STAMPED SELF-ADDRESSED ENVELOPE FOR COMPLETE INFORMATION.

1690

VIRGIN ISLANDS BOARD OF EDUCATION (EXCEPTIONAL CHILDREN SCHOLARSHIP)

PO BOX 11900
ST THOMAS VI 00801
809/774-4546

AMOUNT: $2000

DEADLINE(S): MAR 31

FIELD(S): ALL AREAS OF STUDY

OPEN TO BONAFIDE RESIDENTS OF THE VIRGIN ISLANDS WHO SUFFER FROM PHYSICAL; MENTAL OR EMOTIONAL IMPAIRMENT & HAVE DEMONSTRATED EXCEPTIONAL ABILITIES & THE NEED OF EDUCATIONAL TRAINING NOT AVAILABLE IN VIRGIN ISLANDS SCHOOLS.

NOT FOR STUDY AT THE COLLEGE LEVEL. WRITE FOR COMPLETE INFORMATION.

1691

VIRGIN ISLANDS BOARD OF EDUCATION (TERRITORAL SCHOLARSHIP GRANTS)

PO BOX 11900
ST THOMAS VI 00801
809/774-4546

AMOUNT: $1000 - $3000

DEADLINE(S): MAR 31

FIELD(S): ALL AREAS OF STUDY

GRANTS OPEN TO BONAFIDE RESIDENTS OF THE VIRGIN ISLANDS WHO HAVE A CUMULATIVE GPA OF AT LEAST 'C' & ARE ENROLLED IN AN ACCREDITED INSTITUTION OF HIGHER LEARNING.

300-400 GRANTS PER YEAR. RENEWABLE PROVIDED RECIPIENT MAINTAINS AN AVERAGE OF 'C' OR BETTER. LOANS ARE ALSO AVAILABLE. CONTACT ADDRESS ABOVE FOR COMPLETE DETAILS.

1692

VIRGINIA DEPT. OF VETERANS' AFFAIRS (WAR ORPHANS EDUCATION PROGRAM)

PO BOX 809; 210 FRANKLIN RD SW; #1012
ROANOKE VA 24004
703/857-7104

AMOUNT: FREE TUITION

DEADLINE(S): NONE

FIELD(S): ALL FIELDS OF STUDY

OPEN TO SURVIVING/DEPENDENT CHILDREN (AGED 16-25) OF USA MILITARY PERSONNEL WHO WERE/ARE VIRGINIA RESIDENTS & AS A RESULT OF WAR/ARMED CONFLICT ARE DECEASED; DISABLED; PRISONER OF WAR OR MISSING IN ACTION.

ELIGIBLE APPLICANTS ENTITLED TO UP TO 48 MONTHS OF FREE TUITION AT ANY STATE SUPPORTED VOCATIONAL; UNDERGRADUATE OR GRADUATE INSTITUTION. WRITE FOR COMPLETE INFORMATION.

1693

VIRGINIA STATE COUNCIL OF HIGHER EDUCATION (TUITION ASSISTANCE GRANT PROGRAM)

101 N 14TH ST; JAMES MONROE BLDG
RICHMOND VA 23219
804/225-2141

AMOUNT: $1275

DEADLINE(S): JUL 31; SEP 10

FIELD(S): ALL AREAS OF STUDY

OPEN TO VIRGINIA RESIDENTS WHO ARE FULL TIME UNDERGRADUATE; GRADUATE OR PROFESSIONAL STUDENTS AT ELIGIBLE PRIVATE COLLEGES & UNIVERSITIES IN VIRGINIA.

GRANTS ARE RENEWABLE UP TO 4 YEARS FOR UNDERGRADUATE STUDENTS & UP TO 3 YEARS FOR GRADUATE STUDENTS. WRITE FOR COMPLETE INFORMATION.

1694

VIRGINIA STATE COUNCIL OF HIGHER EDUCATION (COLLEGE SCHOLARSHIP ASSISTANCE PROGRAM)

101 N 14TH ST; JAMES MONROE BLDG
RICHMOND VA 23219
804/225-2141

AMOUNT: $400 - $2000

DEADLINE(S): VARIES

FIELD(S): ALL FIELDS OF STUDY EXCEPT RELIGION

OPEN TO VIRGINIA RESIDENTS WHO ARE UNDERGRADUATE STUDENTS (WITH AT LEAST 6 CREDIT HOURS) AT ELIGIBLE VIRGINIA COLLEGES & UNIVERSITIES. APPLICANTS MAY NOT BE ENROLLED IN A PROGRAM OF RELIGIOUS TRAINING OR THEOLOGICAL EDUCATION.

WRITE FOR COMPLETE INFORMATION OR CONTACT YOUR INSTITUTION'S FINANCIAL AID OFFICE.

1695

VIRGINIA STATE COUNCIL OF HIGHER EDUCATION (UNDERGRADUATE FINANCIAL ASSISTANCE 'LAST DOLLAR' PROGRAM)
JAMES MONROE BLDG; 101 N 14TH ST
RICHMOND VA 23219
804/225-2141
AMOUNT: MINIMUM $200 PER TERM
DEADLINE(S): NONE SPECIFIED
FIELD(S): ALL AREAS OF STUDY

'LAST DOLLAR' IS A NEED-BASED PROGRAM DESIGNED TO ASSIST BLACK VIRGINIA STUDENTS IN ATTENDING STATE SUPPORTED COLLEGES ON AT LEAST A HALF-TIME BASIS. MUST BE VIRGINIA RESIDENT AND ENROLLED IN A VIRGINIA INSTITUTION.

CONTACT THE FINANCIAL AID OFFICE AT YOUR COLLEGE OR UNIVERSITY.

1696

VIRGINIA STATE COUNCIL OF HIGHER EDUCATION (VIRGINIA SCHOLARS PROGRAM)
101 N 14TH ST; JAMES MONROE BLDG
RICHMOND VA 23219
804/225-2141
AMOUNT: $3000
DEADLINE(S): DEC 15 (H.S.); MAY 15 (TRANSFER)
FIELD(S): ALL AREAS OF STUDY

VIRGINIA RESIDENTS. FOR OUTSTANDING HIGH SCHOOL SENIORS OR GRADUATES OF PUBLIC 2-YEAR COLLEGES WHO PLAN TO ENROLL AS FULL TIME UNDERGRADS AT A 4-YR VIRGINIA COLLEGE OR UNIV. MUST BE NOMINATED BY YOUR HIGH SCHOOL OR PUBLIC 2-YR COLLEGE.

GRANTS ARE MERIT BASED. RENEWABLE UP TO 3 ADDITIONAL YEARS. WRITE FOR COMPLETE INFORMATION.

1697

VIRGINIA STATE COUNCIL OF HIGHER EDUCATION (VIRGINIA TRANSFER GRANT PROGRAM)
101 N 14TH ST; JAMES MONROE BLDG
RICHMOND VA 23219
804/225-2141
AMOUNT: FULL TUITION & FEES
DEADLINE(S): VARIES
FIELD(S): ALL AREAS OF STUDY

OPEN TO 'OTHER RACE' STUDENTS WHO ENROLL AT LEAST HALF TIME IN A TRADITIONALLY WHITE OR BLACK PUBLIC 4-YEAR INSTITUTION IN VIRGINIA. MUST BE VA RESIDENTS; MEET MINIMUM MERIT CRITERIA & QUALIFY FOR ENTRY AS FIRST TIME TRANSFER STUDENTS.

CONTACT COLLEGE FINANCIAL AID OFFICE FOR COMPLETE INFORMATION.

1698

VIRGINIA STUDENT ASSISTANCE AUTHORITIES (GUARANTEED STUDENT LOAN PROGRAMS)
411 E FRANKLIN ST; SUITE 300
RICHMOND VA 23219
804/755-4000 OR 800/792-LOAN
AMOUNT: VARIES
DEADLINE(S): NONE
FIELD(S): ALL FIELDS OF STUDY

VARIOUS LOAN PROGRAMS OPEN TO STUDENTS ENROLLED IN APPROVED INSTITUTIONS. ELIGIBILITY GOVERNED BY SEAA & FEDERAL REGULATIONS.

CONTACT COLLEGE FINANCIAL AID OFFICE OR WRITE TO ADDRESS ABOVE FOR COMPLETE INFORMATION.

1699

VON TROTHA EDUCATIONAL TRUST (VON TROTHA SCHOLARSHIP)
TRUST DEPT; PO BOX 1057; 1000 10TH ST
GREELEY CO 80631
303/356-1000
AMOUNT: $300 TO $500
DEADLINE(S): MAR 31
FIELD(S): ALL AREAS OF STUDY

SCHOLARSHIPS ARE OPEN TO GRADUATES OF WELD COUNTY, COLORADO HIGH SCHOOLS WHO ARE IN UPPER 25% OF THEIR CLASS. TO BE USED ONLY AT ACCREDITED COLLEGES AND UNIVERSITIES.

WRITE FOR COMPLETE INFORMATION.

1700

WAL-MART FOUNDATION (SCHOLARSHIP PROGRAM)
702 SW 8TH ST
BENTONVILLE AR 72716
501/273-6878
AMOUNT: $1000
DEADLINE(S): ESTABLISHED BY EACH STORE
FIELD(S): ALL FIELDS OF STUDY
OPEN TO HIGH SCHOOL SENIORS WHO LIVE WITHIN THE ADVERTISING AREA OF A WAL-MART STORE. EACH WAL-MART STORE GIVES ONE SCHOLARSHIP EACH YEAR. CONSIDERATIONS INCLUDE ACADEMIC RECORD; SCHOOL ACTIVITIES; FINANCIAL NEED.
CONTACT SCHOOL COUNSELOR FOR APPLICATION FORMS AND COMPLETE INFORMATION ON ELIGIBILITY REQUIREMENTS.

1701

WALTER S. AND EVAN C. JONES FOUNDATION (EDUCATIONAL ASSISTANCE PROGRAM)
527 COMMERCIAL ST; ROOM 515
EMPORIA KS 66801
316/342-1714
AMOUNT: VARIES WITH NEED
DEADLINE(S): JUN 1 FOR FALL SEMESTER; NOV 1 FOR SPRING
FIELD(S): ALL FIELDS OF STUDY
OPEN TO UNDERGRADUATE AND TECHNICAL SCHOOL STUDENTS WHO HAVE LIVED IN OSAGE; COFFEE OR LYON COUNTY (KANSAS) FOR AT LEAST 1 YEAR PRIOR TO APPLICATION. MUST HAVE 2.0 OR BETTER GPA AND DEMONSTRATE FINANCIAL NEED.
RENEWABLE. WRITE FOR COMPLETE INFORMATION.

1702

WASHINGTON HIGHER EDUCATION COORDINATING BOARD (WASHINGTON STATE NEED GRANT PROGRAM)
PO BOX 43430; 917 LAKERIDGE WAY; GV-11
OLYMPIA WA 98504
206/753-2210
AMOUNT: VARIES
DEADLINE(S): VARIES BY SCHOOL
FIELD(S): ALL FIELDS OF STUDY EXCEPT THEOLOGY
OPEN TO RESIDENTS OF WASHINGTON STATE FOR AT LEAST 1 YEAR PRIOR TO ENROLLMENT. AWARDS TENABLE AT ELIGIBLE WASHINGTON STATE COLLEGES & UNIVERSITIES. FOR UNDERGRADUATE STUDY. MUST ATTEND AT LEAST HALF TIME & BE USA CITIZEN OR LEGAL RESIDENT.
22000 GRANTS PER YEAR. RENEWABLE. DO NOT APPLY DIRECTLY. APPLY AS PART OF REGULAR FINANCIAL AID APPLICATION PROCESS AT ANY WASHINGTON STATE COLLEGE; UNIVERSITY OR TECHNICAL OR PROPRIETARY SCHOOL.

1703

WASHINGTON POST (THOMAS EWING MEMORIAL EDUCATIONAL GRANTS FOR NEWSPAPER CARRIERS)
1150 15TH ST NW
WASHINGTON DC 20079
202/334-5799
AMOUNT: $1000 - $2000
DEADLINE(S): LAST FRIDAY IN JANUARY
FIELD(S): ALL AREAS
OPEN TO CURRENT POST CARRIERS WHO HAVE BEEN ON-ROUTE THE PAST 18 MONTHS. AWARD IS INTENDED TO ASSIST & ENCOURAGE PURSUIT OF HIGHER EDUCATION AT ANY LEVEL.
25-35 AWARDS PER YEAR. WRITE FOR COMPLETE INFORMATION.

1704

WASHINGTON STATE PTA (FINANCIAL GRANT FOUNDATION PROGRAM)
2003 65TH AVE WEST
TACOMA WA 98466
206/565-2153
AMOUNT: $500 - $1000
DEADLINE(S): MAR 1
FIELD(S): ALL FIELDS OF STUDY
OPEN TO WASHINGTON STATE RESIDENTS. GRANT PROGRAM IS DESIGNED TO ASSIST WASHINGTON STATE HIGH SCHOOL SENIORS & GRADUATES WHO WILL BE ENTERING FRESHMEN AT AN ACCREDITED COLLEGE OR UNIVERSITY. FINANCIAL NEED IS PRIMARY CONSIDERATION.
WRITE FOR COMPLETE INFORMATION.

1705

WASIE FOUNDATION (SCHOLARSHIP PROGRAM)
909 FOSHAY TOWER
MINNEAPOLIS MN 55402
612/332-3883
AMOUNT: $1000 - $5000
DEADLINE(S): APR 15
FIELD(S): ALL FIELDS OF STUDY

UNDERGRADUATE & GRADUATE SCHOLARSHIPS OPEN TO QUALIFIED STUDENTS OF POLISH DESCENT WHO ARE OF THE CHRISTIAN FAITH. AWARDS TENABLE ONLY IN MINNESOTA AT 10 SPECIFIED INSTITUTIONS OF HIGHER EDUCATION.

50 AWARDS PER YEAR. WRITE FOR LIST OF MINNESOTA COLLEGES AT WHICH AWARD IS TENABLE. APPLICATIONS ARE SENT OUT IN JANUARY AND MUST BE RECEIVED BY APR 15.

1706

WELLESLEY COLLEGE (ALICE FREEMAN PALMER FELLOWSHIPS)
OFFICE OF FINANCIAL AID; BOX GR; SECRETARY GRADUATE FELLOWSHIPS
WELLESLEY MA 02181
617-235-0320
AMOUNT: UP TO $4000 STIPEND
DEADLINE(S): DEC 15
FIELD(S): ALL AREAS OF STUDY

OPEN TO UNMARRIED WOMEN UNDER 27 YEARS OLD. FELLOWSHIPS ARE FOR GRADUATE STUDY OR RESEARCH AT INSTITUTION OF YOUR CHOICE IN USA OR ABROAD. SHOULD REMAIN UNMARRIED THROUGHOUT AWARD TENURE.

NON WELLSELEY GRADS SHOULD APPLY THROUGH THE INSTITUTION FROM WHICH THEY RECEIVED BACHELOR'S DEGREE. WELLESLEY WILL NOT MAIL APPLICATIONS AFTER NOV 20.

1707

WELLESLEY COLLEGE (FELLOWSHIPS FOR WELLESLEY GRADUATES)
OFFICE OF FINANCIAL AID; BOX GR; SECRETARY GRADUATE FELLOWSHIPS
WELLESLEY MA 02181
617/235-0320
AMOUNT: $1000 - $14000 STIPEND
DEADLINE(S): DEC 15
FIELD(S): ALL FIELDS OF STUDY

NUMEROUS FELLOWSHIP PROGRAMS IN VARIOUS AREAS OF STUDY OPEN TO WELLESLEY COLLEGE GRADUATING SENIORS AND WELLESLEY COLLEGE GRADUATES. FOR GRADUATE STUDY OR RESEARCH AT INSTITUTION OF YOUR CHOICE IN USA OR ABROAD.

APPLICATIONS AVAILABLE FROM SEP 1 TO NOV 24. WRITE FOR COMPLETE INFORMATION.

1708

WELSH SOCIETY OF PHILADELPHIA (SCHOLARSHIPS)
450 S BROADWAY
CAMDEN NJ 08103
WRITTEN INQUIRY ONLY
AMOUNT: $500 - $1500
DEADLINE(S): MAR 1
FIELD(S): ALL FIELDS OF STUDY

OPEN TO UNDERGRADUATE STUDENTS OF WELSH DESCENT WHO LIVE WITHIN 150 MILES OF PHILADELPHIA OR PLAN TO ENROLL IN A COLLEGE WITHIN THAT AREA. MUST PROVE WELSH DESCENT.

5 TO 6 AWARDS PER YEAR; RENEWABLE. SEND SELF-ADDRESSED STAMPED ENVELOPE TO DANIEL E. WILLIAMS; YSGRIFENNYDD CYMDEITHAS GYMREIG/PHILADELPHIA; ADDRESS ABOVE FOR APPLICATION AND COMPLETE INFORMATION.

1709

WEST VIRGINIA DIVISION OF VETERANS' AFFAIRS (WAR ORPHANS EDUCATION PROGRAM)
1321 PLAZA EAST; SUITE 101
CHARLESTON WV 25301
304/558-3661
AMOUNT: $400 - $500 PER YEAR
DEADLINE(S): JUL 15; DEC 1
FIELD(S): ALL AREAS OF STUDY

OPEN TO SURVIVING CHILDREN (AGED 16-23) OF USA MILITARY PERSONNEL WHOSE ACTIVE DUTY SERVICE IN US ARMED FORCES INVOLVED HOSTILE ACTION. DEATH OF PARENT MUST HAVE BEEN THE RESULT OF A DISABILITY INCURRED DURING SUCH WARTIME SERVICE.

STUDENT MUST HAVE LIVED IN WV FOR 1 YEAR PRIOR TO INITIAL APPLICATION. AWARDS TENABLE AT ANY STATE SUPPORTED HIGH SCHOOL; COLLEGE OR UNIVERSITY. WRITE FOR COMPLETE INFORMATION.

1710

WESTERN GOLF ASSOCIATION (EVANS SCHOLARS FOUNDATION)
SCHOLARSHIP COMMITTEE
GOLF IL 60029
708/724-4600
AMOUNT: FULL TUITION & HOUSING
DEADLINE(S): NOV 1
FIELD(S): ALL FIELDS OF STUDY
OPEN TO USA HIGH SCHOOL SENIORS IN TOP 25% OF THEIR CLASS WHO HAVE SERVED AS A CADDIE AT A WGA MEMBER CLUB FOR AT LEAST TWO YEARS. NEED CONSIDERED. APPLICATIONS ARE ACCEPTED FOLLOWING THE JUNIOR YEAR IN HIGH SCHOOL BETWEEN JUL 1 AND NOV 1.
200 AWARDS PER YEAR RENEWABLE FOR FOUR YEARS. CONTACT YOUR LOCAL COUNTRY CLUB OR WRITE TO ADDRESS ABOVE FOR COMPLETE INFORMATION.

1711

WESTINGHOUSE FAMILY SCHOLARSHIP PROGRAM (SCHOLARSHIPS)
11 STANWIX STREET; ROOM 1042
PITTSBURGH PA 15222
412/642-6033
AMOUNT: $3000 - $12000
DEADLINE(S): DEC 1
FIELD(S): ALL AREAS OF STUDY
SCHOLARSHIPS ARE FOR SONS AND DAUGHTERS OF CURRENT WESTINGHOUSE EMPLOYEES WHO ARE PLANNING TO ENROLL IN 4-YEAR COLLEGES. SELECTION IS BASED ON SCHOLASTIC APTITUDE AND ACHIEVEMENT; GENERAL ABILITY AND LEADERSHIP.
SCHOLARSHIP TO BE APPLIED TO A BACHELOR'S DEGREE PROGRAM. WRITE TO CHERYL L. KUBELICK; ADMINISTRATOR; ADDRESS ABOVE; FOR COMPLETE INFORMATION.

1712

WESTPORT-WESTON FOUNDATION (HORACE C HURLBUTT MEMORIAL FUND)
C/O WESTPORT BANK & TRUST CO; PO BOX 5177
WESTPORT CT 06881
203/222-6950
AMOUNT: UP TO $1500
DEADLINE(S): NONE
FIELD(S): ALL AREAS OF STUDY
OPEN ONLY TO RESIDENTS OF WESTPORT & WESTON CT. AWARDS ARE TENABLE AT RECOGNIZED UNDERGRADUATE COLLEGES & UNIVERSITIES.
APPROX 15 AWARDS PER YEAR. WRITE FOR COMPLETE INFORMATION.

1713

WHITNEY BENEFITS INC. (STUDENT LOANS)
PO BOX 691; 403 N JEFFERSON
SHERIDAN WY 82801
307/674-7303
AMOUNT: $2000 - $4000
DEADLINE(S): NONE
FIELD(S): ALL FIELDS OF STUDY
OPEN TO GRADUATES OF SHERIDAN COUNTY WYOMING HIGH SCHOOLS WHO ARE UNDER 25 YEARS OF AGE & MAINTAIN AT LEAST A 2.0 GPA. LOANS MAY BE USED FOR UNDERGRADUATE STUDY ONLY. A PERSONAL INTERVIEW IS REQUIRED.
FINANCIAL NEED IS CONSIDERED. FAMILY INCOME SHOULD BE UNDER $40000 PER YEAR. APPROX 70 AWARDS PER YEAR. WRITE FOR COMPLETE INFORMATION.

1714

WHITTIER COLLEGE (JOHN GREENLEAF WHITTIER SCHOLARS PROGRAM)
13406 E PHILADELPHIA ST
WHITTIER CA 90608
310/907-4238
AMOUNT: $1000 TO $4880 (FULL TUITION)
DEADLINE(S): JAN 15 (MERIT); FEB 15 (TALENT)
FIELD(S): ALL FIELDS OF STUDY
CANDIDATES FOR MERIT SCHOLARSHIPS MUST BE IN TOP 10% OF CLASS AND HAVE A CUMULATIVE GPA OF OVER 3.5 (4.0 SCALE). HALF TUITION SCHOLARSHIPS ARE OFFERED FOR TALENT IN THE AREAS OF ART; MUSIC; THEATER ARTS.

1715

WILLIAM BRADLEY SCHOLARSHIP FOUNDATION INC. (WILLIAM BRADLEY SCHOLARSHIP)
125 OZARK DR
CRYSTAL CITY MO 63019
314/937-2570
AMOUNT: $400
DEADLINE(S): APR 1
FIELD(S): ALL FIELDS OF STUDY
OPEN TO GRADUATING SENIORS OF CRYSTAL CITY HIGH SCHOOL; FESTUS HIGH SCHOOL OR

ST. PIUS X HIGH SCHOOL IN JEFFERSON COUNTY; MISSOURI. MUST RANK IN THE TOP 10 PERCENT OF CLASS.
WRITE FOR COMPLETE INFORMATION.

1716

WILLIAM H. CHAPMAN FOUNDATION (SCHOLARSHIPS)
PO BOX 1321
NEW LONDON CT 06320
203/443-8010
AMOUNT: $200 - $850
DEADLINE(S): APR 1
FIELD(S): ALL FIELDS OF STUDY
OPEN ONLY TO RESIDENTS OF NEW LONDON COUNTY; CT. AWARDS SUPPORT FULL TIME UNDERGRADUATE STUDY AT ACCREDITED COLLEGES & UNIVERSITIES. USA CITIZEN OR LEGAL RESIDENT. MUST DEMONSTRATE FINANCIAL NEED.
APPROX 100 AWARDS PER YEAR. RENEWABLE WITH RE-APPLICATION. WRITE FOR COMPLETE INFORMATION.

1717

WINDHAM FOUNDATION INC. (SCHOLARSHIPS)
PO BOX 70
GRAFTON VT 05146
802/843-2211
AMOUNT: VARIES
DEADLINE(S): MAR 1
FIELD(S): ALL FIELDS OF STUDY
PROGRAM OPEN TO STUDENTS WHO ARE RESIDENTS OF WINDHAM COUNTY VERMONT. SCHOLARSHIPS ARE TENABLE AT RECOGNIZED UNDERGRADUATE COLLEGES & UNIVERSITIES.
APPROX 400 AWARDS PER YEAR. RENEWABLE UP TO 4 YEARS. WRITE FOR COMPLETE INFORMATION.

1718

WISCONSIN DEPARTMENT OF VETERANS AFFAIRS (DECEASED VETERANS' SURVIVORS ECONOMIC ASSISTANCE LOAN/EDUCATION GRANTS)
PO BOX 7843
MADISON WI 53707
608/266-1311
AMOUNT: $4500 MAXIMUM
DEADLINE(S): NONE SPECIFIED
FIELD(S): ALL AREAS OF STUDY
OPEN TO SURVIVING SPOUSES (WHO HAVE NOT REMARRIED) OF DECEASED ELIGIBLE VETERANS AND TO THE MINOR DEPENDENT CHILDREN OF THE DECEASED VETERANS. MUST BE RESIDENTS OF WISCONSIN AT THE TIME OF APPLICATION.
APPROX 5700 GRANTS AND LOANS PER YEAR. CONTACT A WISCONSIN VETERANS SERVICE OFFICER IN YOUR COUNTY OF RESIDENCE FOR COMPLETE INFORMATION.

1719

WISCONSIN DEPARTMENT OF VETERANS AFFAIRS (VETERANS ECONOMIC ASSISTANCE LOAN/EDUCATION GRANTS)
PO BOX 7843
MADISON WI 53707
608/266-1311
AMOUNT: $4500 MAXIMUM
DEADLINE(S): NONE SPECIFIED
FIELD(S): ALL AREAS OF STUDY
OPEN TO VETERANS (AS DEFINED IN WISCONSIN STATUTE 45.35-5) WHO ARE LIVING IN WISCONSIN AT THE TIME OF APPLICATION. THERE ARE LIMITATIONS ON INCOME.
APPROX 5700 GRANTS AND LOANS PER YEAR. WRITE FOR COMPLETE INFORMATION.

1720

WISCONSIN HIGHER EDUCATION AID BOARD (STUDENT FINANCIAL AID PROGRAM)
PO BOX 7885
MADISON WI 53707
608/267-2206; FAX 608/267-2808
AMOUNT: VARIES
DEADLINE(S): NONE SPECIFIED
FIELD(S): ALL AREAS OF STUDY
BOARD ADMINISTERS A VARIETY OF STATE AND FEDERAL PROGRAMS THAT ARE AVAILABLE TO WISCONSIN RESIDENTS WHO ARE ENROLLED AT LEAST HALF TIME AND MAINTAIN SATISFACTORY ACADEMIC RECORD. MOST REQUIRE DEMONSTRATION OF FINANCIAL NEED.
WRITE FOR COMPLETE INFORMATION.

1721

WOMEN OF THE EVANGELICAL LUTHERAN CHURCH IN AMERICA (SCHOLARSHIP PROGRAM)
8765 W HIGGINS RD
CHICAGO IL 60631
312/380-2700
AMOUNT: $500 - $2000

DEADLINE(S): MAR 1
FIELD(S): ALL FIELDS OF STUDY EXCEPT MINISTRY OR CHURCH CERTIFIED PROFESSIONS
OPEN TO ELCA LAYWOMEN AGE 21 OR OLDER WHO HAVE EXPERIENCED AN INTERRUPTION IN SCHOOLING OF AT LEAST TWO YEARS SINCE HIGH SCHOOL. MUST PROVIDE ACADEMIC RECORD OF COURSE WORK BEYOND HIGH SCHOOL AND DEMONSTRATE ABILITY; FINANCIAL NEED; ETC.
WRITE FOR COMPLETE INFORMATION.

1722

WOMEN'S SPORTS FOUNDATION (TRAVEL & TRAINING GRANTS)
342 MADISON AVE; #728
NEW YORK NY 10173
212/972-9170
AMOUNT: UP TO $1500 (INDIVIDUAL); UP TO $3000 (TEAM)
DEADLINE(S): MAR 15; JULY 15; NOV 15
FIELD(S): ALL FIELDS OF STUDY
THIS FUND WAS ESTABLISHED TO PROVIDE ASSISTANCE TO ASPIRING FEMALE ATHLETES & FEMALE TEAMS TO ACHIEVE HIGHER PERFORMANCE LEVELS & RANKING WITHIN THEIR SPORT. USA CITIZEN.
GRANTS ARE AVAILABLE FOR TRAINING; COACHING; EQUIPMENT & TRAVEL TO SCHEDULED COMPETITIVE EVENTS. WRITE FOR COMPLETE INFORMATION.

1723

WOMEN'S WESTERN GOLF FOUNDATION (SCHOLARSHIPS)
348 GRANVILLE RD
CEDARBURG WI 53012
WRITTEN INQUIRY
AMOUNT: $2000 PER YEAR
DEADLINE(S): MAR 15
FIELD(S): ALL FIELDS OF STUDY
OPEN TO FEMALE HIGH SCHOOL SENIORS HAVING HIGH ACADEMIC ACHIEVEMENT; FINANCIAL NEED AND AN INVOLVEMENT WITH THE SPORT OF GOLF. GOLF SKILL IS NOT A CRITERION. FOR UNDERGRADUATE STUDY AT ANY ACCREDITED FOUR YEAR INSTITUTION. USA CITIZEN.
12 TO 15 AWARDS PER YEAR. RENEWABLE IF A 'B' AVERAGE IS MAINTAINED. WRITE FOOR COMPLETE INFORMATION.

1724

YAKIMA INDIAN NATION (SCHOLARSHIP PROGRAM)
PO BOX 151
TOPPENISH WA 98948
509/865-5121
AMOUNT: $1000 PER YEAR
DEADLINE(S): JUL 1
FIELD(S): ALL AREAS OF STUDY
PROGRAM OPEN TO ENROLLED MEMBERS OF THE YAKIMA INDIAN NATION. AWARDS TENABLE AT RECOGNIZED UNDERGRADUATE & GRADUATE INSTITUTIONS. USA CITIZEN.
APPROX 200 AWARDS PER YEAR. WRITE FOR COMPLETE INFORMATION.

1725

YOUTH FOR UNDERSTANDING INTERNATIONAL EXCHANGE (CONGRESS BUNDESTAG YOUTH EXCHANGE PROGRAM)
3501 NEWARK ST NW
WASHINGTON DC 20016
800/883-6243
AMOUNT: NOT SPECIFIED
DEADLINE(S): NOV 26
FIELD(S): ALL FIELDS OF STUDY
FULL YEAR SCHOLARSHIP TO STUDY IN GERMANY OPEN TO ANY HIGH SCHOOL SOPHOMORE OR JUNIOR HAVING A 3.0 OR BETTER GPA (4.0 SCALE). STUDENTS ATTEND A GERMAN HIGH SCHOOL AND LIVE WITH A HOST FAMILY. THERE IS NO LANGUAGE REQUIREMENT.
300 SCHOLARSHIPS PER YEAR. WRITE FOR COMPLETE INFORMATION.

1726

YOUTH FOR UNDERSTANDING INTERNATIONAL EXCHANGE (CORPORATE SPONSORED SCHOLARSHIPS)
3501 NEWARK ST NW
WASHINGTON DC 20016
800/833-6243
AMOUNT: PROGRAM TUITION
DEADLINE(S): NOV 25
FIELD(S): ALL FIELDS OF STUDY
MERIT BASED SCHOLARSHIPS OPEN TO HIGH SCHOOL STUDENTS WHO WISH TO GO OVERSEAS FOR A SUMMER OR FOR A SCHOOL YEAR. MOST CORPORATE SPONSORED SCHOLARSHIPS ARE AVAILABLE ONLY TO CHILDREN OF EMPLOYEES OF SPONSORING CORPORATIONS.

PARENTS OF INTERESTED STUDENTS SHOULD CHECK WITH THEIR PERSONNEL OFFICE AT WORK TO SEE IF THEIR FIRM IS A PARTICIPANT.

1727

YOUTH FOR UNDERSTANDING INTERNATIONAL EXCHANGE (FINLAND U.S. SENATE YOUTH EXCHANGE)
3501 NEWARK ST NW
WASHINGTON DC 20016
800/883-6243
AMOUNT: NOT SPECIFIED
DEADLINE(S): NOV 26
FIELD(S): ALL FIELDS OF STUDY

MERIT SCHOLARSHIPS OPEN TO HIGH SCHOOL JUNIORS FROM CA; FL; MA; MI; MN; OR AND WA FOR STUDY IN FINLAND DURING THE SUMMER MONTHS. A GPA OF 3.2 (4.0 SCALE) IS REQUIRED.

SCHOLARSHIPS GO TO 14 STUDENTS FROM THE SEVEN PARTICIPATING STATES. WRITE FOR COMPLETE INFORMATION.

1728

YOUTH FOR UNDERSTANDING INTERNATIONAL EXCHANGE (FUTURE BUSINESS LEADERS OF AMERICA SCHOLARSHIP)
3501 NEWARK ST NW
WASHINGTON DC 20016
800/833-6243
AMOUNT: NOT SPECIFIED
DEADLINE(S): NOV 26
FIELD(S): ALL FIELDS OF STUDY

PARTIAL SCHOLARSHIP OPEN TO DUES PAYING MEMBERS OF FUTURE BUSINESS LEADERS OF AMERICA FOR SUMMER STUDY IN JAPAN OR GERMANY.

WRITE FOR COMPLETE INFORMATION.

1729

YOUTH FOR UNDERSTANDING INTERNATIONAL EXCHANGE (FUTURE HOMEMAKERS OF AMERICA / KIKKOMAN CORP. SCHOLARSHIP)
3501 NEWARK ST NW
WASHINGTON DC 20016
800/833-6243
AMOUNT: NOT SPECIFIED
DEADLINE(S): NOV 26
FIELD(S): ALL FIELDS OF STUDY

FHA IN PARTNERSHIP WITH KIKKOMAN CORP OFFERS SEVERAL SCHOLARSHIPS TO JAPAN TO FHA MEMBERS.

WRITE FOR COMPLETE INFORMATION.

1730

YOUTH FOR UNDERSTANDING INTERNATIONAL EXCHANGE (MAZDA NATIONAL AND TOYOTA NATIONAL SCHOLARSHIPS)
3501 NEWARK ST NW
WASHINGTON DC 20016
800/833-6243
AMOUNT: NOT SPECIFIED
DEADLINE(S): NOV 26
FIELD(S): ALL FIELDS OF STUDY

MERIT SCHOLARSHIPS FOR SUMMER STUDY IN JAPAN OPEN TO ANY HIGH SCHOOL STUDENT IN THE USA WHO HAS A GPA OF 2.0 OR BETTER (4.0 SCALE).

WRITE FOR COMPLETE INFORMATION.

Helpful Publications

1731

10 STEPS IN WRITING THE RESEARCH PAPER
AUTHOR-ROBERTA MARKMAN; PETER MARKMAN & MARIE WADDELL
BARRON'S EDUCATIONAL SERIES INC.
250 WIRELESS BLVD
HAUPPAUGE NY 11788
COST-$7.95
ARRANGED TO LEAD THE STUDENT STEP BY STEP THROUGH THE WRITING OF A RESEARCH PAPER; FROM FINDING A SUITABLE SUBJECT TO CHECKING THE FINAL COPY. EASY ENOUGH FOR THE BEGINNER; COMPLETE ENOUGH FOR THE GRADUATE STUDENT. 160 PGS.

1732

200 WAYS TO PUT YOUR TALENT TO WORK IN THE HEALTH FIELD
AUTHOR-NHC
NATIONAL HEALTH COUNCIL INC.
350 FIFTH AVE; SUITE 1118
NEW YORK NY 10018
COST-25 CENTS EACH PLUS $3 PER ORDER FOR SHIPPING AND HANDLING
HIGHLY RECOMMENDED. INCLUDES STRAIGHT ANSWERS TO YOUR QUESTIONS ABOUT HEALTH CAREERS PLUS A LISTING OF ORGANIZATIONS WHERE MORE INFORMATION CAN BE OBTAINED ABOUT SPECIFIC FIELDS; FINANCIAL AID AND TRAINING SCHOOLS.

1733

A JOURNALIST'S ROAD TO SUCCESS - A CAREER AND SCHOLARSHIP GUIDE
AUTHOR-DJNF
DOW JONES NEWSPAPER FUND INC.
PO BOX 300
PRINCETON NEW JERSEY 08543
COST-$3 PER COPY
HIGHLY RECOMMENDED FOR PRINT OR BROADCAST COMMUNICATIONS STUDENTS OR JOURNALISTS. COMPREHENSIVE BOOKLET DESCRIBING WHAT AND WHERE TO STUDY; HOW TO PAY FOR IT; WHERE THE JOBS ARE AND HOW TO FIND THEM. TO ORDER CALL 800/DOW-FUND.

1734

ABC'S OF FINANCIAL AID (MONTANA FINANCIAL AID HANDBOOK)
AUTHOR-MONTANA GUARANTEED STUDENT LOAN PROGRAM
MONTANA CAREER INFORMATION SYSTEM
2500 BROADWAY; PO BOX 203101
HELENA MT 59620
COST-FREE
DESCRIBES EDUCATIONAL COSTS AND FINANCIAL AID AVAILABLE IN MONTANA AS WELL AS APPLICATION AND AWARD PROCEDURES AND FINANCIAL AID PROGRAMS.

1735

ACADEMIC YEAR ABROAD
AUTHOR-SARA STEEN; EDITOR
INSTITUTE OF INTERNATIONAL EDUCATION
IIE BOOKS; 809 UNITED NATIONS PLAZA
NEW YORK NY 10017
COST-$39.95 + $3 HANDLING
PROVIDES INFORMATION ON MORE THAN 1900 POST-SECONDARY STUDY PROGRAMS OUTSIDE THE USA.

1736

AFL-CIO GUIDE TO UNION-SPONSORED SCHOLARSHIPS
AUTHOR-AFL-CIO DEPARTMENT OF EDUCATION
AFL-CIO
815 16TH STREET NW
WASHINGTON DC 20006
COST-FREE TO UNION MEMBERS; $3 NON-UNION
COMPREHENSIVE 100-PAGE GUIDE FOR UNION MEMBERS & THEIR DEPENDENT CHILDREN. DESCRIBES LOCAL; NATIONAL & INTERNATIONL UNION-SPONSORED SCHOLARSHIP PROGRAMS. ALSO INCLUDES A BIBLIOGRAPHY OF OTHER FINANCIAL AID SOURCES.

1737

AMERICAN INSTITUTE OF ARCHITECTS INFORMATION POSTER & BOOKLET
AUTHOR-AIA
AMERICAN INSTITUTE OF ARCHITECTS
1735 NEW YORK AVENUE NW
WASHINGTON DC 20006
COST-FREE
PROVIDES LIST OF ACCREDITED PROFESSIONAL PROGRAMS AND CAREER INFORMATION.

1738

ANNUAL REGISTER OF GRANT SUPPORT
AUTHOR-REED REFERENCE PUBLISHING
NATIONAL REGISTER PUBLISHING CO
121 CHANLON RD
NEW PROVIDENCE NJ 07974
COST-$165.00 + $11.55 SHIPPING/HANDLING
COMPREHENSIVE ANNUAL REFERENCE BOOK WHICH CAN BE FOUND AT MOST MAJOR LIBRARIES. DETAILS THOUSANDS OF GRANTS FOR RESEARCH WHICH ARE OPEN TO INDIVIDUALS & ORGANIZATIONS.

1739

ART CALENDAR
AUTHOR-CAROLYN BLAKESLEE; EDITOR IN CHIEF
ART CALENDAR
PO BOX 199
UPPER FAIRMOUNT 21867
COST-$32/ONE YEAR
MONTHLY PUBLICATION CONTAINING ARTICLES OF INTEREST TO ARTISTS INCLUDING LISTINGS OF GRANTS & FELLOWSHIPS; EXHIBITS ETC. SAMPLE COPY IS AVAILABLE FOR $5.

1740

ART SCHOLARSHIP BOOK
AUTHOR-NAEA
NATIONAL ART EDUCATION ASSN.
1916 ASSOCIATION DR
RESTON VA 22091
COST-$12 PLUS $3.50 SHIPPING/HANDLING
LISTING OF SCHOLARSHIPS; FELLOWSHIPS; GRANTS AND OTHER FINANCIAL AID FROM AMERICA'S ART SCHOOLS; COLLEGES AND UNIVERSITIES. 60 PAGES.

1741

BARRON'S GUIDE TO LAW SCHOOLS (10TH EDITION)
AUTHOR-GARY A. MUNNEKE J.D. ISBN 0-8120-4864-4
BARRON'S EDUCATIONAL SERIES INC.
250 WIRELESS BLVD
HAUPPAUGE NY 11788
COST-$14.95
COMPREHENSIVE GUIDE COVERING MORE THAN 200 ABA-APPROVED AMERICAN LAW SCHOOLS. ADVICE ON ATTENDING LAW SCHOOL.

1742

BASIC FACTS ON STUDY ABROAD
INSTITUTE OF INTERNATIONAL EDUCATION
IIE BOOKS; 809 UNITED NATIONS PLAZA
NEW YORK NY 10017
COST-FREE
BROCHURE OFFERING ESSENTIAL INFORMATION ON PLANNING FOR UNDERGRADUATE AND GRADUATE STUDY OUTSIDE THE USA.

1743

CAREER GUIDE FOR SINGERS
AUTHOR-MARY MCDONALD; EDITOR
OPERA AMERICA
777 14TH ST NW; SUITE 520
WASHINGTON DC 20005
COST-$25 NON MEMBERS; $15 MEMBERS
DIRECTORY CONTAINING INFORMATION ON AUDITIONS; GRANTS AND COMPETITIONS FOR YOUNG SINGERS CONTEMPLATING A CAREER IN OPERA.

1744

CFKR CAREER MATERIALS CATALOG
AUTHOR-CFKR
CFKR CAREER MATERIALS INC.
11860 KEMPER RD; UNIT 7
AUBURN CA 95603
COST-FREE
A CATALOG OF SOFTWARE AND VIDEO TAPES COVERING CAREER PLANNING; COLLEGE FINANCING AND COLLEGE TEST PREPARATION. THE CATALOG INCLUDES MATERIALS APPLICABLE TO ALL AGES; FROM THE PRIMARY GRADES THROUGH GRADUATE SCHOOL.

1745

CHRONICLE CAREER INDEX
AUTHOR-CGP; ISBN #1-55631-187-7
CHRONICLE GUIDANCE PUBLICATIONS
AURORA ST EXTENSION; PO BOX 1190
MORAVIA NY 13118
COST-$14.25
COMPREHENSIVE REFERENCE LISTING OF CAREER AND VOCATIONAL MATERIALS FOR STUDENTS AND COUNSELORS. DESCRIBES ABOUT 500 SOURCES OF PUBLICATIONS & AUDIOVISUAL MATERIALS. 90 PAGES.

1746

CHRONICLE FINANCIAL AID GUIDE
AUTHOR-CGP; ISBN #1-55631-186-9
CHRONICAL GUIDANCE PUBLICATIONS
AURORA ST EXTENSION; PO BOX 1190
MORAVIA NY 13118
COST-$19.97
ANNUAL GUIDE THAT CONTAINS INFORMATION ON FINANCIAL AID PROGRAMS OFFERED NATIONALLY & REGIONALLY BY PUBLIC & PRIVATE ORGANIZATIONS. PROGRAMS SUPPORT STUDY AND/OR RESEARCH AT THE UNDERGRADUATE; GRADUATE & POST-GRADUATE LEVELS. 534 PAGES.

1747

CHRONICLE FOUR-YEAR COLLEGE DATABOOK
AUTHOR-CGP; ISBN #1-55631-184-2
CHRONICLE GUIDANCE PUBLICATIONS
AURORA ST EXTENSION; PO BOX 1190
MORAVIA NY 13118
COST-$19.99
EXCELLENT REFERENCE BOOK IN 2 SECTIONS. 'MAJORS' SECTION LISTS 2111 INSTITUTIONS OFFERING 926 4-YEAR; GRADUATE & PROFESSIONAL MAJORS. 'CHARTS' SECTION CONTAINS COMPREHENSIVE INFORMATION & STATISTICS ON EACH OF THE SCHOOLS. 548 PAGES.

1748

CHRONICLE TWO-YEAR COLLEGE DATABOOK
AUTHOR-CGP; ISBN #1-55631-185-0
CHRONICLE GUIDANCE PUBLICATIONS
AURORA ST EXTENSION; PO BOX 1190
MORAVIA NY 13118
COST-$19.96
EXCELLENT REFERENCE BOOK IN 2 SECTIONS. 'MAJORS' SECTION LISTS 2361 INSTITUTIONS OFFERING 963 OCCUPATIONAL; ASSOCIATE & TRANSFER PROGRAMS. 'CHARTS' SECTION CONTAINS COMPREHENSIVE INFORMATION & STATISTICS ON EACH INSTITUTION. 444 PAGES.

1749

COLLEGE DEGREES BY MAIL
AUTHOR-JOHN BEAR PH.D; ISBN 0-89815-379-4
TEN SPEED PRESS
BOX 7123
BERKELEY CA 94707
COST-$12.95 + $2.50 SHIPPING & HANDLING
LISTING OF 100 COLLEGES THAT OFFER BACHELORS; MASTERS; DOCTORATES AND LAW DEGREES BY HOME STUDY. BOOK IS THE SUCCESSOR TO BEAR'S GUIDE TO EARNING NONTRADITIONAL COLLEGE DEGREES. 214 PAGES.

1750

COLLEGE FINANCIAL AID EMERGENCY KIT
AUTHOR-JOYCE LAIN KENNEDY & DR. HERM DAVIS
SUN FEATURES INC
BOX 368-K
CARDIFF CA 92007
COST-$5.50 (INCLUDES POSTAGE AND HANDLING)
40-PAGE BOOKLET FILLED WITH TIPS ON HOW TO MEET THE COSTS OF TUITION; ROOM & BOARD. THIS 1993-94 EDITION TELLS WHAT IS AVAILABLE; WHOM TO ASK AND HOW TO ASK.

1751

COLLEGE HANDBOOK (THE); 1993 EDITION
AUTHOR-CBP; ISBN #0-87447-431-0
COLLEGE BOARD PUBLICATIONS
PO BOX 886
NEW YORK NY 10101
COST-$19
DESCRIBES IN DETAIL OVER 3200 2-YEAR & 4-YEAR UNDERGRADUATE COLLEGES & UNIVERSITIES IN THE USA. INCLUDES INFO ON ADMISSIONS REQUIREMENTS; COSTS; FINANCIAL AID; MAJORS; ACTIVITIES; ENROLLMENT; CAMPUS LIFE & MUCH MORE. 1600 PAGES.

1752

COLLEGE SMARTS - THE OFFICIAL FRESHMAN HANDBOOK
AUTHOR-JOYCE SLAYTON MITCHELL; ISBN 0-912048-92-1.
GARRETT PARK PRESS
PO BOX 190
GARRETT PARK MD
COST-$10.95
COGENT ADVICE FOR THE COLLEGE FRESHMAN COVERING SUCH PRACTICAL SUBJECTS AS WHAT THINGS TO TAKE; COPING WITH DORM LIFE AND YOUR ROOMMATE; REGISTRATION; FRATERNITY/SORORITY RUSH; EVEN YOUR LAUNDRY. ADVICE IS PRACTICAL; TO THE POINT.

1753

COOPERATIVE EDUCATION UNDERGRADUATE PROGRAM DIRECTORY
AUTHOR-NCCE
NATIONAL COMMISSION FOR COOPERATIVE EDUCATION
360 HUNTINGTON AVENUE
BOSTON MA 02115
COST-FREE
EXPLAINS WHAT CO-OP EDUCATION IS; DETAILS ITS ADVANTAGES & LISTS COLLEGES AND UNIVERSITIES THAT OFFER CO-OP EDUCATION PROGRAMS.

1754

CORPORATE TUITION AID PROGRAMS
AUTHOR-JOSEPH P O'NEILL; ISBN #0-87866-482-3
PETERSON'S GUIDES
DEPT 7707; PO BOX 2123
PRINCETON NJ 08543
COST-$14.95
BIENNIAL PUBLICATION WHICH DESCRIBES THE EMPLOYEE TUITION BENEFIT PROGRAMS OF 730 OF AMERICA'S LARGEST BANKS; RETAILERS; UTILITIES; TRANSPORTATION; SERVICE & INDUSTRIAL FIRMS. 208 PAGES.

1755

DENTISTRY AS A CAREER
AUTHOR-AADS
AMERICAN ASSOCIATION OF DENTAL SCHOOLS
1625 MASS AVE NW
WASHINGTON DC 20036
COST-FREE
BROCHURE DISCUSSES DENTISTRY AS A CAREER AND OFFERS ADVICE ON PLANNING FOR A DENTAL EDUCATION.

1756

DESTINATION - COLLEGE
AUTHOR-BARBARA G. HEYMAN
WARNER BOOKS INC.
666 FIFTH AVE
NEW YORK NY 10103
COST-$8.95
UNIQUE 4-STEP WORKBOOK THAT HELPS COLLEGE-BOUND STUDENTS UNDERSTAND THEIR GOALS; CHOOSE THE RIGHT COLLEGE; GET ACCEPTED & FIND FINANCIAL AID. 85 PAGES.

1757

DIRECTORY OF ATHLETIC SCHOLARSHIPS
AUTHOR-ALAN GREEN; ISBN #0-8169-1549-X
FACTS ON FILE INC.
460 PARK AVE SOUTH
NEW YORK NY 10016
COST-$29.95
CONTAINS THE INS & OUTS OF THE RECRUITING PROCESS; SCHOOL BY SCHOOL INDEX; SPORT BY SPORT INDEX & STATE BY STATE INDEX.

1758

DIRECTORY OF COLLEGE FACILITIES & SERVICES FOR PEOPLE WITH DISABILITIES
AUTHOR-CAROL H. THOMAS & JAMES L. THOMAS; ISBN 0-89774-604-X
ORYX PRESS
4041 NORTH CENTRAL AVE; #700
PHOENIX AZ 85012
COST-$115.00
COMPLETE BOOK ON COLLEGE FACILITIES & SERVICES FOR PEOPLE WITH DISABILITIES IN THE USA & CANADA. ALSO CONTAINS INFORMATION ON ASSOCIATIONS; CENTERS; ORGANIZATIONS; SOCIETIES; CLEARINGHOUSES & DATA BASES.

1759

DIRECTORY OF EDUCATIONAL INSTITUTIONS
AUTHOR-AICS
ASSOCIATION OF INDEPENDENT COLLEGES AND SCHOOLS
1 DUPONT CIRCLE; #350
WASHINGTON DC 20036

COST-$5.00
THIS DIRECTORY IS PUBLISHED ANNUALLY TO PROVIDE INFORMATION ON MORE THAN 650 INSTITUTIONS ACCREDITED BY THE AICS. INFORMATION CAN BE OBTAINED ABOUT ANY OF THE LISTED SCHOOLS THROUGH AICS.

1760

DIRECTORY OF FINANCIAL AIDS FOR MINORITIES
AUTHOR-GAIL ANN SCHLACHTER
REFERENCE SERVICE PRESS
1100 INDUSTRIAL RD; SUITE 9
SAN CARLOS CA 94070
COST-$47.50 + $4 SHIPPING
DESCRIBES OVER 2000 SCHOLARSHIPS; FELLOWSHIPS; GRANTS; LOANS; AWARDS & INTERNSHIPS SET ASIDE FOR ETHNIC MINORITIES. COVERS ALL LEVELS OF STUDY. 600 PAGES.

1761

DIRECTORY OF FINANCIAL AIDS FOR WOMEN
AUTHOR-GAIL ANN SCHLACHTER
REFERENCE SERVICE PRESS
1100 INDUSTRIAL RD; SUITE 9
SAN CARLOS CA 94070
COST-$45 + $4 SHIPPING
CONTAINS OVER 1700 DESCRIPTIONS OF SCHOLARSHIPS; FELLOWSHIPS; GRANTS; LOANS; AWARDS & INTERNSHIPS SET ASIDE FOR WOMEN. COVERS ALL LEVELS OF STUDY. 478 PAGES.

1762

DIRECTORY OF NATIONAL INFORMATION SOURCES ON DISABILITIES
AUTHOR-DEPT. OF EDUCATION
U.S. DEPT. OF EDUCATION
CLEARINGHOUSE ON THE HANDICAPPED; OFFICE OF SPECIAL EDUCATION AND REHABILITATIVE SERVICES
WASHINGTON DC 20202
COST-FREE
DIRECTORY WHICH INVENTORIES RESOURCES AT THE NATIONAL LEVEL (PUBLIC & PRIVATE) WHICH HAVE INFORMATION AND/OR DIRECT SERVICES PERTINENT TO THE HANDICAPPED & PEOPLE INVOLVED IN EDUCATING; TRAINING OR HELPING THE HANDICAPPED.

1763

DIRECTORY OF POST-SECONDARY EDUCATIONAL RESOURCES IN ALASKA
AUTHOR-ACPE
ALASKA COMMISSION ON POST-SECONDARY EDUCATION
PO BOX 110505
JUNEAU AK 99811
COST-FREE
COMPREHENSIVE DIRECTORY OF POST-SECONDARY INSTITUTIONS AND PROGRAMS IN ALASKA PLUS INFORMATION ON STATE AND FEDERAL GRANTS; LOANS AND SCHOLARSHIPS FOR ALASKA RESIDENTS (THOSE WHO HAVE LIVED IN ALASKA FOR TWO YEARS).

1764

DIRECTORY OF RESEARCH GRANTS 1993
ORYX PRESS
4041 N CENTRAL AVE
PHOENIX AZ 85012
COST-$125
ANNUAL REFERENCE BOOK WHICH CAN BE FOUND IN MOST MAJOR LIBRARIES. EXCELLENT TOOL FOR ANY PERSON OR ORGANIZATION LOOKING FOR RESEARCH FUNDING. ORGANIZED BY GRANT TITLE WITH EXTENSIVE INDEXES.

1765

DIRECTORY OF SPECIAL PROGRAMS FOR MINORITY GROUP MEMBERS
AUTHOR-WILLIS JOHNSON
GARRETT PARK PRESS
PO BOX 190F
GARRETT PARK MD 20896
COST-$30
COMPREHENSIVE BOOK WHICH DESCRIBES CAREER INFORMATION SERVICES; EMPLOYMENT SKILLS BANKS & EDUCATIONAL FINANCIAL AID SOURCES FOR MINORITY GROUP MEMBERS. 348 PAGES.

1766

DIRECTORY OF UNDERGRADUATE POLITICAL SCIENCE FACULTY
AUTHOR-PATRICIA SPELLMAN
AMERICAN POLITICAL SCIENCE ASSN.
1527 NEW HAMPSHIRE AVE NW
WASHINGTON DC 20036

COST-$35 (NON-MEMBERS); $20 (APSA MEMBERS) PLUS $3.50 POSTAGE

THIS DIRECTORY LISTS NEARLY 600 SEPARATE DEPARTMENTS OF POLITICAL SCIENCE WITH NAME ADDRESS PHONE NUMBER AND NAMES AND SPECIALIZATIONS OF FACULTY MEMBERS.

1767

EDUCATIONAL OPPORTUNITIES IN THE NAVY
AUTHOR-USN
U.S. NAVY
BUREAU OF NAVAL PERSONNEL; PERSONAL EXCELLENCE & PARTNERSHIPS DIV. (PERS-602)
WASHINGTON DC 20370
COST-FREE
VARIOUS NAVY-ORIENTED ORGANIZATIONS SPONSOR SCHOLARSHIPS OR OFFER AID FOR UNDERGRADUATE & GRADUATE STUDY. DEPENDENT CHILDREN OF CURRENT OR FORMER MEMBERS OF THE NAVY; MARINE CORPS OR COAST GUARD ARE ELIGIBLE TO APPLY.

1768

EEO BIMONTHLY
AUTHOR-CRS PUBLICATIONS
CAREER RESEARCH SYSTEMS INC.
1800 SHERMAN PLACE
EVANSTON IL 60201
COST-$42.00/YEAR
BI-MONTHLY PUBLICATION CONTAINING DETAILED CAREER OPPORTUNITY PROFILES ON AMERICAN COMPANIES; GEOGRAPHIC EMPLOYER LISTINGS & OCCUPATIONAL INDEX.

1769

ENCYCLOPEDIA OF ASSOCIATIONS; VOL 1
GALE RESEARCH INC.
835 PENOBSCOT BLDG
DETROIT MI 48226
COST-$320
AN OUTSTANDING RESEARCH TOOL! 3-PART SET OF REFERENCE BOOKS WHICH CAN BE FOUND IN MOST MAJOR LIBRARIES. CONTAINS DETAILED INFORMATION ON OVER 22000 ASSOCIATIONS; ORGANIZATIONS; UNIONS; ETC. INCLUDES NAME & KEY WORD INDEX.

1770

EXPLORING CAREERS IN MUSIC
AUTHOR-PAUL BJORNEBERG; ISBN 0-940796-86-4
MUSIC EDUCATORS NATIONAL CONFERENCE
1902 ASSOCIATION DRIVE
RESTON VA 22091
COST-FREE
INFORMATIVE BOOKLET DISCUSSING CAREERS IN THE PERFORMING ARTS; MUSIC EDUCATION; THE MUSIC BUSINESS; RECORDING INDUSTRY AND ALLIED FIELDS.

1771

FACTFILE 12 - FILM AND TELEVISION GRANTS AND SCHOLARSHIPS
AUTHOR-ANDREA ALSBERG AND DAVID H. CHADDERDON
AMERICAN FILM INSTITUTE
PO BOX 27999
LOS ANGELES CA 90027
COST-$9.95 + $2 SHIPPING/HANDLING. CA RESIDENTS ADD SALES TAX
LISTS 57 SPECIFIC GRANT PROGRAMS GIVING DETAILS ON AMOUNTS GIVEN; DEADLINES; ELIGIBILITY. LISTS SCHOLARSHIP PROGRAMS SPECIFICALLY FOR FILM; TELEVISION AND VIDEO STUDENTS. 56 PAGES.

1772

FACTFILE 2 - CAREERS IN FILM AND TELEVISION
AUTHOR-DEBORAH A. DAVIDSON
AMERICAN FILM INSTITUTE
PO BOX 27999
LOS ANGELES CA 90027
COST-$9.95 + $2 SHIPPING/HANDLING. CA RESIDENTS ADD SALES TAX
LISTS UNIONS; GUILDS AND PROFESSIONAL ORGANIZATIONS AND GIVES INFORMATION IN INTERN AND APPRENTICESHIP PROGRAMS IN DIRECTING; DISTRIBUTION; FILM AND TELEVISION PRODUCTION AND WRITING. 46 PAGES.

1773

FEDERAL BENEFITS FOR VETERANS & DEPENDENTS (S/N 051-000-00198-2)
AUTHOR-VETERANS ADMINISTRATION
SUPERINTENDENT OF DOCUMENTS
U.S. GOVERNMENT PRINTING OFFICE
WASHINGTON DC 20402

COST-$2.75
94-PAGE BOOKLET CONTAINING DETAILS OF ALL FEDERAL BENEFIT PROGRAMS AVAILABLE TO VETERANS & THEIR DEPENDENTS.

1774

FELLOWSHIP GUIDE TO WESTERN EUROPE
AUTHOR-CAROLYN MORLEY; EDITOR
COUNCIL FOR EUROPEAN STUDIES
C/O COLUMBIA UNIV; BOX 44 SCHERMERHORN
NEW YORK NY 10027
COST-$8.00 (PREPAID CHECK TO COLUMBIA UNIV)
THIS BOOKLET IS INTENDED TO ASSIST USA & EUROPEAN STUDENTS IN FINDING FUNDS FOR TRAVEL & STUDY IN THE SOCIAL SCIENCES & HUMANITIES IN EUROPE.

1775

FINANCIAL AID FOR MINORITIES - AWARDS OPEN TO STUDENTS WITH ANY MAJOR
AUTHOR-ISBN 0-912048-93-1
GARRETT PARK PRESS
PO BOX 190F
GARRETT PARK MD 20896
COST-$4.95
THIS BOOKLET LISTS SOURCES OF FINANCIAL AID AND CLARIFIES APPLICATION PROCEDURES. INCLUDES A BIBLIOGRAPHY OF OTHER SOURCES OF FUNDING INFORMATION.

1776

FINANCIAL AID FOR MINORITIES IN BUSINESS & LAW
GARRETT PARK PRESS
PO BOX 190F
GARRETT PARK MD 20896
COST-$4.95
THIS BOOKLET LISTS SOURCES OF FINANCIAL AID AND CLARIFIES APPLICATION PROCEDURES. INCLUDES A BIBLIOGRAPHY OF OTHER SOURCES OF FUNDING INFORMATION.

1777

FINANCIAL AID FOR MINORITIES IN EDUCATION
GARRETT PARK PRESS
PO BOX 190F
GARRETT PARK MD 20896
COST-$4.95
THIS BOOKLET CONTAINS FINANCIAL AID OPPORTUNITIES FOR ELEMENTARY; SECONDARY & ADMINISTRATIVE PROGRAMS. ALSO FIELDS SUCH AS COUNSELING; SPECIAL ED. & SPEECH PATHOLOGY.

1778

FINANCIAL AID FOR MINORITIES IN ENGINEERING & SCIENCE
GARRETT PARK PRESS
PO BOX 190F
GARRETT PARK MD 20896
COST-$4.95
INDIVIDUAL AWARDS AND GENERAL PROGRAMS OFFERED FOR GRADUATE AND PROFESSIONAL STUDY BY PRIVATE ORGANIZATIONS; FOUNDATIONS; FEDERAL AND STATE GOVERNMENTS; COLLEGES AND UNIVERSITIES.

1779

FINANCIAL AID FOR MINORITIES IN HEALTH FIELDS
GARRETT PARK PRESS
PO BOX 190F
GARRETT PARK MD 20896
COST-$4.95
INCLUDES INDIVIDUAL AWARDS AND GENERAL PROGRAMS OFFERED FOR GRADUATE OR PROFESSIONAL STUDY BY PRIVATE ORGANIZATIONS; FOUNDATIONS; FEDERAL AND STATE GOVERNMENTS; COLLEGES AND UNIVERSITIES.

1780

FINANCIAL AID FOR MINORITIES IN JOURNALISM & MASS COMMUNICATIONS
GARRETT PARK PRESS
PO BOX 190F
GARRETT PARK MD 20896
COST-$4.95
THIS BOOKLET LISTS SPECIFIC SOURCES OF FINANCIAL AID FOR MINORITY STUDENTS AND ALSO HELPS TO EXPLAIN HOW TO GO ABOUT APPLYING FOR THEM.

1781

FINANCIAL AID FOR THE DISABLED & THEIR FAMILIES
AUTHOR-GAIL ANN SCHLACHTER & R. DAVID WEBER
REFERENCE SERVICE PRESS
1100 INDUSTRIAL RD; SUITE 9
SAN CARLOS CA 94070
COST-$37.50 + $4 SHIPPING
CONTAINS OVER 800 REFERENCES & CROSS-REFERENCES TO SCHOLARSHIPS; FELLOWSHIPS; GRANTS; LOANS; AWARDS & INTERNSHIPS SET ASIDE FOR THE DISABLED & THEIR FAMILIES. COVERS ALL LEVELS OF STUDY. 310 PAGES.

1782

FINANCIAL AID FOR VETERANS; MILITARY PERSONNEL & THEIR FAMILIES
AUTHOR-GAIL ANN SCHLACHTER & R. DAVID WEBER
REFERENCE SERVICE PRESS
1100 INDUSTRIAL RD; SUITE 9
SAN CARLOS CA 94070
COST-$37.50 + $4 SHIPPING
CONTAINS OVER 900 DESCRIPTIONS OF SCHOLARSHIPS; FELLOWSHIPS; GRANTS; LOANS; AWARDS & INTERNSHIPS SET ASIDE FOR VETERANS; MILITARY PERSONNEL & THEIR FAMILIES. COVERS ALL LEVELS OF STUDY. 300 PAGES.

1783

FINANCIAL ASSISTANCE FOR LIBRARY EDUCATION
AUTHOR-ALA
AMERICAN LIBRARY ASSOCIATION
OFFICE FOR LIBRARY PERSONNEL RESOURCES; 50 EAST HURON ST
CHICAGO IL 60611
COST-$1.00 FOR POSTAGE/HANDLING
AN EXCELLENT SUMMARY OF FELLOWSHIPS; SCHOLARSHIPS; GRANTS-IN-AID; LOAN FUNDS & OTHER FINANCIAL ASSISTANCE FOR LIBRARY EDUCATION. PUBLISHED ANNUALLY EACH FALL FOR THE FOLLOWING YEAR.

1784

FINDING MONEY FOR COLLEGE
AUTHOR-JOHN BEAR; PH.D
TEN SPEED PRESS
PO BOX 7123
BERKELEY CA 94707
COST-$7.95
IN THIS BOOK DR. BEAR BUILDS ON THE EXTENSIVE RESEARCH HE HAS DONE IN EDUCATION TO SEARCH OUT THE UNCONVENTIONAL; THE OVERLOOKED; THE ORDINARY BUT NOT WELL UNDERSTOOD SOURCES OF ASSISTANCE & HOW TO PURSUE THEM. 168 PAGES.

1785

FISKE GUIDE TO COLLEGES
AUTHOR-NEW YORK TIMES BOOKS; ISBN 812-92024-4
TIMES BOOKS
400 HAHN RD
WESTMINSTER MD 21157
COST-$16
DESCRIBES THE TOP-RATED 265 OUT OF 2000 POSSIBLE 4-YEAR SCHOOLS IN THE USA. THEY ARE RATED FOR ACADEMICS; SOCIAL LIFE & QUALITY OF LIFE.

1786

FLORIDA STUDENT FINANCIAL AID - FACT SHEETS
AUTHOR-DEPT. OF EDUCATION
FLORIDA DEPARTMENT OF EDUCATION
1344 FLORIDA EDUCATION CENTER
TALLAHASSEE FL 32399
COST-FREE
BOOKLET CONTAINING INFORMATION ON ALL FLORIDA GRANTS; SCHOLARSHIPS AND TEACHER PROGRAMS.

1787

FOUNDATION DIRECTORY (THE)
FOUNDATION CENTER
79 FIFTH AVE
NEW YORK NY 10003
COST-$150 SOFT COVER; $175 HARD COVER
AUTHORITATIVE ANNUAL REFERENCE BOOK FOUND IN MOST MAJOR LIBRARIES. CONTAINS DETAILED INFORMATION ON OVER

8700 OF AMERICA'S LARGEST FOUNDATIONS. INDEXES ALLOW GRANTSEEKERS; RESEARCHERS; ETC. TO QUICKLY LOCATE FOUNDATIONS OF INTEREST.

1788

GED...THE KEY TO YOUR FUTURE
AUTHOR-GENERAL EDUCATIONAL DEVELOPMENT TESTS (GED)
GED TESTING SERVICE OF THE AMERICAN COUNCIL ON EDUCATION
ONE DUPONT CIRCLE; SUITE 250
WASHINGTON DC 20036
COST-FREE
IF YOU OR SOMEONE YOU KNOW LEFT HIGH SCHOOL PRIOR TO GRADUATION; THIS FREE BROCHURE WILL EXPLAIN WHAT THE GED TESTS ARE & HOW THEY CAN GIVE SOMEONE THE OPPORTUNITY TO EARN A HIGH SCHOOL EQUIVALENCY DIPLOMA.

1789

GET SMART FAST
AUTHOR-SONDRA GEOFFRION
ACCESS SUCCESS ASSOCIATES
PO BOX 1686
GOLETA CA 93116
COST-$6.95 EACH (CA RESIDENTS ADD 7.75% SALES TAX); (POSTAGE $2.50 USA; $4 FOREIGN)
61 PAGE HANDBOOK FOR ACADEMIC SUCCESS WHICH EXPLAINS HOW TO MASTER THE ART OF STUDYING; WRITE ESSAYS; PREPARE FOR AND TAKE TESTS; ETC.

1790

GOVERNMENT ASSISTANCE ALMANAC (6TH EDITION)
AUTHOR-J. ROBERT DUMOUCHEL; ISBN 1-55888-789-5
OMNIGRAPHICS INC
2500 PENOBSCOT BLDG
DETROIT MI 48226
COST-$84
COMPREHENSIVE GUIDE TO MORE THAN 600 BILLION WORTH OF FEDERAL PROGRAMS AVAILABLE TO THE AMERICAN PUBLIC. CONTAINS 768 PAGES AND 1157 ENTRIES DETAILING PROGRAMS OF BENEFIT TO STUDENTS; EDUCATORS; RESEARCHERS AND CONSUMERS.

1791

GUIDE TO SOURCES OF INFORMATION ON PARAPSYCHOLOGY
AUTHOR-EILEEN J. GARRETT LIBRARY
PARAPSYCHOLOGY FOUNDATION
228 EAST 71ST STREET
NEW YORK NY 10021
COST-$2
AN ANNUAL LISTING OF SOURCES OF INFORMATION ON MAJOR PARAPSYCHOLOGY ORGANIZATIONS; JOURNALS; BOOKS & RESEARCH.

1792

GUIDELINES FOR THE PREPARATION OF SCHOOL ADMINISTRATORS
AUTHOR-AASA
AMERICAN ASSN. OF SCHOOL ADMINISTRATORS
1801 NORTH MOORE ST
ARLINGTON VA 22209
COST-$5.00 PREPAID
PEOPLE WHO ARE PLANNING A CAREER IN SCHOOL ADMINISTRATION WILL FIND THIS BOOK HELPFUL IN EXPLAINING THE DEMANDS AND EXPECTATIONS OF SCHOOLS AS WELL AS THOSE WHO PLAY KEY ROLES IN RECOMMENDING OR ESTABLISHING CERTIFICATION REQUIREMENTS.

1793

HANDBOOK OF PRIVATE SCHOOLS
PORTER SARGENT PUBLISHERS INC
11 BEACON ST; SUITE 1400
BOSTON MA 02108
COST-$72.41
ANNUAL REFERENCE BOOK WHICH CAN BE FOUND AT MOST MAJOR LIBRARIES. DESCRIBES IN DETAIL OVER 1800 AMERICAN ELEMENTARY & SECONDARY PRIVATE SCHOOLS. 1495 PAGES.

1794

HANDICAPPED FUNDING DIRECTORY
AUTHOR-RICHARD M. ECKSTEIN; EDITOR
RESEARCH GRANT GUIDES
PO BOX 1214
LOXAHATCHEE FL 33470
COST-$39.50 + $4 HANDLING
COMPLETE GUIDE TO FUNDING SOURCES IN THE USA FOR HANDICAPPED PROGRAMS AND SERVICES.

1795

HAPPIER BY DEGREES
AUTHOR-PAM MENDELSOHN
TEN SPEED PRESS
PO BOX 7123
BERKELEY CA 94707
COST-$8.95 + $1.25 SHIPPING & HANDLING
EXCELLENT BOOK FOR WOMEN JUST STARTING OUT OR RETURNING TO COLLEGE. THIS IS A COMPREHENSIVE GUIDE TO THE ENTIRE PROCESS OF ENTERING INTO A NEW ACADEMIC FIELD INCLUDING FINANCIAL AID; CHILD CARE; ETC. 266 PAGES.

1796

HIGH SCHOOL STUDENT'S APPLICATION WORKBOOK
AUTHOR-KEN & PAT VOAK
KEN & PAT VOAK PUBLICATIONS
230 OLD GRAHAM HILL RD
SANTA CRUZ CA 95060
COST-$5.00
COMPLETE WORKBOOK THAT WILL HELP YOU ORGANIZE THE RECORDING & EVALUATING OF YOUR HIGH SCHOOL YEARS. INCLUDES STANDARDIZED FORMS TO GIVE YOU AN IDEA OF WHAT INFORMATION WILL BE ASKED ON APPLICATIONS FOR COLLEGES; JOBS; SCHOLARSHIPS; ETC.

1797

HOW TO FIND OUT ABOUT FINANCIAL AID
AUTHOR-GAIL ANN SCHLACHTER
REFERENCE SERVICE PRESS
1100 INDUSTRIAL RD; SUITE 9
SAN CARLOS CA 94070
COST-$35 + $4 SHIPPING
A COMPREHENSIVE GUIDE TO MORE THAN 700 PRINT & ONLINE DIRECTORIES THAT IDENTIFY OVER $21 BILLION IN FINANCIAL AID AVAILABLE TO UNDERGRADUATE STUDENTS; GRADUATE STUDENTS & RESEARCHERS.

1798

INDEX OF MAJORS
AUTHOR-CBP; ISBN #0-87447-410-8
COLLEGE BOARD PUBLICATIONS
PO BOX 886
NEW YORK NY 10101
COST-$15.95
DESCRIBES OVER 580 MAJOR PROGRAMS OF STUDY AT 2900 UNDERGRADUATE & GRADUATE SCHOOLS. ALSO LISTS SCHOOLS THAT HAVE RELIGIOUS AFFILIATIONS; SPECIAL ACADEMIC PROGRAMS & SPECIAL ADMISSIONS PROCEDURES. 736 PAGES.

1799

INTERNATIONAL JOBS
AUTHOR-ERIC KOCHER
ADDISON-WESLEY PUBLISHING CO
1 JACOB WAY
READING MA 01867
COST-$12.95
A HANDBOOK LISTING MORE THAN 500 CAREER OPPORTUNITIES AROUND THE WORLD.

1800

INTERNSHIPS
AUTHOR-PETERSON'S
PETERSON'S GUIDES
202 CARNEGIE CENTER; PO BOX 2123
PRINCETON NJ 08543
COST-$28.95 + $5.75 SHIPPING & HANDLING
LISTS ON THE JOB TRAINING OPPORTUNITIES FOR TODAY'S JOB MARKET ARRANGED BY CAREER FIELD & INDEXED GEOGRAPHICALLY.

1801

JOB OPPORTUNITIES FOR THE BLIND
AUTHOR-NFB
NATIONAL FEDERATION OF THE BLIND
1800 JOHNSON ST
BALTIMORE MD 21230
COST-FREE
JOB OPPORTUNITIES FOR THE BLIND PROGRAM IS OPERATED BY THE NATIONAL FEDERATION OF THE BLIND IN PARTNERSHIP WITH US DEPT. OF LABOR. IT IS A LISTING & REFERRAL SERVICE FOR BLIND JOB APPLICANTS.

1802

JOURNALISM AND MASS COMMUNICATION DIRECTORY
AUTHOR-AEJMC
ASSOCIATION FOR EDUCATION IN JOURNALISM & MASS COMMUNICATIONS
1621 COLLEGE ST; UNIV SOUTH CAROLINA
COLUMBIA SC 29208
COST-$20 USA; $30 FOREIGN

ANNUAL DIRECTORY LISTING OVER 350 SCHOOLS AND DEPARTMENTS OF JOURNALISM AND MASS COMMUNICATION; INFORMATION ON NATIONAL FUNDS; FELLOWSHIPS AND FOUNDATIONS; COLLEGIATE AND SCHOLASTIC SERVICES. OVER 2500 INDIVIDUAL MEMBERS.

1803

JOURNALISM CAREER GUIDE FOR MINORITIES
AUTHOR-DJNF
DOW JONES NEWSPAPER FUND INC.
PO BOX 300
PRINCETON NJ 08543-0300
COST-FREE
COMPREHENSIVE GUIDE WHICH LISTS NEWSPAPER RECRUITERS FOR COLLEGE STUDENTS WHO ARE LOOKING FOR WORK AS REPORTERS & EDITORS. ALSO INCLUDES CAREER INFORMATION; JOBS; SALARIES; INTERN PROGRAMS & MUCH MORE. TO ORDER CALL 1-800-DOW FUND.

1804

LEARNING DISABILITY INFORMATION
AUTHOR-ODS
ORTON DYSLEXIA SOCIETY
CHESTER BUILDING/SUITE 382; 8600 LASALLE RD
BALTIMORE MD 21204
COST-FREE
NATIONAL ORGANIZATION FORMED TO HELP LEARNING DISABLED CHILDREN & THEIR PARENTS. THERE ARE LOCAL CHAPTERS THROUGHOUT THE USA. CONTACT ADDRESS ABOVE FOR DETAILS ON MEMBERSHIP; SERVICES OFFERED & LOCATION OF THE NEAREST CHAPTER.

1805

LEARNING DISABILITY INFORMATION
AUTHOR-ODS-CALIF
ORTON DYSLEXIA SOCIETY; NORTHERN CALIFORNIA BRANCH
1244 SIERRA AVE
SAN JOSE CA 95126
COST-FREE
ORTON DYSLEXIA SOCIETY (ODS) IS A NAT'L ORGANIZATION FORMED TO HELP LEARNING DISABLED CHILDREN & THEIR PARENTS. SEND SASE TO ADDRESS ABOVE FOR DETAILS ON MEMBERSHIP AND SERVICES OFFERED BY THE N. CALIFORNIA CHAPTER.

1806

MAKING IT THROUGH COLLEGE
AUTHOR-PSC
PROFESSIONAL STAFF CONGRESS
25 WEST 43RD STREET; 5TH FLOOR
NEW YORK NY 10036
COST-$1.00
HANDY BOOKLET DESCRIBING HOW TO MAKE IT THROUGH COLLEGE. INCLUDES INFORMATION ON HOW TO COPE WITH COMPETITION; GETTING ORGANIZED; FINANCIAL AID; STUDY TECHNIQUES; SOLVING WORK OVERLOADS AND MORE. 14 PAGES.

1807

MEDICAL SCHOOL ADMISSION REQUIREMENTS
AUTHOR-CYNTHIA T. BENNETT
ASSOCIATION OF AMERICAN MEDICAL COLLEGES
2450 N ST NW
WASHINGTON DC 20037
COST-$10 + SHIPPING
CONTAINS COMPLETE ADMISSION REQUIREMENTS OF ALL ACCREDITED MEDICAL SCHOOLS IN USA & CANADA.

1808

MEDICINE - A CHANCE TO MAKE A DIFFERENCE
AUTHOR-AMA
AMERICAN MEDICAL ASSOCIATION
ORDER PROCESSING; PO BOX 109050
CHICAGO IL 60610
COST-$5.00
FOR COLLEGE STUDENTS CONSIDERING A CAREER IN MEDICINE. ANSWERS QUESTIONS ABOUT THE PROFESSION AND MEDICAL EDUCATION INCLUDING PREREQUISITES; ADMISSION REQUIREMENTS AND CHOOSING A MEDICAL SCHOOL.

1809

MUSIC SCHOLARSHIP GUIDE
AUTHOR-SANDRA V. FRIDY; ISBN 0-940796-91-0
MUSIC EDUCATORS NATIONAL CONFERENCE
1902 ASSOCIATION DRIVE
RESTON VA 22091
COST-
LISTS OVER 1300 UNDERGRADUATE MUSIC SCHOLARSHIPS IN THE UNITED STATES AND

CANADA INCLUDING ELIGIBILITY REQUIREMENTS; APPLICATION DEADLINES; CONTACT INFORMATION.

1810

NAEA SCHOLARSHIP BOOK
AUTHOR-NAEA
NATIONAL ART EDUCATION ASSOCIATION
1916 ASSOCIATION DRIVE
RESTON VA 22091
COST-$12
LISTS OVER $12.5 MILLION IN ART SCHOLARSHIPS; AWARDS; FELLOWSHIPS & GRADUATE ASSISTANT PROGRAMS IN THE USA & CANADA.

1811

NATIONAL DIRECTORY OF ARTS INTERNSHIPS
AUTHOR-NNAP
AMERICAN COUNCIL FOR THE ARTS (ACA BOOKS)
ONE E 53RD ST
NEW YORK NY 10022
COST-$35
DETAILED LISTINGS OF MORE THAN 2100 ON-THE-JOB OPPORTUNITIES NATIONWIDE IN THE FIELDS OF DANCE; THEATER; MUSIC; ART; DESIGN; FILM AND VIDEO. 360 PAGES.

1812

NATIONAL DIRECTORY OF CORPORATE GIVING
AUTHOR-TFC; ISBN 0-87954-400-7
FOUNDATION CENTER (THE)
79 FIFTH AVENUE/16TH STREET
NEW YORK NY 10003
COST-$199.50 (INCLUDING SHIPPING/HANDLING)
BOOK PROFILES 2000 PROGRAMS MAKING CONTRIBUTIONS TO NONPROFIT ORGANIZATIONS. A VALUABLE TOOL TO ASSIST GRANT SEEKERS IN FINDING POTENTIAL SUPPORT.

1813

NEARLY FREE TUITION
AUTHOR-ALEXANDER A. BOVE JR; ISBN #0-14-010462-3
PENGUIN USA
345 HUDSON ST
NEW YORK NY 10014
COST-$8.95
OUTLINES HOW TO MEET THE SOARING COSTS OF EDUCATION THROUGH CLEVER (BUT LEGAL) TAX PLANNING. 240 PAGES.

1814

NEED A LIFT?
AUTHOR-AMERICAN LEGION
AMERICAN LEGION EDUCATION PROGRAM
PO BOX 1050
INDIANAPOLIS IN 46206
COST-$2.00
OUTSTANDING GUIDE TO EDUCATION & EMPLOYMENT OPPORTUNITIES. CONTAINS COMPLETE INFO ON THE FINANCIAL AID PROCESS (HOW; WHEN & WHERE TO START); SCHOLARSHIPS; LOANS & CAREER INFORMATION ADDRESSES. 120 PAGES.

1815

NURSING EDUCATION; ENROLLING IN A COLLEGE OR UNIVERSITY
AUTHOR-AMERICAN NURSES ASSOCIATION
AMERICAN NURSES ASSOCIATION
2420 PERSHING ROAD
KANSAS CITY MO 64108
COST-$3.50 MEMBERS; $4.95 NON-MEMBERS
HOW-TO BOOKLET THAT ANSWERS THE MOST COMMON QUESTIONS ASKED BY PROSPECTIVE NURSING STUDENTS. HOW TO CHOOSE A SCHOOL; HOW TO GET INFORMATION FROM SCHOOLS; HOW TO APPLY; HOW TO OBTAIN FINANCIAL AID & THE TYPES AVAILABLE.

1816

OCCUPATIONAL OUTLOOK HANDBOOK
AUTHOR-U.S. BUREAU OF LABOR STATISTICS; STOCK #029-001-03090-8 (CLOTH); 029-001-03091-6 (PAPER)
SUPERINTENDENT OF DOCUMENTS
U.S. GOVERNMENT PRINTING OFFICE
WASHINGTON DC 20402
COST-$26 (CLOTH BOUND); $23 (PAPER)
ANNUAL PUBLICATION DESIGNED TO ASSIST INDIVIDUALS IN SELECTING APPROPRIATE CAREERS. DESCRIBES OVER 200 OCCUPATIONS IN GREAT DETAIL AND INCLUDES CURRENT & PROJECTED JOB PROSPECTS FOR EACH. 492 PAGES.

1817

OCEAN OPPORTUNITIES
AUTHOR-COMPILED BY THE INSTITUTE OF ELECTRICAL & ELECTRONIC ENGINEERS AND THE MARINE TECHNOLOGY SOCIETY.
MARINE TECHNOLOGY CENTER
1828 L ST NW; SUITE 906
WASHINGTON DC 20006
COST-$3 FOR SHIPPING/HANDLING
BOOKLET WHICH EXPLORES CAREER OPPORTUNITIES IN THE MARINE SCIENCES.

1818

OFF TO COLLEGE
AUTHOR-GUIDANCE RESEARCH GROUP
ORDER FULFILLMENT DEPT-95-RSCH
PO BOX 931
MONTGOMERY AL 36101
COST-$5
AN EXCELLENT ANNUAL BOOKLET IN MAGAZINE FORM. IT HELPS PREPARE INCOMING FRESHMEN FOR SUCCESS IN COLLEGE LIVING THROUGH PERSONAL ESSAYS CONCERNING A VARIETY OF CAMPUS EXPERIENCES.

1819

OFFICIAL HANDBOOK FOR THE CLEP EXAMINATIONS
AUTHOR-CBP; ISBN #0-87447-455-8
COLLEGE BOARD PUBLICATIONS
PO BOX 886
NEW YORK NY 10101
COST-$15
OFFICIAL GUIDE TO THE COLLEGE LEVEL EXAMINATION PROGRAM (CLEP) TESTS FROM THE ACTUAL SPONSORS OF THE TESTS. CONTAINS SAMPLE QUESTIONS & ANSWERS; ADVICE ON HOW TO PREPARE FOR TESTS; WHICH COLLEGES GRANT CREDIT FOR CLEP & MUCH MORE. 500 PGS.

1820

PETERSON'S COLLEGES WITH PROGRAMS FOR STUDENTS WITH LEARNING DISABILITIES
AUTHOR-PETERSON'S INC.; ISBN 1-56079-080-6
PETERSON'S INC.
PO BOX 2123
PRINCETON NJ 08543
COST-$22.95
COMPREHENSIVE GUIDE TO OVER 1000 TWO YEAR AND FOUR YEAR COLLEGES AND UNIVERSITIES OFFERING SPECIAL ACADEMIC PROGRAMS FOR STUDENTS WITH DYSLEXIA AND OTHER LEARNING DISABILITIES.

1821

PETERSON'S GUIDE TO FOUR-YEAR COLLEGES 1994
AUTHOR-PETERSON'S INC.; ISBN #1-56079-235-3
PETERSON'S INC.
PO BOX 2123
PRINCETON NJ 08543
COST-$18.95
DETAILED PROFILES OF OVER 1900 ACCREDITED 4-YEAR COLLEGES IN THE USA & CANADA. ALSO INCLUDES ENTRANCE DIFFICULTY DIRECTORY; MAJORS DIRECTORY & COLLEGE COST DIRECTORY.

1822

PETERSON'S NATIONAL COLLEGE DATABANK
AUTHOR-PETERSON'S INC.; ISBN 1-56079-020-2
PETERSON'S INC.
DEPT 7707; PO BOX 2123
PRINCETON NJ 08543
COST-$19.95
THE COLLEGE BOOK OF LISTS CRAMMED WITH FACTS & FIGURES ON SUCH SUBJECTS AS COLLEGE CHARACTERISTICS; ACADEMICS; UNDERGRAD ENROLLMENT DATA; CAMPUS LIFE; ADMISSIONS; ENTRANCE DIFFICULTY; EXPENSES; FINANCIAL AID; INTERCOLLEGIATE ATHLETICS.

1823

PHARMACY SCHOOL ADMISSION REQUIREMENTS
AUTHOR-AACP
AMERICAN ASSOCIATION OF COLLEGES OF PHARMACY
OFFICE OF STUDENT AFFAIRS; 1426 PRINCE ST
ALEXANDRIA VA 22314
COST-$20 PREPAID
114-PAGE BOOKLET THAT IS UPDATED ANNUALLY. IT CONTAINS COMPARATIVE INFORMATION CHARTS AND THE GENERAL HISTORY AND CURRENT ADMISSION REQUIREMENTS FOR ACCREDITED PHARMACY PROGRAMS.

1824

PILOT TRAINING GUIDE
AUTHOR-FAPA
FUTURE AVIATION PROFESSIONALS OF AMERICA (FAPA)
4959 MASSACHUSETTS BLVD
ATLANTA GA 30337
COST-$20.95
BOOKLET DESIGNED TO HELP BEGINNER AND ADVANCED PILOTS MAKE DECISIONS ABOUT THEIR TRAINING. INCLUDES LIST OF FAA APPROVED FLIGHT TRAINING SCHOOLS IN USA.

1825

POWER STUDY TO UP YOUR GRADES AND GPA
AUTHOR-SONDRA GEOFFRION
ACCESS SUCCESS ASSOCIATES
PO BOX 1686
GOLETA CA 93116
COST-$4.95 + $2.50 USA POSTAGE; $4 FOREIGN POSTAGE. CA RESIDENTS ADD 7.75% SALES TAX
ONE OF 5 EXCELLENT BOOKLETS EXPLAINING TECHNIQUES TO DISCOVER WHAT WILL BE TESTED; CUT STUDY TIME IN HALF; PREPARE THOROUGHLY; WRITE ESSAYS; TAKE TESTS. OTHER TITLES COVER MATH; ENGLISH; SOCIAL STUDIES; SCIENCE.

1826

POWER STUDY TO UP YOUR GRADES IN MATH
AUTHOR-SONDRA GEOFFRION
ACCESS SUCCESS ASSOCIATES
PO BOX 1686
GOLETA CA 93116
COST-$4.95 + $2.50 USA POSTAGE; $4 FOREIGN POSTAGE. CA RESIDENTS ADD 7.75% SALES TAX
ONE OF 5 EXCELLENT BOOKLETS EXPLAINING TECHNIQUES TO DISCOVER WHAT WILL BE TESTED; CUT STUDY TIME IN HALF; PREPARE THOROUGHLY; WRITE ESSAYS; TAKE TESTS. OTHER TITLES COVER ENGLISH; SOCIAL STUDIES; SCIENCE AND IMPROVING GRADE POINT AVERAGE.

1827

POWER STUDY TO UP YOUR GRADES IN ENGLISH
AUTHOR-SONDRA GEOFFRION
ACCESS SUCCESS ASSOCIATES
PO BOX 1686
GOLETA CA 93116
COST-$4.95 + $2.50 USA POSTAGE; $4 FOREIGN POSTAGE. CA RESIDENTS ADD SALES TAX
ONE OF 5 EXCELLENT BOOKLETS EXPLAINING TECHNIQUES TO DISCOVER WHAT WILL BE TESTED; CUT STUDY TIME IN HALF; PREPARE THOROUGHLY; WRITE ESSAYS; TAKE TESTS. OTHER TITLES COVER MATH; SOCIAL STUDIES; SCIENCE AND IMPROVING GRADE POINT AVERAGE.

1828

POWER STUDY TO UP YOUR GRADES IN SOCIAL STUDIES
AUTHOR-SONDRA GEOFFRION
ACCESS SUCCESS ASSOCIATES
PO BOX 1686
GOLETA CA 93116
COST-$4.95 + $2.50 USA POSTAGE; $4 FOREIGN POSTAGE. CA RESIDENTS ADD 7.75% SALES TAX
ONE OF 5 EXCELLENT BOOKLETS EXPLAINING TECHNIQUES TO DISCOVER WHAT WILL BE TESTED; CUT STUDY TIME IN HALF; PREPARE THOROUGHLY; WRITE ESSAYS; TAKE TESTS. OTHER TITLES COVER MATH; ENGLISH; SCIENCE; AND IMPROVING GRADE POINT AVERAGE.

1829

POWER STUDY TO UP YOUR GRADES IN SCIENCE
AUTHOR-SONDRA GEOFFRION
ACCESS SUCCESS ASSOCIATES
PO BOX 1686
GOLETA CA 93116
COST-$4.95 + $2.50 USA POSTAGE; $4 FOREIGN POSTAGE. CA RESIDENTS ADD 7.75% SALES TAX
ONE OF 5 EXCELLENT BOOKLETS EXPLAINING HOW TO DISCOVER WHAT WILL BE TESTED; CUT STUDY TIME IN HALF; PREPARE THOROUGHLY; WRITE ESSAYS; TAKE TESTS. OTHER TITLES COVER MATH; ENGLISH; SOCIAL STUDIES; AND IMPROVING GRADE POINT AVERAGE.

1830

PRINCETON REVIEW - COLLEGE ADMISSIONS - CRACKING THE SYSTEM
AUTHOR-ADAM ROBINSON & JOHN KATZMAN; EDITORS
VILLARD BOOKS
201 E 50TH ST
NEW YORK NY 10022
COST-$7.95
OFFERS HIGH SCHOOL STUDENTS BOLD STRATEGIES FOR GETTING INTO THE COLLEGE OF THEIR CHOICE. 153 PAGES.

1831

PROCEEDINGS AND ADDRESSES OF THE AMERICAN PHILOSOPHICAL ASSOCIATION
AUTHOR-APA
AMERICAN PHILOSOPHICAL ASSOCIATION (THE)
UNIVERSITY OF DELAWARE
NEWARK DE 19716
COST-$10
ANNUAL ISSUE CONTAINS LISTS OF GRANTS AND FELLOWSHIPS OF INTEREST TO PHILOSOPHERS.

1832

SAVE A FORTUNE
AUTHOR-PHILLIP GODWIN; ISBN # 0-945332-05-X
AGORA BOOKS
842 E BALTIMORE ST
BALTIMORE MD 21202
COST-$14.95
A COMMON SENSE PLAN TO BUILDING WEALTH THROUGH SAVING RATHER THAN EARNING. INCLUDES INFO ON HOW TO SAVE ON TAXES; EDUCATION; HOUSING; TRAVEL; HEALTH; ETC. 209 PAGES.

1833

SCHOLARSHIPS & LOANS FOR NURSING EDUCATION
AUTHOR-NLN; ISBN #0-88737-505-7
NATIONAL LEAGUE FOR NURSING
350 HUDSON ST
NEW YORK NY 10014
COST-$10.95 + $3.50 POSTAGE
COMPLETE GUIDE TO FINANCIAL AID FOR NURSING AND HEALTH CARE PROFESSIONS. LISTS SCHOLARSHIPS; FELLOWSHIPS; GRANTS; TRAINEESHIPS; LOANS & SPECIAL AWARDS. 82 PAGES.

1834

STUDENT FINANCIAL AID & SCHOLARSHIPS AT WYOMING COLLEGES
UNIVERSITY OF WYOMING; DIV. OF FINANCIAL AID
PO BOX 3335
LARAMIE WY 82071
COST-FREE
DESCRIPTION OF POST-SECONDARY STUDENT AID & SCHOLARSHIP PROGRAMS THAT ARE AVAILABLE TO WYOMING STUDENTS. BOOKLETS CAN BE OBTAINED AT ALL WYOMING HIGH SCHOOLS AND COLLEGES.

1835

STUDENT GUIDE TO FINANCIAL AID
AUTHOR-U.S. DEPARTMENT OF EDUCATION
FEDERAL STUDENT AID INFORMATION CENTER
PO BOX 84
WASHINGTON DC 20044
COST-FREE
LISTS QUALIFICATIONS & SOURCES OF INFORMATION FOR FEDERAL GRANTS; LOANS AND WORK-STUDY PROGRAMS.

1836

STUDY ABROAD (VOL 27; 1992-94)
AUTHOR-UNESCO
UNITED NATIONS EDUCATIONAL; SCIENTIFIC AND CULTURAL ORGANIZATION
UNIPUB; UNESCO AGENT U7154; 4611-F ASSEMBLY DRIVE
LANHAM MD 20706
COST-$24.00 + POSTAGE & HANDLING
PRINTED IN ENGLISH; FRENCH & SPANISH THIS VOLUME LISTS 3700 INTERNATIONAL STUDY PROGRAMS IN ALL ACADEMIC & PROFESSIONAL FIELDS IN MORE THAN 124 COUNTRIES.

1837

TAFT CORPORATE GIVING DIRECTORY
TAFT GROUP
12300 TWINBROOK PKWY; SUITE 450
ROCKVILLE MD 20852
COST-$327.00
THIS REFERENCE BOOK CAN BE FOUND IN MOST MAJOR LIBRARIES. CONTAINS COMPREHENSIVE INFORMATION ON OVER 500 FOUNDATIONS WHICH ARE SPONSORED BY TOP CORPORATIONS. 859 PAGES.

1838

THE A'S & B'S OF ACADEMIC SCHOLARSHIPS
AUTHOR-DEBBIE KLEIN; EDITOR
OCTAMERON ASSOCIATES
PO BOX 2748
ALEXANDRIA VA 22301
COST-$7.50 POSTPAID
PROVIDES INFORMATION ON ACADEMIC SCHOLARSHIPS AT 1200 SCHOOLS. ALSO INFORMATION ON PREREQUISITES.

1839

THE FACTS ABOUT ARMY ROTC
AUTHOR-U.S. ARMY
U.S. ARMY - COLLEGE ARMY ROTC
GOLD QUEST CENTER; PO BOX 3279
WARMINSTER PA 18974
COST-FREE
PROVIDES INFORMATION ON TYPES OF SCHOLARSHIPS AVAILABLE; ELIGIBILITY; DEADLINES; APPLICATION PROCEDURES AND MONETARY VALUE.

1840

THEIR WORLD
AUTHOR-NCLD
NATIONAL CENTER FOR LEARNING DISABILITIES
99 PARK AVE; 6TH FLOOR
NEW YORK NY 10016
COST-$10.00
ANNUAL MAGAZINE DEVOTED TO HELPING PARENTS OF LEARNING DISABLED CHILDREN AS WELL AS PROFESSIONALS IN THE LEARNING DISABILITIES FIELD AND INCREASING PUBLIC AWARENESS OF LEARNING DISABILITIES.

1841

UNIVERSITY CURRICULA IN OCEANOGRAPHY AND RELATED FIELDS
AUTHOR-MARINE TECHNOLOGY SOCIETY
MARINE TECHNOLOGY SOCIETY
1828 L ST NW; SUITE 906
WASHINGTON DC 20036
COST-$5 SHIPPING/HANDLING
A GUIDE TO CURRENT MARINE DEGREE PROGRAMS AND VOCATIONAL INSTRUCTION AVAILABLE IN THE MARINE FIELD. CONSOLIDATES AND HIGHLIGHTS DATA NEEDED BY HIGH SCHOOL STUDENTS AS WELL AS COLLEGE STUDENTS SEEKING ADVANCED DEGREES.

1842

UNLOCKING POTENTIAL
AUTHOR-BARBARA SCHEIBER & JEANNE TALPERS; ISBN #0-917561-30-9
ADLER & ADLER PUBLISHERS INC.
WOODBINE HOUSE; 5615 FISHERS LN
ROCKVILLE MD 20852
COST-$12.95
A STEP-BY-STEP GUIDE ON COLLEGE & OTHER CHOICES FOR LEARNING DISABLED PEOPLE. DISCUSSES CHOOSING THE RIGHT POST-SECONDARY SCHOOL; ADMISSIONS PROCESS; OVERCOMING ACADEMIC HURDLES & MUCH MORE. 195 PAGES.

1843

VACATION STUDY ABROAD
AUTHOR-SARA STEEN; EDITOR
INSTITUTE OF INTERNATIONAL EDUCATION
IIE BOOKS; 809 UNITED NATIONS PLAZA
NEW YORK NY 10017
COST-$31.95
GUIDE TO SOME 1450 SUMMER OR SHORT TERM STUDY-ABROAD PROGRAMS SPONSORED BY USA COLLEGES; UNIVERSITIES; PRIVATE INSTITUTIONS & FOREIGN INSTITUTIONS. 330 PAGES.

1844

WHAT COLOR IS YOUR PARACHUTE?
AUTHOR-RICHARD N. BOLLES; ISBN #0-89815-492-8
TEN SPEED PRESS
PO BOX 7123
BERKELEY CA 94707
COST-$14.95 PLUS $2 POSTAGE
STEP-BY-STEP CAREER PLANNING GUIDE. HIGHLY RECOMMENDED FOR ANYONE WHO IS JOB HUNTING OR CHANGING CAREERS. VALUABLE TIPS ON ASSESSING YOUR SKILLS; RESUME WRITING; HANDLING JOB INTERVIEWS. 464 PAGES.

1845

WORK-STUDY-TRAVEL ABROAD - THE WHOLE WORLD HANDBOOK
AUTHOR-ST. MARTINS PRESS
COUNCIL ON INTERNATIONAL EDUCATIONAL EXCHANGE
205 E 42ND ST; 16TH FLOOR
NEW YORK NY 10017

COST-$12.95

EXCELLENT BOOK ON THE BASICS OF TRAVELING; WORKING AND STUDYING ABROAD. HOW TO FIND OUT ABOUT STUDY-ABROAD OPPORTUNITIES; GRANTS; SCHOLARSHIPS; EXCHANGE PROGRAMS AND TEACHING OPPORTUNITIES. ALSO INFORMATION ON THE CHEAPEST WAYS TO TRAVEL.

1846 ______

WORLD DIRECTORY OF MEDICAL SCHOOLS
AUTHOR-WHO
WORLD HEALTH ORGANIZATION
WHO PUBLICATION CENTER; 49 SHERIDAN AVE
ALBANY NY 12210
COST-$35

COMPREHENSIVE BOOK WHICH DESCRIBES THE MEDICAL EDUCATION PROGRAMS & SCHOOLS IN EACH COUNTRY. ARRANGED IN ORDER BY COUNTRY OR AREA.

1847 ______

YOU...THE DOCTOR
AUTHOR-AMA
AMERICAN MEDICAL ASSOCIATION
535 NORTH DEARBORN ST
CHICAGO IL 60610
COST-FREE

PAMPHLET THAT DESCRIBES OPPORTUNITIES IN THE MEDICAL PROFESSION AND DETAILS THE PREPARATIONS FOR THE PRACTICE OF MEDICINE.

Career Information

1848 'LAW AS A CAREER' BOOKLET
AMERICAN BAR ASSOCIATION
750 NORTH LAKE SHORE DR
CHICAGO IL 60611

1849 ACCOUNTING CAREER INFORMATION
AMERICAN INSTITUTE OF CERTIFIED PUBLIC ACCOUNTANTS
1211 AVENUE OF THE AMERICAS
NEW YORK NY 10036

1850 ACCOUNTING CAREER INFORMATION
NATIONAL SOCIETY OF PUBLIC ACCOUNTANTS
1010 NORTH FAIRFAX ST
ALEXANDRIA VA 22314

1851 ACCOUNTING CAREER INFORMATION
INSTITUTE OF MANAGEMENT ACCOUNTANTS
10 PARAGON DR
MONTVALE NJ 07645

1852 ACCOUNTING CAREER INFORMATION FOR WOMEN
AMERICAN SOCIETY OF WOMAN ACCOUNTANTS
NATIONAL HEADQUARTERS; 1755 LYNFIELD RD; SUITE 222
MEMPHIS TN 38119

1853 ACTUARIAL SCIENCE CAREER INFORMATION
SOCIETY OF ACTUARIES
475 N MARTINGALE RD; SUITE 800
SCHAUMBURG IL 60173

1854 ADVERTISING CAREER INFORMATION
AMERICAN ADVERTISING FEDERATION
EDUCATION SERVICES; SUITE 1000; 1400 K ST NW
WASHINGTON DC 20005

1855 AERONAUTICS CAREER INFORMATION
AMERICAN INSTITUTE OF AERONAUTICS AND ASTRONAUTICS - STUDENT PROGRAMS DEPT.
370 L'ENFANT PROMENADE SW
WASHINGTON DC 20024

1856 AEROSPACE EDUCATION CAREER INFORMATION
AEROSPACE EDUCATION FOUNDATION
1501 LEE HIGHWAY
ARLINGTON VA 22209

1857 AGRICULTURAL ENGINEERING (CAREER INFORMATION)
AMERICAN SOCIETY OF AGRICULTURAL ENGINEERS
2950 NILES ROAD
ST JOSEPH MI 49085

1858 AGRICULTURE CAREER INFORMATION
AMERICAN FARM BUREAU FEDERATION
225 TOUHY AVE
PARK RIDGE IL 60068

1859 AGRONOMY CAREER INFORMATION
AMERICAN SOCIETY OF AGRONOMY
677 SOUTH SEGOE ROAD
MADISON WI 53711

1860 AIR FORCE (CAREER INFORMATION)
HEADQUARTERS; U.S. AIR FORCE
USAF RECRUITING SERVICE
RANDOLPH AFB TX 78148

1861 AIR FORCE ACADEMY/AFROTC (CAREER INFORMATION)
DIRECTOR OF SELECTIONS
UNITED STATES AIR FORCE ACADEMY
USAF ACADEMY CO 80840

1862 AIRLINE (CAREER INFORMATION)
AIR TRANSPORT ASSOCIATION OF AMERICA
1301 PENNSLVANIA AVE NW; SUITE 1100
WASHINGTON DC 20004

1863 ANIMAL BIOLOGY/ZOOLOGIST CAREER INFORMATION
AMERICAN SOCIETY OF ZOOLOGISTS
104 SIRIUS CIRCLE
THOUSAND OAKS CA 91360

1864 ANIMAL SCIENCE CAREER INFORMATION
NATIONAL ASSOCIATION OF ANIMAL BREEDERS INC.
401 BERNADETTE DRIVE; PO BOX 1033
COLUMBIA MO 65205

1865 ANIMAL SCIENCE CAREER INFORMATION
AMERICAN SOCIETY OF ANIMAL SCIENCE
BUSINESS OFFICE; 309 W CLARK ST
CHAMPAIGN IL 61820

1866 ANTHROPOLOGIST CAREER INFORMATION
AMERICAN ANTHROPOLOGICAL ASSOCIATION
1703 NEW HAMPSHIRE AVE NW
WASHINGTON DC 20009

1867 APPRAISER CAREER INFORMATION (REAL ESTATE; GEMOLOGY; MACHINERY & EQUIPMENT; PERSONAL PROPERTY; ETC.)
AMERICAN SOCIETY OF APPRAISERS
PO BOX 17265
WASHINGTON DC 20041

1868 APPRENTICESHIP (CAREER INFORMATION)
U.S. DEPT. OF LABOR BUREAU OF APPRENTICESHIP AND TRAINING
200 CONSTITUTION AVE NW; RM N-4649
WASHINGTON DC 20210

1869 ARCHAEOLOGIST CAREER INFORMATION
ARCHAEOLOGICAL INSTITUTE OF AMERICA
675 COMMONWEALTH AVE
BOSTON MA 02215

1870 ARCHAEOLOGY CAREER INFORMATION
SOCIETY FOR AMERICAN ARCHAEOLOGY
808 17TH ST NW; #200
WASHINGTON DC 20006

1871 ARCHITECTURE CAREER INFORMATION
AMERICAN INSTITUTE OF ARCHITECTS
1735 NEW YORK AVENUE NW
WASHINGTON DC 20006

1872 ASTRONOMY CAREER INFORMATION
AMERICAN ASTRONOMICAL SOCIETY
EDUCATION OFFICER; ASTRONOMY DEPT.; UNIVERSITY OF TEXAS
AUSTIN TX 78712

1873 AUDIOLOGY CAREER INFORMATION
AMERICAN SPEECH-LANGUAGE-HEARING ASSOCIATION
10801 ROCKVILLE PIKE
ROCKVILLE MD 20852

1874 AUTHOR/WRITER (CAREER INFORMATION)
PEN AMERICAN CENTER
568 BROADWAY; SUITE 401
NEW YORK NY 10012

1875 AUTOMOTIVE ENGINEERING (CAREER INFORMATION)
SOCIETY OF AUTOMOTIVE ENGINEERS INC
400 COMMONWEALTH DRIVE
WARRENDALE PA 15096

1876 BANKING (CAREER INFORMATION)
AMERICAN BANKERS ASSOCIATION
LIBRARY & INFORMATION SYSTEMS; 1120 CONNECTICUT AVE NW
WASHINGTON DC 20036

1877 BIOLOGIST CAREER INFORMATION
AMERICAN INSTITUTE OF BIOLOGICAL SCIENCES
730 11TH ST NW
WASHINGTON DC 20001

1878 BIOTECHNOLOGY (CAREER INFORMATION)
INDUSTRIAL BIOTECHNOLOGY ASSOCIATION
1625 'K' STREET NW; SUITE 1100
WASHINGTON DC 20006

1879 BLACK FILMMAKERS (CAREER INFORMATION)
BLACK AMERICAN CINEMA SOCIETY
3617 MONTCLAIR ST
LOS ANGELES CA 90018

1880 BROADCAST NEWS CAREER INFORMATION
RADIO & TELEVISION NEWS DIRECTORS ASSN.
1000 CONNECTICUT AVE NW; SUITE 615
WASHINGTON DC 20036

1881 BROADCASTING CAREER INFORMATION
AMERICAN WOMEN IN RADIO & TELEVISION
1101 CONNECTICUT AVE NW; SUITE 700
WASHINGTON DC 20036

1882 BUSINESS ADMINISTRATION CAREER INFORMATION
AMERICAN ASSEMBLY OF COLLEGIATE SCHOOLS OF BUSINESS
605 OLD BALLAS RD; #220
ST LOUIS MO 63141

1883 BUSINESS EDUCATION (CAREER INFORMATION)
NATIONAL BUSINESS EDUCATION ASSOCIATION
1914 ASSOCIATION DR
RESTON VA 22091

1884 CAREERS IN THE DENTAL PROFESSION
AMERICAN DENTAL ASSOCIATION
211 E CHICAGO AVE; SUITE 1804
CHICAGO IL 60611

1885 CARTOONING CAREER INFORMATION
NEWSPAPER FEATURES COUNCIL
37 ARCH ST
GREENWICH CT 06830

1886 CHEMICAL ENGINEERING CAREER INFORMATION
AMERICAN INSTITUTE OF CHEMICAL ENGINEERS
345 EAST FORTY SEVENTH STREET
NEW YORK NY 10017

1887 CHIROPRACTIC (CAREER INFORMATION)
AMERICAN CHIROPRACTIC ASSOCIATION
1701 CLARENDON BLVD
ARLINGTON VA 22209

1888 CHIROPRACTIC CAREER & SCHOOLS INFORMATION
INTERNATIONAL CHIROPRACTORS ASSOCIATION
1110 N GLEBE ROAD; SUITE 1000
ARLINGTON VA 22201

1889 CIVIL ENGINEERING CAREER INFORMATION
AMERICAN SOCIETY OF CIVIL ENGINEERS
345 E 47TH ST
NEW YORK NY 10017

1890 CLINICAL CHEMIST (CAREER INFORMATION)
AMERICAN ASSOCIATION FOR CLINICAL CHEMISTRY
2029 K ST NW; SEVENTH FLOOR
WASHINGTON DC 20006

1891 COMMUNICATIONS CAREER & SCHOOLS INFORMATION
ACCREDITING COUNCIL ON EDUCATION IN JOURNALISM AND MASS COMMUNICATION
UNIVERSITY OF KANSAS SCHOOL OF JOURNALISM
LAWRENCE KS 66045

1892 COMMUNITY NON-PROFIT ORGANIZATION CAREER INFORMATION
UNITED WAY OF AMERICA
701 NORTH FAIRFAX ST
ALEXANDRIA VA 22314

1893 COMPUTER SCIENCE CAREER INFORMATION
IEEE - USA
1828 L ST NW; SUITE 1202
WASHINGTON DC 20036

1894 CONSTRUCTION CAREER INFORMATION
ASSOCIATED GENERAL CONTRACTORS OF AMERICA
1957 'E' ST NW
WASHINGTON DC 20006

1895 COSMETOLOGY CAREER INFORMATION
ASSOCIATION OF ACCREDITED COSMETOLOGY SCHOOLS
5201 LEESBURG PIKE; SUITE 205
FALLS CHURCH VA 22041

1896 CRAFTSMEN CAREER INFORMATION
AMERICAN CRAFT COUNCIL
72 SPRING ST
NEW YORK NY 10012

1897 CREATIVE WRITING (CAREER INFORMATION)
NATIONAL WRITERS CLUB
1450 S HAVANA; SUITE 620
AURORA CO 80012

1898 DANCE CAREER INFORMATION
AMERICAN ALLIANCE FOR HEALTH; PHYSICAL EDUCATION; RECREATION & DANCE
1900 ASSOCIATION DR
RESTON VA 22091

1899 DATA PROCESSING MANAGEMENT (CAREER INFORMATION)
DATA PROCESSING MANAGEMENT ASSOCIATION
505 BUSSE HIGHWAY
PARK RIDGE IL 60068

1900 DEMOGRAPHY
POPULATION ASSOCIATION OF AMERICA
1722 N STREET NW
WASHINGTON DC 20036

1901 DENTAL ASSISTANT CAREER INFORMATION
AMERICAN DENTAL ASSISTANTS ASSN
919 N MICHIGAN AVE; SUITE 3400
CHICAGO IL 60611

1902 DENTAL HYGIENIST (CAREER INFORMATION)
AMERICAN DENTAL HYGIENISTS ASSN INSTITUTE FOR ORAL HEALTH
444 NORTH MICHIGAN AVENUE; SUITE 3400
CHICAGO IL 60611

1903 DENTAL LAB TECHNOLOGY CAREER INFORMATION
NATIONAL ASSOCIATION OF DENTAL LABORATORIES
3801 MT VERNON AVE
ALEXANDRIA VA 22305

1904 DENTISTRY CAREER INFORMATION
AMERICAN ASSOCIATION OF DENTAL SCHOOLS
1625 MASSACHUSETTS AVE NW; SUITE 502
WASHINGTON DC 20036

1905 DIETETIC CAREER INFORMATION
AMERICAN DIETETIC ASSOCIATION
ATTN MEMBERSHIP DEPARTMENT; 216 W JACKSON BLVD; SUITE 800
CHICAGO IL 60606

1906 DRAMA/ACTING (CAREER INFORMATION)
SCREEN ACTORS GUILD
7065 HOLLYWOOD BLVD
HOLLYWOOD CA 90028

1907 EDUCATION CAREER INFORMATION
AMERICAN FEDERATION OF TEACHERS
PUBLIC AFFAIRS DEPARTMENT - 555 NEW JERSEY AVE NW
WASHINGTON DC 20001

1908 EDUCATION CAREERS INFORMATION
NATIONAL EDUCATION ASSOCIATION
1201 16TH STREET NW
WASHINGTON DC 20036

1909 ELECTRICAL ENGINEERING CAREER INFORMATION
INSTITUTE OF ELECTRICAL AND ELECTRONICS ENGINEERS - UNITED STATES ACTIVITIES
1828 L ST NW; SUITE 1202
WASHINGTON DC 20036

1910 ENERGY CAREERS INFORMATION
AMERICAN GAS ASSOC
1515 WILSON BLVD
ARLINGTON VA 22209

1911 ENGINEERING (CAREER INFORMATION)
NATIONAL SOCIETY OF PROFESSIONAL ENGINEERS
1420 KING STREET
ALEXANDRIA VA 22314

1912 ENGINEERING CAREER INFORMATION
JUNIOR ENGINEERING TECHNICAL SOCIETY INC (JETS)
1420 KING ST; SUITE 405
ALEXANDRIA VA 22314

1913 ENTOMOLOGY (CAREER INFORMATION)
ENTOMOLOGICAL SOCIETY OF AMERICA
9301 ANNAPOLIS ROAD
LANHAM MD 20706

1914 ENVIRONMENTAL STUDIES & CAREER INFORMATION
U.S. ENVIRONMENTAL PROTECTION AGENCY
401 M STREET SW; OFFICE OF PUBLIC AFFAIRS
WASHINGTON DC 20460

1915 F.B.I. CAREER INFORMATION
FEDERAL BUREAU OF INVESTIGATION
DEPARTMENT OF JUSTICE
WASHINGTON DC 20535

1916 FARM MANAGEMENT CAREER INFORMATION
U.S. DEPT. OF AGRICULTURE; FARMERS HOME ADMINISTRATION
HUMAN RESOURCES; 14TH & INDEPENDENCE AVE SW
WASHINGTON DC 20250

1917 FASHION DESIGN CAREER INFORMATION
FASHION INSTITUTE OF TECHNOLOGY
227 WEST 27TH STREET
NEW YORK NY 10001

1918 FIRE SERVICE (CAREER INFORMATION)
NATIONAL FIRE PROTECTION ASSOCIATION
1 BATTERYMARCH PARK; PO BOX 9101
QUINCY MA 02269

1919 FISHERIES (CAREER & UNIVERSITY INFORMATION)
AMERICAN FISHERIES SOCIETY
5410 GROSVENOR LANE; SUITE 110
BETHESDA MD 20814

1920 FLORISTRY CAREER INFORMATION
SOCIETY OF AMERICAN FLORISTS
1601 DUKE ST
ALEXANDRIA VA 22314

1921 FOOD AND NUTRITION SERVICE (CAREER INFORMATION)
U.S. DEPT. OF AGRICULTURE; FOOD AND NUTRITION SERVICE
PERSONNEL DIVISION; ROOM 620 - 1301 PARK CENTER DR
ALEXANDRIA VA 22302

1922 FOOD RETAILING (CAREER INFORMATION)
FOOD MARKETING INSTITUTE
800 CONNECTICUT AVE NW
WASHINGTON DC 20006

1923 FOOD TECHNOLOGY/SCIENCE CAREER INFORMATION
INSTITUTE OF FOOD TECHNOLOGISTS
221 NORTH LASALLE STREET
CHICAGO IL 60601

1924 FOODSERVICE (CAREER INFORMATION)
EDUCATIONAL FOUNDATION OF NATIONAL RESTAURANT ASSOC
250 S WACKER DR; SUITE 1400
CHICAGO IL 60606

1925 FOREIGN LANGUAGES CAREER INFORMATION
MODERN LANGUAGE ASSOCIATION OF AMERICA
10 ASTOR PLACE
NEW YORK NY 10003

1926 FOREIGN SERVICE OFFICER CAREER INFORMATION
U.S. DEPT. OF STATE-RECRUITMENT DIVISION
PO BOX 9317-ROSSLYN STATION
ARLINGTON VA 22219

1927 FOREST SERVICE CAREER INFORMATION
U.S. DEPT. OF AGRICULTURE
14TH & INDEPENDENCE AVENUE; ROOM 801 RPE
WASHINGTON DC 20250

1928 FORESTRY CAREER INFORMATION
SOCIETY OF AMERICAN FORESTERS
5400 GROSVENOR LANE
BETHESDA MD 20814

1929 FUNERAL DIRECTOR (CAREER INFORMATION)
NATIONAL FUNERAL DIRECTORS ASSN.
11121 WEST OKLAHOMA AVE
MILWAUKEE WI 53227

1930 GEOGRAPHY CAREER INFORMATION
ASSOCIATION OF AMERICAN GEOGRAPHERS
1710 SIXTEENTH ST NW
WASHINGTON DC 20009

1931 GEOLOGICAL SCIENCES CAREER INFORMATION
AMERICAN GEOLOGICAL INSTITUTE
4220 KING STREET
ALEXANDRIA VA 22302

1932 GEOPHYSICIST CAREER INFORMATION
SOCIETY OF EXPLORATION GEOPHYSICISTS
PO BOX 702740
TULSA OK 74170

1933 GEOPHYSICS CAREER INFORMATION
AMERICAN GEOPHYSICAL UNION
2000 FLORIDA AVENUE NW
WASHINGTON DC 20009

1934 GRAPHIC ARTS CAREER INFORMATION
EDUCATION COUNCIL ON GRAPHIC ARTS INC.
1899 PRESTON WHITE DR
RESTON VA 22091

1935 GRAPHIC ARTS CAREER INFORMATION
AMERICAN INSTITUTE OF GRAPHIC ARTS
1059 THIRD AVE
NEW YORK NY 10021

1936 HEALTH FIELDS CAREER INFORMATION
NATIONAL HEALTH COUNCIL INC.
1730 M ST NW; SUITE 500
WASHINGTON DC 20036

1937 HEALTH PROFESSIONALS PRACTICE OPPORTUNITY (CAREER INFORMATION)
U.S. DEPT. OF HEALTH AND HUMAN SERVICES-NATIONAL HEALTH SERVICE CORPS
8201 GREENSBORO DR; SUITE 600
MCLEAN VA 22102

1938 HEATING & AIR CONDITIONING ENGINEER CAREER INFORMATION
REFRIGERATION SERVICE ENGINEERS SOCIETY
1666 RAND ROAD
DES PLAINES IL 60016

1939 HOME ECONOMIST CAREER INFORMATION
AMERICAN HOME ECONOMICS ASSOCIATION
1555 KING ST
ALEXANDRIA VA 22314

1940 HORTICULTURE CAREER INFORMATION
AMERICAN ASSOCIATION OF NURSERYMEN
1250 'I' STREET NW
WASHINGTON DC 20005

1941 HOSPITAL ADMINISTRATION CAREER INFORMATION
AMERICAN COLLEGE OF HEALTH CARE EXECUTIVES
840 NORTH LAKE SHORE DRIVE
CHICAGO IL 60611

1942 HOTEL MANAGEMENT CAREER INFORMATION
AMERICAN HOTEL AND MOTEL ASSOCIATION
1201 NEW YORK AVE NW; SUITE 600
WASHINGTON DC 20005

1943 ILLUMINATING ENGINEERING CAREER INFORMATION
ILLUMINATING ENGINEERING SOCIETY OF NORTH AMERICA
345 EAST 47TH STREET
NEW YORK NY 10017

1944 INSURANCE - CAREER INFORMATION
INSURANCE INFORMATION INSTITUTE
110 WILLIAM STREET
NEW YORK NY 10038

1945 INSURANCE CAREER INFORMATION
ALLIANCE OF AMERICAN INSURERS
1501 WOODFIELD RD; SUITE 400W
SCHAUMBURG IL 60173

1946 JOURNALISM CAREER INFORMATION FOR MINORITIES
AMERICAN SOCIETY OF NEWSPAPER EDITORS
PO BOX 17004; MINORITY AFFAIRS DIRECTOR
WASHINGTON DC 20041

1947 LANDSCAPE ARCHITECTURE CAREER INFORMATION
AMERICAN SOCIETY OF LANDSCAPE ARCHITECTS
4401 CONNECTICUT AVE NW; 5TH FL
WASHINGTON DC 20008

1948 LAW LIBRARIANSHIP
AMERICAN ASSOCIATION OF LAW LIBRARIES
53 WEST JACKSON BLVD; SUITE 940
CHICAGO IL 60604

1949 LEARNING DISABLED (EDUCATION & CAREER INFORMATION)
LEARNING DISABILITIES ASSOCIATION OF AMERICA
4156 LIBRARY RD
PITTSBURGH PA 15234

1950 LIBRARY SCIENCE CAREER INFORMATION
AMERICAN LIBRARY ASSN
OFFICE FOR LIBRARY PERSONNEL RESOURCES; 50 EAST HURON ST
CHICAGO IL 60611

1951 MACHINE TECHNOLOGY (CAREER INFORMATION)
AMT - THE ASSOCIATION FOR MANUFACTURING TECHNOLOGY
7901 WESTPARK DR
MCLEAN VA 22102

1952 MACHINE TECHNOLOGY (CAREER INFORMATION)
NATIONAL TOOLING AND MACHINING ASSN
9300 LIVINGSTON ROAD
FT WASHINGTON MD 20744

1953 MANAGEMENT CAREER INFORMATION
CLUB FOUNDATION (THE)
1733 KING ST
ALEXANDRIA VA 22314

1954 MANAGEMENT CAREER INFORMATION
AMERICAN MANAGEMENT ASSOCIATION
135 WEST 50TH STREET
NEW YORK NY 10020

1955 MARINE TECHNOLOGY (CAREER INFORMATION)
U.S. DEPT. OF COMMERCE/NOAA (NATIONAL SEA GRANT COLLEGE PROGRAM; R/OR-1)
1335 EAST-WEST HWY
SILVER SPRING MD 20910

1956 MATHEMATICIAN CAREER INFORMATION
MATHEMATICAL ASSOCIATION OF AMERICA
1529 18TH STREET NW
WASHINGTON DC 20036

1957 MATHEMATICS TEACHER CAREER INFORMATION
NATIONAL COUNCIL OF TEACHERS OF MATHEMATICS
1906 ASSOCIATION DRIVE
RESTON VA 22091

1958 MECHANICAL ENGINEER CAREER INFORMATION
AMERICAN SOCIETY OF MECHANICAL ENGINEERS
UNITED ENGINEERING CENTER; 345 EAST 47TH STREET
NEW YORK NY 10017

1959 MEDICAL LABORATORY CAREER INFORMATION
AMERICAN SOCIETY OF CLINICAL PATHOLOGISTS
CAREERS; 2100 W HARRISON
CHICAGO IL 60612

1960 MEDICAL RECORDS CAREER INFORMATION
AMERICAN MEDICAL RECORD ASSOCIATION
919 NORTH MICHIGAN AVE; SUITE 1400
CHICAGO IL 60611

1961 MEDICAL TECHNOLOGIST CAREER INFORMATION
AMERICAN MEDICAL TECHNOLOGISTS
710 HIGGINS ROAD
PARK RIDGE IL 60068

1962 MEDICINE CAREER INFORMATION
AMERICAN MEDICAL ASSOCIATION
515 N STATE ST
CHICAGO IL 60610

1963 METALLURGY & MATERIALS SCIENCE CAREER INFORMATION
ASM INTERNATIONAL
STUDENT OUTREACH PROGRAM
MATERIALS PARK OH 44073

1964 MICROBIOLOGY CAREER INFORMATION
AMERICAN SOCIETY FOR MICROBIOLOGY
1325 MASSACHUSETTS AVE NW
WASHINGTON DC 20005

1965 MOTION PICTURE (CAREER INFORMATION)
SOCIETY OF MOTION PICTURE AND TELEVISION ENGINEERS
595 W HARTSDALE AVE
WHITE PLAINS NY 10607

1966 MOTION PICTURE CAREER INFORMATION
ACADEMY OF MOTION PICTURE ARTS AND SCIENCES
8949 WILSHIRE BLVD
BEVERLY HILLS CA 90211

1967 MUSIC CAREER INFORMATION
MUSIC EDUCATORS NATIONAL CONFERENCE
1902 ASSOCIATION DRIVE
RESTON VA 22091

1968 MUSIC PERFORMER & COMPOSER CAREER INFORMATION
AMERICAN MUSIC CENTER
DIRECTOR OF INFORMATION; 30 W 26TH ST; SUITE 1001
NEW YORK NY 10010

1969 MUSIC THERAPY (CAREER INFORMATION)
NATIONAL ASSOCIATION FOR MUSIC THERAPY
8455 COLESVILLE ROAD; SUITE 930
SILVER SPRING MD 20910

1970 NAVAL ARCHITECTURE (CAREER INFORMATION)
SOCIETY OF NAVAL ARCHITECTS & MARINE ENGINEERS
601 PAVONIA AVE
JERSEY CITY NJ 07306

1971 NAVAL OFFICER (CAREER INFORMATION)
U.S. NAVAL ACADEMY
CANDIDATE GUIDANCE OFFICE
ANNAPOLIS MD 21402

1972 NAVAL/MARINE ENGINEERING (CAREER INFORMATION)
SOCIETY OF NAVAL ARCHITECTS & MARINE ENGINEERS
601 PAVONIA AVE
JERSEY CITY NJ 07306

1973 NEWSPAPER CAREER INFORMATION
AMERICAN SOCIETY OF NEWSPAPER EDITORS FOUNDATION
PO BOX 17004
WASHINGTON DC 20041

1974 NEWSPAPER INDUSTRY (CAREER INFORMATION)
NEWSPAPER ASSOCIATION OF AMERICA
THE NEWSPAPER CENTER; 11600 SUNRISE VALLEY DR
RESTON VA 22091

1975 NURSE ANESTHETIST CAREER INFORMATION
AMERICAN ASSOCIATION OF NURSE ANESTHETISTS
216 HIGGINS RD
PARKRIDGE IL 60068

1976 NURSING (CAREER INFORMATION)
NATIONAL LEAGUE FOR NURSING INC.
350 HUDSON ST
NEW YORK NY 10014

1977 NURSING CAREER INFORMATION
AMERICAN NURSES ASSN.
600 MARYLAND AVE SW; SUITE 100 WEST
WASHINGTON DC 20024

1978 NUTRITIONIST CAREER INFORMATION
AMERICAN DIETETIC ASSOCIATION
ATTN MEMBERSHIP DEPARTMENT; 216 W JACKSON BLVD; SUITE 800
CHICAGO IL 60606

1979 OCEANOGRAPHY & MARINE SCIENCE (CAREER INFORMATION)
MARINE TECHNOLOGY SOCIETY
1828 L STREET NW; SUITE 906
WASHINGTON DC 20036

1980 OPTOMETRIC ASSISTANT/TECHNICIAN
AMERICAN OPTOMETRIC ASSN
243 NORTH LINDBERGH BLVD
ST LOUIS MO 63141

1981 OPTOMETRIST CAREER INFORMATION
NATIONAL OPTOMETRIC ASSOCIATION
2838 S INDIANA AVE
CHICAGO IL 60616

1982 OPTOMETRY CAREER INFORMATION
AMERICAN OPTOMETRIC ASSN
243 NORTH LINDBERGH BLVD
ST LOUIS MO 63141

1983 ORNITHOLOGIST CAREER INFORMATION
AMERICAN ORNITHOLOGISTS' UNION
SMITHSONIAN INSTITUTION; DIV OF BIRDS
WASHINGTON DC 20560

1984 OSTEOPATHIC MEDICINE CAREER INFORMATION
AMERICAN OSTEOPATHIC ASSN.
142 E ONTARIO ST
CHICAGO IL 60611

1985 PALEONTOLOGY (CAREER INFORMATION)
PALEONTOLOGICAL SOCIETY
DR. DONALD L. WOLBERG; SECRETARY; PO BOX 1937
SOCORRO NM 87801

1986 PATHOLOGY (CAREER INFORMATION)
INTERSOCIETY COMMITTEE ON PATHOLOGY INFORMATION
4733 BETHESDA AVE; SUITE 735
BETHESDA MD 20814

1987 PEDIATRICIAN CAREER INFORMATION
AMERICAN ACADEMY OF PEDIATRICS
141 NW POINT BLVD; PO BOX 927
ELK GROVE VILLAGE IL 60009

1988 PETROLEUM ENGINEERING CAREER INFORMATION
SOCIETY OF PETROLEUM ENGINEERS
222 PALISADAS CREEK DR; PO BOX 833836
RICHARDSON TX 75080

1989 PHARMACOLOGY CAREER INFORMATION
AMERICAN SOCIETY FOR PHARMACOLOGY AND EXPERIMENTAL THERAPEUTICS INC.
9650 ROCKVILLE PIKE
BETHESDA MD 20814

1990 PHARMACY (BOOKLET ON ACCREDITED SCHOOLS)
AMERICAN COUNCIL ON PHARMACEUTICAL EDUCATION
311 W SUPERIOR; #512
CHICAGO IL 60610

1991 PHARMACY CAREER INFORMATION
AMERICAN ASSOCIATION OF COLLEGES OF PHARMACY
OFFICE OF STUDENT AFFAIRS; 1426 PRINCE ST
ALEXANDRIA VA 22314

1992 PHARMACY CAREER INFORMATION
AMERICAN FOUNDATION FOR PHARMACEUTICAL EDUCATION
PO BOX 7126; 618 SOMERSET ST
NORTH PLAINFIELD NJ 07060

1993 PHOTOJOURNALISM CAREER INFORMATION
NATIONAL PRESS PHOTOGRAPHERS ASSN.
3200 CROASDAILE DR; #306
DURHAM NC 27705

1994 PHYSICAL THERAPY CAREER INFORMATION
AMERICAN PHYSICAL THERAPY ASSOCIATION
1111 NORTH FAIRFAX ST
ALEXANDRIA VA 22314

1995 PHYSICS CAREER INFORMATION
AMERICAN INSTITUTE OF PHYSICS
335 EAST 45TH STREET
NEW YORK NY 10017

1996 PILOT (CAREER INFORMATION)
INTERNATIONAL WOMEN PILOTS (99'S)
WILL ROGERS WORLD AIRPORT
OKLAHOMA CITY OK 73159

1997 PODIATRY CAREER INFORMATION
AMERICAN PODIATRIC MEDICAL ASSN.
9312 OLD GEORGETOWN RD
BETHESDA MD 20814

1998 POLITICAL SCIENCE CAREER INFORMATION
AMERICAN POLITICAL SCIENCE ASSN
1527 NEW HAMPSHIRE AVE NW
WASHINGTON DC 20036

1999 PRINTING INDUSTRY CAREER INFORMATION
PRINTING INDUSTRIES OF AMERICA INC.
ATTENTION CAREERS- MEMBER PROGRAMS; 100 DAINGERFIELD RD
ALEXANDRIA VA 22314

2000 PSYCHIATRY CAREER INFORMATION
AMERICAN PSYCHIATRIC ASSOCIATION
1400 'K' STREET NW
WASHINGTON DC 20005

2001 PSYCHOLOGY CAREER INFORMATION
AMERICAN PSYCHOLOGICAL ASSOCIATION
750 FIRST ST NE
WASHINGTON DC 20002

2002 PUBLIC RELATIONS (CAREER INFORMATION)
PUBLIC RELATIONS SOCIETY OF AMERICA
33 IRVING PLACE
NEW YORK NY 10003

2003 RADIOLOGIC TECHNOLOGIST CAREER INFORMATION
AMERICAN SOCIETY OF RADIOLOGIC TECHNOLOGISTS
15000 CENTRAL AVE SE
ALBUQUERQUE NM 87123

2004 RANGE MANAGEMENT (CAREER INFORMATION)
SOCIETY FOR RANGE MANAGEMENT
1839 YORK ST
DENVER CO 80206

2005 REAL ESTATE (CAREER INFORMATION)
NATIONAL ASSOCIATION OF REALTORS
777 14TH ST NW
WASHINGTON DC 20005

2006 REHABILITATION COUNSELING (CAREER INFORMATION)
NATIONAL REHABILITATION COUNSELING ASSOCIATION
633 S WASHINGTON ST
ALEXANDRIA VA 22314

2007 RESPIRATORY THERAPIST CAREER INFORMATION
AMERICAN RESPIRATORY CARE FOUNDATION
11030 ABLES LN
DALLAS TX 75229

2008 RURAL ELECTRIFICATION (CAREER INFORMATION)
U.S. DEPT. OF AGRICULTURE; RURAL ELECTRIFICATION ADMINISTRATION
14TH AND INDEPENDENCE AVE SW; ROOM 4032
WASHINGTON DC 20250

2009 SAFETY ENGINEER CAREER INFORMATION
AMERICAN SOCIETY OF SAFETY ENGINEERS
1800 EAST OAKTON ST
DES PLAINES IL 60018

2010 SCHOOL ADMINISTRATION CAREER INFORMATION
AMERICAN ASSOCIATION OF SCHOOL ADMINISTRATORS
1801 NORTH MOORE STREET
ARLINGTON VA 22209

2011 SCIENCE TEACHER CAREER INFORMATION
NATIONAL SCIENCE TEACHERS ASSN
ATTN OFFICE OF PUBLIC INFORMATION; 1742 CONNECTICUT AVE NW
WASHINGTON DC 20009

2012 SECRETARY (CAREER INFORMATION)
PROFESSIONAL SECRETARIES INTERNATIONAL
PO BOX 20404
KANSAS CITY MO 64195

2013 SOCIAL WORK CAREER INFORMATION
NATIONAL ASSOCIATION OF SOCIAL WORKERS
7981 EASTERN AVE
SILVER SPRINGS MD 20910

2014 SOCIOLOGIST CAREER INFORMATION
AMERICAN SOCIOLOGICAL ASSOCIATION
1722 'N' STREET NW
WASHINGTON DC 20036

2015 SOIL CONSERVATION CAREER INFORMATION
U.S. DEPT. OF AGRICULTURE; SOIL CONSERVATION SERVICE
PO BOX 2890
WASHINGTON DC 20013

2016 SOIL CONSERVATIONIST CAREER INFORMATION
SOIL & WATER CONSERVATION SOCIETY
7515 NE ANKENY ROAD
ANKENY IA 50021

2017 SPECIAL EDUCATION TEACHER CAREER INFORMATION
ASSOCIATION FOR RETARDED CITIZENS (THE ARC)
300 E BORDER ST; SUITE 300
ARLINGTON TX 76006

2018 SPECIAL EDUCATION TEACHER CAREER INFORMATION
NATIONAL CLEARINGHOUSE FOR PROFESSIONS IN SPECIAL EDUCATION
1920 ASSOCIATION DRIVE
RESTON VA 22091

2019 SPEECH & HEARING THERAPIST CAREER INFORMATION
ALEXANDER GRAHAM BELL ASSOCIATION FOR THE DEAF
3417 VOLTA PLACE NW
WASHINGTON DC 23007

2020 SPEECH PATHOLOGY CAREER INFORMATION
AMERICAN SPEECH-LANGUAGE-HEARING ASSOCIATION
10801 ROCKVILLE PIKE
ROCKVILLE MD 20852

2021 SYSTEMS ANALYST/COMPUTER SCIENCE CAREER INFORMATION
ASSOCIATION FOR SYSTEMS MANAGEMENT
24587 BAGLEY ROAD
CLEVELAND OH 44138

2022 TRANSLATOR CAREER INFORMATION
AMERICAN TRANSLATORS ASSN
109 CROTON AVENUE
OSSINING NY 10562

2023 UNITED STATES COAST GUARD OFFICER (CAREER INFORMATION)
U.S. COAST GUARD ACADEMY
DIRECTOR OF ADMISSIONS; 15 MOHEGAN AVE
NEW LONDON CT 06320-4195

2024 UNITED STATES MARINE CORPS OFFICER
HEADQUARTERS; MARINE CORPS
(CODE MRON)
WASHINGTON DC 20380

2025 UNITED STATES MILITARY ACADEMY
U.S. MILITARY ACADEMY
DIRECTOR OF ADMISSIONS; 606 THAYER RD
WEST POINT NY 10996

2026 URBAN PLANNER CAREER INFORMATION
AMERICAN PLANNING ASSOCIATION
1776 MASSACHUSETTS AVE NW
WASHINGTON DC 20036

2027 VETERINARIAN CAREER INFORMATION
AMERICAN VETERINARY MEDICAL ASSOCIATION
1931 N MEACHAM RD; SUITE 100
SCHAUMBURG IL 60173

2028 WATER POLLUTION CONTROL CAREER INFORMATION
WATER POLLUTION CONTROL FEDERATION
EDUCATION DEPT; 601 WYTHE ST
ALEXANDRIA VA 22314

2029 WELDING TECHNOLOGY CAREER INFORMATION
HOBART SCHOOL OF WELDING TECHNOLOGY
TRADE SQUARE EAST
TROY OH 45373

2030 WOMEN AIRLINE PILOT CAREER INFORMATION
INTERNATIONAL SOCIETY OF WOMEN AIRLINE PILOTS
ISA+21; PO BOX 66268
CHICAGO IL 60666

2031 WOMEN PILOT CAREER INFORMATION
NINETY-NINES (INTERNATIONAL ORGANIZATION OF WOMEN PILOTS)
PO BOX 59965
OKLAHOMA CITY OK 73159

2032 YOUTH LEADERSHIP CAREER INFORMATION
BOYS & GIRLS CLUBS OF AMERICA
771 FIRST AVENUE
NEW YORK NY 10017

2033 YOUTH LEADERSHIP CAREER INFORMATION
BOY SCOUTS OF AMERICA
NATIONAL EAGLE SCOUT ASSOCIATION; 1325 W WALNUT HILL LN; SUM 220
IRVING TX 75015

Alphabetical Index